THE EXILE'S COOKBOOK

ALSO BY DANIEL L. NEWMAN

The Sultan's Feast: A Fifteenth-Century Egyptian Cookbook

The Sultan's Sex Potions: Arab Aphrodisiacs in the Middle Ages

An Imam in Paris: Account of a Stay in France by an Egyptian Cleric (1826–1831)

Arabic-English Thematic Lexicon

Co-authored with R. Husni

A to Z of Arabic-English-Arabic Translation

Arabic-English-Arabic Translation: Issues and Strategies

Modern Arabic Short Stories: A Bilingual Reader

Muslim Women in Law and Society

THE EXILE'S COOKBOOK

Medieval Gastronomic Treasures from al-Andalus and North Africa

IBN RAZĪN AL-TUJĪBĪ

Translated and Introduced by
Daniel L. Newman

SAQI

To Whitney,
As ever, with love, for ever

SAQI BOOKS

26 Westbourne Grove
London W2 5RH
www.saqibooks.com

Published 2023 by Saqi Books

A full CIP record for this book is available from the British Library.

Printed and bound by PBtisk a.s.

ISBN 978 0 86356 992 0

eISBN 978 0 86356 997 5

CONTENTS

Preface ix
Note on Transliteration xi
Introduction 1
The Author and His Age 1
The Book 17
The Cuisine 26
Weights and Measures 72
The Translation 74

THE EXILE'S COOKBOOK 79

Introduction 81

Section One 89
1. On breads 89
2. On *tharīdas* 92
3. On porridges and mashed cereal dishes 114
4. On pastries, various types of *mujabbana* (fried cheese buns), *isfanj* (doughnuts), and other similar foods 119
5. Dishes that are soaked in broth, like *tharīdas*, or cooked like pottage 147

Section Two 157
1. On beef 157
2. On mutton 167
3. On lamb 200
4. On kid meat 207
5. On wild and game meats 208
6. On the different uses of meat from quadrupeds used for meatballs 213

Section Three 222
1. On goose meat 222
2. On chicken meat 225

3. On partridge meat 253
4. On squab meat 255
5. On turtledove dishes 258
6. On starling meat 261
7. On sparrow meat 262

Section Four 264
1. On making the *Ṣanhājī* dish 264
2. On making stuffed tripe 265
3. On making *Ṣanhājī* tongue 266

Section Five 267
1. On types of fish 267
2. On ways of making eggs 285

Section Six 290
1. On curd and what to make with it 290
2. Making curdled milk and extracting butter 293
3. On maturing dry cheese in an earthenware jar, what is made with it, and restoring butter and buttermilk 295

Section Seven 298
1. On dishes made with gourd 298
2. On what is made with aubergine 302
3. On carrot dishes 314
4. On how to prepare truffles 314
5. On what to do with asparagus, for which there is only one recipe 316
6. On artichokes, which are called *qannāriya* 316
7. On what to do with mushrooms, for there is only one recipe 317
8. On what to do with spinach, leafy, goosefoot lettuce and other similar things 318
9. On cooking *jināniyya* 319
10. On taro 320

Section Eight 321
1. On fresh and dried broad bean dishes 321
2. On chickpea dishes 325
3. On lentil dishes 326

Section Nine 328
1. Making *mu'assal* and *ghassānī* 328
2. On various kinds of sweets 329
3. Making *Qāhiriyya* and *sanbūsak* 336
4. On making *jawzīnaq* and *lawzīnaq* 339
5. On making sweet cane 340
6. Making *fānīdh* and *ashqāqūl* 340
7. Eastern recipes 342

Section Ten 344
1. On making *ṣināb* 344
2. On preserving olives 346
3. On pickling limes 349
4. On pickling capers 351
5. On pickling aubergines, onions and turnips 352
6. Pickling fish 354
7. Making vinegars 356
8. Making macerated, cooked and other kinds of *murrī* 362
9. Making and restoring olive oil 375
10. On extracting oils required for certain dishes 376
11. Making *qadīd* (jerky) 377
12. Restoring food 379

Section Eleven 380

Section Twelve 383

Bibliography 391
Index of People and Places 407
General Index 409

PREFACE

In the course of my research for what became *The Sultan's Feast* (Saqi Books, 2020), I was fortunate enough to uncover not only an unknown medieval Arabic recipe collection at the Wellcome Library (London), entitled *Taṣānīf al-aṭʿima* ('Categories of Foods'), but also a previously unidentified manuscript copy of al-Tujībī's text, which, though held by the British Library, I accessed through the Qatar Digital Library in November 2018. As it contained information not found in the printed edition of the book, I started to use it for my translation, alongside the edition and the two known manuscripts, held in Berlin and Madrid. To the best of my knowledge, I was the first to report (in *The Sultan's Feast*) on the British Library copy of al-Tujībī's text.

I finished a complete draft by April 2020, but extraneous factors, not least the Covid pandemic, resulted in its publication being delayed.

The present book is a timely addition to the field of food history, where an interest in non-European culinary traditions has been increasing over the years.

In anticipation of the translation, many of those who share my passion have already had a taste of some of the recipes contained in this book through re-creations on various social media platforms (www.eatlikeasultan.com; on Instagram @medieval_arab_cooking). As a result, a thirteenth-century Arabic cookery book has been brought to life in more ways than one.

In the meantime, I have continued working on the above-mentioned Wellcome manuscript, the translation of which will constitute the next – and final – part in the trilogy, in addition to being a valuable contribution to the early history of the Arab culinary tradition. As a result, and thanks to the work of other scholars, such as the indefatigable Charles Perry, before long all of the known medieval Arabic cookery books will be available in translation, thus enabling a wider audience of non-Arabic-speaking scholars and enthusiasts alike to gain access to this amazing heritage. We have indeed come a long way since even the mid-1980s, when a mere two texts were available in an Arabic edition, only one of which had been translated into English.

I'd like to take this opportunity to thank Durham University for granting me research leave, which enabled me to devote time to the present project. However, my biggest debt of gratitude goes to Whitney Stanton, my enthusiastic fellow traveller along historical culinary roads, for her constant support and encouragement.

NOTE ON TRANSLITERATION

The transliteration used in the book is that of the *International Journal of Middle East Studies*.

Initial hamza is not transliterated, no distinction is made between *alif mamdūda* and *alif maqṣūra*, both of which are rendered as *ā*. The *tāʾ marbūṭa* marker is not rendered, except when it occurs as the first element in a *status constructus* (the so-called *iḍāfa*): so *madīna*, but *madīnat al-zahrāʾ*.

In the case of plurals, common sense has been allowed to prevail, with the use of regular plural English endings, rather than the Arabic ones; so, for instance, *mujabbanas*, rather than *mujabbanāt*.

Place names appear in their common historical English forms or in transliteration, usually followed by a modern equivalent in brackets when it involves little-known towns, e.g. 'Tétouan' (not Tiṭwān) but 'Bijāya (Béjaïa)'. In some cases, historical forms are preferred when there is no adequate modern geopolitical equivalent and in the absence of an accurate delineation: e.g. Ifrīqiyā (the eastern part of North Africa), Mashriq (the area corresponding roughly to the present-day terms Near and Middle East), and Maghrib (North Africa, west of Tunisia).

INTRODUCTION

The Author and His Age

The thirteenth century was a period of immense upheaval and change across the Muslim world, from its farthest western outposts to its eastern confines. In the East, the capital city of the Abbasid caliphate, Baghdad, was sacked in 1258, while in Egypt a powerful new dynasty emerged of slave soldiers of non-Muslim origin imported from Central Asia and the Causasus and converted to Islam at a young age. Known in Arabic as *mamlūk* ('owned'), they rebelled against their masters, the Ayyubids, in 1250, and would go on to rule Egypt, Syria, and south-eastern Anatolia. In 1517 they succumbed to the might of the Ottomans, who first emerged at the end of the thirteenth century as a small Anatolian emirate.

At the other end of the Mediterranean, in Muslim-controlled Spain, or al-Andalus as it is known in Arabic, things were not going well either. It was five centuries since a Berber-Arab force crossed the Straits of Gibraltar and ended Visigothic rule in Spain, shortly after North Africa itself had been invaded by Muslim armies coming from the East, who Islamized its native Berber (Amazigh) populations.

The expedition into the Iberian Peninsula started in 711 and was composed almost entirely of Berbers, including its commander, Ṭāriq Ibn Ziyād. His name survives in *Jabal Ṭāriq*, 'Tāriq's mountain', which gave the English 'Gibraltar'. Very early on, Córdoba became the seat for Muslim rule, and it was here that a refugee from the East arrived in 755; his name was 'Abd al-Raḥmān Ibn Mu'āwiya (d. 788), and he was one of the few surviving members of the Umayyad dynasty, which was ousted by the Abbasids.

This inaugurated a period of great splendour for the city, whose stature and monuments, such as the Grand Mosque and the country estate of Madīnat al-Zahrā', rivalled those of Baghdad. It was one of the most advanced cities of its day thanks to to its prosperous industry and infrastructure, with paved and well-lit streets, and running water for its large population, which was probably around half a million at its heyday.

It also became a centre of learning and culture. When it came to the latter, the Mashriq was considered an example to be emulated. In this context, chroniclers invariably mention the name of another refugee from the East as the conduit of Eastern sophistication. His name was Abū 'l-Ḥasan ʿAlī Ibn Nāfiʿ, but he is best known by his nickname Ziryāb (*ca.* 790–852),[1] which means 'blackbird' in Persian, in reference either to his skin colour or his mellifluous voice. Persian by birth, his family were clients (*mawālī*) of the Abbasid caliph and gastronome Ibrāhīm Ibn al-Mahdī (779–839), who is said to have created a number of dishes and even written a cookery book, which unfortunately has not survived. Ziryāb was a gifted musician who had been a pupil of the leading musicians of the day, Ibrāhīm al-Mawṣilī and his son, Isḥāq. However, the latter became so jealous of Ziryāb's extraordinary musical talents that he forced him out of Baghdad. Ziryāb first tried his luck with the Aghlabid ruler in Kairouan, but when he fell out of favour sought his fortune in Córdoba, where he was welcomed with open arms by the Umayyad ruler ʿAbd al-Raḥmān II (822–52).

In addition to establishing his reputation as a musical innovator, Ziryāb became the local Beau Brummell – the ultimate arbiter of fashion, culture and etiquette in Córdoba. His influence also extended to food, and his biographer Ibn Ḥayyān (d. 1076)[2] credited Ziryāb with introducing the following eastern elements to the Andalusian culinary repertoire: asparagus, the *tafāyā* (see recipes Nos. 109–10), *baqliyya* (vegetable stew),[3] *tharīda* (see below), *bawārid* (a kind of sandwich or wrap),[4] *mudaqqaqāt*,[5] *jawzīnaq* (Nos. 55, 410), *lawzīnaq* (Nos. 56,

1 Up until relatively recently, information on this personage relied on a seventeenth-century account (al-Maqqarī 2012: II, 127–8), which drew on the biography written by Ibn Ḥayyān some five hundred years earlier that was thought to be lost before it was discovered a few decades ago (Makkī 2003: 307–35). Also see Reynolds 2008; *idem* 2021: 59–85; Dozy 1861: II, 89ff.; Ibn Khaldūn 2005: II, 331 (trans., II, 405); *EI*[2], s.v. (H. G. Farmer/E. Neubauer).

2 Makkī 2003: 321–2.

3 The anonymous Andalusian treatise contains a recipe for this kind of dish that bears his name, *baqliyyat Ziryāb*, a lamb stew with cabbage; *Anwāʿ*, 134–5 (BNF, fol. 50r.).

4 The word – like the dish – originated in Persia and denoted flat loaves filled with meat and herbs. They were very popular in Abbasid cuisine: al-Baghdādī 1964: 58; al-Warrāq 1987: 57–8; *Waṣf*, 381–2; Lewicka 2011: 160–1, 186, 195–6 (note 292); Steingass 1892: 178, 184. They were said to be heavy on the stomach, slow to digest, and are best eaten at the start of the meal (al-Warrāq 1987: 54).

5 Pounded meat made into balls, or what today we would call burgers; see Ibn Mubārak Shāh 2020: Nos. 25, 85 and note 77.

411), stuffed *qaṭāyif* (No. 60), *fānīdh* (No. 413), *mu'aqqada* (Nos. 402, 405), stomachics (*jawārish*), and conserves (*murabbayāt*). In the field of dining etiquette, he is said to have recommended serving drinks in fine glassware rather than heavy metal goblets, and the use of leather cloths to serve food on.

One can imagine that Ziryāb brought with him cookery books from the East, among them most probably that of his master, Ibrāhīm Ibn al-Mahdī. This explains why, as we shall see, there are often parallels between al-Tujībī's recipes and those of the earliest Abbasid gastronomical tradition. The timing is relevant; the cookery book compiled by al-Kātib al-Baghdādī in the early thirteenth century marks a clear departure from the earlier tradition, which reflects a cuisine from the ninth to tenth centuries, in that a substantial number of dishes and ingredients no longer appear. The fact that some of those are found in the Andalusian manuals would indicate that the Abbasid elements arrived in Spain no later than the end of the twelfth century, presumably much earlier. And so, it is perhaps ironic that some of the earliest aspects of Abbasid gastronomy should have been preserved in al-Andalus long after they had disappeared from their original birthplace.

Opulent Abbasid living (which was itself patterned on that of the Sasanian Persians) was not the only Eastern import. Andalusian – and North African – rulers also filled their botanical gardens with exotic produce from the Mashriq. For instance, the park surrounding the palace of 'Abd al-Raḥmān I (756–88) in Córdoba, al-Ruṣāfa, was home to plants from all over the world, including for the first time a particularly prized variety of Syrian pomegranate, the *safarī*, and the date palm.

Another keen collector, 'Abd al-Raḥmān II (822–52), introduced a kind of fig from Constantinople, while the chief minister at Córdoba, al-Manṣūr (d. 1002), is responsible for the arrival of the sour orange (*nāranj*) and the planting of the Patio de los Naranjos in Córdoba. The ruler of Almería, al-Mu'taṣim Ibn Ṣumādiḥ (1051–91) started to grow bananas and sugar cane in his palace gardens. But it was not mere window dressing the rulers were interested in; the famous botanical garden in Toledo was managed by two of Spain's leading agronomists, Ibn Baṣṣāl (eleventh century) and Ibn Wāfid (1007–1074), who used it as a laboratory for their experiments on grafting, crop rotation, and fertilization.[6] The former scholar even went to the East to collect seeds and plants by order of the Toledan ruler, al-Ma'mūn (d. 1075). His journey took him to Egypt, the Arabian Peninsula, Syria, Iraq, Iran and even northern India. He may have returned with, among other things, a tulip, which would bring forward the date of introduction of this flower in Europe by some 500 years.[7]

Andalusian scholars would complete their education in the East and return to put into practice the knowledge they had acquired. These included the famous physician Abū Marwān Ibn Zuhr (d. 1162) – known in the West as Avenzoar – who had lengthy residences in Kairouan and Cairo, where he practised medicine for many years.[8] Indeed, the traditional narrative of Eastern scientific dominance is belied by a considerable movement in the other direction, with Andalusian scholarship being exported to the East. The two most prominent examples of this were the leading polymaths of the age (and fellow Córdobans born a mere fourteen years apart): the philosopher Ibn Rushd – the Latin Averroës (1126–1198) – and the Jewish physician Maimonides (d. 1204), known in Arabic as Ibn Maymūn.

Once back home, these scholars would maintain contacts with their networks. For instance, the Egyptian physician Nasṭās Ibn Jurajī (*fl.* early tenth century) wrote a *Risāla fī 'l-bawl* ('Treatise on urine') for his Córdoban Christian colleague Yazīd Ibn Rūmān al-Andalusī, possibly at the request of the latter, to assist him in the treatment of his patients.[9] There was also a prolific book trade from East to West as rulers and nobility extended their libraries with precious manuscripts in all fields of learning. For instance, the work by the father of modern surgery, the Cordóban al-Zahrāwī (Abulcasis, d. 1013), was informed by his readings of the works of Near Eastern scholars such as Sābūr Ibn Sahl (d. 869), Qusṭā Ibn Lūqā (d. 912), and al-Rāzī (d. 925 or 935). This is also how the 'Canon of Medicine' (*al-Qānūn fī 'l-ṭibb*) by Ibn Sīnā (known in the West as Avicenna) reached the Peninsula, though this historic event was clearly not viewed with due importance at the

6 Watson 1983: 89, 90, 118, 119.

7 Hernández Bermejo & García Sánchez 2009.

8 Ibn Abī Uṣaybiʿa 2020: 13.60. On this physician, see See *EI*², s.v. 'Ibn Zuhr', (R. Arnaldez), *EI*³, s.v. 'Banū Zuhr' (C. Álvarez Millán); R. Kuhne Brabant & C. Álvarez Millán in Lirola Delgado 2004–17: VI, 352–68; García Sánchez 1995b.

9 Ibn Abī Uṣaybiʿa 2020: 13.14.

time, if we are to believe the account relayed by the historian Ibn Abī Uṣaybiʿa (d. 1270):

> A certain merchant brought a copy of [Ibn Sīnā's] book from Iraq to al-Andalus. It had been executed extremely beautifully, and he presented it as a gift to Abū l-ʿAlāʾ ibn Zuhr as a way of ingratiating himself with him because he had never seen the book before. But when ibn Zuhr examined the *Canon* (*al-Qānūn*) he criticized and rejected it. He did not deposit it in his library, but decided instead to cut it into strips and to use them to write prescriptions for his patients![10]

Ibn Baṣṣāl was not the only Andalusian scholar to conduct scientific research farther afield. A contemporary of al-Tujībī, and author of a monumental encyclopedia of plants, foods and medicines (*al-Jāmiʿ li-mufradāt al-adwiya wa 'l-aghdhiya*, 'Compilation of Simple Drugs and Foodstuffs'), the Seville-born botanist and pharmacologist Ibn al-Bayṭār (d. 1248) undertook multiple expeditions in the East to collect and catalogue plants. The Córdoban physician Ibn Juljul (d. *ca.* 994), for his part, referred to Persian traders as the source for his work supplementing Dioscorides's *De materia medica*.[11]

Subsequent emirs held on to al-Andalus, with varying degrees of success, until the advent of ʿAbd al-Raḥmān III (*r.* 912–61), who also proclaimed himself caliph (929) – that is to say, the successor of the Prophet Muḥammad as leader of the Muslim community, the *umma*. At no point, however, were the Muslims able to control the entire Peninsula, large swathes of which remained under Christian control.

By the start of the second millennium, things took a turn for the worse with the fall of the Córdoban caliphate in 1031. In its final decade, the territory had started to fall apart before disintegrating with the emergence of the so-called 'party kings', known in Arabic as *Mulūk al-ṭawāʾif* (*reyes de taifas* in Spanish), which refers to the rulers of Muslim principalities known as 'party states', some forty in total. This chaotic fragmentation resulted in a dramatic reversal of the power

---

10 *Ibid.*, 13.61.

11 Dietrich 1993: Nos. 40, 50

balance in favour of adjacent Christian rulers, who were aided by the internal conflicts between the *taifas*, while further weakening them by charging them a protection levy. This period marks the beginning of the so-called 'Reconquista', with the loss of a number of cities to the Castilians in the middle of the century.

A turning point came with the conquest of Toledo by the Christian King Alfonso VI (*r.* 1072–1109) in 1085. This was quite the wake-up call for the party states, whose rulers realized that the writing was on the wall, and that it would be just a matter of time before all of them would suffer the same fate. They also realized that they could not solve the problem by themselves, and therefore sought help from their religious brethren in North Africa. The Almoravids (*al-murābiṭūn,* 'those bound together [in truth or piety]') were a Berber confederation of Saharan desert tribes (around seventy in total), the Ṣanhāja, which controlled an area roughly corresponding to present-day Morocco. Their emir agreed to help, but, unsurprisingly, this came at a cost, and under the leadership of the most important tribe, the Lamtūna, who were known for wearing face veils (*lithām*), they quickly gained control of all of the *taifas*, thus marking the end of al-Andalus as an independent – or self-contained – political entity for the first time since the eighth century.

During the Almoravid reign, which lasted some sixty years, the Christians continued their attacks on various fronts, conquering Valencia (1094–1101) and Saragossa (1118), the latter giving the Crown of Aragon control over the Ebro Valley and its agricultural riches. But this was only half of the problem facing the Almoravids. To the south, in their North African homeland, they were threatened by a new, powerful rival – also Berber in origin – the Almohads, *al-muwahhidūn* ('those professing the unity of God'). They were followers of the reformist puritan doctrine of Muḥammad Ibn Tūmart (d. 1130), which was based on the concept of *tawḥīd* ('divine unity'). The fight on two fronts ultimately proved too much, and in 1147 the Almohads took the Almoravid capital Marrakech and established their rule in al-Andalus.

This changing of the guard exemplified the cycle of rise and decline of dynasties as explained by the great Tunisian historian Ibn Khaldūn (1332–1406) as follows: the Almoravids obliterated the party kings as they no longer had a group feeling (*'aṣabiyya*), whereas the

Almoravids, in turn, were overpowered by the Almohads because they had a stronger group feeling and were more deeply rooted in desert life, supported by religion-based power.[12]

The conflict between the Almohads and Almoravids was also an ideological one, in that they opposed the latter's reliance on the books of the Mālikī school of law rather than the Qur'ān and *ḥadīth* (the sayings of the Prophet). The expansionist drive of the Almohads was nothing short of spectacular; starting in 1146, they cut a wide swathe across the Northern African coast, taking Tunis in 1160.

In al-Andalus, earlier victories had emboldened Christian powers, which were able to take advantage of the Almoravid–Almohad power struggle to make more gains, including Tortosa (1148) and Lisbon (1147). It took Almohad reinforcements from across Morocco to consolidate their position and defeat Alfonso VIII's Castilian forces at the Battle of Alarcos (1195).

Throughout these political upheavals, al-Andalus continued to be a centre of learning, culture and science. The region also made significant contributions to Arabic literature, with the creation of new genres of strophic poetry like the *zajal* and the *muwashshaḥ*.[13]

In the early thirteenth century, Christian armies inflicted severe punishment, starting with a humiliating defeat of Muslim forces at Las Navas de Tolosa (known to Arab historians as al-ʿUqāb) in 1212 by a combined force of Castilians, Navarrese and Aragonese. This opened the way to the Guidalquivir valley and marked the end of Almohad rule in al-Andalus. But worse was yet to come, in the shape of a general uprising, the Castilian conquest of Córdoba (1236), and the Aragonese occupation of Valencia (1238). Like dominoes, the Muslim states tumbled in rapid succession – Murcia (1243), Jaén (1246), Seville (1248) and Cadiz (1265) – reducing the Muslim presence to a mere toehold in Granada.

Spain was a multi-faith space that included Jews, Muslims and Christians. As the Reconquista progressed, a new group emerged, known in Spanish as *mudéjar* – a term derived from the Arabic *mudajjan* ('tributary') to denote Muslims who remained in Christian-controlled territory where they were subject to tribute. This mirrored the status of

12 Rosenthal [Ibn Khaldūn] 1986: I, 316, 321. For a recent survey of the Almoravids and Almohads, see Berenson 2016.

13 For an overview, see Menocal *et al.* 2000.

the *dhimmi* in Muslim-controlled territories: non-Muslims guaranteed protection of worship in exchange for the payment of a special tax (*jizya*). The situation of Muslims living within what is known in Islamic law as the *Dār al-Ḥarb* ('House of War') or *Dār al-Kufr* ('House of Unbelief') was, then as now, a fraught topic, as Muslims were enjoined to reside only in Islamic territory, the *Dār al-Islām* ('House of Islam'). It is perhaps telling of the perception of those who remained that the word *mudajjan* also means 'tamed, domesticated', and is a cognate of *dawājin* ('poultry').

The Iberian Peninsula was not the only battleground that pitted Muslim against Christian; this was, of course, still the age of the crusades. After initial Christian victories and the carving out of four states in the Levant during the First Crusade (1096–99), the thirteenth century marked a reversal as a result of crushing punishment meted out by the Mamluks. In the midst of the Mamluk rise, another formidable warrior force swept in from the East. Originally from the steppes of East Asia, the Mongols advanced rapidly across the continent, conquering Iran and laying waste to Baghdad.

In addition to conflict, religion – or, rather, the pilgrimage – was another reason for travel for Christians and Muslims from the Iberian Peninsula, as they headed east towards their respective holy sites. For Andalusian scholars, the pilgrimage was often combined with a quest for knowledge (*ṭalab al-ʿilm*), as they sought instruction in the great Islamic seats of learning, such as Cairo, Damascus and Baghdad. It is therefore no surprise that the region produced a large number of travelogues (*riḥla*), starting with the seminal work of the Valencia-born Ibn Jubayr (1145–1217).[14]

Trade, too, never ceased to connect the Muslim East and South with the Christian North. Merchants of all faiths crisscrossed the Mediterranean, carrying goods from as far east as China, and as far north as Scandinavia. Much of Andalusian trade consisted of manufactured goods, and the region was famous for its linen, silk (including a variety made waterproof with wax), brocades and ceramics. It was also a hub for the fur, gold and slave trades.[15] The importance of al-Andalus as a centre for trade was such that international merchants had local agents to represent them.

14 See Newman 2018.

15 On the trading links of al-Andalus, see Constable 1994.

Enmity between religious communities did not, generally, disrupt trade, and Christian merchants were able to conduct their business without fear of molestation; a ninth-century fatwa (legal opinion), for instance, prohibited the capture of Christian ships with merchants on board. The same safe passage was also afforded to Muslim pilgrims, who often travelled East on Christian ships.

These trading routes coincided with routes of discovery. The thirteenth century saw the European discovery of the Far East, with the extraordinary adventures and accounts of people like the Venetian Marco Polo, who from the 1270s to the 1290s journeyed to Asia along the Silk Road, ending up as a diplomat at the court of the Great Kublai Khan, the Mongol ruler. The Flemish monk William of Rubruck was there before Marco Polo, but with a rather different objective – to convert the Mongols and thus create a lethal ally against the Muslims. However, all of them were preceded by many centuries by Muslim traders, and the earliest descriptions of life in China were written in Arabic, in the ninth century.[16]

The thirteenth century witnessed great scholarship and science in the Christian West as well, including the contributions of Robert Grosseteste, Francis of Assisi, Roger Bacon and Thomas Aquinas. By the end of the thirteenth century, no fewer than twelve universities were in operation in Europe, three of which were on Iberian soil (Salamanca, Coimbra and Valladolid).

Science and culture underpinned many cross-community exchanges. The translation movement from Arabic into Latin started in eleventh-century Italy (Salerno) but reached its acme in Toledo in the twelfth century, before the centre of this activity shifted to Sicily in the thirteenth century, in the reign of Frederick II (1194–1250), who is said to have been conversant in Arabic. Palermo had been the temporary home of possibly Islam's greatest geographer, the Moroccan al-Sharīf al-Idrīsī (1100–1165), who wrote a monumental geography of the known world. This text included a number of maps, which served as a key to a planisphere he had made for the Norman king of Sicily, Roger II (1095–1154) – presumably in pursuit of his expansionist aims. The book is entitled *Kitāb Nuzhat al-mushtāq fi ikhtirāq al-āfāq* ('The Book

16 The account is entitled *Akhbār al-Ṣīn wa 'l-Hind* ('News of China and India'); see Mackintosh-Smith & Montgomery 2014.

of Excursions Across the Horizons') – or, in reference to the author's patron, *Kitāb Rujār* ('The Book of Roger').

Though most of the Latin translations were in the medical field, there was an interest in other areas as well. The university of Bologna, for instance, became a centre of 'Averroism', which related to the commentaries of Aristotle's work by Ibn Rushd. The translation movement introduced Arabic sciences – especially medicine – into Christian Europe, as well as affording access to ancient Greek sources whose originals had been lost.

Not surprisingly in light of its frontier location, it was also on the Iberian Peninsula that the Qur'ān was translated for the first time, by Robert of Ketton (d. 1157), at the instruction of the Abbot of Cluny, Peter the Venerable (*ca.* 1092–1156). Like the translations of other Muslim texts, it was weaponized to serve as a tool to refute Islam as part of the anti-Muslim campaign waged in Latin Christendom at the time. Christian missionaries journeyed to the East to acquire the language and obtain texts and information the better to fight the 'heretics' and support their evangelizing efforts.

One of these was the Dominican missionary pilgrim Riccoldo da Monte Croce (1243–1320), who spent some ten years in Baghdad. He also travelled around the region, even working as a camel-driver in the deserts of Persia and Arabia before returning to his native Italy as a formidable Arabist. He put his experiences and knowledge to use in the writing of virulently anti-Islamic pamphlets, such as *Liber Contra Legem Sarracenorum* ('Book Against the Saracen Law'), a detailed refutation of the Qur'ān.[17]

In Muslim Spain, the Christian translation movement was not exactly viewed favourably. In his book on market regulations, the Seville legist Ibn 'Abdūn al-Tujībī (*fl.* twelfth century) warned his coreligionists not to 'sell scientific books to Jews or Christians, except those that are related to their faiths, as they translate these works and attribute them to their coreligionists and bishops, even though they are written by Muslims!'[18]

---

17 On Riccoldo, see George-Tvrtković 2012.

18 Ibn 'Abdūn [Lévi-Provençal 1955]: 57 (trans., 91). On this author, see *EI*³, s.v. 'Ibn 'Abdūn' (Alejandro García Sanjuán). On regulations regarding the religious communities, see García-Sanjuán 2008.

It was the translation of another polemical religious text that would have a more lasting legacy in European Christian history. Titled *Kitāb al-mi'rāj* ('Book of the Ladder'), the story was based on a Qur'ānic verse (17:1), and described the Prophet Muḥammad's nocturnal journey to the seven heavens. In 1264, King Alfonso X ('the Wise') commissioned a translation into French and Latin of an earlier (now lost) Castilian version, made by his private physician, Abraham of Toledo.[19] The translator selected for the new renditions was the king's notary, an Italian by the name of Bonaventura da Siena. It was through this translation that Tuscany's most famous son, Dante Alighieri (1265–1321), probably became acquainted with the text, which inspired some aspects of the *Divine Comedy*. It is unclear when or how Dante gained access to it, but one of the likely scenarios is that it was through his mentor Brunetto Latini (1220–94), who had been sent to Alfonso on a diplomatic mission and happened to visit Toledo, where his fellow Tuscan Bonaventura was engaged in the translation. It is even less of a stretch to imagine that Dante would have been interested in this text, in light of the number of Arabic and Muslim references in the *Comedy*. These include the Prophet Muḥammad and the fourth caliph of Islam, 'Alī Ibn Abī Ṭālib (656–61), as well as figures such as the ruler Saladin (Ṣalāḥ al-Dīn, 1137–93), Ibn Sīnā, and Ibn Rushd. In fact, it has been suggested that the *Kitāb al-mi'rāj* was not the only Islamic or Arabic source to have inspired Dante.

Translations from Arabic into Latin in the period also covered the culinary arts, thus providing textual evidence of an Arab influence on European cooking. Tantalizingly little is known about the context or motivation driving a physician from Padua by the name of Iambobinus of Cremona in the year 1300 to translate some eighty-two recipes, chosen seemingly at random from a pharmacological encyclopedia, entitled *Minhāj al-bayān fīmā yasta'miluhu al-insān* ('The Pathway of Explanation Regarding that which Human Beings Use'), compiled by the Baghdadi physician Ibn Jazla (d. 1100).[20]

---

19 Both the French and Latin translations have come down to us: *Livre de l'Eschiele Mahomet* (dated 4 May 1264; Bodleian, Laud Misc. 537), *Liber Scale Machometi* (Biblioteca Apostolica Vaticana, *Vat. lat.* 4072; BNF ms. lat. 6064). For a discussion of the relationship between the *Kitāb al-mi'rāj* and the *Divine Comedy*, see, for instance, Wenzel 2014: 52–67; Asín Palacios 1919. For a broader discussion of Islamic aspects in Dante's work, see Ziolkowski 2015.

20 In the early fifteenth century, the recipe collection was translated into German,

Murcia was one of the newly reconquered towns; it was served by the port of Cartagena, and was equidistant between Valencia and Almería – a five-day journey away from each, and ten days from Córdoba.

This is where the protagonist of our story was born, shortly before the death of his fellow Murcian, the mystic Ibn al-ʿArabī (1165–1240), one of Islam's greatest philosophers.

Like so many places, it had seen its fair share of tribulations, particularly as it was the object of desire of the adjacent kingdoms of Almería, Denia, Valencia and Granada. After the fall of the Umayyad Caliphate, Murcia was governed by Almería (1016–38), followed by a brief spell of independence. This ended when it had to submit to Seville (1078) and later on to the Almoravids (1093). In the twelfth century, it once again became a city state, but could not withstand Almohad expansion.

The Murcians were never enthusiastic subjects, to put it mildly. The city was the seat of power of Ibn Mardanīsh (d. 1172), who for several decades was the overlord of the eastern part of al-Andalus and was able to fight off the Almohad onslaught by making common cause with the Castilians. Against this backdrop, it is perhaps not surprising that, after the Almohad defeat at Las Navas de Tolosa, it was in Murcia that the spark was lit for what was to become a general uprising against the Almohads across al-Andalus.

In 1228, Murcia was once again going it alone when Muḥammad Ibn Hūd formally declared independence from the Almohads. This would be the final spell of independence in its history, though, as fifteen years later, in 1243, the city surrendered to the future King Alfonso X and became a Castilian vassal. Under the terms of the agreement, the Muslim population was allowed to continue as before, in terms of their religion, system of justice and way of life. In exchange, they had to accept the payment of tribute, military occupation, and Christian settlers on land sold or relinquished by Muslim owners. However, increasing Christian encroachment led to discontent among the Muslim population, culminating in an uprising by the Mudéjars in 1264. Murcia was briefly ruled by the rebels, but soon found itself under Castilian reign again. This marked the beginning of

under the title *Daz púch von den chósten* ('The Book of Dishes'). See Martellotti 2001; Weiss Adamson 2006.

a redistribution – and conversion – of the Muslim space as it became increasingly Christianized.

The city was also mentioned in the geographical literature. Al-Idrīsī, who probably studied in Córdoba, described twelfth-century Murcia as follows:

> It is the capital of the province of Tudmīr and is situated on a plain on the banks of the White River [Segura river]. The outskirts are flourishing and populous and, like the city, surrounded by robust walls and fortifications. The suburbs are traversed by running water. As for the city, it was built on one of the banks of the river, and can be reached by means of a boat bridge. There are mills constructed on ships, like the mills of Saragossa, which can be moved from one place to another, as well as a number of gardens, orchards, arable land and vineyards planted with fig trees. The city also controls various strong castles, important towns and areas of incomparable beauty.[21]

Writing a little later, the Byzantine-born Yāqūt (d. 1229) included Murcia in his monumental *Muʿjam al-Buldān* ('Dictionary of Countries'). He said it was called Tudmīr, after the Syrian city of Tadmur (Palmyra), and was surrounded by trees and gardens.[22]

The Granadan scholar-traveller Ibn Saʿīd (1214–1286), who would have visited Murcia when al-Tujībī was still there, wrote that it was a great and noble city known for the craftsmanship of its gold-embroidered silk clothes. He also singled out some of its famous landmarks on its outskirts, such as Arrixaca (*al-Rishāqa*) and Lebrilla (*al-Harillā*), as well as an apparently magical mountain, Ayl, which was surrounded by parks.[23] This information was subsequently included in the geographical manual *Taqwīm al-Buldān* ('Survey of Countries') by the Syrian scholar-prince Abū 'l-Fidā' (d. 1331), who compared Murcia to Seville in terms of its large number of gardens and recreational

21 al-Idrīsī 1866: 194–5 (trans., 236–7).
22 Yāqūt 1977: V, 107.
23 Ibn Saʿīd 1970: 140, 167; 1953: II, 245–6.

spaces, identifying it as one of the principal cities in the eastern part of al-Andalus.[24]

Very little is known about the author of the cookery book.[25] His full name is Aḥmad Ibn Abū 'l-Ḥasan ʿAlī Ibn Muḥammad Ibn Abī 'l-Qasim Ibn Muḥammad Ibn Abī Bakr Ibn Razīn al-Tujībī al-Shaqūrī al-Mursī.[26] He was born in Murcia in 626AH/1228–29 CE, but the family's origins went back to Castillo de Segura (Shaqūr). The ethnonym al-Tujībī refers to an affiliation – whether real or alleged – with the Tujīb tribe (Banū Tujīb),[27] an Arab dynasty which rose to prominence in the *ṭawā'if* era. In the tenth and eleventh centuries, they assumed power in the so-called Upper March (*al-thaghr al-aʿlā*) area, and ruled the two city states of Zaragoza and Almería.

Being a member of the *ulamā'* class, Ibn Razīn was trained in the religious sciences by leading scholars of the day before leaving his native town when it fell to the Christians, in 1247–48. As with so many thousands of his fellow Andalusian Muslims, his journey took him to Morocco, where the Almohads had been overthrown by the Marinids, a Berber tribe. He was accompanied by his uncle, Abū 'l-Ḥasan Nabīl al-Rūmī, a freed slave (possibly of Greek origin, as his name would indicate), who was also a religious scholar. Their first stop was Ceuta (Sabta), which was then a scholarly centre and thus allowed the young Ibn Razīn to continue his studies. But after two years he struck out on his own and moved further east to Bijāya (Béjaïa) – more commonly known in history by its French name Bougie – which was then the second-largest port (after Tunis) of the western Mediterranean and was ruled by the powerful Ḥafṣid dynasty,[28] the successors to the Almohads in the region. Its first emir, Abū Zakariyyā' Yaḥyā (1228–49) – a rebel Almohad commander recognized by Andalusian rulers as their liege – took control of large parts of Algeria and Morocco.

24 Abū 'l-Fidā' 1840: 178, 179.

25 The information here relies on Delgado 2004–17: IV, 469–73; Binsharīfa 1983; *idem* 2009.

26 This is the name that appears in al-Marrākushī 2012: I, 729–30 (No. 851). In one of the manuscripts of the text (Gayangos XVI, fol. 1v.), it is given as Abū 'l-Ḥasan ʿAlī Muḥammad Ibn Abī al-Qāsim Ibn Muḥammad Ibn Abī Bakr Ibn Razīn al-Tujībī al-Andalusī.

27 *EI*², 'Tuḏjīb' (P. Guichard).

28 For an exhaustive survey of this dynasty, see Brunschvig 1940–47.

During his stay in Bijāya, al-Tujībī became a part of its thriving scholarly and literary community, and expanded his studies to include the secular arts. It was to the Ḥafṣid capital, Tunis, that he moved at the end of the decade, and there he would remain until his death on 17 July 1293. At the time of his arrival, the city had a large Andalusian community, many of whose members were part of the elite, and occupied leading positions in society. One may speculate therefore that al-Tujībī might have been tempted by the prospects offered to someone with his background and training, which would make him eminently suited for a scribal or secretarial position at the court. The itinerary was a well-trodden one, and among the Andalusian immigrants in this period, there was a family from Seville that included a certain Abū Bakr Muḥammad Ibn Khaldūn, the great-grandfather of the historian. It is certain that the two men would have met, as Abū Bakr was briefly in charge of the finances of the Ḥafṣid state.[29] Praising the many inventions and cultural advances in Muslim Spain, Abū Bakr's descendant explains that these were introduced into Tunis by the Spanish exiles, but that the country had not achieved the required level of civilization to fully benefit from them.[30] He adds that the Andalusian influence commingled with Egyptian customs as a result of the intensive contacts between the two regions.[31] Unfortunately, the young émigré's stay in Tunis did not live up to his aspirations and the scholar Ibn Rushayd (d. 1321), who met al-Tujībī in 1287, reported that the latter never managed to fulfil his potential and was barely able to provide for his family. Why this should have been the case remains a mystery, particularly since his renown as a scholar never waned; the traveller al-ʿAbdarī (d. 1289) offered high praise for the breadth of al-Tujībī's scholarship and the quality of his teaching.

It was during his residence in Tunis that the city became the object of the eighth – and last – Crusade. The backdrop was a familiar one, with deep historical roots and precedents; North Africa – and Tunis, in particular – had been the springboard for the Muslim conquest of Sicily, while Christian rulers feared the threat the region posed to the northern Mediterranean.

This was certainly not a figment of their imagination, particularly in

29 He also wrote a manual for official scribes; see Lévi-Provençal 1955: 280–8.

30 Ibn Khaldūn 2005: II, 284–5 (trans., II, 349–51).

31 *Ibid.*, 225 (trans., II, 290).

light of the expansionist policy of the newly founded Ḥafṣid dynasty. It was a preoccupation particularly for those on the front line, like Charles of Anjou, the king of Sicily, who succeeded in changing the itinerary of the Crusade initiated by his brother Louis IX (St Louis) of France to include a call on Tunis *en route* to the Near East. The conquest of Tunis would have the additional advantage of cutting off a major supply route to its ally, Egypt. Secondly, the self-proclaimed Ḥafṣid caliph al-Mustanṣir (1249–77) maintained very good relations with Christian powers on the other side of the Mediterranean, such as Aragon and the Italian republics – tribute had been paid to Sicily during the reign of Charles's predecessor, King Manfred, as part of a trade agreement that guaranteed the right to maritime trade and the importation of Sicilian wheat.[32]

According to Louis's confessor, the French king was attracted to Tunisia because of the prospect of converting its ruler, since the latter had allegedly let it be known – through his envoys to Paris in October 1269 – that he would be baptized if a Christian army could come and assist him in convincing his population.[33] Though it has been readily accepted for centuries, there is no truth to this fanciful claim; rather, it should be regarded as an expression of a common medieval Christian fantasy in which Muslims innately craved conversion – a fantasy nourished by the highly improbable notion that the caliph had requested crusader troops to invade his territory.

The same period saw the establishment in Tunis of sizeable Christian trading communities, predominantly from Spain and Italy, concomitant with the appointment of the first European consuls to protect the newcomers' interests.

The French and Sicilian Crusader forces could also rely on English and Scottish troops commanded by the heir to the English throne, Edward Longshanks. But things did not exactly get off to a good start; shortly after the French fleet landed at Carthage in July 1270, the troops were crippled by disease, and Saint Louis himself died a little over a month later from dysentery. In the face of the combined armies, al-Mustanṣir decided that a treaty would be the better part of valour; but, in addition to indemnity, he was forced to accept a resumption of tribute to Sicily.

32 *EI*³, s.v. 'Ḥafṣids' (H. R. Idris).
33 Brunschvig 1940–47: I, 55–65; Riley-Smith 1987: 174–6.

Thus was disaster averted. One can only imagine the dread al-Tujībī and his fellow Andalusian exiles, many of whom were eager to take up arms, must have felt at the prospect of Christian forces invading their new home, on Muslim soil.

The Book

The present culinary treatise is entitled *Faḍālat*[34] *al-khiwān fī ṭayyibāt al-ṭaʿām wa ʾl-alwān* ('Remainders on the Table as regards Delightful Foods and Dishes').

It is one of ten known remaining Arabic works of its kind, which span a period of some five centuries (tenth to fifteenth) and a geographical area from al-Andalus to Egypt, Iraq, and Syria; combined, they comprise well over 4,200 recipes.[35] Besides al-Tujībī's text, Muslim Spain produced another, anonymous cookery book, containing 498 recipes, which most probably dates from the same century, or possibly earlier.[36] For many years, it was known through a single manuscript (BNF Ar7009), copied in 1604, and edited by the Spanish Arabist Huici Miranda in 1961–62. In the early 2000s, the Moroccan scholar ʿAbd al-Ghanī Abū ʾl-ʿAzm discovered another copy of the same text from the middle of the nineteenth century, entitled *Anwāʿ al-ṣaydala fī alwān al-aṭʿima* ('Pharmaceuticals in Food Dishes'), which he edited and published in 2003.[37]

In an interesting twist of history, copies of al-Tujībī's text arrived in Europe around the same time, in the middle of the nineteenth century, as a result of purchases made by Spanish and German manuscript scholar-collectors.

---

34 Rather than *fuḍāla* (e.g. van Gelder 2000: 151, 163) or *fiḍāla* (García Sánchez 2007). See Kazimirski 1860: II, 608; Lane 1863–74: VI, 2412. The Arabic *khiwān* refers to a raised table, or one that does not have food on it, in contrast with *māʾida*, which does.

35 See Introduction in Ibn Mubārak Shāh 2020 for an overview and discussion.

36 The text survived in two manuscripts. The oldest copy, which lacks a title, is held at the Bibliothèque nationale de France in Paris (Ar7009) and was completed on 13 Ramaḍān 1012 AH/14 February 1604 CE. The Arabic text was edited by Huici Miranda in 1961–62 (reprinted in 1965) and by Catherine Guillaumond in 1991. The Moroccan manuscript is dated to 18 Dhūʾ l-Qaʿda 1272 AH/21 July 1856 CE. The BNF mss has been translated into Spanish (1966; 2nd edn 2005), English, and French (2017). References to the Arabic text will be to Abū ʾl-ʿAzm's edition (referred to hereinafter as *Anwāʿ*) and the BNF manuscript.

37 See Ibn Mubārak Shāh 2020: xiv–xv, note c.

The first was the Spanish Arabist Pascual de Gayangos y Arce (1809–97), a former pupil of the foremost scholar of Oriental languages in Europe at the time, Silvestre de Sacy (1758–1838) at the École spéciale des Langues orientales in Paris.[38] In October 1848, just a few years after taking up the Chair of Arabic at the University of Madrid (1843–47), Gayangos went to Morocco with a view to acquiring manuscripts.[39] In a handwritten note signed by Gayangos (dated Tangiers, 5 October 1850) and appended to the al-Tujībī manuscript, the text was bought in Tétouan from a 'Moor' (*moro*) called "As-senúsi" (al-Sanūsī), for a price of 25 *mitscales*, equivalent to 250 Spanish reals'. The manuscript, which is held at the Library of the Real Academia de la Historia in Madrid (de Gayangos XVI), is unfortunately undated, but the editor of the text, Muḥammad Ibn Shaqrūn, speculated that it was produced in the reign of the Moroccan Sultan Mawlay Ismā'īl Ibn al-Sharīf (*r.* 1662–1727), based on indications that it was present in Morocco in 1705–6 (1118 AH),[40] though this should more appropriately be viewed as a *terminus ante quem*.

The Gayangos manuscript includes the name of the author as 'the jurist, the man of letters, the masterful scribe, the most erudite' Abū 'l-Ḥasan 'Alī Ibn Muḥammad Ibn Abī al-Qāsim Ibn Muḥammad Ibn Abī Bakr Ibn Razīn al-Tujībī al-Andalusī – may Allah have mercy on his soul' – thus indicating that the copy was made after the death of the author.[41] The manuscript comprises 134 numbered folios (fifteen lines per page) and is written in a careless but very clearly legible Maghribi hand, with occasional vowelling, mostly restricted to titles, and some marginalia. There is a consistent use of catchwords, with headings in black, red or blue ink. It is most likely it was made in Morocco, possibly even in the nineteenth century. Unfortunately, the text lacks a total of eight chapters, six from the seventh section and two from the tenth.

In the same period, but on the other end of the Muslim world, the German Orientalist Johann Gottfried Wetzstein (1815–1905), who was Prussian consul in Damascus (1848–62), was also diligently amassing

38 On Gayangos, see Álvarez Millán & Heide 2008.
39 See Vilar 1997; Terés Sádaba 1975.
40 al-Tujībī 2012: 21.
41 Gayangos XVI, fol. 1v.

manuscripts to send back to Berlin. One of them was al-Tujībī's text, which is still held at the Staatsbibliothek, and was entered in the catalogue[42] as a 'Cookbook (*Kochbuch*) [...] preceded by some remarks on the use of cooking utensils and on the need to eat the heavy dishes first at the table'.

The manuscript, which contains seventy-seven numbered folios and twenty-five lines per page (17×12 cm), is written in a crisp and elegant *naskh* script, with occasional diacritics (gemination of consonants and indefinite accusative endings) but almost no vowelling, and very few marginal corrections. There is a consistent use of catchwords, whereas headings and titles are in red ink. It is significant for a number of reasons, even though it is incomplete, containing about three-quarters of the full text, and only goes up to Section Seven, Chapter Three, with the text breaking off just a few lines into the last recipe (No. 365).

It is dated to the month of Dhū 'l-Ḥijja 1211 AH (June 1797), while the title page mentions that the manuscript entered the library al-Sayyid ʿAlī Qudsī al-Ḥasanī on the tenth day of the month of Shaʿbān 1244 AH (Saturday, 4 February 1829). More importantly, the fact that it is written in an Eastern (Mashriqi) hand and produced at such a late date proves the exchanges of Arab culinary texts continued throughout the centuries, testifying to the enduring interest in such texts among the intellectual elites across the Muslim world.

For nearly a century, al-Tujībī's work remained unmentioned. But in 1949 the French scholar Maxime Rodinson briefly referred to the Berlin manuscript in his seminal article on Arabic cooking-related documents, identifying it as a text 'possibly of Maghribi origin' because it includes 'a dish called *ṣanhājī*' (No. 269).[43]

Things changed dramatically when Femando de la Granja started working on an edition and Spanish translation of al-Tujībī's text as part of his doctoral study at the University of Madrid. When the PhD was submitted in 1960, there had only been one other edition of an Arabic cookery book, published almost forty year earlier, in 1934. De la Granja titled his study, which also included a Spanish translation of the recipes, *La cocina arábigo-andaluza según un manuscrito inédito* ('Arab-Andalusian Cuisine in an Unedited Manuscript'). For many

42 Ahlwardt 1889–99: V, 43–5, No. 5473 (= Wetzstein II 1207).

43 Rodinson 1949: 106.

years, it remained unexplored and, in a rather unusual twist to the tale, the sole submitted copy of the dissertation has since then disappeared from the Madrid University library.[44]

The next important date for the dissemination of the text was 1981, when Moroccan scholar Muḥammad Ibn Shaqrūn published his edition of the Arabic text,[45] which relied on the Madrid and Berlin manuscripts, supplemented with extracts held in private ownership. This edition later formed the basis for translations into French[46] and Spanish.[47]

In 2018 I was able to identify another, until then unknown manuscript copy of al-Tujībī's text in the British Library (Or5927, fols. 101r.–204v.).[48] This copy had remained undiscovered because it contains neither the name of the author, nor the title of the work. It is the third in a collection of four treatises, all of which are anonymous: the first is a pharamacopoeia (fols. 1r.–67v.) with recipes for perfumes, syrups, cataplasms, stomachics, electuaries, sniffing medicines, collyria, preserves, and so on. The second deals with dietetics (fols. 68r.–100v.), and the fourth (fols. 205r.–217v.) with the making of various substances including soaps, dyes and fruit waters. It was purchased by the British Library in 1901 from David Fetto, a manuscript dealer in Baghdad. According to the catalogue it should be dated to the fifteenth or sixteenth century, though this is by no means certain.

The manuscript is generally in good condition, though there is some fading, which in some cases hampers reading. There are thirty lines per page, and no marginalia. It is written in a clear Maghribi hand, with enlarged titles in red or black ink, and with occasional text-stops in the form of a Nautilus shell spiral in some section and chapter titles. There is frequent vowelling, but no catchwords. The numbering is modern, with renumbering throughout, and some mis-ordered folios.

44 Prof. Paradela de Alonso, personal communication.

45 It first appeared in Rabat, with both the second and third editions being published in Beirut (Dār al-Gharb al-Islāmī) in 1984 and 2012, respectively.

46 Mohamed Mezzine & Leila Benkirane, *Fudalat al-Khiwan d'ibn Razin Tujibi*, Fez: Publications Association Fès Saïss, 1997.

47 Manuela Marín, *Relieves de las mesas, acerca de las delicias de la comida y los diferentes platos,* Madrid: Trea, 2007.

48 Ibn Mubārak Shāh 2020: xv–xvi, note g. Ellis & Edwards 1912: 47; Hamarneh 1975: 249–50 (Item II.16).

The most significant feature of this manuscript is that it contains the missing chapters mentioned above, as well as other additional material, in total amounting to about forty-five recipes. On the other hand, the British Library copy does lack a few of the recipes that are found in the manuscripts used for the printed edition, while some of the text is illegible in places. As a result, it, too, is incomplete.

In terms of intent and production, Gayangos XVI reveals a number of interesting features in comparison with the BL Or5927 and Wetzstein 1207 copies. Both in style and language it is more rough-and-ready than the other two; besides a higher incidence of colloquial spellings, instructions in the recipes are often more 'compressed', and religious formulae, for instance, are reduced, or omitted altogether.

The anonymous Andalusian treatise is quite corrupted and lacks a clear structure; recipes are listed in a rather haphazard fashion and there is no table of contents. Conversely, al-Tujībī's work is well organized; it is divided into twelve Sections (*aqsām*), each containing up to twelve Chapters (*fuṣūl*), sixty in all, with a total of 480 recipes. The first section includes chapters on breads, *tharīdas* (bread soaked in a broth topped with vegetables and/or meat), pottages, *mujabbanas* (fried cheese buns), and doughnuts. The second section is devoted to the meat of quadrupeds (beef, sheep, goat, game), meat pies and porridges, and sausages. The third section discusses dishes made with various kinds of poultry (goose, chicken, partridge, turtledove, starling, sparrow). And the fourth one focuses on recipes associated with the above-mentioned *Ṣanhājī* Berber tribes. This is followed by sections on fish and eggs, dairy produce (curds, butter, cheese); vegetables (gourds, aubergines, truffles, asparagus, artichokes, mushrooms, spinach, taro); pulses (broad beans, chickpeas, lentils); sweets; fermented condiments, oils, vinegars and pickles; grasshoppers and shrimp; and, finally, hand-washing powders.

Al-Tujībī probably started compiling the book during his exile. Besides being a recipe collection intended for cooks, it is, like other works in the same tradition,[49] an anthology, preserving the culinary heritage of his homeland which he had been forced to flee. He must also have been a keen amateur cook, as well as gourmet. In the introduction he states that he has collected both his favourite recipes,

49 See Ibn Mubārak Shāh 2020.

'and many dishes' invented by him, though one never learns which are which.

In the course of the work, his pride in his Andalusian identity is almost palpable, while it also includes autobiographical elements in the form of dishes associated with areas he had visited. Given that the book is a record of a culinary legacy, one may wonder whether the recipes contained in it were all still being cooked, or if some were included to preserve Andalusian culinary traditions for posterity, or as a service to the sizeable Andalusian diasporic communities in North Africa. Indeed, in a coda to one of the recipes (No. 32) in one of the manuscript copies, it is specified that, 'even if most of the [recipes] will scarcely be made, they deserve to be added because of their exquisiteness. The same applies to most of the chapters in this book.' Naturally, this comes with the caveat that it is impossible to ascertain when – and by whom – this was added, possibly many centuries after the original work was compiled.

The sources employed by al-Tujībī for his work reveal a mixed picture. The single biggest source is the anonymous Andalusian treatise, with over seventy shared recipes – some identical, while others are variations. The Andalusian manual probably preceded al-Tujībī's, but it is equally plausible that both copied from an earlier – or contemporaneous – source that has not survived. This would also explain some scribal errors such as the repetition of certain recipes (for example, Nos. 13 and 14), where mistakes made by copyists are repeated blindly by others. Directly or indirectly, al-Tujībī also drew on other cookery books, some from the Mashriq, which are clearly marked as 'eastern recipes' in the text (Nos. 415–17). Unfortunately, none of the sources is mentioned by name.

In addition to culinary manuals, al-Tujībī availed himself of scientific sources, which remain for the most part likewise unnamed. These include Ibn Zuhr, who acted as court physician to the Almoravid and Almohad dynasties in Seville and in Marrakech. It was to his Almohad patron, the caliph 'Abd al-Mu'min (1130–63), that he dedicated his influential *Kitāb al-aghdhiya* ('Book on Foodstuffs'), from which al-Tujībī quotes a number of passages in his introduction regarding the most appropriate materials to use for cooking containers, though its author is simply referred to as 'one of the physicians'.

Andalusian agricultural manuals constitute another source. Al-Tujībī drew on Abū ʿAbd Allāh al-Ṭighnarī's *Kitāb zuhrat al-bustān wa nuzhat al-adhhān* ('Splendour of the Garden and Recreation of the Minds'), which was written around 1110 and dedicated to the Almoravid governor of Granada,[50] as well as on the works of the Sevillians Ibn al-ʿAwwām (twelfth century)[51] and Ibn Baṣṣāl.[52]

Similarly unstated is the debt al-Tujībī owed to the Kairouan-born physician Ibn al-Jazzār (d. 1004), who is perhaps best known for his *Zād al-musāfir wa qūt al-ḥāḍir* ('Provision for the Traveller and the Nourishment of the Settled'), which was translated into Greek, Latin and Hebrew in the Middle Ages. In its Latin translation (*Viaticum Peregrinantis*) by Constantinus Africanus (1015–87), it became a key teaching resource at European medical schools.[53] It is, however, from Ibn al-Jazzār's *Kitāb fī funūn al-ṭīb wa 'l-ʿiṭr* ('Book on the Arts of Aromatics and Perfumes') that al-Tujībī lifts almost an entire chapter on hand-washing powders (seven recipes in total).

The only source whose title and author are mentioned by name (recipe No. 466) is the *Kitāb al-talkhīṣ* ('The Book of Abridgement'), a multilingual glossary of simple drugs by the eleventh-century Jewish physician and linguist Ibn Janāḥ, known for his work on Hebrew grammar and lexicography.

The format of the recipes also merits some attention. On the one hand, there are a number of similarities with those in other treatises of the period in terms of their structure, with the ingredients usually listed at the beginning, followed by a chronological 'linear' description of the preparation method. Measures are often not specified beyond 'some' or 'a handful of' this or that ingredient. They are written in informal, non-literary Arabic, in keeping with their practical design and intent. As in other collections, many of the recipes are named after a main ingredient (for example, Nos. 111, 207), method of preparation or presentation (for example, No. 125), purported social, ethnic or geographical origin (Nos. 83, 212, 219), or their alleged originator (for

---

50 See *EI²*, s.v. 'al-Ṭighnarī' (E. García Sánchez); García Sánchez 1987–88, 1988, 1990a, 2001.

51 See Hernandez Bermejo & García Sánchez 1988.

52 Both of them wrote a *Kitāb al-Filāḥa* ('Book of Agriculture'). See Jayyusi 1992: 990 *et passim*; García & Carabaza 2009.

53 See Ammar 1994.

example, No. 220). Often, the titles of the recipes are very descriptive (for example, No. 118). A number of identically named recipes can be found in different chapters, and constitute further proof of the author's eclectic use of sources. More unusually, over 30 per cent of recipes are simply identified as 'a dish' or 'another [similar] dish', whereas another fourteen have no title or description at all.

The book tells us a great deal not only about Andalusian cuisine, but also about the history of the early Arab culinary tradition and thus presents a microcosm of medieval Arab cuisine. The recipes identified by al-Tujībī as 'Eastern' can generally be traced back to the early Abbasid gastronomical tradition. But the influence from that part of the Mediterranean is not as straightforward as it might seem. For instance, the earliest precursor of one of the most popular Near Eastern dishes, the *tharīd*, is found in ancient Mesopotamia.

While it may be tempting to view the inclusion of the Eastern recipes as the symptom of some starry-eyed admiration of the 'wonders of the East', it quickly becomes clear that nothing could be further from the truth. Here, we have a proud Andalusian, who wishes to share his admiration for his culinary heritage, which he feels is superior to that of the Mashriq. Already in the introduction, he nails his colours to the mast when condemning the cookery books from the East because they contain many things that 'disgust the ear and should be dismissed, or almost regarded as filthy for human beings, even if, to them, it is the most refined food!'

Al-Tujībī's book has a high number of typically Andalusian dishes – probably more than any other recipe collection. Among them we find *banij* bread (No. 3), *lakhṭij* (No. 38), *zabzīn* (No. 39), *mujabbanas* (Nos. 77-84), *ra's maymūn* (Nos. 68, 152), *fidāwsh* (No. 90), *balāja* (No. 153), *isfiriyya* (No. 181), *ra's barṭāl* (No. 386), *mushamma'* (No. 301), and *qawqan* (No. 471).[54]

In most instances, we are dealing with variations of Eastern dishes, including *tharīda* (also known as *tharīd*) and *harīsa* (No. 188). In some cases, however, dishes acquired a new name as they moved from one region to the next. For instance, the Near Eastern classic vinegar dish, *sikbāj*, becomes a *mukhallal* (No. 196) in al-Andalus, while the

54 Marín 1997 identifies twelve Andalusian dishes in the two cookery books that are not found anywhere else.

above-mentioned *tafāyā* corresponds to the Abbasid *isfīdhbāj*. Today's *tafāyā* is considered a Fez speciality and comes in various guises, such as a lamb stew with almonds, or a confit of onions and raisins serving as a garnish for meat or couscous.

Some dishes, such as *kawāmikh* (fermented condiments) and *judhāba* (No. 221) bear the same name as their Eastern counterpart, but are prepared very differently. In other cases, the similarity in name may be mere coincidence, as in the case of a stewed offal recipe (No. 154), whose name (*qaliya*) denotes a type of dish found in other cookery books, but also simply means 'fried'. Al-Tujībī's book is also the only one that contains a recipe for a wheat *harīsa* (No. 97) – a sweet vegetarian variant of what is usually a savoury meat porridge. A similar change affected the Mashriqi *sanbūsak* ('samosa'), which was transformed from a savoury meat pastry into a delicate sweetmeat (No. 409).

The *tharīda*[55] recipes exemplify a number of features of the medieval Arab culinary tradition, aside from the cross-regional mobility of dishes. Despite its long history, it is a rarity in Near Eastern cookery books – it is found in only two Abbasid sources.[56] This may be explained by the fact that it was generally considered a peasant dish, and thus not fit for elite dining. In Andalusian cuisine, however, the humble *tharīd* was reinvented as a sophisticated banquet showstopper, and al-Tujībī includes the highest number of recipes of any source – twenty-seven all told (Nos. 6-32) – including sweet milk bread puddings (Nos. 26–9), made in a pan or baked in the oven, which may be likened to the so-called 'hasty pudding' of European cooking.

It also illustrates the existence of a uniform basic diet across the population as dishes were adapted to suit different socio-economic strata. Movement between social milieux was very fluid, and worked in both directions. Elite dishes also freely moved down the hierarchy, ingredients and cooking methods being adapted accordingly.

A clearly recognizable direct descendant of the Andalusian *tharīd* can be found in the modern Moroccan *rfissa*, whose name goes back

55 In Andalusian Arabic, the dish appeared as *tharīd*, *tharīdạ*, or *thurda*, all derived from the verb *tharada* ('to crumble'), in reference to its preparation. In Near Eastern sources, the usual form is *tharīd*. Corriente 1997: 83.

56 al-Warrāq 1987: 162 (Chap. 61, 2 recipes), 204–9 (Chap. 83, 12 recipes); *Taṣānīf*, fol. 68r.–v. (3 recipes).

to the medieval *rafīs*, meaning dough kneaded with butter and dusted with sugar,[57] not unlike the Algerian *rfiss*. The term *rfissa* denotes chicken with some vegetables on shredded bread (usually *msemmen*), or a thin crêpe-like pastry known as *trid*, which is often served by itself with a sweet topping. It is usually served on a *metred*, which is now a clay plate, but goes back to something al-Tujībī knew as a *mithrad* – a tureen associated with the *tharīd*.

Recipes often play a role in both the creation and preservation of collective memory. An example is the inclusion of the opulent Ṣanhājī dishes at a time when this dynasty was long gone – not unlike the Abbasid Golden Age of Hārūn al-Rashīd embedding itself into an increasingly factitious Near Eastern consciousness.

The recipes contain numerous clues to the multi-faith, multicultural and multilingual Andalusian space inhabited by the author. There is a dish said to be Jewish (No. 211), some five 'monk's dishes' – but in neither case are there any identifiably religious elements. If anything, this corroborates the claim that, except for ritual occasions, Iberian Muslims, Jews and Christians shared a common diet.

At the linguistic level, there are a number of non-Arabic words – especially Romance and Berber, as well as Persian – with the author often giving names for ingredients in several dialects and languages.[58] There are several instances of Andalusian and North African Arabic terminology differing from Mashriqi usage: fennel is *nāfiʿ* or *basbās* (instead of *rāziyānaj*), sesame is *juljulān* (rather than *simsim*), and sesame oil is identified as *zayt al-simsim* ('oil of sesame'), rather than *shayraj*. This naturally offers vital clues about the birthplace of a dish.

As a result, the text is a significant historical document not only because of its culinary import as a source for regional Andalusian cuisine, but also for the light it can throw on diachronic Arabic linguistics and dialectology.

The Cuisine

When the Arab traveller ʿAbd al-Basīṭ Ibn Khalīl (1440–1514) visited Tunis in 1462, he was invited to a dinner by one Abū 'l-Qāsim al-Gharnāṭī al-Bunyūlī, the leading merchant in Tunis at the time, who, as

57 Corriente 1997: 213.

58 For a wider discussion on the terminology in the book, see Marín 2010.

his name indicates, had Granadan origins. The event was attended by other members of the Andalusian community, and Ibn Khalīl reports the following:

> They prepared an Andalusian dish called *mujabbana*, which is made by mashing fresh cheese by hand until it becomes like dough. Then, semolina [and water] is kneaded into a stiff dough until it acquires the consistency of our *zulābiyya* dough, or even slightly thicker still. Next, a piece of it is gently and skilfully stretched out in the palm of the hand. A piece of the mashed cheese is put on top of it and the dough is folded so that the cheese becomes the filling. It is flattened a bit and then thrown into a pan with oil which is on the fire. Once the piece is fried, it is taken out and sprinkled with crushed sugar, as well as a bit of cumin. All of this was done in front of the gathering by one of the most distinguished members of the community.[59]

This account not only reveals the enduring Andalusian culinary legacy in the diaspora, but also the extent to which it remained deeply embedded in the consciousness of the expatriate community. Far more than a mere act of hospitality, the ceremonious way it was prepared by the host during the actual meal, rather than by his kitchen staff beforehand, produces a carefully preserved communal experience, a ritual act, 'expressing social relations or symbolising social structure',[60] or a structured social event rooted in 'repeated analogies', to borrow May Douglas's words.[61]

Ibn Khalīl brings the scene alive to his home readership by drawing a parallel with another fried dough dish, the *zulābiyya*, which was actually common in North Africa and al-Andalus as well (see recipe No. 73).

This is not to say that dishes from the western Mediterranean did not travel to the East – quite the opposite. The best-known example is probably couscous, a dish of Berber origin that was introduced in

59 Brunschvig 1936: 21 (trans., 75).
60 Goody 1996, 30.
61 Douglas 2001: 240.

al-Andalus in the twelfth century under the Almohads, and spread eastward very early on.[62] Several recipes using it are already found in a thirteenth-century Syrian cookery book,[63] and the Moroccan traveller Ibn Baṭṭūṭa (d. 1369) even encountered it in the Sudan in the fourteenth century.[64] But it was in Egypt that the dish became most popular, and the seventeenth-century Ottoman traveller Evliya Çelebi counted couscous among Egyptian specialities, together with pilaff, Jew's mallow, okra, taro and cauliflower.[65]

We are fortunate to have another report from the same period, this time by an Andalusian who had travelled in the opposite direction. The Malaga-born poet and legal scholar Abū 'Abdallah Ibn al-Azraq (428–69), sometime *qāḍī* (judge) at Granada, undertook several missions to the East – especially Egypt – in order to muster support against the Castilian threat, and eventually settled in Jerusalem. The Algerian biographer al-Maqqarī (1577–1632) preserved a moving poem in which Ibn al-Azraq lamented his separation from his homeland,[66] with the famous opening verse:

> If fate had been just to me
> perhaps I would not have been expelled from my land.
> Now I have no paradise, no home at all.

What little comfort he finds comes from reminiscing about his favourite native foods, while at the same time bemoaning the decline of al-Andalus. Of the seventeen items listed, all but six can be found in the present text,[67] and he even expands on the synaesthetic experience of eating couscous:

---

62 On the early history of couscous, see Brisville 2020.

63 *Wuṣla*, Nos. 6.130–1. Also see Ibn Mubārak Shāh 2020: 29 (note 109).

64 Ibn Baṭṭūṭa 1853–58: IV, 394.

65 Dankoff & Kim 2011: 398.

66 al-Maqqarī 2012: III, 298–303. Also see García Sánchez 1980. On Ibn al-Azraq, see Harvey 2005: 84, 335.

67 These are *mujabbana*, *muthawwama* (No. 30), *isfanj* (Nos. 74–6), *'aṣīda* (No. 67), *ruqāq* (No. 57), *zabzīn* (No. 39), *tafāyā* (Nos. 109–10), *shāshiya* (No. 13), *tharīd* (Section One, Chapter Two), couscous (Nos. 85–9), rice pudding (No. 93). The other foods he mentions are lentils and the unidentified *samansinī* (Dozy 1881: I, 687), the hindquarters of a yearling ram, and *jildat al-farrūj* (chicken fried in a lot of clarified butter; *ibid.*, I, 206).

an excellent dish, very tasty,
especially when it is well mixed,
from which I would raise balls that [when falling]
would produce a noise that would heal my ears.

The Andalusian immigration wave into Tunis during al-Tujībī's time was the first of three such mass movements. The second occurred in 1492, when the *mudéjars* were faced with the choice of conversion, emigration or death, with those that took the first option becoming known as Moriscos. The third wave took place in 1609-12, when the Spanish authorities expelled all Moriscos; some followed the well-trodden routes of their predecessors and settled in Morocco (Fez), Algeria (Tlemcen, Constantine, Annaba), or Tunisia, while others travelled east, to Italy and thence to the Ottoman Empire.[68]

In Tunis, the Andalusian community built its own mosques, such as the one of Subḥān Allāh (in the modern Bab Souika area of the capital). The Tunisian historian Muḥammad Ibn al-Khūja highlighted the influence of the Andalusians on Tunis in terms of crafts (bookbinding and tile-making) and agriculture, as well as cooking and sweets, attributing to them the introduction of *fālūdhaj*.[69] Subsequent waves of immigration reinforced these elements of Andalusian culture in Tunis, as well as adding new ones.

The present text shows the amazing variety and richness of Andalusian cuisine. However, it should be borne in mind that, like the overwhelming majority of cookery books, it largely reflects the habits of the elite – though it does contain numerous indications regarding the food practices across various strata of the population, and even includes a dish made by itinerant shepherds (No. 156). Before discussing some of the salient features of the cuisine more closely, let us turn our attention to the sources.

Very little is known about the culinary situation of the Iberian Peninsula at the time of the invasion of the North African forces in the early eighth century. The diet of Visigothic Spain continued that of Roman-controlled Spain, with a reliance on wheat, millet and barley,

68 See Latham 1957; Jónsson 2007.

69 Ibn al-Khūja 1939: 82–3 (1985: 142–3); Fathia Skhiri, 'Les traditions culinaires andalouses à Testour', in de Epalza & Petit 1973: 349–58; Gobert 1955: 529ff.

a limited range of vegetables (onions, cabbages), and sheep meat. This diet endured in Christian Spain after the Muslim conquest.[70]

The Romans introduced a number of agricultural techniques that greatly expanded agriculture in Spain, driven to a large extent by a thirst for tribute.[71] Their most significant contribution in terms of food was the establishment of an industrial-scale network of salteries on the Iberian Peninsula that produced the salted and fermented fish sauce called *garum* (from the Greek *garos*) – also sometimes known as *liquamen*[72] – the staple Roman condiment. Due to its geographical location and the plentiful supply of fish, Spain – especially its southern part (Baetica) – was a major centre for salteries producing high-quality *garum*, which was exported across the western Roman Empire.[73]

The most important text produced in Visigothic times – or, as some would have it, of the entire Christian Middle Ages – was the encyclopedic *Etymologies* by the archbishop of Seville, Isidorus (d. 636). It was a work of universal knowledge, including foods, which are discussed in its final section.[74] This is particularly relevant, as it influenced the work of another Sevillian, the Andalusian Muslim botanist and scholar Ibn al-Bayṭār, whose discussion of the various types of bread in his day closely follows Isidorus's list, though misattributing it to the physician al-Rāzī.[75]

At the beginning of the Muslim occupation of Spain, newcomers and indigenous populations shared a common space. But an Arab-Andalusian cultural identity emerged very quickly, as crops and agricultural techniques were developed and expanded, especially through the continuous introduction of elements from both (Berber) North Africa and the Mashriq. The edible crops introduced by the Arabs to the Iberian Peninsula included apricots, artichoke, carob,

70 See García Sánchez 1990b.

71 Kulikowski 2004: 4.

72 Originally, these were two distinct sauces: *liquamen* was made by fermenting the salted intestines of certain types of fish in the sun, *garum* being the strained-off liquid while the sediment in the strainer was known as *allec*. The word *muria* referred to another related product that remains imprecise, but was probably the brine of salted fish. See Grainger 2021; Curtis 1991.

73 See Curtis 1991: 46–63.

74 Isidorus 1911: XX, i–viii (trans., 395–402).

75 Bolens 1980: 465–6; Isidorus 1911: XX, ii.15–19 (trans., 396).

rice, saffron, sugar, jujube, aubergine, parsnip, lemon, orange and carrot.[76]

Many centuries after Isidorus, the historian Ibn Khaldūn described the food of Andalusians as consisting primarily of sorghum (*dhura*) and olive oil.[77] Strikingly, he pointed out the benefits of such a spartan diet since, in times of drought or famine, far fewer died than among those who were used to a life of abundance. Of course, Ibn Khaldūn was writing in the fourteenth century on another continent, and spent only a short time on the Iberian Peninsula, and so his comments were not based on first-hand knowledge.

Besides the two recipe collections, we are fortunate to have a variety of sources which allow us to draw up a detailed picture of Andalusian cuisine, foodways and gastronomy. These include agricultural treatises and calendars, both linked to the emergence of a veritable school of Andalusian agronomy,[78] as well as medical and dietetic manuals. The latter did not limit themselves to specifying the therapeutic benefits of ingredients and dishes, but often also included instructions on how to prepare them.

Of particular relevance are the so-called *ḥisba* manuals. Originally referring to the Muslim's duty to promote what is morally good, the word came to denote the supervision of the market by an inspector (*muḥtasib*) to ensure that practices complied with this injunction.[79] This genre was produced all over the Muslim world, including al-Andalus.

The *ḥisba* texts give a wonderful insight into the food – both produce and dishes – available at markets, and thus of the diet and eating habits at the time.

In some cases, the instructions are of an advisory nature, to enhance the quality and wholesomeness of the product. For instance, Ibn ʿAbdūn said vegetables should not be washed in the ponds of orchards but in the river, since the latter is cleaner.[80] Similarly, Ibn ʿAbd al-Raʾūf (tenth century) prescribed the cutting of meat with a knife rather than with a

---

76 Glick 1979: 77.

77 Ibn Khaldūn 2005: I, 142–3 (trans., I, 180–1).

78 For a good introduction, see García Sánchez 1992: 987–99.

79 *EI*², s.v. 'ḥisba' (Cl. Cahen & M. Talbi); *EI*³, s.v. 'muḥtasib' (Ahmad Ghabin); Yaacob 1996; Cook 2004; Chalmeta 1970.

80 Ibn ʿAbdūn [Lévi-Provençal 1955]: 42.

cleaver – 'which is how the people in the Mashriq do it' – because the latter cut through bones that would then become mixed in with the meat.[81]

Sometimes, the advice is more recondite. Ibn al-Ukhuwwa advises against preparing *murrī* by cooking it over a fire, since this causes leprosy![82] The manuals often give detailed cooking instructions as well on the various ready-made meals available, such as porridges (*harīsa*), sausages (*mirqās*), *qaṭāyif* (crêpes) and doughnuts (*isfanj*), all of which are in al-Tujībī's text as well. A good example can be found in the twelfth-century *Nihāyat al-Rutba fī ṭalab al-ḥisba* ('The Utmost Authority in the Pursuit of Ḥisba') by al-Shayzarī for the making of the famous Ramadan sweet *zulābiyya*:

> [They] should be made from one-third finely ground wheat flour and two-thirds coarsely ground semolina. This is because if there is a lot of semolina, the *zulābiyya* will be too white, too light and will not cook sufficiently. [...] The best oil to fry with is sesame oil, and if this cannot be obtained then some other pure oil. The *zulābiyya* should not be fried until the dough has risen; the sign of this being that it floats to the surface of the oil, while when it has not risen it sinks to the bottom of the frying pan. Also, risen *zulābiyya* become like tubes which stick together when gathered in the hand, while unleavened *zulābiyya* become crushed and are not hollow in the middle. No salt should be put in the dough because *zulābiyya* are eaten with honey and it would make one nauseous if they contained salt.[83]

More often than not, however, the manuals are intended to assist the *muḥtasib* in finding fraudulent practices, whether related to weights and measures, the purity of ingredients, or the preparation of dishes or medicines sold at market. Then, as now, the more expensive the substance, the greater the temptation. Few commodities were more

81 Ibn 'Abd al-Ra'ūf [Lévi-Provençal 1955]: 93.
82 Ibn al-Ukhuwwa 1938: 163 (trans., 40).
83 al-Shayzarī n.d.: 226 (trans., 50).

precious than musk, and the Malagan market inspector al-Saqaṭī (thirteenth century) gave instructions on how to test musk: 'Take a little by putting it in the mouth and dissolving it with saliva; spit it on a white cloth and then shake it. If after this, no stain remains, it means that the musk is pure, and if not, it is adulterated.'[84] This apparently allowed detection of a whole range of corrupting substances such as lead filings, or the blood of gazelle, kid or squab.

However, reading the manuals, one is left with the impression that hardly anything sold was safe from corruption and fraud. The *muḥtasibs* took their role as the arbiters of morality very seriously, and would monitor everyone who visited the market to ensure they did not engage in immoral behaviour such as consorting with the opposite sex. This also extended to religious rituals; for instance, Ibn 'Abdūn's manual prohibits the sale of animals slaughtered by Jews to Muslims, as this would mean the meat was not halal.[85]

Bread was a staple in medieval Andalusian cuisine, as it was in that of the Mashriq, and came in several guises – leavened and unleavened (*faṭīr*), thick (*raghīf*) and thin (*ruqāq*).[86] Ibn Zuhr lists no fewer than eighteen varieties.[87] The loaves came mostly in the form of flatbreads, which were often used as an ingredient in dishes, not just as an accompaniment to appetizer dips – known as *idām* – which included aromatic salts, pickles, olive oil and vinegar. The fifteenth-century Algerian scholar al-'Uqbānī mentioned that in Tunis they sold bread made with only finely ground white flour (*duqāq*), semolina or *khushkār*,[88] and was thus superior to the breads sold in places like Syria and Egypt, where everything was mixed together, extracting only the bran from wheat.[89]

The importance of this staple, emphasized in all treatises, has deep roots in the history of the region; in Jordan, breadmaking is attested over

84 al-Saqaṭī 1931: 46.

85 Ibn 'Abdūn [Lévi-Provençal 1955]: 49.

86 This word goes back to the Biblical Hebrew *ūreqīqē* (Leviticus 2:4) but is ultimately from Akkadian *raqāqu* ('to become thin') and *ruqququ* ('very thin'), related to a root meaning 'hammered metal'. Roth 1956–2010: XIV, 167, 416, 420.

87 Ibn Zuhr 1992: 10–13 (trans., 46–9).

88 Coarsely ground wheat flour with its bran (Dozy 1881: I, 373; Ibn al-Ḥashshā' 1941: 40, No. 378), from the Persian *khushkār*, 'coarse unsifted flour, full of bran' (Steingass 1892: 462).

89 al-'Uqbānī 1965: 115.

fourteen millennia ago.[90] Leavened bread was also made in Neolithic Egypt,[91] which is the site of the oldest remains of dough and loaves. In Ancient Mesopotamia (second millennium BCE), the Assyrians made both unleavened bread and beer using barley and other grains such as millet, emmer wheat and rye.[92]

Like several other medieval Arab recipe collections,[93] al-Tujībī's opening recipes are for various types of bread (six in all), but there are many other recipes requiring flatbreads and doughs, including various sweets that are still around today, such as *kunāfa* (No. 57) and *qaṭā'if* (Nos. 59–60). Cereals were at the heart of the Andalusian diet, whether it be in breads or in porridges, stews (including *tharīds*) or soups, no doubt helped by the fact that the region had been a major producer of wheat and barley since Roman times.[94]

At a time when, in Christian Europe, rye and barley breads were the only types available, wheat was the main cereal used in bread-making in the Muslim world. Nonetheless, the present text includes a millet bread (No. 5), which, 'of all the non-wheat breads', so the author tells us, 'is the most prized among Andalusians and they eat a lot of it when it is millet-harvesting season in their country'. In the present text, barley is also often called for, in recipes for mash and *murrī*. Barley bread was restricted to the poorest or reserved for times of shortage, when recourse would even be had to flour made from dried pulses, chestnuts, acorns or tree roots.[95]

The quality of the bread was linked to both the cereal and the type of flour used. The most prized was the finest white wheat flour, which was known as *darmak*, a borrowing from the Persian *dārmag* ('fine').[96] This is called for in 10 per cent of all recipes. It also received the imprimatur of physicians for its nutritiousness, especially if it was freshly ground.[97]

90 Arranz-Otaegui *et al.* 2018.
91 Darby *et al.* 1977: II, 501–28.
92 Bottéro 1995.
93 Ibn Mubārak Shāh 2020: 9–12; *Kanz*, Nos. 1–6, App. Nos. 1–4.
94 See García Sánchez 1983–86; N. Afif. 'Du blé et des spécialités culinaires à base de céréales au Maghreb et en Al-Andalus au Moyen-Âge', in Stengel & Debbabi Missaoui 2020: 37-54.
95 García Sánchez 1995a: 49.
96 Corriente 1997: 177; Ibn Zuhr 1992: 22 (trans., 46).
97 Ibn Khalṣūn (1996: 156; trans., 81) pointed out that it is slow and difficult to digest, which could be counteracted by careful kneading and cooking, and with the correct

The average family would often make their own dough and then send it to the public oven for baking – though it could also be bought ready-made at the oven, or the market, though the latter was frowned upon.[98] Stale bread would be used to make breadcrumbs, which occur in a large number of recipes, in stuffing, as a thickener, and as part of the egg-crusting layer on top of many savoury dishes.

As it was also the most expensive of flours, *darmak* was often adulterated or simply replaced with flour of poorer quality at markets. At one point, these fraudulent practices reached such proportions that a judge in the city of Toledo in the early eleventh century prohibited the making of *darmak* altogether. However, while the populace was suckered by the low-grade flour, the elite could afford to have the real thing. Rather than forgoing their delicacies, the latter decided they should just do away with the judge![99]

The text also contains three recipes referring to *ḥuwwāra* flour, which denotes the same premium variety, but is the word found in Near Eastern cookbooks.[100] As a result, it is likely that these were recipes that originated in the Mashriq.

The flour available to most people was semolina, which occurs in many recipes here. Bread made with it would be baked in the *tannūr* (clay oven) or *furn* (brick oven), and fried on a *malla* (hot plate) or in a pan. The text also reveals a general preference for leavened bread, including only one recipe for an unleavened loaf (*faṭīr*). Dough is generally made by combining water, salt and yeast, though some of these ingredients are not always included in the recipes.

Semolina is also a core ingredient for cereal-based dishes like couscous, for which al-Tujībī gives the highest number of variations in any medieval cookery book (Nos. 85–9, 91). There are also recipes for two varieties of dried pasta. The first is *fidawsh* (No. 90) – the ancestor of the Spanish *fideos* – which is described as 'the size of a wheat grain' and thus corresponds to the present-day *pastini* of the type variously known as *risi*, *risoni* or *orzo*. The second is called *iṭriyya* (No. 92), and is similar to what today are called noodles (or spaghetti). This is

amount of salt and fermentation.

98 García Sánchez 1981–82: 150.

99 Waines 1992.

100 See Ibn Mubārak Shāh 2020: 76, note 340.

mentioned in other collections, but al-Tujībī and the Abbasid *Taṣānīf*[101] are the only ones to give a recipe, perhaps because it was generally bought ready-made at markets.

Starch (*nashā*) was usually used in its dried form as recipes require it to be dissolved in water. It is used for sealing pastry (No. 60), to make thin flatbreads (Nos. 64, 66) and confections (for example, Nos. 395, 396, 407–8), and also in a lamb stew with honey (Nos. 150, 393). In one recipe (No. 64), it is mentioned as being extracted from semolina and called *lubāb*.[102]

Another category of cereal-based dishes is that of thick vegetable soups (pottages), made with breadcrumbs and flour (Nos. 33–40), which were commonly eaten, especially by the poor,[103] like the *ʿaṣīda* (a gruel with seasonal vegetables). The same is true for various types of mash (Nos. 41–3), known as *jashīsh* in Andalusian Arabic, made with barley, wheat, millet or rice.

As in Near Eastern manuals, the use of rice was quite limited, and it is called for in only four recipes – among them a rice pudding, which was a particular Andalusian favourite and was even considered the food of Paradise dwellers.[104] It is little surprise, therefore, that it was one of the foods that elicited nostalgia in the above poem by al-Azraq.

References to cultivation of the crop in al-Andalus can already be found in the tenth century, in the so-called 'Calendar of Córdoba'.[105] As al-Tujībī points out, it was cultivated mainly around Murcia and Valencia. The low number of recipes may be due to elite attitudes towards rice, since other sources show that rice was frequently eaten in al-Andalus. Rice flour was also used in the making of bread, though this tended to be only in times of scarcity, because it was thought to be inferior to wheat flour, as well as cheaper. In addition, physicians

101 *Taṣānīf*, fol. 81r.

102 According to Ibn Janāḥ, *lubāb* was a synonym of *nashā*, which is an abbreviated form of *nashāstaj*, a Persian borrowing. Starch, which was made only of wheat or spelt, was also known as *amilūn*, *amīlūn*, or *amiyūlūn*; Ibn Janāḥ 2020: Nos. 21, 498; Ibn al-Ḥashshā' 1941: No. 807. It was made by washing and soaking wheat in water before beating it well until it acquired a cottage-cheese-like consistency, and then it was strained and left to dry; *Taṣānīf*, 106v.

103 García Sánchez 1995a: 50.

104 Ibn ʿAbd Rabbih 1983: VIII, 6.

105 Dozy & Pellat 1961: 77 (trans., 76).

claimed that it lacked nutrition, and was slow to digest.[106]

All the cookery books – and al-Tujībī's is no exception – are meat heavy, since this was an expensive, and thus prestige ingredient.[107] A little over 40 per cent of the dishes included are made with some kind of meat – compared to one-third of recipes in Ibn Mubārak Shah, slightly over half in al-Baghdādī, but nearly two-thirds in the other Andalusian cookery book. Even dishes made with vegetables will often include a variation prepared with meat (for example, No. 377).

The present text is the odd one out among the cookery books in terms of the meat ingredients it uses. Firstly, there are the large number of meats not found elsewhere; besides the usual sheep (lamb, mutton) and chicken, there are recipes for rabbit, hare, goose, partridge, pigeon, squab, turtledove, starling, sparrow, deer, bovine antelope, ass, mountain goat, gazelle, and even hedgehog. In many cases, the type of animal within the species is further specified. While other books will generally specify simply 'chicken' or 'lamb', here the recipes will call for, respectively, pullets, poussins or capons, and mutton, lamb, hogget or (yearling) ram. Conversely, in some recipes, especially those using game, the choice of meats is far less specific and one is told to use whatever is available.

Secondly, there are the number of recipes requiring a multitude of meats, the most extreme example being the 'Ṣanhājī dish' (No. 269), which suggests using the prime cuts of some thirteen animals – no wonder one needs the biggest casserole dish one can get in order to cook this meat extravaganza! Its appeal would appear to have crossed borders as it is clearly a precursor of the *oglia potrida* found in the *Opera dell'arte del cucinare* by Bartolomeo Scappi (d. 1577), the private chef (*cuoco secreto*) to Pope Pius V, and later on in Antonius Magirus's *Koocboec oft familieren keukenboec* ('Cookery Book, or the Family's Kitchen Book'), published in Leuven, in the Low Countries, in 1612, where it is known as 'Spanish stew' (*Spaenschen hutspot*).[108]

106 García Sánchez 1981–82: 162–4. Many scholars, however, considered rice nourishing, especially when cooked with almonds and milk, while its constipating and astringent properties could be counteracted if it were soaked in water overnight. According to Ibn Jazla (fol. 15v.), eating rice results in good dreams.

107 On the use of meat in Andalusian cookery books, see the excellent work by Brisville 2013, 2018a, 2018b.

108 Scappi 1570: 65r–v.; Magirus 1612: 46–8 (1663: 49–51).

Thirdly, al-Tujībī for the most part specifies the meat that is required, unlike other authors, who mostly use the generic 'meat' (*laḥm*), usually implying lamb or mutton. Fourthly, a huge number of animal parts – seventeen in total – are mentioned, ranging from breast, ribs, flanks, loins and shanks, to trotters, heads (sheep or goat), the wind-pipe and tail, as well as nearly every part of the intestines. When the part of the animal is not specified, the instruction is often to take 'the best parts', or 'whatever is available'.

The offal dishes merit some attention as these are absent from all Near Eastern cookery books, except Ibn Sayyār al-Warrāq's and *Taṣānīf*, which reflect early Abbasid cuisine. The former contains about ten dishes that call for it – one of them a tripe *harīsa* attributed to Ibrāhīm Ibn al-Mahdī[109] – while the latter has even more (fifteen), and of a greater variety, including a sheep's head cooked inside tripe.[110] The predilection for this type of food probably came from Sasanid Persia, like so many other culinary habits. While it clearly fell out of favour among the Mashriq elites between the tenth and twelfth centuries, it continued in Iran as Bāvarchī's sixteenth-century Safavid cookery book contains a considerable number of offal recipes.[111]

Al-Tujībī, *Taṣānīf* and al-Warrāq are also the only sources that include recipes with game (gazelle, antelope and wild ass),[112] and locusts (or grasshoppers).[113]

The beef recipes somewhat stand out since there are twice as many as in the other Andalusian source. In the Mashriq, beef was either absent from the cookery books (for example, al-Baghdādī, *Wuṣla*, and *Waṣf*) or mentioned very rarely – only twice in Ibn Mubārak Shāh's work, for instance. In fact, in the Near East, beef was almost solely associated with the famous vinegar stew *sikbāj*. In an interesting twist, the Andalusian equivalent of this dish (No. 196) is made not with beef, but with chicken.

The rarity of beef in the recipes may be linked to a number of factors. For one thing, it was not widely available in many areas,

109 al-Warrāq 1987: 130, 135, 139, 224–6.
110 *Taṣānīf*, fols. 70r.–71v.
111 Afshār 1981: 163–8, 172–3.
112 al-Warrāq 1987: 127, 128–9, 130; *Taṣānīf*, fols. 62r.–v., 63r.
113 al-Warrāq 1987: 102.

whereas medically it was considered tough, dry and difficult to digest.[114] Religiously, too, it did not enjoy the favour of lamb (due to its connection with Islamic festivals, especially the Eid al-Adha), and in a famous *ḥadīth* beef is condemned by the Prophet as being a 'disease' (*dā'*), even if cow's milk and butter are 'medicine' (*dawā'*). In the Mashriq, at least, this bad reputation persisted through the ages; the Victorian traveller Richard Burton reported that in the Arabian Gulf region it was viewed as an 'unwholesome food' and that the Bedouin would not even drink cow's milk.[115] Indeed beef is not often found in Middle Eastern dishes even today.

The claim by Ibn Zuhr that in al-Andalus mutton or lamb was the meat eaten by most people is contradicted by the present book, where the preferred meat is clearly chicken – the subject of its own chapter containing forty-one recipes. Additionally, it occurs in many more recipes besides – about a quarter of all cooked dishes, more than double the proportion in Near Eastern culinary treatises. This is echoed by the other Andalusian manual, where it is required in almost 40 per cent of the recipes. The various types of sheep meat account for nearly a fifth of dishes (the majority involving ram), which is markedly lower than in the Mashriq.

Except for a hare recipe in *Taṣānīf*,[116] the use of hare (*arnab*) and rabbit (*qunilya*) in dishes is restricted to Andalusian collections. In the present text, there are only dedicated hare dishes, in some of which rabbit appears as a possible variant. While rabbits were unknown in the Mashriq, hare was already eaten in the pre-Islamic Near East but was not a gastronomical food in the area. Medical opinion on hare meat was divided; the thirteenth-century Andalusian pharmacologist Ibn Khalṣūn said it was very nourishing and fortifying, and recommended it for women who have just given birth.[117] Conversely, al-Rāzī considered it very harmful – except, he said, for the brain, which, if fried, is beneficial for those suffering from tremors, especially if eaten with pepper and mustard.[118] The time of year also mattered;

114 Ibn Zuhr 1992: 57.
115 Burton 1893: II, 17.
116 *Taṣānīf*, fol. 63r.
117 Ibn Khalṣūn (1992; 160; trans., 85).
118 al-Rāzī 1881: 22.

according to Isḥāq Ibn 'Imrān, a physician in the city of Kairouan (d. early tenth century), hares should never be eaten in December.[119]

Despite being lawful in Islam, rabbit could not be sold around mosques, only at a location specified by the market inspector, so that the slaughtering and skinning of the animals could be monitored to ensure their freshness.[120] Interestingly enough, abstaining from hare or rabbit – as well as shellfish and pork – became a liability after the Reconquista as it was one of the outward signs that gave away those of the Jewish faith to the Inquisition.[121]

Al-Tujībī's text provides the full gamut of meat practices and processing methods in Andalusian cuisine. The recipes detail the various stages, starting with slaughtering the animal and, where appropriate, gutting, scalding, plucking, washing and cleaning before being carved, chopped, pounded, sliced, and so on. Some of the techniques are very modern, such as the butterflying of chicken so as to ensure even cooking. Meat is often boiled to tenderize it before being fried, stewed or roasted.

The recipes show the great variety of ways in which meat was cooked in the Andalusian culinary tradition – in stews, fried, and as sausages or meat cakes. A more unusual cooking method is found in the *aknāf* recipe (No. 140) for roasting a ram by burying it in the ground and covering it with a casserole dish, while a fire is lit around it. In another recipe, meat slices are stuck around the sides of a *tannūr*, like loaves of bread, for roasting (No. 174). There are several recipes requiring the removal of meat that is then mixed with herbs, spices, breadcrumbs, and so on, before it is stuffed back into the animal. This would become a very popular cooking method in Europe as well; there are more than passing similarities between, for instance, Robert May's recipes for *Stuffings of the Brawn of a Capon, Chickens, Pigeons, or Any Tender Sea Foul*[122] and some of the recipes in the present text (for example, No. 69). Of course, one might even extend the analogy to modern meat stuffings, including that used for Christmas turkey! Another stuffing favourite, so to speak, involved

119 Ibn 'Abd Rabbih 1983: VIII, 46.
120 Ibn 'Abdūn [Lévi-Provençal 1955]: 43 (trans., 72).
121 Alpert 2001: 144; Gitlitz & Davidson 2000: 18.
122 May 1685: 29–30.

a plethora of poultry (pullets, squabs, turtledoves, sparrows, and so on) stuffed inside a lamb or ram which is then roasted (for example, Nos. 148, 164).

Terminologically the text makes interesting use of the word *maraq* (or *marqa*), which in Standard Arabic and Near Eastern Arabic varieties denotes 'broth', but in Andalusian Arabic meant a sauce, as indeed in Tunisia today *marqa* (also *marga*) refers to any kind of stew, generally quite spicy, a sugared variety of which (*marqa ḥluwa*) is a speciality in the Testour region.

The sausage recipes also display Andalusian features in terms of variety and use. In the Near Eastern tradition, the *laqāniq* sausages made from small intestines (No. 184) are found only in an Abbasid cookery book,[123] while the *mirqās* variety (Nos. 183–4) is peculiar to the western Mediterranean. However, while the Abbasid sausages are filled with uncooked meat and immediately fried or stored, the Andalusian variety require the meat to be fried before stuffing, after which the completed sausages are either dried or smoked before being stored for later use, at which point they are fried. Another way in which meat was preserved was as jerky (No. 466) – though this method goes back to pre-Islamic Arabia and may thus have been an import from the Mashriq.

Meatballs are another Andalusian speciality, and were widely sold at markets. Known in Andalusian Arabic as *bunduq* ('hazelnut') – possibly because of their usual size – they were made originally with mutton or lamb, but also appear prepared with chicken, pigeon or partridge. They are always liberally seasoned with a variety of spices, including mastic, spikenard, ginger and cloves, and are required in nearly forty dishes, often in conjunction with other types of meat, as a garnish (alongside split eggs, for instance), or even as part of a stuffing (inside a ram).

Snails are probably the most unusual ingredient in the book, and no other recipes using them have been found in medieval Arabic culinary sources. It is likely that this was an Andalusian and/or North African food that went back to the Romans, who took snail eating to a whole new level, even breeding and fattening them for food (the fourth-century Roman cook Apicius recommended doing so in milk). The use of

123 al-Warrāq 1987: 87–9.

the Berber word for snails, *aghlāl*, would support the theory that the origins of dishes that include them are in Roman North Africa, as does the fact that snails are not mentioned in the other Andalusian manual. In all likelihood, al-Tujībī came into contact with this dish during his stay in Morocco, where snails prepared in a similar way, albeit with a spicier sauce, have remained a very popular street food to this day, and are still known as *ghlāl* (or *bābūsh*).

In the medieval Arab culinary tradition, the use of fish constitutes another difference between the Near East, on the one hand, and al-Andalus and North Africa, on the other. In the former – at least as far as the elites were concerned – fish was used far less, for reasons of availability, prestige (it was not considered a luxury item), and the fact that it was thought to be difficult to digest. In general, fresh (and salted) sea fish were much preferred over river fish, while those from lakes were considered harmful.[124]

Like their Mashriq counterparts, the Andalusian upper classes did not hold fish in high esteem, and it tended to be eaten far more among the lower classes. García Sánchez points out that socio-religious issues may have played a greater role, since Muslims may have used it as a way of distinguishing themselves from the Christian population, who consumed a great deal of fish during Lent or on days of abstinence.[125] Interestingly enough, fish was not eaten all that much among Christians outside these periods.[126]

The Andalusian cookery books stand out not just because of the higher number of fish recipes they include – al-Tujībī has no fewer than thirty-three (Nos. 272–305) – but also because of the varieties used. The present text is the only one with recipes for eel, anchovy, tuna (both fresh and dried) and the use of a variety of fish in a single dish (for example, No. 272).

The higher number of fish recipes is linked to the abundance of fish in the region, with its long coastlines and many rivers. The Andalusian geographer Abū 'Ubayd al-Bakrī (d. 1094) reported on the unparalleled number of fish varieties in Tunis, with several species found nowhere else, and its people enjoying fish throughout the year as different

124 See, for instance, al-Samarqandī 2016: 95–8; Ibn Sīnā 1999: I, 605–7.

125 García Sánchez 1995a: 52.

126 García Sánchez 1986: 265.

species became available during every month.[127] Al-Idrīsī mentions proudly that in his birthplace, Ceuta, 'there is a lot of fishing and there are about 100 types of fish, among them many large tuna, which are caught by throwing barbed spears the fish cannot get out of'. He also refers to tuna fishing along various towns on the north coast of Sicily (Trabia, Caronia, Trapani and Castelammare del Golfo) where it was caught with nets.[128]

The way in which fish was cooked also received a lot of attention from physicians since it might be potentially harmful, as Ibn Zuhr explains in some detail:

> The best way to prepare the fish is as follows: blanch it in hot water, then put it in a clay or glazed earthenware casserole with a little oil. When it is cooked, it is left to simmer, and a broth prepared with vinegar and ginger is added. If this dish is to be improved, soups are added to the broth, which does not detract from its quality, but if coriander and eggs are added, it is tastier. If saffron is added, it not only adds flavour but also looks better; however, it alters the food and generates harmful elements in it, some of which fill the brain with harmful vapours, clog the veins and cause disease.[129]

In addition, fish should not be cooked with vinegar or garlic, since both cause damage to the brain and increase the harmfulness of the fish, while frying fish in olive oil is dangerous because 'the heat of the fire transmits a sulphurous substance to the fish'. Cheese, too, should never be cooked with fish.

Ibn Zuhr's prescriptions do not appear to have been heeded, as several of al-Tujībī's recipes (for example, Nos. 279, 288, 299) use these combinations. But opinions varied. According to al-Warrāq, frying fish is better than roasting it because the oil makes it less dense.[130]

---

127 al-Bakrī 1857: 41 (trans., 89); *idem* 2003: II, 216.

128 al-Idrīsī 2002: II, 529, 594, 595, 602; *idem* 1866: 201. The same account is repeated by the geographer al-Ḥimyarī (1984: 303).

129 Ibn Zuhr 1992: 36–7 (trans., 66).

130 al-Warrāq 1987: 28.

The anonymous Andalusian cookery book quotes the Sasanian ruler Anūshirwān (Khosrow I) on the subject of not leaving fish, fried or prepared in some other way, in a copper container, since this would make it go off.[131]

The fish was usually scaled, gutted, washed in water and sometimes salted, and then possibly left overnight. If it was a large fish, it was cut into smaller pieces. It was then boiled before being cooked with spices in a casserole over a fire, and finally browned in the oven – though this latter stage could be omitted. There is also a recipe for very modern-sounding fish cakes, which are made by pounding the fish, and sometimes coating it with egg whites and flour.

The most interesting fish recipe is a battered fried fish, aptly called 'the protected' (No. 290), which may well be the direct ancestor of the British classic fish dish – it is even eaten with vinegar! The claim is reinforced by the fact that the modern dish indeed entered the country from Spain, courtesy of Sephardic Jewish immigrants in the sixteenth century.[132]

Perhaps it is the above-mentioned Roman-Visigothic *garum* heritage that explains why a fish *murrī* (fermented fish sauce) is found only in an Andalusian recipe collection; it is unattested in cookery books from the Mashriq, where *murrī* only denotes a fermented sauce made with rotted barley.[133] It is worth pointing out though that the use of the same word for different sauces actually goes back at least to the ninth century, as Ḥunayn Ibn Isḥāq (809–73) rendered the Greek *garos* in Galen's 'On the Powers of Foods' (*De Alimentorum Facultatibus*) as *murrī*.[134]

In terms of preparation, the Andalusian sauce differed considerably from its Roman counterpart. The latter was made with salted fish intestines and small fish left in the sun before being strained, while the recipe here (No. 461) uses salted sprats, augmented with sweet grape juice, oregano, quince and onions before being left to ferment. When served separately, it was topped with olive oil and onions, or even fried eggs, fried fish and olives.

131 *Anwāʿ*, 57 (BNF, fol. 24r.–v.).
132 Panayi 2014: 109–12.
133 See, for example, Ibn Mubārak Shāh 2020: No. 91.
134 Ibn Iṣḥāq 1997.

In light of the flourishing and varied agriculture, vegetables and fruit played a significant part in the diet of Andalusians across all social classes, and a variety of produce was available throughout the year. The region was mostly self-sufficient, with very few items being sourced from outside its borders. The population lived in perfect organic harmony with the land, as revealed by the Calendar of Córdoba. January and February were for the planting of olive and pomegranate trees, as well as saffron, the harvesting of sugar cane, the sowing of summer vegetables, and the gathering of truffles, asparagus and fennel.

In March and April, aubergines, cucumbers, lemon balm, cauliflowers, beans and rice were sown, while carrots and cucumbers were ready to harvest. Apples, pears, apricots, cherries, figs and sour grapes were harvested in May and June.

The summer months were the time to harvest wheat, barley, nigella, mustard, oregano, rue and grapes. September was the season for peaches, jujubes, pomegranates, quinces, walnuts and pine nuts, while October saw the harvesting of fennel and lettuce, and the start of the onion-sowing season, which lasted until January. In November, acorns, chestnuts and saffron were gathered, whereas in December it was time to sow quinces, aubergines, leeks and garlic.[135]

Nothing went to waste as any surplus vegetables and fruit were pickled, cured, or turned into jams and conserves. This book contains no fewer than five chapters on preserving various kinds of produce (Nos. 420–32).

In al-Tujībī's recipes, vegetables are used more than in the Mashriq. However, the Arabic word for 'vegetables', *buqūl*, merits some clarification. It is used here in its modern sense, which does not exactly correspond to medieval Arabic usage, which denoted a broad category of leaf vegetables and herbs. In some cases, this applied only to fresh herbs, whose dried counterparts were classed as spices. According to Najīb al-Dīn al-Samarqandī (d. 1222), when vegetables 'are dried, their qualities are enhanced and they gradually pass from being food (*ghadhā'*) to being medicines (*dawā'*), suitable only for seasoning (*taṭyīb*) food'.[136] In keeping with this statement, he classified fresh herbs such as mint, fresh coriander, fenugreek, dill and rue as

135 Dozy & Pellat 1961; García Sánchez 1995a: 51–2.
136 al-Samarqandī 2016: 174.

vegetables (*buqūl*), and dried herbs and seeds – such as cumin, thyme, ginger, pepper and salt – as spices. Confusingly, however, dill for some reason appears in both categories. Often there was little consensus among authors; for instance, Ibn Baṣṣāl's *buqūl* list does not include any aromatics.[137]

The present recipe collection mentions a total of some twenty-five vegetables. The most frequently used are onions, aubergine, chickpeas, gourds and broad beans, which together appear in about 40 per cent of the recipes. Onions are used in the majority of savoury dishes. A comparison with, for instance, Ibn Mubārak Shāh's and al-Baghdādī's cookery books reveals that al-Tujībī contains not only more, but also different varieties of vegetables such as artichoke, asparagus, truffles, cauliflower and taro. Conversely, rhubarb, leek, Jew's mallow, lupine and mung beans are found only in the Egyptian collection. As for those the present book has in common with the others, the frequency of use is generally higher; a telling example is aubergine, which is used in less than 1 per cent of al-Kātib al-Baghdādī's recipes, but was an Andalusian favourite, required in almost one-fifth of savoury recipes. Taro is rather the odd one out; introduced by the Arabs, it was cultivated in al-Andalus by the twelfth century, but was especially associated with Egypt, where it was a staple crop.[138] It is not called for in the anonymous Andalusian treatise, but occurs in three of al-Tujībī's recipes, one of which is qualified as 'Eastern'.

Bean dishes also stand out, and they are found much less frequently in the Mashriq. For instance, there are only four dishes requiring them in a thirteenth-century cookery book from Aleppo (*Wuṣla*), five in al-Baghdādī's, and seven in Ibn Mubārak Shāh's, as opposed to 5 per cent of al-Tujībī's recipes. As beans were part of the non-elite's diet in the Near East, the difference may be due to the fact that Andalusian elites were also partial to these kinds of vegetables, or that al-Tujībī included them because of their widespread use among the general population. One may also suspect a Maghribi predilection, since to this day there are more bean dishes in Moroccan cuisine, for instance, than in Levantine cuisines.

137 Ibn Baṣṣāl 1955: 151–62 (cabbage, cauliflower, orache, spinach, purslane, wild amaranth, chard, lesser bindweed, summer savory, lettuce, chicory, absinthe).

138 Watson 1983: 66–9; Ibn Mubārak Shāh 2020: 27 (note 100).

There are a number of vegetarian – even vegan – dishes in the present collection. In Near Eastern cookery books, vegetarian recipes were called *muzawwarāt* ('counterfeit'),[139] and were intended for sick people. The name is linked to the dishes being made to look as though they included meat in order to make them more attractive to diners – just as today a veggie burger, for instance, may be said to be a counterfeit burger. Al-Samarqandī defined *muzawwarāt* as follows:

> dishes that do not contain meat and are prepared with oils instead. They are food for the sick. There are those made with cold and moist vegetables, which are suitable for hot, dry ailments and are useful against chest and bladder diseases. There are also soups and porridges made from flours, grains, almond milk, poppy seeds, starch and other things – sweetened with sugar or unsweetened – for such diseases.[140]

The *muzawwarāt* were sometimes also known as *kadhdhāb* ('false, deceitful') dishes – especially, it seems, when they simulated fish.[141] Another key target group for dishes of this kind were Christians, during Lent and on meat-free days. In one Abbasid cookery book, recipes for the two groups appear in different chapters since the vegetarian dishes for the sick contained ingredients not found in the 'Christian' *muzawwarāt* (most notably eggs and milk).[142] The absence of any reference to this category of dishes, or of their religious aspect, in al-Tujībī's recipes is quite interesting in the light of his close contacts with Christians. On the other hand, the number of vegetarian dishes in the text suggests that they were part and parcel of the Andalusian Muslim diet. In addition, the absence of *muzawwarāt* may also be due to the fact that al-Tujībī was writing his text in a Muslim society without native Christians.

Fruits were eaten on their own, fresh or dried, and in the form of juices, conserves or jams. Medical opinion on fresh fruits was not unanimous, but they were often considered harmful, of little nutritional value, and flatulent. Some scholars suggested eating fruit before the meal,

139 Ibn Mubārak Shāh 2020: xxxvii–viii.
140 al-Samarqandī 2016: 246.
141 *Kanz*, Nos. 255, 257, 259.
142 al-Warrāq 1987: 119–24 (Christians), 281–4 (sick people).

prior to the digestion of other foods, whereas others claimed it should be eaten after the meal because it requires the full digestive powers of the stomach, removes the bad taste of greasy food, and purifies the upper digestive tract. Al-Rāzī, who thought of all fruit as medicine, argued against the one-size-fits-all approach, as it did not take into account differences between fruit varieties and people's individual temperaments. As a general rule, however, he warned against eating fruit frequently, irrespective of the time.[143] The Andalusian physician Ibn al-Khaṭīb (d. 1374) advised travellers against eating vegetables or fruit or fruit, except out of need or for medical reasons, since they generate raw humours.[144]

The recipes in the present collection reveal the wide variety of fruit available in the region, though most are required in only very few recipes; Andalusians clearly lacked their Mashriqi counterparts' predilection for sweet-and-sour fruity meat stews, except for some made with quince (No. 129), apples (No. 130), sour grapes (No. 207), and two with a variety of plums, known as 'cows' eyes' (Nos. 102–3), which were imported from 'the land of the Christians' (northern Spain).

Instead of fruit, the majority of Andalusian stews were made with vegetables, such as turnips, broad beans, cauliflower, chard, and so on. Pomegranates occur only once, and then only in the form of juice. Dates are used only in sweets, and figs in cheese and curd dishes, as well as in a vinegar, whereas sour grapes are used to make verjuice (*ḥisrim*). There are a number of surprising omissions from the text, starting with sour oranges, bananas, watermelon, apricots and cherries – all of which were already grown in al-Andalus in the tenth century.

The Andalusian palate was very partial to citrus fruit – another Arab introduction – as evidenced by the varieties that occur in the recipes.[145] Citron (*utrujj*) is called for in some 10 per cent of the recipes; in food dishes, only the leaves are used, whereas the peels are ingredients in hand-washing powders.

Al-Tujībī is the only one to include references to a citrus fruit known as *zanbūʿ*, which appears in four recipes, one of them a vinegar. In Ibn al-ʿAwwām's agricultural treatise it is defined as being similar

143 Kuhne Brabant 1996; *idem,* 'Al-Rāzī on when and how to eat fruit', in Waines 2002: 317–27.

144 Ibn al-Khaṭīb 1984: 130 (trans., 261).

145 See Watson 1983: 42–50.

to the *nāranj* tree, except that the fruit is wide, granular (*muḥabbab*) and yellow; it is edible inside and out, and 'very sour'.[146] The botanist Abū 'l-Khayr al-Ishbīlī (*fl.* eleventh–twelfth centuries) added more confusion by referring to it as a species of the citron, 'but with wider and greener leaves, and larger, spotted fruit, grainy like the skin of the neck of the *sharkī* goat (...) as well as another species whose fruit [has] a colour tending to yellow, larger than any other, and another species known as *lāmūn, līmūn* or *laymūn*'.[147]

The modern identification of this fruit has eluded consensus in the literature, with suggestions ranging from its being the colloquial word for *nāranj* (sour orange),[148] a Berber word meaning a type of citron,[149] or even grapefruit (which *zanbūʿ* denotes today in Tunisia and Egypt).[150] In Andalusian agricultural sources it is often equated with a fruit known by a variety of names: *bustanbū* (also *bustanbūr, bustanbūn, bastanbūn*), *astayūb* (*astayūn*), *astanbūdh* (*asanbūdh*) and *istinbūnī* (*istibūtī*).[151]

The physician Dā'ūd al-Anṭākī (d. 1599) defined *istabūn* as 'a Persian word meaning *zanbūʿ* in Arabic, explaining that it is 'a graft of the citron tree on the sour orange tree and is also called *kubbād*'.[152] The latter word is used in both Egyptian and Syrian cookery books, and is thought to refer either to the trifoliate orange or the pomelo.[153] In the definitive study on the fruit, Aubaile-Sallenave (1992) traced the word back to the Sanskrit *jambū(la)*, which denotes the Malabar plum. Descendants of the term subsequently spread across South and East Asian languages, where it often meant pomelo, as in the Malaysian *jambūwa*, which may be the Arabic etymon. The identification remains uncertain and *zanbūʿ* probably referred to a hybrid citrus fruit, cognate with the citron, as the Castilian Spanish *azamboa* does.[154]

146 Ibn al-ʿAwwām 1802: I, 323.

147 al-Ishbīlī 2004–10: No. 545.

148 Renaud &. Colin 1934: 124–5 (No. 279); Ibn al-ʿAwwām 1802: I, 323.

149 Dozy 1881: I, 605; Dozy & Engelmann 1869: 363; Corriente 2008: 50; al-Ishbīlī 2004–10: No. 545.

150 Issa Bey 1930: 51 (No. 12).

151 al-Ishbīlī 2004–10: Nos. 650, 1067; Ibn al-ʿAwwām 1802: I, 323; Carabaza Bravo *et al.* 2004: 255–7; al-Ṭighnarī 2006: 287.

152 al-Anṭākī 1890–91: I, 47.

153 Ibn Mubārak Shāh 2020: 35–6 (note 134).

154 Carabaza Bravo *et al.* 2004: 255–7; de Eguílaz y Yanguas 1886: 294.

The second-most-used citrus fruit in this text, after citron, is *līm*, which usually means 'lime' but was often used interchangeably with 'lemon', known as *laymūn* (also *līmūn*, *lāmūn*).[155] Both were grown in al-Andalus, where the latter word could also denote oranges, as it does in some Moroccan dialects today, where 'lemon' is *ḥāmiḍ* ('sour'). The terminological ambiguity is also found in the sources; Ibn al-Raqqām (1250–1315),[156] al-Ṭighnarī,[157] Ibn al-ʿAwwām[158] and al-Ishbīlī[159] only mention *laymūn* not *līm*, whereas Ibn Zuhr[160] includes *līm* but not *laymūn*.

In the translation, *līm* is consistently rendered as lime, even though in some cases the author may have been referring to lemons – or, equally likely, allowing for the possibility of either being used in the recipe. This may explain why in some cases al-Tujībī felt the need to specify, using *līmūn* in connection with a vinegar (No. 106), and 'green' *līm* in a recipe for stewed aubergine (No. 352). Limes and lemons are used mostly pickled and for their juice, as well as in vinegars and as a garnish (together with olives).

This issue illustrates a much more general problem when dealing with plants and fruits mentioned in medieval resources. In many cases, identification is necessarily tentative at best, since the terminology does not reflect modern hierarchic taxonomies or any consistent approach to botanical description.

Almonds (*lawz*) are the most frequently encountered nut variety, and are called for in over a quarter of the dishes, as an ingredient, thickener or garnish, with all kinds of meat and fish, and in nearly all sweets, usually as a filling combined with sugar. They can be added to the dish whole, but are often blanched, skinned, pounded ('to a brain-like consistency'). Rather more unusual are an almond-and-bran pottage (No. 37) and a dish with ram (No. 124), which requires unripe green almonds. The almonds from the Jerez area were particularly prized.[161]

155 Corriente 1997: 490; Carabaza Bravo *et al.* 2004: 243.
156 Ibn al-Raqqām, fol. 41r. A fellow Murcian, this scholar also resided in Bijāya at some point, and is known for astronomical tables and a treatise on agriculture.
157 al-Ṭighnarī 2006: 287ff. (*līmūn[ī]*).
158 Ibn al-ʿAwwām 1802: I, 323–4.
159 al-Ishbīlī 2004–10: No. 5044 (*lāmūn*).
160 Ibn Zuhr 1992: 65.
161 García Sánchez 1995a: 54.

Walnuts (*jawz*) are used a third less frequently, occurring in savoury dishes, even as ingredients in one variety of *murrī*, and also pickled. One recipe (No. 468) mentions another purpose for both walnuts and almonds; in order to get rid of foul meat odour, a whole pierced walnut (or almond) is dropped into the pot in which meat is being cooked and left there until the meat is done.

The use of pine nuts (*ṣanwabar*) in a total of twenty recipes is another characteristically Andalusian practice; they are rarely used in Near Eastern medieval cookery books, and usually only in sweets. Hazelnuts (*bunduq*) and chestnuts (*qasṭal*) appear in only two recipes, while acorns are limited to one (No. 233), where they are cooked in a poultry dish together with almonds, pine nuts, chestnuts and walnuts. Pistachios (*fustuq*) are used only in sweets, either as an ingredient or in a garnish, in one case with almonds, spikenard and cloves (No. 220). Despite being the alleged principal ingredient in a dish called *fustuqiyya* (No. 140), recipes for which are found in several Near Eastern cookery books, pistachios are conspicuous by their absence. Although this may have been an adaptation of a dish that originally did contain pistachios, it is interesting to note that an Egyptian treatise also has a *fustuqiyya* without pistachios, albeit with very different ingredients.[162]

The most important ingredients in the creation of the flavours of medieval Arab cuisine are, of course, the spices, which were used in significant quantities. The recognition of 'spices' as a separate category occurs for the first time in Arabic sources; there was no such division in the Greek medical literature. But, as we have seen, the boundaries between vegetables, herbs and spices were often blurred in the medieval botanical tradition. The most generic term is *abāzīr* (or *abzār*), meaning 'seeds' (singular *bizr*). But one encounters other terms, such as *tawābil*, *afāwīh* and *ṭīb*, whose usage is often overlapping, sometimes interchangeable.[163]

The first of these is a plural of *tābil*, which is, lexicologically at least, synonymous with *abāzīr* as both mean 'seeds used for seasoning food'.[164] Indeed, al-Rāzī suggested a combined category of *tawābil* and *abāzīr*, which included salt, vinegar, *murrī*, pepper, coriander, cumin,

162 Ibn Mubārak Shāh 2020: 39.
163 See Ibn Mubārak Shāh 2020: lii–iv.
164 Lane 1863–74: I, 199, 296.

caraway, root of lovage (*kāshim*), thyme, asafoetida, cassia, galangal, cinnamon and the root of asafoetida (*maḥrūth*).[165] Ibn Khalṣūn had a separate category for 'hot spices' (*tawābil ḥārra*): pepper, ginger, galangal, mustard (*ṣināb*) and *murrī*.[166] The inclusion of *murrī* and vinegar with spices is somewhat unusual, and is supported only by the Jewish Andalusian physician Isḥāq al-Isrā'ilī (d. *ca.* 955). Usually they are classified as sauces (*ṣibāgh*) and/or pickles (*mukhallalāt*).

For his part, the tenth-century physician Abū Manṣūr al-Qumrī contrasted *tawābil* – 'things that season (*yuṭayyib*) the pot (*qidr*), such as salt, vinegar and saffron – with *abāzīr*, 'of which there are fresh ones like coriander, mint, and dry ones like coriander seeds, cumin, caraway, etc.'[167] The anonymous author of an Andalusian cookery book refers to 'premium' *tawābil* as being a mix of pounded and sifted pepper (one part), caraway (two parts), and coriander seeds (three parts),[168] explaining its importance as follows:

> You should be aware that knowing how to use spices (*tawābil*) is the cornerstone of cooked dishes; in fact, it constitutes the foundation on which cooking is built since among the spices there are things that particularly suit the various recipes, such as vinegar dishes, 'feminine' dishes such as various types of *tafāyās*, *baqliyyas*, and the like. Spices distinguish between foods, giving them flavour, while also bringing benefits and protecting from harm.[169]

Ibn Khalṣūn usefully drew up a list of what he called *abāzir* – that is to say, pepper, ginger, cassia, cloves, saffron, cumin, caraway, spikenard, fennel, aniseed, nigella, coriander and mastic.[170]

Aromatics, which provide both flavour and fragrance, tended to be referred to as *afāwīh* or *ṭīb*. Al-Rāzī identified the following *ṭīb*: musk, ambergris, camphor, sandalwood, *sukk*, agarwood, saffron, mahlab, rose water, cloves, storax, ungues odorati, costus, cyperus

165 al-Rāzī 1987: 144–5.
166 Ibn Khalṣūn 1996: 153 (trans., 77).
167 al-Qumrī 1991: 86.
168 *Anwā'*, 87 (BNF, fol. 35v.).
169 *Anwā'*, 53 (BNF, fol. 22v.).
170 Ibn Khalṣūn 1996: 163–4 (trans., 92–3).

and saltwort.[171] Conversely, Ibn Khalṣūn divided *ṭīb* into those that are hot (*sukk*, saffron, amber, liquorice and narcissus), cold (camphor, sandalwood, musk, rose, violet, nenuphar and myrtle), and 'balanced' (*ghāliya*, agarwood, nutmeg, spikenard, white musk rose, jasmine, chamomile and wallflower).[172] The fact both lists include items such as saltwort and perfume compounds not used in food, like *sukk* (Nos. 472, 473, 474) and *ghāliya*,[173] shows that scent, rather than taste, was held to be the defining characteristic. In addition, the medium (roots, herbs, liquids) seemed not to be considered a distinguishing factor.

One of the earliest subdivisions is that by the caliphal physician Ibn Māsawayh (777–857), who listed the following primary aromatics (*ṭīb*): musk, ambergris, aloes, camphor and saffron.[174] These are contrasted with *afāwīh* (also *afwāh*), the plural of the word *fūh* (also *fūha*), which usually means 'mouth', but also 'perfume' and a 'fragrant substance used in cooking' (also *fuwwaha*).[175] Rather confusingly, this word is sometimes combined with *ṭīb* as *afwāh al-ṭīb* – which often denotes a popular spice blend (known also as *aṭrāf al-ṭīb*), comprising spikenard, betel leaf, bay leaf, nutmeg, mace, cardamom, cloves, rosebuds, ash tree fruit, long pepper, ginger and black pepper.[176]

Ibn Māsawayh added a second list of aromatics, *afāwīh* – twenty-four in total – which includes things like spikenard, cloves, sandalwood, nutmeg, cardamom, but also mahlab, mastic, laudanum, ungues odorati and civet. The tenth-century historian ʿAlī Ibn Ḥusayn al-Masʿūdī adopted both of Ibn Māsawayh's lists, though without acknowledging the latter, and with only a few amendments to the *afāwīh*, including the addition of sweet flag.[177]

This classification was subject to considerable change over time and according to the region. The author of a fourteenth-century Egyptian cookbook listed the following as *afāwīh*: cloves, cardamom, spikenard,

171 al-Rāzī 1987: 158–9.
172 Ibn Khalṣūn 1996: 164 (trans., 92).
173 A perfume whose key ingredients were musk and ambergris, and which was often used on hair.
174 Sbath 1936: 9; Levey 1961: 397–8.
175 Lane 1863–74: VI, 2464–5. The related participle, *mufawwah* (*ibid.* 2466) denotes 'seasoned with *afāwīh*', as well as 'being eloquent' and 'ravenous'.
176 *Wuṣla*, No. 4.4.
177 al-Masʿūdī 1861–77: I, 367.

cassia, ginger and saffron.[178] The list of 'premium' *afāwīh*, on the other hand, provided in the anonymous Andalusian treatise consists of cinnamon, cassia, spikenard, pepper, galangal and nutmeg.[179]

Al-Tujībī most often refers to *abāzīr*, but on occasion also uses *afāwīh*, as well as the more unusual *'aqāqīr* (singular *'uqqār*), which appears here in its Andalusian Arabic sense of aromatic spice, but usually referred to medicinal plants and roots.[180] Aromatic spices could also be coloured with saffron or with fresh coriander juice before being used.

In the Iberian Peninsula, including al-Andalus, the use of herbs and spices represented a continuation of native Iberian, Roman and Visigothic practices, combined with imports from the Mashriq as part of a more general trend of emulating the splendours of Eastern courts. Thanks to agricultural advances, several of these new spices were grown locally with great success, to the extent that the fourteenth-century chronicler Shihāb al-Dīn al-'Umarī claimed that in al-Andalus one could find medicinal herbs not found in India or anywhere else.[181] A prime example is saffron; it was produced in several regions, including Toledo and Valencia,[182] but especially in the town of Basṭa (the modern Baza), which, according to al-'Umarī, not only produced the best earthenware cookware in the world, but also enough saffron to satisfy the demand of the whole of the Muslim population (*al-milla al-Islāmiyya*) of al-Andalus.[183] Already in the tenth century, Spain was an exporter of saffron, as well as ambergris and ginger,[184] whereas it was self-sufficient in cumin, coriander, oregano and caraway.

Many other spices, however, needed to be imported, often from as far afield as India. These included pepper, cinnamon, cloves, rose water, spikenard, myrrh and musk.[185] It was by all accounts a very prolific trade as the market inspector al-Saqaṭī noted that over 3,000 spice varieties were available in the country.[186]

---

178 *Kanz*, No. 146.
179 *Anwā'*, 67 (BNF, fol. 28v.).
180 Lane 1863–74: V, 2110. The word is a borrowing from Syriac, meaning 'root'. See Löw 1881: 298 (No. 240).
181 al-'Umarī 2010: IV, 117.
182 García Sánchez 1995a: 53; *idem* 1997: 47.
183 al-'Umarī 2010: IV, 127.
184 al-Mas'ūdī 1861–77: I, 367.
185 Constable 1994: 151–9.
186 al-Saqaṭī 1931: 43.

Andalusian cuisine shared a number of features with the Near Eastern tradition, such as the sheer number of spices used (twenty-nine in the case of al-Tujībī), and the combination and often large quantities of various spices in order to create a highly complex combination of flavour notes.

At the same time, the selection and proportions of spices used in al-Tujībī differed significantly from those in other cookery books from across the Muslim world, such as al-Baghdādī's or the anonymous ones from Aleppo (*Wuṣla* – thirteenth century) and Egypt (*Kanz* – fourteenth century). Salt is used in nearly 80 per cent of dishes, which is a quarter more than in al-Baghdādī, almost four times more than in *Kanz*, and eight times more than in *Wuṣla* recipes. Coriander is used in almost 70 per cent of dishes, mostly in the form of seeds but also fresh, or as a juice. Sometimes all three occur in one and same recipe, as in the case of a green *tafāyā* (No. 110). In third position we find pepper, the most traded spice on the medieval international market, which is called for in about 60 per cent of dishes, twice the amount in al-Baghdādī, and five times that of Egyptian cookery books. Cinnamon appears in over one-third of recipes, and saffron in nearly a quarter. The latter is frequently bloomed as well for colouring the food.

While we find similar, though generally slightly lower, proportions of saffron in Near Eastern cookery books, there is a stark contrast in the use of cinnamon, which appears in less than 10 per cent of Mashriqi dishes. Conversely, the use of mint (about 15 per cent of dishes) was quite similar in Baghdad and Syria at the time, but considerably lower than in Egypt. The most striking Andalusian feature is the significant use of mint juice, which accounts for more than half of the dishes with mint. Similarly, spices like ginger, spikenard, oregano, fennel and cloves are required far more frequently in the present text than in Near Eastern manuals. Conversely, the latter make heavier use of cumin, salt and cassia (almost 60 per cent of al-Baghdādī's dishes). Sumac was very popular in the Mashriq but is hardly used in Andalusian sources, and in the present book occurs only once (No. 208), and then only in what is clearly a dish imported from the East. Nutmeg is called for in three hand-wash recipes, but only once in food – in a sweet of Eastern origin (No. 406).

Although there are many similarities between the two Andalusian cookery books, there are also some marked differences. The most striking of these is that al-Tujībī uses almost three times as much ginger as the anonymous treatise, and more than twice the amount of mint and mastic. While differences between the two texts may reflect regional Andalusian cuisines, they are more likely the result of influences absorbed by al-Tujībī during his sojourns in Morocco, Algeria and Tunisia.

The use of large quantities of pepper can be traced back to the Roman substratum in Andalusian cuisine, as it was one of the defining flavours of Roman cuisine – it is used in over 80 per cent of dishes in Apicius's cookery book. Similarly, one may point to the use of cumin, coriander and ginger in a significant number of recipes in the same source. On the other hand, it contains very little spikenard (two recipes), and no cinnamon or cloves. The Roman use of saffron also contrasts with that in Arab cuisine in that it tended to be limited to medicinal recipes, and there are no references to its use as a colouring,[187] which is very frequent in Arabic sources.

Another feature that sets Andalusian gastronomy apart from its Near Eastern counterparts is its use of certain spices as a garnish sprinkled on certain dishes, both savoury and sweet. Often, it involves combinations of cinnamon, ginger, pepper and spikenard. In some cases, other items are added as well; one *tharīda* (No. 16) is served with a sprinkling of peeled almonds, walnuts, green olives, seasoned black olives, grated cheese, cinnamon and spikenard. Cinnamon and sugar was also a popular combination, and one that influenced European cuisine until the seventeenth century. In Lancelot de Casteau's *Ouverture de Cuisine* (1604), this combination is found in nearly 80 per cent of the recipes, often sprinkled on before serving.

The author of the anonymous Andalusian cookbook tells us that spices and seasonings help distinguish between foods – rather, foods are differentiated by the use of different spices and combinations.[188] The most frequently used spices in al-Tujībī's *tharīdas*, for instance, are salt, pepper, coriander, ginger, cinnamon and cumin. An 'Eastern' variant stands out in its use of spikenard, caraway and cloves, alongside the pepper, ginger and cinnamon of the others.

187 Laurioux 1983: 22.
188 *Anwāʿ*, 53.

Fish dishes, on the other hand, tend to call for pepper, salt, coriander, cumin, mastic, garlic, ginger, cinnamon and galangal. This differs somewhat from the Near Eastern fish spice selection which, besides pepper and coriander, often include caraway, sumac and saffron. Al-Tujībī's fish recipes are unusual in that several of them require hardly any spices, except for salt or garlic.

The present text contains the highest number of recipes of all cookery books of the fermented condiment *murrī* – a total of thirteen (Nos. 449–62), with unusual variations and methods, such as an instant ready-to-use variant for those who could not wait three months, which is how long it usually took to make the sauce. Barley *murrī* would start to be made at the end of March each year. As in Near Eastern cooking, *murrī* was used in a large variety of dishes, except sweets. Only three of the *tharīdas* are made with the sauce. Those wishing to get a taste of this condiment might be interested to learn that a modern recreation of *murrī* revealed it is similar to soya sauce.

Vinegar is one of the staple condiments in the medieval Arab culinary tradition, in both the eastern and western Mediterranean. It was not only used as an ingredient but was also a popular dip (eaten with bread), and a particular favourite of the Prophet. Its popularity was such that the physician al-Uryūlī included vinegar among the spices, since it is used so often alongside them in dishes.[189]

Its significance in al-Tujībī's recipes becomes apparent from the sheer number of recipes containing vinegar (over 30 per cent of savoury dishes), as both an ingredient and a marinade. More importantly, the text stands out for its inclusion of recipes for no fewer than sixteen different vinegars (Nos. 433–48) found nowhere else, as well as for its wide variety of ingredients: sweet grapes, figs, pepper, chickpeas, raisins, squill, limes (or lemons), sour grapes and mint. Yet, in spite of this array of vinegars, very few of them appear in the recipes, which usually just require the generic 'vinegar'. Naturally, this does not mean that they were not used, only that it was left to the cook's judgement to decide which vinegar to use in which dish. In a handful of recipes (Nos. 106, 132, 174, 301), a selection of three vinegars (lime or lemon, sour grapes, and *zanbū*') is mentioned in dishes with a variety of ingredients (tuna, game, sheep, fish and beef); strangely

189 al-Uryūlī 1983: 64 (trans., 22).

enough, no recipe is given for two of the vinegars – lemon (*khall līmūnī*) and *zanbū'* – in the chapter on vinegar making. The most startling omission is wine vinegar, which was a frequent ingredient in cookery books in the Near East, as well as in the pharmacological literature. Although wine vinegar is considered lawful in Islamic law because it does not have the intoxicating properties associated with wine, it is possible that as a religious scholar Ibn al-Tujībī preferred to err on the side of caution.

Some recipes incorporate some unusual uses of vinegar – added towards the end of the cooking process while the pot is left to simmer, boiled and poured on before serving (for example, No. 173), included as part of a basting sauce together with *murrī* and olive oil, in a sauce with saffron to cook meat in, or drizzled on with olive oil before eating. When crushed garlic is used as a garnish, it is often first cooked in vinegar – though, as we have seen, this particular combination was subject to medical restrictions.

In terms of cooking oils, Andalusian cuisine consistently uses olive oil, which appears infrequently in the Near East, where sheep's tail fat was favoured in the period. In post-Reconquista Spain, olive oil came to be viewed as a sign of Moriscos clinging to their Islamic traditions, like abstaining from wine or pork. For instance, in 1502 'the morisca Leonor de Morales's husband denounced her before the Inquisitorial authorities for cooking meat in oil rather than in fat'.[190] Sesame oil, another favourite in the Near East – in a fifteenth-century Egyptian cookery book, it is called for in a quarter of the recipes[191] – is used only once by al-Tujībī, in a cheese dish (No. 327).

Al-Tujībī's work reveals the differences in the use of dairy between Andalusian and Mashriq cuisines, both in terms of the number of recipes and varieties of processed products. Dairy was widely consumed by all social classes, and was the object of a bustling market trade. Milk was drunk by itself but was also used in a number of savoury dishes, including stews, pottages and porridges and, less commonly, in *tharīdas* (Nos. 12, 26–9), as well as in sweets, such as *qaṭā'if*, *mujabbanas* and rice pudding. Many other sweets, however, were made without

190 Gerli & Giles 2021: 298. In this context, the reference was to lard, rather than to sheep's tail fat.

191 Ibn Mubārak Shāh 2020: lv.

milk, including cakes, puddings and doughnuts, such as *khabīṣ*, *fālūdhaj*, *zulābiyya* and *isfanj*. The most popular varieties were sheep's and goat's milk. Milk enjoyed both medical and religious sanction, and in the Qur'ān (16:66), it is said to be a beneficence of Allah, and 'pleasant to drink'. As we have seen, this did not apply to cow's milk, and al-Tujībī suggests it as an alternative to sheep's milk only when the latter is not available (for example, No. 93). Sour milk appears in a number of Eastern dishes, such as *maḍīra* (Nos. 168–9). Milk was also used to make yoghurt, curds, butter and, most importantly, cheeses. Over time, milk was increasingly used in the Near East as well. In Ibn Mubārak Shāh's cookery book, for instance, it is occurs in about 15 per cent of the recipes.

Butter, made from cows' or goats' milk, was also very much part of Andalusian gastronomy – both fresh butter (*zubd*) and clarified butter (*samn*) – and is called for in over one-sixth of the recipes. Conversely, in the Near Eastern cookery books, fresh butter is a rarity. It is used only once in al-Warrāq and not at all in al-Baghdādī, though it is found in two recipes in *Taṣānīf*.[192] Clarified butter, on the other hand, was clearly preferred in the eastern Mediterranean. In Egypt, for instance, it was typically used in the preparation of egg recipes such as omelettes and sweet dishes such as rice pudding, sometimes made with flour and often combined with sesame oil.[193] Both types of butter were used as an ingredient, but they were also poured onto dishes like *tharīdas* and couscous before eating. In other recipes, the dish is served with a small bowl of butter placed in the middle, to be eaten with the food. This practice was not entirely new, as al-Mas'ūdī had already described a *harīsa* served with a bowl (*sukurruja*) of chicken broth being placed in the middle.[194]

But one may question the extent to which the frequent use of clarified butter by al-Tujībī is representative of the whole of Andalusian cuisine, since it does not occur in the other Andalusian manual. And so its use may betray a Mashriqi – or North African – influence on the author. The Eastern connection is supported by the fact that the Andalusian physician Ibn Biklārish (*fl.* late eleventh and early twelfth centuries) referred

192 *Taṣānīf*, fols. 75v.–76r., in a *maḍīra* (see recipe No. 168 below), and in a sweet pudding (fols. 85v.–86r.).

193 Waines 2012: 168, s.v. 'clarified butter' (J. Ruska/Waines).

194 al-Mas'ūdī 1861–77: VIII, 244.

to clarified butter as *samn ʿarabī*, adding that it is butter made from goat's milk, cooked with a bit of salt, known in Romance as *unbūra*.[195] Further evidence is provided by Ibn Khaldūn, who noted that the Andalusians lack *samn*, whereas the rural regions of the Maghrib do not use it either, because of its tastelessness (*tafāhatuhu*).[196]

Cheese was another Andalusian favourite both in the home and as a market food, but was not used very often in Mashriq sources of the period. Al-Tujībī's text not only contains the largest number and variety of cheese recipes, including some for maturing cheese, but also many recipes that require it as an ingredient in various forms – dry or fresh, young or aged, grated or powdered – added at different stages of the cooking process, including as a garnish. One of the recipes (No. 13) even has some elements that a modern reader might associate with a cheese fondue. Cheese was eaten as a side as well, which was not the case in the Mashriq at the time. This clearly changed over time, however, at least in Egypt, where, so a fifteenth-century cookery book tells us, 'some people do not consider a meal complete without there being cheese'.[197] Finally, fresh cheese was also added to milk to prevent it from going sour (No. 330).

The most famous Andalusian cheese dish is the fried cheese bun called *mujabbana*, which translates literally as 'filled with cheese' (*jubn*). Al-Tujībī's book contains no fewer than eight variations, three more than in the other Andalusian collection. The *mujabbana* does not seem to have made it to the Mashriq, as no recipes are found in Eastern manuals. They were considered a speciality of the western part of al-Andalus, especially the region of Jerez, due to the quality of the cheeses available there, which gave rise to the saying that 'Anyone who enters Jerez without eating *mujabbanas* is an outcast (*maḥrūm*)!'[198] Physicians held that they were very heavy and difficult to digest, but this clearly did not deter Andalusians.[199]

They were made with milk, or with hot water, and sometimes served with fresh melted butter, a sprinkling of sugar and cinnamon, and a

195 Ibn Biklārish, fols. 102v.–103r.
196 Ibn Khaldūn 2005: I, 142 (trans., I, 180).
197 Ibn Mubārak Shāh 2020: No. 182.
198 al-Maqqarī 2012: I, 113.
199 al-Uryūlī 1981: No. 28. Also see Marín 1997: 14.

little dish with honey to dip the *mujabbanas* in. The modern Spanish *almojábana*[200] denotes a popular Colombian cheese bread and, in Spain, a type of cheesecake, or even a fritter made without cheese.

Mujabbanas were also a very popular market food, but, if the *hisba* manuals are anything to go by, they were subject to all manner of fraud. As a result, market inspectors closely monitored all aspects of their preparation. And for good reason, it seems. Al-Saqaṭī, for instance, warned that 'fried *mujabbana* makers' were among the biggest cheats when it came to using the scales. Their tampering included adding flour to the cheese, mixing in inferior flours, increasing the amount of dough, and artificially bloating the cheese with hot water.[201]

He imposed proportions for the ingredients (one *rub*ʿ of cheese, half a *rub*ʿ of flour, a quarter of a *rub*ʿ of olive oil), and gave the following instructions on how *mujabbanas* were to be made, specifying that vendors

> should bring cheese that is washed and clean. The kneading [of the dough] must be done in a clean place, with the tubs for the dough covered with a lid. The frying pan must be tinned to prevent the formation of rust on the copper. When unleavened dough is used, the buns are very oily, weigh heavy on the scales but are not tasty.[202]

Eggs are probably the single most important food in Andalusian cuisine, and they are found in the overwhelming majority of recipes. Eggs were a staple for all socio-economic strata, albeit with notable differences, 'for if they were a basic foodstuff at the popular level, on refined tables they appeared as another element of luxurious dishes, or simply as decorative objects'.[203]

Chicken eggs were by far the most popular variety, although Ibn Zuhr reported that duck eggs were also appreciated, while eggs of partridge, pigeon, ostrich, and even peacock were eaten as well. He recommended the yolk rather than the white, and soft-boiled eggs

---

200 Maíllo Salgado 1991: 407–9; de Eguílaz y Yanguas 1886: 234–5: *almojábana* (also *almoiavana*).

201 al-Saqaṭī 1931: 36–7; ʿAbd al-Raʾūf [Levi Provencal 1955]: 98.

202 al-Saqaṭī 1931: 31, 36–8.

203 García Sánchez 1986: 267.

as they were beneficial for the stomach. The best recipe is apparently the one given by the great translator and physician Ḥunayn Ibn Isḥāq: 'Break and beat ten eggs in a glazed earthenware vessel, and add a tablespoonful each of olive oil, vinegar and macerated *murrī*. Put over the fire, and stir until the eggs curdle, and then remove from the fire.'[204]

Andalusians also prepared eggs in other ways: fried, or cooked in a sauce with breadcrumbs and coriander. Ibn Zuhr adds that some people fried a mixture of eggs and fresh cheese, eating it with honey sprinkled on top, though this was harmful and caused serious illnesses that were difficult to cure. Even worse, apparently, was adding eggs to fish and cooking them together, which was more harmful than poison. Nevertheless, some of al-Tujībī's recipes do call for both fish and eggs (for example, Nos. 293–5).

In Near Eastern cookery books, eggs tend to be used mostly in omelettes, or with yolks floating on top of a dish known as *narjisiyya*, from the Arabic word *narjis* ('narcissus'), in reference to their appearance. In Andalusian cuisine, eggs were used in a bewildering variety of ways (stewed, poached, boiled, fried) and dishes, as well as in huge quantities – one chicken recipe (No. 233) requires an incredible thirty eggs for each bird used in the dish. In some cases, the use of eggs is decidedly modern, as a binding agent in stuffings.

It is not unusual to have 'eggs on eggs', with eggs being used in a dish and then also as a garnish – which could be egg yolks or split hard-boiled eggs, or even both (for example, No. 17). Eggs were also involved in another typically Andalusian cooking technique, known as *takhmīr*, which literally means 'fermentation', but in the present text refers to a layer of eggs beaten with a number of spices – such as pepper, ginger or coriander – and sometimes breadcrumbs, or even crushed walnuts.

The sweet recipes also throw up a number of interesting points. Firstly, there is the fact that they are not all in one chapter. The largest number (thirty-nine) are pastries and puddings, which are grouped in in the fourth Chapter of the first Section, with recipes for *ka'k* (ring-shaped biscuits), *mujabbanas*, *isfanj* (doughnuts), and so on. (Nos. 44–83). Another twenty-five – confections – are located towards the end of the book (Nos. 392–417). A staple at the tables of the elite,

204 Ibn Zuhr 1992: 19–21 (trans., 54–6).

sweets figure prominently in most of the medieval Arab cookery books. The proportion of such recipes in al-Tujībī's book is equal to that in al-Baghdādī's, but markedly lower than in *Wuṣla*, which dates from the same period. The exception are the Egyptian cookery books, in which sweet recipes account for less than one-tenth of the total number; Ibn Mubārak Shāh has less than half the proportion of sweets than al-Tujībī. Equally significantly, the Egyptian tradition contains fewer Abbasid sweets.

As we have seen, diners and cooks were inspired by the Near East, and a number of the Andalusian recipes bear the name of sweets also found in cookery books from that region, though often with numerous local variations in terms of preparation and ingredients. For instance, *ka'k* (Nos. 44–6) was a dry biscuit in the Mashriq but was often stuffed with sweets (sugar, almonds, honey) in al-Andalus (Nos. 44–5). In some cases, multiple variations coexisted, as in the *fālūdhaj*, which is both a pudding (No. 67) and a confection (No. 395).

Some of the sweets have withstood the test of time, as their homonymous descendants can still be found in many cuisines. In some cases, the modern version is quite different, as in the case of *kunāfa* (Nos. 57–8) or *khabīṣ*, but in others, such as *qaṭā'if* (Nos. 21, 59, 60), *zulābiyya* (No. 73) and *ka'k*, there are clear similarities. Like other dishes from the Mashriq, sweets also sometimes underwent a name change, which could be minor, as in the case of *mu'aqqad* – a relation of the Egyptian *'aqīd* – or more drastic, as in *qubbayṭ majbūdh* (pulled honey taffy) – a variation of the Abbasid *nāṭif* – or 'al-Mutawakkil's Brains' (No. 415), a type of *fālūdhaj*. The case of the *rukhāmiyya* (No. 404) is interesting, as this was a very popular dish in the Mashriq, and can be found in almost all Near Eastern cookery books – where, however, it was a meat stew, rather than a marbled candy. More mysteriously, *zumurrudī* (No. 416) appears as an 'Eastern' recipe, but no such recipe can be found in the existing sources. The often confusing terminology may be attributable, at least in some cases, to the fact that recipes were culled from different collections and compiled at different times.

In addition to the 'transcreation' of Mashriqi classics, the Andalusian chefs contributed a fair number of their own inventions to the medieval Arab sweets repertoire, such as *juljulāniyya* (No. 397) and *Ra's maymūn*

(No. 68). What is more, this text also contains the oldest recipe for the North African favourite *maqrūḍ* (date-filled pastries), both a plain and filled version (No. 71).[205] Equally Andalusian is the use of pepper as an ingredient in some sweets (for example, No. 55) and the fact that several are served with a dusting of pepper, alongside cinnamon and sugar (No. 59) – though the last two are by far the most frequently used. On a side note, sprinkling ground pepper over food before eating was considered by some to be a Christian and Berber habit.[206]

Most of the sweets from the Near East are part of early Abbasid gastronomy, many of them originating in Persia, as in the case of *jawzīnaq* (Nos. 55, 410), *fālūdhaj*, and *lawzīnaq* (Nos. 56, 411). Others reveal an Egyptian connection – most notably pastries such as *kaʿk*. The marzipan biscuits known as *Qāhiriyya* ('the Cairene'), for which there are three recipes (Nos. 407–9), are found in the anonymous Andalusian treatise, as well as in three other cookery books – one from thirteenth-century Syria and two from Mamluk Egypt. Although the end result might have looked similar across all sources, there is considerable variation in the number of ingredients, which ranges between seven (Syria), eleven (Egypt) and fifteen (al-Andalus). Out of a total of twenty-six ingredients, only three are used across all five sources: sugar, rose water and flour. There are ten ingredients that appear in only one book; these vary from spices such as musk and nutmeg, to sweeteners like syrup and honey. More significant is the difference between the two Andalusian sources, which use the same number of ingredients, but different ones; only al-Tujībī uses walnuts, spikenard, camphor and yeast.

In the Near East, sugar was the elite's sweetener of choice; Andalusian gastronomy, however, preferred honey. Leaving aside the dishes of Eastern origin, al-Tujībī's recipes require honey almost twice as much as sugar. Sugar cane probably entered the Iberian Peninsula soon after the Muslim conquest, and was widely grown there, as well as in North Africa.[207] The prestige of sugar was linked, on the one hand, to its being a scarce – and thus expensive – product at the time, and, on the other, to the favour it enjoyed among some sections of the medical profession.

205 Also see al-Dabbābī al-Mīsāwī 2017: 152–4.
206 *Anwāʿ*, 54–5 (BNF, fol. 23v.).
207 Watson 1983: 28–9; Ouerfelli 2008: 179–222.

One of the voices in the opposing camp was Ibn Zuhr, who devoted a treatise to 'The Preference for Honey over Sugar' (*Tafḍīl al-ʿasal ʿalā ʾl-sukkar*),[208] in which he explained that the preference for sugar over honey in the making of beverages and medicines ran counter Galenic principles. He criticized the royal courts' love of sugar as being part of their relentless quest for rare and exotic products to distinguish themselves from their subjects. The royal seal of approval, in turn, promoted the spread of sugar among the elites keen on emulating courtly habits. However, most of his ire was reserved for his colleagues – physicians and pharmacologists – who promoted this new-fangled and expensive product for their own selfish reasons, for profit, and to curry favour with rulers. That is not to say that sugar should be eschewed entirely, and Ibn Zuhr preferred it to honey in the preparation of syrups for specific ailments, especially those affecting the oesophagus, stomach and bladder. More surprisingly, despite his praise for honey, he strongly advised against using it in combination with olive oil to cook meat, as this would make it tough, slow to digest, and lacking in flavour, even though it produced a good broth.[209]

The prevailing medical framework of the period was a system which went back to Greek physicians, especially Hippocrates (*ca.* 460–*ca.* 375 BCE) and Galen of Pergamon (d. *ca.* 216). It centred on the so-called 'humours', which were fluids – yellow and black bile, blood and phlegm – regulating bodily health. The same framework underpinned the medieval Arab culinary tradition.[210] Food was medicine, and medicine was food; the latter was, in fact, more important, as expressed in al-Rāzī's famous saying: 'Don't treat with medicines what you can treat with foods.'[211]

Many of the cookery books contain medical information about both ingredients and dishes, but its extent and detail varies greatly. Al-Tujībī's work is at the lower end of the spectrum. The Introduction discusses the role of food in a balanced temperament, the medically most beneficial order of dishes in a meal, and the properties of various materials used in cooking vessels.

208 al-Khaṭṭābī 1988: I, 310–11; Kuhne Brabant 1995; Kuhne Brabant & da Silva 1997.
209 Ibn Zuhr 1992: 138 (trans., 149). Also see Ouerfelli 2008: 519–20.
210 For more details, see Ibn Mubārak Shāh 2020: xxix–xxxiii.
211 Ibn Khallikān 1968–72: V, 158.

Besides the Introduction, there are a few other instances where medical information is offered: a *jūdhāba* engendering 'good humours' (No. 221); *tharīdas* to restore the strength of those suffering from exhaustion (No. 18) or increase sexual potency (No. 19); a barley mush that cools fevers and hot temperaments (No. 42); a sauce with 'innate heat' (No. 107); a mustard dish for weak cold stomachs (No. 145); a gourd *fālūdhaj* that loosens the bowels (No. 341); the laxative properties of chickpeas (No. 390); or the fact that perfuming food with musk, ambergris, rose water and camphor strengthens the soul and gladdens the heart (No. 129). Some dietetic advice is also proffered for fish: its potential harm, how to counter any nefarious effects by means of certain drinks, as well as a strict prohibition against engaging in any physical exertion either before or after eating fish.

Humoral theory also affected the method used to cook food – whether it was fried, roasted, stewed, and so on. The fact that many of al-Tujībī's recipes specify leaving the pot on embers to 'balance' the flavours also goes back to humoral theory, which has the concept of 'balance' at its core. When the humours are balanced and working together, there is *eucrasia*, or 'good mixture', known in Arabic as *iʿtidāl al-mizāj*.

The order in which dishes should be eaten was determined by the properties of the food. In his introduction, al-Tujībī follows Ibn Zuhr (though without acknowledging him):

> One should first eat heavy foods so that they can settle at the bottom of the stomach, which has greater digestive strength than its upper part. Similarly, dairy produce, *tharīds*, cheese, *harīsa*, *iṭriyya*, fatty beef and lamb, jerky, fish, toasted seeds and the like should also be eaten first, in order to improve digestion. Vegetables should be served to soften the stomach. Everything with a pronounced salty flavour should be eaten in the middle of the meal, whereas sweets, fruits and roasts – provided they are well cooked – should come at the end. Start with things that have just been prepared. First serve sweets with eggs that have solidified, and everything made with sesame or flax seeds, unless the stomach has a bilious humour, in which

> case you must avoid these; if you can't, then eat them last. Those with a very weak stomach should select foods that are easily digested.

It is interesting to contrast this with the recommended order for courses – seven in total – in the Andalusian culinary tradition, as set forth in the other Andalusian treatise, which starts the meal with 'a feminine dish, such as *baqliyya mukarrara* and the various kinds of *tafāyās* (Nos. 109–10, 191–2, 283) or after this the *jamali* dish' (No. 99). Then come the following successive dishes: a *muthallath* (No. 101), a dish of *murri* (Nos. 449–62), *mukhallal* (No. 196), *muʿassal* (Nos. 150, 392), *farṭūn* (No. 68) and, finally, another *muʿassal*.[212] The author adds that this sequence of dishes was the practice of rulers and the nobility in both al-Andalus and the Maghrib. Interestingly enough, Ibn Khalṣūn held that all sweets except pulled taffy (recipe No. 398) should be eaten before the meal.[213] The ordering of distinct courses was an Andalusian contribution to the Arab culinary tradition, since the concept of a succession of clearly delineated courses was alien to the Mashriq, and the literature does not discuss the order of individual dishes in this kind of detail.

When it comes to religious references, al-Tujībī's work is once again an exceptional case, in that there are far more of them than in any of the other cookery books. Indeed, generally speaking, the medieval Arab cookery manuals do not contain many religious references. In fact, aside from the 'counterfeit' dishes specifically linked to Christians during Lent, one would be hard put to find anything regarding foods linked to religious practices or festivals. The answer, as we have seen, is, of course, that there were no differences in the day-to-day diet between the religious communities.

In this book, the first glaring religious motif is the use of the phrase 'Eat and enjoy, Allah the Exalted willing' which ends almost every single recipe. In addition to showing the author's Islamic credentials, it also conveys that he is writing exclusively for a Muslim readership. Al-Tujībī is always mindful of ingredients that might be unlawful in Islam; for instance, in a recipe for making fish *murrī* with grape juice

---

212 *Anwāʿ*, 58 (BNF, fols. 24v.–25r.).

213 Ibn Khalṣūn 1992: 166 (trans., 96).

(No. 461), he reassures the reader that the fermentation of the must will completely cancel out the effect of the wine. The effect of ritual purity – or rather the lack thereof – is mentioned in a couple of recipes, as the author warns against letting any man – or woman – who is in a state of impurity handle, or even go near foods being pickled, cured or fermented (for example, Nos. 323, 425). This prohibition was shared by scholars and often referred to women on their menses. The agronomist Ibn al-ʿAwwām, for instance, advised that they should not be allowed to get close to vinegar, olives, capers or any other preserved vegetables, for fear of spoiling them.[214]

One can ascribe the increased religious references in the text partly to the fact that al-Tujībī was a legal scholar, but we cannot exclude an element of 'overcompensation' on the part of a newcomer from a multi-faith area onto Muslim soil. References to his native land understandably elicit a strong reaction – the mere mention of using plums imported from Christian Spain requires the imprecation: 'May Allah destroy it!' Meanwhile, the names of formerly Muslim towns like Valencia and, of course, his hometown Murcia, are followed by the supplication to Allah to 'restore them to Islam!' On the other hand, the use of a type of mustard from Christian territory does not provoke any comment. On one occasion he even praises a recipe that is 'eaten a lot by Christians' (No. 107), especially the use of *jalja* (sauce). He also includes several dishes (Nos. 105, 202, 248, 281, 302) known as *rāhibī*, from the Arabic *rāhib* ('monk'). However, it is unclear why they should bear this name in the absence of any identifiably Christian, or non-Muslim, features. In fact, there is nothing in the nature of the ingredients that sets them apart from any of the other dishes. And then there is the use of the Julian, rather than the Hijra calendar when discussing crops, and so on.

Marín connects the incorporation of Christian elements in al-Tujībī's book with the Murcian court of Ibn Mardanīsh, which was considered a place where the imitation of Christian customs was the rule.[215] This statement exaggerates the Christian element in the book. If anything, it might explain al-Tujībī's anti-Christian comments and consistent use of Islamic formulae, as a way of pre-empting suspicions of having been 'tainted' by living among Christians. The use of the Julian months,

214 Ibn al-ʿAwwām [Clement-Mullet 1866:] II:1, 415; *idem* 1802: I, 689; 2012: III, 533.
215 Marín 2010: 42.

on the other hand, may be attributed to the sources from which they were borrowed, most notably agricultural calendars, where this was common practice.

There is one reference to a chicken dish being called 'Jewish' (No 212), which not only lacks any Jewish elements, but is also included in a section with Mashriq dishes. One may draw a comparison with the handful of so-called Jewish dishes in the anonymous Andalusian cookery book, which are similarly devoid of any features that might be considered Jewish.[216]

Some ingredients in al-Andalus would become associated with Christians – most notably parsley – while coriander would come to be regarded as the quintessential Muslim herb.

The sophistication of many of the dishes in the present book, as shown by the number and variety of ingredients as well as the often complicated methods and tools, obviously required an extensive *batterie de cuisine*. It comprised all manner of specialized implements. The most frequently used piece of equipment was the mortar, which we are told is best made out of wood, followed by stone, while copper should be used only if the other two are not available. Other implements included skewers; slabs for kneading sweets and pounding spices; knives and cleavers; moulds for making cheese or *kaʿk*; juicing presses; chisels used in the making of biscuits; strainers and sieves; different sizes of jars (earthenware, leather) to store liquids, condiments and pickles; kneading tubs; rolling pins; graters; a special hook to manipulate food (especially *mujabbanas*) as it is cooking; a *kunāfa* griddle; a *qaṭāʾif* pan; and a ring for cleaning intestines. The generic cooking pot was the *qidr* ('pot'), which could be made of (glazed) clay, copper (in which case it would be tinned), iron or stone, and appears in almost every single recipe. Other cookware included the cauldron (*ṭanjīr*), frying pans (*miqlā*); and, of course, the *ṭājin*, a shallow earthenware stewing pan or casserole dish that was used for oven cooking, but could be put directly over the fire.[217] There is also a description of a special pot to make couscous, which is very easily

216 See Ibn Mubārak Shāh 2020: xxxv–xxvi.

217 The word entered Arabic from Aramaic, but goes back to the Greek *tágenon*, though its etymon may actually be the ancient Egyptian *ʾīkn* ('vessel') – possibly related to the Babylonian *akunu* – and the Coptic *aca/on*, a metal or wooden vessel. Erman & Grapow 1971: I, 140; Crum 1939: 26.

recognizable as the modern *couscousier*. Pots often had a perforated lid, or were covered with a sieve to allow the steam to escape, since it was thought to be harmful to the food. In other cases, the pot was sealed with dough or soaked paper, as were lids with clay, and olive oil was poured onto condiments to seal them during storage. Recipes often use alternate layers of dough with other ingredients, both in savoury and sweet dishes (for example, Nos. 28, 69).

The majority of the dishes require multiple cooking stages, such as boiling, frying, stewing and, finally, baking or roasting in the oven. In some cases, several stints in the communal oven were required (for example, No. 28). Dishes were consistently left to simmer down before serving, and so they were eaten lukewarm rather than scalding hot – often, the cook is told to wait for something to cool down entirely. Several dishes were eaten cold.

Some of the methodology is decidedly modern, in that it reveals 'modular' features, best illustrated by the garniture pot (No. 108), or the use of one pot as a heating source for another whose contents are added later on.

Naturally, the full kitchen arsenal would not have been available to the general population in urban areas, who would often eat out, not least because only the well-off had kitchens to speak of, and so stews, processed food – whether sausages, rose water or pasta – were purchased from the market. Some other sections of the population – one is tempted to use the anachronistic term 'middle classes' – would have been able to heat up food on a home stove, which is sometimes given as an option in the recipes.

Bread was baked at the *furn* (from the Latin *furnus*), the communal brick oven, with the dough being prepared in the home – a practice that is still found in some areas to this day. It also served to heat dishes that would be prepared at home. It was by far the most popular heating method and is used in half of the recipes. In order to regulate the heat, dishes could be moved closer or farther away from the fire inside the oven.

Another kind of oven was the conical *tannūr*, which was made out of clay. Its history can be traced back to ancient Egypt and Mesopotamia, where it was known as a *tinūru*. It retained its form through the ages and many people today will recognize it as the *tandoor*. The *tannūr* is only required in about fifteen recipes – mainly for breads, in which loaves (usually unleavened) are stuck to the sides. It is also used for roasting a whole skewered lamb or ram, as well as game meat and chickens. More unusually, it is also recommended for roasting aubergines by placing them in the middle of the embers (No. 364). Interestingly enough, neither the *tannūr* nor the *furn* oven is required in any of the fish recipes.

Two other devices appear in only one recipe: a brazier (*kānūn*) to make *qaṭā'if* (No. 59), and a small bread oven (*kūsha*) for *ka'k* (No. 83). The former was used quite extensively in the Near East and came in a portable version as well. It could also denote a two-chambered oven made of red pottery; embers in the lower chamber heat up the upper chamber, which is fitted with a grate and can also support a pot or casserole. Known in Spanish as *anafe*, it was particularly prevalent in Murcia. This was probably the oven called for in a thirteenth-century Iraqi recipe for smoked olives (*zaytun mubakhkhar*).[218]

The most enigmatic cooking method in the book involves the *malla*. In Near Eastern cookery books it referred to a pit filled with ashes and stones, whereas in Spain it could also denote an oven distinct from both the *furn* and *tannūr*.[219] Neither of these appears to fit the recipes here where the *malla* is clearly a hotplate of some kind, which could be made out of iron, copper or even (unglazed) earthenware, and was sometimes also put in the oven. The word, and indeed the use of this implement, cannot have been very widespread since it is not attested in this sense in any other source. One of al-Tujībī's contemporaries, and fellow Tunis resident, the physician Ibn al-Ḥashshā', who composed a medical glossary commissioned by the Ḥafṣid caliph al-Mustanṣir, described *malla* in the Mashriqi sense, as hot ashes and embers in which dough is placed for baking bread.[220] The anonymous Andalusian also uses *malla* in the sense of roasting in ashes, noting that it was loved by the Bedouins (*al-bādiyya*).[221]

218 al-Baghdādī 1964: 69; G. Rosselló Bordoi, in Marín & Waines 1994: 51–2; Lewicka 2011: 94. It could apparently also denote a six-foot-high coal-fired stove used for heating in winter (Dozy 1881: I, 491).

219 Dozy 1881: II, 608; Guillermo, in Marín 1994: 74.

220 Ibn al-Ḥashshā' 1941: 74 (No. 688).

221 *Anwā'*, 51. A thirteenth-century Syrian cookery book has no name for it, but the process described is very similar and is also said to be a Bedouin speciality (*Wuṣla*, No. 617). Today, the practice still exists in some communities, and is known as the

Going by the description and use of the *malla* in the present text, it is probably similar to the Near Eastern *ṣāj*, which is a metal disc placed over a fire that serves as a griddle or baking tray.[222] It is used to this day in many countries, with the resultant bread being known by a variety of names, including *ṣāj* (Lebanon), *sharāk* (Jordan) and *raqāq* (Iraq and UAE). In Turkey, it is called *saç ekmeği*, whereas this type of griddle is also widely used in India to make roti and chapati.

Dining in the medieval Muslim World was very much a 'holistic' experience that appealed to all of the senses, including the visual. This was very important as eating was a highly communal activity. This is reflected in the variety of tableware that was used to serve and present the food. The serving dish of choice in al-Andalus was the *ghaḍāra* (also *ghiḍāra*), a large glazed ceramic bowl, which al-Jāḥiẓ claimed was sometimes made of briar wood (*khalanj*) as well as in a Chinese glazed variant.[223] The text also refers to a range of bowls and dishes of varying sizes that would be put on the table, including a special tureen for *tharīdas* (*mithrad*), though not infrequently the generic *wiʿā* and *inā'* were used, both meaning 'container, vessel'.

Weights and Measures

One of the challenges of researching medieval Arab cooking revolves around the issue of weights and measures. Usually, they are not given, and the cook is expected to know by experience or instinct. On the other hand, this may perhaps also have been a way of withholding vital information and safeguarding 'intellectual property'. More importantly, the recipes in the literature never specify the number of diners they are supposed to cater for.

In some cases, basic guidance is given about quantities – 'a little' (*yasīr*, *qalīl*), 'a lot' (*kathīr*), 'enough', or 'enough to add/remove/enhance the flavour of', and so on. Often, the instruction is simply to take 'a sufficient quantity' of this or that ingredient.

One would imagine that in those few cases where precise measures

'bedouin barbecue'.

222 Shafer-Elliott 2013: 119.

223 Ahsan 1973: 212. The term (also *ghuḍār*, *ghiḍār*) may come from the Persian *ghadāra*, which denoted a copper vessel. See Steingass 1892: 881; Dozy 1881: II, 216; Corriente 1997: 380.

are given, all problems are resolved. In fact, nothing could be further from the truth, since there was no uniform system of weights across the Muslim Mediterranean, and there were often substantial differences between regions as well as periods. The table below lists approximate correspondences, taking into account the area and time in which the book was written – that is to say, thirteenth-century Muslim Spain and Tunisia.[224]

The book uses a number of measures. Some, like *raṭl* and *ūqiya*, are used across the board, whereas others are restricted to specific recipes (for example, *dirham* and *mithqāl* in hand-washing powders and perfumes), or for certain ingredients – *mudd* for flour and salt, *qadaḥ* for milk and grape juice. Some appear only once: *qādūs* (for semolina), *qafīz* (for vinegar).

MEASURE	NO. (RECIPES)	VALUE
dirham	11	3.3g.
mithqāl	5	4.4g.
mudd	5	*ca.* 1 kg.
qadaḥ	2	*ca.* 1 litre
qādūs	1	3.159 pounds
qafīz	1	44 litres
raṭl	59	454.5g.
rubʿ	4	8.16 litres/pounds
ūqiya	26	31g.

In addition, recipes also include more imprecise, generic measures such as *juz'* ('part') and *shibr* ('hand span'), while both *qubḍa* and *kaff* denote a handful.

Equally sparse in the cookery books is the length of time ingredients and/or dishes are supposed to be cooked. In the few instances where the timing is specified, the reader is told to leave something 'for an hour' (*sāʿa*), but this was not, in fact, to be taken literally, and simply

224 The list is based on Brunschvig 1935; Hinz 1955; Rodríguez Lorente 1988; Vallvé Bermejo 1976, 1977, 1984; Ibn Wāfid 1980.

meant 'a while'. More often than not, the instruction is simply to cook something 'until it is done'.

The Translation

This translation is based on the 2012 Beirut edition and the three known surviving manuscripts.

In order to reduce the number of notes and make the text accessible to as wide an audience as possible, the translation amplifies and compresses where appropriate, without, of course, detracting from the intended meaning of the text.

I have avoided anachronistic 'translations' of dishes, so the *kunāfa* here is a thin flatbread, rather than a 'crêpe'; the latter would mislead the modern reader since no eggs are used in the recipe. Similarly, as the measures used are approximate, they appear in the original Arabic, rather than converted into their modern equivalents. This also conveniently circumvents the need for multiple systems.

In the translation, 'milk' means fresh milk, and *samīd* has been rendered as 'semolina', but is also sometimes used to refer to semolina flour. The Arabic *zayt* has been consistently translated as 'olive oil'.

The word *maghrafa* is rendered consistently as 'ladle', which is what it means in modern Arabic. But in Andalusian Arabic – and indeed in some North African vernaculars, such as Tunisian – it can also mean 'spoon'. A look at some of the recipes will show that in some cases the quantity of a ladle would probably have been too much. Contemporaneous cooks would of course have been aware of this, and amended instructions accordingly.

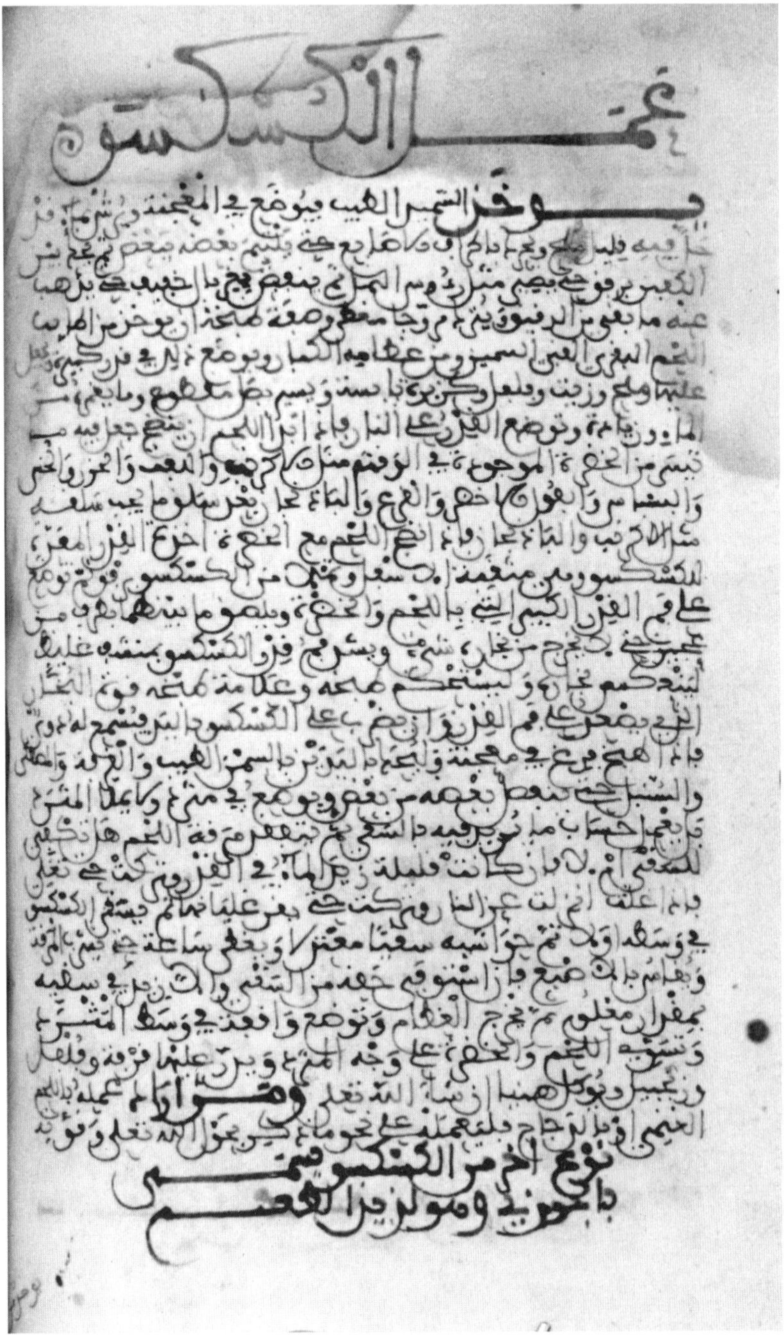

British Library Or5927, fol. 121v. (couscous recipe, No. 85)

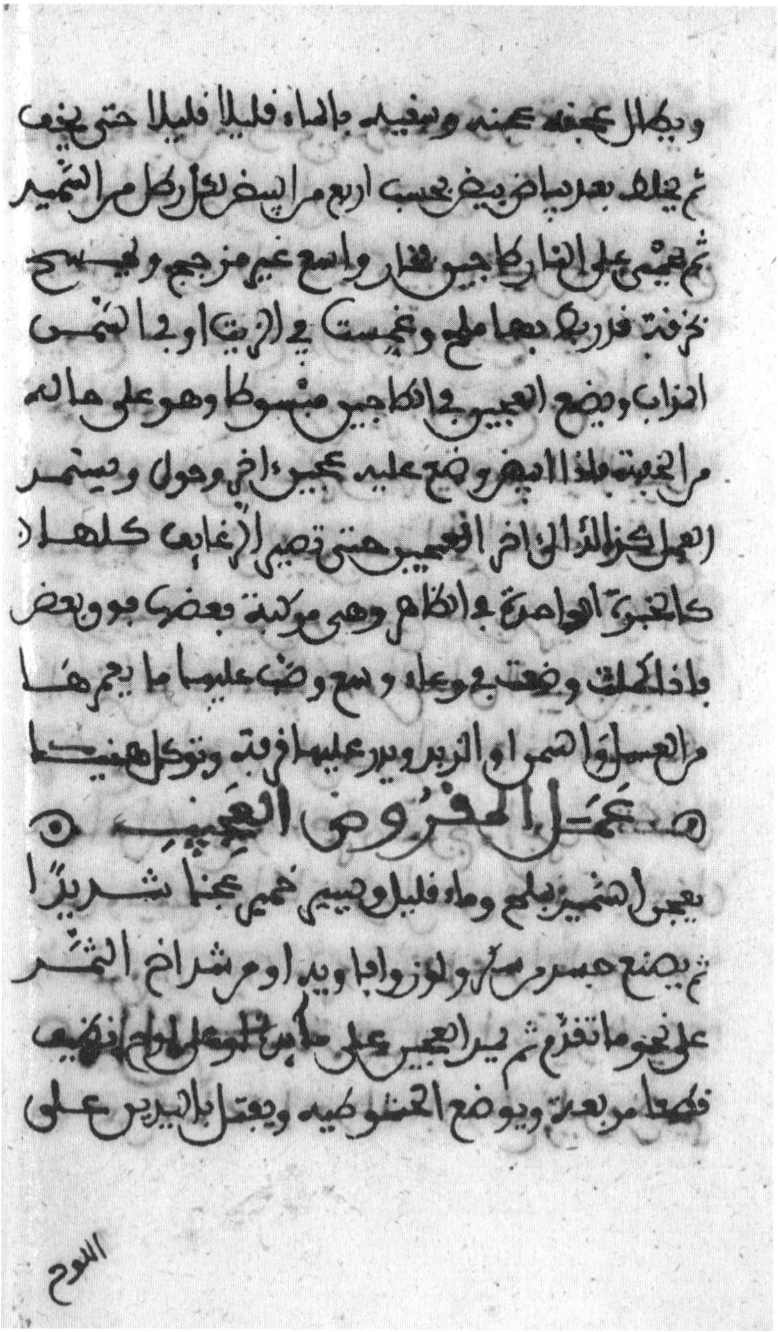

Gayangos XVI, fol. 36v. (*maqrūḍ* recipe, No. 71)

قد ازيلت رغوته ويترك فيه حتى تستوفي حقها من العسل ثم تزال منه وتوضع
على لوح او شباك من قصب حتى تجف وان ظهر العمل رقيقا زيد فيه الدقيق
وترك حتى يختمر وصنع منه ذلك واستعمل ان شاء الله تعالى **عمل الاسفنج**
يبل السميد الطيب بماء سخن وملح وخمير ويترك حتى يرطب ثم يعجن قويا
ويسقى بالماء قليلا قليلا ويطال حتى يصير خفيفا ويرفع كله في اثناء عجنه عجنه
من المعجنة باليدين وينزل بسرعة حتى يخرج عنه الريح ويترك يختمر حتى
يظهر عليه اثر الاختمار ثم توضع على النار مقلاة من نحاس او حديد مقصدرة
نظيفة بمقدار معلوم من الزيت فاذا غلى الزيت اخذ من العجين باليد اليسرى
وشددت عليه الكف حتى يخرج بعضه فوق الابهام والسبابة ويقطع قطعا
يوضع منها في المقلاة ما يعلوها لمن شاءها كبارا وهي المسماة بالاقصاد
فلا يغمرها بالزيت احمر والنصف الاعلى ابيض وليحركها برفق فاذا انضجت
اخرجها واستعملها ومن ارادها صغارا وهي المسماة بالمغدر فليكثر من الزيت
في المقلاة وليقطع العجين بالعصر في كفه على نحو ما ذكر على القدر الذي يريد من الصغر
فاذا امتلأت المقلاة وبدا الاسفنج في الاحمرار اخرجها ووضعها في اناء وملأ المقلاة
باسفنج آخر فاذا بدا احمرارها اضاف اليها الاسفنج المعمولة اولا وحرك الجميع حتى
تنضج وتجف وبعد ذلك يخرجها ويضعها في وعاء من عود بعد وضعها في اناء
آخر قبله ليجف زيتها ويوكل ذلك ان شاء الله ويختبر العجين اولا بان يصنع
منه كعكة فان بقيت مفتوحة على صفتها وعلت على وجه الزيت بعد طبخها
وظهر داخلها منقبا فذلك علامة اختماره والا فليترك حتى يختمر بحول الله
تعالى **عمل اسفنج الريح** يعجن دقيق الدرمك بالماء والملح والخمير
والزيت العذب عجنا محكما ثم يحل بالماء شيئا شيئا حتى يصير اقرب منه
الى الخفة ويترك حتى يختمر ثم توضع على النار مقلاة بزيت كثير ويوخذ
من العجين بالاصبع ويطرح فيها ويعمل كذلك الى اخر العجين ومن شاءها
منتفخة فليعجن العجين بالبيض ويعمل على ما تقدم **عمل اسفنج القلة**
يعجن السميد او الدرمك على نحو ما تقدم من اللين والخفة ويوخذ قلة

جديدة

Wetzstein 1207, fol. 19r. (*isfanj* recipes, Nos. 73-5)

REMAINDERS ON THE TABLE AS REGARDS DELIGHTFUL FOODS AND DISHES

In the name of Allah, the merciful, the compassionate

Allah's blessings and peace on our lord Muḥammad, his family and companions[1]

PRAISE BE TO ALLAH, Who put human beings above all creatures and favoured them with merit – 'Say: "Who has forbidden the ornaments Allah has produced for His servants and the good things that He has provided for you?"';[2] Who increased beneficences on His servants and lavished various dishes upon them; Who introduced differences in their desires for foods through diversity in their composition and preparation, and made it lawful for them to be enjoyed in abundance as a blessing ('Eat of the good things we have provided for you!').[3] Blessings upon our lord Muḥammad, His Messenger, the master of intercession and the blessed lake[4] and the most noble before Allah of all the people on earth; may Allah bless him, his family and his companions, with prayers to preserve them until the Day of Judgement.

Among the things that move a generous person and distinguish the people of rank is an unwavering interest in food, which is the cornerstone of physical health and the primary cause of a balanced temperament, as well as in the refinement of cooking it in accordance with tried and tested methods of precision and mastery.[5] This applies especially to those of noble character, who eschew greed and sweeten the nobility of the soul through generosity; who dine by the flickering of the fire without shirking the debt owed to their neighbours, and show patience in their homes; who are content with half the pot and are not satisfied unless they share it. It also applies to those whose call

1 This is where the author's name appears in Gayangos XVI, fol. 1v. (see Introduction).

2 Qur. 7:32.

3 Qur. 2:57.

4 *Ṣāḥib al-ḥawḍ*, 'master of the lake' (also pond, basin), which refers to the place where believers will go on the Day of Resurrection, and when they drink from the (musk-scented) water they will never again become thirsty.

5 The preceding passage in this paragraph is very different in Gayangos XVI (fols. 1v.–2r.), which has: 'When I wrote this book and Allah the Exalted inspired me to gather the various culinary branches for people of discernment, I called it 'The Book of What Remains on the Tables by way of Delicious Dishes', and related wondrous foods, seasonings, condiments, how to restore spoilt foods, hand-washing powders. This has been done with due care and attention for tried and tested methods of precision and mastery.'

is not, as in the proverb, a mirage in the salty desert and about whom it is not said that their chef's apron is the whitest there is.[6]

The best introduction is like the vinegar dip, which is the most excellent appetizer there is.[7] The blessing that excels all is that of *tharīd*.[8] If I had wanted to expand this chapter, I would have mentioned al-Ma'mūn[9] and barley bread, or Būrān, who has given her name to an influential culinary invention. I would have also listed curiosities of unparalleled utility[10] and anecdotes from the gatherings of gluttons and gourmet boon companions. Rather, I have decided to be concise and restrict myself to the best cooking recipes, since I have found that many people have composed cookbooks but limited themselves to what is famous, and failed to mention many [important] things. Those from the East contain much that disgusts the ear and should be dismissed, or almost regarded as filthy for human beings even if, to them, it is the most refined food. This may be due to the water and air there, as well as the nature of their intentions and desires.

I have always been partial towards Andalusian food, and I can safely say that in this area the Andalusians and those like them are zealous and progressive, even though they have come late to gastronomic invention. This is due to the small size of their territory and its proximity to the enemies of Islam who are so close that they can see

6 This goes back to a saying that when food becomes expensive and/or scarce (e.g. in winter), the chef's apron becomes white, as he does very little cooking.

7 The author cites a famous *ḥadīth* by the Prophet Muḥammad: 'vinegar is truly the perfect dip (*idām*).'

8 This echoes the *ḥadīth* according to which the Prophet Muḥammad called it 'the Lord of food' and that its superiority over all food is like the superiority of A'isha (his favourite wife) over all other women (*faḍl 'Ā'isha 'alā 'l-nisā' ka-faḍl al-tharīd 'alā sā'ir al-ṭa'ām*).

9 Abbasid caliph (813–33) and son of Hārūn al-Rashīd (766–809). He was known as a great patron of the sciences and arts. He himself is said to have written a cookery book, and inspired – or created – several dishes (especially sweets) bearing his name. These were known as *ma'mūniyya*, and very early on one of the recipes entered Christian Europe as *mamonia*. See Ibn Mubārak Shāh 2020: 88–9; Rodinson 1962. Al-Ma'mūn's wife Būrān gained culinary fame in her own right through her signature fried aubergine dishes (known as *Būrāniyya*, though frequently misspelt as *Burāniyya* in the present text), an example of which can be found in recipe No. 100 below. See Ibn Mubārak Shāh 2020: 33 (note 125); Perry [Rodinson *et al.* 2001]: 241–50; Marín 1981; *EI*^{2}, s.v. (D. Sourdel).

10 Both Gayangos XVI (fol. 2r.) and BL Or5927 (fol. 101r.) have 'benefits of meals' (*fawā'id al-mawā'id*).

each other's fires.[11]

In this book I have collected recipes I deem the most pleasing, as well as many dishes that I have invented. I have included many Andalusian recipes, and a small selection of dishes from the Mashriq. I have added the usual and well-known things connected in any way to various types of dishes, such as fermented condiments, vinegars and other similar things, which are included in many chapters.

I believe that the first rule of cooking is to avoid dirty and unpleasant places. You should not cook twice in the same earthenware pot. One of the physicians insisted on this point, saying that, if possible and allowed by religious law, it is best to cook in gold or silver containers.[12] He also advised against using earthenware and glazed clay containers; the former should not be used more than once, the latter only five times.[13] Copper containers are not to be used either, because they are harmful.[14] He recommends cooking in iron containers, provided they are washed and cleaned, and kept free from rust. He mentioned that one of the properties of these vessels is that the more you cook with them, the greater their benefit, the least of which is the strengthening of the limbs in all actions. He added that there is no problem in using

11 This references another *ḥadīth*, according to which Muslims should not be so close to non-Muslims that they can see their fires, and is part of the prohibition for Muslims to reside in non-Muslim territories.

12 The physician in question is Ibn Zuhr, who added that food cooked in gold vessels strengthens the heart and is useful against low spirits and weakness of any organ (1992: 108, 136, 140; trans., 124, 147, 149). Ibn al-Khaṭīb specified that the best vessel is made of gold, followed by silver, clay and ceramic (1984: 61; trans., 137). Others subscribed to the religious objection, and in his market-inspector manual Ibn al-Ukhuwwa (1938: 76; trans., 25), for instance, prohibited even the making of vessels of gold or silver, as well as drinking from them.

13 This is a verbatim quote from Ibn Zuhr (1992: 136; trans., 148), who explains that it is 'because the remains of the last food prepared in them penetrate into the pores, remain there and will later become corrupted'.

14 Cf. Ibn Zuhr (1992: 138; trans., 149), who said that 'everything that is prepared in copper pans is harmful, especially fatty foods, such as sausages (*mirqās, laqāniq*) and fried foods, because they are very strong foods and, if they are already easily altered on their own, even more so if they come into contact with copper'. This was, of course, due to the risk of verdigris poisoning. Copper vessels were used, provided they were tinned, though Ibn Zuhr (1992: 137; trans., 148) adds that 'copper utensils, even if they are tinned, will always leave some traces of the constituent matter of copper which, when the pots are regularly used in cooking, reappear, in the same way that the constant dripping of water on stones leaves traces on them'.

tin pots and pans. Others have said that it is best to use glass containers for eating, drinking and even cooking, if possible.[15]

They also advise against covering the food in pots after preparing it, except with something that allows the steam to escape, such as a sieve. This is because they allege that if the vapours are locked in and cannot escape, they produce a harmful effect on food, especially fish and anything eaten grilled. So, whenever you cook food in a pot, it should be covered with a very finely pierced lid.[16] For frying, the best containers are those made of silver or gold, followed by tin and lead. Copper ones are not good and everything that is fried in them goes bad, especially if it involves food with a high fat content, such as *mirqās* sausages, fried foods, and so on, because they have a sharp and unbalanced temperament, which is not easily rectified. So, just think of what will happen if the bad humours of the copper are added![17]

You should first eat heavy foods so that they can settle at the bottom of the stomach, which has greater digestive strength than its upper part. Similarly, dairy produce, *tharīds*, cheese, *harīsa*, *iṭriyya* (noodles), fatty beef and lamb, jerky, fish, toasted seeds and the like should also be eaten first, in order to improve digestion. Vegetables should be served to soften the stomach. Everything with a pronounced salty flavour should be eaten in the middle of the meal, whereas sweets, fruits and roasts – provided they are well cooked – should come at the end. Start with things that have just been prepared. First serve sweets with eggs that have solidified, and everything made with sesame or flax seeds, unless the stomach has a bilious humour, in which case you must avoid these; if you can't, then eat them last. Those with a very weak stomach should select foods that are easily digested.[18] There are many examples of this, but this goes beyond the scope of my book.

15 Ibn Zuhr (1992: 137; trans., 148) has the following: 'lead and tin vessels, whether pots or dishes, are very good, and so are glazed earthenware vessels, although food is prepared very slowly in them. Glass ones are very good, and even though you cannot cook in them because they break easily, it is highly recommended to use them as tableware.' According to Ibn al-Khaṭīb ((1984: 61; trans., 137), cooking in copper pots alters the temperament, especially when frying in them, and while tin pots are excellent for cooking, they slow down the cooking process.

16 Cf. Ibn al-Khaṭīb, *ibid*.

17 This entire paragraph is for the most part taken from Ibn Zuhr (1992: 137–8; trans., 148–9).

18 The introduction in BL Or5927 ends here and misses the table of contents up to and including Section 10, which starts on fol. 102r.

I have called this book *Remainders on the Table as regards Delightful Foods and Dishes*[19] and divided it into twelve Sections.

Section One: on breads, *tharīds*, soups, dishes with bread, and similar things. It consists of five chapters:
- Chapter One: on breads
- Chapter Two: on *tharīdas*
- Chapter Three: on pottages and mashed cereal dishes
- Chapter Four: pastries, various types of *mujabbanas* (fried cheese buns), *isfanj* (doughnuts) and other similar foods
- Chapter Five: on dishes that are soaked in broth like *tharīdas*, or cooked like soups

Section Two: on the various kinds of meat from quadrupeds. It consists of six chapters:
- Chapter One: on beef dishes
- Chapter Two: on dishes with sheep meat
- Chapter Three: on lamb meat dishes
- Chapter Four: on kid meat dishes
- Chapter Five: on wild game meat dishes
- Chapter Six: on the use of quadruped meat in the making of meatballs, *mirqās* sausages, meat pies,[20] *harīsa*, etc.

Section Three: on poultry. It consists of seven chapters:
- Chapter One: on goose meat dishes
- Chapter Two: on chicken meat dishes
- Chapter Three: on partridge meat dishes
- Chapter Four: on squab meat dishes
- Chapter Five: on turtledove meat dishes
- Chapter Six: on starling meat dishes
- Chapter Seven: on sparrow meat dishes

19 Gayangos XVI (fol. 3v.) has *Faḍālat al-khwān fī ṭībat al-alwān* (instead of *Faḍālat al-khiwān fī ṭayyibāt al-ṭaʿām wa 'l-alwān*), which translates as 'Remainders of the Choicest Dishes on the Table'.

20 The Arabic text has *ajrash*, which is clearly a spelling mistake for *aḥrash*, which is the form that also occurs in the relevant passages. Corriente 1997: 121.

Section Four: on the so-called *Ṣanhājī* dish and on the cooking of tongue and tripe. It consists of three chapters:

Chapter One: on the *Ṣanhājī* dish
Chapter Two: on tongue
Chapter Three: on tripe

Section Five: on fish and eggs. It consists of two chapters:

Chapter One: on fish
Chapter Two: on egg dishes

Section Six: on dairy products and everything that is made with them. It consists of three chapters:

Chapter One: on milk curd and what to make with it
Chapter Two: on making curds and extracting butter
Chapter Three: on making dry cheese, what is prepared with it, and on restoring butter and milk

Section Seven: on vegetables and similar things. It consists of ten chapters:

Chapter One: on gourds
Chapter Two: on aubergine dishes
Chapter Three: on carrot dishes
Chapter Four: on truffle dishes
Chapter Five: on asparagus[21] dishes
Chapter Six: on dishes with artichokes (*ḥarshaf*,[22] *qannāriya and afzān*)
Chapter Seven: on cooking mushrooms
Chapter Eight: on dishes with spinach, leafy goosefoot,[23] lettuce and things of that kind
Chapter Nine: on *jināniyya*
Chapter Ten: on taro

---

21 *isfārāj*, which is incorrectly copied as *isfarānaj* in Gayangos XVI (fol. 4v.).

22 Gayangos XVI (fol. 4v.) has the variant spelling *khurshuf* (see recipe No. 126).

23 The text has the nonsensical *yarbūn*, which was amended to *yarbūz* (which is written as *yarbūr* in Gayangos XVI, fol. 4v.). See Corriente 1997: 576; Renaud &. Colin 1934: No. 67.

Section Eight: on types of pulses, such as broad beans, chickpeas and others. it consists of three chapters:
Chapter One: on dishes with dried and fresh broad beans
Chapter Two: on chickpea dishes
Chapter Three: on lentils

Section Nine: on honeyed rice puddings and other sweetmeats. It consists of seven chapters:
Chapter One: on making *mu'assal* and *ghassānī*
Chapter Two: on varieties of *ḥalwā* (sweetmeats)
Chapter Three: on *Qāhiriyya* and *sanbūsak*[24]
Chapter Four: on *jawzīnaq* and *lawzīnaq*[25]
Chapter Five: on making sweet cane
Chapter Six: on making *fānīdh* and *ashqāqūl*[26]
Chapter Seven: on Eastern recipes

Section Ten: on fermented condiments, vinegars, types of *murrī*, the extraction of oils, and on restoring olive oil and other foodstuffs that have gone off. It consists of twelve chapters:
Chapter One: on making *ṣināb*
Chapter Two: on making olives
Chapter Three: on pickling limes
Chapter Four: on pickling capers
Chapter Five: on pickling aubergine
Chapter Six: on pickling fish
Chapter Seven: on making vinegars
Chapter Eight: on making various types of *murrī*
Chapter Nine: on making olive oil from various seeds, and on restoring olives

24 The *sanbūsak* of the edition (2012: 34) is omitted from the entry in Wetzstein 1207 (fol. 2r.) and Gayangos XVI (fol. 4v.).

25 The order of entries 4–6 is that found in Wetzstein 1207 (fol. 2r.) and Gayangos XVI (fol. 4v.), rather than in the edition, which has been jumbled up, and has the chapter on sweet cane followed by those on *fānīdh* and *jawzīnaq*. The same order will also be followed in the text later on.

26 Here and elsewhere in the text, the edition has the incorrect *ashfāfūl*. The correct spelling appears in Gayangos XVI (fol. 4v.), whereas Wetzstein 1207 (fol. 2r.) omits the word altogether.

Chapter Ten: on extracting oils
Chapter Eleven: on making jerky
Chapter Twelve: on restoring food, and other things

Section Eleven: on cooking grasshoppers and shrimp

Section Twelve: on hand-washing powders

SECTION ONE

On breads, *tharīdas*, pottages, dishes with bread, and similar things

It consists of five chapters.

Chapter One: on breads

1. Type of bread baked in a brick oven (*furn*)[1]

Take semolina,[2] moisten it [with water], add salt, and leave it long enough for the moisture to be absorbed. Rub well and then add yeast. Knead while gradually adding water until the dough is ready and has the right consistency. Coat it with some very finely ground flour[3] and shape into discs of the desired size. Put them inside a linen or woollen cloth and cover them with sheepskins, or something like that. Leave the dough to rise. You can tell the fermentation is done when you hear a sound when you hit the loaves with your hand. Next, bake them in the oven, but keep an eye on them. Once they are ready, clean and put them in a container until they are required.

If you use *darmak*[4] flour or another kind, it is not necessary to moisten it and leave it to stand. Instead, you can just add yeast and salt, and knead it immediately. In all cases, the water must be sufficiently hot, Allah the Exalted willing.

2. Type of bread baked in the *tannūr*

Moisten semolina and knead into a dough, as mentioned above, and then leave it to rise. When it has almost fully risen, light the fire in the *tannūr* and kindle it until the oven is white hot. Extract the smoke and

---

1 According to al-Rāzī, bread from a *furn* was not as good as that baked in the *tannūr* because the inside is not cooked as well as the outside (2000: 3016).

2 *samīd* (more correctly *samīdh*); on this term, see Ibn Mubārak Shāh 2020: 29 (note 109). It could also sometimes be synonymous with *darmak*; Ibn Janāḥ 2020: No. 677.

3 Both the edition (2012: 36) and Wetzstein 1207 (fol. 2v.) have *ruqāq* ('thin flatbread'), which does not make sense in this context, and unfortunately this particular word is omitted from Gayangos XVI and illegible in BL Or5927 due to fading. It is very likely that it is an instance of graphemic confusion, and should be read as *duqāq*, whose translation was taken from Corriente 1997: 181.

4 See Introduction.

shape the dough into round flat loaves. Quickly stick the loaves to the sides of the *tannūr*, one by one, after rubbing them with wet hands. Put water-moistened vine leaves on the top of the loaves so that they get a glaze. Cover the top of the *tannūr* and the holes at the bottom of it to prevent the heat of the fire from escaping, and outside air from entering the oven. If the fire is very strong, move it to the middle of the *tannūr* and put stones underneath the bread to stop it getting burnt. Keep an eye on the bread until it is done baking. Then, take it out, wipe clean, and eat, Allah the Exalted willing.

3. Type of bread baked on a malla[5] or in an iron casserole dish

Take semolina and knead it into a dough as mentioned. Leave it to rise and then put the *malla* over a moderate fire. When it is hot, shape the dough into round flat loaves and place them on it, one by one. Watch them, and turn them over when necessary until they are done.[6] Then, eat, Allah the Exalted willing.

4. Type of unleavened bread[7]

Take semolina and knead it, as described, but without yeast and only a little water. Work the dough very well, shape it into round flat loaves – as thin as you can make them – and then pierce holes in them. Rub the top of the loaves with water, and bake them in a brick oven. Proceed in the same way if you are using a *tannūr* or *malla*.

---

5 See Introduction.

6 Scholars stressed the need for this type of bread to be well done, as it is hard to digest and causes stomach aches otherwise; al-Rāzī, BNF2866, fol. 35r.

7 *al-khubz al-faṭīr*: according to Ibn Khalṣūn (1996: 156/trans., 82), unleavened bread is very hard to digest but highly nutritious, and is most suited for those doing hard physical labour. However, it generates phlegm and black bile, and causes colic. This echoes the views of other physicians, such as Ibn al-Bayṭār (1992: II, 315) or al-Rāzī (2000: 3016; BNF arabe 2866, fol. 35r.), who advised against eating it as it causes wind, and causes (liver) blockages and kidney stones. The latter author claimed that it does not agree with anyone, not even peasants, who are able to digest all dense foods. And while leavened bread does not have any of these drawbacks, its use was not recommended either, since it provides little nourishment and weakens those who engage in physical exertion, who should combine it with heavy and viscous foods, such as lamb, *harīsa*, *'aṣīda* (wheat-flour porridge), or spices (*tawābil*) and pungent vegetables, *murrī*, fermented condiments (*kawāmikh*), and old wine, alongside hot baths (Ibn al-Bayṭār, *ibid.*).

5. Type of millet bread[8]

Put millet flour in a kneading tub, add salt and knead into a firm dough but use only a little water because too much of it is not good. Then shape into thick round loaves if you bake them in a brick oven, or thin ones if you are using a *tannūr* or *malla*. Sprinkle sesame, aniseed and fennel [seeds] on top. Bake them quickly, otherwise they will go bad.

Of all the non-wheat breads, this is the most prized among Andalusians, and they eat a lot of it when it is millet-harvesting season in their country.

8 *banīj* (also *banij*): Ibn al-ʿAwwām (1802: II, 78–82) says millet bread is as nutritious as rice bread, but tastes better, and should be eaten with fatty meats or butter. According to Ibn Zuhr (1992: 12; trans., 48), the taste of millet bread is surpassed only by that made with wheat and barley. Other terms for millet in Arabic are *jāwars* (also *jāwarsh*, from the Pahlavi *gāwars*), *dukhn* and *dhura* (which more properly denotes sorghum). Ibn al-Ḥashshāʾ (1941: 29, No. 264) states that *banij* was the Romance (*ʿajamiyya*) word for *jāwars*, which in Berber is also known as *inīl*. A variant of *banij* has survived in the Moroccan Arabic for millet, *bansha*. The word ultimately goes back to the Latin *panicium* ('millet'). Ibn Luyūn (1988: No. 120) remarks that millet was commonly known as *dukhn*, which is very similar to *dhura* (sorghum) and is fed to animals to strengthen them. According to al-Ishbīlī (who also gives the form *banajju*), *jāwarsh* comes in three varieties: *dhura* (the largest), *zahina* (medium) and wild millet (*dukhn barrī*) (2004–10: Nos. 645, 1388, 1935). Ibn al-Raqqām (fol. 44v.) said that *jāwars* should be eaten with milk and oils, and that it is very difficult to digest. Also see Lewicki 1974: 26–7; Marín 1997: 11–12; Ibn Khalṣūn 1996: 98 (note 17), 157 (trans., 84). Ibn Janāḥ 2020: No. 207.

Chapter Two: on *tharīdas*[9]

6. Calf's head *tharīda*

Take the head of a fatty calf, and put a copper cauldron[10] over a fire with enough water to cover it entirely. When the water has come to a boil, put in the head and leave it for a while. Then, use your hand to test whether you can easily remove the hairs; if you can, take the head out of the water and quickly pluck the hairs. If some remain, return the head to the hot water until it is clean and free of hairs. If you do not scald the head with water, you can scorch[11] it over a fire. Afterwards, put it in a large container with enough water to cover it, and leave it to soften. Then, wash and rub it until you get rid of the scorched smell. Cut it into pieces, wash them, and put them in a large pot with salt, olive oil, pepper, coriander seeds and cut-up or pounded onions. Put the pot over a fire after pouring in enough water to more than cover the meat, and leave until everything is cooked. Then crumble leavened bread as finely as you can. Skim off the fat that has gathered on the surface, and put it aside in a bowl. Pour the broth on the breadcrumbs and leave to stand for a while. Check whether the crumbs are absorbing the broth;

9 On this type of dish, whose name is derived from a verb meaning 'to crumble (bread)', see Ibn Mubārak Shāh 2020: 7 (note 18); al-Dabbābī al-Mīsāwī 2017: 105–16. This was already a Bedouin favourite in pre-Islamic Arabia; indeed, it was known as 'the food of the Arabs', and much loved by the Prophet Muḥammad, who recommended eating only the sides (rather than the centre) and also liked it to be made with *ḥays* (a mixture of dates, clarified butter and breadcrumbs). In his book on Prophetic Medicine, Ibn Qayyim al-Jawziyya (1927: 198) referred to *tharīd* as the food of those in Paradise. According to tradition, its creation is attributed to Hāshim Ibn 'Abd Manāf, the Prophet's great-grandfather, whose first name is a gerund of a verb meaning to crumble, *hashama*. Al-Jāḥiẓ (1990: 74; trans., 62) said it was most suited to the old, young and toothless. The dish was not part of the elite cuisine in the East, where it was seen as peasant food, but gained popularity in the Muslim West, with the anonymous *Andalusian* treatise also having seven recipes. According to Ibn Zuhr (1992: 14; trans., 50) all *tharīda* varieties produce thick phlegm. Those prepared with fried bread are slow to digest, and generate a sulphurous temperament (*mizāj kibrītī*). Al-Uryūlī (1981: No. 21), on the other hand, held that *tharīds* are less nutritious and quicker to digest and evacuate from the stomach than bread eaten with broth. Those who exercise a lot should avoid it, and one should not drink water after it until digestion is complete.

10 *burma*, which Corriente (1997: 49) describes as 'cauldron' (also *qudayr burmī*), and Dozy (1881: I, 77) as 'an earthenware water pot.'

11 *shawwaṭa*: this word is associated with the cooking of calves' heads, and in this context can also mean 'to (half-)roast'; Corriente 1997: 295.

if not, add some more, as required, but take care that the *tharīda* does not become too runny. Next, pour the fat over the crumbs and layer the pieces of head on top. Finish off with a dusting of cinnamon, and eat, Allah the Exalted willing.

If you like, you can make it with dough kneaded again after rising,[12] in which case the semolina is kneaded, as described, and left to rise. When it has, knead the dough again and shape it into thin round loaves, and perforate them. Rub their surfaces with water and, after they have been baked in the oven or *tannūr*, crumble them as finely as possible and pour the broth over them, as explained before.

If you want, you can use laminated pastry;[13] cut it into large pieces and pour on enough broth to completely drown them.

7. *Tharīda* with the heads and other parts of sacrificial sheep[14]

Take the heads and scald them, as we have described, in boiling water together with the trotters. If you do not scald them, scorch them over a fire until all the hair is gone. Put the heads in a container with enough water to cover them, and let them soak and tenderize. Scrape the heads with a knife, and rub them with your hands to clean them thoroughly. Beat the noses of the heads against a stone so that any worms that are hidden inside fall out. Cut the heads into pieces and place them in a large pot after thoroughly cleaning and washing them with water. Take tripe and boil it in hot water. Scrape it with a knife until it is white and cleaned. Then, take (caul) fat from inside the belly of a ram – this is called *mansij* or *ridā'*[15] – cut it into pieces, fold a piece of tripe inside each, and tie them

12 *khubz muʿād*: Corriente 1997: 370.

13 *muwarraqāt*; see recipes Nos. 61 and 78. The text here, and in the next recipe, refers to sheets of *muwarraqāt* of *isfanj*, instructions for which are found in Nos. 74–6, below. This would suggest that it is *muwarraqa* from *isfanj* dough, which is made slightly differently.

14 *ghanam al-aḍāḥī*; the practice of sacrificing an animal (usually a sheep, but it can also be a camel or goat) is associated with the last day of the Muslim pilgrimage (*ḥajj*), on the tenth day of the month of *Dhū 'l-Ḥijja*, which is known as *'Īd al-aḍḥā* ('feast of sacrifice'), *'īd al-qurbān* ('feast of the offerings') or, in the Maghrib, *'īd al-kabīr* ('the Great Feast'). It commemorates Ibrāhīm (Abraham) being instructed by Allah to sacrifice his son.

15 Both terms denote the 'fat of the intestines' (Corriente 1997: 206, 527). The word for 'ram', *kabsh*, is an adult sheep or ram; the one-year-old sheep is called *ḥawlī*, the one with its first teeth is *al-kabsh al-thanīy*, but sometimes *thanīy* denotes suckling lamb (*kharūf*). The oldest mutton comes from *al-kabsh al-harīm*. See al-Uryūlī (1983:

together with intestines after thoroughly cleaning the insides. Then, roll these into large sausages[16] and put them in the pot with the heads. Add salt, olive oil, coriander seeds, pepper and a few cut-up onions. Pour in enough water to cover everything and then cook it in the communal oven, or at home, until it is done. Then, cut up layered pastry into large pieces into a bowl. Pour in a lot of broth, much more than can be absorbed. Sprinkle on cinnamon, and eat and enjoy.

If you like, you can also make it with unleavened or leavened bread, in the way we have described, with the power of Allah.

8. *Tharīda* with kid goats' heads

After cleaning and washing the heads, put them in a pot and add salt, olive oil, pepper, coriander seeds and some pounded onion. Pour on enough water to cover everything, and then place the pot over a fire. When it is almost done, clean some spinach[17] by washing it thoroughly, cut it up and add it to the pot. Let it boil twice and then remove the pot from the fire. Add some boiled clarified butter. Crumble bread as finely as you can and pour on the broth – use your fingers to see whether the crumbs are fully soaked. Then remove the heads from the pot and

---

47–8; trans., 5–6).

16 The Arabic *ʿuṣub* (also *ʿuṣbān*) is the plural of *ʿaṣīb*. A recipe for meat strips wrapped in fat and tied with intestines is already found in al-Warrāq (1987: 225). The word is derived from a verb meaning 'to bind, wind round'. Lane 1863–74: 2059–60 ('lights of an animal bound round with guts, and then roasted, or broiled').

17 al-Tujībī has quite a few recipes (Nos. 119, 170, 171, 374, 375) calling for spinach (*a/isfanākh*). The vegetable, which was unknown in the ancient world, probably hailed from Nepal, from where it moved to Persia and was introduced into Europe by the Arabs. It was quite popular, and Ibn al-ʿAwwām even called it 'the lord of vegetables' (*raʾīs al-buqūl*). It was also known in al-Andalus as *baqla dustiyya* or *dustī*. See al-Ishbīlī 2004–10: Nos. 962; Ibn al-ʿAwwām 1802: I, 1316, II, 160–1; Ibn Baṣṣāl 1955: 154–5 (trans., 197–8); Watson 1983: 62. Dishes requiring spinach can be found in almost all medieval Arabic cookery books: two in al-Warrāq (1987: 146, 157, 265–6); three in al-Baghdādī (1964: 27, 41, 68); eight in *Waṣf* (330, 331, 348, 349, 355, 399, 443–4, 446–7); five in *Wuṣla* (Nos. 6.40, 6.48–51); one in Ibn Mubārak Shāh (2020: No. 243); four in *Kanz* (Nos. 204, 205, 215, 221); two in Ibn al-Mubarrad (1937: 372/trans., 471; 375/trans., 474); two in *Taṣānīf* (fols. 74v., 77v.–78r.), and four in the *Andalusian* (*Anwāʿ*, 133–4, 148–9, 160–1; BNF, fols. 50r., 54v., 57v.–58r.). Medicinally, spinach was thought to be laxative (Ibn Sīnā 1999: I, 375; al-Rāzī 2000: 2932), useful against jaundice (Ibn Khalṣūn 1996: 161; trans., 89), as well as coughs and back pains, but harmful to people with cold temperaments (Ibn Jazla, fol. 16v.). Ibn Khalṣūn (*ibid.*) recommended cooking it with fatty meat.

arrange them on the bread. The vegetables should be placed underneath and around the heads. Then, eat and enjoy, Allah the Exalted willing.

9. *Tharīda* with fattened beef and winter cabbage[18]

Take choice cuts of beef, such as the brisket and shanks, as well as honeycomb and thick-seam tripe after washing it in hot water and scraping it until it is clean and turns white. Then, wash and clean everything again and put it in a large pot, together with salt, olive oil, pepper, coriander seeds and some cut-up onions. Pour on enough water to immerse all of the ingredients, and put the pot on the fire. Cut thick cabbage heads into quarters and add as many tender cabbage leaves as possible. Put both into another pot with only water over a fire, and bring to a boil three times. Check the cabbage, and when it is nearly done and it no longer tastes bad, remove it from the pot, rinse with hot water, and add it to the meat. Next, crumble the bread of your choosing, and when the meat and cabbage are cooked, crush[19] a small quantity of fresh coriander leafstalks in the pot. Bring to a boil once, and then remove from the fire. Leave it on the embers for a little while for the fat to gather on the surface. When it does, skim it off and then pour the rest of the broth over the crumbled bread. Once it has been absorbed, remove the meat and cabbage and arrange them on top of the *tharīd*. Pour on the skimmed-off fat, and then sprinkle on cinnamon and ginger. Eat and enjoy, Allah the Exalted willing.

If you like, you can also make this dish using fatty sheep meat.

10. *Tharīda* with fattened beef, gourd and aubergine

Take prime beef cuts and bones, such as the hip bone, and others like it. Cut up the meat and clean it together with the bones. Put all of it in a large pot with olive oil, salt, pepper, ginger, coriander seeds, cumin,

18 Andalusian agronomists identified two kinds of cabbage. The first is grown (and eaten) in summer and is a closed, tender cabbage, with intertwining leaves or branches. The other variety has its leaves separated, and is grown only in winter. Al-Ishbīlī 2004–10: No. 2557; Ibn al-ʿAwwām 1802: II, 162; al-Ṭighnarī 2006: 500. According to Ibn Waḥshiyya (1993: 859), the cabbage that grows in summer is very pungent, salty and bitter, much more so than that grown in winter.

19 The edition (2012: 41) has *dhūba* ('dissolved'); this has been amended with the help of BL Or5927 (fol. 103v.), which has the more logical *duqqa* ('pounded').

cut-up onion, a bulb of garlic with its peel, soaked white chickpeas, citron leaves and a fennel stalk. Pour enough water in the pot to cover everything and put it over a fire. Then, peel the aubergines and cut each into quarters, without fully separating the parts. Boil them in another pot with water and salt until they lose their bad taste. When the aubergine pieces are nearly done, take them out of the pot, rinse with hot water and then leave to dry. Next, scrape the outside of the gourd, clean out the pulp, and cut it into pieces of about three fingers in width. Put them in a container with the aubergine. Then, pound saffron in a mortar and thoroughly colour the gourd and aubergine with it. Add both of them to the meat and, when everything is done, pour in an appropriate amount of good-quality vinegar. Next, crumble as finely as possible whatever amount of leavened bread you have decided to use. When everything is ready, remove the pot from the fire and leave it on the embers to allow the fat to gather, and then skim it off. Remove the hip bone and then the citron leaves, fennel, and garlic bulb before pouring the broth over the bread, using your fingers to test whether it has been fully absorbed. Now pour the skimmed-off fat in the tureen, fully immersing its contents. Finally, sprinkle on ginger and cinnamon. When you start to eat, take out the bones from the centre of the tureen, extract their marrow and beat them against the bottom of the mortar. Blow inside the bone and then repeatedly strike it as hard as you can. Do this with every bone until all the marrow inside has been expelled into the bowl. Turn the tureen as you are doing this so that the marrow can spread everywhere. Then eat and enjoy, Allah the Exalted willing.

11. The 'beloved'[20] *tharīda*

Take fatty mutton, cut it up into large pieces and clean them before putting them in a large pot. Add salt, pepper, coriander seeds, cut-up or pounded onion and a lot of olive oil. Fry the meat for a while, until it turns white and has released its juices. Pour hot water over it, and leave to cook until it is done. Next, take dough made with yeast and leave until it is close to rising before kneading again with a bit of flour. Thoroughly work it, and then shape into thin round flat loaves. Bake them in a brick

---

20 *al-maqbūla* (Corriente 1997: 414), which is the name in the edition (and Wetzstein 1207, fol. 4v.), whereas in BL Or5927 (fol. 104r.) and Gayangos XVI (fol. 9v.) it is called *al-mardūda* ('the returned').

oven or a *tannūr* and, when they are ready, crumble them as finely as you can. When the meat is done, colour it with a little saffron and then remove it from the pot. Strain the broth and return it to the pot. Add the crumbled bread to it, followed by fresh strained butter or good-quality clarified butter. When it is done, transfer the contents of the pot to a tureen and layer on the meat, or hindquarters if there are any [as is the habit of both townsfolk and country-dwellers].[21] Finally, sprinkle on cinnamon and pepper, and eat it, Allah the Exalted willing.

12. *Tharīda* with mutton and milk[22]

Cut fatty full-grown lamb into large pieces, and throw them in a large pot with pepper, salt, coriander, one cut-up onion and a sufficient amount of water. Cook over a fire and, when the meat is done, take it out of the pot and cover it with a sieve, or something else that is thin enough to allow the steam to escape. Then, strain the broth and remove the sediment. Wash the pot and return the strained broth to it. Next, crumble unleavened bread as finely as you can and mix it into the broth in the pot. Put it over a gentle fire and stir with the handle of a ladle so that the breadcrumbs do not get stuck to the bottom of the pot. Then, gradually pour milk over the crumbs until they can absorb no more. Transfer to a tureen, layer on the meat and pour fresh strained butter over it. If you like, you can use a plump chicken or capons instead of lamb, in which case, cook the crumbs and the milk in the broth, and then add more butter. Dust with sugar and then eat and enjoy, Allah the Exalted willing.

21 The passage enclosed in brackets is found only in Gayangos XVI (fol. 9v.).

22 Though unknown in the Mashriq, *tharīds* made with milk were quite common in al-Andalus. According to Ibn Zuhr (1992: 31; trans., 62), if the milk is boiled, they are tastier and milder, but very harmful.

13. *Tharīda* called *Ibn al-Waḍī'’s chechia*[23]

Take the finest cuts of fatty fully-grown lamb or a suckling kid, whichever is available. Cut them up, clean, and then put them in a large pot. Add salt, olive oil, pepper, coriander, a few cut-up onions, and enough water to immerse the meat. Put the pot on a fire, and when it is nearly done, take lettuce, fennel, fresh broad beans, truffles and a little fresh coriander. Clean everything separately and take the most tender bits. Remove the outer peel of the broad beans, and peel the truffles. Cut and clean everything and put it in the pot with the meat. When everything is cooked, crumble any kind of bread you like[24] as finely as possible. Take the pot off the fire and leave it on the embers (to simmer down). Cut up some fresh cheese and throw it in the pot. Drench the breadcrumbs with broth until they can absorb no more. Then, boil fresh butter in an earthenware casserole and strain. Remove the vegetables from the pot and use them to cover the surface of the *tharīda*. Put the meat and the cheese on top, pour on butter to cover the surface of the dish, and then dust with cinnamon. Eat and enjoy, Allah the Exalted willing.

14. Unleavened bread *tharīda* made with chicken

Slaughter and scald plump chickens and capons, cut open their bellies, remove the entrails, and then joint them. Put the pieces into a large pot after washing and cleaning them, and then add salt ....[25]

---

23 The name of the person is given as Ibn al-Rafī' in the edition (2012: 44) but this is clearly a misreading, as 'Ibn al-Waḍī'' is found in the *Andalusian* (*Anwā'*, 160; BNF, fol. 58r.) and BL Or5927 (fol. 104v.). The chechia (*shāshiyya*) is the traditional red woollen hat worn in Tunisia, but hailed originally from al-Andalus. In other parts of the Arab world, similar headgear was called *ṭarbūsh* (known in English as tarbouch or fez). The Andalusian manual (which has different cooking instructions and adds spinach and turnips) explains that this type of *tharīda* is characteristic of the people from Bijāya, and that the dish derives its name from the fact that the butter added at the end drips down the sides like the tassel of the chechia. Nothing is known about the person after whom the recipe is named. For Andalusian influences on the cuisine of Bijāya, see Rouighi 2005.

24 Gayangos XVI (fol. 10v.) prescribes 'leavened bread' (*khubz mukhtamar*).

25 The remainder of the recipe has been left out since it is identical with the previous one (No. 13) in the printed edition (2012: 44), Wetzstein 1207 (fol. 5r.) and BL Or5927 (fol. 104v.). Gayangos XVI (fols. 7v.–8r.) has only one recipe.(No. 15).

15. Unleavened bread *tharīda* with chicken

Slaughter and scald[26] plump chickens and capons, cut open up their bellies, remove the entrails, and then joint them. Put the pieces into a large pot after washing and cleaning them. Add salt, olive oil, pepper, coriander, halved and quartered onions and soaked chickpeas, and cook over a fire. Then, take semolina, moisten it, add salt and knead with a little water into a firm dough. Take an iron casserole dish or an unglazed earthenware *malla* and put it over a gentle fire. When the casserole has heated up, take a piece of dough, smear it with clarified butter and rub it with your hands. Then, roll it out with a rolling pin, fold it over, and add some more butter. Roll it out as thinly as possible and then put it in the casserole for as long as it takes for it to whiten and dry. When this happens, remove it and strike it with both hands so that it is separated into layers [like for *musammana*].[27] Cut them into medium-sized pieces and put them in a bowl. Take another piece of the dough and do the same thing until you have used it all. At this point, take all of it and put it in a couscous[28] pot, which is placed on top of the one containing the chicken. Join the two pots together with a strip of dough applied all around the connecting area. Cover the top of the bottom pot with a piece of cloth in order to prevent the steam from escaping. Leave until it is cooked in the steam rising from the pot underneath, through the perforations in the couscous pot.

The rolling pin is a stick of turned agarwood that is thick in the middle and thin at the ends.

If you like, you can shape the dough into small discs with clarified butter; put them on top of each other – no more than three, though – and then, as described above, roll them out with the rolling pin. Dry them in the casserole dish and finish cooking them in the couscous pot. When the chicken is done, check the amount of fat in the pot; if there is not enough of it, add some good clarified butter and fresh butter, and leave in the pot to boil. Then, transfer the pot from the fire to the embers in order for the fat to collect on the surface. Skim off the fat and put it in a separate container. Pour the [remaining] broth on the unleavened bread, but do not add too much because otherwise the loaves

---

26 Gayangos XVI (fol. 10v.) has 'pluck [the feathers]' (*tuntaf*).

27 The phrase in brackets is found only in Gayangos XVI (fol. 8r.). See recipe No. 61.

28 See recipes Nos. 85–9, below.

will fall apart and be spoilt. Remove the chicken pieces, onion and chickpeas, and put them on top of the loaves, in the middle of the bowl. Line the edges with boiled eggs, good olives and preserved limes. Pour on all of the set-aside fat from the container, and sprinkle on cinnamon and ginger. Eat and enjoy, Allah the Exalted willing. This unleavened bread recipe is typical of the people of Ifrīqiyā, especially those from the capital, Tunis. They eat it a lot at celebrations and compete over who makes the best one during feasts.

16. *Tharīda* with unleavened bread, called *sabāt*[29]

Take plump chickens, fattened capons and any other poultry you like, such as geese, squabs, partridges or sparrows. Slaughter the animals you will use, clean them and split their breasts open, and then put them in a pot with salt, olive oil, pepper, coriander and a cut-up onion. Put the pot over a gentle fire and, when the meat is fried, pour on enough water to cover everything, and let it cook. When the birds are nearly done, take them out of the pot and thread them on spits. Make a basting sauce with vinegar, *murrī* and olive oil, and brush it on the meat. Roast the birds over embers until they are golden. Then shape some flat loaves out of a firm semolina dough and prick holes in them with a fine stick so they bake well in the brick oven or *tannūr*. When they are done, take them out and break them into large *dinar*-coin-sized pieces. Then, grate a sufficient amount of good dry cheese into the pot, together with enough pounded garlic for its flavour to come through. When the pot comes to a boil, pour the broth over the unleavened bread until it is fully absorbed, and then layer on the jointed birds. Garnish[30] the dish with hard-boiled eggs sliced in half with a thread, and sprinkle on peeled almonds, walnuts, green olives, seasoned black olives, grated cheese, cinnamon and spikenard. Then eat, with the power and strength of Allah the Exalted.

29 This dish was always made with poultry, whereas the word is linked to *shabbāba* and *shabbāt* (this the form that appears in BL Or5927, fol. 105r.), a type of loaf. The name is a lexical offspring of Romance and Germanic words like *sopa* or *suppa*, meaning 'sop' or 'broth'. Corriente 1997: 241, 271; Dozy 1881: I, 719.

30 The Arabic uses the Andalusian Arabic verb *najjama*, which is related to the word for star, *najm*, and thus conjures up the image of the eggs being dotted about on the surface like stars in the firmament. Corriente 1997: 522.

17. *Tharīda* made with chicken[31]

Clean and joint chickens in the way described above. Put the pieces in a large pot over a fire with salt, a generous amount of olive oil, pepper, coriander, cumin, a few cut-up or pounded onions, soaked white chickpeas, blanched almonds, citron leaves, a fennel stalk and a clove of unpeeled garlic. Take finely milled flour or semolina and knead with water and yeast. Leave the dough in the kneading tub until it rises. Then, knead some more and shape into medium-sized round flat loaves. Prick holes in them, rub the surfaces with water, and bake in the oven. Once they are done, crumble them up as finely as possible. When the chicken is nearly done, dissolve a sufficient quantity of saffron in cold water, but not too much, so that it does not get spoilt. Put it in the pot and stir until the saffron has coloured all of the contents. Let it stand for a while, pour in as much good vinegar as you like, and bring to a boil. Next, take enough eggs to crust the dish, and crack them into a bowl with salt, pepper, ginger and cinnamon. Beat with a ladle until everything is mixed, and colour with saffron dissolved in water. Add to the pot, stir and then leave it over a gentle fire. Boil the eggs, quarter them with a thread and put them in a separate bowl. Pound the gizzards and livers until you get a marrow-like consistency, and then add pepper and any aromatic spices to the egg whites. Make flat round loaves with this mixture and fry them in sweet olive oil until they turn golden brown. Once they are ready, cut them up lengthwise and put them with the split eggs. Fry four egg yolks in sweet olive oil until they turn golden and add them to the quartered eggs. Then skim off the fat that collects on the surface and put it in a separate dish. Pour the remaining broth over the crumbs and, when it has been absorbed, layer the meat on top and garnish with the split eggs and egg yolks, and the loaves made from the gizzards. Drench everything with the fat and then sprinkle on cinnamon and ginger. Eat and enjoy, Allah the Exalted willing.

If you like, you can also make this recipe in exactly the same way with leavened bread.

31 Gayangos XVI (fol. 11v.) adds that it is 'amazing' (*'ajīb*).

18. *Tharīda* called *al-mukarrara*[32]

Clean and joint plump poussins, and put the pieces in a new pot with olive oil, pepper, ginger, coriander, and onion juice. Fry the meat and then pour on lots of water to stew until everything is cooked through and the meat falls off the bones. [Strain the broth and cook other chickens in it until they are also fully cooked and then strain the broth again.] Cook some more chickens with as much of the appropriate spices as you like, and when they are [more or less] done, remove them from the pot. Next, take grated breadcrumbs, put them in an earthenware bowl and pour in the broth. Then layer the pieces of chickens on top. Move it close to the fire again and leave until all the ingredients have melded together, and then sprinkle on cinnamon, pepper and spikenard. Garnish with eggs.

This *tharīda* greatly increases the blood and restores the strength of those who suffer from exhaustion.

19. *Tharīda* which increases sexual potency[33]

Clean and joint a plump poussin, and sauté it in a new pot with olive oil, salt, cinnamon and coriander seeds. Add the water in which white chickpeas have been soaked overnight, as well as the chickpeas themselves, and also pour in a sufficient amount of juice squeezed out of pounded onions. Next, add clarified butter, and when everything is done throw in egg yolks and *ḥuwwārā* breadcrumbs.[34] Sprinkle on spikenard, cloves, ginger, pepper and cinnamon, and cover the dish so the broth can be absorbed. If you use sparrows instead of chicken – or the two combined – it will be even better. Carrots can also be cooked in the pot if they are available, and this will make the dish extremely delicious [and beneficial].[35]

---

32 This recipe can be translated either as 'the repeated' or 'the refined', the former being perhaps the more logical since two batches of chickens are cooked. The passages enclosed in square brackets are additions from Gayangos XVI, fols. 12v.–13r.

33 Gayangos XVI (fol. 13r.) adds that it is 'amazing'.

34 See Introduction.

35 This addition is found only in Gayangos XVI, fol. 13r. The use of carrots is also connected to the fact that the (white) wild variety (known as *dūqū*), in particular, was considered a powerful sexual stimulant (with enhanced effect when pickled in vinegar), even though they were said to be very difficult to digest and to generate bad blood. It was recommended that they should be boiled several times and then eaten with vinegar, or with fatty meat in an *isfīdhbāj*. Al-Idrīsī 1995: 84; Ibn Buṭlān 1990:

20. *Tharīda* called *al-shāqūma*, which is eaten by some Berbers[36]

Cook lamb which has been cut into medium-sized pieces with salt, olive oil, pepper, coriander and a large amount of halved or quartered onions. Put enough water in the pot to make a *tharīd* after the meat is fried. Next, knead milk-soaked, finely-milled flour or semolina into thin flat loaves. Bake them on a *malla* and then crumble them as finely as you can. Once the meat is done and the pot has come to a boil, pour the broth over the bread and layer the meat on top. Pour on lots of strained fresh butter, and eat, Allah the Exalted willing.

21. Eastern *tharīda* with *qaṭā'if* (crêpes), known as al-*mushahhada* ('the honeyed')[37]

Take a plump poussin, gut it, but leave it whole, and tuck the legs inside the vent. Clean it and put it in a large pot over a fire with salt, lots of olive oil, pepper, coriander and plenty of whole onions if they are small, or cut up if they are large. Next, pound the breast of another chicken and shape it into meatballs with spices and one egg white before putting them in the pot with the chicken. When the chicken is done, remove it from the pot and take it to the oven in an earthenware casserole dish.

84–5 (trans. 170–1); Ibn Sīnā 1999: I, 429–30; al-Ṭūsī 2014: 134.

36 The Berber reference is taken from BL Or5927 (fol. 106r.), and does not occur in the edited text, whereas Gayangos XVI (fol. 13r.) adds that 'it is tasty' (*ladhīdha*). As regards the name of the dish, Corriente (1997: 264) has the variant *sānūma*, and suggests it may be a Berber dish. The latter word is cognate with *sinām* ('hump') and perhaps refers to the way in which the meat is layered on top.

37 This word is derived from *shuhd* (also *shahd, shahda*), 'comb honey', and is the Andalusian word for what in Eastern cookbooks are known as *qaṭā'if*: Corriente 1997: 293; Dozy 1881: I, 794; Lane 1863–74: III, 160. *Qaṭā'if* – the plural of *qaṭfa* (from a verb meaning 'to pluck, pick') – are still a favourite all over the Middle East (especially during Ramadan) today, with its modern version being folded pancakes filled with cream or nuts, and then deep-fried. According to al-Rāzī (1987: 139), *qaṭā'if* are dense and difficult to digest, but very nutritious. Al-Isrā'ilī (1992: 210) considered the sweet very harmful to the liver and spleen because of its viscosity and coarseness, which causes blockages, though the nefarious effects are attenuated if it is eaten with honey. For medieval recipes of this sweet, which is also mentioned in the 1001 Nights (Mahdī 1984: I, 127), see: Ibn Mubārak Shāh 2020: 123; *Wuṣla*, No. 7.42; *Kanz*, Nos. 281, 282, 293, 323–4, 328–9, 331, 335; al-Baghdādī 1964: 80 (trans., 103–4); *Waṣf*, 428, 434–5, 439, 460; al-Warrāq 1987: 274–5; al-Dabbābī al-Mīsāwī 2017: 131–3. For another *mushahhada* recipe, see No. 59, below. Al-Rāzī suggested *qaṭā'if* with walnuts are digested more quickly, and are thus suited for old people with cold temperaments, while those with almonds agree more with hot temperaments (1881: 51).

Leave it in long enough for the meat to turn golden. Alternatively, you can fry it in a pan with good-quality clarified butter. Cook[38] three eggs in the broth, and then boil three more eggs and quarter them. [Stuff a large intestine[39] with the pounded meat][40] mixed with salt, pepper, ginger, cinnamon, spikenard, cloves, blanched almonds and three eggs, as well as the boiled egg yolks. Sew the intestine up with thread, and put it in a wide pot over a fire with water, salt, olive oil and a bit of *murrī*. When it is done, take it out and put it in an earthenware casserole dish. Add a little of the strained broth and send it to the oven. Regularly turn the intestine sausage over to brown it. Then, take the *qaṭā'if*, and fold them so that the holes are on the inside.[41] Place them on an iron grill over a moderate fire, flipping them over regularly until they turn golden. Then put them in a tureen, and open them so that the holes are facing up so they can absorb the broth. Evenly pour the broth over them in the tureen. Put the onions and chicken on top, surrounded by the meatballs and eggs (that were cooked in the broth). Cut the intestine sausage into pieces and, together with the split eggs, place them around and on top of the dish. Sprinkle on cinnamon, pepper and ginger. Eat and enjoy, Allah the Exalted willing.

22. Eastern *tharīda*, called *al-falyāṭil*[42]

Take a large plump chicken, slaughter it and, while its feathers are still on, inflate it with great force until all the skin across the body comes off the bones. Then tie the neck with thread and pluck the feathers using hot water. Scour the skin with a grater[43] and salt to clean it. Next, undo the thread, cut off the chicken's neck, and remove the crop and

---

38 The form *tuḥammar*, which appears here and further down in the recipe in the edition, is clearly a misreading, and has been corrected to the more logical *tukhammar*, which is also the form found in BL Or5927 (fol. 106r.) and Gayangos XVI (fol. 13 v.).

39 See recipe No. 187. Also see Nasrallah [al-Warrāq 2011]: 187ff., 612, 718.

40 The passage in brackets is an addition from Gayangos XVI, fol. 14r. The edition and the other manuscripts refer to the intestine being cut only at the end of the recipe.

41 There are little holes on the side that is not cooked since the yeast in the batter results in spongy bubbles.

42 This has been corrected from the misreading *fayāṭil*, which appears in the edition (2012: 49), as well as in BL Or5927 (fols. 106r.-107v.) and Wetzstein 1207 (fol. 7v.). The correct form is, however, used later, in recipe No. 29, and also occurs in Gayangos XVI (fol. 14v.). The vowelling is taken from Gayangos XVI and BL Or5927, while Corriente suggests *fulyāṭil* (1997: 406, 'dish of poultry with waffle').

43 The implement is specified only in Gayangos XVI (fol. 14v.).

gizzard. Cut the wings underneath the skin but leave the ends intact. Do the same with the thighs. Also remove the entire breast from underneath the skin, but leave the end of the rump in the skin. Gingerly remove all of the flesh and bones from underneath the skin, but take care not to tear the skin. Strip all the meat from the bones and pound it together with the meat of another chicken, mixed with pepper, ginger, cinnamon, spikenard, cloves, caraway seeds, salt, olive oil, fresh coriander juice, mint juice and a bit of onion juice. Go easy on the clove and spikenard. Knead all of this with eight eggs, to which you add boiled egg yolks, skinned almonds and meatballs. Check the skin of the chicken and, if any of it is torn, repair it with thread and then stuff it with the meat mixed with the broth, egg yolks and meatballs. Stuff the thighs, wings, rump and belly until the skin is filled and the chicken has been restored to its original form. Sew up the area around the chicken's neck and then put it in a pot. Take two squabs and fill their bellies and the space between the flesh and the skin with the meat of another squab and some eggs. Sew up their bellies and the areas that have been stuffed, put them in the pot with the chicken and add salt, lots of olive oil, pepper, coriander, a small cut-up onion, soaked chickpeas, two ladlefuls of skinned almonds and good vinegar. Put the pot over a fire and pour in enough water to moisten the *tharīd* (the breadcrumbs) later on. Then, moisten semolina and knead it into a firm dough without yeast and only a little water. Shape the dough into ultra-thin discs and smear each one of them with clarified butter. Stack them up one by one on an earthenware *malla* and bake them only slightly in the oven, rather than all the way through. Then cut them into medium-sized pieces into a bowl. Colour the chicken and squabs with saffron and put them in an earthenware casserole dish together with a little broth, and then send it to the oven. Turn them over from time to time to make sure they brown [all over]. Crack eggs, separate the yolks and put them in a pot with some fresh cheese and almonds. Beat the egg whites with salt, cinnamon, pepper, ginger, spikenard, fresh coriander juice and mint juice, and then colour with saffron. Pour everything into the pot, remove it from the fire and leave on the embers to simmer down. Cut up and pound the gizzards and livers, add salt and any aromatics available, together with the egg whites. Use your hands to thoroughly mix everything together. Shape into an *isfāriyya* (meat loaf)[44] disc and put it in a frying pan with olive oil that has been brought to a boil. Gently turn them over from time to time to brown. [When they are ready, take them out,] cut them lengthwise and put them in a vessel with boiled eggs that have been halved or quartered, and add three fried egg yolks. Once you have done this, get the casserole dish from the oven and gradually pour in the broth until it has been fully absorbed by the breadcrumbs. Put the chicken and squabs on top and remove the threads from them. Put what remains of the crusting on the top and sides of the pot, together with the meatballs, chickpeas, eggs, almonds, boiled eggs, fried egg yolks and the *isfāriyya* strips. Sprinkle on any aromatics you have to hand and then eat and enjoy, Allah the Exalted willing.

23. *Tharīda* stuffed with chicken[45]

Gut a plump tender chicken and chop the meat as finely as you can. Add salt, pepper, coriander leaves and seeds and a bit of cut-up onion. Then knead semolina or *darmak* flour with water, salt, fresh melted butter and three eggs until the dough is soft. Mix it with the meat and season with a sufficient amount of salt and pepper. Next, pour melted butter into a new pot and stir until the butter coats the sides and some remains at the bottom. Make another dough, shape it into a round, flat loaf and stretch it along the bottom and sides of the pot. Put the dough mixed with the chicken meat in the pot and cover it with the other dough in order to prevent the former from sticking to the sides of the pot. Then pour in enough butter to cover the dough and let it cook in the oven away from the fire until it is done. Roast another plump tender chicken on a spit, with the fire on the sides of it, not underneath. This should be done beforehand so that, when the pot returns from the oven, the roasted chicken is ready. Then, transfer what is in the pot into a bowl. Carve up the roasted chicken and layer the pieces on top. Eat and enjoy, Allah the Exalted willing.

24. *Tharīda* stuffed with squabs

Clean the squabs and cut open their bellies. Chop up the gizzards and mix them with salt, coriander seeds, fresh coriander, pepper, a bit of

---

44 See recipe No. 181.

45 Gayangos XVI (fol. 15v.) adds that it is 'amazing'.

crushed onion, a dribble of *murrī* and two eggs. Stuff this mixture inside the bellies of the squabs and in the space between the skin and the flesh. Sew the birds up and put them in a wide pot with two ladlefuls of good-quality vinegar, one ladleful of olive oil, a bit of pepper, coriander, some coarsely cut onion and enough salt. Cook over a fire. Next, pound the breast of a chicken and add cinnamon, ginger, pepper and two egg whites. Shape the mixture into meatballs and add them to the pot with the squabs. When they are done, colour with saffron, and crust with five eggs. Crumble leavened bread as finely as you can and put it in a bowl. Boil another chicken breast, using only water and salt. When it is done and the meat has been pounded, mix it with the breadcrumbs in the bowl. Pour the squab broth over the crumbs, followed by fresh melted butter. Put the squabs and meatballs on top and then add on split boiled eggs. Finish it off with a dusting of pepper and cinnamon. Eat and enjoy, Allah the Exalted willing.

25. *Tharīda* with squabs[46]

Take squabs, split open their bellies, and clean them. Cook them in a pot with salt, olive oil, pepper, coriander, a dash of cumin, and two ladlefuls of good-quality vinegar. When it has come a boil, pour in onion juice and then leave until the squabs are done. Crust with three eggs and continue to cook over the fire, but make sure there is enough water in the pot.[47] Crumble unleavened bread as finely as possible and put it in a bowl. Next, put an iron or glazed earthenware casserole[48] with olive oil on the fire. When the oil comes to a boil, crack six eggs and whisk them with salt until the whites and yolks are mixed and then fry everything in the casserole until the omelette is golden on both sides. Lift the omelette out in one piece. Take a bit of the cooked broth and some good-quality honey, and pour over it the crumbs in the bowl.

46 According to Gayangos XVI (fol. 16v.) this was also an 'Eastern' dish.

47 This rather incongruous instruction is found in the edition (2012: 52), as well as in Wetzstein 1207 (fol. 9r.) and BL Or.5927 (fol. 108r.). In Gayangos XVI (fol. 16v.) the water is more appropriately added after the vinegar, at the start of the cooking process.

48 This amends the clearly corrupted *juz'* ('part') in the text to *ṭājīn*, by analogy with instructions in other recipes. Gayangos XVI (fol. 17r.) instructs using a frying pan (*miqlā*).

Remove the squabs from the pot. Pour the remainder of the broth on the bread until it has been fully absorbed. Sprinkle on pepper and put the omelette on top of the crumbs. Then, place the squabs on top of the eggs, and finish off with pepper. Eat and enjoy, Allah the Exalted willing.

26. *Tharīda* with milk only

Dissolve a lump of dough in water and put it in a large pot over a low fire. Make sure you stir it continuously. Then, strain fresh milk and put it in a pot. Stir it gently[49] and top up the milk as it reduces. When it is ready, remove from the fire and transfer to a bowl. Sprinkle on some sugar and eat.

If you like to have it with honey, put some honey in a glass or earthenware dish in the middle of the bowl and eat it with a small spoon.

If you want to make it with uncooked bread, start by kneading semolina without yeast, but with a splash of water so that you get a firmer dough. Then, make small and ultra-thin discs out of the dough and leave them on a sieve in the sun to dry out. When the milk is almost cooked,[50] crumble the discs into it and gingerly stir with the handle of a ladle. Gradually add more milk until the crumbled bread has absorbed all the milk it can. Serve in a bowl, pour on fresh butter, and dust with sugar. Eat and enjoy, Allah the Exalted willing.[51]

27. Another *tharīda* with milk

Take some fresh milk and put it in a pot over a low fire. Stir gently and, when it comes to a boil, pour in extremely fine crumbs from firm unleavened bread. Make sure that you pour the milk on little by little until the bread has softened and the milk starts to spill over the crumbs. Sprinkle on sugar and cinnamon. Put a dish with fresh butter at the centre of the bowl. [It is the height of sophistication to eat this with small spoons.][52] Eat and enjoy, Allah the Exalted willing.

---

49 Gayangos XVI (*ibid.*) adds: 'When it starts to thicken, add crumbs from either leavened or unleavened bread.'

50 According to Gayangos XVI (fol. 17v.), it is 'when the milk begins to boil'.

51 Gayangos XVI (fols. 17v–18r.) includes a recipe for another 'milk *tharīda*, which is delicious', which repeats most of this recipe's instructions.

52 The passage in brackets is an addition in Gayangos XVI (fol. 18r.).

28. Milk *tharīda* baked in the oven

Take two *raṭls* of semolina or *darmak* flour and knead into a firm dough. Make extremely thin loaves out of it and bake them for a bit in the oven. Then take one-and-a-half *qadaḥs* of milk and stir in eight eggs with a dash of flour. Cook over a moderate fire. Next, take a good-quality casserole dish, put butter and milk at the bottom, and a loaf on top. Cover with another layer of butter and milk, followed by a loaf, and so on. Continue doing this until you have run out of loaves and butter and milk. Then, put a thick loaf on top of the thin ones and send the dish to the oven for baking. When it is almost done, take it out, pour in some more milk and return to the oven. Do this once or twice until the loaves have absorbed all the milk they can. When it is fully done, gingerly break the dish and you will be left with the loaves, which will look as if they have merged together and turned into one large cake. Split it with a knife and cut into pieces. Dust with sugar and then eat and enjoy, Allah the Exalted willing.

29. Falyāṭil *tharīda*[53]

Knead semolina with water and salt into a firm dough, and shape it into thin round loaves. Rub them with clarified butter and put them on top of one another on a *malla* so that they look like one thick loaf. Take it to the oven and, when the loaves are almost done, remove them before they are fully baked. In the meantime, take some milk, strain it, put it in a pot over a low fire and stir continuously. When it starts to curdle, break up the loaf into medium-sized breadcrumbs and pour on as much milk as they can absorb. Pour any remaining milk over the crumbs, add melted butter and finish off with a dusting of sugar. Eat and enjoy, Allah the Exalted willing.

53 See recipe No. 22. According to Gayangos XVI (fol. 18v.), this was a Near Eastern (*sharqiyya*) dish.

30. Garlic *tharīda* made on Nayrūz[54]

Take plump chickens and capons, cut open their abdomens and remove the entrails after plucking them and washing them with water and salt. Then, clean them inside and out, and tuck the ends of the legs into the cavities. Put them in a pot with water and salt only, and heat over a fire. You will already have cracked and shelled good-quality walnuts and put them in hot water in order to make them easier to peel. Skin them until they are all white, and wash them in cold water. Peel and boil garlic to get rid of the smell. Use a specially made iron grater to grate dry cheese into powder. Add whatever remains ungrated to the walnuts and garlic, and thoroughly crush everything. Then, knead semolina with water and salt, but without yeast. Work it well with a dash of water and shape into flat loaves. Rub them with water, prick holes into them, and bake them halfway through in the oven. When the chickens are nearly done, remove them from the pot, thoroughly rub them with olive oil, and then send them to the oven in glazed earthenware casseroles. Turn them over at regular intervals so that they turn golden, and take care not to burn them. Meanwhile, do what has been mentioned in terms of crushing the garlic with the leftover cheese and the walnuts until you get a marrow-like consistency. Dissolve this mash in a kneading tub with hot water and add lots of olive oil. Divide the flatbreads up into parts when they come out of the oven and put them in the tub with the mixture. Cut the loaves into medium-sized pieces

---

54 (*tharīda*) *muthawwama*, which literally translates as 'garlicked' (*thūm*, 'garlic'). In Gayangos XVI (fol. 19r.), the title is simply 'Garlicky *tharīda*, amazing'. The word *nayrūz* is a variant form of the Persian *nawrūz* (*now*, 'new'; *rūz*, 'day), which marks the date of the spring equinox on 21 March and was already celebrated on that day in Abbasid Baghdad. In Egypt, it became an important festival among Copts, for whom it marked the beginning of their year (the first day of the Coptic month of Thout), coinciding with 11 September of the Gregorian calendar, and was linked to the flooding of the Nile. Like the Persian *nowruz* today, it was associated with specific foods, such as the *harīsa*, but also the drinking of wine and beer, as well as general rowdiness and debauched behaviour, which explains why it was eventually banned in 1354. In Muslim Spain, where Nayrūz was the first of January, this feast was also known as *yanāyir* or *nurūs/z*, and marked the beginning of the solar year. According to the Calendar of Córdoba, it was the feast of Jesus's circumcision and one of the so-called bad, 'Egyptian' (*jibsiyāqū*) days among the Greeks – a reference to the *dies Aegyptiaci* in Greek astrology, which were thought to bring bad luck. See Shoshan 1993: 40–61; Lewicka 2011: 166 (note 145), 542 (note 254); Corriente 1997: 525. Dozy & Pellat 1961: 27 (trans., 26), 131 (trans., 130).

– they should be on the larger, rather than smaller side. Put some of the grated cheese at the bottom of a bowl and put the broken-up flatbreads on top. Gradually sprinkle on more cheese until the tub and the bowl are filled up. Then, take the mash and, if there is not enough cheese in it, add some more grated cheese until it is thickened again, and has turned white because of the high cheese content. Pour the mixture on the crumbs, and then add good sweet olive oil. Boil, and then gradually pour in all of the broth in which the chickens have been cooked, until it is finished and there is broth at the bottom of the bowl. If there is not enough broth, add boiling water prepared especially for this purpose. In the meantime, stir the bread mixture from the bottom of the bowl upwards so as to ensure that the broth is fully absorbed. Then, sprinkle on the powdered cheese, and layer the meat from the tub on top of the dish. Scatter on more finely grated cheese and then pour on olive oil. Eat and enjoy, Allah the Exalted willing. [This dish is mostly served by Andalusians at Nayrūz days, as is customary in their country.][55] You can roast chickens on spits instead of cooking them in the oven, whereas the dish can also be made with rabbits, hares or partridges instead of chickens. [However, rabbits are rarely found outside al-Andalus.]

31. Pigeon *tharīda* made during the summer with a variety of vegetables[56]

Take a tender gourd, clean it inside and out and chop it up. Peel small aubergines and cut each into quarters, without fully dividing them. Stuff with salt and leave them until their bad juices have been expelled. Then, wash them in fresh water and put them in a pot together with the gourd pieces and add a generous amount of both salt and olive oil, as well as pepper, coriander, one cut-up onion, and enough water to cover everything. Put the pot over a fire. Then take whatever vegetables are available at the time of year, as well as vine tendrils and those of serpent melons, cucumbers[57] and gourd. Clean all of them, cut them

55 The passages enclosed in brackets are additions from Gayangos XVI (fol. 20r.).

56 The name of the dish is clearly at odds with the recipe, which is devoid of pigeon, or indeed any other meat. Gayangos XVI (fol. 20r.) has the more logical title of *jināniyya* (see recipe No. 377).

57 Though denoting different varieties, *qiththā'* (serpent melon) and *khiyār* (common cucumber) were – and still are – often used interchangeably for 'cucumber'. According to Ibn Zuhr (1992: 61–2; trans., 88), the cucumber provides comfort in

into the smallest possible pieces, and wash them. When the gourd and aubergine are nearly done, add the other vegetables. Then, make flat loaves from leavened dough in the kneading tub, bake them in the oven or *tannūr*, and crumble them. Next, cut up good-quality dry cheese and put in a pot, but also grate a little of it. Crush mint, fresh coriander and cloves of garlic, and also put this in the pot. When the pot has come to a boil, pour the broth on the breadcrumbs. Now remove the gourd and aubergine and all of the vegetables from the pot and layer them all on top of the bread. Finally, scatter on some grated cheese, and then eat and enjoy, Allah the Exalted willing.

32. *Tharīda* of broad beans (*baysār*), also known as *fūl*[58]

Take ground broad beans and rinse them once with hot water. Smear them with olive oil and put them in a pot with enough fresh water to cover them, as well as a clove of garlic. Place the pot on the fire and then take the stomach of a young fatty ram, boil the tripe in hot water and scrape with a knife until it turns white. Clean it together with the small coiled intestines[59] and cut into pieces. Also cut up the caul fat and use everything to make small sausages and put them in another pot with salt, lots of olive oil, pepper, coriander, cumin, a cut-up onion, and enough water to fully cover everything. Place the pot over a fire. Then crumble leavened bread as finely as possible. When the sausages are done, take them out of the pot and set them aside in a bowl. Strain the broth in which they have been cooked. When the broad beans are done, remove the garlic from the pot and use a large ladle to stir the beans until they are dissolved and the mixture obtains a marrow-like

---

case of fainting, but causes heartburn, when eaten, and is more 'cooling' than the serpent melon. It was considered an anaphrodisiac – Maimonides even claimed it was extremely harmful for coitus. See Ibn Janāḥ 2020: No. 190; Schmucker 1969: 337 (No. 562); Renaud & Colin 1934: No. 347; al-Ishbīlī 2004–10: Nos. 1804, 1241, 3881, 3947; Kircher 1967: 170–1; Dietrich 1988: II: 283, 656, 692 (note 14); Meyerhof 1940: Nos. 343, 388; al-Isrā'ilī 1992: 355, 358.

58 In Gayangos XVI (fol. 20v.), the recipe is titled '*tharīda* of *baysār*, which is amazing'. Though *baysār* was a vernacular variant of the standard word for broad beans (*fūl*), in the present text it denotes dried broad beans, as in other recipes that require them (Nos. 89, 141), whereas it was also the name of a dish (No. 387). Also see Schiaparelli 1871: 381 (*baysār, faysār*).

59 *Dawwāra* (also *duwwāra*); Nasrallah [al-Warrāq 2007]: 716–7; Corriente 1997: 187; Lane 1863–74: III, 932.

consistency. Then, add a sufficient quantity of water for the dish. When the pot has come to a boil, add the breadcrumbs little by little, and stir. Gradually pour in enough of the broth of the sausages to be absorbed by the breadcrumbs. Season with enough salt. Put the sausages in the pot with the breadcrumbs, and gently stir with a ladle. Serve them in a bowl immediately afterwards, and put good olives on top. Eat and enjoy, Allah the Exalted willing.

You should cook this *tharīda* over a low-to-moderate fire and take care it does not get burnt. If you like, you can make it without sausages. Or, if you want, you can place clarified butter, fresh butter or olive oil with turnips and onions in the centre of the bowl when you eat the dish. I have heard that some people pour milk in after the broad beans have dissolved and the breadcrumbs have been added. When the breadcrumbs have absorbed all they can, the dish is served with a dusting of sugar, and a bowl of honey on the side. I have not cooked or eaten it this way, but anyone who wishes to try it should do so, Allah the Exalted willing. This concludes the *tharīda* recipes that need to be mentioned. [And even if most of them will scarcely be made, they deserve to be added because of their exquisiteness. The same applies to most of the chapters in this book.][60]

60 The passage enclosed in brackets is an addition from Gayangos XVI (fol. 21v.).

Chapter Three: on pottages[61] and mashed cereal dishes[62]

33. Breadcrumb pottage made with chicken broth

Take a tender plump chicken or rooster,[63] cut open its belly and clean inside and out. Bruise it and put it whole in a new pot with salt, olive oil, a stick of cinnamon, a grain of mastic, ginger, coriander, a small piece of onion and enough water. Cook over a fire. Crumble leavened semolina or *darmak* flour bread and rub the pieces very finely with your hands until they become like flour. Next, sift them onto a tray or sieve, and then rub them again with the hands until all the breadcrumbs are equally fine. Put them in a bowl and place a lid on top of it. When what is in the pot is done, take it out and strain the broth through a thick cloth. Then clean the pot and return the broth to it. When it comes to a boil, gradually throw in the rubbed breadcrumbs with one hand, using the other to stir the pot, and continue this until you have no crumbs left. Make sure to keep stirring until you see that the mixture has coagulated and it is done to a turn. Then take down the pot and transfer the contents to a large ceramic bowl. Dust with cinnamon or add a drizzle of sour grape vinegar. Eat and enjoy, Allah the Exalted willing.

---

61 *aḥsā'*, the plural of *ḥasā'* (also *ḥasw*). In the Near Eastern culinary manuals this word referred to soup; Corriente 1997: 127; Nasrallah [al-Warrāq 2007]: 617. According to Ibn Khalṣūn (1996: 161; trans., 89), *ḥasw* could also be made with *ka'k*, in which case it is a very fattening dish.

62 *jashā'ish*, the plural of *jashīsh/a* (usually denoting coarsely ground wheat), with the frequent variant of *dashīsh* (Dozy 1881: I, 442; Corriente 1997: 179; Lane 1863–74: I, 426). The *Andalusian* has only one *jashīsha* recipe (*Anwā'*, 173; BNF, fol. 61v.), which does not, however, correspond to any of al-Tujībī's. Ibn Khalṣūn (1996: 157/trans., 82; also Lane, *ibid.*) held that *jashīsh* made with grains that are toasted before being crushed is the basis for *sawīq* (grain gruel), which is very nutritious. He added that the mashed wheat was also used to make round, flat loaves, which, together with honey, made an excellent travel provision. Unfried *jashīsh*, on the other hand, resembles wheat *harīsa*. According to al-Uryūlī (1981: No. 24), both *jashīsh* and semolina (*samīd*) generate good blood and fortify the body; however, if abused, they cause a hardening of the bowels, and kidney stones. These harmful effects can be counteracted by drinking oxymel (honey and vinegar) after eating it. Also see Ibn Mubārak Shāh 2020: 79 (note 354); al-Dabbābī al-Mīsāwī 2017: 44–5.

63 *farrūj* (pl. *farārīj*): in contemporary Arabic, it generally refers to a young chicken or pullet, but in Andalusian Arabic denoted either a rooster (*dīk*) or cockerel, the latter – like capons (*makhṣī, khaṣī, kabbūn*) – being preferred, as their meat is more tender.

34. Another breadcrumb pottage

Take a new pot and pour in enough freshwater, together with some olive oil. Use a clean cloth to make a sachet with salt, ginger, a stick of cinnamon, a grain of mastic and a piece of onion. Add it to the pot and then place it over a fire. Take leavened breadcrumbs and proceed in the same way as in the previous recipe, grating them, etc. When the water has come to a boil twice, take out the sachet and put the crumbs in, as in the previous recipe. When everything is cooked, take the pot down from the fire. Then, crack one egg and whisk it in a bowl until the white and yolk are mixed. When the pottage is transferred to a large ceramic bowl, pour in the egg and stir until both are thoroughly mixed together. Sprinkle on cinnamon and then eat, Allah the Exalted willing.

You can also have it without the egg, while those who wish to eat it with fresh coriander and mint should lightly pound their leafstalks and squeeze the juice into the pottage. Those who do not want to use the juice should finely chop up the mint and coriander and put them in the pot when the pottage is nearly done. There are people who add fennel seeds, aniseed and clarified butter to the pottage at the start of the cooking. Remember this.

35. Another flour pottage

Take a new pot, pour in enough water and salt, and put it over a fire. Take wheat flour and put it in a bowl, moisten it with water and stir with a ladle until it is dissolved and the mixture is entirely smooth, without any lumps. When the pot has boiled, pour in the dissolved flour and gently stir, but take care that it does not get stuck to the bottom of the pot. Leave to cook until the mixture begins to thicken, and then remove the pot from the fire. When it simmers down, pour the pottage in a large ceramic bowl and eat. If you wish, you can add breadcrumbs, in which case use a knife to cut a loaf of bread in half, and toast it over a fire; once it turns golden, crumble it, pour olive oil on the crumbs, and add them to the bowl.

36. Yeast pottage

Take a new pot, pour in enough water and salt, and add a small amount of fennel seeds, aniseed, caraway and a clove of unpeeled garlic. Put the pot over a fire. Then, take as much yeast as necessary to make the dough rise, and dissolve it in a bowl of hot water while stirring it with a ladle. When the garlic is nearly done, pour the dissolved yeast into the pot and continue stirring for the usual time it takes for the dish to be finished, but do not overdo it since this particular type of pottage should not be thick. Transfer the pottage to a large ceramic bowl, and eat. You are free to either remove the garlic, or eat it.

37. Almond and bran pottage

Take coarse bran and pour a lot of hot water over it. Vigorously rub it with your hands until it has released its strength. Then squeeze it with your hands before straining it through a cloth. When a cloudy liquid appears on the surface, pour it away. Pour the strained broth into a new pot. If you need to add water, do so. Then, crush blanched almonds to a marrow-like consistency. Dissolve the almond mixture in water, strain, and then put it in the pot with the bran broth. Keep stirring until everything is mixed and thickened. When it is ready, take it out of the pot and eat, Allah the Exalted willing.

38. Flour and milk[64] pottage, called *lakhṭij*[65] by the people of al-Andalus

Dissolve flour in water and put it in a new pot over a moderate fire. Strain milk and add it to the dissolved flour in the pot. Stir until it thickens and then serve it in a bowl, Allah the Exalted willing.

---

64 The edition (2012: 60) has the misreading *laban wa ḥalīb*, which has been corrected with the help of BL Or5927 (fol. 111r.) to *laban ḥalīb*.

65 This Andalusian Arabic word is related to a root meaning 'slime', and Corriente (1997: 478) traces its origin to the Latin *lac* (lacquer), with *-ṭij* being a pejorative suffix. According to Dozy (1881: II, 523), it is 'clay which thickens water', which could explain the name of the dish, as the end result has a similar appearance. Also see Marín 1997: 12.

39. Pottage known to Andalusians as *zabzīn*[66] and to North Africans[67] as *barkūs*[68]

Put flour into a kneading tub and sprinkle on water into which salt has been dissolved. Whisk it with your hands until it is mixed and becomes granulated. Then, gently roll the dough with your palms into small chickpea-shaped balls. Sift them in a fine-meshed sieve to remove any of the remaining flour, and then put them on a tray to dry. Take a new pot and, before putting it over a fire, pour in enough water and salt, as well as a dribble of olive oil, pepper, coriander and cut-up onion segments. Put the pot over a fire and, once it has come to a boil, gingerly add what is on the tray and stir until you see that that water has dried out, and the mixture has thickened. Then, cut small pieces of good-quality dry cheese into the pot and also add finely chopped fresh coriander. When the pot comes to a boil, serve and eat, Allah the Exalted willing.

40. Millet flour pottage

Thoroughly dissolve millet flour in a bowl with water. Then put a new pot over a fire with enough water and salt. When it comes to a boil, gently put in the dissolved flour and stir continuously with a ladle until the water is reduced and the pottage has thickened. Serve and eat, Allah the Exalted willing.

41. Wheat mush

Sieve good-quality wheat, pick it over and grind. Sift the grounds and extract the flour and bran. Wash and put it in a new pot. Add an eighth of its content in macerated fenugreek. Pour on a lot of water and cook over the fire. When it is ready, transfer to a large ceramic bowl, sprinkle

---

66 A variety of coarse couscous (often combined with legumes), which is well known in North Africa, where it denotes various kinds of cereal porridges; Marín 1997: 12; Corriente 1997: 226. This variety of couscous is also called *muḥammiṣ* (see recipe No. 91), with *abāzīn* and *avāzīn* as variants of *zabzīn*.

67 *ʿidwa*, short for *ʿbarr* ('land') *al-ʿidwa*', which literally translates as 'embankment' or 'shore', but in Andalusian Arabic referred to the North African coast. Corriente 1997: 347; Dozy 1881: II, 105.

68 This is a variant of *barkūkas(h)*, which is the word that appears in Gayangos XVI (fol. 22v.), and may derive from the Latin *praecox*, 'done hurriedly' (Corriente 1997: 48). In present-day Morocco, *barkūkash* (*berkoukech*) is a soup prepared with couscous grains, vegetables and meat. See al-Dabbābī al-Mīsāwī 2017: 67–70.

on a bit of hand-rubbed saffron,[69] and then eat. If you want to make this recipe with milk, do not put in fenugreek and reduce the amount of water, replacing it with milk. Let the mashed wheat cook in the milk until it has fully absorbed it.

42. Barley mush

Pound good-quality barley in a large wooden or stone mortar until the husks come off, and then sieve and crush the kernels. Sift the grounds and extract the bran and flour. Wash it and put it in a new pot, filled to three-quarters capacity with water. Cook in the oven overnight until the liquid has browned. Drain off the broth, and serve it. This dish cools those with fevers and hot temperaments. If you like, you can have both the broth and the mash. You could also add fennel seeds and aniseed to the dish at the beginning of the process, to reduce its coldness [in temperament].

43. Rice mash[70]

This is not a common mash, except in my hometown of Murcia, or Valencia – may Allah restore them to Islam! – which are known for the growth and abundance of rice, unlike the other regions of al-Andalus.

During the crushing of the rice to dehusk it, some of the grains break, which constitutes the base for the mash. Remove them from the hulled rice, and then cribble them in a wide-meshed sieve. Store until needed. The recipe for cooking it is as follows: thoroughly wash the crushed rice with fresh water and put it in an iron pot with six *raṭls* of water for each *raṭl* of rice. Cook over a moderate fire and, when it is done, add a sufficient quantity of crushed salt before serving, Allah the Exalted willing.

---

69 The text has the Andalusian word *ʿabīr* (which in standard Arabic means 'fragrant'), rather than the more customary *zaʿfarān*. However, both BL Or5927 (fol. 111v.) and Gayangos XVI (fol. 23v.) have *ghubayrā* ('pennyroyal'), which is equally possible.

70 Gayagangos XVI (*ibid.*) adds that it is 'amazing' in the title but omits the first paragraph of the recipe relating to its geographical distribution.

Chapter Four: on pastries, various types of *mujabbanas* (fried cheese buns), *isfanj* (doughnuts) and other similar foods

44. Making *kaʿk*[71] (ring-shaped biscuits) stuffed with sugar and almonds[72]

Moisten *darmak* flour with olive oil and rub it well in between your hands. Knead into a firm dough with water, salt and a little yeast. Do not add a lot of water all at once, but pour it in little by little so that it can be fully absorbed. You will know the dough is ready when you tear off a piece and it stretches but does not break. Finely crush sugar with the same amount of ground almond kernels in a copper mortar, and mix the two. If the sweetness of the sugar predominates, add enough almonds to balance the flavours. Add rose water, ginger, spikenard, cinnamon, cloves, pepper and a little camphor to the almonds and sugar, and knead it all together by hand into a tight dough. Use your hands to make pieces the size of fingers, or slightly longer and thinner, depending on the desired thickness of the biscuits and whether you want them big or small. Prepare a clean table or board and smooth out part of the dough on it. Spread the rolled filling lengthwise along the inside of the dough, folding the ends of the dough over the filling and using your hands to roll it on the table so that it is tightly packed, with

71 Usually, *kaʿk* were dry biscuits: *Wuṣla*, Nos. 7.97–99; *Kanz*, Nos. 2–6, Appendix, No. 4; *Anwāʿ*, 188–9. According to Ibn al-Ḥashshāʾ (1941: 66, No. 616) and others (e.g. al-Farāhīdī 2008: I, 67), *kaʿk* simply denoted dry bread (*al-khubz al-yābis*). Ibn Zuhr (1992: 13; trans., 49) alleged that because both *kaʿk* and another kind of biscuit known as *bishmāṭ* were kneaded with oil, they become flammable when baked, as a result of which they have a sulphurous strength (*quwat kibrīt*), which makes them harmful for people with a hot temperament and those suffering from fevers. Ibn Khalṣūn (1996: 161; trans., 89) said that *kaʿk* were dense, slow to digest and constipating, but very nutritious. When made with pottage (*ḥasw*), they are very rich and fattening, but any negative effects can be counteracted by eating *kaʿk* with sweetmeats. Ibn al-Bayṭār (1992: II, 317) reported that *kaʿk* was also known as *khubz Rūmī* ('Byzantine bread'), or *baqsamāṭ*, which 'is called *bishmāṭ* among the common people in the Maghrib'. Ibn al-Khaṭīb (1984: 59), for his part, held that *kaʿk* included various sweets such as *zulābiyya* (recipe No. 73) and *qanāniṭ* (recipe No. 48), but that they were not known in the Maghrib as *bishmāṭ*, but as stuffed (*maḥshuw*) *kaʿk*. Also see Ibn Mubārak Shāh 2020: 123, note 559. In Tunisian Arabic, the word *bishmāṭ* is applied to the dried pieces of bread served as a topping for the *tbkikha*, a lentil soup. Also see al-Dabbābī al-Mīsāwī 2017: 97–100.

72 There is a similar – but highly abridged – recipe in *Anwāʿ*, 218.

the desired length and thickness. Then shape the dough into a circle, with the ends stuck tightly together. Crimp with a copper chisel made for this purpose. Then, spread out another piece of the dough and repeat the process. Continue making rings, one after another, until you run out of dough and filling. Layer them on a board lightly dusted with flour, and bake them in the oven. Keep a close eye on the baking, and when they are ready carefully remove them from the board one by one. Then rub them with a clean cloth and drizzle on mastic-infused rose water. Sprinkle rose water in the container in which the biscuits will be stored and scent it with good Indian agarwood.[73] Put the biscuits inside when they are freshly made and leave them there until it is time to eat them, Allah the Exalted willing.

45. Another recipe, with a honey filling[74]

Take a sufficient amount of honey and boil it over a moderate fire after skimming off the froth. Then, pound previously made unfilled *kaʿk* together with peeled almond kernels. Add the mixture to the honey, together with rose water and the requisite aromatic spices, and thicken the honey with it. When it is done, remove from the fire and leave to cool down. Smear your hands with olive oil, mould the filling into thin rolls and put them in a bowl. Then, knead the flour dough as described before, spread out a piece on the table, fill it with one of the honeyed rolls, and then shape into *kaʿk*, as described in the previous recipe. If you like, you can fill the *kaʿk* with dried dates instead of honey, in which case you should clean and de-stone *shadānaj*[75] dates, and pound them to a marrow-like mixture before adding the spices and completing the process, as described.[76]

73 BL Or5927 (fol. 112r.) has 'Mandalayan (*mandala*) agarwood' instead of 'Indian' (*Hindī*).

74 In Gayangos XVI (fol. 24v.), the recipe is titled 'another kind, mixed (*mashūb*) with honey'.

75 According to the editor of the text (2012: 64, note 1), this is a variety of tender succulent dates which are particularly eaten in Marrakech and the south of Morocco. The word (also *shadhanj*, *shadhāna*) denotes 'hematite' (Corriente 1997: 276), and may have been applied to the dates in question in reference to their colour. Gayangos XVI (fol. 25r.) has *shaddakh* dates, which is a variant of *shaddākh* (also *shudhdhākh*), and denoted a type of date used mainly in confectionery (Corriente 1997: 276, 277).

76 Gayangos XVI (*ibid.*) adds: 'This is how most people make it.'

46. Plain *ka'k*, without a filling[77]

Take *darmak* flour, rub with olive oil, add fennel seeds and then knead into a firm dough with hot water into which salt and a little yeast have been dissolved. Divide the dough into the desired *ka'k* size and thickness. Roll them out on a table one by one and shape into rings, as described. Put them on a tray lightly dusted with flour and then bake them in the oven. When they are done, wipe them down and store them in a container until such time as they are served, Allah the Exalted willing.

47. Gazelle's ankles[78]

Moisten flour with a little olive oil and knead into a firm dough with hot water in which you have dissolved salt but no yeast,[79] and then add fennel seeds, aniseed, pepper and ginger. Pound sugar and almonds together until they are thoroughly mixed, and then transfer the mixture to a bowl. Add rose water and the customary aromatic spices and knead so that everything becomes thoroughly blended. Then, smear your hands with olive oil and mould the mixture into rolls, as thin as you can make them. Spread the dough out on the table, fold the filling inside, wrap the ends [of the dough] in, and then roll by hand as you do for the *ka'k*, except that in this recipe they are left elongated instead of being shaped into rings. Put them on a *malla* and use a knife to cut them crosswise into similar-sized pieces.[80] Place the *malla* in the oven and bake the biscuits as they are. When they are ready, separate them and store them in a clean jar until they are eaten. This type of biscuit is prized because it is unusual. Some refined people[81] add crushed hulled pine nuts to the filling, and

77 These biscuits bear an uncanny resemblance to the Italian fennel *taralli*.

78 A modern iteration of this sweet is primarily associated with Morocco, and is often referred to by its French name, *cornes de gazelle* ('gazelle's horns'), a crescent-shaped biscuit filled with almond paste scented with orange-blossom water. In the Middle Ages, the biscuits were also sold at markets, with unscrupulous confectioners apparently adulterating the filling with crystallized sugar cane juice (Buckley [al-Shayzarī 1999]: 63).

79 Addition in Gayangos XVI (fol. 25r.).

80 According to Gayangos XVI (*ibid.*), the pieces should resemble broad beans (*ḥabb al-fūl*).

81 The author uses the word *ẓurafā'* (singular *ẓarīf*), which denoted a particular class of individuals in medieval society who combined the literary and social dictates of refinement, within which food, or gastronomy to be more precise, played a big part. See *EI*², '*ẓarīf*' (J. Montgomery); von Grunebaum 1953: 221–58; Ghazi 1959.

when cutting the rolls they put a hulled pine nut in each one. This can only be done with patience and skill. If you do not want any filling, put the usual aromatic spices in the dough when you are kneading it, and then shape it into the above-mentioned rolls. Remember this.

48. Stuffed cannoli[82]

Knead unleavened *darmak* flour with only water until you get a firm dough. Wrap the dough around cane reeds, covering them entirely, and roll them on the table with the palm of the hand to smooth out the dough. Cut only the dough into small tubes and keep them apart from one another. Leave them to dry on the reeds. Then put honey in a cauldron and skim off the froth as it is heated on the fire. Mix in good-quality pounded skinned almonds and any of the usual aromatic spices you have to hand. If any of the dough breaks off, crush it and also mix it in. Thicken the mixture with honey. Then gingerly remove the dough tubes from the reeds and fry them in an earthenware pot with good-quality olive oil until they turn golden brown. When they are ready, stuff them with the above-mentioned filling and put a blanched almond at the ends of each of them. Dust with cinnamon and sugar, and then serve, with the strength of Allah the Exalted.

49. The Judge's morsels[83]

Crush sugar with three times the amount of finely pounded almonds, and add the usual aromatics. Then knead the dough in the same way

82 *qanāniṭ* (singular *qannūṭ*, 'tube'). Recipes for this sweet can be found in a number of other works from the Near East. In *Kanz* (Nos. 285, 308), they appear as 'Zaynab's fingers' (*aṣābiʿ Zaynab*), whereas in al-Warrāq's cookbook (1987: 276) they are called *ḥalāqim* (the plural of *ḥulqūm*, 'wind-pipe'), and are made with a filling of walnuts and sugar, with the ends dipped in syrup and sprinkled with dyed sugar candy. Ibn al-Khaṭīb (1984: 59) defined them as a kind of *kaʿk*, 'bread tubes filled with sugar, almonds and spices'. In modern Arabic, *ḥulqūm* (also *rāḥat al-ḥulqum*, 'comfort for the throat') refers to what is known in English as Turkish delight, the abbreviated form *luqum* becoming the English *lokum*. In some countries (e.g. Lebanon), it is called *malban*. Though today cannoli is associated with Sicily, the evidence clearly points to an Arab origin.

83 *luqmat al-Qāḍī*: this is a variation of a very well-known sweet for which recipes can be found in al-Baghdādī 1964: 81 (trans., 104); *Waṣf*, 430; *Wuṣla*, No. 7.82. It even makes an appearance in the famous tale of 'The Porter and the Three Ladies' in the 1001 Nights (Mahdī 1984: I, 127). Today's sweet by this name is more similar to the *isfanj* recipe in the present text (No. 74).

as for *kaʿk*, and roll it out rectangularly. Insert the filling as explained above and mould the dough into walnut shapes. Fry them in sweet olive oil and then sprinkle on sugar before eating them, Allah the Exalted willing.

50. Stuffed ears[84]

Knead *darmak* flour, as described above. Roll it out and fold in the shape of ears before frying them in good-quality olive oil. Immediately after taking them out of the pan, stuff them with the kind of filling you use for the cannoli. Dust with sugar and cinnamon, and eat cold, Allah the Exalted willing.

51. A kind of pastry

Crush sugar and almonds, as described, and knead with the usual spices. Then, knead *darmak* flour into a *kaʿk* dough and mould it in the shape of walnuts, almonds and pine nuts, and so on, in all sizes. Stuff them with the usual filling. Carefully deep-fry them in a pot with olive oil. Every now and then stir them about with a ladle until they turn golden brown. When they are done, put them in glazed bowls, and pour on skimmed honey that has been thickened with good-quality rose water. Perfume them with aromatic spices and musk, and eat them when they are cold, Allah the Exalted willing.[85]

52. Stuffed *muqawwara* (loaf cake)[86]

Knead one-and-a-half *raṭls* of *darmak* flour with fifteen egg yolks, a little yeast and enough milk into a thick firm dough. Shape into round thin loaves and then leave to rise. Put a pan on the fire with sweet olive oil

---

84 Ear-shaped bread is already attested in ancient Mesopotamia, where it was called *khashistu*, which may also have been stuffed; Roth 1956–2010: VI, 126, X–2, 109.

85 The result brings to mind modern descendants such as the Italian *cartellate* or *castagnole* (which derive their name from the fact that they are shaped like chestnuts), or even the Spanish (Mallorcan) *ensaïmadas*, though these are baked rather than fried.

86 Derived from a verb meaning 'to excavate, hollow out', it refers to the fact that the loaves are hollowed and stuffed (Corriente 1997: 447). This recipe is also found in the *Andalusian* (*Anwāʿ*, 71; BNF, fol. 29v.), which, however, is somewhat more elaborate: the result is similar to a pie in that, after pouring in the honey and butter, the top crust (i.e. the lid) that is removed to open up the loaf is put back on, followed by more honey and butter, and only then is the sugar sprinkled on.

and, when the oil has come to a boil, put the loaves in and turn them over, one after another, so that they brown slightly, but do so carefully (so they do not break apart). Then remove the loaves from the pan and hollow them out as you do for a *muqawwara*. Remove the toasted crumb and finely grate it by hand. Crush and mix sugar with peeled almonds and walnuts, and gradually put them inside the loaf in layers alternating with the grated crumbs until it is full. Apply a dusting of sugar to every other layer and simultaneously sprinkle on rose water. Then, boil clarified butter and honey, and pour this over the *muqawwara* until it has absorbed as much as needed. Finally, sprinkle on sugar and eat, Allah the Exalted willing.

53. Stuffed round loaves

Knead two *raṭls* of *darmak* flour with water, yeast, olive oil and salt into a tender dough. Make a filling of sugar and almonds, as described above, and spread out half of the dough with half of the filling. Press down [the dough], while adding some olive oil, and shape into small loaves. Leave them to rise, and then bake them in the oven using an iron casserole dish[87] that has been greased with olive oil. When the loaves are golden brown, transfer them to a large ceramic bowl. Pour on hot honey after having made holes into the loaves with your fingers so as to allow the honey to be absorbed. Sprinkle on pine nuts and perfume with musk. Use the remaining half of the dough to make thin circular loaves, and stuff them with the remaining filling before frying them in sweet olive oil. When they are done, put them in a bowl, pour on boiled honey, and top with crushed walnuts. Perfume with musk and eat all of it together, Allah the Exalted willing.

87 According to Gayangos XVI (fol. 27r.), it should be a new glazed earthenware casserole dish.

54. A similar recipe, known as 'The Emir's *thurda*'[88]

Knead *darmak* flour with water, salt, yeast and a drizzle of oil into a firm dough. Mould into four thin, round loaves and fry them in a pan with a lot of sweet olive oil until they are golden brown. Then, pulverize them. Mould the remainder of the dough in the shape of small hollow *mujabbanas* with (removable) lids, and fry off both in sweet olive oil. Then, finely crush sugar, almonds, pine nuts and peeled pistachios, and add aromatic spices and rose water mixed with the ground loaves. Use the mixture as filling for the *mujabbanas*, and then cover with their lids. Take care the lids remain intact and in place. Arrange the *mujabbanas* in a bowl, place the rest of the filling in between them, and drizzle on rose water. Before serving, dust everything with caster sugar and pour on very thick honey-infused rose-water syrup.

55. *Jawzīnaq*[89]

Finely pound good-quality walnuts in a wooden mortar. Extract their oil by rubbing the crumbs in between your hands and drizzle on hot water. When you are almost done with this, add a little comb honey and resume rubbing the walnut crumbs with your hands until all of their oil has been released. Strain the oil, add good comb honey and mix them together. Take some more walnuts and soften them in hot water before skinning them. Cool them down in cold water and then wipe them with a clean cloth before pulverizing them in a wooden mortar. Mix in enough ground sugar and pepper.[90] Then, knead *darmak* flour and water into a light dough (i.e. batter) and mix in a sufficient amount of egg whites.

---

88 Both the printed edition (2012: 68) and BL Or5917 (fol. 113v.) have *mithrada* ('bowl'); however, *thurda* (a variant of *tharīda*) is the word used in Gayangos XVI (fol. 27r.) – albeit in the colloquial form of *turda* – as well as in the title of the near-identical recipe in the *Andalusian* (*Anwāʿ*, 71). The latter has several *thurda* recipes, and thus it is likely that this was the established name of the dish (Corriente 1997: 83). The word can also be found in al-Baghdādī's cookery book from the same period (1964: 53). In addition, the preparation has a number of features in common with the *tharīda*. Also see Lane 1863–74: I, 335.

89 This sweetmeat (for which another recipe is included later on – No. 410) is Persian in origin, as its name indicates, and is already mentioned in a sixth-century Persian text (Unvala 1921: 23; al-Thaʿālibī 1900: 707), alongside *lawzīnaq* (recipes Nos. 56, 411). It also commonly appears as *jawzīnaj* (*jawz*, 'walnut'). The *Andalusian* (*Anwāʿ*, 193) contains a recipe by the same name, but it is very different, and the result would have been stuffed biscuits in various shapes, such as flowers or rings.

90 According to Gayangos XVI (fol. 28r.), the weight should be that of the walnuts.

Heat a *kunāfa*[91] pan over a fire and, when it is hot, rub some wax on it and wipe with a clean cloth. Pour in the batter mixed with the egg whites and swirl it around the pan so that it spreads evenly across its surface. If the batter looks too thick or lumpy, add a splash of water. In order to prevent the batter from sticking to the bottom of the pan, coat it with wax, and then wipe. Finish frying all of the batter into thin loaves, but leave a little batter to one side. Mix this with egg yolks and make some more thin (round) loaves with it, which you cook like the first batch. Then, gather all the loaves, put the filling lengthwise inside each one, fold them at the ends, and then twice more. Next, cut into discs and layer them in a glazed bowl. Pour on olive oil mixed with honey, and sprinkle caster sugar on top and underneath the discs before serving, Allah the Exalted willing.

56. *Lawzīnaq*[92]

This is made the same way as *jawzīnaq*, except that there is no pepper in it. Bear this in mind.

---

91 See recipe No. 57. Gayangos XVI (*ibid.*) is the only one to use *mallat al-kunāfa* for the pan, whereas the other manuscript copies all have *miqlāt al-kunāfa*.

92 This is an unusually terse description of this sweet, which is better known as *lawzīnaj*. It is actually an almond confection (*lawz*, 'almond') of thin sheets of dough stuffed with nuts (pistachios and almonds) and sugar, and sometimes drenched in almond oil and/or syrup. According to Ibn al-Khaṭīb (1984: 59), *lawzīnaj* – and all other fried sweets made with dough and honey, such as *khabīs* (recipes Nos. 63-6), *zulābiyya* (see recipe No. 73), and *qaṭā'if* (see recipes Nos. 59, 60, 416) – are excellent for the old and those with cold temperaments, but are very harmful to youngsters and people with hot temperaments, and can even cause death or fevers. It was far better known than *jawzīnaq*, with multiple recipes in other cookery books (especially those from the Near East): *Waṣf*, 418–19, 456; al-Baghdādī 1964: 76 (trans., 99–100); al-Warrāq 1987: 37, 265–6; *Anwā'*, 193; *Taṣānīf*, fol. 58r. Ibn Jazla (fols. 199v.–200r.) and *Taṣānīf* also refer to a Persian variety which is uncooked (*bi-ghayr/bi-lā nār*, 'without fire') and made with equal amounts of ground skinned almonds, sugar and rose water, and flavoured with camphor and musk. Ibn Zuhr (1992: 95; trans., 116) qualified it as both an electuary and a sweet. When used as a drug, it produces a peaceful and restful sleep and nourishes the brain, to such an extent that doctors alleged that its fundamental property is to increase brain substance. It also ripens phlegm in the chest and lungs, making it easier to expectorate. When eaten as a dessert in excessive quantities, it is harmful to the stomach and spoils the appetite. If eaten on an empty stomach, it upsets it and, after a large meal, causes vomiting. *Lawzīnaj* may be the precursor of both lasagne (the *lasagne al forno* from the Veneto region being an extant sweet descendant) and baklava.

57. *Kunāfa*[93]

Knead two *raṭls* of prime semolina that has been picked over into a firm dough after moistening it with hot water. Cover the dough to soften it up, and set aside. Then pour water on the dough and wash it the way you do when making clothes starch,[94] until it releases all of its gluten. Strain the batter through a thick cloth so as to get rid of all of the semolina. Filter out the water so that you are left with something resembling a bready mixture. Pour on enough water so that the consistency is neither too runny nor too thick. Take the special *kunāfa* griddle and put it over a coal fire which should not have any flames. When it is hot, rub it down with a clean cloth soaked in sweet olive oil, and pour in as much as will fit of the batter. Leave it for a bit until it turns into a crêpe-thin flatbread and then transfer it to a bowl. Pour in a little more of the dough and do the same thing. Keep making one flatbread after another until all of the batter is finished. Every time you make one, wipe the pan with the oil-soaked cloth and scrape it with a knife to prevent the loaf sticking to the edges, which will spoil it. Then, melt one quarter of a *raṭl* of butter or clarified butter on a fire with two *raṭls* of honey until both are mixed together. Those who like can also add a bit of pepper. Arrange the flatbreads evenly and pour on the melted butter and honey. Serve while they are hot. Clarified butter is better than fresh butter. If you want to keep and save the flatbreads, cut them as thinly as you can with scissors. Put a new pot on the fire with sufficient honey and, when it comes to a boil, skim off the froth and add the flatbread strips to the pot. Cook to

---

93 Unlike today's *kunāfa* (*kanafeh, knafeh*), which is usually made with shredded filo pastry soaked in syrup and layered with cheese, the medieval variety was a very thin unleavened flatbread. This was an Egyptian invention originally, and the name itself goes back to the Coptic (*kenefiten*), which denoted a kind of loaf or cake (Crum 1939: 113). For recipes in other cookery books, see: Ibn Mubārak Shāh 2020: 62 (No. 141), 68 (No. 153); *Wuṣla*, Nos. 7.19–24; *Waṣf*, 436–7, 453; *Kanz*, Nos. 277, 290, 298, 325, 330, 332–3; *Anwā'*, 178; al-Dabbābī al-Mīsāwī 2017: 125–30.

94 *talbīna*, which can also denote 'semolina paste' or 'porridge' (made with milk or honey); Corriente 1997: 476; Kazimirski 1860: II, 962; Dozy 1881: II, 515. In pre-Islamic times, *talbīn* was a thin soup (*ḥasā'*), which could also be used as the broth for *tharīd* (Ibn Qayyim al-Jawziyya 1927: 80–1). Also see recipe No. 183. Ibn Ḥabīb (1992: 46–7; trans., 79) quotes a *ḥadīth* about *talbīn* containing a blessing, explaining that the word means 'the hated useful one (*al-baghīḍ al-nāfi'*)', and that it is finer than *ḥarīra* (see recipe No. 450). *Ḥadīths* also refer to the psychologically uplifting effect of *talbīna*, which was said to 'relieve the heart of the sad and gladden the heart of the sick'.

a turn and, when the mixture is almost set, pour in a sufficient amount of clarified butter or olive oil. When it is ready, take the pot down from the fire but leave the contents inside until it is time to eat it. Serve hot or cold, whichever you prefer, and dust with sugar or cinnamon[95] before eating, Allah the Exalted willing. [It is more appropriate to use clarified butter instead of fresh butter in this recipe. If you prefer, you may also use good-quality olive oil instead of fresh butter or clarified butter, as this this is what most people use in cooking.][96]

58. A similar recipe

Moisten the best and purest kind of semolina in hot water and leave for a while before kneading it with *darmak* yeast, salt and half a *raṭl* of *darmak* flour. When everything is thoroughly blended, gradually pour on hot water, and work the dough with your hands until it rises and becomes like silk. Put it in a new pot and leave it to rise. You can tell when it is ready when you see some moistness and holes appear. Heat up a tinned frying pan over a fire and then tie up ground salt into a clean cloth and soak it in olive oil. Wipe the pan down with the cloth several times. Pour in as much of the batter as the pan can accommodate, moving it about right and left so that it gets evenly distributed and you obtain something resembling *khabīṣ*[97] sheets. Cook the batter through, but take care not to let it brown. Each time you finish a sheet, transfer it to a board or table. Continue frying the flatbreads one after another, until you run out of batter. Make sure to wipe the pan with the salt bag each time you fry a flatbread. Then stack them in a bowl and cut them into pieces with a knife. Pour on a mixture of boiled honey and butter or clarified butter, and then dust with sugar before serving, Allah the Exalted willing.

59. *Qaṭā'if* (crêpes) called *mushahhada*[98]

Sift semolina in a wide-meshed sieve and pour on hot water into which yeast and salt have been dissolved. Work the dough by hand until it has

95 BL Or5927 (fol. 114v.) has 'crushed sugar and cinnamon', whereas Gayangos XVI (fol. 29r.) only has 'crushed sugar'.
96 The passage in brackets is an addition from Gayangos XVI (*ibid.*).
97 See recipes Nos. 63–6, 399.
98 See recipe No. 21. For a similar recipe, see *Anwā'*, 184 (BNF, fols. 64v.–65r.).

firmed up, and add milk. Whisk with your hand until the dough starts to stick to it, but make sure that it does not become too thin. Put the dough in a clean pot and put it close to the edge of the brazier[99] so that it gets some heat without being directly touched by the fire. Leave it until it rises. Then, take a specially prepared casserole[100] with narrow perforations at the bottom. Heat over the fire and rub with a clean cloth into which salt soaked in good-quality clarified butter has been tied. Gradually drop batter into the casserole in the form of small crêpes the size of common *qaṭā'if*. When bubbles appear (on the surface of the uncooked side), remove them, and fry others. Taste the dough and if it is too sour, add sufficient amounts of semolina, salt and milk, and then stir as much as needed. When all the crêpes have been made, arrange them in a bowl and pour on boiled honey to which either melted butter or clarified butter has been added. Finally, drizzle on pepper, cinnamon and sugar, and then eat, Allah the Exalted willing.

60. Abbasid *qaṭā'if*

Knead semolina with hot water, salt and yeast, as described in the previous recipe. Crush sugar and almond kernels as stated above, and perfume with the usual aromatic spices and a little rose water. When you have cooked the crêpes in the usual way, dissolve starch into water. Turn over each crêpe, fill them with the crushed sugar-and-almond stuffing and bring the edges together. Fold them with the bubble side facing outwards, and then drag the edges through the dissolved starch. Fry the crêpes in a pan with sweet olive oil so that they set quickly. Carefully take them out and arrange them in a bowl. Sprinkle on sugar, cinnamon, spikenard, and a dribble of almond oil – in fact, it is better if they are fried in almond oil as well – and then serve.

It is also possible to crush and dry the almonds like semolina. Pound them with the same amount of white sugar, and add cloves and spikenard. When the crêpes are cooked in the casserole, as described above, sprinkle the filling on them, and fold each crêpe over it, in the shape of a semi-circle. Seal the ends with dough dissolved in rose water, and fry in good-quality olive oil until golden. Drain the crêpes of the oil in which they have been fried, and then drench them in rose syrup,

99 *kānūn*: see Introduction.
100 Gayangos XVI (fol. 30r.) specifies that it should be glazed earthenware.

rose-water syrup or mastic syrup, and then eat.

You can also stack the crêpes one on top of the other with the filling in between them, in which case you should seal the edges with dough before frying them in a pan until golden, and then eat them, Allah the Exalted willing.

61. *Muwarraqa* (laminated flatbread), known as *musammana*[101]

Knead semolina or *darmak* flour with water and salt, and thoroughly work it. Melt clarified butter, smear it on a piece of dough and stretch it out in the kneading tub as thinly as possible. Smear clarified butter on the inside and fold it over itself. Then, stretch it out again and push it down by hand. Put the dough in a frying pan or on a *malla* over a fire. The *malla* should be coated with a little bit of clarified butter to prevent the dough from burning. When the loaf is done, remove it from the fire and hit it with your hands to make [the layers] come apart. Put it in a bowl and cover it with a cloth. Do the same with the remainder of the dough. Then pour on hot honey, dust with cinnamon and sugar, and eat, Allah the Exalted willing.

If you like, you can make it with small round loaves smeared with clarified butter, and then put one on top of the other. Afterwards, roll them all out extremely thinly with a rolling pin, or by hand. Cook them on the *malla*, as described, and pour on honey before eating them. Remember this.

62. A similar recipe[102]

Knead *darmak* flour [with water] into a moist dough. Moisten it some more by pouring on olive oil. Add yeast, roll it out and then form it into a round flat loaf with thin edges. Fold it and then blow inside. Twist

101 'the buttered one' (*samn*, 'clarified butter'), while *muwarraqa* means 'consisting of sheets' (*waraq*, 'sheet'). The *Andalusian* (*Anwāʿ*, 179; BNF, fol. 63r.-v.) has a similar recipe. Both *musammana* and *kaʿk* were sold ready-made at market, and were subject to tampering through the use of inferior flour and the inclusion of honey and semolina in the filling, rather than the more expensive sugar (al-Saqaṭī 1931: 39–40). The *musammana* still exists today as *msemmen* (also *rghā'if* in some dialects), and is particularly associated with Morocco, where it is eaten for breakfast, or as a snack, often with honey or jam, and cheese. There are equivalents in Tunisia (*mlewi*) and Algeria (*msemmen*), as well as in Egypt (*feteer meshaltet*) and India (*paratha*). Also see al-Dabbābī al-Mīsāwī 2017: 130–1.

102 Gayangos XVI (fol. 31r.) specifies that it is 'amazing, like the previous one'.

the edges so that the air is locked within. Do this several times, with different folds. Then, make a thick (round) loaf from the dough, and put it in an earthenware casserole dish. Add olive oil and then push your fingers into the bread until it looks like *madhūn*.[103] Pour olive oil on it and bake it in the oven until it is golden brown. When it is done, take it out, pour hot honey over it, dust with cinnamon, and then eat. If you want to make it with tallow, you should put it in the dough before rolling it out and blowing and baking, as described. You should pour on boiled honey because of the hardness of the tallow. Remember this, with the power and strength of Allah.

63. Making *khabīṣ*[104]

103 The text uses the plural *madāhin* (literally 'greased'). The word *madhūn* (cf. Spanish *almodón*) is found only in Andalusian texts, and denoted fine baking flour and, by extension, high-quality bread (Corriente 1997: 186), which Ibn Khalṣūn (1996: 156/ trans., 81) called the best food there is. From the text, it would appear that it also had some markings or pattern on the surface. According to other sources, however, it is a medium wholemeal bread or a bread made with wheat flour previously soaked in water. As a result, García Sánchez suggests that it corresponds to 'washed bread' (*khubz maghsūl*), which Ibn Jazla (fol. 78v.) explains as being made with the crumb of stale bread being soaked in hot water until it becomes like yeast and has fully risen. Al-Saqaṭī reports that sometimes *madhūn* was mixed with *darmak* or fine semolina flour (1931: 29, 37). See García Sánchez 1983: 146–7, 157; Dozy & Engelmann 1869: 169–70; De Eguílaz y Yanguas 1886: 231; Corominas & Pasqual 1984: I, 154; Corriente 1997: 422.

104 The name of the dish goes back to ancient Mesopotamia as the etymon of the Arabic *khabaṣa* ('to mix, mingle') is the Akkadian verb *khabāsu* ('to break into pieces'); it was either borrowed directly, or possibly through Aramaic. See Roth 1956–2010: VI, 9; Fraenkel 1886: 36; Löw 1881: 124. Varieties of this sweet are found in other cookery books as well: see Ibn Mubārak Shāh 2020: 65, note 284; *Kanz*, Nos. 288, 316, 318–9; *Anwāʿ*, 72; *Taṣānīf*, fols. 81v–82r. (including a no-bake variety). According to Lewicka (2011: 247), *khabīṣ*-type puddings in Mamluk Egypt were made by boiling a mixture of sesame oil, syrup, flour and, optionally, chopped vegetables. Ibn Jazla (fols. 79v.–81r.) included recipes for a number of *khabīṣ* varieties (with almonds, gourd, carrots, quince and pears), claiming it was less viscid than *fālūdhaj* (see recipes Nos. 67, 337 and 385 below) and better for the brain as well. However, he warned that it is harmful to those with a thick liver, and quickly causes putridity in the stomach because it is very slow to digest (though this can be counteracted with cucumbers or lettuce). al-Rāzī (1987: 139) said that it was lighter and less nutritious than *fālūdhaj* (see recipe No. 67), and less likely to produce obstructions. Conversely, al-Uryūlī (1983: No. 142) claimed it produces more obstructions than *fālūdhaj*. Ibn al-Khaṭīb (1984: 107; trans., 192) recommended it during spring because of its balanced nature. The modern *khabīṣ* is a sweet porridge (made with toasted flour and often containing nuts and raisins), mostly associated with the cuisines of a number of countries in the Arabian

Sift crushed wheat and macerate it in water for two days. On the third day, rub it vigorously with both hands until the liquid thickens. Then, strain it little by little until you are left with a broth that has a curd-like consistency (i.e. a batter). Place a tinned iron frying pan on the fire and, when it is hot, coat it lightly with wax and rub it down with an unused cloth. Then, return it to the fire and pour in enough of the batter to cover the bottom of the pan. When it has set into a white crêpe and the liquid has dried out, gently remove it from the pan and put it out in the sun on a clean sieve. Wipe the pan with wax and make another crêpe in it. Continue doing this until you run out of batter, but smear the pan with wax two or three times before making a new crêpe, and take care that there is no dirt or ash in the pan. If you like the crêpes to be yellow, use saffron to colour the batter. When the crêpes are ready, dry them out in the sun for two days on a sieve placed over a vessel, which, in turn, should be on a mat. Once they are dry, boil enough clarified butter over a fire and put the crêpes in it. If they immediately rise above the clarified butter, this is a sign that they are ready, that is to say, dried. They can also be dried on the fire as long as one makes sure they are not damaged. When they are ready, put them in a clean kneading tub and gingerly turn them over so that they release all of the clarified butter. Then rub them between your hands and sift the pieces over a clean bowl with an esparto[105] sieve to make sure there are no crumbs left. If the holes in the sieve become blocked, strike it with the hand to open them up again. Return what remains in the sieve to the kneading tub, and then pound and sift it. Collect all of it, put the sieve on top of the bowl and cover it to protect it from dirt and store it. Put enough strained comb honey for the *khabīṣ* (i.e. the crumbled loaves) in a tinned copper pot. Make sure the honey is not too red. Add enough egg whites to make the *khabīṣ* and whip them together with the honey until they are fully blended and the mixture has taken on the colour of the egg whites. Put everything over a gentle fire, but keep stirring until it is cooked to a turn and the mixture has thickened. At that point, add

---

Gulf. Also see recipes Nos. 64–6, 393.

105 *ḥalfā'*, also known as *gharaz, ṭawj*, or *dīs muljī*. This fibre was used on the Iberian Peninsula well before the Arab invasion, and would be dried, often after soaking it in water. In the present text, it is mentioned as being used in fans, moulds, baskets and sieves. Al-Ishbīlī 2004–10: Nos. 74, 1565, 1940, 2281.

the *khabīṣ*, together with pepper, and stir over the fire for a little while. When fat appears on the surface, remove it from the fire, and push [the *khabīṣ*] to one side [of the pot] with a ladle before storing it in a clean dish, Allah the Exalted willing.

64. Another similar recipe[106]

Use (water-)dissolved starch with a curd-like consistency to make thin flatbreads (*ruqāq*), like those for a *jūdhāba*,[107] and then let them dry before finely crumbling them [until you are left with something resembling fine breadcrumbs].[108] Then, boil sweet olive oil in a frying pan and fry the *khabīṣ* (crêpes) in it, stirring quickly so that the crumbs do not burn. Strain and drain off any oil they contain. Then, pour them over honey that has been cooked in a separate pot over a low fire, and leave it on the heat so that it remains liquid. Every time *khabīṣ* are removed from the pan, strain off the oil and add them to the honey when they are still hot. Fold them in with a ladle and stir, so that the honey becomes fully absorbed and it becomes a homogeneous mixture. Finally, throw in almonds, and apply saffron so that you are left with red dots, if that is the effect you are aiming for. It is better to make the flatbreads with starch extracted from strained semolina than with (dried) starch, as this rots and goes mouldy.

65. Another similar recipe[109]

Take one part of good-quality honey for three parts of water, and put both in a cauldron over a moderate fire until the honey starts to foam. Colour with saffron and add equal parts of cinnamon and pepper, as well as one-sixth of that amount in spikenard. Leave over a fire until the water evaporates and the honey is ready. Gradually add good-quality semolina, well-sifted of bran and flour, to the honey and stir until you obtain the consistency of a thick pottage. Remove the semolina pot and pour in olive oil in three stages. When the honey mixture has absorbed as much oil as it can and spits it out, remove the pot from the fire and leave it to cool before serving, Allah the Exalted willing.

106 According to Gayangos XVI (fol. 32v.) it is 'pleasant' (*mustaḥsan*).
107 See recipe No. 221.
108 The passage in brackets is an addition from Gayangos XVI (fol. 32v.).
109 Gayangos XVI (fol. 33r.) adds that it is 'exquisite' (*mustaṭraf*).

For each *qādūs* of semolina use two *dirhams* of saffron and three *raṭls* of honey. Bear this in mind.

66. Making *khabīṣ* flatbreads[110]

Take the required amount of starch and dissolve it in cold water until it gains the consistency of molten wax. Then, put a *kunāfa* pan over a gentle fire and use a clean cloth to smear it with olive oil. Pour on dissolved starch and then make crêpe-thin flatbreads as you would for *kunāfa*.[111] Gather and air-dry them on a clean rope. Remove them and store until needed, with the power and strength of Allah the Exalted.

67. Making *fālūdhaj* (pudding)[112]

Thoroughly sift the chaff out of mashed wheat, and put the grains in a tub. Wash them five or six times, until the water runs clear, and then fully immerse them in water. Leave to soak for a long time. Then, scoop out the water by hand, without stirring. Again pour water over the grains, and rub them with your hands [into a mash]. Place a fine-meshed sieve on another sieve and put both on top of another basin. Pour in the mash and strain it until no water remains. Rub some more

110 Gayangos XVI (fol. 33v.) specifies that it is for 'good' (*jayyida*) flatbreads.

111 See recipe No. 57.

112 This is a rather unusual variation of a classic sweet, which usually includes starch; also see recipes Nos. 341, 395–6. According to al-Isrā'ilī (1992: 22, 38), *fālūdhaj* made with oil and wheat is very dense and viscous, and harmful to the liver, spleen and bones. *Fālūdhaj* – also *fālūdhaq* or *fālūdh* – was an early import from Persia; the word goes back to the Middle Persian *pālūdag*, meaning 'purified'. There are a number of recipes in the medieval cookery books; see Ibn Mubārak Shāh: note 23 (note 83). Ibn Zuhr (1992: 45; trans., 97) was clearly undecided about it, pointing out that, although it is slow to digest and a little nauseous, *fālūdhaj* tastes great and is very nutritious. Al-Uryūlī (1983: No. 141) considered it the best and most nutritious of all sweets, but because of its starch content it causes obstructions in the liver, though this can be counteracted with sour pomegranates and oxymel. Similar comments can already be found in al-Rāzī (1987: 139), who said that it was good for the throat and lungs, and for those who exerted their bodies. Ibn Buṭlān (1990: 122) recommended eating a very sweet *fālūdhaj* made with honey after having fish to counter the viscous fat that they introduce into the stomach. There are several literary and religious references to the dish, including a famous *ḥadīth* according to which the Prophet is said to have heard about it for the first time from the archangel Gabriel. See van Gelder 2000: 24–5, 43–4. The modern Persian variant *f/pālūdeh* is starch vermicelli swimming in rose-water syrup, and is particularly associated with the Indian subcontinent, where it is known as *falooda*. In the Arab world, it is mainly restricted to countries with large Indian migrant populations, especially those on the Arabian Peninsula.

grains with your hands in a new batch of water in the first basin, and strain it as you did before. Repeat this three times. Afterwards, thoroughly wash the sieve and tub, and rub and strain the strained mash three more times, draining off all of the water until you are left with only a thick purified pulp. Colour with saffron, stir, and add a pinch of salt. Put good-quality comb honey over a fire in a tinned copper cauldron and, when it starts to foam and is about to curdle, add a lot of premium clarified butter. When it starts to boil with the honey, add the strained mash. Leave over a gentle fire and stir from the bottom of the cauldron so that nothing gets burnt. When the mixture is about to coagulate and stick together, remove it from the fire, and leave on embers [to simmer down]. Stir with a ladle as you do *ʿaṣīda*.[113] If you see that it is too thick, pour on a little hot water. If is not fatty enough, add some clarified butter and return the pot to the fire to let the clarified butter cook through and blend with the rest. Take care not to burn it. Sprinkle with some pepper and transfer to a clean bowl. Eat and enjoy, Allah the Exalted willing.

68. Making *Ra's Maymūn* ('the blessed head')[114]

Moisten semolina with hot water, knead into a firm dough, and then add a bit of *darmak* flour, yeast and salt. Pour the water in little by little until the dough acquires a medium consistency. Add clarified butter and four eggs for each *raṭl* of dough. Leave to rise, and continue to beat it with water and clarified butter so that it rises. Then, take a

---

113 On this type of thick gruel or porridge, made by stirring flour in boiled water and then adding honey and vegetables, see Ibn Mubārak Shāh 2020: 32–3 (note 118). According to Ibn Khalṣūn (1996: 157; trans., 82), it is an undercooked, condensed, hard-to-digest and fattening food. It is improved by prolonged cooking, and should be accompanied by honey and melted butter. Ibn Zuhr (1992: 129; trans., 142) concurred, and warned that it should not be given to children, as their stomachs cannot deal with it.

114 The word *maymūn* is a Persian borrowing, still found in use today in Egypt, where it means a street-performing monkey. It is also the colloquial Andalusian form of the Classical Arabic *ma'mūn*, on which the translation is based, since the recipe specifies that the result should resemble a human head. The *Andalusian* has recipes with the same names as Nos. 68 and 69 here (*Anwāʿ*, 69, 72; BNF, fols. 29v.–30r., 31r.), as well as other similar ones called *fart/ṭūn* (also denoting a conical cooking vessel and, by extension, the dish prepared in it) or *shāshiyya* (*Anwāʿ*, 7, 160-1; BNF, fols. 3v., 58r.), which also appears in another recipe in the present book (No. 13). For a discussion of the dish, see Marín 1997: 12–14; Perry [Rodinson *et al.* 2001]: 193–4; Laurioux 2005: 293–4. Also see recipes Nos. 108 and 152 below.

new glazed (earthenware) wide-bellied pot with a neck, and coat the inside with clarified butter and olive oil. Fill it with dough up to the neck only, and in the middle put a reed of sugar cane[115] smeared with clarified butter. You will know when the dough has risen when small holes start to appear in it. When this happens, take the pot to the oven, place it at a distance from the fire and leave until it is cooked to a turn. When it is ready, remove the pot from the oven and shake it gently to loosen the dough from the sides. Break the pot and gingerly dislodge the dough little by little until you are left with one single lump. If this is difficult to do, pour in a little clarified butter and soften the dough with it so that it comes away whole, because it is essential that it comes out in one piece, in the shape of a human head. Then remove the reed and fill the hole with clarified butter and honey, or fresh butter and honey. Put the dough head in a bowl and 'plant' blanched pine nuts, pistachios and almonds on it. Pour over some clarified butter and melted honey. Dust with caster sugar, and eat, Allah the Exalted willing.

69. A similar recipe, but stuffed

Knead one *raṭl* of *darmak* flour until it is slightly soft. Resume kneading after adding one *raṭl* of clarified butter and water, and ten eggs. The dough should be tender and smooth at the end. Then clean a squab and remove its entrails. Take breadcrumbs and skinned almonds, and mix them with five eggs, adding pepper, cinnamon, cassia,[116] spikenard, the juice extracted from fresh coriander and mint, as well as some pounded onion, and enough salt. Chop up the gizzards and liver, and then stuff the squab with the mixture. Also put in a boiled egg. Then put the bird in a wide pot with water, salt, olive oil, coriander seeds and cut-up onion, and cook it over a fire. Take another wide-bellied pot with a neck and pour in olive oil, swirling it around the inside. Place some of the dough at the bottom, put the squab on top, and cover it with the remainder of the dough. Leave to rise for a while, and then take it to the oven. When it is cooked, carefully break the pot after having shaken it gently so as to loosen the dough. Then, transfer the loaf whole to a bowl and pour on clarified butter and boiled honey.

115 Gayangos XVI (fol. 34v.) specifies that it is 'pierced at both ends'.

116 *dār ṣīnī*, a borrowing from Persian, meaning 'Chinese wood'. In the literature, it is often used as a synonym of (true) cinnamon (*qirfa*).

Decorate with toasted pine nuts, dust with sugar, and eat, Allah the Exalted willing. You can make it another way as well: cut the squab into small pieces and put them over a fire in a pot with salt, olive oil, pepper, coriander seeds and a bit of cut-up onion. When the meat is done, remove from the pot and place it in a clean frying pan with fresh coriander juice, mint juice, eight eggs, salt, pepper, cinnamon, cassia, spikenard, cloves and *murrī*. Mix everything in with the meat. Put the strained broth of the squab in another pan with a bit of olive oil. When it comes to a boil, add the meat mixed with the eggs and stir the pan until the mixture turns golden and solidifies. Take care not to burn it. Then, pound peeled almonds, pistachios and sugar until they are all blended together. Knead the resultant mixture with rose water and aromatic spices, as described above, and place it at the bottom of the pot. On top of it, put half of the meat-and-egg mixture and cover it with the dough. Then, layer the second half of the pounded meat with eggs and almonds on top, followed by another layer with the remainder of the dough. Do not forget to first pour olive oil or melted clarified butter into the pot so that the dough does not stick to the sides. Take it to the oven and put it in at a distance from the fire. When it is done, gently break the pot, as described above. Then pour clarified butter and molten honey over it, and dust with sugar. Eat and enjoy, Allah the Exalted willing.

70. Making *murakkaba*[117]

Knead good-quality semolina with hot water into a strong dough, after having moistened it with water, salt and a little bit of yeast. Make sure to keep adding water, and knead into a light dough. Add egg whites – for each *raṭl* of semolina, take four egg whites – and knead some more until they are thoroughly mixed into the dough. Then, put it in a wide-bottomed unglazed earthenware casserole dish over a fire. Once it is hot, rub with a cloth in which salt has been wrapped, and which has been soaked in olive oil or melted clarified butter. Spread

117 The name of this dish translates as 'the compound one', in reference to the layering of dough. The *Andalusian* has two recipes by this name (*Anwāʿ*, 184–5; BNF, fols. 65r.–v.); the one similar to this one (*ibid.* 184) is said to be a speciality of the Constantine region, and is also known as *Kutāmiyya*. This links it to the Berber Kutāma tribe from Kabylia, whose heartland was in the Titteri range and who came to prominence during the rise of the Fatimid caliphate in the tenth century. See Brett 2017.

the dough out[118] in the casserole and, when it turns white, add some more dough, and flip it over. Continue doing this until there is no more dough left, and it looks like loaves layered on top of one other to form a single composite loaf. When you are finished with this, put it in a wide container and pour on enough honey and clarified butter to cover it. Scatter on cinnamon, and then eat and enjoy, Allah the Exalted willing.

71. Making *maqrūḍ*[119] (fried semolina pastries)

Knead semolina, as described, with yeast and a little water into a strong dough. Make a filling of sugar and almonds, as mentioned before. Roll the dough on a table in the form of a square and place the filling inside, stretching it with your hands as you do with *kaʿk*. Gently smooth it out so that it is even, and then use a sharp knife to cut it into pieces, each one with a length of one finger and the width of two. Fry in oil until golden brown, and put in a bowl to dry and to drain the oil. Afterwards, put them on a glass plate, dust with sugar and eat, Allah the Exalted willing.

If you like, you can stuff them with dates. Proceed in the same way as with the *kaʿk* filling[120] and cook as in the recipe above. Remember this.

72. Making Zubayda's *mushāsh* (flaky biscuits)[121]

Grind good-quality semolina until it becomes like *darmak*, and then knead into a dough with yeast. Work it well, and then take good fresh kidney suet, remove the veins and skin, and pound it in a mortar until it looks like marrow. Roll out the dough into thin round loaves, smear them with the suet and roll them like a scroll.[122] Cut each into three pieces and gather the ends. Then flatten out each sheet of dough with a rolling

118 The recipe in *Anwāʿ* (184; BNF, fol. 65r.) specifies that the dough should be shaped into a thin flatbread.

119 Gayangos XVI (fol. 36v.) adds that it is 'amazing'. Also see Introduction.

120 See recipes Nos. 44–5.

121 According to Ibn al-Ḥashshā' (1941: 72, No. 676), the word actually refers to the ends of bones that can be chewed, and the dish is so named because it resembles a bone in shape. The *Andalusian* (*Anwāʿ*, 191–2; BNF, fols. 67v.-68r.) has three *mushāsh* recipes, but none fully matches the instructions of this one. Interestingly enough, there is also a recipe bearing the same name in a fourteenth-century Egyptian cookery book (*Kanz*, No. 284), but this is for a type of sugar candy made into various figures. The only other cookery book with a *mushāsh* recipe is *Taṣānīf* (fols. 82v.–83r.). Also see al-Dabbābī al-Mīsāwī 2017: 150–2.

122 Addition from Gayangos XVI (fol. 37r.).

pin and use a knife to cut them into four pieces, or however many you like. Heat a lot of olive oil and pour it over them in the cauldron, making sure they are immersed. When the biscuits are ready and have puffed up, remove them and put them on wooden sticks or a sieve to drain off the oil. Next, layer them in a bowl, and pour on a lot of boiled skimmed honey. Peel and lightly pound walnuts and almonds. Add pepper, ginger, cinnamon, and hulled and unhulled sesame seeds. Finish off with a dusting of sugar, and eat and enjoy, Allah the Exalted willing.

73. Making *zulābiyya*[123]

Take a sufficient amount of yeast and soak it in water until the mixture starts to resemble curdled milk. Strain into a pot and add sifted *darmak* flour. When it has dissolved, add flour until you are left with a batter of medium consistency, neither light nor thick. Then use a small thimble-sized cup with a small hole in the bottom to scoop up the batter. Prepare a frying pan with a lot of olive oil and put it over a fire. Cover the hole in the cup with your finger. Hold the cup over the pan and then remove your finger from the hole to let its contents flow out. Move the cup around with your hand and form lattices,[124] and other shapes

123 Gayangos XVI (fol. 37v.) adds that it is 'amazing'. On this sweet (also *zalābiyya*), see Ibn Mubārak Shāh 2020: 67 (note 291). In al-Warrāq's recipe for a *zulābiyya mushabbaka* ('latticed'), a cut-off coconut shell is used as the funnel for the batter (1987: 268). In the *Andalusian* (*Anwāʿ*, 199) recipe, the *zulābiyya* (which is, however, quite dissimilar) is called a *shubbākiyya* (< *shubbāk*, 'window') sweet, though this description is not present in the earlier manuscript copy of that text (BNF, 'Colin', arabe 7009, fol. 69v.). According to al-Uryūlī (1983: No. 144), it is the fastest to digest of all sweets because of the yeast it contains. It was a popular market treat, then as now, with regulations specifying that it should be made in a red copper pan (Ibn al-Ukhuwwa 1937: 112; trans., 36). Al-Rāzī claimed *zulābiyya* is highly heating and thirst inducing (1881: 51; 1987: 139), whereas the oils released from the dough generate dense humours (2000: 3018). Al-Isrā'īlī (1992: 211) said that they came in two forms, a Greek one called *layārābā* (presumably a transliteration of the Greek *lalagia* – a variant of *laganon*, a kind of cake in ancient Greece, but today referring to doughnuts) and the actual *zulābiyya*. Both are slow to digest, very harmful to the liver, spleen and kidneys, and cause blockages. He recommended eating *zulābiyya* with honey to counter some of these harmful properties. The modern descendants of this sweet include the North African *zlabia*, the Levantine *mushabbak*, the Indian *jalebi*, or the North American funnel cake. In other places, such as Egypt, the word refers to a deep-fried doughnut (whose preparation is actually closer to the next *isfanj* recipe), which in Spain and Latin America is known as *buñuelo*. Also see al-Dabbābī al-Mīsāwī 2017: 142–6.

124 *sarājīb* for *sharājīb*, 'windows': Corriente 1997: 248, 278.

like circles. When the frying makes the *zulābiyya* pieces rise [to the surface],[125] quickly remove them, drain off the oil, and immerse them in boiled skimmed honey. Leave them in until they have absorbed the honey, and then transfer them to a wooden board or reed lattice to dry. If they look too thin, add some more flour [to the dough], leave it to rise, and repeat what has been said. Then, eat, Allah the Exalted willing.

74. Making *isfanj* (doughnuts)[126]

Moisten good-quality semolina in hot water, salt and yeast, and leave it until tender. Then, knead into a strong dough, adding water little by little. Keep working the dough until it becomes light. As you are doing this, use both hands to lift up the dough from the kneading tub, and in a rapid movement slap it back down in the kneading tub to expel the air. Then leave the dough to proof. When the dough has risen, put it in a clean copper or tinned iron frying pan with the usual amount of olive oil, and heat it up over a fire. When the oil starts to boil, take some of the dough with your left hand and make a fist so that some of the dough protrudes from between your thumb and index finger. Then, cut it up into pieces and put those into the pan, as many as it can take. If you like the doughnuts to be big (these are called *aqṣād*), then do not cover them with oil, and the bottom halves will be golden, while the top halves will be white. Gently stir and remove them when they are done and ready to be eaten.

---

125 Gayangos XVI (fol. 37v.) refers to the pieces turning white, rather than rising to the surface.

126 Gayangos XVI (*ibid.*) adds that it is 'good and nice'. The *Andalusian* contains a number of *isfanj* recipes (*Anwāʿ*, 61–2, 77–8, 111–2; BNF, fols. 26r., 32r., 43v.), among them a *tharīda* with milk (*Anwāʿ*, 77–8; BNF, fol. 32r.), as well as an *isfanjiyya* (*Anwāʿ*, 215–6; BNF, fol. 74r.–v.), none of which fully corresponds to the recipes here. The end result is very similar to the modern Arab sweet variously known as *ʿawwāma* ('floater'), *luqmat al-Qāḍī* (recipe No. 49), *zulābiyya* or *luqayma* ('little morsel'), depending on the region, or the Greek *loukoumades* – though all of these are also drenched in syrup or honey after frying. Market inspectors would be on the lookout for *isfanj* made with bad flour and which have been overoiled so that the *isfanj* break off in the customer's hands, leaving them dripping with oil (al-Saqaṭī (1931: 38). Interestingly enough, Ibn ʿAbdūn ([Lévi-Provençal 1955]: 45) uses *isfanj* in the sense of *mujabbana,* since he refers to the fraudulent practice (*ghishsh*) of flour being mixed in with the cheese, and stipulates that the butter (*zubd*) must be pure. These are still a delicacy across North Africa, whether it be the Moroccan and Algerian *sfenj*, the Tunisian *bambalunī* (< Italian *bombolone*), or the Libyan *sfinz*. See al-Dabbābī al-Mīsāwī 2017: 137–42.

If you want small doughnuts known as *mughaddar*,[127] pour a lot of olive oil in the frying pan and cut the dough by squeezing it in your fist, as described above, and make the pieces as small as you like. When the frying pan is full and the doughnuts have started to turn golden, take them out and place them in a bowl. Then, fill the pan with more doughnuts and, when they start to turn golden, add the first batch you have made. Stir them all together until they are done and have a crust. Take them out, drain off their oil in a separate dish, and put them in a wooden bowl. Then, eat, Allah the Exalted willing. Make sure to test the dough by first shaping it into a *kaʿk*; if the hole remains open, and the dough rises to the surface of the oil after cooking, and the inside becomes perforated, that is the sign that the dough is fully proofed. If not, then leave it a bit longer until this is the case, by the power of Allah the Almighty.

75. Making 'wind' *isfanj*

Knead *darmak* flour with water, salt, yeast and sweet olive oil into a dough. Then moisten with water little by little so that it becomes thinner, and then leave to rise. Heat a frying pan with a lot of olive oil over a fire. Take some of the dough with your fingers, and drop it in the pan. Continue doing this until you run out of dough. If you like the *isfanj* puffed, knead the dough with eggs and then proceed in the manner described.

76. Making jar *isfanj*[128] (honeyed cake)

Knead semolina or *darmak* flour as described, into a smooth and light dough. Take a new jar, pour in a lot of olive oil and also rub some along the sides so that it can be absorbed with some being left at the bottom. When the dough has risen, fill the jar up to the neck, and in the middle stick a palm frond stalk or cane reed without its knots, after smearing it with olive oil. Take the jar to the oven and place it at a distance from the fire to cook. When you remove it, gently shake to extract the reed, and then pour honey and clarified butter or fresh butter into the resultant hole. Leave it to settle for a while and then gingerly break the jar so that the *isfanj* comes free, but remains whole. Dust with cinnamon, pour in

127 Also *mughaddara* (Corriente 1997: 375), which is related to a verb meaning 'to betray', perhaps in reference to the fact that the diner feels cheated by the size!

128 Cf. *Anwāʿ*, 215/BNF, fol. 74r.-v. (*isfanjiyya*).

clarified butter and honey, and then eat it, Allah the Exalted willing.

MAKING *MUJABBANAS* (FRIED CHEESE BUNS)

77. Recipe for a fried *mujabbana*

Moisten semolina with cold water in summer, or hot in winter. Then, make a dough like that for *isfanj*, and leave it to settle. Take fresh cheese and, if it is soft, wash it with water and massage it with the palm of your hand in the kneading tub until it acquires a marrow-like consistency. Once it is dry and has become salty, cut it into pieces and leave in water to soften it and expel the salt. Try the cheese, and if it does not taste salty enough, add some more. If it is too dry, moisten it with milk – or hot water if you have no milk. Use one part of dough to four parts of cheese. Add a little aniseed, mint juice and fresh coriander juice and knead everything together until it forms a single mass. Then place a tinned frying pan over a fire with a lot of olive oil. When the oil comes to a boil, the cook should wash his hands with water. Cut a piece of the dough, flatten it in the left hand, and with the right one take a piece of the cheese mixture and place it in the centre of the dough. Close the left hand over it until it comes out between the thumb and index finger. Cut off the bits that stick out, and then smooth the *mujabbana* over the thumb with the back of the right hand. Make a hole in the centre of each *mujabbana* and put them in the pan one by one, until it is full. Keep turning them over with an iron hook until they are done and golden. If you see that one of them is floating in the oil, place another one that is ready on top so they all get done equally. Then, take them out and put them in a dish to let them rest before transferring them to a bowl. Pour on fresh strained butter or melted honey, and then dust with sugar and cinnamon. Eat and enjoy, Allah the Exalted willing.

If you want plain *mujabbanas*, without pouring anything on – which is how the Andalusians prefer it – then put them in a big serving bowl and sprinkle on cinnamon, crushed aniseed, and sugar. Put a dish with honey in the middle of the bowl and dip each piece of *mujabbana* into it as you eat them. You can also mix in egg whites – seven or eight for each *raṭl* of semolina. This will further enhance the taste and delight.

78. Recipe for making *mujabbanas* known as *makhāriq*,[129] *muthallatha* ('trebled')[130] or *muwarraqa* ('multi-layered')[131]

Knead the required amount of semolina with milk and a dribble of rose water. Take the same amount of fresh cheese and of fresh butter. Grate the cheese very well and mix it with the butter. If it is a dry and salty cheese, soak it in water for one day and one night. Add the cheese and butter to the dough, thoroughly knead everything together, and leave it in the tub. Put a pan over a fire with enough olive oil to immerse the *mujabbanas*. Cut [the dough] into small, round, flat loaves and puncture a small hole in the middle of each one. Place them in the pan until it is full, and turn them over with a hook. When they are done and golden brown, remove them from the pan and place them in good honey. Leave them for a little while, and then transfer them to a glazed earthenware dish. Sprinkle sugar and cinnamon on top. Eat and enjoy, Allah the Exalted willing.

79. How to make *mujabbanas* with milk in the oven, known as *qayḥāṭa*[132]

Knead *darmak* flour with water and salt[133] into a firm dough, let it rise a bit, and then make ultrathin round loaves (*ruqāq*). Bake them in the oven but keep them away from the flames of the fire. When you take them out, wipe off any dust and ashes from the oven. Finely grate fresh

---

129 The word is the plural of *makhrūq* ('perforated'), but can also mean 'delights' (Dozy 1881: I, 366;). The present-day Tunisian Ramadan speciality by the same name is a finger-shaped honeyed deep-fried doughnut with perforations, commonly associated with the town of Béja, east of the capital Tunis.

130 This word usually referred to a dish requiring three ingredients, as in recipe No. 101. A similar recipe (*mujabbana muthallatha*) can be found in the *Andalusian* (*Anwāʿ*, 182; BNF, fol. 64r.–v).

131 This name is missing from the title in Gayangos XVI (fols. 39v.–40r.).

132 This is a corruption of the more logical *qayjāṭa* (from *qayjāṭ*, 'milk curds'), which form only appears in Gayangos XVI (fol. 40r.). Usually pronounced *qījāṭa*, the word is of Hispanic origin and its cognate, *qayshāṭa*, was the Arabic name of the present-day town of Quesada, on the Spanish Costa Blanca. According to al-Idrīsī (1866: 203; trans., 249), it was densely populated and a centre for the making of wooden tableware (bowls, plates, etc.), which was famous across al-Andalus, as well as North Africa. The *quesadilla* is a descendant of this dish. There is a similar recipe in the *Andalusian* (*Anwāʿ*, 183; BNF, fol. 64v.), where it is spelled *fayjāṭa*, and is said to be called *sabʿ buṭūn* ('seven bellies') by the Andalusians, in reference to the fact that it would have contained seven layers. Marín 1997: 14; Corriente 1997: 450; Corominas & Pasqual 1984: IV, 721.

133 Gayangos XVI (fol. 40r.) also includes 'a little yeast'.

cheese and add mint juice, fresh coriander juice, pepper and cloves. If the cheese is dry, pour on milk after heating it up a little.[134] Then, shape the dough into a good-sized round loaf (*raghīf*), put hazelnuts on top[135] and place it at the bottom of a casserole dish. Add enough of the cheese to cover it, and then put one of the *ruqāq* on top of the cheese. Continue alternating the *ruqāq* and cheese layers until you run out of both. Pour on milk which has been slightly heated over the fire, and cover everything with a thick, round, flat loaf of the dough and then send it to the oven, but watch over it. If the milk is reduced and has been absorbed by the loaves, pour on some more milk, accordingly. It is crucial that you continue doing this until all of the milk you put in has been absorbed. When it is done cooking, and the top loaf has turned golden, take the dish out of the oven and remove the lid, that is to say the uppermost thick loaf, and pour on hot honey to which you have added pepper and cassia after quartering the *mujabbana*. Leave covered for a while until it becomes lukewarm and the honey has been absorbed. Then, serve. It is the most delicious thing.

These *mujabbanas* can also be made plain, without cheese, in which case you cook them in the same way as described, and put the *ruqāq* in the casserole dish, one on top of the other, but without including the cheese layer in between them. Then, pour on milk and cover with a thick loaf before sending it to the oven. Gradually add milk and, when it has finished cooking, take it out of the oven. Pour on honey, and eat, as mentioned.

80. Another *mujabbana* recipe[136]

Knead the required amount of *darmak* flour, once with water, and once with olive oil. Add yeast and milk until it acquires an *isfanj*-like consistency, and let it proof. Coat a casserole dish with olive oil and

134 The Arabic *yusḥaq* ('it is pounded'), which appears in both the edition (2012: 83) and BL Or5927 (fol. 120r.), has been corrected to the more logical *yusakhkhan* ('it is heated up').

135 Though *banādiq* usually means 'meatballs' in the text, this would appear highly unlikely here. Nevertheless, the addition of hazelnuts – the only time they are called for as an ingredient – also appears somewhat incongruous, and is missing from the recipe in the *Andalusian*.

136 This recipe is repeated in BL Or5927 (fol. 120v.), as well as in one of the manuscripts used for the edition (2012: 84, note 1).

stack flattened sheets of the dough, alternating each layer with cheese until you run out of both. Cover with some more cheese, just as in the preceding recipe, and bake in the oven, as described. After taking it out, pour on honey and scatter on cinnamon and pepper. Then, eat, Allah the Exalted willing.

81. Another *mujabbana* recipe

Take one *raṭl* of *darmak* flour and half a *raṭl* of fresh cheese and knead both until they are thoroughly mixed. Add five eggs, enough salt and a little bit of water, if necessary, and continue kneading the dough. Shape into very thin round sheets and fry in a pan with a lot of olive oil so that they come out white. Then boil pounded walnuts with honey and pour the mixture on them. Chop up pine nuts and pistachios and sprinkle them on with sugar before eating, Allah the Exalted willing.

82. Another recipe for an oven *mujabbana*

Knead *darmak* flour with water, salt and olive oil into a dough of medium consistency. Add three-quarters the amount in grated cheese, and knead both until you obtain a marrow-like consistency. Mix in aniseed, mint juice and fresh coriander juice. Roll the dough into large, thin, round loaves and coat them with olive oil or clarified butter. Place cheese in the centre of each loaf and fold the sides inwards until the cheese is entirely covered, except for a coin-sized (*dīnār*) hole in the middle. Gently smooth the dough, but be careful that the cheese does not spill out, and without increasing the size. Make other parcels like it, as many as you need, and then moderately bake them in the oven at a distance from the flames until they are almost golden, while keeping an eye on them. When you take them out, clean off any dust and ash, and transfer them to a wooden or earthenware bowl. Pour on melted honey and fresh butter, and dust with cinnamon, sugar and a bit of the usual aromatic spices. Eat and enjoy, Allah the Exalted willing.

If you do not have fresh cheese, use cheese that has started to dry and then moisten it, as explained above, by the power and strength of Allah the Exalted.

83. How to make Toledan *mujabbana*[137]

Knead *darmak* flour with water, salt and olive oil, as mentioned in the previous recipe. Add three-quarters the amount in fresh cheese mixed with aniseed, mint juice and fresh coriander juice, and work it into the dough, as mentioned. Then, roll out the dough into round, flat loaves with a rolling pin. In each loaf, put in enough grated cheese and then fold in the sides. Carefully smooth out the loaves, as described, and put them on a copper or earthenware *malla*. Bake them in an oven[138] used for making *ka'k*,[139] or things like it. When the buns begin to turn golden, take them out and put them in an earthenware or wooden container,[140] one on top of the other. Then, pour on enough honey and fresh melted butter to cover them. Sprinkle on sugar and cinnamon, and then eat and enjoy, Allah the Exalted willing.

84. Making a pie stuffed with meat, chicken, sparrows, starlings, fresh cheese or fish

Take any of the above fillings that you like and cook them in the way you like. Then, knead flour, water and yeast into a firm dough. When it is close to rising, shape the dough into a round, flat loaf and raise the edges so as to protect the filling. Take the stuffing you will cook and add eggs mixed with aromatic spices coloured with saffron or with fresh coriander juice. Then put the mixture in the centre of the loaf. Take another, smaller flatbread to serve as the lid for the first one, and gather the edges of the bottom loaf together with those of the second loaf. Twist tightly to prevent the filling from spilling out during baking in the oven. When it is done, take it out and eat, Allah the Exalted willing.

If you use a fresh cheese filling, crumble the cheese as finely as you can and add enough eggs, mint juice, fresh coriander juice, and as many

137 The 'Toledan' *mujabbana* in the *Andalusian* (*Anwāʿ*, 182; BNF, fol. 64v.) is referred to as a *furniyya* (i.e. baked in a *furn*, 'brick oven'), but is actually closer in preparation to the preceding recipe (No. 82).

138 Both the edition (2012: 85) and BL Or5927 (fol. 121r.) have the nonsensical *k*rsha*, which is clearly a misspelling for *kūsha* ('baker's oven'), the form that appears in Gayangos XVI (fol. 42r.). It is sometimes also spelt *qūsha*, and denotes a small oven (Corriente 1997: 447, 470). The word has Romance origins, and Dozy (1881: II, 499) links it to the Vulgar Latin *c(h)ochia* ('kitchen'); the *kūsha* was different from the *furn* in that the former was heated up from underneath. In modern Tunisian Arabic, *kūsha* is the usual word for oven.

139 See recipe No. 44.

140 Gayangos XVI (fol. 42r.) specifies that it is *mukhfiya*, 'a glazed bowl' (Corriente 1997: 161).

of the usual aromatics as you have to hand. Mix everything together and put it in the centre of the loaf, and cover it with another one, as described. Cook in the oven. Bear this in mind, with the strength of Allah the Almighty.

Chapter Five: dishes that are soaked in broth, like *tharīdas*, or cooked like pottage

These include the following:

85. Making couscous *(al-kuskusū)*[141]

Take fresh semolina and put it in a kneading tub.[142] Sprinkle on water in which you have dissolved a little bit of salt, and stir with the tips of your fingers until it has been absorbed. Then rub the dough gently in the palms of your hands until you obtain something resembling ant heads. Shake the granules in a fine sieve to get rid of all the flour, and then leave them to rest after covering.

Cooking instructions: Take the best meat and big bones from a fat calf. Put it all into a large pot and add salt, olive oil, pepper, coriander seeds, a few cut-up onions and enough water to cover everything. Place the pot over a fire and, when the meat starts to become tender, add whichever vegetables you have to hand at the time, such as cabbage, turnips, carrots, lettuce, fennel, green broad beans, gourd and aubergine. When the meat and the vegetables are done, take a couscous pot, which has perforations in the bottom, and gently fill it with the couscous granules. Place it on top of the big pot containing the meat and

141 Linguistically, the use of the definite article *al-* here is unusual, since the dish is generally known as *kuskusū*, as it still is in Algeria (also *kuskus*), whereas in Morocco and Tunisia it is, respectively, *suksū* and *kuskusī*. The word *kaskās*, which classical dictionaries (e.g. *Tāj al-ʿArūs*) give as a synonym of *kuskusū*, is more properly the upper (perforated) steam-cooking pot. According to al-Uryūlī (1981: No. 25), couscous is only good if it is fully digested and leaves the stomach quickly, because of its heaviness. If abused, it causes obstructions in the intestines, and one should take an aniseed electuary after eating it. The *Andalusian* also has two couscous recipes (*Anwāʿ*, 158–9; BNF, fol. 57r.–v.). Also see: al-Dabbābī al-Mīsāwī 2017: 70–86; Arié 1974–75: 302–3.

142 BL Or5927 (fol. 121v.) calls for 'good-quality' (*ṭayyib*) semolina, whereas Gayangos XVI (fol. 42v.) omits the reference to both the kind of semolina and the kneading tub.

vegetables, and join both pots together with a strip of dough so that no steam can escape. Cover the mouth of the couscous pot with a thick cloth to contain the steam and let it cook thoroughly. You can tell it is done by the strength of the steam rising from the pot and by the noise you hear when you strike the couscous pot with your hand.

When it is done, transfer the couscous to a kneading tub and use your hands to rub it with good-quality clarified butter, cinnamon, mastic and spikenard until the grains are all separated from one another. Then, put them in a bowl but do not fill it entirely; rather, leave room for what will be added afterwards. Check whether there is enough meat broth [in the bottom pot]. If there is not enough, add some water to the pot and bring to a boil. When it is boiling, remove from the fire and leave to simmer down. Then, gently pour some broth on the couscous, first in the middle and then along the sides. Cover and leave it for a while until the broth is absorbed. Use your fingers to check whether this is the case. If not, add some more broth, in moderate measure. Then, remove the bones [from the pot], place them vertically in the middle of the bowl, and arrange the meat and the vegetables around them. Sprinkle on cinnamon, pepper and ginger. Eat and enjoy, Allah the Exalted willing.

If you like, you can make it with lamb or chicken, in the manner described, with the power and strength of Allah.

86. Another kind of couscous, known as *al-jawziyya* ('the walnutty one')[143]

This is delicious. Take as many choice cuts of fatty beef, mutton or chicken as you need and cook them with the usual spices, as described. Add peeled uncut aubergines that have been boiled in water and salt, and then rinsed with cold water and dried. When the meat and vegetables are almost done, cook the couscous in the pot, as described above. Then take it out and rub with crushed walnut kernels which have been boiled and picked over, as well as cinnamon, spikenard and a bit of mastic. Gradually pour the broth over the couscous, and layer the meat and vegetables on top. Sprinkle on cinnamon and spikenard, and then eat, Allah the Exalted willing.

---

143 This is the name of the dish in BL Or5927 (121v.) – the printed edition (2012: 89) has *al-jawzī* and Gayangos XVI (fol. 43r.) the rather odd *al-jawzā'* ('Gemini').

87. Another couscous that does not involve pouring the broth over it[144]

This is a dish where you remove the meat and vegetables from the pot once they are done, and then strain the bones and other things out of the broth. Throw couscous in the pot and leave it in until it absorbs the broth. Then transfer to a bowl, layer the meat and vegetables on top, and eat. This kind of couscous is known as *ghassānī*.[145] You can also pour on the broth of meat cooked in vinegar and saffron, as you do for a vinegar *tharīd*,[146] in which case you should use aubergines and gourds as vegetables. If you wish, you can rub *ḥuwwārā* breadcrumbs until they become like flour. Then, hand-roll them into granules with a little water before cooking them in a special pot. When the steam starts to come out and the granules are cooked, remove them from the pot and rub with clarified butter or meat fat, and then pour on the broth, as usual.

88. Another couscous recipe, which is extremely delicious

Take a fatty lamb, skin it, cut open its belly, remove the entrails and clean it. Coat the inside with suet crushed with the spices used in the making of meatballs.[147] When the couscous is done, rub it with clarified butter, spikenard, cinnamon and a little mastic, and stuff the lamb with it. Sew it up from the belly to the throat and put it in a *tannūr* to roast until done. Then, remove the couscous, pour it in a tureen and shred the lamb on top. Sprinkle with cinnamon and spikenard before eating, Allah the Exalted willing.

---

144 In the *Andalusian* (*Anwāʿ*, 158; BNF, fol. 57r.–v.), it is called *kuskusū al-fityān* ('the eunuchs' couscous').

145 The other recipe with this name in the book is a honeyed rice pudding (No. 393), whereas its feminine form, *ghassāniyya* (No 151), refers to a meat-and-honey dish.

146 *tharīd al-khall*, for which there is a recipe in the *Andalusian* (*Anwāʿ*, 158; BNF, fol. 57r.), where it is said to be one of the finest *tharīds* there is. It is made with 'the fatty meat from the fattest parts' of the animal, seasoned with salt, onion, pepper, saffron, cumin, garlic, very sour vinegar, and olive oil. The recommended vegetables are turnip, aubergine, and gourd. All of this is then poured onto the crumbled bread. Save for the last step, this dish has a great deal in common with the Near Eastern *sikbāj* (see recipe No. 196).

147 These are: salt, pepper, ginger, cinnamon, mastic, spikenard, cloves and caraway (see recipes Nos. 179–80).

89. A type of couscous with dried ground broad beans *(baysār)*[148]

Roll semolina and flour into couscous and cook as described above. Take dried ground broad beans and cook them in a new pot with enough freshwater or rainwater, without salt, to cover them. Make sure that the beans have been cleaned and repeatedly washed with hot water and rubbed with sweet olive oil. When they are done and have disintegrated, use a ladle to squash the beans along the sides of the pot so that you obtain a marrow-like mass. Then add a sufficient amount of hot water in which you have dissolved enough salt to season the dish. When the beans have come to a boil in the pot, rub the couscous with a large amount of good-quality clarified butter. Put the couscous in the pot with the beans and leave until both are mixed together, and the couscous has absorbed the broth. Remove from the pot, and eat, Allah the Exalted willing.

If you like to have the dish with tripe sausages,[149] cook them with the customary spices in another pot, by themselves. When you put the couscous with the beans in the pot, add the sausage broth. When it is cooked, transfer the couscous to a bowl, put the sausages on top, and in the centre pour some good-quality clarified butter, boiled fresh butter, or sweet green olive oil. Eat and enjoy, Allah the Exalted willing.

90. Making *fidāwsh*[150]

Knead one quarter of a *raṭl* of semolina with water and salt into a strong dough. Work it vigorously and put it in a container with a lid. Then, rub very finely in between the fingers to the size of a wheat grain. Make sure that each grain is very thin, its ends thinner than the middle. Put

---

148 See recipes Nos. 32, 141 and 379.

149 *ʿuṣub;* see recipe No. 7.

150 The variant *fidawsh* is found in Gayangos XVI (fol. 44v.). The word is a borrowing from Romance that passed from al-Andalus to North Africa, and is the etymon of the modern Spanish *fideos* (vermicelli). There is also a recipe in the *Andalusian* (*Anwāʿ*, 161–2; BNF, fol. 58r.), which informs us that it is food for women, cooked like *iṭriyya* (see recipe No. 92), and, most importantly, that it could come in three varieties – long like wheat grains, round like coriander seeds (called *ḥummayṣ*, 'little chickpeas', in the Bijāya region), and sheets as thin as paper (*kāghīd*). In Morocco, the word today denotes vermicelli, though it is also sometimes used as the generic word for pasta, just as *iṭriyya* is in Tunisia. See Ibn Mubārak Shāh 2020: 103 (note 490); Marín 1997: 14–15; al-Dabbābī al-Mīsāwī 2017: 167–8. Al-Uryūlī (1981: No: 26) believed they are very good and nutritious food, especially for those suffering from dysentery. They can be cooked with meat and with milk, but are more nourishing with meat. Eaten to excess, however, they cause intestinal obstructions (which can be remedied with a ginger electuary).

all of the ones you make on a tray in front of you and, once you have finished all of the dough, leave the grains to dry in the sun. Make another dough, and repeat what you have done, until you have got all the grains you require. When you need to cook them, take the best cuts of fatty mutton, such as the breast, sides, tail, and so on, and carve into medium-sized pieces. Clean the meat and put it in a large pot with plenty of water, salt, olive oil, pepper, coriander and a few cut-up onions. Hang the pot over the fire and, when the meat is done, transfer it to a covered tureen. Strain the broth, clean the pot and return the broth to it.

If you have enough broth, cook the *fidāwsh*; if not, add more water. When the pot has come to a boil, gingerly add the *fidāwsh* and cook over a moderate fire until they are done. Meanwhile, put a small pot filled with hot water on top of the other one. If some of the *fidāwsh* water has dried out, add a little from the small pot. When the *fidāwsh* are done, add the same amount of fresh butter or clarified butter, and leave to cook for a little while longer. Carefully stir with the end of the ladle so that the *fidāwsh* remain whole. In the meantime, fry the meat in a casserole with butter or clarified butter until it turns golden. When the *fidāwsh* are done, transfer them to a tureen and place the meat on top. Sprinkle on cinnamon and ginger, and eat, Allah the Exalted willing.

If you like, you can also make the dish with plump chickens, using the same method, with the power of Allah.

91. Making *muḥammaṣ*[151] (large-grained couscous)

Knead semolina the way you do *fidāwsh*, and shape it with your fingers into small pellets, like peppercorns. Dry them in the sun and cook them as you do *fidāwsh*, with beef, mutton or chicken, and then eat. If you are in a hurry, you can roll all of the pellets at the same time in a kneading tub as when making *zabzīn*.[152]

---

151 The word (also *muḥammaṣa*) is derived from *ḥimmiṣ* (or *ḥimmaṣ*), 'chickpea', in reference to its shape and size. It is still used in this sense in North Africa, alongside others like *barkūk, barkūkash, barkūkas,* (see recipe No. 39) *'aysh,* or *mardūd*. *EI*², s.v. 'kuskusū' (A. Cour-Pellat); Dozy 1881: I, 323. This type of couscous is also similar to the Levantine variety, known as *maftūl* or *maghribiyya*.

152 See recipe No. 39.

92. Making and cooking *iṭriyya*[153] (noodles)

Cook the *iṭriyya* as described above with your choice of meat, and add more suet. You can either fry the meat or not, whichever you prefer. If there is no *iṭriyya* available, knead semolina or flour with water and a pinch of salt into a strong dough. Stretch it out on a table or elongated wooden board. Roll the *iṭriyya* as thinly as possible with your hands, and then let them dry in the sun. Cook in the above manner.

93. Making rice pudding (*al-aruzz bi 'l-laban al-ḥalīb*)[154]

Wash white rice with hot water many times until the water runs clear and clean. Put it in a bowl and let it dry fully until there is no water left in it. Strain sheep's milk through a thick cloth. This is the best milk to use for this dish, followed by cow's milk. If you have neither, then you can use goat's milk. The required amount of milk is six *raṭls* for one *raṭl* of rice. Put the rice in a large pot with a little hot water, and pour on all of the milk if the pot is large enough. Leave the pot over a fire until the milk is hot, and then remove the fire underneath and leave it on the embers, or another heat source of that strength. Cover the pot with a clean cloth. If the heat dies down, add some embers, and if the milk dries out in the pot, add some more. Check up on it occasionally until the rice is fully done. Then put in the required amount of salt that has been washed and crushed in a wooden mortar and dissolved in a little bit of milk or water. If you want, you can also just sprinkle the salt on directly. Gently stir the rice with the handle of a ladle so that the salt infuses and perfumes it. Transfer it to a tureen, and in the middle put a bowl filled with honey. Those who like it with sugar can sprinkle some

---

153 For other dishes, see Ibn Mubārak Shāh 2020: 102–3 (note 490); al-Dabbābī al-Mīsāwī 2017: 157–65. According to al-Uryūlī (1981: No. 22), *iṭriyya* are cold and coarse, but very nutritious. They are good for those with a cough, especially if they are cooked with fresh or clarified butter. Al-Rāzī said that *iṭriyya* are very nutritious once they have been digested, but that they thicken weak spleens and generate kidney stones. (2000: 3018).

154 For other recipes of this medieval favourite, see *Waṣf*, 367; al-Warrāq 1987: 143; Ibn Mubārak Shāh 2020: 32, 107; *Wuṣla*, No. 7.110. Very early on, meat (often chicken) was added into the mix, resulting in a name change to *muhallabiyya*, which became the medieval European staple *blancmanger*. The present-day *muhallabiyyas* (a milk pudding made with rice or flour) are all made without meat. The closest descendant of the medieval variation is the Turkish *tavuk göğsü*.

on as well. It is eaten with clean boxwood[155] spoons, with the strength of Allah the Exalted.

If you want to cook it with mutton or chicken, you should boil the rice in water only and, when it is done, add clarified butter or butter and bring it to a boil twice.[156] If you want, you can also boil it in water alone, and eat with honey. This is like cooking *jashīsha*.[157] Remember this.

94. Making *mu'allaka*[158] called *bāzīn*

Knead semolina with water, salt and yeast, and leave to rise in the kneading tub. Take the meat you like – beef or lamb – and put it in a clean pot with water, pepper, salt, olive oil, coriander, and a few cut-up onions. Put the pot over a fire and, when the meat is tender, throw on seasonal vegetables such as cabbage, turnip, gourd and others like them. Let everything cook together. Then, use half of the dough to make round, flat loaves and bake them in the oven for half the required time, or a bit more. Make (little) balls out of the remainder of the dough. Remove the meat from the pot and throw the dough balls into the broth. When they are done, become light and have risen to the surface of the broth, break the flat loaves in a bowl and pour on enough broth to cover them. Press with a large ladle so that the pieces become thoroughly mashed. Then add the dough balls one by one and also mash them until the dough and the bread form a single mass and can no longer be distinguished from one another. If the broth has dried up after mashing, gradually add some more to restore it, but make sure that it is not too liquid. When you have finished all of this, shape it

---

155 *buqs/baqs* (from the Greek *púxos*): also known as *shimshār*, the wood was commonly used for implements due to its hardness. Al-Ishbīlī (2004–10: No. 923) explains that there are two varieties, one the size of the pomegranate tree and another one, grown in high mountains and known as 'country box' (*baqs baladī*), with leaves like the strawberry tree (*janā aḥmar*). It is the latter that was used for truncheons, combs and spoons.

156 According to Gayangos XVI (fol. 45v.), it should be cooked 'for an hour' (*sā'a*).

157 See recipes Nos. 41–3.

158 The word is related to a verb meaning 'to make chewy, viscous' (*'allaka*). The two terms indeed denoted the same dish, though Corriente (1997: 51, 362) conflates this term with *mu'allak* (see recipe No. 156), a dish of lamb seasoned with cheese, while explaining *bāzīn* as 'a dish of couscous, meat and vegetables, more complicated than *zabzīn*'. Dozy (1881: I, 82), for his part, considers *bazīn(a)* to be merely an abbreviated form of *zabzīn* (see recipe No. 39). Also see al-Dabbābī al-Mīsāwī 2017: 55–60.

into a large ball,[159] place it in the middle of a tureen and arrange the meat and vegetables around it. Dig one or two holes in the middle, and fill one of them with sweet olive oil and the other with fresh butter or clarified butter. Dust with pepper and cinnamon, and eat and enjoy, Allah the Exalted willing.

95. Making *marmaz*,[160] that is mashed unripe barley

Take green barley, and beat it with a stick to release its grains. Fry them in an earthenware casserole dish until some of the moistness dries out, and then rub them with both hands to loosen the hulls. Dry the barley in the sun, grind it to a mash, and sieve. If you need to cook it, take the required quantity of fatty young beef or mutton, cut it up, clean it, and put it in a large pot with a lot of olive oil, salt, pepper, coriander, half an onion and aniseeds. Put the pot over a fire and, when the meat is done, remove it and fry it in butter or clarified butter. Wash the mashed barley and put it in the pot with the meat broth. When it is cooked, add fresh butter, bring to a boil, and serve. If there is not enough broth, add some hot water to the pot. Before serving, place the meat on top of the barley and pour on some butter before sprinkling on cinnamon and ginger. Eat and enjoy, Allah the Exalted willing.

If you like, you can cook it with milk in the meat broth, or without meat. If you make it without meat, it is cooked like rice. Remember this.

96. Making *taltīn*[161]

Knead flour with water, salt and a little yeast into a firm dough. Roll it out as thinly as possible on a table, and then use a knife to cut it into square pieces, two fingers wide, and dry them in the sun. If you need to cook them in winter, clean cabbage by removing any mould

159 *jumjuma*, which in addition to a ball of dough, also denoted '(sugar) loaf'; Corriente 1997: 101.

160 Unripe barley, or a dish made with it; Corriente 1997: 218.

161 The origin or meaning of this word is unclear. It may be a dialectal pronunciation of *thalathīn* ('thirty'), which is how it appears within the recipe, whereas Ibn Khalṣūn (1996: 15; trans., 83) lists a dish called *talūtīn* together with *bulyāṭ* and *zabazīn*, 'all dense dishes, slow to digest, which generate phlegm and cause colic; the densest is *talūtīn*, followed by *zabazīn*, and then *bulyāṭ*. They can only be eaten by those who engage in strenuous physical exercise.' The *bulyāṭ* (pl. *balāwīṭ*) was a kind of porridge, eaten with olive oil, which was also sold ready-made at markets by the aptly named *bulyāṭī*; Dozy 1881: I, 115–16; Arié 1974–75: 302; Corriente 1997: 65.

and chop up the soft parts and the leafstalks. Wash them and put them in a large pot. Pour on enough water, salt, olive oil, pepper, coriander and a chopped onion wedge. When the cabbage and onion are cooked, gently cut the *thalthīn* pieces in the pot, and stir with the handle of a ladle so that they do not stick to the pot. Cook them to a turn and then add clarified butter or fresh butter. Also pour butter or clarified butter over it and then eat and enjoy, Allah the Exalted willing.

If you cook this in summer or autumn, clean a gourd inside and out, and cut it into small pieces. Cook it as you do the cabbage, and use the same spices as well as others. If you want to cook it with milk, add only salt and a splash of water. Then, place it in a pot with hot water and leave until it is moist. Then pour in the milk, little by little, until it is absorbed. When everything is done, remove the pot from the fire and transfer the contents to a tureen. Sprinkle on sugar and pour on fresh butter. Eat and enjoy, Allah the Exalted willing.

97. Making wheat *harīsa* (porridge)[162]

Thoroughly soak good-quality sifted wheat in not too much water. Leave it for a little while, and then pound it in a large stone or wooden mortar to remove the husks. Sieve the wheat a second time, and shake before putting it in a large pot with enough water to cover it. Leave the pot in the oven overnight. When you take it out the next day, check whether it is done. Stir vigorously with a ladle to thoroughly blend the wheat with the remaining water. Add a sufficient amount of crushed salt, and then transfer to a tureen. Put a dish with honey in the middle of it, and eat with box-wood spoons, Allah the Exalted willing.

162 The name comes from a verb meaning 'to crush', but was usually made with meat (see recipe No. 188). The editor of the printed text adds that this dish is known as *herbel* (more correctly *herrbel* – Harrell *et al.* 2007: 36) or *herben* in Morocco (94, note 1). It is the only *harīsa* variation in the medieval culinary literature that is a sweet porridge, which could also include orange-blossom water. It would appear that this was an earlier variation, since Ibn 'Abdūn ([Lévi-Provençal 1955]: 55) instructs that *harīsa* makers should 'return to the old habit of selling the dish with butter and honey'. For a full discussion, see Brisville 2017.

98. Making white emmer wheat[163] mash

Pound the white emmer wheat in a wooden mortar to remove the husks. Then sift, pick over and grind into a mash. Sieve the mash and wash it with water several times, until the water runs clear. Put the wheat in boiling water in a large pot and leave to cook. When it is done, and the water has been absorbed, transfer the contents of the pot to a tureen and pour on butter. Put a dish with honey or the inspissated juice (rob)[164] of sweet grapes in the centre of the bowl, and eat and enjoy.

If you want, you can put grated dry cheese, crushed cooked garlic and sweet olive oil in the middle, or you may macerate the cheese and garlic in hot water. Eat and enjoy, Allah the Exalted willing.[165]

163 *quṭniyya bayḍā'* (*Triticum turgidum*), the word being related to *qīṭnīt*, 'small fruit, pulse beans' (Corriente 1997: 435). However, *quṭniyya* (pl. *qaṭānī*) also denoted a category of legumes and pulses, which, according to Ibn Khalṣūn (1996: 157–8; trans., 83–4), comprised chickpeas, broad beans, millet, lentils, lupine beans, green beans, sorghum (*dukhn*), flax seeds (*bizr al-kattān*), hemp seeds (*bizr al-qunnāb*) and sesame (*juljulān*), whereas al-Ishbīlī (2004–10: No. 4219) included broad beans, chickpeas, garden vetch, lentils, garden peas, green peas, chickling vetch, green beans, 'and other similar things'. Ibn Luyūn (1988: No. 120) held that the seeds of *dukhn* ('millet') have pods that are known as *quṭniyya*. In the sixteenth-century Castillian-Arabic lexicon by Pedro de Alcalá (1505: fol. 123r. [qIIIr]), *quṭniyya* appears in the form of *escandia*, 'a type of wheat' used in bread, whereas Dozy (1881: II, 377) suggests it also referred to buckwheat.

164 *rubb* (plural *rubūb*) is the thick residue after fruit is pressed and cooked. Robs were primarily used in medicinal compounds. Ibn Jazla (fol. 105v.) said it was made by boiling pressed and strained grape juice down to about a third or quarter and then letting it dry out in the sun. The Andalusian scholar al-Ṭighnarī (2006: 133–4) explains that the common peasants would also make *rubb*, which he, however, deemed of a very poor and malodorous quality. He adds that it should be made by putting the sweetest grape juice possible in earthenware vessels and leaving them for a day and night. Then, the juice should be transferred to brass pots (though earthenware produces a better-tasting result), which is then heated up, together with water (one *raṭl* of water for each three *raṭls* of juice). As it is cooking, the froth should be skimmed off, and the end result should have a syrupy consistency. Also see Lev & Amar 2008: 187, 566; Lane 1863–74: III, 1004; Ibn Janāḥ 2020: Nos. 38, 216, 246, 261, 520.

165 The invocation is missing from the printed edition (2012: 94), but included in BL Or5927, fol. 124v.

SECTION TWO

On the various types of meat from quadrupeds

It consists of six chapters.

Chapter One: on beef

99. A dish called *jamalī*[1]

Take choice cuts of beef, thick-seam tripe, and other similar parts. Cut everything into medium-sized pieces, and clean them. Pour sweet olive oil into a new pot and put the meat in with salt, pepper, coriander, cumin, a few cut-up onions, soaked white chickpeas, blanched almonds, citron leaves, a fennel stalk, cloves of garlic and macerated *murrī* – use the usual amounts of each. Continuously stir the pot with both hands to blend the meat with the spices and other ingredients, and until it releases its juices. When the meat begins to turn white, pour on just a little hot water from the small pot.[2] Stir the pot some more and leave it to cook over the fire. Then take thigh meat, remove the veins and thoroughly crush it in a wooden mortar. Add salt, pepper, ginger, cinnamon, spikenard, cloves and one egg white, and knead until the pounded meat is mixed with the aromatics. Then, shape into meatballs, put them in the pot with the meat and add three or four egg yolks. When the meat is done, colour the dish with a bit of saffron crushed in a copper mortar and bloomed. Leave the pot and then pour in enough good-quality vinegar to flavour the dish. Take enough eggs to crust the dish and break them into a bowl. Add salt, crushed saffron and aromatic spices. Stir everything with a ladle so that all the ingredients are mixed together, remove the pot from the fire and pour in the beaten eggs. Boil two eggs, and quarter each

---

1 The dish could also be made with fish (see recipes Nos. 284, 288); Corriente 1997: 103. The anonymous *Andalusian* includes has several *jamalī* (*Anwāʿ*, 6, 151; BNF, fols. 3r., 55r.) and *jamaliyya* (*ibid.*, 92, 120, 151; BNF, fols. 37v., 38r.–v., 46r.) recipes, but none corresponds to this one.

2 It is not clear which 'small pot' is being referred to here; presumably it is a small pot of hot water that would always have been kept to hand to replenish broth, etc., as, in those days, it would have taken too much time to heat up water.

of them. When the pot has finished cooking and the meat has been coated[3] with the eggs, transfer everything to a large ceramic bowl and remove the citron leaves, fennel and garlic. Move the meat balls and egg yolks on top and garnish the dish with the egg quarters and mint leafstalks. Sprinkle on cinnamon, ginger and pepper. Eat and enjoy, Allah the Exalted willing.

100. Another dish called *Burāniyya*[4]

Take the same meat as in the previous recipe (i.e. beef), and proceed in the same way, that is to say, clean it and boil the tripe in hot water until it turns white. Add the spices, egg yolks and meatballs, etc., and put everything in a pot over a fire. Then, take large aubergines, cut them into medium-sized slices, neither thin nor thick, and stack them on a wooden board. Put salt in between each piece and press the stack down with something heavy to make them release their black juice, and to remove their harmfulness. Then, wash with fresh water and leave to drain.[5] Fry the pieces in a pan with a generous amount of olive oil until they turn golden, but be careful not to break them up. When the meat is done, take enough eggs to crust the dish, as described above. Then, remove from the fire and leave to rest for a while. When the crust has formed and the fat has gathered on the surface, make a bed of fresh citron leaves in a large ceramic bowl and put half of the aubergine pieces on top. Next, add the meat and on top of that place the remainder of the aubergines. Decorate the dish with egg yolks, meatballs, split eggs and mint leafstalks. Sprinkle on cinnamon and ginger. Eat and enjoy, Allah the Exalted willing.

[It is possible to make additions to this recipe so that it becomes

3 The Arabic verb used here is *'aq(q)ada,* which means 'to curdle, coagulate'.

4 See note 9

5 The safe cooking of aubergines was something addressed by several authors. Ibn al-'Awwām (1866: II:1, 240–1), for instance, said that aubergines should be eaten only in winter and autumn, and that to make them salubrious they should be boiled in water and lightly salted before draining off their water. Afterwards, they should be cooked with sweet almond and sesame oil mixed together, or a mixture of oil and butter, as these oils remove the bitterness from the aubergine. Al-Samarqandī (2017: 164–6) recommended first lightly boiling them and making them into a *Būrānī* with sweet oil, such as almond oil or sesame oil, which removes their pungency and ability to generate black bile. He added that the dried stalks are useful against haemorrhoids if they are sprinkled, coated or smoked with them.

another kind of dish.][6]

If you want, you can take aubergines, peel them, slice them up and put them in a pot over a fire with water and salt. When they are nearly done, take the slices out of the pot, wash them with hot fresh water, and leave to dry. Take meat and pound it in a mortar. Add aromatic spices like those for meatballs, and one egg white. Knead well until everything sticks together. Then, take a frying pan and put it over a fire with olive oil. When the olive oil has come to a boil, throw in the aubergine slices and gently flip them over while frying. Remove them before they are completely fried. Take the pounded meat and cover it with the aubergine. Rub both your hands with olive oil and flatten the meat and aubergine until everything is very smooth and the aubergine is entirely coated (with the meat). Return the pieces to the pan, and fry them gently, making sure to turn them over so that they can brown on all sides. Remove and do the same as you did with the aubergine by itself, with alternating layers of aubergine and meat.

If you like, you can boil and wash the aubergine, and then crush it in a mortar until you get a marrow-like consistency, before thoroughly mixing in the pounded meat and spices. Then rub your hands with olive oil, shape the mixture into thin discs and fry them. Afterwards, proceed as described at the beginning of the recipe. Bear this in mind.

If you want to make the dish with mutton or chicken, proceed in the same way.

You can also put the meat in a casserole dish and layer the aubergine slices underneath it, in the centre, and all over on top. Send the dish to the oven after pouring in the egg-crusting mixture and aromatics, and leave it until it sets and browns.[7] You can also cook it at home, in which case you put the casserole over a fire with another one on top until the mixture thickens and the surface is browned. Then, carefully transfer it to a large ceramic bowl. Remember this.

Another way of preparing the dish is to split the aubergines in half and remove the pulp. Stuff the halves with pounded meat seasoned

6 Addition from Gayangos XVI (fol. 48r.).

7 This sentence is taken from Gayangos XVI (fol. 48v.) as the edition (2012: 97) and BL Or5927 (fol. 125v.) have the nonsensical *ghamara* ('to douse, soak'), rather than *khammara*. For the crusting mixture, see the preceding recipe.

with aromatics and combined with an egg white. Dust[8] them with *darmak* flour and fry in sweet olive oil until done and golden brown.[9] Then make a *Būrāniyya* with them.

101. Another dish called *al-muthallath*[10] ('the trebled')

Take the cuts of the above-mentioned meat (beef), wash them and season with salt and spices, as described earlier, and also add olive oil, *murrī*, and other things. Put the pot over a fire until the meat starts to turn white, and then pour on a sufficient amount of hot water. Leave to cook. Take fresh tender turnips, remove their outer peels and cut lengthwise, the size of a finger. Wash the pieces with water, colour with crushed saffron and throw them in the pot with the meat. Dissolve saffron in water and throw it on the meat. When the pot has come to a boil, add enough good-quality vinegar to flavour it, as well as meatballs, if you like. Then, take some eggs and crack them in a bowl and add salt, pepper, ginger and a little crushed saffron on top. Thoroughly whisk everything together with a ladle until the eggs and spices are blended. Check to see if the meat and turnips are cooked to a turn, and then apply the seasoned egg-mixture. Remove the pot from the fire, and let it rest so as to allow the eggs to set and crust the dish.[11] Transfer to a large ceramic bowl and add split eggs and mint leafstalks before sprinkling on cinnamon and ginger. Eat and enjoy, Allah the Exalted willing.

8 The Arabic *yughayyar* ('changed'), which also appears in BL Or5927 (fol. 125v.) does not make sense in this context, and should be corrected to *yughabbar* ('dusted').

9 The translation is based on BL Or5927 (*ibid.*), which has *yuḥammiru*, rather than the clearly erroneous *yamurr* ('passes through' or 'becomes bitter') of the printed edition (2012: 97).

10 Though the name originally refers to the fact that the dish is made with three ingredients, the author of the *Andalusian* (*Anwāʿ*, 204; BNF, fol. 71r.) defines *muthallath* dishes as being those 'cooked with meat, saffron, vinegar, and vegetables such as turnips, aubergines, gourds, carrots, or heads of lettuce without their leaves'. The *Andalusian* has a few recipes with the same name: a 'Persian *muthallatha*' (*Anwāʿ*, 116; BNF, fol. 45r.), a type of meat stew with aubergine or lamb and lettuce (*Anwāʿ*, 206; BNF, fols. 49v.–50r.), and even a fish *muthallath* (*ibid.*, 155; BNF, fol. 56r.). In al-Warrāq's cookbook the dishes by this name (also *thulāthiyya*) involve the use of three grains and pulses (1987: 145). In the pharmacological literature, the word *muthallath* referred to wine cooked down to a third. Also see recipe No. 78, above.

11 The text has been supplemented with Gayangos XVI (fol. 48v.) here, as it is the only copy that specifies when the egg mixture is added.

If you like, you can also make the dish with mutton, Allah the Exalted willing.

102. *Murūziyya*[12]

Take as many choice parts of fatty calf as you need. Wash and cut the meat, and then put it in a new pot with salt, olive oil, pepper, coriander seeds, cumin, soaked chickpeas, peeled almonds, cloves of garlic, a bit of cut-up onion, citron leaves and a fennel stalk. Put the pot over a fire, without water. Regularly flip the meat and, when it releases its juice and has turned white, add enough hot water to make a broth, and then leave to cook. Then, take a small glazed earthenware casserole dish and put premium vinegar in it, together with plums[13] imported from the land of the Christians[14] – may Allah destroy it![15] – which are called 'cows' eyes'. Take as many as you want, and then wash and clean them. Also take good red raisins, wash off any dirt and put them in with the vinegar and plums. Put this casserole on top of the pot to heat up the vinegar and tenderize the raisins and plums. If you find that the plums and raisins taste like vinegar, tip them into the pot, and add saffron for colour. Then, taste the meat. If it does not taste vinegary enough, add some more. When the meat is done, leave it on a low fire until it

---

12 The name of the dish is a corruption of *marwaziyya*, which suggests a Persian origin (the city of Merw), but the author of the *Andalusian* (*Anwāʿ*, 19; BNF, fol. 8r.) says that it is the food of Tunisians and Egyptians. There is indeed one *marwaziyya* recipe in *Kanz* (No. 65), but this is quite different, in that it is a fruity meat stew made with raisins, jujube and myrobalan plum. In contemporary Moroccan cuisine, *murūziyya* denotes a honeyed spiced lamb tajine with raisins and almonds, but sometimes also includes plums. See Ibn Mubārak Shāh 2020: xxxix.

13 The Arabic *ihlīlaj* (also *halīlaj*) usually referred to the fruit of myrobalan (*Terminalia chebula*), but in the Andalusian Arabic vernacular it denoted plums, also known as *ʿayn al-baqar* ('cows' eyes') or *ijjāṣ* (in Syrian Arabic this denotes the pear, with 'plum' being *khawkh*), which in Egypt (where plum is *barqūq*) means 'peach' (*durrāq* in Syria). It has also been identified as the damson plum. See Ibn Janāḥ 2020: 263 (No. 59); al-Ishbīlī 2004–10: Nos. 192, 3354; Ibn al-Ḥashshā' 1941: 130; Dozy 1881: I, 43; Dietrich 1988: I, 185 (note 2); Kazimirski 1860: I, 149. According to other authors (for instance, Ibn Jazla, fol. 158r.), *ʿayn al-baqar* referred to a type of grape.

14 *Rūm*, which in the Near East denoted 'Greek' or 'Byzantine', but in al-Andalus referred to Christians in general, and more specifically those of the Iberian Peninsula and north of it.

15 This imprecation (*dammarahā Allāh*) is included in BL Or5927 (fol. 126r.), but not in the edition (2012: 98). The phrase has Qur'ānic origins, as the verb *dammara* occurs several times as a divine penalty (e.g. 7:137, 25:36, 27:51).

is browned.[16] Then transfer to a large ceramic bowl and sprinkle on cinnamon and ginger. Eat and enjoy, Allah the Exalted willing.

103. Dish cooked with 'cows' eyes' plums and onions

Take choice cuts of the above-mentioned meat (beef) of your choice, and cut it up. Wash the pieces and put them in a pot with salt, a copious amount of olive oil, pepper, coriander seeds, cumin, lots of cut-up onion, and a sufficient amount of good-quality *murrī*. Put the pot over a fire without adding water. Stir occasionally and, when the meat is hot and its juice and that of the onions have been released, pour in enough hot water to make a broth, but make sure you do not add too much. Then, take the plums, wash them and put them in a small casserole with vinegar. Put it on top of the pot with the meat, and leave until the vinegar is hot and the plums have softened. Crush saffron in a mortar and then bloom it. Add some of it – not too much – to the pot to colour the meat and onions. When the pot has come to a boil, put in the plums and vinegar after checking whether the onions are done. If the onions are soft, add the vinegar. If not, then leave it to cook for a while longer and only add the vinegar when it is done. Then taste it and, if it is to your liking, leave it. If it is not quite right, add some more vinegar. Leave the pot over a gentle fire until all the flavours are balanced, the surface of the dish is browned, and the fat has appeared on the surface. Then, transfer to a large ceramic bowl. Eat and enjoy, Allah the Exalted willing.

If you like, you can make this dish with plums but without onions. In this case, add peeled almonds, soaked chickpeas and cloves of garlic, and proceed as described above, adding all of the spices, as well as saffron and vinegar. Bear this in mind and act, accordingly, Allah the Exalted willing.[17]

16 *yataḥammar*; BL Or5927 (fol. 126r.) has *yatajammar*, which means being set on embers for simmering (Corriente 1997: 101). The discrepancy occurs in other recipes as well, and has sometimes been amended accordingly in the translation.

17 The religious formula is included in BL Or5927 (fol. 126v.), but is missing from the printed edition.

104. Another dish, called *al-arnabī*[18]

Take the required amount of choice cuts of the aforementioned meat (beef). Chop it up and then wash and clean. Put the meat in a large glazed earthenware casserole dish, together with water, salt, lots of olive oil, pepper, coriander seeds, cumin, some cut-up onions, pounded and whole cloves of garlic, hand-rubbed oregano, soaked chickpeas, peeled almonds, citron leaves, a fennel stalk and a sufficient amount of *murrī*. Put the pot over a fire until everything is done and then colour with crushed saffron. Afterwards, put in enough good-quality vinegar to enhance the flavour, and leave on the fire until most of the broth has reduced and the fat remains. Then remove the pot from the fire and leave aside to cool down. Transfer the contents to a large ceramic bowl. Eat and enjoy, Allah the Exalted willing.

105. *al-Rāhibī* ('the monk's dish')[19]

Take choice cuts of the aforementioned fatty meat (beef), such as the brisket, honeycomb and thick-seam tripe, shanks, and so on. Cut into medium-sized pieces and wash them. Boil the stomach in hot water and clean it. Put the meat in a new pot and add salt, lots of olive oil, pepper, coriander seeds, citron leaves, a fennel stalk and a little *murrī*. Put the pot over a fire and leave to cook, occasionally stirring until the meat releases its juices and starts to whiten. Add a little hot water to make a broth. Then, take onions, remove the outer peel and chop

---

18 The name of the dish is somewhat mysterious, since it is the adjective related to *arnab* ('hare'), but is made either with other meat, or fish (recipe No. 303). The other Andalusian treatise contains a vegetarian dish by this name, made with aubergine (*Anwāʿ*, 143; BNF, fol. 52v.).

19 Both BL Or5927 (fol. 126v.) and the *Andalusian* (*Anwa'*, 136–8; BNF, fols. 50v.–51v.; Huici-Miranda 1961–62: 161–3) have the meaningless *dhāhabī*. However, the word is clearly spelled *rāhibī* in Wetzstein 1207 and Gayangos XVI. The monastic or Christian connection with dishes by this name is unclear; the *rāhībīs* in the *Andalusian* are all made with lamb or beef, whereas those in the present work can have beef (No. 105), chicken (No. 203), pigeon (No. 248), or even fish (Nos. 281, 301). The anonymous author of the *Andalusian* provides some interesting background to the dish, saying that it is made in various ways, but that its taste should be improved with the smell of onions, sweetened with rose syrup. It was also made with syrups of other fruits like pomegranates, apples or grapes, or with vinegar and preserved plums. One of the customs among the people was to make the dish with the meat of fatty animals. It must be cooked in a brick oven (rather than a *tannūr*). It should be sweet and sour, and because the dish already has colour no saffron is required.

them up. Wash with fresh water and set them aside. Check the meat and, if you see that it is close to being done, throw in the onions. When the onions are done, colour the meat with crushed saffron and pour it in the pot with some good honey – enough to sweeten it – or some honey-infused rose jam. If you like, you can use some good-quality vinegar instead of honey. Then, put the pot in the oven until the meat is browned and the broth has reduced, and then remove. You can also do this in a *tannūr*.

If you want to make the dish at home, transfer the meat and the onions to a glazed casserole dish and cook them over a moderate fire. Then take another casserole, made of iron or glazed earthenware, and light a strong fire in it. Put it on top of the first casserole and regularly check whether the side of the meat has browned and the liquid has dried out. Then, remove from the fire and let it sit to cool down. After you take it out of the oven, or wherever you cooked it, sprinkle on fragrant pure rose water to perfume the dish.

If you like, you can stew the meat in onion juice, in which case the dish is called *al-mufarrij*[20] or 'rays of sun'. Cut and wash the onions before cooking them separately in a pot. When they are cooked, squeeze them tightly until they release all of their juice. Then, strain and add it to the meat. When the meat is done, colour with saffron and add enough honey or honey-infused rose jam to sweeten it, as mentioned before, but also add rose water. If you wish, you can make both variations with mutton or all kinds of edible birds, Allah the Exalted willing.

106. Another dish, fried with *murrī* and garlic

Take the required amount of the aforesaid meat (beef), cut it up, wash and put the pieces in a clean pot with water, salt, plenty of olive oil, pepper, coriander seeds, good-quality *murrī* and peeled garlic. Put the pot over a fire until the meat is cooked and browned, and its juices have evaporated. Remove from the fire and perfume with some lemon, *zanbūʿ*[21] or sour grape vinegar. Eat and enjoy, Allah the Exalted willing.

---

20 This was a well-known dish, essentially a meat (beef or chicken) stew with onions (see recipes Nos. 24, 249, 257); Corriente 1997: 392. The name can be translated as 'the consoler' or 'comforter'.

21 See Introduction.

107. Another dish

Take meat (beef) from the thigh and the backstrap,[22] without the suet, and carve it up into large pieces. Wash and put them in a clean pot with enough water, salt, pepper and coriander seeds. Put the pot over a fire to cook. Then, take garlic and cook it in water to the strength you would like it to be. When it is done, clean it, and then crush in a wooden mortar. Transfer the crushed garlic to a large ceramic bowl. Take fresh coriander and parsley, which is called *būshīn*[23] in Romance, crush them both and squeeze their juices onto the garlic. Sprinkle on a lot of pepper and pour fresh sour grape vinegar and water on the garlic. Whip everything together until all the ingredients are blended. If you cannot find sour grape vinegar, then take good-quality tart vinegar. When you have finished this and the meat is done, transfer it to a separate large ceramic bowl and take everything to the table. Dip the bread in the sauce of your choosing, and then use a knife to cut the meat into small pieces and throw them in the *jalja*,[24] which is the sauce. If you want, you can dunk each individual piece [in the sauce] with your hands. Eat and enjoy, Allah the Exalted willing.

This recipe is eaten a lot by Christians[25] with roast chicken, roasted

---

22 *sinsin* (pl. *sanāsin*), an anatomical term which referred to 'protrusions along the middle of the spine' or 'bones connected to the vertebrae, neck of the ribs'. This is the only cookery manual that uses this term. See Dozy 1881: I, 693; Ibn al-Ḥashshā' 1941: 114 (No. 1061); Kazimirski 1860: I, 1151.

23 This word is not attested anywhere else, and is most likely a misspelling of *barshīn* (also *barshīl*), which does indeed mean 'parsley'. Corriente 1997: 46; Dozy 1881: I, 72 (*barrishīn*). In de Alcalá's glossary (1505: fol. 293v. [CIIIv]), the Castilian *perexil* is listed as the translation of the Arabic *perrixín*, which would corroborate Dozy's spelling.

24 The text adds that it is written with the 'dotted *jīm*' (*bi 'l-jīm al-muʿjama*). Corriente (1997: 99) traces this word back to the Latin *salsa*. Later on in the text (No. 276) the word appears in the variant pronunciation of *shalsha*. In Near Eastern cookery books, the word *ṣalṣa* – or *ṣalṣ* (plural *ṣulūṣ*) – denoted a condiment made with ground nuts, some kind of souring agent, and herbs, often accompanying fried fish. While in al-Andalus, the word and the dip came in through their Christian neighbours, in the Mashriq its origin is linked to the Crusades. It seems the sauces were extremely popular in fourteenth-century Egypt, as evidenced by the large number of recipes and variations in *Kanz* (Nos. 442–3, 486–95), but had evidently fallen out of favour there by the fifteenth century, as no recipes appear in a cookery book from that time. See Ibn Mubārak Shāh 2020: xxxviii; Marín 1997: 15; Perry [Rodinson *et al.* 2001]: 499–502.

25 The edition (2012: 102) and BL Or5927 (fol. 127v.) have *Rūm*, except for Gayangos XVI (fol. 50v.), which has *Naṣārā*.

and boiled meats, or fish. This broth is called *jalja* and is one of their best foods because of its innate heat. Keep this in mind, and act according to your wishes, Allah the Exalted willing.[26]

108. Garniture[27] pot, when an abundance of food is served

Take a big pot and add boiled thick-seam tripe, plus small coiled intestines and large intestines after cleaning and cutting them up into pieces in the size of your choosing. These will be used to decorate food coloured with saffron and cooked with vinegar. When you put the meat in the pot, also add peeled almonds and the spices that are used for the above-mentioned *jamalī*.[28] Leave in the pot until cooked, and then add a lot of meatballs and egg yolks, as well as crushed fresh suet. Thoroughly colour everything in the pot with saffron. When it is done, set the pot aside. When you serve it in bowls containing dishes like *jamalī*, *muthallath*[29] or *Ra's Maymūn*,[30] use a ladle and put the meat pieces on top. Garnish with split eggs and sprinkle on aromatic spices, Allah, the Mighty, the Venerable willing.[31]

26 The religious formula is included only in BL Or5927 (fol. 127v.).

27 Both the edition (2012: 102) and BL Or5927 (fol. 127v.) have *(qidr al-) m-f-r-sh*, which can be vowelled as *mafrash* ('grid-iron') or *mufarrash*, 'spread out' (from the verb *farrasha*, 'to cover, pave'), in reference to the meat being layered on top. However, Gayangos XVI (fol. 50v.) has the more correct *farsh*, which also appears in recipe No. 152, and means 'food garniture' (as well as 'bed'); see Corriente 1997: 394–5.

28 See recipes Nos. 99, 285, 289.

29 See recipe No. 101.

30 See recipes Nos. 68, 152.

31 The religious formula is included in BL Or5927 (fol. 127v.), but missing from the printed edition.

Chapter Two: on mutton

109. White *tafāyā*[32]

Choose meat from the breast, trotters and sides of a yearling ram. Carve it up, clean it, and put it in a new pot with water and olive oil. Take a new cloth and put in ginger, salt,[33] coriander seeds and a few cut-up onions. Tie it up into a parcel and throw it in the pot with the meat. When it is clear that the pot has been infused with all its flavours, remove the parcel from the pot so that it does not alter the broth. Leave the meat until it is done. If you like, you can add meatballs to the pot. When the meat is done, leave it over a gentle fire to simmer down and to allow the fat to rise to the surface. Then serve and eat, Allah the Exalted willing. If you want to make the dish with suckling kid, pullets or chickens, proceed as described above, with the strength of Allah the Exalted.

110. Green *tafāyā*[34]

Take meat from the desired prime cuts of a yearling ram, carve it up, wash and clean it, and then put the pieces in a new pot with a sufficient amount of olive oil. Add salt, pepper, coriander seeds, skinned almonds and a bit of sliced onion. Put the pot over a fire and on top of it place a small pot filled with freshwater which is then heated up by the

32 The *Andalusian* has nine recipes for this dish (*Anwāʿ*, 59, 60, 89, 90, 150, 151; BNF, fols. 25r.–v., 36r.–v., 54v., 55r.), which, according to Ibn Zuhr (1992: 138; trans., 149), was one of the best ways to cook meat. This was allegedly imported by Ziryāb (see Introduction) and was known in the Near East as *isfīdhbāj(a)*, a Persian borrowing which translates as 'white stew' because it was originally made with cheese. According to Ibn Ḥayyān (2003: 322), Andalusians were very quick to adopt the *tafāyā*, and even served it as the first course of every meal. As for its medicinal properties, it was said to be purifying, highly nutritious, and a recommended medicine for paralytics, the elderly and the phlegmatic, as well as being one of the foods that can balance the temperament after epidemics or famine (Ibn Zuhr 1992: 139, 145; trans., 149, 155). Al-Samarqandī 2016: 198) held that *isfīdhbāj* was particularly useful for people with cold temperaments. Also see Ibn Mubārak Shāh 2020: 6 (note 15).

33 BL Or5927 (fol. 128r.) specifies that it is 'washed' (*maghsūl*) salt.

34 This was a popular variant of the preceding recipe. According to al-Maqarrī (1968: III, 127), it was made with fresh coriander juice and garnished with samosas (*sanbūsak*) and kebabs. Al-Uryūlī (1983: No. 69), too, omits mint, and adds that the dish tends towards coldness if a lot of coriander is used, but is balanced if there is only a little coriander in it.

steam of the pot containing the meat. When it has released its juices and starts to whiten, add enough hot water to make a broth and leave to cook. Next, pound meat in a mortar, and add salt, cinnamon, ginger, pepper, spikenard, a sufficient amount of cloves and egg whites. Knead the mixture well until all of the ingredients are blended, and then make meatballs with it and put them in the pot. Take some fresh coriander, pound it in a wooden mortar, use your hand to squeeze out the juice, and put it in a bowl by itself. If you happen to have some chard to hand, take its green leaves and pound them before squeezing out their juice and adding it to the coriander. Then, crack some eggs in a large bowl, and add fresh coriander juice, mint juice, salt and aromatic spices, and beat everything well. Check on the meat and, if it is done, add the coriander and chard juice to the pot. Then, take some of the fresh suet, remove the veins, and crush it with the leafstalks of fresh coriander and mint until the suet turns green. Throw it in the pot, followed by three or four egg yolks, and brown. Then remove the fire underneath but leave it on the embers until it thickens and the (egg) crust has formed on top. Take two eggs and boil them in water. When they are done, peel and quarter them. When all of this is done, transfer the meat to a large ceramic bowl and put the meatballs and yolks on top. Finally, garnish with the quartered eggs. If you wish, you may fry the egg yolks in the pan. Sprinkle on cinnamon and ginger, and serve in the name of Allah. Eat and enjoy, Allah the Exalted willing.

If you want to make the recipe with aubergines, take as many small ones as you like, remove their outer peel and quarter them, but only cut up to the calyx, and do not separate the pieces. Put them in a pot with water and salt, and take it to the fire. When the aubergines are cooked, remove, rinse with hot water, and gently squeeze them. Put them with the meat and leave everything to cook. When you make it this way, include only the fresh coriander juice, the chard juice, the crushed suet with coriander and mint leafstalks, and leave out the eggs and crusting, since they are not needed.

You can make this variant of the recipe with white (milk) veal, or just the first one with suckling kid and plump chickens, so act accordingly, Allah the Exalted willing.[35]

35 The religious formula is included only in BL Or5927 (fol. 128v.).

111. Another recipe, called *kurunbiyya*[36] (cabbage stew)

Take the best parts of meat you like from a young, fatty ram, cut them up, and wash and clean them. Put the meat in a new pot with enough olive oil for the quantity of meat you have, and add salt, pepper, coriander seeds and a bit of sliced onion. Put the pot over a fire and on top of it a small pot with fresh water. Stir the pot from time to time so that the meat releases its juices and starts to whiten. Add enough water from the top (water) pot, but not too much, to make the broth. Then, take winter cabbage,[37] thoroughly clean it, and take the tender leaves. Remove the small leaves and cut the tender ribs after stripping the outer layer. Put the cabbage in a pot with water and salt and take it to the fire for boiling, as this is the best way to get rid of its harmful properties.[38] If you want, you can wash it with hot water and put it in the pot with the meat. When everything is cooked, take a little suet, pound it, and put it in the pot with fresh coriander leafstalks. Take a little caraway and lightly pound it in a mortar, and then add it to the pot after everything is cooked. Set on embers for a little while to simmer down and let the flavours infuse the dish. Transfer to a serving bowl and eat, Allah the Exalted willing.

---

36 According to al-Uryūlī (1983: Nos. 78), stews with cabbage (*kurunb* <Greek *krambídion*) produce black bile, while its broth loosens the bowels. He adds that cabbage dishes can be harmful to the eyesight. Ibn al-Raqqām (fol. 73r.) held that cabbage is only eaten cooked since this makes it easier to digest; the garden variety is cooked with meat, which strengthens eyesight, the brain and nerves. Additionally, Ibn Jazla (fol. 186r.) says that *kurunbiyya* is made like an *isfīdhbāj* (see recipe No. 109), and that the best one is made with chicken fat. He adds that it slows down intoxication and is good for a hangover, but dries out the body.

37 See recipe No. 9

38 Ibn Khalṣūn (1996: 162; trans., 90), for instance, said that cabbage may produce black bile and cause leprosy (*judhām*). He recommended eating tender short-stemmed cabbage, preferably with the meat of a fatty yearling sheep. According to Ibn Sīnā (1999: I, 531), it is laxative, slow to digest, harmful to the stomach, and low in nutrients. Its quality can be improved, however, by cooking it with fatty meat and chicken. Though concurring on its negative properties, al-Samarqandī (2016: 182) states that it is useful against hangovers, while the broth serves as a diuretic and emmenagogue, as well as providing relief against back and knee aches. Al-Ṭighnarī (2006: 501) recommended cabbage seeds as an anthelmintic, whereas al-Ishbīlī (2004–10: No. 2557) prescribed a poultice of cooked cabbage leaves (or its roots with pig or donkey fat) to dissolve tumours, and a poultice of its roots kneaded with sour milk to remove skin blemishes.

If you want to make this dish with summer cabbage,[39] first peel and clean it; it must be cooked in all cases because of its acridity. Once it is cooked, wash it with hot fresh water and then put it in the pot with the meat. Then, pound some meat, remove the veins, and add salt, pepper, ginger, coriander seeds, cinnamon, cloves and a sufficient amount of spikenard, as well as egg whites. Thoroughly knead the mixture until all the ingredients are blended. Make meatballs out of it and put them in the pot with the meat. Crack eggs and add salt, spices and fresh coriander juice. Whisk very well until everything is thoroughly mixed, and set aside. Pound some suet with fresh coriander and mint leafstalks until it turns green, and then put it in the pot. When it has come to a boil, crust the pot [with the eggs], stir and then remove the fire from underneath. Leave it on the embers for the dish to thicken.

If you like, you can use egg yolks and peeled almonds. When the dish has turned golden brown, serve and garnish with split (boiled) eggs. Sprinkle on cinnamon and ginger, and eat, Allah the Exalted willing.

You can also make the dish with veal in the two ways we have described.

112. Another recipe called *liftiyya*[40] (turnip stew)

Take meat from the best cuts you like of a young, fatty ram. Cut it up, wash and clean it, and put the pieces in a new pot with olive oil. Add salt, pepper and coriander seeds – some people also include a bit of cumin and a bit of sliced onion. Place the pot over a fire to cook, and on top of it put a small pot filled with fresh water. Stir occasionally until the meat has released its juices and starts to whiten. Take enough hot water from the top pot to make a broth. Leave to cook. Then, take

39 See recipe No. 9.

40 The name of the dish is derived from the Arabic word for turnip, *lift* (also *laft* or *shaljam/saljam*, the latter being a Persian borrowing). The *Andalusian* has two *liftiyya* recipes, though, confusingly, only one – called *sādhija* ('plain') – actually contains turnips (*Anwāʿ*, 205; BNF, fol. 71r.–v.), the other being a sweet-and-sour meat stew with walnuts and sugar (*Anwāʿ*, 115–16; BNF, fol. 44v.). Ibn Jazla (fol. 198r.–v.) said that *liftiyya* is made with rice, turnip and meat, and that it invigorates coitus, but is difficult to digest (though nourishing once it is digested), and causes wind. The recipe in *Taṣānīf* (fol. 78v.) also includes chickpeas, onions and carrots. Conversely, al-Uryūlī (1983: No. 77) praised the dish for being nutritious, producing little gas and being beneficial for weak eyesight.

turnips, remove the outer peel, and wash them before putting them in the pot with the meat. When everything is done, remove the pot from the fire and let it simmer down. Transfer to a large ceramic bowl and dust with cinnamon. Eat and enjoy, Allah the Exalted willing.

If you want it to make it with summer turnips,[41] peel them well, cut into round pieces and wash. Put them in the pot with the meat and leave until done. Then, pound the meat and remove the veins. Add salt, pepper, ginger, cinnamon, spikenard and a sufficient amount of cloves, as well as egg whites, and knead everything well into a dough. Make meatballs out of it and put them in the pot with the meat. Next, take suet and pound it together with fresh coriander and mint leafstalks, and put it in the pot. When it comes to a boil, crack some eggs into a bowl and add the coriander juice and spices as described above. Beat everything well with a ladle until the ingredients are all blended together. Check the pot with the meat, and if you find that everything is done, pour in the beaten eggs and stir by hand. Then, remove the fire underneath the pot and leave it on embers until the dish has set and crusted. Transfer to a serving dish, garnish with split (boiled) eggs and a sprinkling of cinnamon and ginger. Eat and enjoy this, Allah the Exalted willing.

41 The 'summer turnips' are the 'early' white elongated (*bakīr*) turnips – sometimes known as 'Toledan' – which Ibn al-ʿAwwām (1802: II, 177ff.) says were planted from the middle of July until the end of August, and were 'the usual variety eaten by people in our country'. Turnips sown in summer would be eaten in autumn and winter, and those sown in spring were eaten in May and June. Ibn Baṣṣāl (1955: 141) restricts the sowing season to August, and praises these turnips for being tastier. Ibn al-Raqqām (fol. 50v), for his part, places it in September and October. According to al-Ishbīlī (2004–10: No. 2747), turnips were particularly abundant in the Seville and Córdoba regions; medicinally, they were said to increase semen and act as a diuretic. Ibn Khalṣūn (1996: 162; trans., 91) restricts *lift* to the elongated variety of *saljam* – known sometimes as 'Christian' (*Rūmī*) – as opposed to the round one, and states that it is eaten with fatty meat, pepper and mustard. Turnips were often eaten with carrots, and al-Ṭighnarī (2006: 130) recommended using the red turnip for cooking. According to Ibn Waḥshiyya (1993: 543–4), turnips are best eaten after they have been boiled twice, dried and sprinkled with vinegar (or sumac juice or verjuice), *murrī*, olive oil, rue, verjuice, salt, pounded caraway seeds, cassia, mint, sweet basil, asafoetida, and other herbs like it. They should be eaten with bread, or perhaps together with boiled carrots. Ibn al-ʿAwwām (1802: II, 181–2) and Ibn al-Raqqām (fol. 50v) have similar recipes, albeit with some variations: the former has only salt, caraway and cinnamon as the dry seasonings, but adds mustard, whereas the latter advises using vinegar and sumac juice as well as verjuice, but with only caraway seeds and cassia sprinkled on.

If you like, you can put in a bit of fresh coriander juice before adding the crusting. You can also make both recipes with veal, if you prefer.

113. Another dish, called *qunnabīṭiyya*[42] (cauliflower stew)

Take the meat of your choosing from a young fatty ram, cut it up, wash and clean it. Then, put it in a new pot and add salt, generous amounts of olive oil and pepper, coriander seeds and a bit of cut-up onion. Put the pot over a fire and on top of it place another small pot with fresh water. Stir until the meat releases its juices and is about to whiten. Pour in enough hot water from the smaller pot to make a broth. Then, take a fresh cauliflower and cut off the head with your hand, but discard its stalk. Thoroughly clean and wash the cauliflower. Check on the meat and, if it is tender, add the cauliflower to it and leave until everything is done. Then, remove the fire from underneath the pot and set it on embers to simmer down and balance the flavours. Transfer to a large ceramic bowl and sprinkle on cinnamon and ginger. Eat and enjoy, Allah the Exalted willing.

42 There is only one other cookbook that has cauliflower (*qu/annabīṭ*) recipes: *Wuṣla*, Nos 8.109–14. According to al-Uryūlī (1983: No. 79), meat stews with cauliflower generate phlegm, are bad for those with a cold temperament, and produce gas and colic. To reduce the potential harm, they should be cooked with a lot of caraway seeds. Ibn Jazla (fol. 180r.) said that the best *qunnabīṭiyya* is made with the white of a moist cauliflower. It can be cooked with a variety of things, but mostly with rice. In addition to causing flatulence, it obscures vision and causes gripes, black bile and phlegm, though these can be counteracted with cooked grape juice. Ibn Māsawayh (fol. 145v.) recommended boiling cauliflower in water and salt several times before cooking it with fatty meat, while one should add cumin, pepper and caraway in order to speed its digestion. However, the dish can also be lethal, since the poet Makhāriq is said to have dropped dead on the spot after eating a cold *qunnabīṭiyya*. Ibn al-Raqqām (fol. 74v.–75r.) said that cauliflower was sown in April, and that it was eaten cooked with fatty meat, suet and olive oil. In Andalusian texts, cauliflower was known by a variety of names: *qarrabīṭ*; *qurbīṭ*; *kurunb nabaṭī* (Nabataean), *kirmānī* (Kermani) or *shāmī* (Syrian); and *asfāraj ṣīnī* ('Chinese asparagus'). See al-Ishbīlī 2004–10: Nos. 2557, 2561–3, 4073.

114. Another dish, called *silqiyya*[43] (chard stew)

Take the meat of prime cuts of your choosing from a fatty ram. Cut it up, wash and clean, and then place the pieces in a new pot, adding salt, good olive oil, pepper, coriander seeds, a bit of cut onions, soaked chickpeas and peeled almonds. Put the pot over a fire, and on top of it place another small pot with fresh water in order to make a broth. When you have poured the water from the smaller pot into the lower pot, let it cook. Take tender fresh chard, strip the leaves from the ribs and cut them up. Put the chard ribs in a clean pot with water and salt and put it over a fire in order to expel any bitterness in the chard, and to tenderize them. Then take them out and check on the meat. If you see that it is almost done, add the chard to it. When everything is cooked, remove the fire from underneath the pot and set it on embers to simmer down and balance the flavours. Transfer to a large ceramic bowl and eat and enjoy, Allah the Exalted willing.

115. Another dish, called *basbāsiyya* (fennel stew)[44]

Take the required amount of meat from a young fatty ram. Cut it up, wash, and put the pieces in a new pot with salt, olive oil, pepper, coriander seeds, and a bit of sliced onion. Put the pot over a fire to cook. Stir occasionally until the meat has released its juices and starts to whiten. Pour on hot water, as described above, in order to make the broth. Then, take tender, fresh fennel and clean it. Cut up the tender parts as finely as you can or, if you prefer, you can crush them, and then wash them. Check the meat and, if you see that it is done, add the fennel and let everything cook together. Pound suet with fresh coriander and fennel leafstalks, and put it in the pot with the meat. Add a bit

---

43 This is another unusual dish, and *Wuṣla* is again the only other cookery book that has *silqiyya* recipes: Nos. 8.105–8. The Arabic *silq* refers to Swiss chard and goes back to the Akkadian word for mangelwurzel (*Beta vulgaris macrorhiza*) – a type of beet – *silqu* (Roth 1956-2010: XV, 67). According to Ibn al-Raqqām (fol. 58r.), it came in three sizes (small, medium and large), all of which were sown in summer and spring. He stated that it was boiled three times and then dried before being ground and turned into bread, while it was also used to make a *khabīṣ* pudding. Chard was considered to increase sexual potency and semen. Also see al-Kindī 1966: 284–5; Dietrich 1988: II, 269–70; Rodinson *et al.* 2001: 22.

44 The *Andalusian* (*Anwāʿ*, 134, 150; BNF, fols. 50r., 54v.–55r.) is the only other cookery book to have fennel (*basbās*) recipes by this name, but *Wuṣla* has a few similar dishes (Nos. 123–4). Also see recipe No. 284, below, for a fish *basbāsiyya*.

of fresh coriander juice. When everything is done, leave the pot over a gentle fire to simmer down. Serve the dish in a large ceramic bowl, and eat and enjoy, Allah the Exalted willing. [If you want to have an egg crusting, you can prepare it as in the already-mentioned green *tafāyā* dish, but this requires a little liquid.][45]

116. A dish called *naʿnaʿiyya*[46] (mint stew)

Take meat from the prime cuts of your choosing from a young fatty ram. Cut it up, and then wash and clean before putting it in a new pot with salt, olive oil, pepper, coriander seeds and a bit of cut onion. Put the pot over a fire and, on top of it, place a small pot with fresh water to be heated up by the steam. Stir continually until the meat releases its juices and is about to whiten. Add water – not too much – from the small pot to make a broth. Then, take fresh and tender mint, and clean the leaves and leafstalks, making sure you wash off any sand or dirt that clings to them. Put them in a clean pot with fresh water and boil them. When they are done, take them out of the water and drain it. If you like, you can use this liquid, instead of hot water, to make a broth, as it is better and more beneficial. Take the cooked mint leaves, pound them into a dough, and put it in the pot with the meat. Then, take suet and pound it with fresh coriander and mint leafstalks. Put it in the pot with some fresh coriander juice and leave to cook. When it is done, remove the fire from underneath the pot, and leave it on embers to simmer and balance the flavours. Then serve the dish in a large ceramic bowl and eat, Allah the Exalted willing.

117. Another dish, called *turunjāniyya*[47] (lemon-balm stew)

It is made exactly like the previous recipe – no more no less. Bear this in mind.

---

45 The sentence in brackets is an addition from Gayangos XVI (fol. 52r.).

46 Although mint (*naʿnaʿ, naʿnāʿ*) was used extensively in both the Mashriq and Maghrib, *Taṣānīf* (fol. 76r.–v.) is the only other cookery book that has a recipe by this name. Also see recipe No. 205, below.

47 Besides *turunjān*, lemon balm (*Melissa officinalis*) is known as *bādaranjbūja* (a Persian borrowing) – with the variants *bādharanjūya, bādharanbūya* and *bādharanjbūja* – *utrunjī* (also *utrunjiyya*); Ibn Janāḥ 2020: 325, No. 129; Ibn Jazla, fol. 32v.; al-Ishbīlī 2004–10: Nos. 680, 998, 1593, 3000; Corriente 1997: 4, 41. According to Ibn Zuhr (1992: 67), it was used like fennel or celery. Al-Rāzī (1987: 155) claimed it loosens the bowels and soothes the throat.

118. A dish cooked with borage (*abū khuraysh*),[48] which is also known as 'ox tongue' (*lisān al-thawr*)

Take young fatty ram meat and cut, wash and clean it. Then put it in a new pot with salt, olive oil, pepper, coriander seeds and a bit of cut-up onion, and put it over a fire. Stir occasionally until the meat releases its juices and starts to whiten. Add a sufficient amount of hot water. Take borage, cut and wash it, and put it in a clean pot with a little salt and water. Put it over a fire to cook. Then, remove the borage and put it on a wooden board before beating it with the back of a knife until it is all broken up and forms a pulp. Check the meat and, if it is done, add the pounded borage. Crush suet with fresh coriander leafstalks and add it to the pot with a bit of fresh coriander juice. Leave it for a while over a low fire to simmer down and to balance the flavours. Serve in a large ceramic bowl, and eat and enjoy, Allah the Exalted willing.

119. Another dish, cooked with spinach

Take the required amount of prime cuts of your choosing from a young, fatty ram. Cut, wash, clean and put the meat in a new pot with salt, olive oil, pepper, coriander seeds and a bit of cut-up onion.[49] Put the pot over a fire and stir from time to time, until the meat releases its juices and starts to whiten. Add hot water in order to make a broth. Then, take spinach, especially the tender parts, and clean it. Put it in a clean pot with water and place it over a fire. When it is done, remove and put it on a wooden board and beat it with the back of a knife to hack it up and turn it into a mash. Check the meat and if it is done, add the spinach to the pot. Crush suet with fresh coriander and mint

48 This is the North African and Andalusian Arabic word, with *lisān al-thawr* (a loan translation from the Greek *boúglōsson*) being the usual technical term, though it was also known as *būghallisūn, haraqān* or *kuḥaylā'*; Renaud & Colin 1934: 110 (No. 246); Ibn al-Ḥashshā' 1941: No. 644; Ibn al-Bayṭār 1992: IV, 382; al-Ishbīlī 2004–10: Nos. 400, 827, 1497, 2517, 2713. This is the only time borage appears as an ingredient in a food dish, as it was used primarily in medicinal compounds (often its water in beverages), most notably in stomachics, anti-nausea drugs, and to delay intoxication; see *Kanz*, Nos. 373, 375, 435, 438, 440, 448, 450, 671; *Wuṣla*, Nos. 2.5–7, 2.12. The best borage was said to come from the Levant (*shāmī*) and Khorasan, and according to Ibn Jazla (fol. 196v.) has anti-inflammatory properties, gladdens the heart, and is beneficial for palpitations and black bile ailments.

49 BL Or5927 breaks off here (fol. 130v.), skips over fifty recipes and two whole chapters, and continues (fol. 131r.) with recipe No. 172. The spinach recipe is completed on fol. 137r.

leafstalks and put them in with the meat, together with fresh coriander juice. Leave the pot over a gentle fire to prevent the vegetables from turning yellow. Serve the dish in a large ceramic bowl, and eat. When making a large quantity for banquets, the dish is garnished with fresh cheese before serving, Allah the Exalted willing.

If you want, you can make it with kid's meat, which suits this dish. If you cook it with yearling ram meat, orache[50] and leafy goosefoot,[51] make it separately as with spinach. Bear this in mind [and act accordingly, Allah the Exalted willing].[52]

120. Another dish, made with lettuce heads

Take the required quantity of prime cuts of your choosing from a young fatty ram. Cut, wash, and clean the meat, and then put it in a new pot, together with salt, olive oil, pepper, coriander seeds and a bit of cut-up onion. Put it over a fire and stir from time to time until the meat releases its juices and starts to whiten. Pour on hot water, but not too much,[53] to make a broth. Then, peel and cut up the lettuce. Remove all of the green leaves and boil them in a clean pot with water until they are done. Then, take them out and pound them in a wooden mortar until they turn into a pulp with a marrow-like consistency. Check whether the meat is done; if so, add the lettuce to it and bring to a boil once or twice. Then apply the egg crusting to the dish, as described earlier.

---

50 *qaṭaf* (*Atriplex hortensis*), which was also called *baqla dhahabiyya* ('golden herb'), *baql al-Rūm* ('Greek/Christian herb'), *sarmaq*, or *sakhbar*. See al-Ishbīlī 2004–10: Nos. 947, 3914, 4331, 4575; Ibn al-Bayṭār 1992: IV, 272–3. Ibn Khalṣūn (1996: 162/ trans., 90) considered it useful against jaundice and poisons, but harmful to the stomach, and advised eating it with strong aromatics. According to al-Samarqandī (2016: 182–4), it is a laxative, and particularly suitable for people suffering from a fever.

51 The edition (2012: 110) has the nonsensical *yarbūn*, which should be corrected to *yarbūz*, as it appears in BL Or5927 (fol. 137r.). The plant is a member of the amaranth family, and was also known as *baqla Yamāniyya* ('Yemeni herb'), *bulīṭun* or *ruyūzī*. See al-Ishbīlī 2004–10: Nos. 948, 2063, 3999, 5106; al-Ṭighnarī 2006: 498; Ibn al-Bayṭār 1992: I, 142; IV, 516. According to Ibn Khalṣūn (1996: 162; trans., 90) and al-Samarqandī (2016: 184), it has laxative properties, and is useful against coughs and thirst, but harmful to the stomach, whereas the former recommended preparing it with almond oil.

52 The section enclosed in brackets was taken from BL Or5927, fol. 137r.

53 The edition (2012: 110) has *lā yutrak* ('do not leave'), but the translation renders the more logical *lā yukhtar* from BL Or5927 (fol. 137r.) since a similar instruction can be found in other recipes.

Remove the fire from underneath the pot and leave it on the embers for it to simmer down and the flavours to balance, and then serve. Eat and enjoy, Allah the Exalted willing.

If you want to make it like a *qarʿiyya*[54] (gourd stew), take the meat and proceed in exactly the same way as stated at the beginning of the recipe. Then, take lettuce and peel it very well before cutting the heads into thin slices. Take the leafstalks with their small leaves and split them. Wash everything and add it to the pot with the meat and, when it is done, put in hand-rubbed oregano and leave to brown over a gentle fire. Serve in a large ceramic bowl and eat and enjoy, Allah the Exalted willing.

If you want to, you can make it with suckling kid's meat, which is suitable for this dish, with the strength of Allah the Exalted.

121. Another dish, called *rijliyya*[55] (purslane stew)

Take the required amount of meat from two yearling rams, as described previously. When you take the pot to the fire, take fresh and tender purslane without the seeds and chop it up as finely as you can. Then gingerly wash it with salt and rub it with both hands to remove the slime. Put it in the pot with the meat. When everything is done, take some eggs, crack them and add what has been described above.[56] Beat them well and then put them in the pot. Stir gently and leave the pot on embers to simmer down and thicken. Serve in a large ceramic bowl, and eat, Allah the Exalted willing.

---

54 See recipes Nos. 128, 207, 250, below.

55 *rijl(a)* was the Andalusian Arabic for 'purslane'; it was usually stewed with the meat and was associated with the regions around Córdoba and Jaén. Al-Ishbīlī traced the origin of the word back to the Prophet, who beseeched God to help his men who had complained about burning their feet (*rijl*) on the hot earth; as a result, they were made to grow purslane so they could walk on that instead. It is most commonly known as *baqla ḥamqāʾ* (the 'stupid vegetable'), which the same author attributed to the fact that the plant grows in people's paths (and is thus often trampled). Medicinally, purslane was thought to suppress yellow bile and to be beneficial for the stomach, liver and fevers, but harmful to the libido. According to a *ḥadīth*, purslane is a remedy against ninety diseases, but is especially effective against headaches (Ibn Ḥabīb 1992: 46; trans., 78). See Ibn al-Ḥashshāʾ 1932: 15 (No. 131); al-Kindī 1966: 244–5; Ibn Jazla, fols. 40v., 107r.; Nasrallah [al-Warrāq 2007]: 784; Dietrich 1988; II, 270–1; al-Ishbīlī 2004–10: Nos. 90, 2098, 3608–9.

56 Recipe No. 17 specifies salt, pepper, ginger and cinnamon, whereas No. 99 has salt, crushed saffron and aromatic spices. Presumably, any combination of these would be acceptable.

122. Another dish, cooked with asparagus[57]

Cut up the required amount of meat from a fatty yearling ram, and then wash and clean it before putting it in a pot with plenty of olive oil, salt, pepper, coriander seeds and a few cut-up onions. Put the pot over a fire and stir, as described earlier. Add enough water to make a broth. Then, take the tender parts of asparagus and clean them before putting them in a clean pot with water and salt. Place the pot over a fire and leave until the asparagus is cooked, and the water has evaporated. Taste it to make sure that there is no bitterness left, which is what you want. If it has not, add some more hot water and let it boil some more until the bitterness is gone. Then, remove the asparagus, wash it in hot water and put it in a sieve to drain their water. Check the meat and, if you find that it is cooked, add the asparagus to the pot and leave until done. Pound suet with fresh coriander and mint leafstalks and add it to the pot with some fresh coriander juice. When the suet has boiled once or twice, crack some eggs and add aromatic spices and coriander juice, as described previously. Crust the pot [with the egg mixture] and then remove the fire from underneath and leave it on the embers to thicken, simmer down, and to balance the flavours. Transfer to a large ceramic bowl and garnish with split (boiled) eggs, as stated earlier. Sprinkle on cinnamon and ginger, and then eat it, Allah the Exalted willing.

If you want to cook it with vinegar and colour it with saffron, add cumin, cloves of garlic, a little *murrī* and citron leaves to the spices. When you put the pot on the fire, take the asparagus, and clean and boil it, as described earlier, to remove its bitterness. Then, wash and dry it before cutting it up into medium-sized pieces. Check the meat and, if you see that it is done or near to it, add the asparagus and leave until everything is cooked. Then, crush saffron, dissolve it in water, and add it to the pot to colour the meat and asparagus, but do not put too

57 *asfarāj*, the Andalusian vernacular variant for the standard *hilyawn*, which was also known as *māsūnaj* (Ibn Janāḥ 2020: 744, No. 576), *alasmarāgh*, *ashbāraj* (al-Ishbīlī 2004–10: Nos. 260, 4969) or *marjuniq* (Ibn Biklārish, fols. 47v.–48r.). See Dietrich 1988; II, 271–2. According to Ibn Biklārish, who gives *ashbāraghūsh* as the Romance (*'ajamiyya*) term, it increases semen, acts as a diuretic, and is useful against jaundice, liver blockages and colic. Ibn Jazla (fol, 236r.–v.) adds that it is beneficial for sciatica, and that its decoction can kill dogs. It can also be harmful to the stomach, and should be cooked with meat, as well as *murrī* and olive oil. Also see recipe No. 370.

much in. When the pot has come to a boil, add the requisite amount of good-quality vinegar to enhance the flavour. Then, take as many eggs as are needed, crack them, and add aromatics, as mentioned, and a little saffron. Beat everything well and crust the dish with it. Then, remove the fire from underneath the pot and leave it on the embers to thicken, simmer down, and to balance the flavours. Serve in a large ceramic bowl and garnish with split (boiled) eggs. Finally, sprinkle on cinnamon and ginger, and eat, Allah the Exalted willing.

If you want to make this dish as a *muṭajjan*,[58] take the abovementioned meat of your liking, and cut it up into small pieces before washing and cleaning it. Then, place it in a new pot and add salt, plenty of olive oil, pepper, coriander seeds, cumin, a few onions, cloves of garlic, citron leaves, fennel stalks and a sufficient amount of good-quality *murrī*. Put the pot on the fire and stir, as described earlier. Pour in enough hot water to make the broth. Then, take asparagus and proceed as described above, but without cutting it. When it has been boiled and is done, crush and bloom saffron, and add it to the pot. Once the pot has come to a boil again, take some good-quality vinegar and pour enough of it on the meat to enhance the flavour. Leave the pot on the fire. Then, crust it, as mentioned, and leave to thicken. Next, take a glazed casserole dish

58 The passive participle of a verb (*ṭajjana*) meaning 'to fry in a pan', called a *ṭājin* (ultimately from the Greek *tēganon*, 'pan'), usually made of copper. This preparation was sometimes contrasted with *qalāyā*, that is, dishes fried in a frying pan (*miqlā*), often in sesame oil, with prior boiling of the meat (for a *qaliyya*, see recipe No. 154). According to one cookery book (al-Warrāq1987: 74), *muṭajjanas* were made with jointed chickens with the bones, as opposed to a dish called *ṭabāhija* (see recipes below Nos. 137–9), which contained boneless and sliced meat, with coriander not being used in either. In the course of history, things changed dramatically, though. For one thing, the semantic link between the cooking process and the utensil weakened, and *muṭajjan* dishes also sometimes required a *miqlā*. Secondly, other things could also be prepared *muṭajjan*, i.e. fried in sesame oil, such as eggs (*Waṣf*, 384; al-Baghdādī 1964: 58–9; trans., 80) or spinach (al-Baghdādī 1964: 68/trans., 89; *Waṣf*, 399). In the Muslim West, the *muṭajjan* recipes of the anonymous Andalusian treatise (*Anwāʿ*, 103–4; BNF, fols. 41r.–v.) are made with eggs and are essentially meat omelettes. According to al-Rāzī (1987: 137), both *muṭajjan* and *qalāyā* are harmful and provide little nourishment. Ḥunayn Ibn Iṣḥāq (1997: 64; trans., 108) considered that both *muṭajjanas* and roasts (*shuwāʾ*) provided only dry nourishment to the body. Also see *Waṣf*, 357–8, 377, 384 (*muṭajjan* eggs); al-Baghdādī 1964: 56 (trans., 77); Ibn Mubārak Shāh 2020: 105 (note 496). There is also a parallel with the Persian *muṭanjan*, which means 'fried or boiled in a pan', as well as 'stew' (Steingass 1892: 820, 1262).

with olive oil and put it over a fire. When the oil comes to a boil, take enough eggs and crack them in a bowl with a small amount of aromatics. Then, pour the eggs in the pan – the mixture should cover the bottom. Take the asparagus and gently squeeze out the juice with your hands and layer it on top of the eggs, followed by a layer of meat. Continue alternating the asparagus and meat layers until you have run out of both. Strain the meat broth and add it to the casserole. Crack more eggs, beat them with aromatics and a bit of dissolved saffron, and pour the mixture on the dish. Put egg yolks on top before taking the casserole to the oven to set, but take care not to burn it. If you like, you can take it out of the casserole, garnish with split [boiled] eggs, and sprinkle on cinnamon and ginger. Eat and enjoy, Allah the Exalted willing.

123. Another dish, which is made with unripe tender garlic

Take the best meat from a fatty ram, such as the breast and sides. Cut and clean it, and then put in a new pot with salt, lashings of olive oil, pepper, coriander seeds, cumin, soaked chickpeas, a bit of onion, citron leaves, a fennel stalk and *murrī*. Place the pot over a fire and then proceed as described earlier in terms of stirring and making a broth. Take the garlic, remove the outer peel, cut off the green parts with the leaves, and leave the heads with the white parts. Score them and colour with crushed saffron before putting them in the pot with the meat to cook. Add saffron to the meat in the pot. Check the meat and, when it is almost done, add the requisite amount of good-quality vinegar. Seal the top of the pot with dough or soaked paper,[59] take it to the oven and leave it until the liquid has dried out. When it is ready, take it out of the oven.

If you want to cook it at home, transfer the contents of the pot to a glazed casserole dish and layer the meat and garlic in it. Add the strained broth and put the pot over a fire. Take another, unglazed casserole, light a strong fire inside it and place it on top of the dish with the meat. Check regularly to see if it is done and to your liking. Then,

59 *kāghad* (a borrowing from Persian *kāghadh*); paper was introduced in the medieval Muslim world in the eighth century, and was made with linen, flax or hemp. The Andalusian paper industry, with its centre in Jativa in the Valencia region, was already famous for its high-quality outputs in the tenth century. Lévi-Provençal 1932: 185; *EI*[2], s.v. 'kāghadh' (Cl. Huart-A. Grohmann).

remove it from the fire and leave to cool down before serving. Eat and enjoy, Allah the Exalted willing.

This dish can also be made with veal, doeling or buckling meat.[60]

124. Another dish, made with unripe green almonds[61]

Take the best pieces of fatty ram meat and cut, wash and clean them before placing them in a new pot with salt, olive oil, pepper, coriander seeds, cumin, a sufficient amount of *murrī*, a bit of cut-up onion, cloves of garlic, citron leaves, a fennel stalk, and soaked chickpeas. Put the pot over a fire and stir from time to time until the meat releases its juices and starts to whiten. Add hot water in order to make the broth. Leave on the fire to cook. Then, take green almonds and shell them before cleaning and washing them. Add them to the pot with the meat and, when the meat and almonds are almost done, colour both with saffron, as described above. Add a ladleful of good-quality vinegar in order to enhance the flavour, and leave on a low fire to simmer down.

You can crust it with eggs if you like, and then transfer everything to a large ceramic bowl, sprinkle on ginger, and eat and enjoy, Allah the Exalted willing. If you want, you can also make the dish with veal, with the strength of Allah.

125. Another dish, called *narjisiyya*[62]

Take meat of a young, fatty ram, carve, wash and put it in a pot with salt, olive oil, pepper and coriander seeds, and cook halfway through. Then scrape good-quality carrots and cut them lengthwise, about half a finger long. Place them on the meat with a bit of water, vinegar and saffron. Sprinkle on a bit of washed rice and, when it is done, pour on enough eggs whipped with saffron to thicken the dish. Leave to cook. Once it is ready and has cooled down, use a knife to cut what is in the

60 This variation is found only in BL Or5927, fol. 138v.

61 In Gayangos XVI (fol. 67r.), where it is called an 'amazing *lawziyya* dish' (see No. 135), the recipe is highly compressed, but includes that the almonds should be pierced before adding them to the meat.

62 This recipe, which is called 'amazing' in Gayangos XVI (fol. 67r.), is also found in the *Andalusian* (*Anwāʿ*, 136; BNF, fol. 50v.), with the more specific name of '*narjisiyya* with carrots'. It was a popular medieval dish which originally got its name from egg yolks being added at the end, creating the impression of floating narcissi (*narjis*). See Ibn Mubārak Shāh 2020: 33 (note 126). Also see recipe No. 215, below.

pot and the pieces will look like narcissi. It is also possible to cook this dish in the oven, Allah the Exalted willing.

126. Another dish, cooked with artichokes[63] called *afzān*

Take the required amount of fatty ram meat, cut it up, wash and clean it, and put the pieces in a new pot. Proceed in the way described above. Put it on the fire, and do the same things as in the previous recipes. Take artichokes, remove their thorns and other parts, and boil them in water until they are done. Then, remove them from the pot and wash them with hot water. Chop them up and put the pieces in the pot with the meat, and leave to cook until done. Then, add saffron and vinegar, as described above. When everything is done and you want to crust the pot, do so according to the instructions above, and leave the pot so it can be crusted. Then, serve in a large ceramic bowl, and eat and enjoy, Allah the Exalted willing. You also use this method to cook cardoon[64] and garden artichokes.[65] If you want to cook it like a *Būrāniyya*,[66] cut them into slices, add meatballs, and fry the varieties of artichokes after boiling them. You can also make the dish with veal. Remember this.

---

63 *ḥarshaf* (also *ḥurshuf*), which according to al-Ishbīlī (2004–10: No. 1631) denoted various species of thorny plants, cultivated or wild, some of which people eat in spring, the cultivated variety being known in Berber as *afzān*. Later on (recipes Nos. 368–70), al-Tujībī uses the more usual word for (wild) artichoke, *khurshūf* (also *khurshuf, kharshaf*), whereas Gayangos XVI (fol. 67r.) has *khurshuf* in the title of the present recipe. The word probably goes back to the Persian *kangarzad* (also *kangar*), via Syriac (*kangar*), and entered Spanish as *alcachofa*. Also see Ibn Janāḥ 2020: 564–5 (No. 395); Dietrich 1988: II, 360–1; Renaud & Colin 1934: 95–6 (No. 213); López y López 1990: 280–2; Ibn al-Ḥashshā' 1932: 39 (No. 367); Löw 1881: 293 (No. 234).

64 *laṣīf*, also known as 'artichoke thistle'; according to al-Ishbīlī (2004–10: No. 2772) it is 'a variety of wild artichoke (*kankar barrī*), [also known as] the "camel thistle" (*shawk al-jimāl*), which the Berbers call *tākā'*. Also see al-Ishbīlī Nos. 500, 1099, 1631, 2447, 2655, 2772, 4853. Corriente (1997: 480) identifies it as the wild artichoke (*Scolymus hispanicus*).

65 *qannāriya* (from the Greek *kinára*) often referred to cardoon, but not in Andalusian Arabic, where it is the garden or globe artichoke, also known as *kankar*, which Ibn al-Ḥashshā' (1932: 66, No. 216) defines as the cultivated artichoke (*ḥarshaf bustānī*), known as *qannāriya*. al-Ishbīlī 2004–10: Nos. 219, 2591, 4025, 4027; López y López 1990: 339–41; Meyerhof 1940: 76 (No. 154).

66 See recipe No. 100.

127. Another dish, cooked with truffles, called *tirfās*[67]

Cut up and wash the meat of a fatty yearling ram. Put the pieces in a new pot with salt, olive oil, pepper, coriander seeds and a sufficient amount of *murrī*. Put the pot over a fire and stir until the meat releases its juices and starts to whiten. Pour in hot water to make a broth, but not too much. Take truffles and peel them, after washing them and removing any dirt and other impurities. Then break them up with your hands – do not use a knife – and put the pieces in the pot with the meat to cook. When it is ready, remove the fire from underneath the pot and set it on the embers to simmer down. Then, serve in a large ceramic bowl with a sprinkling of pepper and ginger. Eat and enjoy, Allah the Exalted willing.

128. Another dish, called *qar'iyya*[68] (gourd stew)

Take the meat from, for instance, the breast and sides of a fatty yearling ram. Cut it up and wash it before putting it in a new pot with salt, good-quality olive oil, pepper, coriander seeds and a few cut-up onions. Put the pot on the fire and proceed as explained earlier. Then take a fresh, tender gourd, remove its outer peel and scoop out the

67 Gayangos XVI (fol. 67v.) adds that it is 'amazing'. Of Berber origin, the word is Andalusian and North African Arabic for 'truffles' (*kam'a*), which, according to Ibn Zuhr (1992: 63; trans., 89-90), occur in manure and sandy soil and are intermediate between plants and animals. They cause stomach pains prior to digestion, and engender many ailments. The nefarious effects of truffles can be counteracted by cooking them with plenty of pepper. Interestingly enough, Ibn Zuhr believed mushrooms are much worse than truffles, as 'there is nothing good about mushrooms, especially those that grow spontaneously on dung heaps, which can lead to death by poisoning or suffocation. They do not really have any good properties, so it is not advisable to eat them.' According to the legist Ibn 'Abdūn (Lévi-Provençal 1955: 32), *tirfās* should not be sold around mosques because it is 'a fruit of depravity'! Ibn Qutayba (1925–30: III, 297) claimed truffles were cooked in water and salt and then eaten with thyme and pepper.

68 There is a similar recipe in the *Andalusian* (*Anwā'*, 204–5; BNF, fol. 71r.), where it is said that it is called a *sādhija* ('plain') or *mu'annatha'* ('feminine') *qar'iyya*, 'according to cooks' lore'. In other recipe books, dishes by this name tend to be sweets: Ibn Mubārak Shāh 2020: Nos. 145–6; *Kanz*, Nos. 312–14. For other recipes, sometimes called *yaqṭīniyya*, after another word for 'gourd' (*yaqṭīn*), see Ibn Mubārak Shāh 2020: 64–5; *Waṣf* 350–1 (an identical dish is titled *būrāniyyat al-qar'* in al-Baghdādī (1964: 43–4; trans., 62). According to al-Uryūlī (1983: No. 76), *qar'iyya* is cold, moist, and suitable for young people and those with a hot temperament. However, it should not be eaten with thyme. Also see recipes Nos. 207 and 250 below.

seeds and pulp inside, cleaning it well inside and out. Cut into squares, wash and put them in the pot with the meat to cook. When everything is done, add a sufficient amount of summer savory[69] sprigs. If savory is not available, use hand-rubbed oregano, but not too much. Leave the pot over a gentle fire to simmer down. Serve in a large ceramic bowl, and eat and enjoy, Allah the Exalted willing. If you like, you can also make this recipe with veal.

129. Another dish, which is made with sour and sweet apples[70]
Take the required amount of meat from a fatty yearling ram, carve it up, wash and clean it. Put the pieces in a new pot with salt, olive oil, pepper, coriander seeds, a little cumin and some onions. Put the pot over a fire and stir until the meat releases its juices and starts to whiten. Pour on hot water to make a broth. Then, take apples, peel them and remove cores, seeds and stems. Cut them any way you like, and put the pieces in the pot with the meat to cook everything together. Then, add a little saffron, followed by good-quality vinegar – a little if you are using sour apples, and a ladleful, or any other amount you like, for sweet apples. Leave the pot to simmer down, and then transfer to a large ceramic bowl. Sprinkle on cinnamon and ginger before serving. Eat and enjoy, Allah the Exalted willing. If you like, you can perfume the dish with musk, ambergris, rose water and camphor, which strengthens the soul and gladdens the heart.

69 *shaṭriyya*; identified as a variety of thyme, it was also known as *tarāghurīghānīs* and Persian thyme, as well as Slav thyme or pepper. See al-Ishbīlī 2004–10: Nos. 2296, 3201, 3209, 3802, 4627.

70 This kind of dish was usually known as a *tuffāḥiyya* (*tuffāḥ* 'apples'); it is also the title in Gayangos XVI (fol. 67v.), which adds that it is 'good'. In the next recipe (No. 130), it is actually referred to as such. Also see *Taṣānīf*, fol. 47v.; al-Baghdadi 1964: (trans., 34-5); *Kanz*, Nos. 119, 138; *Waṣf*, 311, 352. According to Ibn Jazla (fol. 49r.–v.), the best *tuffāḥiyya* is one made with fragrant apples, and is useful against a hot liver and weak stomach, but can cause cough, colic, as well being harmful to sexual potency and the joints. Its harmful effects can be counteracted by eating a fatty chicken, prepared in the juice of sour apples.

130. Another dish, cooked with quince[71]

This is made like the previous recipe, neither more nor less, including perfuming it with fragrant aromatics, mentioned in the apple stew (*tuffāḥiyya*). Remember this[, and proceed accordingly, Allah the Exalted willing].[72]

131. Another dish, called *faḥṣī*,[73] which is cooked with pickled lime and whole cinnamon

Take however much you need from the meat and suet of a fatty ram, cut it up and wash it before putting it in a new pot with salt, plenty of olive oil, pepper, coriander seeds, a few onions and cinnamon sticks. Put the pot on the fire and stir from time to time until the meat releases its juices and starts to whiten. Add hot water to make the broth, but not too much. Leave the pot to cook and, when the meat is nearly done, add as much pickled lime as you want, but not too much. The best kind is pickled in vinegar. Put the limes in with the meat and leave on a moderate fire until they are done, their juice has dried out and nothing remains in the pot except the olive oil and the fat. Serve in a large ceramic bowl, and dust with cinnamon. Eat and enjoy, Allah the Exalted willing. This kind of dish can also be made with a plump chicken or veal, with the strength of Allah the Exalted.

132. Another dish, fried in a pot

Take the desired amount of meat and suet of a fatty ram, cut it up and clean it before placing it in a pot with salt, olive oil, pepper, ginger, coriander seeds, a few onions, and a bit of water and *murrī*. Place it over a fire until everything has gently cooked, and the liquid has dried out. Stir the meat until it has browned. Then, take the pot down from the fire and transfer the contents to a large ceramic bowl. Pour lime,

---

71 The quince stew was commonly known as a *safarjaliyya* (< *safarjal*, 'quince'); see Ibn Mubārak Shāh 2020: 79 (note 148). This recipe appears earlier on in Gayangos XVI (fol. 55r.), which completes this chapter with five hare recipes (fol. 69v.), which correspond to recipes Nos. 177 and 178 below.

72 The section in brackets is omitted from the edition, and was taken from BL Or5927, fol. 140r.

73 The name of the dish means 'of the fields, or countryside' (*faḥṣ*, 'field, meadow', but also 'district' or 'suburb'), as well as 'peasant'. Corriente 1997: 391; Dozy 1881: II, 243. Also see recipe No. 204.

zanbūʿ or fresh sour grape vinegar on the meat. Eat and enjoy, Allah the Exalted willing.

133. Another dish, which is made with macerated *murrī*

Take the required amount of fatty ram meat, and cut it up into small pieces. Clean and put the pieces in a new pot with salt, olive oil, pepper, coriander seeds, a bit of cut onion, a sufficient amount of *murrī* and good-quality water. Put the pot over a fire to cook. When everything is done and the meat is tender, set the pot on embers to simmer down. Transfer to a large ceramic bowl and add any of the above-mentioned vinegars that you like. Eat and enjoy, Allah the Exalted willing.

134. *Shiwā' qidr* (pot roast)[74]

Take the required amount of meat from the best cuts of a fatty yearling ram and add some parts with suet as well as some of the coiled small intestines and the large intestines. Cut the meat into small pieces, clean them without washing, and put them in a new pot. Take the small intestine, split it open, wash the insides and clean it. Chop it up into small pieces and put them in the pot with the meat. Take the large intestine, turn it inside out, and then scrape, clean and wash it before cutting it up and adding it to the meat. [Seal the top of the pot with dough or soaked paper][75] and take it to the oven, but make sure you keep stirring it. When you know that everything is done, take the pot out of the oven. You will have prepared crushed cinnamon, pepper, ginger and salt. Open the pot and add these to it in sufficient amounts, but not too much. Stir the pot until the meat, aromatics and salt are mixed together. Then, transfer the contents of the pot to a large ceramic bowl and sprinkle on cinnamon and ginger. If you want, you can also add one of the vinegars we have mentioned. Eat this and enjoy, Allah the Exalted willing.

74 Gayangos XVI (fol. 55v.) adds that it is 'good'. According to al-Uryūlī (1983: No. 82), oven roasts are slow to digest, very nutritious, and constipating, especially if they are made with lean meat, but less so if fatty meat is used. Al-Qumrī (1001: 79) defines *shiwā* as 'any meat which is hung in the *tannūr*, or something like it, and becomes roasted'.

75 The instruction in brackets is an addition from Gayangos XVI (*ibid.*).

135. Another dish, called *lawziyya*[76] (almond stew)
Carve up the required amount of meat and suet of a fatty yearling ram. Wash and clean the pieces, and put them in a new pot. Make a cloth sachet with clean salt, plenty of ginger, or coriander seeds and a bit of onion. Tie up the cloth and put it in the pot with a generous helping of olive oil. Put it over a fire, and stir it from time to time until the meat releases its juices and starts to whiten. Add hot water – not too much – in order to make a broth, and leave the pot on the fire. Then, take sweet peeled almonds which have been washed in cold water and dried in a cloth, and pound them in a clean wooden mortar until you obtain a mass with a marrow-like consistency, and they have released their oil. Remove the mixture and put it in a covered container so as to protect it from dust. Take the pot, transfer the contents to a large bowl and put the meat piece by piece in a separate vessel.[77] Strain the broth through a clean cloth. Wash the pot to get rid of whatever is in there, and then return it to the fire. Put the strained broth and meat back in. When it has heated up, add the crushed almonds and carefully stir to dissolve them. Continue to cook until the fat rises to the surface, and then remove the fire from underneath the pot. Leave it on embers to simmer down before serving in a ceramic bowl. Eat and enjoy, Allah the Exalted willing. Feel free to also add meatballs, if you wish.

If you like, you can make the dish with lime juice, in which case you should pour it in the pot after the almonds have been cooked. Leave until it has come to a boil once or twice, and then let the pot simmer down on embers before serving. Eat and enjoy, Allah the Exalted willing.

76 *Wuṣla* is the only other cookery book that contains a recipe by this name, but it is very different, and made with chicken (No. 5.62).

77 This sentence was amended with the help of BL Or5927 (fol. 141r.) as the edition (2012: 118) has the erroneous 'transfer to a large bowl in a separate vessel'.

136. Another Eastern dish cooked with taro[78]

It is made exactly like the meat-and-turnip dish, except that you use thin and young taro, which is peeled, cleaned, cut into small slices and then boiled in water and salt. Wash the slices and add them to the meat. After everything is done, add a bit of lime juice, which enhances the flavour. Eat and enjoy, Allah the Exalted willing.

137. Another Eastern dish, called *ṭabāhijiyya*[79]

Take fatty ram meat and cut it into thin finger-length pieces, and then chop those up into smaller chunks. Separate out the fat and lean meat.[80] Take the fatty meat chunks on the bottom of the pot and cook until the fat oozes out and melts, after which you add the lean meat on top. Do not stir, so that it boils in its own juices. When the meat has come to a boil, add salt, pepper, caraway and coriander seeds. Stir, and cover the pot. It is ready to be eaten very quickly.

If you want it to be sour, add sour pomegranate juice to the meat. Eat and enjoy, Allah the Exalted willing.

---

78 *qulqās*; this is one of only three occurrences of taro in the Western Muslim cookbooks (also see recipes Nos. 378, 392). Though it is found in a Syrian cookbook (*Wuṣla*, Nos 6.40–4) and *Taṣānīf* (fol. 5r.), the taro is mainly associated with Egypt, where it was an important crop. See Ibn Mubārak Shāh 2020: Nos. 41 (also note 100), 304; *Kanz*, Nos. 56, 69, 70, 88–90, 746, App. Nos. 10, 24; *Waṣf*, 310, 325–6, 327, 328, 340, 349, 364. It was also known as *banṭīqus* or *tirās al-Turk* ('Turkish shields'), while *saysārūn* denoted the root. According to al-Ishbīlī (2004–10: No. 4222), it 'grows in salt marshes and is used in orchards for its beautiful appearance and large leaves'; also see *ibid.*, Nos. 911, 4460. Al-Isrā'ilī (1992: 442–3) held that it is slightly astringent, difficult to digest and bloating. However, if one drinks its flour in a broth, it strengthens the stomach and suppresses diarrhoea.

79 These fried slices of meat (also *ṭabāhija)* were very popular in the Near East, and there are recipes in almost all of the culinary treatises. See Ibn Mubārak Shāh 2020: 105 (note 496). Ibn al-Ḥashshā' (1932: 61, No. 571) stated that it was equivalent to *kabāb*, i.e. 'meat fried with sheep's tail fat or sesame oil which is spiced and used either rolled into chickpea-sized balls, or not'. Al-Qumrī (1991: 80) defined it as 'what is cut from meat and then roasted in any kind of fat, whether it be olive oil, clarified butter, walnut oil, etc.' According to al-Warrāq (1987: 219), the difference between *ṭabāhija* and *maqlī* ('fried') dishes is that the former contain a sauce and vegetables (esp. aubergine), while the meat is sliced, whereas *maqlī* is made with meat chopped to the size of a hazelnut and without vegetables.

80 *laḥm aḥmar* ('red meat'), which denoted meat without fat; Ibn al-Ḥashshā' 1932: 68 (No 638).

138. Another Eastern *ṭabāhijiyya*, to suit all temperaments
Take meat, cut it into small strips and put them in a bowl with vinegar. Leave it for a while, until the meat has absorbed the vinegar. Then take it out and squeeze it well with both hands to expel all of the vinegar. Take a pot, pour in olive oil, and put it over a fire. When the oil starts to boil, add the meat and fry it until golden. Put vinegar, *murrī*, coriander seeds, oregano and saffron in a bowl. Leave for a little while and strain. Pour the resultant liquid over the meat. Gently stir the pieces of meat so that they absorb the broth. Remove from the fire, and eat, Allah the Exalted willing.

139. Another Eastern dish, called a covered (*maghmūma*) *ṭabāhijiyya*[81]
Take meat of a fatty ram and cut the lean parts into medium-sized strips, and those with suet into small strips. Take a new pot and pour in a generous amount of olive oil. Layer the pieces with the fat at the bottom, and place the lean meat on top of it. Add salt, pepper, coriander seeds, caraway, good-quality vinegar and a little *murrī*. Chop up some dry cheese into small pieces and spread them all over the meat. Do not stir until everything is done, and then eat and enjoy, Allah the Exalted willing.

81 Gayangos XVI (fol. 56v.) praises it as being 'amazing'. The *maghmūma* was also a dish in its own right, the term referring to the fact that the pot was covered with bread at the end of the cooking process, thus 'hiding' the content, as the cheese does in this particular recipe. See Ibn Mubārak Shāh 2020: 112 (note 503). The *Andalusian* also has a 'covered *ṭabāhijiyya*' (*Anwāʿ*, 124; BNF fol. 47r.), which is slightly different, however, and contains no eggs. Also see recipe No. 221. The same manual has several other *maghmūm* dishes (*Anwāʿ*, 23, 96–7, 200–1; BNF, fols. 9v., 15r., 39r.), one of which (23; fol. 15r.) is attributed to the already-mentioned Abbasid caliph and gastronome Ibrāhīm Ibn al-Mahdī (779–839). Also see recipe No. 222.

140. Another dish cooked with green broad beans, called *fustuqiyya*[82]
Take what you have selected from the best cuts of the meat and suet of a fatty yearling ram. Cut them up, wash and clean them, and put them in a new pot with salt, olive oil, coriander seeds, a little cumin, and a bit of onion. Put the pot on the fire and stir until the meat releases its juices and starts to whiten. Add hot water to make a broth and leave to cook. Then peel and wash fresh, tender green broad beans, and put them in a clean pot with fresh water. Put the pot over the fire and leave it until the beans are cooked. Put a small pot on top of it, and if the water with the beans dries out before they are done, pour in some hot water (from the smaller pot) and leave to cook. When you see that the beans are done, remove the pot from the fire. Use a large ladle to vigorously stir the beans until you obtain a marrow-like consistency, and then set aside. Check the meat and, if you find that it is done, add the beans, stirring gently. Remove the heat from underneath the pot and let it cook some more over a gentle fire. Then, crush fresh suet with fresh coriander or mint leafstalks and add it to the pot with the meat and the beans. Also add some fresh coriander juice. Bring it to a boil and leave it on embers to simmer down. Serve in a large ceramic bowl. Eat and enjoy, Allah the Exalted willing.

141. Another dish cooked with ground dried broad beans called *baysār*
Take the meat, suet and small intestines of a fatty yearling ram, and cut, wash and clean them. Put everything in a new pot with salt, olive oil, pepper, coriander seeds, cumin and a cut-up onion. Put the pot over a fire and stir from time to time until the meat releases its juices and starts to whiten. Add hot water to make a broth and leave the pot on the fire to cook. Then, wash the broad beans[83] several times with

---

82 Gayangos XVI (fol. 56v.) includes that it is 'good'. Derived from *fustuq* ('pistachio'), it originally denoted a pistachio stew, for which several recipes can be found in the Near Eastern cookery books. The thirteenth-century physician 'Abd al-Laṭīf al-Baghdādī (2021: 116; trans., 117) was particularly taken by it, though he said it was fattening. He attributed the preference of Egyptians for pistachios (rather than almonds) to the fact that they clear obstructions in the liver. However, in al-Andalus and North Africa, the word was applied to bean stews in reference to a similarity in appearance. Ibn Mubārak Shāh 2020: 19 (note 62), 26, 28, 122; al-Mālikī 1994: II, 101. Also see recipe No. 379 below.

83 Gayangos XVI (fol. 57r.) uses the word *baysār* here, as opposed to *fūl* in the other

hot water, coat them with olive oil and put them in a new pot which has been rubbed with olive oil. Add hot water, a whole onion, a whole garlic bulb, cumin and fennel. Put the pot over a fire to cook but do not stir until the broad beans are done. If the water dries out before they are cooked, add some more hot water and leave until done. [Remove the onion and garlic.][84] Then, take salt and put it in a bowl. Take a ladle to the pot, stir the broad beans and add salt to it. Stir the beans with the bowl of the ladle until they have dissolved and absorbed the salt. Set aside and then check whether the meat is done. If it is, add the broad beans bit by bit so they fully blend with the meat. Leave the pot on embers for a while until it cools down, and then serve in a large ceramic bowl. Eat and enjoy, Allah the Exalted willing.

142. Another dish, cooked with ground chickpeas[85]
Take meat from a yearling ram such as the tailhead, tail fat, or the breast. Cut it up and wash it, and place it in a new pot. Peel and grind chickpeas and add them to the pot with the meat, together with hot water, plenty of olive oil, salt, pepper and a crushed onion. Put the pot over a fire to cook. When it comes to a boil, reduce the fire underneath and leave over a gentle heat until the chickpeas are dissolved, after which remove the meat. Whisk the chickpeas with a ladle until they have completely dissolved, and then put the meat back in, together with as much good-quality vinegar as desired. Leave the pot on embers for a while. Serve in a large ceramic bowl, and eat, Allah the Exalted willing.[86]

copies.
84 Addition from Gayangos XVI (fol. 57v.).
85 This recipe is missing from Gayangos XVI.
86 The religious formula is included in BL Or5927 (fol. 142v.), but missing from the printed edition.

143. Another Eastern dish called *ṭifshīla*[87]

Take yearling ram meat like in the previous recipe, and cut it up into small pieces. Wash the meat and put it in a new pot with salt, plenty of olive oil, pepper, coriander seeds and a sliced onion. Place the pot on a fire and stir from time to time until the meat releases its juices and starts to whiten. Add a medium amount of hot water to make a broth, and leave the pot to cook. Then, take chickpeas, crush them until you obtain the consistency of *darmak* flour, and then sift with a hair sieve. Next, remove the meat from the pot piece by piece, place them in a large ceramic bowl, and cover it. Strain the broth with a clean cloth. Then, wash the pot clean and return it to the fire. Throw in the strained broth and meat, and add saffron which has been crushed and dissolved in water, crushed cinnamon and as much good-quality vinegar as desired. When everything is cooked to a turn, use a ladle to gradually add chickpea flour and stir until it is fully absorbed and the mixture has thickened. Take care not to burn or spoil it. Then, remove the pot from the fire, and serve the dish in a large ceramic bowl. Eat and enjoy, Allah the Exalted willing.

144. The Arab (*ʿArabī*) dish[88]

Take the required amount of fatty ram meat, cut it up, wash, clean and place in a new pot with salt, olive oil, pepper, coriander seeds, a little cumin, soaked chickpeas, a lot of peeled almonds, a medium amount of *murrī*, a sliced onion, citron leaves and a fennel stalk. Put the pot over a fire and stir until the meat releases its juices and starts to whiten. Pour in hot water to make a broth and leave the pot on the heat to cook. When the meat and chickpeas are done, crush saffron in a copper mortar and throw it in the pot to thoroughly colour the meat

---

87 In Gayangos XVI (fol. 57v.), it is called *mishliyya*, which is not attested elsewhere. This kind of dish was also known as *ṭafshīl*, and recipes can be found in al-Warrāq (1987:170–1) and al-Baghdādī (1964: 54; trans., 74–5). Usually, it contained lentils and chickpeas, and various types of beans. Ibn al-Ḥashshāʾ (1932: 61, No. 571) said that it was food made with pulses such as broad beans or chickpeas. Corriente (1997: 331) traces the origin of the word to a blend of *ṭabshīlā* and *ṭassa* ('wooden bowl'). It was still eaten in the eighteenth century, and is described by al-Shāṭirī (fol. 38v.) as 'any kind of food made from legumes (*al-qattānī*), that is to say, pulses such as lentils and grass peas, etc.' Kazimirski (1860: II, 89) identified it as a lentil soup.

88 Gayangos XVI (fol. 57v.) adds that it is 'good'. In the *Andalusian* (*Anwāʿ*, 114; BNF, fol. 52v.), a recipe by this name is an aubergine dish which does not contain chickpeas.

and the chickpeas. Remove the fire from underneath the pot, and set it on embers to simmer down. Then serve and eat, Allah the Exalted willing.

You can also make this dish with veal if you like. At banquets, this variant is decorated with a garniture[89] and split eggs. Remember this.

145. A mustard dish (*ṣinābī*),[90] which is good for a weak, cold stomach

Take young fatty ram meat, clean and cut it, and put the pieces in a clean pot with salt, olive oil, coriander seeds, pepper, some garden rue, a little bit of onion and a ladleful of vinegar. Put the pot over a gentle fire. When [the meat] is fried, pour on enough water and cook until it is done. Then, take grated crumbs of leavened bread, beat them with eggs and two spoonfuls of excellent mustard, and use this mixture to crust the dish. When it has set, remove the pot from the heat and leave until the fat gathers at the surface. Serve and then enjoy, Allah the Exalted willing.

146. Another dish

Take the side of a yearling ram with the breast, and cut the ribs with a cleaver until they are broken from one end to the other, but without separating them. The ribs should be broken in three places. Thoroughly rub the side with salt and pepper, and put it in a large, glazed, wide-bottomed casserole dish. Put it in the oven away from the fire until the meat is done and browned. Then turn it over onto the other side so that it can also brown. Afterwards, take it out of the oven and eat, Allah the Exalted willing. If you like, you can also add some of the aforementioned vinegars, or eat it with mustard.

If you prefer to spit-roast the ram, put it on an iron or wooden spit with fire around it, but at a distance from it. Gently roast the meat until it is done and leave it intact, in its original shape. If you wish, you can cut it up and break the ribs with a cleaver and cut [the side] lengthwise before skewering it on the spit and roasting it after gingerly rubbing in

89 See recipe No. 108.

90 *ṣināb* (< Latin *sinapi*) denoted either 'mustard' (more usually *khardal*) or, especially in the Near East, a mustard-raisin paste (see recipes Nos. 409–10), which was used as a dip (*ṣibāgh*). Ibn Khalṣūn (1996: 163; trans., 92) included it in his list of *kawāmikh* (fermented condiments). There is a similar recipe in *Anwāʿ*, 5 (BNF, fol. 3r.).

salt and pepper until it is done. Eat and enjoy, Allah the Exalted willing.

147. Another variation

Take fatty ram meat from the thighs and the backstrap with the suet. Cut it into thin strips with a knife and add crushed salt, a sufficient amount of crushed oregano, and pepper. Turn the meat over with your hands to make sure the pieces absorb the salt and spices. Then, take a gridiron prepared for roasting strips and put it over a medium fire that does not produce flames or smoke. Layer the strips on the gridiron and, when they have browned on one side, turn them over to cook them on the other side until they are all done. Then remove the strips and put others on until you have used all of them. Do not cover them, except with something that allows the steam to escape. When the meat is ready to eat, place a bowl with macerated *murrī* and another with mustard on the table, and dunk the strips in either one, in accordance with your taste. Eat and enjoy, Allah the Exalted willing.

If you want to roast a yearling ram in the *tannūr*, skewer the entire animal, from tail to neck, on a wooden spit. Cut the forelegs at the joints, and the hind shanks at the hock. Also cut off the tailhead, tail fat and haunches.[91] Then, take the tripe, intestines and heart, and clean everything. Cut these up, fashion into a large roll on a spit, wrapped with caul fat and intestines tied around it.[92] Then, take a spit and put the animal on it so that it will be roasted on both sides. Put the tail and its fat on it, and stuff the legs and shanks inside the cavity. Heat up the *tannūr* until it is white hot and then put an earthenware casserole dish at the bottom of it. Insert the ram into the *tannūr*, placing one end of the spit in the casserole. Do the same with the spit with the tripe roll. Cover the *tannūr* and seal the lid with mud so that the steam cannot escape. Close off all the vents in the same way and leave it closed until you know that the ram is cooked. Then, open up the *tannūr*, remove the animal and put it on whatever you like by way of mint, fennel, myrtle, etc. After you take the ram out of the oven, you can also sprinkle on mint vinegar, if you like, and season with aromatics. Put crushed salt in front of the diners when serving. Eat

91 The edition (2012: 124) has the singular *warakahu*, rather than the more logical dual *warakayhu*, which appears in BL Or5927 (fol. 143v.).

92 See recipe No. 7.

and enjoy, Allah the Exalted willing.

148. Another dish, called *al-kāmil* ('the complete')[93]

Take a fatty yearling ram, slaughter it and skin it. Make a narrow opening in between its thighs that is big enough to put your hand through to remove everything that is inside. After washing the blood away[94] and cleaning the carcass, set it aside. Take as many plump pullets as you need, as well as fatty squabs, turtledoves and sparrows, and cook them in any way you like. Then, make a pottage[95] with grated breadcrumbs beaten with egg whites and all the spices (you have to hand). Stuff everything inside the birds that have been prepared for this. Then, take the birds one by one and put them inside the ram until it is full. Add the remainder of the pottage, together with the usual (boiled) egg yolks, meatballs, pickled limes and olives. Tightly sew up the opening with thread. Put the ram as it is in the *tannūr*, cover it [and seal with clay],[96] and leave for a little while. Then, take the animal out, and grease it from top to bottom with marinated *murrī* vinegar, a little saffron, pepper and oregano. Also remember to sprinkle the inside of the ram with this mixture before filling it with the stuffing. Then, return it to the *tannūr*, [seal it with clay,][97] and leave until it is done. Serve after taking it out, Allah the Almighty willing.

149. Another dish, called *aknāf*[98]

Take a yearling ram, cut its joints and ribs into three equal parts. Dig a hole in the ground [and put live coal in it.][99] Place the neck in and, on top of it, the meat, piece by piece. Then, take a large casserole dish and cover the meat with it. Pack soil along the sides of the casserole

93 Gayangos XVI (fol. 58v.) adds that is 'amazing'. A similar recipe is found in the *Andalusian*: *Anwāʿ*, 10 (BNF, fols. 4v.–5r.).

94 This is the only recipe where the removal of the animal's blood is mentioned, which has great ritual importance since it is specifically prohibited as food in the Qur'ān (2:173), alongside 'carrion, pig's meat and animals over which any name other than God's has been invoked'.

95 *ḥasw:* see recipes Nos. 33–40 above.

96 Addition from Gayangos XVI (fol. 59r.).

97 Addition from Gayangos XVI (*ibid.*).

98 This is the plural of *kanaf* ('side'). The recipe precedes the *kāmil* in Gayangos XVI (fol. 58v.), where it is called *kabāb*.

99 Addition from Gayangos XVI (fol. 58v.).

so that the steam from the meat cannot escape. Put firewood along the sides of the casserole and set it alight. Leave the pot for as long as you reckon it takes for the meat to turn golden brown on top. Then move the firewood aside, lift the casserole and turn over the meat so that the bottom is now on top. Cover it again with the casserole dish, and return the firewood. Leave until you know that the meat is done roasting and browning, and then remove the fire and lift the casserole. Transfer the meat to a dish, sprinkle on salt and pepper and then eat and enjoy, Allah the Exalted willing.

150. Another dish, cooked with honey and called *al-muʿassal* ('the honeyed')[100]

Take fatty ram meat from the tailhead, breast and other similar parts with fat, as well as kidney suet. Cut it up into small pieces, clean them and place them a new pot with salt, plenty of olive oil, coriander seeds and a sufficient amount of water. Take the pot to the fire for cooking. Next, take enough good-quality honey and heat it up in a cauldron so that it releases its foam, and then skim and strain it. Remove the meat from the pot and set it aside. Strain the broth and put it to one side. Wash the pot to clean it, and return it to the fire. Pour the honey in, followed by the meat and the broth. Then take one and a half *ūqiyas* of starch for every *raṭl* of honey and dissolve it in water. Carefully strain it into a pot while stirring continuously to make sure that the starch does not curdle. Colour with a bit of saffron and leave the pot on embers to simmer down and until the fat appears on the surface. Then, eat this and enjoy, Allah the Exalted willing.

100 In Gayangos XVI (fol. 58v.), the title is simply 'dish with honey'. There is a similar recipe in the *Andalusian* (*Anwāʿ*, 197–8; BNF, fol. 49r.). Also see recipe No. 390 for a sweet *muʿassal*. The word simply means 'added or thickened with honey'.

151. Another dish, known as *al-ghassāniyya*[101]

Take the aforementioned meat, and clean it before placing it in a new pot with water, salt, plenty of olive oil, coriander seeds and skimmed honey. Put the pot on the fire and cook until the meat is done. Then, take semolina, wash it several times with hot water, and gradually add it to the pot with the meat while stirring it, until you have used it all. Taste it, and if it is not sweet, add some honey. If it is runny, add some semolina until you have the right consistency. Stir and, if the oil rises to the surface, leave it; if not, add more oil (and leave) until the semolina is done. Move the pot away from the fire and colour with a bit of saffron before serving.[102] Eat and enjoy, Allah the Exalted willing.

152. Another dish, called *Ra's Maymūn* ('the blessed head')[103]

Take meat from a fatty ram, from the loins and coiled small intestines, and cut it up into small pieces. Wash and clean them and then put them in a new pot with salt, plenty of olive oil, pepper, coriander seeds, cumin, a few sliced onions, peeled almonds, soaked chickpeas, a ladleful of *murrī*, cloves of garlic, citron leaves and a fennel stalk. Put the pot on the fire and stir until the meat releases its juices and starts to whiten. Add hot water to it and leave on the fire until cooked. Then, crush saffron in a copper mortar and bloom it in fresh water before adding it to the pot with the meat for colouring. Afterwards, pour in the requisite amount of good-quality vinegar. Take the usual number of eggs for the pot and crack them in a bowl. Separate out the yolks and put them in

---

101 The *Andalusian* (*Anwāʿ*, 197; BNF, fol. 69r.) has a vaguely similar dish, incorrectly named as *al-lawz al-ghassānī* ('*ghassānī* almonds'), instead of *al-lawn al-ghassānī* ('the *ghassānī* dish'). In Gayangos XVI (fol. 59v.), it is called *al-ghassānī*, which in the present text also denotes a sweet (No. 393) and even a type of couscous (No. 87). As a result, one may conjecture that there were two types of *ghassāniyyas*, one made with meat, and the other a sweet. The former was more common in al-Andalus (Corriente 1997: 370). The latter variety was the usual one in North Africa, and Abū Bakr al-Mālikī (eleventh century) recounts that it was made with semolina, honey and saffron (1994: II, 448–9). The origins of the name of the dish are unknown but in all likelihood reflect a link – either real or imaginary – to an individual by that name, though there may also be a connection with the famous Ghassanids, a tribal group from the Arabian Peninsula who ruled the Hejaz and parts of the Levant until the Muslim conquest of the area.

102 Gayangos XVI (fol. 59v.) adds that it should be left for a bit (*qalīlan*) before serving, but omits colouring it with saffron.

103 Also see recipe No. 68.

the pot. Add salt, pepper, ginger, cinnamon and a little crushed saffron to the remainder (of the eggs). Once the meat is done, transfer it to a dish by itself, and strain the broth. Remove the citron leaves, fennel stalks and the sediment from the pot. Then, take glazed earthenware vessels that are especially made for this dish; they should be narrow at the bottom and wide at the top. Put them over a fire with two *ūqiyas* of olive oil. When it has come to a boil, take the meat, chickpeas and almonds, and mix them with the eggs. Put the resultant mixture in the earthenware vessels on top of a solid egg yolk you have put into each of them. Do not completely fill the vessels. Take the fat from the strained broth and put it with the olive oil. When the eggs have set and the olive oil and fat have almost dried out, remove the dishes from the fire [and leave them on hot embers].[104] When serving in a large ceramic bowl, tip the contents of the earthenware vessels in the middle of it, and you should be left with something that looks like a sugar loaf. Finally, take a ladleful of the garniture pot, as mentioned above,[105] and pour it on top. Decorate with split eggs, sprinkle on aromatic spices and then eat, Allah the Exalted willing.

153. *Balāja*[106] (tripe casserole)

Take the wind-pipe[107] together with everything else, except the spleen; cut everything into large pieces, and clean them. Take the coiled small intestines, wash them, and cut them up. Put everything in a new pot with water, salt, olive oil, pepper, coriander seeds and onions split in half, as many as you want. Put the pot over a fire. When it is almost done, remove the contents of the pot and place it on a wooden board.

---

104 Addition from Gayangos XVI (fol. 60r.).

105 See recipe No. 108.

106 In Gayangos XVI (fol. 60r.), the name of the recipe is given as *al-balajiyya al-asadiyya*, the lion's (*asad*, 'lion') *balāja*. There is a similar recipe in the *Andalusian* (*Anwāʿ*, 27; BNF, fol., 11r.), where it is explained that this dish is typical of Córdoba and Marrakech, and the areas in between them. This was sold ready-made at market, but was subject to a great deal of corruption, as unscrupulous vendors (*ballājīs*) reportedly used rotten meat they boiled repeatedly in water to make it look acceptable, bulking it up with bread, using turmeric, safflower, hairy onosma or dyers' buckthorn instead of saffron to colour the dish (al-Saqaṭī 1931: 39–40).

107 The only other cookbook that has a wind-pipe recipe is al-Warrāq's (1987: 224), though *Taṣānīf* (fol. 71v.) has one for *tannūr*-roasted sheep's lungs.

Cut everything as finely as possible [with scissors].[108] Then, take a sufficient number of eggs, and crack them into a bowl. Add salt, lots of pepper, cinnamon, ginger (or, if you do not have ginger, use pellitory[109] instead), saffron and breadcrumbs. Beat everything together well. Take the strained broth, the chopped heart and the other meat, and put everything with the eggs. Then, take a glazed earthenware casserole dish and put olive oil into it. Add the egg-and-meat mixture and garnish the surface with egg yolks and almonds. Add some fat and then take it to the oven. Place it at a distance from the fire and leave until it is done and golden brown. After you take it out, let it cool down, and serve, Allah the Exalted willing.

If you want to make it with meat, [use the thighs and backstrap].[110] Do not cut it up and cook it in a new pot with salt and water. When it is done, take it out of the pot and tear it with your hands until it looks like the meat used for *harīsa*.[111] Put it in a glazed casserole dish and pour on eggs beaten with spices, as mentioned before. Throw in saffron and lots of good-quality olive oil, and then take it to the oven for cooking until it is done and golden brown. Add a lot of pepper, pellitory and ginger, and then serve, Allah the Exalted willing.

---

108 Addition from Gayangos XVI (fol. 60v.).

109 *'āqir qarḥā* (from Syriac, meaning 'bald root') was also known as *kundus* and, in the Islamic West, by its Berber name *tāghandasht*. The plant is native to Northwest Africa and was already used medicinally (especially its root) in Antiquity. In Arabic pharmacological literature it was sometimes confused with tarragon. Pellitory was thought to be useful against blockages and sciatica. In present-day Middle Eastern folk medicine, it is prescribed for toothache (in which case it is chewed) and even epilepsy. In cooking it was used very rarely – in fact, there is only one other recipe in the culinary literature that requires it (*Kanz*, No. 521). See Dietrich 1988: II, 421–3; al-Ishbīlī 2004–10: Nos. 1157, 3315; Ibn Janāḥ 2021: Nos. 422, 696, 1008; al-Kindī 1966; 301–2; Dalby 2003: 25; Ibn Jazla, fol. 151v.

110 Addition from Gayangos XVI (fol. 60v.), which is the only copy to specify the cuts that need to be used.

111 See recipe No. 188.

154. Another dish, which the Andalusians call *qaliyya*[112]

Take the wind-pipe, as described above, as well as the tripe and small intestines. Boil the tripe in hot water until it has turned white. Clean, wash and split the intestines. Chop up the wind-pipe, tripe and intestines and put them in an earthenware or iron casserole dish. Add water, salt, olive oil, pepper, coriander seeds, a spoonful of macerated *murrī*, cumin and a sliced onion. Put the casserole dish over a fire for cooking. When it is done, add the required amount of good-quality vinegar, and leave the pot on the fire until the vinegar has boiled once or twice. Then, remove the dish from the fire, and eat and enjoy, Allah the Exalted willing.

Chapter Three: on lamb meat

155. A dish called *al-badīʿī* ('the wondrous')[113]

Take the breast, sides, tail and other similar parts of a lamb. Chop them up into small rather than medium-sized pieces and place them in a new pot with salt, water, plenty of olive oil, pepper, coriander seeds and a few cut onions. Put the pot over a fire and, when the meat is almost done, take fresh cheese that is two or three days old. Wash it with fresh water and cut it up into thin, square slices, the size of your palm. Take as many eggs as you like and crack them in a bowl. Remove five or

112 This term (plural *qalāyā*) is derived from the verb *qalā* ('to fry') and is used for a number of dishes with fried meat in culinary treatises: *Anwāʿ*, 41–2, 123 (BNF, fols. 17r., 47r.); al-Warrāq 1987: 210–15 (a total of twenty-seven dishes). According to al-Uryūlī (1983: No. 81), when meat is fried with fat or clarified butter it is moist, very nutritious, but slow to digest; when fried in oil it is lighter and more easily digestible, and strengthens the body. Any harmful effects can be counteracted with mustard and brine. Al-Qumri (1991: 80) explains it as follows: 'It is meat that is cut up and fried in a pot, after which water is poured and it is left to boil until the water has reduced and the meat remains, moist and broken up. Then, all of the necessary vegetables and herbs (*buqūl*), spices (*abāzīr*) and aromatics (*afāwīh*), in accordance with the (diner's) condition and time, are added.' According to Corriente (1997: 441), *qaliyya* denoted a fricassee of rabbits' livers and lights. In Persian (Safavid) cooking, *qaliye* tended to refer to fruity, sweet-and-sour meat stews; Afshār 1981: 145–56.

113 A similar recipe for this meat-topped omelette dish can be found in a thirteenth-century Syrian cookery book (*Wuṣla*, No. 6.133), where it is called a *badīʿiyya* and is said to be a North African speciality. It is similar in its use of cheese, eggs and spices, but also includes meatballs. The *Andalusian* has three *badīʿī* recipes (*Anwāʿ*, 11, 25–6; BNF, fols. 5r., 10r.–v.).

more yolks and set them aside. Then, add the eggs, pepper, ginger, cinnamon, saffron, fresh coriander and mint juice to the meat and beat everything well to mix. Take the cheese, put it in a bowl and stir it with the eggs and with saffron to colour it. Colour the meat with saffron, but do not use too much. Check the meat and, if it is done, remove it from the pot and set it aside. Strain the broth and put it to one side as well. Take a large, glazed casserole dish, pour in olive oil and put a layer of cheese at the bottom, with one of cooked meat on top of it. Continue alternating the cheese and meat layers until you run out of both. Carefully skim the fat from the broth and put it in the casserole. Pour in the beaten eggs, immersing the meat and cheese, and garnish with the egg yolks and peeled almonds. Add a little broth and sprinkle on aromatic spices of your choosing. Take the dish to the oven, and place it out of reach of the flames. Let it cook and brown. Once it is browned on top and the liquid has dried out, stir and let the pot cool down. Eat and enjoy, Allah the Exalted willing. You can also make this recipe with suckling kid meat or a plump chicken. Remember this, and act according to your preference.

156. Another dish, called *muʿallak*[114]

Take a whole fatty suckling lamb, but do not use the head, tripe and intestines. Cut the animal from joint to joint, clean and place the parts in a large earthenware or iron cauldron with salt. Rub the meat until it grows tender and releases its liquid. Then, take fresh cheese that is about three days old, clean it, cut it up and put it in with the meat, stirring the pot with a ladle. Keep stirring until the meat and cheese are thoroughly mixed together. If the meat is fatty, you can use its fat, rather than olive oil or butter, which is best; if not, add olive oil or butter, whichever is the most suitable, and leave until the meat is done and starts to brown. At that point, do not add any more butter and leave on a moderate fire to simmer. Serve in a tureen and eat, Allah

114 A similar recipe is found in the *Andalusian* (*Anwāʿ*, 167; BNF, fols. 59v.–60r.), which also includes breadcrumbs and milk. Its name is related to *ʿilk* ('gum', with *ʿilk al-Rūm*, 'Byzantine gum', or *ʿilk al-Anbāṭ*, 'Nabataean gum', denoting mastic), and *muʿallak* would translate as 'added with gum', in reference to the sticky white sauce in the dish. Ibn Janāḥ 2020: Nos. 83, 562, 715, 721; Dietrich 1988: II, 354; al-Ishbīlī 2004–10: Nos. 3429, 3479–82; al-Kindī 1966: 306; Corriente 1997: 362 ('bird-lime'); Nasrallah [al-Warrāq 2007]: 653.

the Exalted willing. Dust with cinnamon and pepper if these spices are available. This type of food is mostly made by itinerant shepherds. Remember this.

157. Another dish

Take whatever good parts of a lamb you like, clean them, and place them in an iron casserole dish with water, salt, olive oil, pepper, coriander seeds, a piece of onion and as much macerated *murrī* as you like. Put the casserole over a fire and, when the meat is nearly done, add some saffron dissolved in water if you want to colour the dish. Then, take it to the oven to complete the cooking and brown it. When you remove the casserole from the oven leave it until it has lost some of its heat, and then eat and enjoy, Allah the Exalted willing. If you like, you can make it with fish *murrī* instead of macerated *murrī*, as this goes well with it, with the strength of Allah.[115]

158. Another dish

Take whatever good parts of a lamb you like, and cut and clean them before placing them in a new pot with salt, olive oil, pepper, coriander seeds, a bit of cut-up onion and macerated *murrī*. Put the pot over a fire and, when the meat has started to release its juices and is almost done, pour in hot water. Take truffles, wash them, remove the outer peel, and pull them apart with your hands. Add the pieces to the meat to cook and, when everything is done, set the pot on embers to cool down. Eat and enjoy, Allah the Exalted willing. If you like, you can boil the truffles in water and salt before adding them to the meat. In fact, this is a better way of doing things. Or, if you prefer, you can make the dish with fish *murrī* instead of macerated *murrī*, Allah the Exalted willing.

159. Another dish

Deep-score a leg of lamb and put it in a new pot with salt, pepper, coriander seeds, two ladlefuls of vinegar, half a ladleful of *murrī*, and one ladleful of olive oil. Put the pot on a fire to cook. When it is half done, remove the leg from the pot and fry it in olive oil in an iron or glazed earthenware casserole dish. Then, take five eggs, some flour and

115 The religious formula is included in BL Or5927 (fol. 146v.), but missing from the printed edition.

breadcrumbs, and beat everything together. Return the leg to the pot with a little of the broth and add the eggs. Leave to cook. When it is done, return all of the broth to it and set it on embers to simmer down. Serve in a large ceramic bowl and then eat and enjoy, Allah the Exalted willing.

160. Another dish

Deep-score a leg of lamb and place it in a pot with salt, olive oil, vinegar, pepper, coriander seeds, and crushed almonds dissolved in water. Put the pot on a fire to cook. When the meat is done and browned, crust it with eggs and breadcrumbs. Leave the pot on the embers to simmer down. Eat and enjoy, Allah the Exalted willing.

161. Another dish

Take a side of ribs of a fatty lamb and push a knife in between the meat and ribs and gingerly separate them, but without cutting them entirely. Rub with salt, and set aside. Then, pound[116] meat from the legs and other parts and add a ladleful of olive oil, half a ladleful of macerated *murrī*, peeled almonds, a ladleful of fresh coriander juice, pepper, eggs and breadcrumbs. Crack the eggs and mix them with spices, breadcrumbs, and the rest. Take an earthenware or iron frying pan and pour in olive oil. When it is sizzling, take the pounded meat mixed with the eggs and the other ingredients, i.e. the stuffing, and put it in the pan over a moderate fire until it is done. Make sure not to overcook it. Carefully put the stuffing in the side of ribs of the lamb, in between the ribs and the flesh. Smear with *murrī*, place in a casserole dish, and take it to the oven. If you want to cook it at home, use a wide-mouthed pot. Wash the container in which you have made the stuffing with water and put it on top of the side of ribs in the pot. Place it so that the ribs face upwards and the meat and stuffing face downwards. Leave until everything is cooked, and then eat and enjoy, Allah the Exalted willing.

162. Another dish

Cut up and wash whatever meat you like of a fatty ram, and place the pieces in a new pot with sugar, good-quality honey, rose water, whole

116 Gayangos XVI (fol. 62v.) is the only manuscript which specifies that the meat should be pounded; in the other copies, the instruction is simply 'to take'.

crushed almonds, and hulled sesame seeds. Put the pot over a moderate fire and stir continually until the meat is done. Take two biscuits (*ka'k*), thoroughly crush them and put the crumbs in the pot, which should then be set on embers. Stir with a ladle until it sets, Allah the Exalted willing. Eat and enjoy, with the strength of Allah.

163. Another dish

Take a fatty tender lamb, cut open its belly but leave it whole, and then clean it. Smear with olive oil, salt, pepper and coriander, and leave for a little while. Then, take fresh cheese and rub it with your hands until you are left with crumbs. Add fresh coriander juice, pepper, cinnamon, mint juice and leafstalks, sweet olive oil and salt. Beat everything together well and stuff the mixture inside the lamb in between the thighs and underneath the sides of ribs. Take a bit of water, dissolve cheese into it and add eggs and spices before beating everything well. Put the lamb in a large casserole dish and add the water with the cheese and eggs to it. Take it to the oven and place it away from the fire. Once it is cooked and browned, take it out. Remember to sew up the abdomen of the lamb after stuffing it.

164. Another dish

Slaughter and skin a fatty lamb, and then make a small opening in the abdomen to remove the entrails. Clean it and then set aside. Next, take plump sparrows, starlings, plump turtledoves and squabs. Boil the turtledoves and squabs, remove the innards, and put them inside the lamb with macerated *murrī* in which saffron and pepper have been dissolved. Put the lamb in a large enough casserole dish and pour on a sauce made with olive oil, *murrī*, onion juice, fresh coriander juice, pepper, coriander seeds, saffron and whatever is left over from the stuffing. Put it in the oven and leave until it is done and the sides have browned. Then, remove from the oven, and eat, Allah the Exalted willing. This dish can also be made with kid, if you wish.

165. Another dish

Take a side of ribs of a fatty lamb and rub it with salt after separating the meat from the ribs, especially in the middle. Then, pound some other meat and add crushed almonds, breadcrumbs, a ladleful of fresh fennel juice and an egg. Beat everything together and add pepper, ginger, salt and cinnamon. Stuff this mixture in the lamb, between the meat and the ribs. Take some of the pounded meat, immerse[117] it in water, beat with two yolks, and stir. Put the side of ribs in an earthenware casserole dish and put the pounded meat mixture on top. Cook it for a while at home first, before sending it off to the communal oven. When it is done and has turned golden, remove it from the oven, and eat, Allah the Exalted willing.

166. Another dish

Take a side of ribs and the breast of a lamb and use a knife to separate the meat from the bones, but make sure that they remain in place. Then, take other meat and pound it with almonds, breadcrumbs, mint juice, salt and pepper. Stuff this mixture in between the meat and the ribs, and then put the lamb in a glazed casserole dish. Next, take the intestines, wash and chop them up. Add egg yolks and spices, and whisk. Take the casserole to the fire and pour on a sauce made with water, olive oil, pepper, coriander seeds, a few onions, and a ladleful of macerated *murrī*. When it is cooked, add the eggs with the minced intestines, but leave the broth aside. Then, take the casserole to the oven and place it away from the fire. When it is done, the water has dried out and the surface of the dish has turned golden, remove it from the oven, and leave to cool down. Eat and enjoy, Allah the Exalted willing.

167. Another dish

Take a whole fatty lamb, remove the entrails, wash and clean them, and make a sausage coil[118] with them. Take a large casserole dish or a small basin and put the lamb and the sausage coil in it. Take to the oven, but put it at a distance from the fire until it is done and turned golden. Remove from the oven, gently turn over the meat slab, and return it to the oven to brown the other side and head. Once it is golden brown, take it out, sprinkle on the aromatic spices of your choosing, and serve with crushed salt. Eat and enjoy, Allah the Exalted willing.

If you want to make it in the *tannūr*, put the lamb on an iron or wooden spit before roasting it in the *tannūr*. Use another skewer for

117 The Arabic text refers to 'dissolving' it (*taḥulluhu*).

118 See recipe No. 7.

the tripe coil. Put the ends of the skewers in a casserole dish at the bottom of the *tannūr* with a little bit of water so that it collects the lamb and intestinal fat. When the meat is done and has turned golden, open the *tannūr*, remove the dish and eat, Allah the Exalted willing.

168. Another Eastern dish, called *maḍīra* (sour milk stew)[119]

Take the head, breast, tailhead, backstrap and small ribs of a fatty lamb and put everything in a large new pot with enough water and salt to cook. When it is done, remove the meat and place it in a bowl. Take peeled almonds and crush them until you obtain a marrow-like consistency. Take freshly milked milk, strain it into a new pot and add two mashed onions to it. Put the pot over a fire and, when the milk has come to a boil, add the meat and let everything boil again before adding the crushed almonds. Top the dish with two eggs that have been whisked into a smooth mixture. Sprinkle on pepper when serving the meat and milk from the pot. Eat and enjoy, Allah the Exalted willing.

169. Another Eastern dish, also called *maḍīra*[120]

Take the head, breast, backstrap, tailhead, trotters and small ribs of a fatty lamb. Cut the meat up into medium-sized pieces and place them in a new pot with salt, butter and whole onions. Put the pot over a fire until it is cooked and the butter is boiling. Then, take thickened and soured buttermilk from the day before, and add it to the pot with the meat. Leave it on a moderate fire until it comes to a boil, and then crust the pot with yeast dough and fresh coriander. Serve with a sprinkling of pepper. Eat and enjoy, Allah the Exalted willing.

---

119 This was a very popular dish in the Near East, with a number of recipes across the cookery books; see Ibn Mubārak Shāh 2020: 157 (note 713). It was already well known in al-Andalus at the time al-Tujībī was writing, and was commonly sold in markets, where unscrupulous sellers would thicken the dish by adding some kind of flour (Buckley [al-Shayzarī 1999]: 58). Ibn Zuhr (1992: 21; trans., 56) considered it a harmful way of preparing lamb, since this should be cooked in a way that reduces its moisture content, with *murrī* or with plenty of oil or vinegar. Al-Uryūlī (1983: No 73), on the other hand, claimed that it is very nourishing, and suitable for the young but harmful for the phlegmatic and the old, and recommended making it with a lot of 'hot' spices (for example, pepper, cloves or cassia). According to Ibn Qutayba (1925–30: III, 298), it was cooked with mint, rue and celery.

120 Gayangos XVI (fol. 64r.) specifies that it is 'amazing'.

170. Another Eastern dish, called *muballaqa*[121]

Take the best meat from a fatty lamb, as described earlier, but not the head. Clean the meat and then put it in a new pot with salt, three onions, and lots of strained butter. Put the pot over a fire and, when the meat is done, add fresh strained milk. Stir the pot over a gentle fire until it comes to a boil. Then, take semolina bread, or whatever suits the milk broth, and crumble it as finely as you possibly can. Sift the crumbs with an esparto grass sieve before putting them in a clean wide-mouthed pot, and then add the broth with the milk. Pour in the butter until the mixture can no longer absorb any more. Transfer to a tureen and put the cooked meat on top. Eat and enjoy, Allah the Exalted willing.

If you want, you can cook the lamb meat in a white or green *tafāyā*,[122] or with spinach, leafy goosefoot, lettuce or purslane, as described in the above recipe, Allah the Exalted willing.

Chapter Four: on kid meat

171. Dish

Take any meat you like of a fatty suckling kid, clean it, and place in a glazed earthenware casserole dish with water, salt, olive oil, coriander seeds, and a sufficient amount of macerated *murrī*. Put the casserole over a fire and, when the meat is done, add a little crushed and dissolved saffron, if you like. Otherwise, just leave it and take the casserole to the oven for further cooking until it turns golden brown and the broth has reduced slightly. Then, remove from the oven and eat, Allah the Exalted willing.

If you want to cook suckling kid meat in a white or green *tafāyā*;[123] with mint, lemon balm, fennel, spinach, leafy goosefoot, lettuce, or

---

121 Gayangos XVI (fol. 64r.) has the nonsense form *ma/ulaqqabiyya*, and adds that it is 'good'. The edition (2012: 135) and other manuscripts (Wetzstein 1207, fol. 41r.; BL Or5927, fol. 148r.) have *muballaqa* (lit. 'speckled'), as does Corriente (1997: 64). However, this spelling is probably the result of metathesis, as the spelling *mulabbaqqa* can be found in al-Warrāq's treatise, which contains two recipes by this name (1987: 137, 206–7) for a type of fat-soaked *tharīda*. Further support for the latter spelling is the link with the verb *labbaqa*, which means 'to soften, tenderize' (with fat, for instance); Kazimirski 1860: II, 961.

122 See recipes Nos. 109–10, 191–2, 282–3.

123 See recipes Nos. 109–10, 191–2, 282–3.

purslane; in a *badīʿī*[124] with fresh cheese and truffles; or with green broad beans in a *fustuqiyya*,[125] then proceed as described in the two previous chapters, Allah the Exalted willing.

If you want to roast it whole in the brick oven or *tannūr*, do exactly the same things you did with the lamb above, Allah the Exalted willing.

Chapter Five: on wild and game meats[126]

172. Dish

Take meat from the breast, ribs and trotters, as well as parts with suet and fat from a deer,[127] bovine antelope,[128] ass, mountain goat,[129] or gazelle – whichever is available to you. Cut, wash and clean the meat before putting it in a large casserole with water, salt, olive oil, pepper, coriander seeds, cumin, a few cut onions, crushed and whole garlic, oregano or soaked chickpeas, peeled almonds or citron leaves, a fennel stalk, and a ladleful of good-quality *murrī*. Put the pot over a fire until the meat is done, and then add dissolved saffron. When it comes to a boil with the saffron, add as much good-quality vinegar as you like. Leave the casserole over a moderate fire until some of the liquid is reduced and the fat appears on the surface. Then, remove from the fire and let it cool down. Eat and enjoy, Allah the Exalted willing. This dish can also be made this way with hare, rabbit or hedgehog.[130] Bear this in

---

124 See recipe No. 155. This section has been amended slightly with BL Or5927, fol. 148v.

125 See recipes Nos. 140, 377.

126 Physicians such as Ibn Zuhr (1992: 25; trans., 58) held that all wild animals have a hot and dry temperament, are slow to digest, and constitute a harmful food, for which reason it is not advisable to eat their meat, especially that of the old ones. Game occurs infrequently in medieval Arab gastronomy, and no recipes can be found in the Egyptian and Syrian collections.

127 *a/iyyal*; this usually denoted a mountain goat (Kazimirski 1860: I, 74), but not in Andalusian Arabic; Corriente 1997: 34.

128 *baqar waḥsh*, 'wild cows', which, depending on the area, could denote a number of animals, most often a species of bovine antelope, such as members of the oryx family (for example, the North African scimitar oryx), or the Bubal hartebeest. Dozy 1881: I, 102; Lane 1863–74: I, 234.

129 *waʿl*, which could also refer to a deer, but not in Andalusian Arabic. Corriente 1997: 567; Dozy 1860: II, 822; de Alcalá 1505: fol. 119v. [VIIv] (*guâāl*); Kazimirski 1960: II, 1569.

130 This is the only cookery book that has a recipe calling for hedgehog (*qunfudh*). According to Ibn Zuhr (1992: 25–6; trans., 58), its meat has a pleasant taste, its tallow

mind and act accordingly.

173. Another dish

Take any meat that is available from the thighs, trotters, backstrap, loins or flanks. Cut the meat into slices and beat them on a wooden board with an iron stick made for *aḥrash* (flat minced meat cakes)[131] and *mirkās* sausages, or with a cleaver, until all the meat has been mashed up and you are left with a dough-like mixture. Add suet if you have it, and cut it up with the meat. Add sufficient amounts of salt, pepper, coriander seeds, cumin and vinegar. Then, take garlic and a little cut onion, pound them, and add water. Strain the water, add it to the minced meat in the kneading tub and thoroughly mix the meat, spices, etc. Take some of this meat and roast it over a fire. Taste it and, if everything is to your liking, leave it as is. If you do not like the taste, add whatever is lacking until you get the best flavour. Next, take a clean frying pan and put it over a fire with olive oil. When it comes to a boil, smear your hands with olive oil before taking the meat, and shape it into discs in the size you like, big or small. Fry them in the pan, making sure you turn them over. When they are done and have turned golden, transfer them from the pan to a bowl. Once you are done with this, take a small earthenware casserole and add crushed garlic and a bit of water. When the garlic is cooking, add a sufficient amount of good-quality vinegar, and when this comes to a boil take the meat discs, transfer them to a large ceramic bowl and pour on the boiled vinegar. If you want you can add macerated *murrī* to some of them, leaving others as they are. This is the way to prepare all kinds of game and wild meat, hare and rabbit. Remember this.

174. Another dish

Take the thighs and backstrap of any kind of game meat you have to hand. Cut into slices in whichever size you like and add crushed salt, oregano and pepper. If you want to roast the meat in the *tannūr*, heat it until it turns red hot, and then stick the slices to the sides of the oven and put a lid on top. When you think the meat slices are done

---

is useful against tetanus and facial paralysis, while a drink made with the dried and crushed sexual organ of the male is highly aphrodisiac.

131 See recipe No. 185.

and browned, lift the lid and remove them, after having prepared a bowl with sweet olive oil and cooked crushed garlic. When you take the meat out of the *tannūr*, immediately cut it up and put it in a large ceramic bowl with the olive oil and garlic. Once this is done, eat and enjoy, Allah the Exalted willing.

If you want to roast it in a brick oven, put the slices with salt in an earthenware casserole dish and add olive oil and crushed garlic before taking it to the oven.[132] When the meat is done and browned, remove it from the oven and cut it up in a large ceramic bowl. Pour on olive oil and garlic, and eat and enjoy, Allah the Exalted willing.

If you like, you can also add a bit of vinegar made from lime, *zanbūʿ* or sour grapes. You can also roast the slices on an iron grill, in which case you should prepare the fire, put the grill on top of it and then place the slices on the grill. Make sure to turn them over so they are fully cooked and both sides have turned golden. Then, remove the slices from the grill and cut them up in a large ceramic bowl with olive oil and garlic. When it is ready, eat and enjoy, Allah the Exalted willing.

If you want to roast the meat on a spit, cut the slices up into small pieces, thread them on the spit and roast at a distance from the fire. Take a bowl and add vinegar, olive oil, *murrī*, crushed garlic, pepper and cinnamon to it. Then, take a feather from a chicken wing, wash it and dip it in the bowl and gradually baste the skewered meat with the mixture until the meat is done and has turned golden. Continue until there is no sauce left, and then transfer the meat from the spit to a large ceramic bowl. Eat and enjoy, Allah the Exalted willing.

If you want to roast the meat on live coal, light a fire and remove the smoke, flames and ashes emanating from it. Put the meat slices on the coal and keep an eye on them. Remove any ash that gets stuck to them, and when the meat is ready and has turned golden, cut it up in a large ceramic bowl that contains garlic and olive oil. Once this is done, eat and enjoy, Allah the Exalted willing.

132 According to the anonymous *Andalusian* treatise (*Anwāʿ*, 8; BNF, fol. 1v.), this is the ideal roasting method 'as the fat and moisture remain at the bottom of the pan and nothing goes into the fire, contrary to when the spit or *tannūr* are used'.

175. Another dish[133]

Take a hare, and wash, clean, joint and bone it. Place the bones in a new pot with plenty of water, salt, olive oil, pepper, coriander seeds, soaked chickpeas, a few onions, garlic cloves, cumin, a spoonful of *murrī*, two ladlefuls of good-quality vinegar and a little dissolved saffron. Put the pot over a fire to cook. Then, take the meat, pound it very well in a mortar and add a pinch of salt, pepper, cinnamon, ginger, a dash of crushed saffron, coriander seeds, cumin and egg whites. Knead the meat and spices into a dough, thoroughly mixing everything together. Remove the bones from the pot and wrap the meat mixture around them to restore them to their original shape.[134] Next, take an earthenware casserole, put some of the broth from the pot in it, and bring to a boil. Gingerly place the bones with the meat into the pot one by one, and leave them until they set and are close to being done. Take an iron or earthenware frying pan and put olive oil in it. Once it starts to boil, take the meat and fry it carefully so that it browns. When it is done, take it out and transfer to a large ceramic bowl. Take the broth, strain it and return it to the pot. Then crack eggs and add salt, aromatics and saffron. Put everything, including the yolks, in the pot with the broth. Take some more egg yolks and fry them. Additionally, boil an egg or two in water, and when they are done, peel them and cut them into quarters. If there is pounded meat left over, make small meatballs with it and cook them. When everything is finished, take the bowl with the fried meat and add the strained broth, together with the chickpeas, almonds,[135] eggs and the yolks from the pot, as well as the fried yolks and the peeled eggs. Sprinkle pepper, ginger and cinnamon on top, and then eat and enjoy, Allah the Exalted willing.

If you like, you can make this dish the same way with rabbit.

176. Another dish

Wash and clean a hare, cut it into pieces and place them in a glazed earthenware casserole dish. Add water, salt, olive oil, pepper, coriander

---

133 In Gayangos XVI (fol. 66v.), the recipe is called *mughaffar* (see recipes Nos. 199, 355).

134 This vital instruction was missing from the edition and has been taken from BL Or5927, fol. 132r.

135 It is unclear when the almonds are to be added to the dish, as they are not mentioned earlier.

seeds, cumin and macerated *murrī*, and colour with saffron. Put the pot over a fire to cook and, when the meat is done, add a spoonful of good vinegar and take it to the oven. Once the meat is golden brown and the liquid has dried out, take it out and leave it to cool down. Eat and enjoy, Allah the Exalted willing.

If you like, you can also cook this dish in exactly the same way with rabbit.

177. Another dish

Cut up a hare, and wash and clean the pieces before putting them in a new pot with water, salt, olive oil, pepper, coriander seeds and a bit of sliced onion. Place the pot over a fire, and when the meat is done, remove it. Then take a tin-plated iron frying pan, pour some olive oil in it and put it over a fire. When the oil comes to a boil, put the pieces of hare in the frying pan and gently turn them over so that they can brown on all sides. When they are done, take them out of the pan and put them in a large ceramic bowl and do the same with other pieces until you have finished frying all of the meat. Next, take a casserole dish and add a splash of water to it. Crush garlic and cook it in the casserole dish. When it is done and the liquid has dried out, pour the vinegar in with the garlic and then add the strained broth. Leave it on the fire and, when it comes to a boil, sprinkle lots of pepper on the meat and pour on the vinegar and everything with it. Eat it and enjoy it, Allah the Exalted willing.

If you like, you can make the dish with dry cheese. In this case, pound the cheese with the cooked garlic and dissolve it all with the strained broth. Then pour it on the fried meat that is in the ceramic bowl. Eat and enjoy, Allah the Exalted willing.

178. Another dish[136]

Take a hare, wash and clean it, and skewer it whole on an iron or wooden spit. Roast it over a moderate fire that should not be too close. Prepare a bowl with salt dissolved in rose water, as well as crushed garlic, pepper, cinnamon and macerated *murrī*. Use a feather to continually baste the hare with this sauce until it is done and golden brown.

136 In Gayangos XVI (fol. 69r.), this recipe is titled 'another roasted dish, which is amazing'.

Remove it from the spit and cut up the meat, removing all the bones. Place the meat in a large ceramic bowl with garlic and olive oil. If you like, you can smear the hare with fresh butter to keep the meat moist and tender. Instead of just olive oil and garlic, you can use macerated *murrī*, grated oregano and olive oil for the basting sauce. If you want to use another one, grate dry cheese and dissolve it in hot water before adding crushed cooked garlic and olive oil, and then put the meat in it. Alternatively, you can use the juice of fresh coriander and of parsley, and add crushed garlic, pepper and vinegar. Pour all this into a bowl and put the meat in it.[137] Whatever you do with the hare you can also do it with a rabbit.[138] Remember this.

If you want to roast the rabbit in a brick oven and ensure that it is still tender, put it whole in a clean pot and pour plenty of olive oil and garlic over it. When it is done, take it out, cut it up in a large ceramic bowl and then pour on what remains in the pot. Add any of the above-mentioned vinegars[139] to make it even more delicious and fragrant.[140] Eat and enjoy, Allah the Exalted willing.

Chapter Six: on the different types of meat from quadrupeds used for meatballs

179. A dish[141]

Take meat from the thighs and backstrap, and remove the nerves. Pound the meat in a wooden mortar until it becomes like dough. Place it in a bowl and add a sufficient amount of salt, pepper, ginger, cinnamon, a little bit of mastic, spikenard, cloves – not too much – and egg whites. Knead everything until thoroughly mixed [and it becomes

137 According to BL Or5927 (fol. 132v.), the meat should be 'dunked' or 'moistened' with the sauce (*yuṣbagh al-laḥm fihi*), rather than 'put in'. Both are possible in this context as, earlier on in the recipe, the meat is indeed put in a sauce.

138 In Gayangos XVI (fol. 69v.), this is a new recipe: 'Cooking a rabbit (*qunayna*). If it is available, cook it in the same way as hare in all dishes.'

139 See recipe No. 174.

140 This paragraph is a separate recipe in Gayangos XVI (fol. 69v.).

141 In Gayangos XVI (fol. 53v.), the dish is titled 'meatballs'.

one single mass].[142] If you have to prepare a lot of food, for instance for wedding banquets and similar occasions, you should take a new pot with water, olive oil, coriander seeds, pepper and a bit of cut-up onion. Put it over a fire and, when the water has come to a boil, coat your hands with olive oil and use a mould to make balls with the meat in the size you want, big or small. Add the meatballs to the boiling water until you have used all of the meat, and let them cook until the liquid has dried out. Then fry them in olive oil and fat until they are golden brown. Leave them to cook in the pot, on embers, until they are to your liking.[143] If you are making the dish for a small number of people, and you are using, say, one or two pots, make the meatballs and then put them in the pot. When serving the food in large ceramic bowls, make sure the meatballs are visible on top, Allah the Exalted willing.

180. Recipe for a nourishing dish[144]

Take fatty meat, pound it as mentioned before and also add the same spices listed above as well as some macerated *murrī*, a little onion juice, caraway and egg whites. Make large meatballs, the size of meat chunks. Then put *murrī*, vinegar, olive oil, onion juice, saffron and peeled almonds in a clean pot. When the sauce comes to a boil, throw in the meatballs. When they are done, brown them in the olive oil and spices, and let the pot simmer down on embers.[145]

181. Making *isfiriyya*[146]

Take the meat mentioned above, remove the veins, and beat it on a wooden chopping block with an iron rod used for pounding meat.

142 Addition from Gayangos XVI (*ibid.*).

143 Gayangos XVI (*ibid.*) states here that it should be 'until such time as you use them to garnish bowls at wedding banquets'.

144 In Gayangos XVI (*ibid.*), it is titled 'dish with meatballs'.

145 The last sentence is quite different in Gayangos XVI (*ibid.*), but more in keeping with other recipes: 'When they are done, crust them with eggs and spices, and leave the pot on embers until serving.'

146 It is flattened meat cut into strips which was used for decorating certain dishes, and sold ready-made at market. The Andalusian includes no fewer than seven *iṣfiriyā* (as it is called there) recipes: *Anwāʿ*, 3, 4, 91, 110, 146 (BNF, fols. 2r.–v., 37r., 43r.–v.). The spellings in the present text vary between *isfīriyya*, *isfiriyya*, and *isfāriyya*. The earliest attested reference to this dish goes back to the middle of the tenth century. See Marín 1997: 15–16; Corriente 1997: 15.

When it is well pounded and cleaned of its veins, put it in a bowl with salt, pepper, cinnamon, a little mastic, spikenard, a sufficient amount of cloves, and egg whites. Knead this well until it resembles bone marrow.[147] If it needs to be pounded more, do so in a wooden mortar with the spices and egg whites. Then take a frying pan, grease it with olive oil, and heat it up a little. Put the meat in the pan, spread it out it with your hands, and coat it with olive oil.[148] Proceed gently, making sure the disc is made thin and smooth and, once it is done, put it on a board. Then, cut it lengthwise with a knife and place it in a large ceramic bowl until it is time to garnish food when serving it, Allah the Exalted willing. The *isfiriyya* is put on the surface of dishes together with split eggs, Allah the Exalted willing.[149]

182. Making *mirqās*[150] sausages

Take meat from the thighs, backstrap, and other similar parts, and use the above-mentioned iron rod to beat it with great force on a wooden chopping block, until it falls apart and is devoid of veins. When you are done with this, put the meat in a large kneading tub. Take fresh suet, about a third of the quantity of meat, or a little more. Remove the veins and cut it as finely as you can with a knife. Add it to the meat, to which you have already added salt, pepper, ginger, cinnamon, a little mastic, spikenard, cloves, slightly crushed aniseed, and cumin. Pound a few onions and one or two cloves of garlic, and put the mixture in water. Then strain and pour the liquid on the meat. Also add sufficient amounts of macerated *murrī* and vinegar, as well as rose water and

147 Gayangos XVI (fol. 54r.) specifies that it should 'become a single mass'.

148 Gayangos XVI (*ibid.*) adds that it should be 'turned over', to ensure browning on both sides.

149 The religious formula is included in BL Or5927 (fol. 133v.), but missing from the printed edition.

150 The variant spelling *mirkās* also occurs in the text, whereas Gayangos XVI (fol. 54r.) has *mirqāsh*. The word, which according to Dozy (1881: I, 555) goes back to the Greek *mázès kreas*, is a North African vernacular term for a particular type of sausage. It was a typical market food – very much like our hotdogs today – and was often the object of unscrupulous practices, including the addition of wood shavings in the minced meat, and the use of suet or tripe instead of meat, etc. They should only be made with fresh meat from a healthy animal; al-Saqaṭī 1931: 36; Ibn 'Abdūn [Lévi-Provençal 1955]: 45 (trans., 74). Today, the word is mainly associated with Morocco, and refers to the red, spicy lamb sausages commonly known by their French form *merguez*. Also see al-Dabbābī al-Mīsāwī 2017: 174–6.

chopped mint leaves. Knead it all in the tub until everything is thoroughly mixed, and beat again with the suet included. Take some of the meat and roast it over a fire. Try it, and if you think it tastes nice, that is fine. If it lacks salt or anything else, add what is required until the meat tastes as it should do. Then, set it aside and take some intestines, which should be from a large nanny goat or large ram as theirs are wider and firmer. Take a ring, fold it and put the intestine inside it. Pull it through in order to strip away any dirt and fully clean it. Put the intestine in a bowl of water. Take one end of the intestine and put it at the end (i.e. the tube) of a funnel.[151] Grab hold of the funnel with the thumb of your left hand, and push the meat into the funnel (cone) with the thumb of your right hand so that the intestine comes out of the other end of the funnel with the meat inside it. If the meat is too hard, soften it by adding a little water. Continue in this way until you have used up all the meat. When you have finished stuffing an intestine, clean it and make sausage links in the size you want – large or small – separating each by removing the meat between them and tying off the ends. Fold the intestine and hang it up to dry in the sun, or smoke it.

A recipe for cooking *mirqās* at wedding banquets: separate the sausages and put them in a pot with a medium amount of water and a pinch of salt. Put the pot over a fire, stirring constantly until they release their juices and fat. Remove from the high heat and set the pot on a low fire to fry and brown the sausages. At wedding banquets, you should serve ten or so in each ceramic bowl. When you cook them at home, make them with green unripe garlic or onion, like a *rāhibī*[152] or a *jamalī*,[153] crusted with eggs. This is how the wedding banquet chefs on the North African coast prepare them.

You can also oven-bake or fry the sausages in a casserole dish with vinegar or *ṣināb* (mustard sauce).[154] If the sausages are roasted on a spit, they should be eaten hot because of the fat they contain. Remember this, and do as you please.

151 The instructions in Gayangos XVI (fol. 54v.) are more detailed in relation to this stage, and specify that the liquid from the intestine is drained through an esparto sieve, that the funnel should be coated with olive oil on the inside, and that most of the funnel tube should be inserted into the intestine.

152 See recipes Nos. 105, 190, 202, 248, 281.

153 See recipes Nos. 99, 284, 288.

154 See recipes Nos. 409–10.

If you want to keep the sausages, cook them until you see that any moisture has been absorbed, and then put them in a new pot. Melt good-quality fresh suet with salt to remove all moistness, and then pour it over the sausages, covering them completely. Put them in a dry place and, whenever you want to eat some of them, take them out of the pot and heat them up over a fire, adding a sufficient amount of vinegar. Eat and enjoy, Allah the Exalted willing.

If you want to include aubergines with the meat and suet, take fresh aubergines, peel them and boil them in water until they are done. Pound them until they fall apart, add eggs, and mix them in. Then make the stuffing with it. It is very good, Allah the Exalted willing.

183. Another recipe

Take meat and add all the other things I have mentioned. Also include a little *darmak* flour and yeast, and put everything in water so that it becomes like a semolina porridge.[155] Put the frying pan on the fire with a drizzle of olive oil. Once it is hot, put in enough of the pounded meat mixture to fill the pan. When you see that it starts to brown, take it out and fry another batch of the meat after adding olive oil. Continue until you have cooked as much as you wanted to. Make a sauce of vinegar, macerated *murrī* and mustard, and immerse the meat in it. Eat and enjoy, Allah the Exalted willing.

184. Making *laqāniq*[156] sausages

They are prepared in exactly the same way as *mirqās*, except that they are not made with *murrī*, but with pounded onion and fresh coriander. They should also be larger than *mirqās*. As a result, the intestines used

---

155 *talbīna*; also see recipe No. 57.

156 In the Mashriq, this was the usual word for (small) spicy sausages (also *maqāniq*, *naqāniq*) made with small intestines (al-Warrāq 1987: 87–9), though their name goes back to the Roman *lucanicae* (sausages from Lucania), which appear in several recipes in Apicius's cookery book (Vehling 1977: Nos. 61, 140, 174, 186, 192, 195, 199, 378). Today, the Levantine *naqāniq* (also *maqāniq*) denotes small mutton sausages. When referring to sausages in general, including the ones common in European cuisines, the Arabic word *sujuq* (cf. Turkish *sucuk*) tends to be used, but this actually is a kind of dry spicy sausage often made with ground beef. In the Maghrib, *mirqās* was the usual lexical equivalent for *laqāniq*, which, as becomes apparent here, denoted sausages that were larger as well as made with different ingredients. Ibn al-Ḥashshā' (1932: 70, No. 653) has the form *laqāliq*, which is also the plural of *laqlaq* ('stork').

must be wider, and so must be especially selected. When you finish making the sausages, boil them slightly in water, and then take them out, and hang them in an airy place. When you want to eat them, cut them up one by one and put the pieces in an earthenware frying pan or casserole dish, without olive oil, over a moderate heat. Stir them so that they release their fat. If you want, you can add vinegar. Eat it and enjoy, Allah the Exalted willing.

If you wish to cook them with other things, as mentioned for the *mirqās*, do so, with the strength of Allah the Exalted.

185. Making *aḥrash* (thin minced meat cakes)[157]

It is made by pounding the meat and with the same spices as for *mirkās* sausages; everything is exactly the same. If you want to make it without suet, crack eggs over the meat and beat it all together until the eggs are mixed in and no yolks ('eyes') are visible. Then take a tin-plated iron or glazed earthenware frying pan, pour some olive oil in it and place it over the fire. Take the meat mixture and shape it into small cakes. Put them in the olive oil once it has come to a boil, and carefully turn them over. When they are golden brown, take them out, put them in a large ceramic bowl, and pour macerated *murrī* or hot vinegar over them.

If you want, you can make them another way, by taking two small frying pans and placing one [...][158] your hand. Take some of the meat and shape it into small *ka'k*-like shapes, and place them in the centre [of the pan]. Then take some more of the meat and mix it with finely ground *darmak* flour and egg whites. Shape the resultant mixture into meatballs, and place them around the meat on all sides, packing them tightly, one next to the other, until it looks like a flat cake. Put the pan over a low heat and add olive oil. When you see that the cake has browned, turn it over into the other pan and grease it again with olive

157 Corriente (1997: 122) states that the 'standard type [was] defined as hashed spiced meat mixed with flour into cakes, then made into balls, fried and served with a sauce of vinegar, oil, garlic and *murrī*'. He adds that there was another kind identified with '*aṣfīriyā*' (i.e. the *isfāriyya* of the present text). The word *aḥrash* is actually an adjective meaning 'rough, harsh', presumably in reference to the appearance of the meat cakes, as in the case of the Moroccan pan-fried semolina bread *ḥarsha*. The *Andalusian* has three recipes, including one with fish; *Anwā'*, 2, 31, 154. Also see al-Dabbābī al-Mīsāwī 2017: 173–4.

158 This is blank in both the printed edition and BL Or5927 (fol. 134v.).

oil. Pack the meat in the pan a second time, until it is done on that side, and then flip it from pan to pan. Whenever a cake is browned on both sides, transfer it to a ceramic bowl and, when you have finished, pour on macerated *murrī* or boiled vinegar. Eat it and enjoy, Allah the Exalted willing.

If you want to make it with suet, take good fresh suet – about half the amount of the meat. Chop it as finely as you can and put it with the meat in a kneading tub, mixing them together very well. Then take an iron frying pan and put it over the fire with a drizzle of olive oil. When the oil comes to a boil, shape the meat mixture into small loaves, and put them in the frying pan, carefully turning them until they are well done and golden brown. Then take them out and put them in a large ceramic bowl. Eat and enjoy, Allah the Exalted willing. They are delicious because of the hot suet inside them.

If you want to make a sauce for them, cook vinegar, olive oil and garlic.

If you want to store them for later, do the same as with the *mirkās*.

186. Making omasum tripe[159]

Take the omasum, reverse it and wash it with vinegar and salt, cleaning it very well. Then take good cuts of meat from the thighs or similar parts, and pound it very well in a wooden mortar. Add salt, pepper, coriander seeds, cinnamon, ginger, spikenard, cloves, a little bit of mastic, a spoonful of *murrī*, fresh coriander and mint juice, peeled almonds, pine nuts and a little bit of chopped suet. Then take eggs and crack them into the meat, beating everything very well. Add boiled egg yolks and one peeled boiled egg. Put some pounded meat in the omasum, distribute the yolks in it, and make sure to put the whole egg in the middle. Then, add what is left of the meat and the remaining yolks. Tie the two ends of the omasum together and put it in an earthenware cauldron or a large pot. Add water, salt, olive oil, pepper, coriander

159 *qibā* (also *qabāwa*), a corruption of *qibba* (< Persian *gīpā*); Dozy 1881: II, 307; Steingass 1892: 951. The omasum (also known as leaf, book, or Bible tripe) is the third compartment (after the rumen and reticulum and before the abomasum) of a ruminant's stomach. The only other Arabic cookery book to include this is *Taṣānīf* (fol. 70r.–70v.). Also see Afshār (1981: 163–8) for similar Safavid recipes. Modern descendants include the Syrian *qabawāt*, Lebanese *fawārigh* and the Egyptian *mombār*.

seeds and a small chopped onion. Put the pot over the fire to cook and, when it is almost done, take the tripe out, put it in a large casserole dish, and colour with a little pounded saffron. Collect the fat that is in the pot or cauldron and put it in the casserole with a little lime juice. Take it to the oven and have someone turn it over so that it browns on all sides. [Once it is done] remove from the oven. When you want to serve it, cut it with a knife the way you like. Eat it and enjoy, Allah the Exalted willing.

187. Making stuffed large-intestine sausages[160]

This recipe is exactly the same as the previous one, except that the eggs cannot be put in whole, but have to be split into halves. However, if the intestine is wide enough, leave them whole, and also add boiled eggs. Keep this in mind and proceed accordingly, Allah the Exalted willing.

188. Making *harīsa* (meat porridge)[161]

Take as much fatty veal thigh meat as you like, put it in an unglazed

160 *ḥashw al-mib'ar*; there are several variations of this dish in *Taṣānīf* (fol. 71r.). The basic recipe is a stuffing consisting of pounded meat, honey, *murrī*, vinegar, sesame oil, pepper, coriander seeds, cumin, thyme and celery juice. The main difference with al-Tujībī's is that the intestine is suspended in the *tannūr* for cooking. In another recipe, it is prepared like a *judhāba* (see No. 221), with a stuffing including almonds, pistachios and sugar. When it is made with boiled liver, walnuts, pepper and saffron are added.

161 The meat *harīsa* was extremely popular in the Mashriq; Ibn Mubārak Shāh 2020: 34–5 (note 131). It was typically sold in markets but was subject to considerable forgery, ranging from using insufficient meat, old meat, offal (sheep's heads), to thickening it with taro (Buckley [al-Shayzarī 1999]: 60). In Seville, *harīsa* sellers (*harrāsūn*) were instructed to provide clarified butter and honey, and not to make the porridge too thick, since this is harmful to the stomach (Ibn 'Abdūn [Lévi-Provençal 1955]: 55; trans., 88–9). Al-Rāzī (1987: 138) said it was the most nutritious of all dishes, especially when eaten with milk, and recommended it for those suffering from exhaustion, individuals with hot temperaments, or in need of gaining weight. For others, however, it can be harmful and can cause joint pains, kidney stones and tumours. Ibn Jazla (fol. 235v.) also praised this dish, which he said increases sexual potency and semen, as it is one of the most balanced foods, very nutritious, and suitable for people who are hard-working and active. According to Ibn Māsawayh (fol. 146r.) the wheat should be thoroughly hulled and then cooked with meats and chicken, with the addition of some milk. If the dish is too heavy, one should eat it with *murrī* and have ginger preserve afterwards. According to the ninth-century author Ibn Qutayba (1925–30: III, 298), *harīsa* was eaten with a lot of pepper, and *murrī*, but was never prepared with clarified butter. Also see recipe No. 97.

earthenware pot, and add soaked wheat – one-third of the quantity of meat – which has been ground in a mortar so that it is husked. Pour a lot of water over it and take it to the oven. Leave it overnight to cook. The next morning, take it out of the oven and put it on the fire at home until any remaining water has evaporated. Then take a large knife or an iron skewer, put it in the pot and stir the meat until it is shredded and falls apart. Take some flour, dissolve it in water and put it in the pot with the meat. Whisk vigorously with a ladle to mix it and obtain a gluey consistency. Then take fresh suet, pound, clean, and melt it in an earthenware pot. When it is ready, serve the *harīsa* in a ceramic bowl and pour the melted suet on top.

If you want, you can take some of the *harīsa*, fry it with olive oil in a frying pan for *isfanj* (doughnuts),[162] and put it on top of the ceramic bowl. Also add egg yolks, fried sparrows and a sprinkling of cinnamon.

You can cook it at home, but take care that it does not burn.

The dish can also be made with mutton or chicken, and rice[163] instead of wheat. Bear this in mind.

162 See recipes Nos. 74–7.

163 I am following BL Or5927 (fol. 135v.) since the edition's 'or with geese' (2012: 149) would not make sense as a contrast with 'wheat'.

SECTION THREE

On various kinds of poultry

It consists of seven chapters.

Chapter One: on goose meat

189. Dish

Slaughter a goose that is tender and fat, grab it by the feathers, and inflate it by blowing in order to separate the skin from the meat. Use whatever method you need to separate the parts that do not come off easily. Then tie its neck with a string, pluck its feathers in hot water, and clean it. Cut the goose open, take out the entrails and wash it thoroughly. Put it in a container and cover it. Then take another goose, slaughter it, clean it, open up the abdomen and take out its entrails. Remove the meat from the bones and pound it in a wooden mortar until it falls apart, and then add salt, pepper, coriander seeds, ginger, cinnamon, cloves, spikenard and semolina breadcrumbs. Crack enough eggs in the mixture to make it set, and then add macerated *murrī* and peeled almonds. Knead well by hand until everything is thoroughly mixed, and then add a little saffron. Stuff both the inside of the goose and the gap between the skin and the meat, and use string to sew up the opening. Keep some of the stuffing to one side, without breadcrumbs, to make meatballs. Take a large cauldron and pour in clear water, plenty of olive oil, salt, pepper, coriander seeds and half a chopped onion. Put the pot on the fire and, when the water is almost boiling, carefully take the goose, which has now been tied with twine around the skin of the neck, and lower it in. Monitor it by gently moving it around. You should have a large needle ready to prick the skin when the pot starts to boil to prevent any tearing, and to release the steam[1] while keeping the skin intact. When it is clear that the goose is done, remove it [the pot] from the heat and carefully take it out, transfer it to a large casserole dish, and colour with saffron. Take (some of) the strained broth with its fat and pour it into the casserole. Take it to the oven but

1 The edition omits the word *bukhār*, which is present in BL Or5927 (fol. 136r.).

place it away from the fire so that it browns, and have someone turn it over carefully so that it browns on the bottom as well. Then, take what is left of the broth and put it in a clean pot, adding olive oil, pepper and a little *murrī*. Then take ten or more eggs and crack them into a bowl with salt, pepper, cinnamon, ginger and a little bit of saffron.[2] Beat them vigorously with a ladle until the egg whites and yolks are mixed with the aromatic spices. Then, take five yolks and put them in the pot. When you know they are cooked, pour enough good vinegar over them. When the pot comes to a boil, cast in the beaten eggs, and stir. Then remove the fire from under the pot and set it on embers until the eggs set, and there is only a little liquid left. Take the gizzards and livers and thoroughly pound them in a mortar. Add salt and aromatic spices, and then knead with the egg whites. Take a frying pan and put it over the fire with olive oil. Shape the pounded mixture into a flat loaf and put it in the frying pan. When it is golden brown, turn it over to brown on the other side. When it is done, gently remove it from the pan, put it on a board and cut it with a knife into long strips. Prepare them together with split (boiled) eggs and fried egg yolks. Check on the goose in the oven and, if you find that it is browned and done, take it out – if not, leave it a little while longer until it is browned. When you take it out, put the goose in a serving dish with a wide base, and pour the broth, the egg yolks, the egg crust layer and the meatballs on top. Garnish with the *isfīriyya*[3] meat strips, the split boiled eggs, and the fried yolks. Sprinkle on cinnamon and ginger, and serve topped with mint leafstalks, Allah the Exalted willing.

190. Another dish

Take a fat, tender goose, slaughter it, pluck it,[4] cut open its abdomen, and wash it. Then skewer it on an iron or wooden spit. Kindle a fire on the sides of the goose, none underneath it. Raise the ends of the spit on a stone to avoid exposure to dust or soil. Continuously turn the spit with your hand, and do not be remiss in relighting the fire if it goes out.

---

2 Gayangos XVI (fol. 70v.) has somewhat different instructions: '(a little *murrī*). Cook the aforementioned meatballs in the sauce with five yolks. When the meatballs are done, add ten eggs beaten with pepper, salt, cinnamon, ginger and saffron.'

3 See recipe No. 181.

4 Here I follow BL Or5927 (fol. 136v.), rather than the edition's 'clean it' (2012: 152), as removing the feathers is the more logical step here.

Prepare a bowl with water, salt, a dribble of olive oil, crushed garlic, and aromatic spices. Take a goose feather, wash it and put it in the bowl. Baste the goose with the feather when you see that it is drying out, and continue to do so until it is golden brown and fully cooked. On long days, this will take from morning to noon or so, but it is best to be patient. One of the signs that tells you it is done, is that, when you take a thigh or wing and pull it towards you, it comes off easily. Another sign is that, if you shake it with your hands, the meat falls away from the bones, or you can remove it easily. All of these indicate that the goose is done. Then take dry cheese and grate it until it is like mill dust. Now take garlic, cook it in any pot you want, and then pound it very well.[5] Take hot water, dissolve the cheese and garlic in it, and then pour it in a ceramic bowl with good olive oil. Then take the goose meat, rip it apart with your hands and put it in the bowl. Whisk it with your hands so that it becomes mixed with the cheese, garlic and olive oil. Eat it and enjoy, Allah the Exalted willing. If you like, you can make the sauce just with olive oil and garlic, or, if you prefer, with some macerated *murrī*, ground oregano and olive oil. It is entirely up to you.

If you want to roast the bird in the oven, salt it and put it in a large casserole dish with olive oil and crushed garlic, and sprinkle on pepper. Then take it to the oven and place it away from the fire. Turn it over until it is done and golden brown. When it is ready, take it out, carve it up and serve it, Allah the Exalted willing. If you want to make it like a *jamalī*[6] or *rāhibī*,[7] proceed as I have described in the first chapter of the second section, Allah the Exalted willing.[8]

---

5 This sentence is omitted from the recipe in the edition (2012: 153), and was taken from BL Or5927, fol. 136v. The manuscript is interrupted here, and the remainder of this recipe is on fol. 149r., with fol. 137r. containing the final part of recipe No. 119.

6 See recipes Nos. 99, 284, 288.

7 Also see recipes Nos. 105, 182, 202, 248, 264, 281.

8 The religious formula is included in BL Or5927 (fol. 149v.), but missing from the printed edition.

Chapter Two: on chicken meat

191. Dish (white *tafāyā*)[9]

Take a fattened pullet, slaughter it, and pluck it in hot water. Rub the outside of the skin with salt, and clean the insides. Cut it in the way you like but, if you want it whole, only sever the neck. Put the ends of the legs in the cavity and then place the bird in a new pot[10] with ginger, a grain of mastic, a cinnamon stick, coriander seeds, washed salt and a bit of onion – all of which should be tied into a bundle. Put the pot over a fire to cook and, when the essence[11] of the spices has been released in the pot, take them out so that the broth is not altered. If you want to, take the breast of another chicken, pound it with aromatic spices and egg whites, and shape the mixture into meatballs. You can also add egg yolks if you wish. If you want to crust it with egg whites and bread-crumbs, do so. Tend to the meat and, if you see that it is done, remove the fire from under the pot and set it on embers to simmer down. Then transfer it to a ceramic bowl, and add some pounded cinnamon or mint leafstalks on top, if you wish. Eat it and enjoy, Allah the Exalted willing. This dish is called a white *tafāyā*, and has already been mentioned in the second chapter of the second section of this book.[12]

192. Another dish, called a green *tafāyā*[13]

Its preparation has already been described in the above-mentioned chapter.

193. Another dish, called *lawziyya* (almond stew)[14]

This has been mentioned in the above-mentioned chapter.

---

9 The title is given only in Gayangos XVI (fol. 71v.). Also see recipes Nos. 109, 282.

10 The version in Gayangos XVI (fol. 72v.) is slightly different, in that the pot should contain water and olive oil, after which ginger and coriander seeds are pounded before adding the other spices for the sachet.

11 Gayangos XVI (*ibid.*) refers to the 'fragrance and flavour'.

12 See recipe No. 109.

13 See recipe No. 110.

14 See recipe No. 135.

194. Another dish, called *kāfūriyya* (camphor stew)[15]

It is made exactly like *lawziyya* in every way. The difference is that when you see the almonds are done – use four *ūqiyas* for each chicken – you should pour enough good-quality lime juice into the pot to enhance the flavour, and then bring it to a boil. Remove the fire from underneath the pot and set it on embers to simmer down before serving it in large ceramic bowl. Eat and enjoy it, Allah the Exalted willing.

195. Another dish, called a sweetened *zīrbājiyya*[16]

Take a large plump pullet, slaughter it and do as mentioned above in terms of cleaning it, and so on. Leave it whole and sever its neck. Take the ends of the legs, and push them inside its cavity. Put the bird in a large new pot with salt, sweet olive oil, pepper, coriander seeds, a little cumin and a bit of sliced onion, citron leaves and a sufficient amount of fresh water. Put the pot over a fire to cook and, when it is almost done, colour with a little pounded saffron dissolved in water. Then, pour good vinegar in the pot, as much as you want. Pound four *ūqiyas* of peeled almonds in a mortar until you get a paste. Check the chicken and, if it is done, add the crushed almonds and stir to dissolve them. Leave the pot on a moderate heat until the almonds have been brought to a boil once or twice. Take good-quality sugar – the same weight as the almonds– and dissolve it in rose water or fresh water. Strain, and pour it into the pot. Taste it and, if you find it too sweet, add vinegar. If it is not sweet enough, add sugar until it is to your liking. Leave the pot on embers to simmer down and to balance the flavours. If you like, you

15 The *Andalusian* also has a similar dish by this name, though the recipe is much more elaborate (*Anwāʿ*, 18; BNF, fol. 7v.), and has the missing camphor, which is included at the simmering stage after being first dissolved into rose water and then added to the juice of two or three limes. Also see al-Dabbābī al-Mīsāwī 2017: 184–5.

16 This was another staple in cookery books in the Mashriq, where it was known as *zīrbāj*; see Ibn Mubārak Shāh 2020: 18 (note 60). The *Andalusian*'s recipe for a *zīrbāja* (*Anwāʿ*, 17–8) is slightly different, in that it does not require cumin, onions or citron leaves. In addition, the author adds that the dish regulates the humours, is nutritious, good for the stomach and liver, and combines the benefits of vinegar stew (*sikbāja*) and sour milk stew. He includes the story about the translator and physician Ḥunayn ibn Isḥāq, who allegedly cured a sick woman with a *zīrbāja*, and referred to it as a balanced dish and the oxymel (*sikanjabīn*) of food, whereas others call it 'the apple of the kitchen', as it has no harmful properties.

can add split eggs after serving the pullet in a large ceramic bowl. Eat it and enjoy it, Allah the Exalted willing.

196. Another dish, called *mukhallal*[17]

Take a plump pullet, slaughter it, and proceed in the same as in the previous recipes in terms of cleaning it, and so on. Put it in a new pot with water, salt, olive oil, pepper, coriander seeds, caraway, a bit of sliced onion, garlic cloves, peeled almonds, soaked chickpeas, a little macerated *murrī*, citron leaves and a fennel stalk. Put the pot over a fire to cook. When it is almost done, colour with saffron that has been pounded and dissolved [in water]. Then add the amount of good vinegar you like. Take a small cooking pot, coriander seeds and pepper, and pound a chicken breast in a mortar. Shape into meatballs in the way described in the sixth chapter of the second section of this book.[18] Put them in the small pot, and add egg yolks. Take some eggs, crack them into a bowl and add salt, spices and saffron, beating everything well with a ladle until it is mixed. Pour the mixture in the pot and leave over a low heat until it sets slightly. Take one or two eggs, boil them in water, and then peel and cut them into quarters. Tend to the chicken and, if it is done, transfer it to a ceramic bowl, add the contents of the small pot on top, and garnish with the quartered eggs and mint leafstalks. Sprinkle on cinnamon and ginger, and then eat and enjoy it, Allah the Exalted willing.

197. Another dish, which is called *al-mufattit* ('the crumbler')[19]

Prepare a chicken as in the previous recipes by slaughtering it, and washing and cleaning it before cutting the joints in the way that suits you best. Put it in a clean pot and add all of the above-mentioned

17 Loosely translatable as 'the vinegared' (*khall*, 'vinegar'), this is the Maghribi name for one of the most famous and prized dishes in medieval Arab cuisine, a vinegar stew known as *sikbāj* (a Persian word consisting of *sik*, 'vinegar', and *bāj*, 'stew'), for which recipes can be found in all cookery books. The *Andalusian* has three *mukhallal* recipes (*Anwāʿ*, 6, 7, 90), as well as two for *sikbāj* (*Anwāʿ*, 67, 83; BNF, fols. 28r., 34r.). The latter is praised for its nutritional value and the fact that the dish keeps for many days without going off, whereas it is called wedding food in western Iberia because it is one of the seven courses (see Introduction) prepared at banquets in Córdoba and Seville (*Anwāʿ*, 6). See Ibn Mubārak Shāh 2020: 15 (also note 49 for recipes in other treatises), 102; Ibn al-Ḥashshā' 1932: 119 (No. 1098).

18 See recipes Nos. 179–80.

19 Corriente 1997: 388 ('a dish of chicken with meatballs').

ingredients. Put the pot on the fire to cook and add a sufficient amount of water. Then take the meat from another chicken, pound it, season it, and make meatballs with it as described earlier. When the chicken in the pot is almost done, add the meatballs. Pound the gizzard and liver, and shape the mixture into a flat loaf. Fry it in a frying pan with a splash of olive oil, and then transfer it to a board (and cut into strips), as described in the preparation of the *isfīriyya*.[20] Put the pieces in a ceramic bowl and keep it separate. Crack ten eggs into a bowl, remove three of the yolks, and set them aside. Add salt, all the aromatic spices you have and some pounded saffron to the eggs, and beat with a ladle to thoroughly mix everything together. Take a small, glazed earthenware stewing pan and pour in water, vinegar, *murrī* and a sufficient amount of olive oil. Put it over a fire and bring to a boil. Pour the beaten eggs into it, and stir with a ladle until they are well set and thickened (into an omelette). Take the yolks that were set aside and fry them in a pan with olive oil until golden brown, and then put them in with the *isfīriyya*. Also boil an egg or two, peel and quarter them, and then put them with the yolks and the *isfīriyya*. Check on the chicken and, if you find it is done, take it out of the pot and fry it briefly in good olive oil. Take a large ceramic bowl, layer it with fresh citron leaves, and on top of them place the omelette, and then the chicken. Also insert the remainder of the omelette in between the chicken parts. Make sure the meatballs are visible. On top of the chicken meat put the fried egg yolks, *isfīriyya* pieces, the split eggs and a little of the strained broth from the chicken. Finally, sprinkle on cinnamon and ginger. Eat and enjoy, Allah the Exalted willing.

198. Another dish, called *al-mughaffar* ('the protected one')[21]

Take two chickens as described, slaughter them and proceed in the same way as before by cleaning and washing them before cutting them up. Remove the bones, but leave the skin hanging off each piece. Thoroughly pound the meat in a wooden mortar, and remove any nerves. Then take the bones and put them in a new pot with salt, water, lots of olive oil, pepper, coriander seeds, lots of cumin, chopped

20 See recipe No. 181.

21 According to Corriente (1997: 381), the term denoted 'a very sophisticated way of cooking chicken which is submitted to many operations but finally looks as if untouched'. For other recipes by this name, see Nos. 175, 289 and 355.

onions, cloves of garlic, peeled almonds, soaked chickpeas, half a ladleful of *murrī* and a ladleful of good vinegar. Put the pot over a fire to cook. Take the pounded meat and add salt, pepper, ginger, coriander seeds, cinnamon, a little macerated *murrī*, and egg whites. Beat it all together and thoroughly mix everything with your hands. Then take the chicken bones and put the meat on it, piece by piece, until all have been covered. If you can, put the skin back on each piece, which would be ideal. Take some of the broth and put it in a large pot over a fire. Carefully place the chicken pieces in the casserole and cook on a low heat until they are set and done. Then take them out and put them in a clean frying pan over a moderate fire, and fry them, turning them carefully until they are golden brown on all sides. Before frying, you will have taken the meat you have left to make meatballs, and cooked them with the broth in the pan until they are done. Now take the gizzards and livers and pound them in the mortar with aromatic spices and egg whites. Use this mixture to make an *isfīriyya*, as explained above, and also add split eggs and fried yolks. Remove the bones that are left in the pot. Crack about five eggs, beat them together with the aromatic spices, and then strain the broth, and clean the pot. Return the purest of the strained broth from the pot and from the casserole in which the meat, meatballs, almonds and chickpeas were cooked. Also return the meatballs, almonds and chickpeas to the pot. Apply the egg crusting while the pot is over a low fire. Take a ceramic bowl, and put in a layer of fresh citron leaves and a few bay leaves. Place the chicken parts on top of the leaves, and pour on whatever else is in the pot. Top everything off with the *isfīriyya* pieces, the split eggs and the fried yolks. Sprinkle on cinnamon and ginger, and scatter on some mint leafstalks. Eat and enjoy, Allah the Exalted willing.

If you like, you can cook the chicken halfway in the pot before taking it out to remove the meat from the breast and thighs. Pound it and mix with spikenard, cinnamon, pepper, coriander and egg whites, which you then smear over the breast and thighs. Fry the meat and return it to the pot with the broth, as stated. If you cook it in a casserole dish in the oven, without frying, this also produces a wonderful result.

199. Another dish, called *al-ḥūtiyya* ('the fishy one')

Take a chicken as described above, slaughter it and do all the other things as before. You can cut it into pieces or leave it whole, as you like. Place it in a new pot with water, salt, olive oil, pepper, coriander seeds and a bit of sliced onion. When the chicken is done, take it out and put it in a clean frying pan with a dribble of olive oil. Fry it – whole or in pieces – gently over a low fire until golden brown. Then take an earthenware casserole dish and add three cloves of crushed garlic. Take the strained broth, that is to say the fat, and pour it into the casserole, which you place over a fire so that the garlic cooks. Add as much good vinegar as you like. Taste it and, if you find it too strong, add some of the strained broth until it is to your taste. If it is too weak, then add vinegar. Finally, put the chicken in a ceramic bowl, dust with pepper, and pour in the strained broth cooked with vinegar and garlic. Eat and enjoy, Allah the Exalted willing.

If you like, you can garnish it with split eggs and mint leafstalks. This is the most appropriate method, especially at wedding banquets, when the chickens are kept whole. Remember this.

200. Another dish, called *al-jaʿfariyya*[22]

Take a chicken as described, slaughter, it and proceed in the same way as before. Put it in a new pot and add water, salt and a lot of olive oil, as well as pepper, coriander seeds and a bit of cumin. Also put in onions, peeled almonds, soaked chickpeas, cloves of garlic, a sufficient amount of macerated *murrī*, citron leaves and a fennel stalk. Place the pot over a fire to cook until everything is done. Add a ladleful of good vinegar after colouring the pot with saffron. Bring to the boil and remove from the fire. Gently take the chicken out and put in a glazed casserole dish, together with the strained broth, almonds and chickpeas. Put the casserole in the oven and remove it when the dish is completely done, that is to say, when the chicken is golden brown all over, the broth has dried out and only the olive oil and fat remain. Serve it in a large ceramic

22 In Gayangos XVI (74v.), it is called *al-jaʿfarī*. There is a similar and identically named recipe in the Andalusian treatise (*Anwāʿ*, 19; BNF, fol. 8r.), where its name is explained as follows: 'It is called *jaʿfariyya* because of the quantity of saffron it contains, which makes it look like *jaʿfari* gold. It is also said that it was invented by a certain Jaʿfar, who gave it his name.' The term *jaʿfar* denoted gold of the finest quality. The two meanings came together during the reign of al-Ḥakam II, Jaʿfar Ibn ʿUthmān al-Mushafī, when gold coins struck in this period were known as *jaʿfariyya*. Corriente 1997: 97.

bowl, and arrange some split eggs over it, along with some mint leaf-stalks. Eat and enjoy, God the Exalted willing.

If you wish, you can take the chicken out of the pot after it is completely done[23] and then fry it in a pan so that it browns all over. Then return it to the pot after cleaning it, adding some of the fat [and broth][24] in which it has been cooked, as well as a ladleful of vinegar, a ladleful of *murrī*, olive oil, meatballs, soaked chickpeas, pepper, saffron, ginger, and citron leaves. Leave on the fire until it is fully cooked, and then crust with a layer of eggs beaten with spices. Leave on hot stones[25] until it releases its fat.

201. Another dish, called *murūziyya*[26]

Take a chicken of the kind described above, slaughter it, and proceed as before. Cook it in the manner explained in the first chapter of the second section of this book, Allah the Exalted willing.

202. Another dish, called *rāhibī*[27]

Take a chicken of the kind described above, slaughter it and proceed as before. Cook it in the manner explained in the first chapter.

203. Another dish, called *al-mufarrij* ('the consoler') or 'rays of sun'[28]

Take a chicken of the kind described above, slaughter it and proceed as before. Cook it in the manner explained in the first chapter, Allah the Exalted willing.

204. Another dish, called *faḥṣī*[29]

Take a chicken of the kind described above, slaughter it, and proceed

23 According to Gayangos XVI (74v.), the chicken should be taken out before it is done.

24 Addition from Gayangos XVI (*ibid.*).

25 The Arabic word *raḍf* denotes both red-hot stones for keeping food warm and embers. Corriente 1997: 210.

26 See recipe No. 102.

27 Also see recipes Nos. 105, 182, 190, 248, 264, 281, 301.

28 The text has the erroneous *al-mufarriḥ*, which has been corrected to *al-mufarrij*, as it appears in recipe No. 105 (also see recipes Nos. 249, 257). Interestingly enough, *mufarriḥ* has a related meaning, in that it can be translated as 'the gladdener', and was also used in the pharmacological literature to denote a type of cordial (Levey 1973: 87).

29 Also see recipe No. 131.

as before. Cook it in the manner explained in the second chapter of the second section of this book.

205. A dish called *na'na'iyya*[30] (mint stew)
Take a chicken of the kind described above, slaughter it, and proceed as before. Cook it in the manner explained in the second chapter of the second section, Allah the Exalted willing. You can cook it in exactly the same way with lemon balm.

206. Another dish, called *qar'iyya* (gourd dish)[31]
Take pullets or poussins, slaughter them, and proceed as before. Cook them in the way explained in the second chapter of the second section of this book.

207. Another dish, called *ḥiṣrimiyya* (verjuice stew)[32]
Take a plump pullet, slaughter it, and wash and clean it. Put it whole – without the neck – or cut into pieces if you prefer, in a new pot. Add water, salt, olive oil, pepper, coriander seeds and a bit of sliced onion. Place the pot over a fire to cook. When it is done, add juice from strained, fresh sour grapes, or sun-dried ones, as much as you like. Leave the pot over a low fire to simmer down and to balance the flavours. Serve the chicken in a large ceramic bowl, and then eat and enjoy it, Allah the Exalted willing.

208. Another dish, called *summāqiyya* (sumac stew)[33]
Take a chicken of the kind described above, slaughter it, and proceed

30 Also see recipe No. 116.
31 Also see recipes Nos. 128, 250.
32 This was a very popular dish in the Mashriq, with recipes in all cookery books; Ibn Mubārak Shāh 2020: 36 (note 135), 119.
33 It was said to be the caliph Hārūn al-Rashīd's favourite dish and a staple of the early Arabic culinary tradition, but seems to have fallen out of favour by the fifteenth century, as only one recipe appears in cookbooks from that period. It also never managed to embed itself in Andalusian or North African cuisine, since this is the only recipe in sources from that area. For other recipes, see Ibn Mubārak Shāh 2020: 19 (note 66), 27. On the importation of sumac in al-Andalus, see García Sánchez & Ramón-Laca 2001. The dish first became known in Europe (Italy) through a thirteenth-century Latin translation of a recipe by Ibn Jazla (fols. 126v.-127r.; Iambobinus of Cremona, fol. 159r.).

as before. Put it in a new pot with water, salt, good-quality olive oil, pepper, coriander seeds and a bit of onion, and put it over the fire to cook. When it is almost done, take good sumac, devoid of mould, clean and pound it, and then put it in a clean cloth and tie it up. Throw it in the pot with the chicken to cook. Taste it, and if you think that the sumac flavour is noticeable, take the sumac parcel out of the pot and leave it over a low heat to balance the flavours. Serve in a large ceramic bowl and then eat and enjoy it, Allah the Exalted willing.

209. An Eastern dish

Take a chicken as described above, slaughter it and proceed as before, washing and cleaning it. Cut it up in the way you like and put it in a new pot with water, salt, olive oil, pepper, coriander seeds and a little cut-up onion. Put the pot over a fire to cook. When the chicken is done, take forty good raisins, wash them with water to remove any sand on them, and then pound until you get a marrow-like consistency. Take fresh coriander, pound it and extract its juice. Dissolve the raisins in it,[34] strain, and put the resultant liquid in the pot with the chicken, together with half a ladleful of vinegar. Then, take four eggs and crack them into a bowl with salt, pepper, ginger, fresh coriander juice and mint juice. Beat the eggs with a ladle to mix everything together, and pour the mixture in the pot for the crusting. Remove the fire from underneath the pot, and leave it on embers to simmer down and to balance the flavours. Serve in a large ceramic bowl, and dust with cinnamon. Eat and enjoy, Allah the Exalted willing.

210. Another Eastern dish, called the chicken of ʿAmrūs[35]

Take a chicken as described above, slaughter, it and proceed as you did before. Roast it whole. Skewer it on any kind of spit you have to hand and roast it, as described above, away from the fire. When it is almost done, remove it from the spit and chop up the meat as finely as you can. Put it in a new pot with salt, olive oil, coriander seeds and

---

34 The edition (2021: 162) has the rather incongruous 'dissolve olive oil (*zayt*) in it', rather than 'raisins' (*zabīb*).

35 This may be a reference to ʿAmrūs Ibn Yūsuf al-Muwallad, a famous military commander of the Emir of Córdoba al-Ḥakam I, and governor of the Upper March (802) and Toledo (807). Dozy 1861: II 63–7 (trans., 246–8); Collins 2012: 32–3, 217–18.

a bit of onion.[36] When the chicken is fully cooked and the pot has come to a boil, take fresh milk, strain it, and pour it into a bowl. Break eggs into this milk and add a little yeast. Whisk well, until everything is thoroughly mixed. Then pour it into the pot with the chicken and gently stir it. Remove the fire from underneath and leave it on embers to simmer down and to balance the flavours. Eat and enjoy, Allah the Exalted willing.

211. Another dish

Take a large chicken, slaughter it, and wash and clean it as described above, but leave it whole. Softly boil eggs.[37] Take breadcrumbs, put them in a bowl, and add the eggs, as well as salt, ginger, pepper, cinnamon and coriander seeds. Knead everything well and add some saffron, peeled almonds, chopped mint leaves, cooked egg yolks and half a ladleful of olive oil. Stuff this mixture inside the chicken, and also apply it along the sides, and then sew it up. Carefully place it in a large, wide-mouthed pot, and add water, salt, olive oil, pepper, coriander seeds and a bit of cut-up onion. Put the pot over a fire to cook. Once the water has come to a boil, stir the chicken with the ladle handle and flip it from side to side so that it does not stick to the sides of the pot. Make sure you have a large needle to hand, ready to pierce the skin to let the steam out, so that the skin remains intact. When it is done, remove the pot from the fire, take the chicken out, and colour it slightly with saffron. Then put it in a casserole with the strained broth and the fat that was in the pot. Take it to the oven and place it away from the heat, so that it browns. Carefully turn it over so that it browns on the other side as well. When it is done, take it out and transfer it to a large ceramic bowl, along with the fat that is left in the casserole. Garnish with split eggs and mint leafstalks, and sprinkle on cinnamon and ginger. Eat and enjoy it, Allah the Exalted willing. This dish is called *al-Yahūdiyya* (the 'Jewish one').[38]

---

36 Gayangos XVI (fol. 75v.) adds 'and the rest of the spices'.

37 According to Gayangos XVI (*ibid.*), the eggs should be parboiled – 'half-boiled'.

38 This sentence is omitted from the printed edition, and was taken from BL Or5927 (fol. 153r). In Gayangos XVI (fol. 75v.), it is actually the title of the recipe. According to Corriente (1997: 553), *yahūdiyya* referred to a way of cooking chicken (rather than a particular recipe).

212. *Al-Turkiyya* (The 'Turkish' dish)
Take a large chicken, and proceed in exactly the same manner as described above, except that the stuffing also includes ten or less premium olives – either split or whole – and two good-quality pickled limes. Keep this in mind, and do it this way, with the power of Allah the Exalted.

213. Another dish
Take a large chicken, slaughter it, and proceed in the manner already described above. Blow from its neck downwards until the skin comes away from the flesh. Cut the pullet open from the neck down to the bottom of the breast. Remove the skin from the thighs, tailhead and wings. Carefully pick off the meat, but leave the bones as they are. Take the meat of another chicken or a large rooster, whichever you have available, and pound it in a mortar with the meat of the first chicken until you obtain a dough-like consistency, and remove the nerves. Throw on salt, pepper, cinnamon, a grain of mastic, and coriander seeds. Crack about six eggs into this and knead with your hands until everything is mixed together. Stuff the inside of the chicken with this mixture, and also add a pickled lime and five olives. Put the meat on top of the thighs, breast and tailhead. Next, carefully put the skin back on. Sew the chicken back up and also sew the neck. Place the bird in a wide-mouthed pot with water, salt, olive oil, pepper, coriander seeds and a bit of cut-up onion. Put the pot over a fire to cook. Gently turn the chicken over to cook it through and, once it is done, remove it from the pot and put it in a large casserole dish. Colour with saffron and add a little of the strained broth from the pot. Then take it to the oven and have someone there keep an eye on it and turn over the chicken to ensure it is golden brown on all sides. Remove from the oven when it is done and transfer to a large ceramic bowl, together with any broth left in the pot. Garnish with split eggs and mint leafstalks. Eat and enjoy it, Allah the Exalted willing.

214. Another dish
Take a large, plump pullet and slaughter it. Blow from its neck down in order to make the skin come away from the flesh. Tie its neck with twine and gingerly pluck it in hot water. Use your hands to rub the skin with salt to remove all the dirt. Cut it open and remove the intestines

and red lungs. Clean and wash the animal. Next, take the gizzard, thoroughly wash it, and cut it up into small pieces. Put it in a bowl and crack three eggs over it. Also add some breadcrumbs, salt, pepper, coriander seeds, a little bit of pounded onion, fresh coriander juice, mint juice and a little macerated *murrī*. Stuff all of this mixture inside the chicken and sew it up. Then take the breast of another chicken and cut it up into small pieces. After rubbing them with salt, put them in an earthenware frying pan, and fry in oil until done and golden brown. Remove the pan from the fire, transfer the meat to a bowl, and add chopped fresh coriander, coriander seeds, pepper, a bit of pounded onion, a little *murrī* and three eggs. Beat and mix everything together, and then stuff it in between the skin and meat of one side of the chicken. Next, take tender meat, pound it in a mortar, and make a similar stuffing to put in on the other side, and the neck. Tie the neck with twine and put the chicken in a casserole dish. Place it in the oven, away from the fire so that it can roast. Have someone turn it from time to time so that it can cook and brown. Then take a small pot into which you put vinegar, *murrī*, pepper, coriander seeds, fresh coriander juice, a bit of pounded onion, olive oil and a sufficient amount of water. Put it over a fire to cook. Take a chicken breast, pound it in a mortar, and remove the nerves. [Shape into meatballs, as described previously, and cook them in the small pot over a fire.][39] Crust the pot with three eggs, coriander juice, salt and [other] spices. Next, check on the chicken in the oven and, if you see that it is done and golden brown, take it out and transfer to a large ceramic bowl. [Add the meatballs and] pour on what is left in the small pot. Garnish with split eggs and mint leafstalks, and then sprinkle on whatever you like. Eat and enjoy, Allah the Exalted willing.

215. Recipe for *narjisiyya*[40]

Take a plump chicken, slaughter it, clean it, and cut it up, so you are left with two thighs, two breasts and two wings. Put all the pieces in a pot with salt, olive oil, *murrī*, pepper, coriander seeds and oregano. Fry the meat without water until golden brown. Next, take onions and fresh coriander, chop up both and extract their juices in a pot, enough to cover the meat. Let it boil for a while, and then take a bit of grated

39 The passages enclosed in square brackets are additions from Gayangos XVI (fol. 77r.).

40 See recipe No. 125.

crumb of a leavened loaf, and beat it together with two or three eggs, pepper and saffron. Crust the dish with it, and leave it to simmer down on hot stones until its fat is released, and then serve.

216. Recipe for a *Qurashiyya* dish[41]

Take a plump, cleaned chicken, and cut it up as described above, and then put it in a pot with salt, olive oil, a bit of cut-up onion, pepper and a splash of water. Bring to a thorough boil over a fire. Then take the meat out and fry it in a frying pan with olive oil so that it browns all over. Take a clean pot and add two ladlefuls of *murrī*, as well as olive oil, pepper, coriander seeds, saffron, cumin and a little oregano. Put the pot over a fire, and when it has come to a boil throw in the chicken. Prepare a crusting layer by beating six eggs with saffron, and pour it on top. When it is set, remove the pot from the fire, and serve.

217. Dish called *jalīdiyya*, made with a chicken, goose or capon[42]

Take whichever of these animals you have to hand, slaughter and clean it, and then put it in a pot. Next, take two *raṭls* of raisins, pound them smooth and pulp them in water to release their sweetness. Strain and put the juice in a pot, and add a sufficient quantity of vinegar, two ladlefuls of olive oil, pepper, coriander seeds, half a chopped onion and salt. Cook until the sauce thickens. Then take peeled and pounded almonds and walnuts, grated bread crumb, and pepper. Beat all of this with six eggs. Crust the pot with this mixture after everything is cooked to a turn. Finally, garnish with whole egg yolks and then leave on hot stones until it releases its fat, before serving.

---

41 The word is an Andalusian Arabic variant of the more correct *Qurayshiyya*, which is the adjective derived from *Quraysh*, the name of the Prophet Muḥammad's tribe. Corriente (1997: 422) describes the dish as a 'spiced stew of chicken'.

42 The same recipe can be found in the *Andalusian* (*Anwāʿ*, 23–4; BNF, fol. 9v.), which also has a variant, called '*jalīdiyya* with chicken' (Huici Miranda 1961–62: 152, where it is erroneously copied as *jalidiyya*; *Anwāʿ*, 126; BNF, fols. 47v.–48r.). This dish and the next one appear in the same order in both cookery books. The name translates as 'the icy (frosty, congealed) one'.

218. Recipe for a *thūmiyya* ('garlic dish)[43]

Take a plump chicken, remove the entrails and put them to one side. Next, take four *ūqiyas* of peeled garlic, and crush it until you obtain a paste that looks like brains. Mix the garlic in with the entrails and then deep-fry everything in olive oil until the smell of garlic is gone. Add the entrails to the chicken, which you have put in a pot with salt, pepper, spikenard, cardamom, cinnamon, ginger, cloves, saffron, pounded and whole blanched almonds, plenty of olive oil, and a little water so that it does not burn. Seal the pot with dough, and put it in the oven. Once it is done, it is ready to eat.

219. Recipe for a chicken dish called *al-badawiyya* ('the peasant dish')

Take a plump cleaned chicken, joint it and put the pieces in a pot with olive oil, salt, pepper, coriander seeds and vinegar. Cook it halfway through and then fry it in a pan until golden brown. Afterwards, return it to the pot with the broth and squeeze the juice of fresh coriander and white onions over it. Crust with eight eggs when it is entirely done, and then garnish with whole egg yolks. Leave on hot stones until the fat is released, after which it is ready to eat.

220. *Ibrāhīmiyya* recipe[44]

Take a chicken or lamb. Clean the chicken and cut it up into small pieces, two from each limb. Put all the pieces in a pot and pour on a ladleful of olive oil, one ladleful of very sour vinegar, and five ladlefuls of rose syrup sweetened with sugar, pepper, saffron, coriander, salt and a little bit of onion. Put it over a low fire and cook until done. Sprinkle on peeled and broken-up almonds, pistachios, spikenard and cloves. Take a bowl and dissolve a little *ḥuwwārā* flour with rose water, and perfume it with a little camphor dissolved in rose water. Beat four eggs into the bowl and use the resultant mixture to crust the pot. Leave on

43 This dish is near-identical to the one in the *Andalusian* (*Anwāʿ*, 24; BNF, fols. 9v.–10r.), which adds that it was prepared for the Catalan Muslim convert and governor of Marrakech, *sayyid* Abū 'l-Ḥasan (d. 1187), who was in the employ of the Almohad sultan Yaʿqūb al-Manṣūr (d. 1199).

44 This is one of several dishes named after the caliph Ibrāhīm Ibn al-Mahdī (*vide ante*). For other *Ibrāhīmiyya* recipes, see: al-Warrāq 1987: 152–4; al-Baghdādī 1964: 14 (trans., 31); *Anwāʿ*, 24 (BNF, fol. 40r.); Ibn Mubārak Shāh 2020: 15.

hot stones until the fat has been released, and then it is ready to eat, Allah the Exalted willing.

221. Recipe for making *jūdhāba*[45]

Take a fattened pullet, clean it, and split open the breast. Throw it in a pot as it is, with sweet olive oil, salt, pepper, cinnamon, spikenard and cardamom. Cook it over a fire until done. Instead of water, add good-quality rose water, and cook the dish dry, without any broth. When it is done, take two thin flatbreads (*ruqāq*), which will be

---

45 The *Andalusian* has four *jūdhāba* (in the Mashriq more often *jūdhāb*) recipes (*Anwāʿ*, 103, 175–8; BNF, fols. 41r., 62r.–63r.), one of which contains very similar instructions (*Anwāʿ*, 176; BNF, fol. 62r.–v.). It was one of the most famous medieval dishes, though this particular variation differs considerably from the usual drip pudding method of the Near Eastern manuals, which involved a chicken being roasted over a fruit pudding; see Ibn Mubārak Shāh 2020: 26 (note 94). The Eastern method would appear to have been the standard, however, as al-Tujībī's contemporary Ibn al-Ḥashshā' (1941: 29, No. 267) explained, the *jūdhāba* was a type of food made with rice and thin flatbreads (*ruqāq*), with bread and vegetables being optional. It is put in the *tannūr* with a fatty animal like a lamb, goose or kid being roasted above it, its fat dripping onto the bread. Indeed, 'if it is not made this way it is not a *jūdhāba*'. The dish here clearly shows some similarities with the modern Moroccan *basṭīla* (*pastilla*, *bstila* in English) – though lacking the pastry element of the modern dish – and some scholars (for example, Gaul 2018) have traced the origins of the latter to the present text, albeit it to the wrong recipe (No. 252). According to Būhīla (2012: 128–30), *basṭīla* is one of the foods imported by Algerians (who originally got it from the Turks) settling in Tetouan in the nineteenth century, and even brought with it its name. The two views are not incompatible, of course, and one can easily imagine that the basic method, as described in the medieval Andalusian cookery books, continued without interruption with the addition of filo pastry later on (whether through Algerian immigration or not). The Tetouan connection would appear to be an important one, though, since Sultan Ḥasan I sent a group of female kitchen servants to the city in 1889 to acquire a number of dishes for which it was famous, among them several *pastillas* (al-Mannūnī 1992). Despite somewhat of a consensus that this dish was imported into Morocco by Andalusian refugees from the Reconquista (Brunot 1952: II, 52), it has been suggested that it actually travelled in the opposite direction and originated in Morocco (Roden 2000: 150). According to Ibn al-Khaṭīb (1984: 59), it was also known as *muʿassal* (see recipes Nos. 150, 392). The sixteenth-century Persian scholar al-Harawī (1830: 88) claimed it is made with meat, bread, milk, sugar, spices and seasonings, but that it can also be made without meat. Al-Rāzī praised it for its nutritiousness, but suggested taking a nap afterwards to facilitate digestion (1881: 51). He warned it could cause colic, especially if one eats a lot of vegetables with it and drinks water after it (*idem* 1987: 138). In his book on poisons, Jābir Ibn Ḥayyān (eighth century) prescribed a very fatty *jūdhāb* after taking arsenic medication and theriacs (Siggel 1958: 192, 199).

mentioned shortly, and flatten them out on the bottom of a stone or earthenware pot, whose sides and bottom have been coated with clean kidney suet that has been pounded to a marrow-like consistency. The edges of the flatbreads should hang over the sides of the pot and will be used to cover others later. On the bottom flatbreads, you should throw sugar, broken and pounded almonds, cloves, spikenard, and a fair amount of sweet olive oil. Dust with sugar and sprinkle on rose water in which some camphor and musk have been dissolved – just enough to moisten the sugar. Then spread two flatbreads – or just one – on top of this, and then scatter on sugar, almonds, spices and olive oil. Also sprinkle with rose water as before. Then spread another flatbread on, and continue layering until the stack is halfway up the pot. Take the prepared chickens,[46] which you will have rubbed with saffron dissolved in rose water, and place them in the centre of the pot. Cover them with flatbreads on which you sprinkle sugar and almonds, as before, and continue adding successive layers until you have filled up the pot. The chickens should be buried in the middle. When all this is finished, sprinkle on a lot of sugar and add a generous amount of olive oil and rose water. Next, cover it with the flatbreads hanging over the sides of the pot, put a lid on the pot, and seal it with dough. Place it in the oven at a moderate temperature, and leave for as long as you would a pot with meat. When you think it is ready, take it out and break the seal of the lid. When it exudes a nice fragrance, you know that it is fully cooked. Now remove the flatbread that covers the top if it is touched by the fire, as well as anything else that is stuck to the sides of the pot. Then, transfer as is to a bowl, and serve. This is a wonderfully crafted dish, fit for kings. It is very nutritious, causes good humours, and has a wonderful composition.

This *judhāba* can also be made without chicken or meat, with layers of flatbreads alternating with layers made up of broken and pounded almonds, sugar, Indian spices, and saffron. Pour on rose water and fine olive oil. When it is ready, put it in a bowl and eat with rose syrup sweetened with sugar and fresh butter.[47] If you prefer, you can also

---

46 I follow BL Or5927 (fol. 155v.) in using the plural, rather than the singular of the edition (2012: 168).

47 At this point, Gayangos XVI (fol. 79v.) is the only copy to include the instructions for making *ruqāq* that are signposted at the beginning of the recipe: 'As for *ruqāq*,

omit the syrup.

222. Recipe for a dish called *maghmūm*[48] ('covered'), which is made with a chicken, goose, squabs or turtledoves

Take a cleaned chicken and put it whole with its breast cut open in a pot containing salt, olive oil, pepper, coriander seeds and a bit of onion. When it is cooked halfway through, remove it and transfer to another pot, and add its fat, macerated *murrī*, saffron, spikenard, oregano, and citron leaves. Put a lime inside the abdominal cavity. Sprinkle on halved almonds and seal the mouth of the pot with dough. Bake in the oven until done, and then serve.

223. Another dish

Take a chicken, as described above, slaughter it, and proceed as before.[49] Next, take the gizzard, clean it and cut it into small pieces. Add salt, pepper, chopped fresh coriander, coriander seeds, a little *murrī* and three cracked eggs. Mix it all together and stuff the inside of the chicken with it, and then sew it up. Afterwards, take the breast of another chicken and pound it in a mortar with peeled almonds, a little coarse semolina and clarified butter. Add pepper, coriander seeds, *murrī* some onion, fresh coriander and mint juice, and a cracked egg. Whisk everything together, and then stuff the mixture in between the skin and the meat. Salt the outside of the chicken and carefully skewer it on a spit. Roast it at a sufficient distance from the flames, rotating it,[50] and from time to time rub it with olive oil and salt until it is done and golden brown. Then take a small pot and add a sufficient amount

---

making them is not unknown. Moisten semolina, knead well with salt and a little water, and then shape into as many *ruqāq* as required for this recipe. If you want a more elegant way of making it, cook it with *darmak* flour and butter, etc.'

48 This recipe is near-identical to one in *Anwāʿ* (18; BNF, fols. 7v.–8r.), which calls for two limes being stuffed inside the chicken, and recommends the dish for being nutritious and agreeable to the stomach. Also see recipe No. 139.

49 The instructions in Gayangos XVI (fol. 80r.) are more detailed, and are similar to those in other recipes (e.g. Nos. 215, 231): 'Take a large plump chicken, slaughter it but leave the feathers. Blow from the neck downwards to remove the skin from the meat, and then tie the neck with twine. Gently pluck the feathers in hot water, and rub it with salt to clean it. Open up the insides, remove the innards and lungs, and clean the animal inside and out.'

50 This translation is based on the word in Wetzstein 1217 (fol. 53v.), i.e., *tudīruhā*, rather than the clearly misspelt *tudharruhā* ('sprinkle it') in the edition (2012: 169).

of water, salt, vinegar, a sufficient amount of *murrī*, some sugar, fresh coriander, coriander seeds, pepper and chopped *laqāniq* sausages,[51] as well as meatballs made from the breast of another chicken. When everything in the pot is done, apply a crusting of five eggs mixed with peeled and pounded almonds, as in the above recipe. Kindle a fire underneath the pot and leave it on the embers. Check on the chicken and, if it is done and browned, gently remove it from the spit and place it in a large ceramic bowl. Pour the contents of the small pot over it, and dust with cinnamon. Eat and enjoy, Allah the Exalted willing.

224. Another Eastern dish

Take a chicken and proceed in the manner described above. Next, take its gizzard and cut it into small pieces, after cleaning it. Add fine olive oil, pepper, chopped fresh coriander, coriander seeds, salt, a bit of cut-up onion, finely chopped peeled almonds, and three eggs. Beat everything together, stuff the mixture inside the chicken, and sew the chicken back up. Next, put it on a spit, and roast over a low fire, away from the flames. When it is done and golden brown, mix together vinegar, *murrī*, coriander seeds, caraway, fresh coriander juice and oregano. Then take the chicken off the spit, put it in a ceramic bowl and pour the sauce mixture over it or, alternatively, leave it on the side as a dip for bread and meat. Eat and enjoy, Allah the Exalted willing.

225. Another Eastern dish

Take a chicken and proceed in the manner described above. Next, take the gizzard and cut it into small pieces. Add spices and eggs, and then stuff the resultant mixture inside the chicken, after which you sew it up. Then, take the gizzard from a goose and put it in a pot with salt, *murrī*, vinegar, pepper, caraway and coriander seeds. Put it in the pot with the chicken, and place it inside the oven. Have someone keep an eye on it and turn the chicken over from time to time. Taste the broth and, if it is to your liking, so much the better. If not, add what you think is missing from the dish, but make sure it does not burn. When it is done and golden brown, remove the pot from the oven, transfer the meat to a large ceramic bowl and pour the broth over it. Eat and enjoy, Allah the Exalted willing.

---

51 See recipe No. 184.

226. Another Eastern dish

Take a chicken and proceed in the manner described earlier, blowing and cleaning it. Then take the gizzard, cut it up into small pieces, and add salt, olive oil, coriander seeds and chopped coriander leaves, pepper, some cut-up onion, and three eggs. Mix all this together, stuff it inside the chicken, and then sew it up. Take another chicken, remove the bones, thoroughly mash the meat in a mortar, and add salt, pepper, cinnamon, a little spikenard, fresh coriander juice and three eggs. Beat it all together until it is thoroughly mixed, and then stuff the mixture on one side of the chicken, between the skin, the meat and the bones. Next, take the breast of another chicken, cut it into small pieces, and then salt and fry it in a pan with olive oil until done. Then, take it out of the frying pan and add *murrī*, pepper and two eggs. Beat until everything is well mixed, and then apply the mixture to the other side of the chicken. Tie the neck of the chicken, and then put it in a casserole dish. Take it to the oven and leave it until it is roasted, positioning it away from the flames. Regularly turn the chicken over until it is fully cooked and golden brown. Next, take three eggs and boil them in water. When they are done, take them out, peel them and remove the coagulated yolks. Take fresh coriander, chop it up and crush it until it becomes like marrow. Mix it with the yolks, and add vinegar, *murrī*, pepper, caraway, coriander seeds and olive oil. Stir until everything is well mixed. Put the chicken in a large ceramic bowl and pour the sauce over it. Eat and enjoy, Allah the Exalted willing.

227. Another Eastern dish

Take a chicken and proceed in the manner described above. Next, take the gizzard, cut it into small pieces, and add salt, pepper, coriander leaves and seeds, *murrī*, a bit of cut-up onion, and pounded tender meat. Crack two eggs in, and beat all the ingredients together until everything is mixed. Stuff this mixture inside the chicken, and sew it up. Next, take *laqāniq* sausages,[52] split them lengthwise, and add fresh coriander juice, coriander seeds, olive oil, *murrī* and pepper, and beat in three egg yolks. Stuff this mixture on one side of the chicken. Then, take the breast of another chicken, pound it in a mortar, and add chopped fresh coriander, coriander seeds, pepper, olive oil, two

52 See recipe No. 184.

crushed walnuts, *murrī* and two eggs. Beat it all together and stuff the other side of the chicken with it. Next, take tender meat, pound it, add spices as described above, and stuff the mixture in the neck of the chicken before sewing it up. When all this is done, take the chicken and put it in a wide-mouthed pot or cauldron, and add vinegar and *murrī* – more of the former than the latter – olive oil, whole *laqāniq*, *isfīriyya*, meatballs, salt, pepper, coriander seeds and a bit of cut-up onion. Colour the chicken with saffron, and add enough water to cook it. Put it over a fire to cook and carefully turn it over, making sure that the skin does not tear away. When it is done, take it out of the pot and put it in a casserole dish with the broth. Finally, apply a layer of eggs mixed with crushed walnuts, and take it to the oven for this to crust. After removing dish from the oven, transfer it to a ceramic bowl, and throw on split eggs and aromatic spices of your liking. Eat and enjoy, Allah the Exalted willing.

228. Another Eastern dish

Take a chicken as described above, and clean it very well inside and out. Next, take the gizzard, clean it and then cut it into small pieces. Add salt, chopped fresh coriander, coriander seeds, pepper, a bit of pounded onion and two eggs. Beat everything together and stuff it inside the chicken. Sew it up, tie its neck with twine, and then put it in a wide pot with salt. Put it over a fire to cook and, when the chicken is done and tender, transfer it to a large ceramic bowl, and top with split eggs. Then, take the yolks of three eggs, put them in a bowl and pour on some of the broth in which the chicken was cooked. Rub the yolks with your hands until they dissolve and the broth turns yellow. Pour the liquid onto the chicken from which you have removed the thread at the breast and neck. Scoop out the stuffing and mix it with the broth. Dust with pepper and cinnamon, and then eat and enjoy, Allah the Exalted willing.

229. Another Eastern dish

Take a plump chicken, as described above, and do the same as before. Next, take the gizzard, cut it into small pieces, and mix it with a breast, also chopped up. Add salt, pepper, coriander seeds, chopped fresh coriander, a bit of pounded onion and two eggs. Beat it all together, stuff the mixture inside the chicken, and sew it up. Put it in a wide pot with a sufficient amount of water and salt, and put it over a fire to cook. Take boiled eggs and the boiled liver of the chicken, and crush both in a mortar. Add fresh coriander leafstalks, some rue and a clove of garlic, and crush everything. Take cooked egg yolks and pound them separately, adding sweet vinegar, *murrī*, pepper, coriander seeds and caraway. Stir everything, and then tend to the chicken; if it is done, take it out of the pot and transfer it to a ceramic bowl. On top of it, put the crushed eggs and livers, as well as everything else that has been mentioned. Eat and enjoy, Allah the Exalted willing.

230. Another Eastern dish

Take a large, plump chicken, slaughter it and blow from the neck downwards to make the skin come away from the meat. If any of the skin sticks to it, gently remove it with your fingers, or whatever else you have to hand. Then tie the neck while it is still inflated and pluck it in hot water, taking care not to tear the skin. Next, slice open the skin of the neck and gingerly remove all the meat and bones, but leave the skin on the tailhead, parts of the thighs, and the ends of the wings near the joints. Strip the meat from the bones. Take the meat from another chicken, and pound the meat of both animals in a mortar, while removing the veins. Afterwards, add salt, pepper, ginger, cinnamon, coriander seeds, fresh coriander and mint juice, a little bit of cut-up onion, sweet olive oil, and macerated *murrī*. Then take six eggs and boil them in water. When they are cooked, peel and crush them in a mortar until you obtain a fully smooth mixture, and work this in with the meat. Take four coagulated yolks and one boiled egg, and stuff the skin with the meat pounded with the spices and the eggs, after kneading it into a dough. Shape it like a chicken and sew up the neck and the parts of the skin that have been torn. Place it in a new wide pot. Then take two squabs and do the same with them as you did with the chicken. Add water, salt, olive oil, pepper, coriander seeds, a bit of cut-up onion, vinegar and a sufficient amount of *murrī*. Cut the chicken and squab gizzards into small pieces and put them in the pot, together with *mirqās* sausages[53] cut in half. Add all of this to the chicken. Put the required amount of water in the pot and put it over a

53 See recipes Nos. 182, 183.

fire to cook. Cautiously turn the chicken and squabs from time to time, and keep an eye on them. When they are done, colour with saffron, but do not overdo it. When the pot has come to a boil after putting in the saffron, remove it from the fire and transfer the contents to a large bowl, into which you also put the squabs. Pour the strained broth over everything, and also scatter on split boiled eggs and mint leafstalks. Finally, sprinkle on aromatic spices of your choice. Eat and enjoy, Allah the Exalted willing.

If you like, you can bake it in the oven until it has turned golden brown. The aim here is that the chicken and squabs should remain intact, without tearing the skin, and that they are served whole in the bowl until they are carved and eaten, with the power and strength of Allah the Exalted.

231. Another Eastern dish

Take a chicken as described above, and clean it very well. Next, take the gizzard, clean it, cut it into small pieces, and add salt, pepper, coriander seeds, crushed fresh coriander, *murrī*, a bit of sliced onion, olive oil, the pounded meat of another chicken, and three broken eggs. Beat all of these ingredients until everything is mixed together. Stuff this filling inside the chicken and then sew it up. Put it in a wide pot with good vinegar, a sufficient amount of *murrī*, olive oil, what remains of the stuffing, and caraway. Put it over a fire to cook with good clear water and stir from time to time to prevent anything from sticking to the pot. Add fresh coriander juice or onion juice.[54] Next, take two quinces free from rot and worms, clean them inside and out, and put them in the pot to cook with the chicken. When the quinces are done, take them out and crush them in a mortar with fresh coriander, breadcrumbs, three eggs and pounded chicken meat. Add a sufficient amount of spices and beat with the eggs until everything is mixed. Then take some of the strained broth from the pot, add it to this mixture, and stir until it has been absorbed. Crust the dish with the egg mixture, and then remove the fire from underneath the pot so that it can simmer down, before transferring the contents to a large ceramic bowl. Eat and enjoy, Allah the Exalted willing.

54 According to BL Or5927 (fol. 158v.), the juice of both is included.

232. Another dish

Take as many chickens and fattened capons as you like. Slaughter them, pluck them and clean them thoroughly. Cut the breast, tailhead and thighs in half, and put the pieces in a new wide pot with water, salt, plenty of olive oil, pepper, coriander seeds, a bit of sliced onion, peeled almonds, and pine nuts. Put the pot over a fire to cook and, when it is done, add enough crushed and dissolved saffron to colour the dish, but do not use too much. Then take a lot of eggs, twenty or so for each bird, and crack them into a bowl. Add salt, pepper, ginger, cinnamon, cloves, a sufficient amount of spikenard, a bit of onion, mastic, fresh coriander and mint juice, and a little saffron. Beat everything together, but first separate out as many yolks as you want. Next, take a large casserole dish and put the strained broth and fat in it. Take the pot and tip its contents into another bowl. Take the pieces of meat, dip them in the beaten eggs and then place them in the casserole. Pour the eggs on top. Make sure that the bottom of the pan has previously been covered with beaten eggs. Layer the pieces of meat, covering them with what is left over from the egg mixture. Garnish the surface of the dish with the egg yolks, almonds and pine nuts. Add the remaining fat to the broth, and sprinkle on cinnamon and ginger. Take the dish to the oven and place it away from the flames until it sets and browns. When it is ready, take it out and eat it, Allah the Exalted willing, when it has lost some of its heat, since it tastes better that way.

233. Another dish

Take fattened chickens and capons of your choice, and proceed in the above manner. After cleaning and cutting them up, put the pieces in a large new pot with water, salt, plenty of olive oil, pepper, coriander seeds, a bit of sliced onion, peeled almonds, pine nuts, fresh acorns and chestnuts, and picked-over and blanched skinned walnuts. Put the pot over a fire to cook. Next, break and put salt on eggs – thirty for each bird – and add pepper, ginger, cinnamon, spikenard, cloves and a sufficient amount of saffron. After removing and setting aside about ten yolks, vigorously beat the eggs with a ladle so that they are mixed in with the aromatic spices. Next, check on the chicken meat and, if you find that it is done, transfer it to another bowl. Take a large tinned frying pan, put it over a fire with olive oil and some strained broth. Remove it from the heat, layer the meat in it, and pour enough eggs over to cover it – as much as the pan will hold. Then, put it over a moderate fire and, when the eggs are about to set, take a knife to cut away any egg batter that clings to the chicken pieces. Cautiously turn them over in the frying pan and fry them until they are golden brown and fried to a turn, but take care not to burn them. Once you have finished the frying, remove the pieces and place them in a ceramic bowl, and on top layer some of the fried egg batter you cut earlier. Do the same with the remaining meat and batter, until you have nothing left, Allah the Exalted willing. Next, take the egg yolks and fry them. If you want, you can take the livers, pound them and make an *isfīriyya*, as described above. The same applies if you want to make meatballs. After layering the meat in the ceramic bowls, garnish it with the egg yolks, *isfīriyya*, split eggs, and meatballs. Pour in the remaining fat, and sprinkle with the aromatic spices of your liking. Note that almonds, pine nuts, walnuts, acorns and chestnuts should be mixed with the egg batter when pouring them in the frying pan. Some people add small pieces of good-quality dry cheese to the batter. Eat and enjoy, Allah the Exalted willing.

234. Another dish[55]

Take a plump pullet, thoroughly clean it, and apply salt inside and out before skewering it on an iron or wooden spit. Light a fire on either side, but make sure that the animal is away from the flames. Gently roast until it is done and golden brown. Make sure that you rotate[56] and baste it throughout with a mixture of olive oil, *murrī* and crushed garlic. Be patient, and keep on basting until the meat has had its fill. Next, put pepper, caraway, coriander seeds, oregano, vinegar, a sufficient amount of *murrī*, and olive oil into a small pot and place it over a fire to cook. When it has come to a boil, taste it, and if it tastes nice, put four whole eggs in the pot. Once the eggs are cooked, remove the pot from the fire. Carve the chicken in a bowl and add the mixture as well as the peeled eggs. For the sauce, you may, if you like, also use olive oil and crushed cooked garlic, and carve the hot chicken in it. You could

55 In Gayangos XVI (fol. 83v.), the dish is called *maḥshuw*, which is used here in the sense of dressing, rather than stuffing, as is the case in other recipes (e.g. No. 354).

56 Addition from Gayangos XVI (*ibid.*).

also put crushed cloves of garlic in the sauce first. Eat and enjoy, Allah the Exalted willing.

Or, if you prefer, you may use olive oil, macerated *murrī* and oregano crumbled with your hands.

If you wish, you can use good-quality dry cheese and grate it to powder. Next, take garlic, cook it in water, crush it, and then put it in a bowl. Dissolve the powdered cheese in hot water and mix it with the garlic. Carve up the chicken and douse the pieces in the cheese mixture. Finish it off with a splash of olive oil.

Instead of cheese, you can use *shīrāz* (cottage cheese)[57] or thick *rā'ib* (curdled milk),[58] which would be the best with cockerels roasted in a *tannūr*.

If you want to roast chickens in a *tannūr*, you need to thread them on a spit, heat the *tannūr* by piling up the embers, and, once it is white-hot, put the spit inside. At the bottom of the *tannūr*, put a casserole filled with water and olive oil, into which you place one end of the spit. Cover the *tannūr*, and seal off with mud. When the chicken is done, take it out and carve it in a bowl with a dressing of your choice from those already mentioned.

---

57 See recipe No. 319.

58 See recipes Nos. 320-1 for making *rā'ib* (more often *rāyib*), which in the Mashriq usually denoted yoghurt made without rennet. See Nasrallah [al-Warrāq 2007]: 587; C. E. Bosworth, in Waines 2011: 168. García-Sánchez (1986: 275, note 175) rightly points to the distinction made by medieval sources between *rā'ib* and *'aqīd* (recipe No. 317); the former denotes coagulated milk, after the cream and fat have been removed, whereas the latter is the result of adding rennet to fresh milk which has been previously heated. Al-Uryūlī (1983: No; 129) recommended *rā'ib* for a hot stomach, though it is harmful to the nerves and to those suffering from colic. Its negative effects, like those of all sour milks, can be counteracted with fresh milk. Ibn Zuhr (1992: 31; trans., 62) added that it has a laxative effect and disturbs the brain, while Ibn Khalṣūn (1996: 160; trans., 88) held that *rā'ib* was particularly suitable for hot and bilious temperaments and young people, but not for old people and phlegmatics. According to al-Rāzī (1987: 142), it suits those with hot temperaments and stomachs, and is less bloating than *māst* (soured milk). Opinions varied on the latter Persian word, meaning 'sour, coagulated milk' (Steingass 1892: 1140). Maimonides and others said it was *rā'ib*, while Ibn al-Ḥashshā' (1941: No. 689) and Ibn al-Bayṭār (1992: IV, 373, 421) claimed it was a mildly sour variety of *rā'ib*. Al-Isrā'ilī (1992: 130, 141, 558) also equated the two, adding that *dūgh* (another Persian borrowing, meaning buttermilk and thus the equivalent of the Arabic *makhīḍ*) was sour (*ḥāmid*) milk which had matured longer than the coagulated (*rā'ib*) milk called *māst*. See Ibn Janāḥ 2020: Nos. 435–6, 557–8, 727–9; Dozy 1881: II, 564; al-Rāzī 1881: 33; *idem* 1987: 141. Today, *rā'ib* (made from cow's milk) is still popular throughout the Maghrib.

If you want, you can roast the bird in a pot inside a brick oven, in which case you should skewer the chicken on a small spit, apply salt, and place it in a pot with olive oil and crushed garlic. Put a lid on the pot and seal it with dough. Place it inside the oven, away from the flames. When you think it is done, take the pot out, and eat it in the manner you like. Similarly, if you want to roast it in a casserole dish in the oven, rub the chicken with olive oil and salt, put it into the dish, and add olive oil and crushed garlic. Put the dish inside the oven, away from the flames, and have someone turn the chicken over until it is done and golden brown. When it is ready, take it out and serve, Allah the Exalted willing.

235. Another dish[59]

Take a plump pullet and thoroughly clean it, but leave it whole. Salt and rub with olive oil, macerated *murrī*, pepper, and oregano before putting it in a casserole dish with a little water. Place it in the oven until it is roasted and golden brown. Next, thoroughly mix about six egg yolks with pepper, cinnamon and ginger. Check on the chicken and, if you see that it is done, remove it from the oven and baste with the egg mixture. Make sure you fully coat the chicken with it. Return the chicken to the oven for the egg mixture to set. Turn the chicken over to ensure it browns completely, but take care not to burn it. When it is all ready, take it out and serve it, Allah the Exalted willing.

236. Another dish

Take a plump pullet and clean it very well. Put it whole in a new pot and add two ladlefuls of honey dissolved in rose water, three ladlefuls of olive oil, a sufficient amount of salt, pepper, peeled almonds and a little water. Put the pot over a low fire to cook. Next, take *darmak* flour and knead it well with some yeast. Moisten it with a bit of water, and then use a rolling pin to roll the dough out as thinly as you can into flat loaves. Put the sheets into a casserole dish, brushing each one with olive oil, and stacking them one on top of the other until all the dough has been used up. On top of the stack, put a thick loaf made from another dough. Now, take the casserole to the oven and bake it away from the fire. When you see that the thick top loaf is golden brown,

59 In Gayangos XVI (fol. 84v.), the recipe is called a 'roast' (*mashwī*).

remove the casserole from the oven. Next, take the chicken after it has been cooked, and put it in a large ceramic bowl. Break the flatbreads and put the pieces on top, followed by the broth. Dust with caster sugar. Eat and enjoy, Allah the Exalted willing.

237. Another dish

Take cockerels and thoroughly clean them, but leave them whole. Place them in a new pot with three *ūqiyas* of rose water in which three *ūqiyas* of sugar have been dissolved, as well as pepper, pine nuts, peeled almonds, two ladlefuls of good-quality olive oil, and a little water. Put the pot over a fire to cook. Next, take *khabīṣ*[60] flatbreads, the making of which is explained in the first section of this book, and fry them in a clean frying pan with olive oil until they are golden brown. Then take them out, break them, and add them to the pot with the chickens. Cook over a low heat until it has thickened and is done. Transfer the chickens[61] and everything else that is in the pot with them into a bowl, and give it a dusting with caster sugar and cinnamon. Eat and enjoy, Allah the Exalted willing.

This recipe can also be made with squabs, with the power and strength of Allah the Exalted.

238. Another Eastern dish

Take a chicken breast, pound it very well, and shape into meatballs, as explained above. Add fresh coriander juice to the meat mixture, and put the meatballs to one side, in a bowl. Take fresh chestnuts, if possible – if you have to use dry ones, boil them first to soften them. Then take a small pot into which you put water, salt, coriander seeds, pepper, onion juice, fresh coriander juice, and olive oil. Place it over a fire and, when it comes to a boil, add the meatballs and leave them until they are done. Take the chestnuts, crush them and put them in with the meatballs. Then, pour a little vinegar in the pot and apply a layer of eggs on top to crust the dish, as explained before. When the flavours have balanced, eat and enjoy, Allah the Exalted willing.

---

60 See recipe No. 63.

61 It is unclear whether there is a scribal error here, or in the reference to cockerels at the beginning of the recipe.

239. Another Eastern dish

Take fresh chicken breast[62] meat and cut it up. Also cut up mushrooms, that is to say *fuqqaʿ*,[63] and then thoroughly wash everything. Mind you do not use too much meat. Put it all in a pot with water, salt, olive oil or fresh butter, a chopped onion, fresh coriander juice and pepper. Put the pot over a fire to cook. When it is done, add a little *murrī* and crust the dish with two eggs, as explained before. Serve in a ceramic bowl, and sprinkle on pepper. Eat and enjoy, Allah the Exalted willing.

240. A roasted dish[64]

Clean plump chickens and place them on sticks raised in the bottom of a pot. Seal its lid with clay and insert it in the oven away from the fire. When the chickens are done, remove the pot, and the fat will have gathered at the bottom of the pot. Pound salt, pepper, cinnamon and ginger, and mix them with the fat. Pour the mixture on the chickens when serving them.

62 BL Or5927simply has 'chicken'.

63 This borrowing from Italian was the Andalusian Arabic word for 'mushroom' (*fuṭr*). Al-Ishbīlī (2004–10: No. 2580) says that *fuqqa*ᶜ is the name of a variety of plants, more specifically the desert truffle (ᶜ*usqul*), which is very big – larger than the palm of the hand. Elsewhere (*ibid.*, No. 3790), he says that it refers to white and black mushrooms, with *fuṭr* being restricted to the black variety, 'the worst species'. The more common variant form is *fuqqā*ᶜ (*ibid.*, No. 3791; Colin & Renaud 1934: No. 320), which was also pronounced *fuggā*ᶜ. This term also denoted a kind of beverage made with yeast, honey and spices, for which there are several recipes in the Eastern cookbooks, but none from the Maghrib, even though it was known there, as evidenced by Ibn al-Bayṭār (1992: III, 225–6, 213). Also see Ibn Mubārak Shāh 2020: xxv, Nos. 166–70.

64 This recipe is only included in Gayangos XVI (fol. 85v.).

Chapter Three: on partridge meat[65]

241. Dish[66]

After skinning, thoroughly washing and cleaning a partridge, put it in a new pot with water, salt, olive oil, pepper, coriander seeds, a bit of cut-up onion, peeled almonds, a ladleful of macerated *murrī* and a little vinegar. Put the pot over a fire to cook. When it is done, take the partridge out, put it in a casserole dish together with the strained broth in which it was cooked, and brown it in the oven. When it is ready, take it out and serve it, Allah the Exalted willing.

242. Another dish

Skin a partridge, wash it inside and out, and put it in a pot with water, salt, pepper, coriander seeds, cumin, a bit of cut-up onion, garlic cloves, soaked chickpeas, peeled almonds, citron leaves, a fennel stalk and some *murrī*. Put the pot over a fire to cook and, when it is almost done, take the breast meat of another partridge, pound it very well and make meatballs out of it, as explained earlier. Add them to the partridge, and then colour the dish with saffron. Finally, pour some good-quality vinegar into the pot, as much as you like. Take eggs and crack them into a bowl, and add a little saffron, salt and aromatic spices, as described above, and use this mixture to crust the dish. Remove the pot from the fire and set it on embers to simmer down and for the crusting layer to

---

65 *ḥajal* (also *qabj* or *ṭayhūj* – though these more properly denoted, respectively, the male partridge and the male chick). The eating of partridge is mostly associated with Andalusian gastronomy, and the anonymous treatise from the same period has a staggering seventeen recipes requiring it, two of them so-called 'Jewish' dishes (see Introduction). It is absent from all Near Eastern cookery books, except al-Warrāq's, which contains two recipes (1987: 286), both of them medicinal stews. According to Ibn Zuhr (1992: 15; trans., 51), partridge meat is astringent if it is boiled before being stewed, while its broth before it has boiled has laxative properties. Ibn Jazla (fols. 168v.–169r.) called it one of the most pleasant meats, as well as being aphrodisiac and very nutritional provided it is well cooked, since otherwise it is slow to digest. It was suggested to leave the meat for a day after slaughtering the animal to increase its benefits (*Taṣānīf*, fol.53r.). Ibn Khalṣūn (1996: 159; trans., 85) said that the male partridge is the best to eat. Its meat prevents diarrhoea and strengthens the stomach, but can cause fevers to those suffering from colic, though this can be remedied by frying the bird in sweet almond oil and crusting it with egg yolks. Also see Brisville 2018a: I, 402–6; Ibn Janāḥ 2020: Nos. 421, 825.

66 In the title of this dish and the next, Gayangos XVI (fol. 86r.) adds that it is 'amazing'.

set. Serve in a large ceramic bowl, garnish with split eggs, and sprinkle on cinnamon and ginger. Eat and enjoy, Allah the Exalted willing.

243. Another dish

Clean and wash a partridge, leave its skin on, and inflate it before plucking it. Next, take the meat of another partridge or of a small lamb and pound it well in a mortar. Add peeled and pounded almonds, whole almonds, pine nuts, breadcrumbs, pepper, ginger, salt and cinnamon. Crush two boiled eggs with your hands and add them to the meat. Next, take raw egg yolks and fold them into the mixture until everything is thoroughly mixed. Stuff this filling into the partridge, in between the skin and the meat, as well as inside. Sew it up and put it in a casserole dish with water, salt, olive oil, pepper, and coriander seeds. Put it over a fire to cook. When the partridge is almost ready, colour it with saffron, add a ladleful of macerated *murrī*, and then put it in the oven. Once it is golden brown all over, remove the casserole from the oven and leave it to settle and cool down. Eat and enjoy, Allah the Exalted willing.

244. Another dish[67]

Skin, wash and thoroughly clean a partridge, leaving it whole. Put it in a new pot, and add water, salt, pepper, coriander seeds, olive oil and a ladleful of white vinegar. Take the breast of another partridge and pound it very well. Take half of this to make an *isfīriyya*, as explained in Chapter Six of Section Two in this book,[68] and put it to one side. Pound the other half with peeled almonds, soak in water and add it all to the partridge. When it is done, coat it with egg whites mixed with a little flour and breadcrumbs. Leave on embers to set and simmer. Transfer to a ceramic bowl and add the *isfīriyya* strips on top. Sprinkle on ginger, and then eat and enjoy, Allah the Exalted willing.

245. Another dish

Skin a partridge and skewer it on an iron or wooden spit. Light a fire on the sides, but do not put the bird close to the flames. Turn the spit by hand until the partridge is done and golden brown. In the meantime,

---

67 Gayangos XVI (fol. 86v.) adds that it is 'good'.

68 Recipe No. 181.

you will have been rubbing it with olive oil, salt, macerated *murrī* and crushed garlic. Once it is done and golden brown, remove it from the spit and carve it up in an earthenware bowl, with the dressing of your choice from the ones mentioned in Chapter Two of Section Three in this book.[69] Eat and enjoy, Allah the Exalted willing.

Chapter Four: on squab meat[70]

246. Dish

Take a squab, slaughter it, and gently pluck it. Cut it open and remove the entrails. Wash and clean it before putting it in a new pot with a little water, salt, a generous amount of olive oil, pepper, coriander seeds, cloves of garlic, a bit of sliced onion and some good *murrī*. Put the pot over a fire to cook. When it is done and the water has evaporated, leave it over a low fire, while stirring the squab in the pot to fry it in the olive oil and brown it. When it is ready, remove the pot from the fire and transfer the contents to a serving bowl. Eat and enjoy, Allah the Exalted willing. You can proceed in the same way if you are making two or more squabs by amending the instructions according to the quantity of birds, with the power of the Allah the Exalted.

---

69 See recipe No. 234.

70 *firākh al-ḥamām*. Pigeon dishes appear frequently in the Western manuals – the anonymous *Andalusian* has no fewer than fourteen. Conversely, in Near Eastern treatises, pigeon meat was a rarity, and recipes can be found only in *Kanz* (Nos. 82, 102, 133, 201; Appendix, No. 29). As in the present text, it is squab meat that is used in those recipes. One of the reasons for the discrepancy may be linked to the differences in judgement regarding its properties between the Muslim East and West. In the East, its hot temperament was considered harmful (e.g. Ibn Jazla, fol. 75v.). Andalusian pharmacologists were much more favourable to it. Ibn Zuhr (1992: 94; trans., 51) praised its extraordinary moistness, even though it can produce migraines. Al-Uryūlī (1983: No. 58) added other virtues, including as 'jewellery polishers' because of the speed of the pigeon's digestive system: 'It is said that those who want to burnish jewellery feed them to the chicks, which they kill immediately after feeding them, so that the jewellery comes out polished, albeit somewhat diminished in size and quantity.' Furthermore, they are beneficial for hemiplegia, with their healing ability being such that sufferers get relief simply by putting pigeons underneath their beds or keeping them in the house. And, of course, like all poultry, they increase the memory, sharpen intelligence, strengthen the senses, and are highly aphrodisiacal.

247. Another dish

Take squabs, clean them very well, and put them in a glazed casserole dish with water, salt, olive oil, pepper, coriander seeds, a little cumin, cloves of garlic, peeled almonds, a ladleful of good *murrī* and half a ladleful of vinegar. Place the dish over a fire to cook and, when the squabs are done, take it to the oven. Leave it in until some of the broth has dried out and the squabs are browned. Then remove the casserole, and leave it to simmer down. Eat and enjoy, Allah the Exalted willing.

248. Another dish, called *al-rāhibī*[71]

Take squabs, clean them very well, and cook them as described in the recipe in the first chapter of the second section in this book.[72]

249. Another dish, called *al-mufarrij*[73]

Take squabs and proceed as explained above, cooking them according to the recipe from the first chapter of the second section in this book.[74]

250. Another dish, called *qar'iyya* (gourd stew)[75]

Take squabs, prepare them as described above, and cook according to the recipe in the second chapter of the second section in this book.[76]

251. Another dish

Take pigeons,[77] clean them well and put them in a new pot with water, salt, pepper, coriander seeds, a bit of sliced onion, and olive oil. Put the pot over a fire to cook. When the water is boiling and the squabs are done, take a clean frying pan and put it over a fire with good olive oil. When the oil is boiling, transfer the squabs from the pot to the pan and fry them, gingerly turning them over so that they brown on all sides. Next, take a small earthenware casserole dish with crushed cloves of garlic. Pour in

71 Also see recipes Nos. 105, 183, 191, 203, 248, 281, 301.

72 Recipe No. 105.

73 Once again, the text has the defective '*al-mufarriḥ*' (see recipe No. 203).

74 Recipe No. 105.

75 Also see recipes Nos. 128, 207.

76 Recipe No. 128.

77 This is clearly a scribal error (which is also found in BL Or5927, fol. 162v.), as only 'squabs' are mentioned afterwards in the recipe. The (much-abridged) recipe in Gayangos XVI (fol. 86v.[–87r.]) does refer to squabs (*firākh*).

some of the strained broth and put the casserole on the fire. When the garlic is done, add some good vinegar. Once it has come to a boil, pour it over the squabs. Eat and enjoy, Allah the Exalted willing.

252. Another dish

Take squabs, clean them well, and put them in a new pot with water, salt, olive oil, pepper, coriander seeds, a bit of cut-up onion, and peeled almonds. Colour the squabs with saffron and put the pot over a fire to cook. Next take eggs – five or six for each squab – and crack them into a bowl. Add breadcrumbs, salt, pepper, cinnamon, ginger, fresh coriander juice and mint juice, and whisk it all together with a ladle or with your hands. Make sure to put aside any egg yolks you may need later on before you start whisking the mixture. Check up on the squabs and, if you find that they are done, remove them from the pot and put them breast-side up in a large casserole dish. Pour on enough of the egg mixture[78] to cover the meat, and then add the fat that has been left in the pot. Garnish the surface with the egg yolks and almonds, sprinkle on cinnamon and ginger, and then put the casserole in the oven. Place it away from the flames until it sets and browns, and its broth has dried up. Then take it out and let it simmer down. Eat and enjoy, Allah the Exalted willing.

253. Another dish

Thoroughly clean squabs, and take the meat of some of them, together with the gizzards and livers. Pound everything in a mortar with salt, pepper, ginger, cinnamon, coriander seeds and a bit of cut-up onion. Break three eggs and beat them together with the meat and seasonings, adding peeled almonds. Stuff this mixture inside the squabs and in between the skin and the meat. Sew them up, and put them in a new pot with water, salt, olive oil, pepper, coriander seeds and a bit of cut-up onion. Put the pot over a fire to cook and, when the squabs are ready, transfer them from the pot to a large casserole dish. Colour them with saffron and pour strained broth over them before taking the dish to the oven. Place it away from the flames, so that the squabs can brown all over. When they are ready, remove the casserole from the oven and put the squabs in a ceramic bowl. Serve with a garnish of split

---

78 The translation is based on BL Or5927 (fol. 163r.), rather than the edition (2012: 185), which has water being poured on.

eggs and mint leafstalks, and a sprinkling of cinnamon and ginger. Eat and enjoy, Allah the Exalted willing.

254. Another dish

Take squabs, slaughter them, and blow hard in them to separate the skin from the flesh. Tie their necks, and then pluck them in hot water. After cleaning them, gut them and wash them thoroughly. Strip away the skin of the neck, sever the neck and throw it away. Cautiously remove the animals' bones, but leave the skin on the tailheads and half of the thighs and wings. Then pound the meat with that of other squabs and proceed as described in the second chapter of the third section in this book, Allah the Exalted willing.

255. Another dish[79]

Take as many squabs as you have available, clean them well, and skewer them on an iron spit. Roast them as explained above and, once they are done, remove them from the spit, and carve them up in a ceramic bowl. Pour thick yoghurt, crushed cooked garlic[80] and good olive oil over the meat, and mix everything together. Eat and enjoy, Allah the Exalted willing.

Chapter Five: on turtledove meat[81]

256. Dish

Take as many turtledoves as you want, slaughter them, clean them, cut open their abdomens, wash and thoroughly clean them. Put them in a

79 In Gayangos XVI (fol. 88r.), the dish is called 'a roast' (*mashwī*).

80 The reference to garlic is taken from BL Or5927 (fol. 164v.); the edition (2012: 186) and Gayangos XVI (fol. 88r.) have the nonsensical 'thick cooked crushed yoghurt' (*laban khāthir maṭbūkh madrūs*).

81 Gayangos XVI (fol. 88v.) specifies that it is the meat of 'fat' (*musmina*) turtledoves; Lane 1863–74: III, 1433; Kazimirski 1860: II, 1143. However, in BL Or5927, the vowelling in this chapter's recipes is *musammana*, i.e. 'fattened (up)'. Besides *yamām*, it was also called *shifnīn* (Ibn al-Bayṭār (1992: III, 85). The anonymous Andalusian treatise has two turtledove recipes (one of which is a *tharīda*), but it is absent from any of the Near Eastern cookbooks. According to Ibn Zuhr (1992: 15, 16; trans., 51, 52), the turtledove was the best of all poultry meat and, like the others, increases the memory, sharpens the intellect and strengthens the senses. Also see Brisville 2018a: 406–7.

new pot with water, salt, plenty of olive oil, pepper, coriander seeds, a bit of sliced onion, and peeled cloves of garlic. Put the pot over a fire to cook and, when the liquid has dried out and the turtledoves are done, set the pot on a low heat, gingerly flipping the turtledoves with a ladle until they are golden brown all over. Then, remove the pot from the fire and transfer the turtledoves to a ceramic bowl. Sprinkle on cinnamon and ginger, and then eat and enjoy, Allah the Exalted willing.

257. Another dish, called *al-mufarrij*[82]

Take as many fattened turtledoves as you like and prepare them as explained above. Cook them as described in the recipe in the first chapter of the second section in this book, with the power of Allah the Exalted.

258. Another dish, called *naʿnaʿiyya* (mint stew)

Take as many fattened turtledoves as you wish, and then proceed as before. Cook them as explained in the recipe in the second chapter of the second section,[83] Allah the Exalted willing. And if you cook it with lemon balm, do exactly the same as well.

259. Another dish

Take as many fattened turtledoves as you want, and do the same as you did before. Put them in a new pot with water, salt, olive oil, pepper, coriander seeds and a bit of sliced onion. Put the pot on a fire to cook. When the turtledoves are done, take a clean frying pan and put it over a fire with olive oil. When the oil comes to a boil, transfer the turtledoves from the pot to the pan and fry them, turning them over to brown them on all sides. Next, take them out of the frying pan and place them in a ceramic bowl. Take some crushed garlic and put it in the frying pan, and pour on some strained broth from the turtledoves. When the garlic is done cooking in the broth, pour both onto the turtledoves. Eat and enjoy, Allah the Exalted willing.

260. Another dish

Take as many fattened turtledoves as you like. Clean the outside and

---

82 The text has the defective '*al-mufarriḥ*' (see above, recipe No. 203). Also see recipes Nos. 105, 249.

83 Recipe No. 116.

their crops, but leave the birds' innards intact and do not split them open. Next, take cloves of garlic, peel them, and in each turtledove put one inside the beak and one inside the vent. Take an iron skewer as fine[84] as a packing needle, and put the beaks onto it. Place them in a large pot, and cover the bottom with a bread crust. Pierce the neck of the pot and insert the skewer so that the turtledoves are suspended in the air. Next, cover the pot and seal it with dough. Take it to the oven, and place it away from the fire. When the dough has turned black or almost black, remove the pot from the oven, and take out both the turtledoves and the bread crust. Sprinkle on ginger, pepper and cinnamon, and then eat and enjoy, Allah the Exalted willing. Before putting the turtledoves on the skewer, rub them with salt, olive oil, *murrī*, pepper and cinnamon, and then put them in the oven, by the power and strength of Allah the Exalted.

261. Another dish[85]

Take as many fattened turtledoves as you like, and do as described above. Then take good crushed salt and use it to cover the bottom of an earthenware glazed – or unglazed – casserole dish. Layer the turtledoves in, facing them upwards. Then take more salt and entirely cover the the birds with it, so none of them is visible any more. Take the casserole to the oven and leave it there until the salt sets and the turtledoves are completely hard. At this point, take them out of the pan and use a knife to strip away the salt. Sprinkle on cinnamon and ginger, and eat and enjoy, Allah the Exalted willing. If you like, you can also make this recipe with squabs.

262. Another dish, called *al-maḥshī* ('the stuffed one')[86]

Take as many fattened turtledoves as you like, cut open the abdomens and thoroughly clean them. Cook them in the manner described in the second chapter of the third section in this book. Use four eggs for each turtledove. Remember this.

---

84 This is specified only in Gayangos XVI (fol. 88v.); the other copies simply refer to a skewer like a needle (*mithl al-misalla*).

85 In Gayangos XVI (fol. 89r.), the recipe is titled: 'Another dish, roasted (*mashwī*)'.

86 In Gayangos XVI (*ibid.*), it is called *maḥshuw*. Also see recipe No. 267.

263. Another dish[87]

Take as many fattened turtledoves as you want, and thoroughly clean them. You are free to cut them open and gut them, or to leave them whole. Skewer them on an iron spit, and then take a bowl and add salt dissolved in water, olive oil, macerated *murrī*, crushed garlic, pepper, ginger and cinnamon. Take a chicken feather, wash it, and put it in the pot. Then light the fire on the sides of the spit – there should be no fire in the middle – and place the spit on something high,[88] turning it with your hand as you baste it with the feather from time to time. When the turtledoves are done and golden brown, remove them from the skewer, and eat and enjoy, Allah the Exalted willing.

If you like, you can make a sauce like the ones described in the second chapter of the third section in this book.

Chapter Six: on starling meat[89]

264. Dish

Take plump white starlings, pluck and clean them, and then cut them open and wash them. Put them in a new pot with water, salt, olive oil, pepper, coriander seeds, and a bit of cut-up onion. Put the pot over a fire to cook and, when the starlings are done, take a clean tinned frying pan and pour some olive oil in it. When the oil has come to a boil, transfer the starlings from the pot to the pan and fry them, gingerly turning them every now and again so they will be golden brown all over. Then, take garlic, crush it, and put it in the frying pan, after

87 In Gayangos XVI (*ibid.*), the recipe is titled 'another dish, roasted (*mashwī*)' but is incomplete, while the manuscript jumps chapters six and seven of the present text and continues on 89v., in the middle of the first sentence of recipe No. 269.

88 Gayangos XVI (*ibid.*) specifies that the skewer is put on stones.

89 Starlings were an Andalusian delicacy, since they are not found in any of the Near Eastern cookery books. Ibn Zuhr (1993: 17–18; trans., 53) states that starlings slow down digestion, and because they feed on all kinds of poisonous insects their meat is sometimes harmful, like that of quail. For this reason, starlings must be kept alive for two or three days to allow them to digest any food that may remain in their bodies. They were indeed kept in captivity for their meat, and al-Uryūlī (1983: No. 57) refers to starlings (and sparrows) being fattened in houses. Ibn Khalṣūn (1996: 159; trans., 85–6) advised eating only the fat ones, with turnips, carrots and a lot of olive oil, whereas they should be followed by a theriac, or dried figs and walnuts.

removing the starlings. Also add some strained broth and, once the garlic is cooked, pour this sauce on the starlings. Eat and enjoy, Allah the Exalted willing. Everything you do to cook turtledoves, you can also apply to starlings. [If you like, you can also make a *rāhibī*,[90] or a *jamalī*[91] with them, in which case you should cook them according to the recipe in the first chapter of the second section of this book.][92]

Chapter Seven: on sparrow meat[93]

265. Dish

Take as many sparrows as you want; gut, clean and wash them very well. Put them in a new pot with water, salt, olive oil, pepper, coriander seeds and a few onions. Place the pot over a fire to cook. When the birds are ready, take a clean frying pan and put some olive oil in it. When the oil is boiling, transfer the sparrows from the pot to the pan, and fry them. Next, take some crushed garlic and put it in the frying pan with the sparrows, adding some strained broth. Leave the pan on the fire until the garlic is cooked and the broth has dried out. Then, transfer the birds to a serving dish with the remaining stock and the garlic. Eat and enjoy, Allah the Exalted willing.

---

90 Also see recipes Nos. 105, 183, 191, 203, 248, 281, 301.

91 See recipes Nos. 99, 284, 288.

92 The section in brackets is omitted from the edition, and was taken from BL Or5927 (fol. 164v.). Also see recipe No. 99.

93 The title was taken from BL Or5927 (fol. 165r.), as the edition (2012: 191) only has 'sparrows' (*'aṣāfīr*; singular *uṣfūr*). The word often refers to various small birds in Arabic, whereas in Andalusian Arabic cooking terminology, *'aṣāfīr* also referred to (lamb) meat pieces (or mince) shaped like small birds and threaded on a skewer (Corriente 1997: 355). Sparrows were not often called for, except in one fourteenth-century Egyptian collection, which includes ten recipes (*Kanz*, Nos. 140–9), though this dwindled to only one by the fifteenth century (Ibn Mubārak Shāh 2020: No. 90). In thirteenth-century Syria, they were eaten salted and seasoned (*Wuṣla*, Nos. 8.62–3). In terms of their medical properties, sparrows were thought to be a strong aphrodisiac, as well as being useful against hemiplegia, facial paralysis and some types of dropsy (Ibn Zuhr 1992: 15; trans., 52). Ibn Khalṣūn (1996: 159; trans., 86) recommended fatty sparrows and young ones, since they are particularly nutritious and should be cooked with vinegar and gourd (for people with hot temperaments) or with aromatic spices and olive oil (for those with cold temperaments).

266. Another dish

Take as many sparrows as you want, clean and wash them, and then put them in a new pot with water, salt, olive oil, pepper, coriander seeds, a few chopped onions, and a sufficient amount of good *murrī*. Put the pot over a fire to cook. If there is not enough water, leave the pot over a low fire, stirring the birds until they are golden brown. Transfer them to a dish with verjuice or lime vinegar. Eat and enjoy, Allah the Exalted willing.

267. Another dish, called *al-maḥshī* ('the stuffed one'), which is made in a casserole dish in the oven.

Take as many sparrows as you like and clean them very well before cooking them as described in the recipe in the second chapter of the third section in this book. Use as many eggs as there are sparrows, Allah the Exalted willing.[94]

268. Another dish

Take fat sparrows, clean them, and skewer them on a wooden stick. Coat them with seasonings mentioned in the fifth chapter of the third section in this book, Allah the Exalted willing.[95]

94 Similar recipes for sparrow omelettes can be found in: *Kanz*, No. 142; *Anwāʿ*, 21 (BNF, fol. 8v.); al-Warrāq 1987: 198.

95 See recipe No. 260.

SECTION FOUR

On cooking the dish called *al-Ṣanhājī*, stuffed tripe and *Ṣanhājī* tongue

It consists of three chapters.

Chapter One: on making the *Ṣanhājī*[1] dish

269.
Take a glazed casserole dish, the biggest you can get, fill it with choice cuts of whatever meat you have to hand: beef, mutton, suckling kid, any kind of game meat you can find, hare, rabbit, chicken, goose, partridge, squabs, plump turtledoves, fat white starlings, or fat sparrows. Cut any of these that require cutting into medium-sized pieces and leave the rest whole. Add *mirqās* and *laqāniq* sausages, *aḥrash,*[2] pickled limes and olives, peeled almonds,soaked chickpeas, citron leaves, and a fennel stalk. Next, add water, salt, olive oil, pepper, coriander seeds, chopped fresh coriander leaves, mint leaves, garlic cloves, half a chopped onion and a spoonful of *murrī*. Colour the meat with saffron and put the casserole over the fire to cook. Then take good-quality tender cabbages, turnips, aubergines, fennel and carrots (if they are available). Clean and wash all of these vegetables, colour with saffron, and place them in the casserole. When everything is cooked, add chopped apples and cleaned quinces from which you have removed the outer peel. Finally, add as much good vinegar as is deemed fit. Leave the casserole on the fire until the vinegar comes to a boil once or twice. Then remove and place it over a low heat to let it cool down. Eat and enjoy, Allah the Exalted willing.

---

1 The *Andalusian* also contains a similar dish (*Anwa'*, 138; BNF, fol. 51r.–v.), as well as a 'royal' (*muluki*) one (*Anwa'*, 4; BNF, fol. 2v.).

2 See recipe No. 185.

Chapter Two: on making stuffed tripe[3]

270.

Blanch the tripe of a fatty ram in hot water, and scrape it with a knife to whiten it and to clean all the dirt away. However, leave it whole without splitting it, and remove the rumen.[4] Then take good meat, pound it well, and put it aside. Next, take a tender chicken and stuff it as described in the second chapter of the third section of this book.[5] Also take two squabs – equally stuffed – *mirqās* sausages, meatballs, *isfiriyya* and boiled (coagulated) egg yolks. Take the meat of a young ram, from the breast, tailhead and the such,[6] and cut it into medium-sized pieces. Put them in a new pot with water, salt, olive oil, pepper, coriander seeds and a bit of cut-up onion. Place the pot over a fire to cook. Take fresh tender cabbages, clean them and take the inner leaves, [as well as chard leaf stalks,][7] and put them in the pot with the meat. Then take the chicken and the squabs and put them in a pot with water, salt, olive oil, pepper, coriander seeds and a bit of pounded onion. Place this pot over a fire to cook. Put the *mirqās* and meatballs in a small pot and pour on a little water and olive oil. Cook it over a fire, and leave until the liquid has dried out, after which you gently fry the meat in the remaining oil. Once this is done, remove the (small) pot from the fire, and check on the pot with the meat. If you find that it is done, add fresh coriander juice and remove the pot from the fire as well. Do the same thing with the pot containing the chicken and squabs. Return to the meat that you pounded at the start, and add salt, pepper, cinnamon, ginger, a little bit of mastic, spikenard and cloves dissolved in a little water. Next, take ten eggs and a small amount of grated breadcrumbs, and mix them in with the meat and the aromatic spices. Then, take the tripe and stuff it with some of the meat mixed with the eggs, followed by the cooked meat, the cabbage and chard, and then a squab, a chicken, the second squab, the meat and the vegetables – which should also include a lot of peeled almonds and pine nuts – the egg yolks, the *mirqās*, the meatballs

3 Gayangos XVI (fol. 91r.) adds that it is 'amazing'. For similar recipes, see *Taṣānīf*, fol. 70v.

4 *rummāna*, also 'pomegranate'.

5 See recipe No. 211.

6 Gayangos XVI (fol. 91r.) refers to 'the best parts of mutton, such as the breast, etc.'

7 Addition from Gayangos XVI (*ibid.*).

and, finally, the *isfiriyya*, after having fried it. Distribute the stuffing throughout. Then take what is left of the stuffing, add the strained broth from the chicken and the squabs to it, and pour the mixture over the tripe. Tie the tripe up with a piece of strong twine and place it in a large casserole dish. Pour on the remainder of the broth with water, so that the tripe is entirely covered. Put the casserole over a fire to cook and, when you see that everything is done, remove the tripe and broth from the casserole. Gather the remaining fat and put it back into the casserole after having cleaned it. Then, return the tripe to the casserole, add a little macerated *murrī*, and take it to the oven for browning. When the tripe is golden brown, take it out of the oven and put it in a ceramic dish. Split it open, and dust with cinnamon. Eat and enjoy, Allah the Exalted willing.

Chapter Three: on making *Ṣanhājī* tongue[8]

271.

Take the meat from the thighs and backstrap of a ram. Pound it on a board with an iron rod and remove the veins. Pound it well in a mortar and add salt, pepper, coriander seeds, fresh coriander and mint juice, a little onion juice, and some good *murrī*. Beat it all together until it is thoroughly mixed. Crack in two eggs and mix everything well. Next, take some of the caul fat of the intestines[9] and spread it out on a board. Add the pounded meat to it, and then proceed to roll the fat over the meat so that you end up with a long roll. Let it dry on a sieve. Once it is dry, skewer it onto a spit and grill it as described above until it is done and golden brown. When it is ready, remove it from the spit, and eat and enjoy, Allah the Exalted willing.

8 In Gayangos XVI (fol. 91v.), the title is 'Cooking tongue'.

9 *mansij* – see recipe No. 7. Gayangos XVI (fol. 92r.) has 'fat inside the belly of the ram'.

SECTION FIVE

On various fish and egg recipes

It consists of two chapters.

Chapter One: on types of fish

You should know that all fish, especially the large ones, must be scalded in boiling water, then removed, washed and left to drain off the water.[1] It is only then that they are cooked, with the power of Allah the Exalted.

272. Dish

Take large fish, such as sturgeon,[2] shad,[3] seabass,[4] *k*mūn,*[5] and large striped mullet,[6] and scale them. Split them open, clean and wash them, and then throw them in boiling water. Cut the fish into medium-sized pieces. Next, take a glazed earthenware casserole dish with a generous amount of olive oil, vinegar, *murrī* and cloves of garlic. Take a large

---

1 A similar general statement on fish is found in the *Andalusian* (*Anwāʿ*, 149; BNF, fol. 40r.), which adds that they should be lightly boiled (*silqa khafīfa*) after being scaled and cut into pieces. However, according to Ibn Ibn ʿAbdūn (Lévi-Provençal 1955: 44; trans., 74) fish, whether salted or fresh, should not be washed in water, as this would spoil it. Nor should salted fish be soaked in water beforehand, as this would also make it go off and rot.

2 *Shūlī*; Dozy 1881: I, 806. According to the calendar of Córdoba (Dozy & Pellat 1961: 63 trans., 62), both sturgeons and shads would start their migration from the sea to the rivers in the month of March.

3 *shābal*, Correinte 1997: 273; Dozy 1881: I, 724. According to Ibn al-Ḥashshāʾ (1941: 123, No. 1140), it is the word used in the Maghrib for the fish also known as *shabbūṭ*, which could also refer to the Atlantic stargazer or the common carp. Ibn Janāḥ 2020: No. 996.

4 *manānī;* Corriente (1997: 513) identifies this fish as *Epinephelus alexandrinus*, which is a kind of seabass (known as *mennani* in Tunisia), with *mānūn* denoting salted (small) fish (especially anchovy). Al-Isrāʾilī (1992: 509) said that physicians used the liquid extracted from *mānūn* in the treatment of putrefied mouth ulcers.

5 It is unclear which fish is meant here. Perry (Rodinson *at al.* 2001: 480) suggests the spelling *kammūn*, i.e. 'cumin, probably referring to its colour'. It is omitted from the recipe in Gayangos XVI (fol. 92r.).

6 The translation is based on Gayangos XVI (fol. 92r., '*al-būrī al-kabīr*'); both the edition (2012: 197) and BL Or5927 (fol. 166v.) have the clearly misspelt *nūri jabjīl*, the latter word possibly being a scribal error for *jalīl* ('huge').

bowl and throw in pepper, coriander seeds, a few cumin seeds, crushed saffron and a little mastic. Dissolve all the spices in a bit of water and pour it into the casserole. Then dredge each piece of fish separately in the mixture until they absorb the spices and the rest. Once you have done this with all the pieces, layer them in the casserole, add a little water and put it over a fire to cook. When it is done, send the casserole to the oven to brown the surface of the dish.

If you want to make this dish at home, you can. You need to put an unglazed clay pot on the casserole dish with the fish, and place it over a strong fire so that the heat can reach the fish so as to dry out the broth and brown the pieces. Once the fish is done, remove the casserole from the fire to let it cool down. Eat and enjoy, Allah the Exalted willing.

If you prefer, you can make it with fresh coriander juice, in which case you should not include vinegar and *murrī*. Everything else is the same. [It is best eaten cold.][7] If you make it with shad, add crushed [or uncrushed] walnuts, Allah the Exalted willing.[8]

273. Another dish of gilt-head bream[9] and striped mullet[10]

Take either of these two fish, clean it inside and out, and wash it thoroughly after boiling it in water. Cut it into medium-sized pieces and put them in a glazed casserole dish with salt, plenty of olive oil, pepper, coriander seeds, a few cumin seeds, a grain of mastic, a little macerated *murrī*, a splash of water and a citron leaf. Add saffron and then whisk the fish pieces and the spice mixture so it can be absorbed, and colour them. Take onions, clean them, cut them into medium-sized pieces, and throw them in a pot with a little water. Put the pot over a fire and, when the onions are cooked, transfer them to a casserole dish, after colouring them with saffron. Check the amount of broth in

7 The passages in brackets are additions from Gayangos XVI (fol. 92v.).

8 The religious formula is included in BL Or5927 (fol. 167r.), but missing from the printed edition.

9 *jarrāfa*; the identification is uncertain, but the word usually refers to a large fish net. Corriente 1997: 94; Dozy 1881: I, 187.

10 *būrī* (also *mūl*), is also known in English as flathead grey mullet or black mullet. Al-Uryūlī (1983: No. 110) said it was fished in the river in Orihuela and is one of the best fish, with little waste and a pleasant taste. The only recipes from Eastern manuals that require mullet are those from Egypt: Ibn Mubārak Shāh 2020: No. 136; *Kanz*, Nos. 241, 254; *Waṣf*, 389, 395. To this day, it is a highly popular fish in Egypt, especially salted.

the casserole; if it has reduced and the fish is not yet done, add some of the onion broth. Once the fish is done, add a little honey or cooked grape syrup and take it to the oven for browning. If you want to do it at home, proceed as above and, once it is ready, leave the casserole to cool down. Then, eat and enjoy, Allah the Exalted willing.

274. Another dish called *murawwaj*[11]

Take any kind of fish – large, small, smooth or rough, whatever you happen to have to hand. Scrape the outside of the fish, cut them open, and clean and wash them after boiling them in water. Cut them into small pieces, add a sufficient amount of salt, and put them to one side. Next, take a casserole dish and add vinegar, *murrī*, good olive oil, pepper, coriander seeds, a few cumin seeds, cloves of garlic and a little oregano. Place it over a fire and, when it has come to a full boil, put the fish in and cover the casserole with a bowl. Leave until done – which does not take long – and remove the dish from the heat. Eat and enjoy, Allah the Exalted willing. This recipe can also be made with small sardines[12] and anchovies,[13] in which case you should use fresh coriander juice, peeled cloves of garlic, and a little vinegar. Remember this.

275. Another dish (fish cakes)

Take any kind of fleshy fish you can find, scale them and then boil them in water. Skin them, take the flesh and get rid of the bones and thorns.

---

11 It is the passive participle of a verb (*rawwaja*) meaning 'to circulate' or 'to expedite, hurry', possibly in reference to the quick preparation of the dish. The *Andalusian* (*Anwāʿ*, 152–3) contains a similar recipe, where it is added that this is a dish that people from Ceuta and Western al-Andalus used to make.

12 *sardīn* (also *sardhīn*), probably of Romance origin. The present text has the highest number of recipes with this fish (the other Andalusian treatise has only this one). The Near Eastern cookery books do not contain any recipes calling for sardines. According to the calendar of Córdoba (Dozy & Pellat 1961: 133 trans., 132), sardines were particularly plentiful in August. Ibn al-Bayṭār (1992: III, 165) quotes Ibn Juljul as saying that *sardīn* was the term used in the Maghrib for the fish called *ʿarm*. Elsewhere, Ibn al-Bayṭār (Dietrich 1991: 98, No. 28) stated that there is a smooth fish called *smaris*, the size of a span or smaller, known as sardines on some coasts. In other sources, the form *smarīdās* is also found. Dietrich 1988: 214 (No. II.26); Ibn Janāḥ 2020: No. 714; Dozy, 1881: I, 648.

13 *shaṭṭūn*, which has survived in the Moroccan Arabic *shṭun* (Corriente 1997: 283; Harrell *et al.* 2007: II, 9). This is the only medieval Arabic culinary text that mentions this fish.

Pound the flesh in a mortar and remove the veins. Once the meat is thoroughly mashed, put it in a bowl with salt, pepper, cinnamon, ginger, a crushed grain of mastic, a few cumin seeds, saffron, coriander seeds, a little onion juice, garlic, mint juice, macerated *murrī* and olive oil. Vigorously knead the mixture into a dough. Next, take a clean frying pan and put olive oil in it. When the oil has come to a boil, make small and large discs as well as balls out of the fish meat and fry them, gingerly turning them so that they can brown on all sides. When they are ready, take them out and replace them with others until you have used up all of your fish. It you want, you can mix egg whites and powdered *darmak* flour into the fish paste.[14] You can also put cheese into the ceramic bowl, as well as lime juice or macerated *murrī*, or[15] a dressing made with vinegar, plenty of olive oil, macerated *murrī* and crushed garlic. All this is cooked in a glazed earthenware casserole dish. Make it the way you like it. Eat and enjoy, Allah the Exalted willing.

276. Another dish

Take any kind of fleshy fish you can find, scrape the outside, and boil them in water to clean the inside. Next, cut them into medium-sized pieces, add salt, and set them aside. Take a bowl in which you put dissolved salt, *murrī*, olive oil, pepper, cinnamon, crushed garlic, and ginger. Take a feather, wash it and put it in the bowl. Thread the pieces of fish on an iron spit and light a fire nearby, along the sides, putting the ends of the spit on stones so that it is raised above the ground. Turn it by hand, basting the pieces of fish with the feather until they are done and golden brown. Then, take a ceramic bowl and put olive oil and crushed cooked garlic in it. Remove the fish from the spit, cut it up into smaller pieces and place them in the oil and garlic. Eat and enjoy, Allah the Exalted willing.

If you want to grill small fish over coals, such as sardines that appear in May (*māya*) and October (*uktūbir*),[16] the *jarkam*,[17] which come out

---

14 This sentence is missing from the edited version, and has been taken from BL Or5927, fol. 167v.

15 The edition (2012: 199) has 'and', rather than the more logical 'or' of BL Or5927 (fol. 167v.)

16 In the Calendar of Córdoba, August is said to be sardine season; Dozy & Pellat 1961: 132 (trans., 133).

17 The vowelling of the word is tentative, and denotes a hitherto unidentified small fish

in September (*shitinbir*), or any other fatty fish as they start to appear, you should light the fire and spread it out, fanning away the flames and smoke. Salt the fish if this has not already been done, and layer them on the coals, turning them over until they are cooked and golden brown. If you like, you can add garlic and olive oil, though you can also eat it without, whichever you prefer. Eat and enjoy.

If you want to roast shad and other similar fish, take a new tile and cover it with salt.[18] Put the fish on it, bury it in salt, and then place it in the oven. When you see that the salt has hardened or is beginning to harden, take the tile out, and remove the salt from the fish. In front of you, you should have one bowl with salt, pepper, ginger, cinnamon and other aromatic spices, a second one filled with olive oil and garlic, a third one containing macerated *murrī*, and a fourth one with a sauce[19] made as described in the fifth chapter of the second section of this book. Similarly, if you want to roast and brown fish like sardines, or any other small fish like it, in the oven, put them on an earthenware *malla* before putting it in so that they will be roasted and browned. Once the fish are ready, remove the *malla* from the oven and eat them how you like, by the power of Allah the Exalted.

277. Another dish

Take small sardines and clean, wash and salt them. Next, take fresh coriander, fresh mint, fresh fennel, and onions. Chop all of these as finely as you can and wash them. Next, put a bed of the chopped herbs and vegetables at the bottom of a casserole dish. Put a layer of sardines on top, followed by a layer of vegetables, and continue alternating them until you have filled up the casserole. Throw some cinnamon, ginger, and a little bit of mastic on top, and then put the casserole in the oven until it is done and golden brown. Once it is ready, take it out and eat, Allah the Exalted willing.

---

that would appear only from September onwards. Corriente 1997: 94.

18 In Gayangos XVI (fol. 94r.), this is a separate recipe ('Another dish, roasted').

19 *shalshala*, see recipe No. 107.

278. Another dish[20]

Take any kind of mackerel or other prime-quality fish[21] you can find, gut and clean it, and remove its skin. Take the flesh but leave the spine whole. Pound the flesh very well, and add breadcrumbs, salt (unless the fish is already salty), pepper, ginger, cinnamon, spikenard, cloves, a sufficient amount of mastic, crushed saffron, coriander seeds, a few cumin seeds, and enough eggs – not too many, mind you – to bind the fish mixture. Place the mixture on the spines, shaping it like a fish, and then line the fish up alongside each other in a casserole. Add peeled almonds and pine nuts to some of the remaining fish meat and shape into balls. Add coriander juice to the left-over stuffing to make it more liquid,[22] and then place the mixture in amidst the fish in the casserole. Pour on plenty of olive oil, and then take the dish to the oven to bake until it is done, the oil has dried out,[23] and the fish is golden brown. When everything is ready, take the casserole out of the oven, and serve, Allah the Exalted willing.

If you want to use a smooth fish[24] and bake it in the oven in a casserole, you should take the fish, cut it open at the back, remove the spine, and throw away the head.[25] Leave the rest of the fish whole, and then wash it. Next, take a casserole and put in a little water, olive oil, pepper, coriander seeds, cumin, rubbed oregano, whole and crushed garlic,

20 There are some interesting similarities between this recipe and that found in al-Warrāq (1987: 78).

21 I have amended the edition's *al-sardha al-ẓardhānis* (2012: 200), which is also found in BL Or5927 (fol. 168r.), with Gayangos XVI (fol. 94r.), where it is *al-sarda wa 'l-ṭardanis*. This is similar to the recipe in the *Andalusian* (*Anwāʿ*, 152; BNF, fol. 55r.), which has *sarda* or *tardani/as*, both being described as 'good-quality fish'. The word *sard(h)a* is a variant of *sarāda*. See Corriente 1997: 248 ('horse mackerel'), 327; Díaz García 2000: 28–30, Nos. 112–13. Perry (*Anonymous Andalusian cookbook*) identifies *sarda* and *tardanis* as, respectively, 'pilchard' and 'red mullet', but the latter is, in fact, *ṭarastūj*. One may also speculate that the reference here is to 'sardine'.

22 The edition (2012: 201) repeats the instruction to make meatballs (*tuḥabbab*), but the translation follows the more logical *tukhaffaf* found in BL Or5927 (fol. 168r.) and Gayangos XVI (fol. 94r.).

23 Perhaps this instruction should be corrected to 'until the liquid/broth has dried out and only the oil remains', like in recipe No. 280.

24 One without scales; those available at the time would probably have included lamprey, swordfish, sturgeon and catfish.

25 The head was considered the worst part of the fish; according to Ibn Zuhr (1992: 41; trans., 67), the healthiest parts are the heart and the liver, whereas the back part of the fish (the tail), is better than the front part, because of the movement it makes.

saffron, *murrī* and vinegar. Put the fish in, turning it over a couple of times so it fully absorbs all the flavours of the mixture. Roast the fish in the casserole with plenty of olive oil, and then take it to the oven, but place it away from the flames to cook and brown, and for the broth to dry out. Once it is ready, take it out and let it cool down. Eat and enjoy, Allah the Exalted willing.

279. A fried fish dish

Take any kind of fish you like – big or small, scaly or smooth. Gut and clean it, and boil in water. Then wash it and, if it is big, cut it up. If it is small, leave it as it is. If it is unsalted, salt it and then leave it on a sieve.[26] Next, take a clean frying pan and add olive oil in proportion to the amount of fat of the fish. When the oil is hot, fry the fish, carefully flipping it over. If you see that it might break, dust it with flour and then fry it in the pan. If the fish is large, split the pieces open, remove the bones, and then fry it. It should be done over a moderate fire. Once it is fried and golden brown, take it out and put it in a ceramic bowl. If the fish is scaly, take an earthenware casserole dish, cook some crushed garlic in it, and add vinegar. Once it has come to a boil, pour it over the fish in the bowl. If you want, you can take leafstalks of celery known as parsley,[27] mint leafstalks or rue leafstalks, and crush them all with garlic. Then put the mixture in a casserole dish with vinegar and bring it to a boil over a fire. Once it has come to a boil, pour this sauce over the fish and leave it until it cools down and the fish has absorbed it. Eat and enjoy, Allah the Exalted willing.

If you make it with a smooth fish, you should heat water and olive oil in a frying pan with crushed garlic and let it cook until the liquid has dried out, and then pour the garlic and oil over the fish. If you use the

26 The translation is based on BL Or5927 (fol. 168v.), as the edition (2012: 201) omits the verb (*tatrukuhu*), while the fish is salted on a sieve rather than being left there to dry, as is done, for instance, in recipe No. 279.

27 *maqdūnis* (a corruption of the Greek *makedonikós*, as it was thought to come from Macedonia) is indeed a close relative of celery (*karafs*) and 'wild/Roman/mountain celery' (*k. waḥshī, Rūmī/jabalī*) all denoted parsley, as did the borrowing *baṭrasālinūn* (from the Greek *petrosélinon*); Ibn Janāḥ 2020: Nos. 152, 447, 540; Ibn al-Bayṭār 1992: IV, 455). Clément-Mullet ([Ibn al-ʿAwwām 1866]: II:1, 295–6) suggested that *karafs* was used for celery with large leaves, whereas *m/baqadūnis* denoted the small-leafed variety of the vegetable. It follows that the highly aphrodisiacal qualities attributed to celery also apply to parsley. Also see Ibn Mubārak Shāh 2020: 49–50 (note 50).

fish known as red mullet,[28] you should add coarsely pounded walnuts to the vinegar and garlic.

280. Recipe for cooking a large fish

Take whatever fish is available, scale and clean it, and then briefly boil it in water. Cut it up, sprinkle on a large amount of salt, and leave it for a while. Wash it thoroughly with boiling water, and then let it drain. Next, take large onions and pound them in a wooden mortar, squeeze them through a cloth and put their juice in a glazed casserole dish, enough to cover the fish with. Add macerated *murrī*, plenty of olive oil, pepper, ginger, coriander seeds, cumin, saffron, a drizzle of vinegar, some mastic, spikenard, cinnamon, cardamom, galangal and oregano. Layer the pieces of fish in this mixture, let them steep in it, and then place them in the oven. Leave until the liquid has dried out, the fish is browned and only the oil remains. Then, remove from the oven, and eat.

281. Another *rāhibī* dish[29]

Scale a fresh fish, sprinkle salt on it, and leave it overnight with stones on top. The next morning, wash it, boil it in water until it goes white, and then wash it in cold water. Next, cook it in a casserole dish with a generous amount of olive oil (use four *ūqiyas* for every *raṭl* of fish), macerated *murrī*, oregano, fennel stalks, citron leaves, pepper, saffron, spikenard, ginger and a little mastic. Chop a sufficient number of onions after boiling them in water and salt; you should have one-third of a *raṭl* of onion for each *raṭl* of fish. Cook everything in the oven until the broth has dried out and the fish has browned on top. Then remove and serve.

282. Another dish made like a *tafāyā* with various kinds of large fish[30]

After cleaning and scaling the fish, boil and cut it up. Place the pieces in a pot with salt, lots of olive oil, spices, galangal, a little mastic and the juice of a pounded onion. Crush peeled almonds, walnuts and pine

28 *mull* (also *mūl*), a borrowing from the Latin *mullus*. See Corriente 1997: 510; Dozy 1881: II, 608, 624.

29 Gayangos XVI (fol. 95r.) adds that it is 'amazing'. Also see recipes Nos. 105, 203, 301.

30 This recipe, which is actually for a white *tafāyā*, is found only in Gayangos XVI (fol. 95v.). For other recipes, see Nos. 109, 192.

nuts until you obtain a marrow-like consistency. Dissolve the mixture in water, and then pour it on the fish in the pot, together with fennel leaf stalks. It is indispensable to have meatballs, which are made like mutton ones.[31] Put the pot in the oven to cook.

283. A green *tafāya* dish[32]
Scale and wash a large fish, cut it up and boil it in hot water and salt, as described. Place the pieces in a casserole dish and immerse it in mint juice, fresh coriander juice, plenty of olive oil, a little pounded onion juice, pepper, coriander seeds, ginger, salt, a bit of mastic, and fennel leafstalks. Cook in the oven until it is golden brown and the liquid has dried out. Once it is done, take it out, and serve.

284. Another dish: a *basbāsiyya*[33]
Scale and wash a large fish, cut it up, and slightly boil it in water and salt. Then, take the pieces out and put them in a casserole dish. Next, pound fresh fennel and squeeze out the juice, enough to completely cover the fish, and then add an ample amount of olive oil, pepper, coriander seeds, ginger, salt, onion juice and a bit of mastic. Cook it in the oven until it is browned on top and the liquid has dried out, after which you can take it out and serve it.

285. Another dish, made like a *jamalī*[34]
Scale some large fish and leave them overnight in salt with a weight stacked on top. In the morning, wash and boil them in salted water. Next, wash, dry and layer them in a casserole dish. Add two ladlefuls of vinegar, one ladleful of macerated *murrī*, pepper, saffron, ginger, cumin, mastic, celery seeds, citron leaves, bay leaves, fennel stalks, oregano, garlic and a large quantity of olive oil. Cook it in the oven until the liquid has dried out, and remove when it is browned on top.

31 See recipe No. 179.

32 The translation is based on Gayangos XVI (*ibid.*), rather than on the edition (2012: 203) and BL Or5927 (fol. 169r.), where the name of the dish is given as 'white *tafāyā*', even though the presence of coriander and mint juice makes it a green *tafāyā* (see recipe No. 110).

33 Gayangos XVI (fol. 95v.) adds that it is 'amazing'. See recipe No. 115 for a meat *basbāsiyya*.

34 See recipes Nos. 99, 290.

286. Another dish

Take some large fish, scale them, and proceed in the same way as before. Layer them in a casserole dish with vinegar, a sufficient amount of macerated *murrī*, cloves of garlic stuck on oregano stalks, plenty of olive oil, saffron, citron leaves, split almonds, pepper, coriander seeds, a pinch of salt if required, a little mastic, spikenard and cardamom. Put the dish in the oven and leave it until the liquid has dried out and it is browned on top, and then serve.

287. Another dish

Take good-quality fish and scale them. If they are large, cut them into pieces or slice into strips. Sprinkle with salt and lightly boil in water. Then wash them, put them in a casserole dish, and rub them with saffron and salt in order to colour[35] them. Pour on plenty of olive oil, and immerse the fish in the juice of fresh coriander and mint. Also throw in mint leafstalks, pepper, coriander seeds, ginger, cinnamon and a little mastic. Put it in the oven and cook until the liquid has dried out and it is browned on top. Once it is ready, serve, Allah the Exalted willing.

288. Another dish[36]

Take sardines or a similar type of fish, and scale, clean and boil them in salted water. Transfer them to a bowl and remove the bones. Gather the sardine meat and pound it until it resembles the mixture used for meatballs. Add pepper, coriander seeds, cinnamon, ginger and spikenard. Then squeeze on mint and coriander juice, and dust with some *darmak* flour. Beat it all together and shape into sardines, or any other shape you like. Coat them with flour and fry in a pan with olive oil until done. Then make a sauce by boiling vinegar, olive oil and pounded garlic in an earthenware casserole dish. When it is done, pour it over the sardines, and then serve.

---

35 The translation of the verb is based on BL Or5927 (fol. 169v.) rather than the edition (2012: 204), which has the incongruous 'until it is done/tender' (*ḥattā yanḍija*, instead of *yanṣabigha*).

36 *Anwāʿ*, 152 (BNF, fols. 55v.–56r.) has a very similar recipe, called *al-munashshā*. In BL Or5927, the next twelve recipes (up to No. 300) are placed after the washing powders, at the end of the manuscript (fols. 203r.–204v.).

289. Another dish, stuffed[37]

Take good-quality fish, and scale and boil them in salted water before cutting them up. If it is a big fish, split it lengthwise and remove the spine and the other bones, and fry it in a pan with olive oil until golden brown. Take a casserole dish, crack eggs into it, and add breadcrumbs, pepper, saffron, cinnamon, spikenard, ginger, coriander seeds, a lot of olive oil, and some macerated *murrī*. Sprinkle on split almonds, and beat everything together. Bury the prepared pieces of fish in this batter, and then cook in the oven until it has set and the surface is golden brown. Once it is ready, take it out of the oven, and serve. It is amazing.

290. Another dish, known as *mughaffar*[38]

Take any good-quality fish you have available, scale it, and then wash[39] with water and salt. Cut it open lengthwise and remove the bones. Next, beat the meat with eggs in a bowl, and add powdered *darmak* flour or grated breadcrumbs, as well as pepper, cinnamon, ginger, saffron, coriander seeds and macerated *murrī*. Coat the fish with this batter and fry in a pan with olive oil until golden brown. Then make a sauce for it by cooking vinegar, *murrī* and olive oil; pour it over the fish and serve. If you want to make a fish *Burāniyya*[40] or *muthallath*,[41] proceed in the same way as you would when using meat, and cook it in a casserole in the oven, as described above[, Allah the Exalted willing].[42]

291. Another dish

Take any kind of fleshy fish you like, clean, wash, and cut it into large pieces. Take a large pot with water and add salt if the fish is not already salted. Heat the pot over a fire and, when it comes to a full boil, put the fish in. Keep a close eye on it until you see that it turns white and is about to fall apart. Then, transfer the pieces to a ceramic bowl, and

---

37 The translation is based on BL Or5927 (fol. 169v.) and Gayangos XVI (fol. 96v.), which have *al-maḥshī*; in the edition (2012: 203) and Wetzstein 1207 (fol. 66r.), it is called *al-jamalī al-maḥshī* ('stuffed *jamalī*').

38 In Gayangos XVI (fol. 97r.), it is misvowelled as *al-mighfar*. See recipes Nos. 199, 352. A similar but slightly more detailed recipe can be found in *Anwāʿ*, 154 (BNF, fol. 41r.).

39 According to Gayangos XVI (*ibid.*), it should be 'boiled' in water and salt.

40 See recipe No. 100.

41 See recipe No. 101.

42 Addition in BL Or5927, fol. 203r.

add whatever aromatic spices and sauce you like. Eat and enjoy, Allah the Exalted willing.

292. Another dish

Take a fish called *al-kaḥla* ('the black one'),[43] clean it inside and out, wash it, and gingerly remove the skin from the head downwards, but leave the skin hanging by the tail. Remove the flesh and the bones. Thoroughly pound the flesh with salt, pepper, coriander seeds, cumin, cinnamon, ginger, spikenard, cloves, a little mastic, and egg whites. Use this mixture as a filling to stuff inside the skin of the fish and reconstruct its original shape. Then fry in a pan with olive oil until it is done and golden brown, carefully turning it over so that it does not break up. Once it is ready, serve in a ceramic bowl. Eat and enjoy, Allah the Exalted willing.

293. Another dish

Take a fish, clean, wash and salt it, and then set it aside. Take the flesh of another fish, which has also been cleaned and boned, and thoroughly pound it in a mortar. Add vinegar, *murrī*, coriander seeds, cinnamon, onion juice, breadcrumbs and cracked eggs. Gingerly whisk everything with your hands into a thick, smooth batter. Next, put a frying pan with olive oil over a fire and fry the batter,[44] stirring and turning it until it is done. Then take the whole fish and fry it in the frying pan until it is golden brown; if it is large, cut it into pieces so that you can fry it. When it is ready, transfer the fish to a bowl and top it with the fried batter before serving, Allah the Exalted willing.

294. Another dish

Take a fish, and clean, scrape and salt it. Next, take peeled almonds, pine nuts, the pounded meat of another fish, crushed garlic, breadcrumbs, olive oil, egg yolks and salt. Stir everything together and put it

---

43 Also *al-kaḥlā'* (Gayangos XVI, fol. 97r.), or *al-kuḥayla* ('the small black one'); it has been variously identified as sargo (white seabream) or grey mullet (Dozy 1881: II, 447), grey-lipped mullet (Perry in Rodinson *et al.* 2001: 480), or the black conger eel (Corriente 1997: 456, linking it to the Spanish *negrilla*). It is mentioned by al-Idrīsī (2002: 289) as one of the fish in the lake of Tunis.

44 The Arabic uses the word for 'stuffing' or 'filling' (*ḥashw*), which is, however, not appropriate here, since the mixture is not actually placed inside the fish.

in a pot with the fish. Then, put the pot over a low fire until it is cooked, Allah the Exalted willing.

295. Another dish

Take a fish, and clean, scrape and salt it. Next, take whole and crushed almonds and pine nuts, olive oil, breadcrumbs and eggs, and beat everything together until mixed. Pour the batter in a casserole dish, and put the fish in the middle of it.[45] Top with egg yolks and olive oil. Send it to the oven for cooking, but place the casserole away from the flames so that nothing gets burnt. When the batter has set and the fish is done, take the casserole out of the oven and leave it to cool down. Eat and enjoy, Allah the Exalted willing.

296. Another dish

Clean, gut and salt a fatty fish. Next, take the flesh from another fish and thoroughly mash it. Add a handful of finely ground *darmak* flour, salt and pepper, and beat it smooth. Then, take a new pot and put in olive oil, pepper, coriander seeds, two ladlefuls of fresh coriander juice, oregano, crushed garlic cloves, and an egg. Put the pot over a fire to cook. Take the mashed fish meat and make balls out of it, as described in the sixth chapter of the second section of this book.[46] Put the balls in a pot to cook. Apply a crusting of breadcrumbs and eggs, and add yolks to the pot as well. Take the salted fish and pan-fry it in olive oil, turning it around in the pan until it is browned all over. When it is ready, transfer the fish to a serving bowl and put whatever else is in the pot on top. Eat and enjoy, Allah the Exalted willing.

45 The instruction regarding the position of the fish is taken from BL Or5927 (fol. 203v.).

46 See recipe No. 179.

297. Another dish

Take thick- or medium-fleshed eels,[47] known as *anqila* or *silawwar*,[48] whichever you prefer. Rub their tails with ashes to skin them. Scrape off the skin from the tail upwards, cut off the heads, and slice the remainder into medium-sized pieces. Wash them thoroughly so that there is no dirt left on them. Put the eel pieces in a glazed casserole dish and add salt, plenty of olive oil, pepper, coriander seeds, cumin, crushed saffron, *murrī*, vinegar and whole garlic cloves. Bring the casserole to a boil with a little water. When the liquid is about to dry out, take it to the oven to brown the surface of the dish.

If you want to do this at home, follow the instructions given above.

If you want to fry the eel in a pan with olive oil and garlic, skin, clean and salt it. Next, take a clean frying pan with olive oil and put it over a fire. When the oil is boiling, take the eel, which you have previously cut into medium-sized pieces, and put it in the pan to fry, gently turning the pieces over to make sure they brown on all sides. When it is done, take the fish out of the pan. Then, crush garlic and put it in the pan. When it is cooked, add some olive oil and return the pieces of fish to the pan so that they can absorb the flavour of the garlic. When everything is ready, remove the pan from the fire and transfer its contents to a serving bowl. Eat and enjoy, Allah the Exalted willing.

298. Another dish

Take a fresh tuna,[49] a small one if possible, split it open at the back, and remove the bones. Put it in a large dish, and cover it with vinegar,

---

47 *silbāḥ* (plural *salābīḥ*); according to al-Uryūlī (1983: No. 115), eels raised in fresh water and running rivers are better than those in stagnant water, and are good for people suffering from pulmonary conditions. The ones that are bred in ponds, marshes and swamps have a pleasant taste, but are not very nutritious. He adds that, in order to reduce their harmfulness, the eels should be baked in the oven after flaying, salting and seasoning them with oil and *murrī*.

48 Both of these are vernacular words for 'eel', the former a borrowing from the Latin *anguilla*, the latter from the Greek *sílouros* ('catfish'); Corriente 1997: 31, 258; Dozy 1881: I, 673.

49 Ibn Khalṣūn (1996: 160; trans., 87) said that, like all salty fish, tuna is of no value, that it causes yellow bile and phlegm, and that it spoils the temperament. He strongly advised against using it as food, especially if it is fried. Red (bluefin) tuna is like sea fish, and if it is fatty, it has laxative properties.

ground cumin and crushed garlic. Leave it overnight, and the next morning take it out, wash it well and cut it into medium-sized pieces. Then, take a glazed casserole dish with salt, pepper, coriander seeds, cumin, saffron, *murrī* and vinegar. Mix everything together. Take the pieces of tuna and put them in the casserole one by one, using your hands to coat them with the sauce so that the fish absorbs the flavour of the spices. Arrange the pieces of tuna in the casserole, add plenty of olive oil, sour plums or sour apples, citron leaves and garlic cloves. Put the casserole in the oven and, when [the fish] is cooked and the plums are fully done, remove the dish from the oven, and serve, Allah the Exalted willing.

The tuna fillets should be cut from the loin to the belly.

299. Another dish

Take whichever pieces you like from a tuna, except the loin, and cut, wash and salt them. Next, take a frying pan, clean it, and put it over a fire with olive oil. When the oil has come to a boil, start frying the pieces of fish, gently turning them over so that they can brown on all sides. When they are done, transfer them to a ceramic bowl and serve. Eat and enjoy, Allah the Exalted willing.

If you like, you can make it with a sauce of vinegar, crushed garlic, and caraway. Put the vinegar in a small casserole with the garlic and bring it to the boil. Afterwards, pour it over the fried pieces of tuna in the ceramic bowl. Eat and enjoy, Allah the Exalted willing. [Those who wish to fry the loin and belly should be patient when doing so.][50]

300. Another dish[51]

Take as much tuna as you want, [scale it and slice it,][52] and put the pieces on an iron skewer. Grill as described above. Coat the tuna with dissolved salt, olive oil, macerated *murrī*, crushed garlic, pepper and cinnamon. Grill until it is golden brown. Eat it like this. If you like, you can have the fish with a dressing of olive oil and crushed cooked garlic. Eat and enjoy, Allah the Exalted willing.

50 Addition from Gayangos XVI (fol. 98v.).
51 In Gayangos XVI (*ibid.*), the recipe is called *mashwī* ('roasted').
52 Additional instruction from Gayangos XVI (*ibid.*).

301. Another dish made with dried tuna, called *mushamma*ʿ[53]

Take as much [dried] tuna as you want and cut it lengthwise into thin strips. Put them in an earthenware pot with water, and put it over a fire. When it has come to a boil, take out the tuna strips, remove any sand and salt on them, and wash them. After cleaning them, take a clean frying pan, pour olive oil in and put it over a fire. When the oil is boiling, fry the pieces, and carefully turn them over to ensure they will be golden brown on all sides. Once the fish is done, take it out of the frying pan, and put some crushed garlic in it and fry it. Add more olive oil, and then return the tuna strips to the frying pan so that they can soak up the flavour of the garlic. When that is done, transfer them to a ceramic bowl, and pour on vinegar from either fresh limes, *zanbūʿ*, or verjuice. Eat and enjoy, Allah the Exalted willing.

If you want, you can add a sauce made with vinegar and crushed garlic, in which case you should put vinegar in a small casserole dish and cook the garlic in it. When it is done, pour it over the tuna.

If you like, you can return the tuna pieces to the pot so that they cook, become tender, and acquire the flavour of the garlic, with the power and strength of Allah the Exalted.

302. Another dish, called *rāhibī*[54]

Take as much dried tuna as you like, and do the same with it as in the previous recipe. Then cook it in a casserole dish, according to the recipe mentioned in the first chapter of the second section of this book, and use plenty of olive oil. [If you want, you can use boiled inspissated grape juice instead of honey.[55] When the dish has finished cooking in the oven and is ready, take it out and serve it, Allah the Exalted willing.][56]

---

53 The word is derived from a verb meaning both 'to wax' and 'to dry (meat and fish)', and denoted a dried and salted tuna dish peculiar to the Muslim West. The word has endured in Spanish as *mojama* and is a speciality of Huelva and Cádiz. Corriente 1997: 291; Marín 1997: 16.

54 Also see recipes Nos. 105, 203, 248, 281, though those are all made with meat.

55 This is the usual sweetener for that dish; see recipe No. 105.

56 The passage enclosed in square brackets is missing from the edition, and was taken from BL Or5927, fol. 170r.

303. Another dish, called *al-arnabī*[57]

Take as much dried tuna as you like and cook it like an *arnabī*, as mentioned in the first chapter [of the second section]. This is the end of the recipe.

304. Another dish[58]

Wash and clean dried tuna as before,[59] and cut it up as finely as you can. Put a drizzle of oil into a clean frying pan, add the tuna, and lightly fry it over a fire, gently turning it over until some of the moisture it contains dries out. Next, take a casserole dish and pour some olive oil in it. Take a bowl, and put a small amount of soaked breadcrumbs in it, together with pepper, coriander, ginger, spikenard, cloves, a bit of mastic, crushed saffron, and coriander seeds. Crack some eggs into it as well, but extract some of the yolks and set them aside. Beat everything together well until all the ingredients are thoroughly blended, and then mix in the tuna. Put the mixture in a casserole dish and arrange the set-aside egg yolks on the surface. Drench the dish with olive oil and sprinkle on cinnamon and ginger before taking it to the oven. Place it away from the fire, and leave it to cook and brown on top. When it is ready, take it out and leave it to cool down. Eat and enjoy, Allah the Exalted willing.

305. Another dish

Take dried tuna and do the same things as described above. Cut it into medium-sized pieces and lightly fry them after boiling. Next, take aubergines, remove their outer peels, and split them lengthwise, cutting out the calyces. Boil them in water and salt to release their harmful juices. Leave the aubergines until they are entirely done, then remove them and wash with hot water. Cut up onions and cook them in a pot until they are done, and then take them out and put them in a casserole

---

57 See recipe No 104, for an *arnabī* dish made with meat. This recipe and the next two are found only in BL Or5927 (fol. 170r.–v.) and Gayangos XVI (fols. 99r.–100r.). This recipe is not titled in the latter manuscript.

58 The translation follows the division in Gayangos XVI (fol. 99r.), where this is a separate recipe (unlike in BL Or5927, fol. 170r.), as the result is very different from the *arnabi*. However, the text of the recipe in BL Or5927 is more detailed, and served as the source text.

59 See recipe No. 301.

dish to which you add the aubergine, the tuna, a large quantity of olive oil, pepper, coriander seeds and cumin; if you leave out the onion, add peeled garlic, macerated *murrī* and vinegar. If you include onion, then omit the garlic, vinegar and *murrī*, and instead add the cooked onion juice. Put the dish over a fire to cook, and when it is done take it to the oven so it can brown on top. When it is ready, take it out, and leave it to cool down. Eat and enjoy, Allah the Exalted willing.

If you want, you can also cook pickled tuna like a *rāhibī*[60] in a casserole dish with olive oil, *murrī* and saffron, as mentioned before. However, after soaking the fish in water, wash it until you are sure that you have got all the salt out. Remember this, and act accordingly.

If you wish, you can make the recipe with salted (cured) sardines.

You could also boil the fish in water and fry it afterwards, adding vinegar, crushed garlic and caraway seeds. The same can be done if you are using pickled tuna, Allah the Exalted willing.

You should know that all fish are harmful to moist and cold temperaments, and they spoil quickly if they have not been well digested. After eating them, it is necessary to drink either undiluted wine,[61] inspissated grape juice, spiced honey syrup, some macerated *murrī*, or squill vinegar.[62] You should not engage in physical exertion either before or after having fish, nor should you drink much water when eating it. If it makes you very thirsty, mix water with one of the above-mentioned beverages, Allah the Exalted willing.[63]

60 See recipes Nos. 105, 203, 248, 281, 302.

61 *sharāb ṣirf* ('pure wine'); according to al-Rāzī (1881: 17), undiluted wine is very good for the stomach and aids digestion. However, it is very harmful to the head because of the rising vapours of the wine and its (intoxicating) effect.

62 See recipe No. 443.

63 In the printed edition, this general section on fish appears at the end of recipe No. 302, but the translation follows BL Or5927 (fol. 170v.), from which the religious formula is also taken, as the passage is clearly intended to close the chapter on fish. A similar section is found in the *Andalusian* (*Anwāʿ*, 155; BNF, fol. 56v.), and there are a number of similarities with al-Rāzī's work (1881: 25–6). Both al-Rāzī and Ibn Buṭlān (1990: 122, 123; trans., 255) recommend eating fish only on 'vomiting' days, adding that there is nothing more harmful than drinking iced water after it.

Chapter Two: on ways of making eggs

306. Dish [*isfīriyya*][64]

Take as many eggs as you like and break them into a bowl. Add salt, pepper, coriander seeds, fresh coriander juice,[65] mint juice, a little saffron, a little leavened dough, cumin, crushed garlic and cinnamon. Thoroughly whisk it all with your hands until everything is mixed. Next, take a clean frying pan and put olive oil in it. When the oil has come to a boil, spread the batter over the entire surface of the frying pan. Once the eggs have set into an omelette, roll the disc so that it looks like a reed.[66] Cut it into pieces of the size you want, and fry them over a low fire, gently turning them over so that they brown on all sides. If the frying pan is too small, remove some of the pieces to make some room in the pan. Whenever a piece is done, take it out and put it in a ceramic bowl, until you have finished them all. [Do not pour too much of the *isfīriyya* into the frying pan, since this will make it difficult to fold.][67] If you want, you can add some boiled vinegar. Eat and enjoy, Allah the Exalted willing.

You can also make this *isfīriyya* another way by putting macerated *murrī* and vinegar into the egg mixture, instead of the fresh coriander and mint juice, and by not including yeast. Beat the eggs with your hands to mix them, and add crushed saffron, a lot of pepper, ginger, cinnamon, spikenard, cloves, a bit of mastic, crushed garlic, coriander seeds and cumin. Leave it alone for a while to settle. Then, take a frying pan, pour in a sufficient amount of olive oil and, when it starts boiling, pour in the eggs. Use a ladle to push the batter away from the sides of the pan. Fold the pancake three times if you have a lot of eggs, so that it does not get too thick to fry. How you fold it depends on the thickness.[68] Then cut it with a knife into large or small pieces, depending on the size you want. If the frying pan is too small, remove some of the

64 The title is added only in Gayangos XVI (fol. 100r.).

65 The translation follows BL Or5927 (fol. 171r.) as the edition (2012: 210) has the clearly incorrect 'dried coriander juice' (*mā' kuzabara yābisa*).

66 *qannūṭ*; Corriente 1997: 422, 444.

67 Addition from Gayangos XVI (fol. 100v.).

68 The folding instructions were taken from BL Or5927 (fol. 171r.), as some details are missing or erroneous in the edition (2012: 210–11), which, for instance, talks about the difficulty of folding rather than frying.

pieces to create space to fry them, and carefully turn them over so that they do not break up. Fry them until they are done and golden brown on all sides. Once they are done, transfer them from the frying pan to a ceramic bowl, and position them side by side. Continue doing so until all the pieces have been fried. Finally, pour on boiled vinegar or vinegar with cooked garlic, though you can also just eat them as they are. This is entirely up to you. Eat and enjoy, Allah the Exalted willing.

307. Another dish[69]

Take as many eggs as you want. Next, take a clean tinned frying pan and put it over a fire with a sufficient amount of olive oil. When the oil starts to boil, take the eggs and crack them one by one into the frying pan, adding salt and pepper if you like. Fold the egg whites over the yolks, so that you end up with a disc. Gently turn the eggs over so that they brown on both sides. In the meantime, continue cracking the rest of the eggs until you have finished all of them. Each time you fry one, remove it from the pan and transfer it to a ceramic bowl. Continue until all have been fried.

If you want, you can add boiled vinegar or vinegar with garlic, as mentioned before, or macerated *murrī*, but you can also leave them plain. Feel free to do as you like. Eat and enjoy, Allah the Exalted willing.

308. Another dish[70]

Take as many eggs as you want and put them in a pot with just water to boil them. When they are done and set, take them out, and throw them in cold water to let them cool down. Next, peel them and leave them to cool further. Then use a thread to cut them across the middle. Gingerly remove the yolks and put them in a bowl. Add a sufficient amount of crushed salt, pepper, ginger, cinnamon, cloves, spikenard and a little mastic. If you like, you can add a bit of fresh coriander juice and mint juice, though you may instead choose to pour in a little *murrī* – it's entirely up to you. Knead the yolks and spices with your hands, making a good dough. Then shape the dough into yolk shapes and place them back inside the eggs. Use a clean twine – or a thin stalk of oregano – to

69 Gayangos XVI (fol. 100v.) adds that it is 'amazing'.

70 There is a very similar recipe in *Anwāʿ*, 107.

keep the two egg halves together so that they do not fall apart. Coat the eggs with egg whites and finely ground *darmak* flour. Once you have done this, take a clean frying pan and pour in some good-quality olive oil. When the oil starts to boil, gently put the eggs in, taking care to keep them together. Fry them and carefully turn them over so that they are golden brown on all sides. When they are done, remove them from the pan and use them in any dish you like, Allah the Exalted willing. Also dust them with cinnamon.

309. A dish called *nīmbirisht*[71] (poached eggs)

Take as many eggs as you want, and put them in a small pot with water and salt. Put it over a fire and bring to a full boil. Then, take the eggs one by one and crack them into the water. When an egg is partly set, remove it with a small ladle, but take care that you do not break it and let the yolk flow out. Put it in a bowl with vinegar and olive oil. Then crack another egg and do the same thing as before, until you have done all of them. Eat and enjoy, Allah the Exalted willing.

310. Another dish

Take a glazed casserole dish with olive oil, vinegar, *murrī*, pepper, coriander seeds, cumin, a clove of crushed garlic, and salt. Beat all this with a ladle to mix it together. Next, take as many eggs as you want, and crack them into the casserole one after the other until you have done them all. Take the dish to the oven, but place it away from the flames until the eggs have set and are golden brown, and the broth has dried

---

71 Gayangos XVI (fol. 100v.) and BL Or5927 (fol. 172r.) have the variants of *numayrashāt* and *nīmarasht*, respectively. The term is a borrowing from Persian, meaning 'half' (*nīm*) 'roasted/fried' (*birisht*, the imperative form of the verb *birishtan*). In Arabic, it usually denotes a soft-boiled egg. Al-Isrā'ilī cites Galen as the source for its other name, *al-murta'ish* ('the trembling one'), 'because it quivers when it is ready' (1992: 173). Ibn Janāḥ (2020: No. 626) also refers to Galen as saying that it is an egg that can be slurped (*tataḥassā*) and that 'it is boiled in water until it becomes hot'. Al-Qumrī (1991: 83) defines it as 'eggs heated over a fire until they are close to coagulation, and are then sipped'. According to Ibn Jazla (fol. 46r.), it is the best way to prepare eggs, and one should boil them in hot water and count up to 300 before taking them out. If there is not enough water, then one should count to 100 before taking them out. Soft-boiled eggs were also said to have many medical advantages, in that they are digested quickly, very nutritious, useful against coughs, and increase semen. Ibn al-Bayṭār (1992: I, 177), however, argued that, because soft-boiled eggs pass quickly through the digestive system, they are the least nutritious.

out. When it is ready, take it out and serve, Allah the Exalted willing.

If you want to make this recipe at home, take a casserole and put in any of the above seasonings. Place it over a fire and, when it has come to a full boil, crack the eggs into it, one by one, but make sure they are kept apart. When they are set and the broth has dried out, remove the pot from the fire, and then eat and enjoy, Allah the Exalted willing.

311. Another dish

Take a casserole dish and add olive oil, fresh butter, or clarified butter, whichever you prefer. Also throw in salt, pepper, and coriander seeds. After putting the casserole over a fire, take as many eggs as you need, and break them into a bowl. Whisk them together with your hands to mix them, and then pour the mixture into the casserole. Stir the eggs with a ladle to separate them and keep them apart. Keep doing this until they are cooked and set, and the liquid has dried out. When they are done, remove the casserole from the fire and serve dusted with cinnamon. Eat and enjoy it, Allah the Exalted willing.

312. Another dish

Take as many eggs as you want, and put them in a pot with just water over a fire. If you want them to be only lightly boiled, so they can be sipped, let them boil, and then take them out of the pot. Serve them with salt and pepper. If you want them coagulated, leave them to cook until the liquid has dried out and they start to rise to the surface. Take them out, peel them, and eat them with bread. Dip in salt and pepper, and eat and enjoy, Allah the Exalted willing.

313. Another dish

Take as many eggs as you like and break them into a bowl. Add a lot of fresh coriander juice, breadcrumbs, pounded almonds and walnuts, salt and pepper. Vigorously beat everything together. Put a frying pan with plenty of olive oil over a fire and pour in the batter. When you see that there is no longer enough olive oil, add some more until the eggs are cooked. Gently turn the omelette over so it can brown on both sides. When it is ready, remove the pan from the fire, and serve in a bowl. Eat and enjoy, Allah the Exalted willing.

314. Another dish

Take a small pot and put in water, vinegar, olive oil, *murrī*, pepper, coriander seeds, fresh coriander, and salt. Put it over a fire and bring it to a boil. Take as many eggs as you want, gently crack them into the pot,[72] and leave it over a low fire. When they are done, crust the pot with eggs and finely ground *darmak* flour. Leave on a low fire until the crusting has set, and let it simmer down before serving. Eat and enjoy, Allah the Exalted willing.

315. Another dish

Take a small pot in which you have put water, pepper, olive oil, coriander seeds, fresh coriander juice, soaked chickpeas, and a bit of cut-up onion. Put it over a fire to cook. When the chickpeas are done, take as many eggs as you want, and crack them into a bowl with a little salt, pepper, fresh coriander juice and mint juice. Thoroughly beat it all together until everything is mixed. Put the mixture in the pot over a low fire, and stir it with a ladle until it is cooked. When it is ready, transfer to a bowl, and dust with cinnamon. Eat and enjoy, Allah the Exalted willing.

If you like, you can make this dish with vinegar and saffron, in which case add cumin to the spices, and instead of coriander and mint juice use vinegar and macerated *murrī*. In addition, throw cloves of garlic and a little crushed saffron in the pot. You can also add saffron to the eggs at the time you break them and start beating them. Then continue in the same way as before. Eat and enjoy, Allah the Exalted willing.

316. Another dish[73]

Take as many eggs as you want and put them in the ashes, so that they are fully exposed to the heat of the fire. If you want them to be lightly boiled so they can be sipped, you should turn them over so that they are heated on all sides. Eat them with salt and pepper, Allah the Exalted willing. If you want them to be fully coagulated, leave them in the ashes and turn them until you know they are done. Then put them in cold water and peel them. Eat them with salt, pepper and cinnamon, Allah the Exalted willing.

---

72 Gayangos XVI (fol. 102 r.) specifies that the eggs should be whole when cooked.

73 This recipe is missing from Gayangos XVI, which instead states that 'there are many other varieties [of dishes] that I have left out' (fol. 102r.).

SECTION SIX

On dairy and everything that is made with it

It consists of three chapters.

Chapter One: on curd[1] and what to make with it

317. [Making curd]

Take freshly milked sheep's, cow's or goat's milk, strain it into an earthenware vessel and leave near the fire so that the heat can reach it. Next, take lamb or kid goat's rennet in proportion to the milk and put it in a clean cloth inside the vessel. Squeeze it with your hand until it dissolves, and leave it for a while until the milk has curdled.[2]

318. Recipe for making cheese

Take a fan made of esparto grass similar to the ones used for fanning a fire. In the middle of it, fashion a ring-shaped strip of esparto, similar to a *ka'k* biscuit, and sew it up. Make it small – one span wide and two or more spans long – and shape it in a circle on top of the fan. Take the curd out of the container in which it was made and press it with your hands to squeeze out the water. Keep adding and squeezing the curd until the fan is full. Then take another fan like the first and put it on top of the curd that is [already] in the mould. Once again, squeeze it with your hand until all the water comes out. Return the mould to where it was, and put it to one side. Then, take another fan and do the same as before, until you have finished making the amount of cheese you want to make. Leave to stand until they have dried – for a whole day if you make it in the morning, or overnight if you make it in the evening. Lift the upper fan, unfasten the smaller strip, and put it to one side. Put the

1 *'aqīd*; according to al-Uryūlī (1983: No. 131), it is intermediate between the nature of fresh cheese and that of milk, but thicker and more nutritious, whereas it causes blockages. In Arabic culinary terminology in the Mashriq, the word also denoted syrup or juice boiled down to candy. See Ibn Mubārak Shāh 2020: 162–4; *Kanz*, Nos. 348, 371.

2 According to Gayangos XIV (fol. 102v.), 'it can be curdled with the flowers of wild artichokes, known as cardoon'. Also see recipe No. 322.

cheese on a board and remove the bottom fan. Salt it if you want it to last. If you are going to make *mujabbanas* or a *badīʿī*[3] with this cheese, leave it unsalted.

If you want to make a cheese-and-egg casserole, the recipe is as follows. Take as much cheese as you want, wash it, and crumble it into a bowl. Crack eggs into it – in an appropriate ratio to the amount of cheese – and add salt (if the cheese is not salted), crushed saffron, pepper, coriander seeds, fresh coriander juice, mint juice and cinnamon. Whip it all together by hand until everything is blended. Next, take a glazed casserole dish and drizzle in a little olive oil before adding the cheese-and-egg batter. Flatten and smooth it out in the dish with your hands. Decorate[4] the surface of the dish with egg yolks and pour on enough olive oil to cover it. Dust with cinnamon and take the dish to the oven. Place it away from the fire until it sets and browns. When it is ready, remove from the oven and let it cool down a bit. Eat and enjoy, Allah the Exalted willing.

You can also make this recipe by frying everything in a pan, rather than sending it to the oven, in which case make a thick rather than runny batter. Take a clean frying pan and pour in a medium amount of olive oil. After it has come to a boil, make small, round, flat loaves out of the cheese-and-egg batter, put them in the pan, and fry them. Gently turn them over until they are done and golden brown. If you see that they are breaking up, add some dough and mix it with the cheese and eggs. Keep this in mind and do it this way.

If you want to fry the cheese without the eggs, you should take cheese that was curdled about five days before and is salty and dry. Wash away the salt, and cut the cheese lengthwise into pieces, about three fingers in width. Then take a frying pan and add a dribble of olive oil. When it starts to boil, put the cheese in the pan and fry it until it is done and golden brown. Gingerly turn the pieces so that they brown all over. Take them out when they are ready, and transfer them to a porcelain bowl. Dust with pepper and cinnamon, and eat and enjoy, Allah the Exalted willing.

If you want to eat this fresh cheese with honey or figs, you should

---

3 See Recipe No. 155.

4 Only Gayangos XVI (103r.) uses the verb *najjama*, 'decorate, garnish', while the other copies simply refer to putting the eggs on top of the cheese.

cut it into strips and dip them in the honey. Eat and enjoy, Allah the Exalted willing. [This is something that is considered delicious.][5]

319. How to make *shīrāz*[6] (cottage cheese)

Take as much curd as you want, put it in an esparto basket, and cover it. Suspend the basket so as to drain the whey. When this is done, take the curd down and rub it with your hands over a horse-hair sieve until it goes into the bowl that has been placed underneath. Add a sufficient amount of salt, and stir with a ladle until the salt is mixed in with the curd. Put it in a new earthenware pot that has not been touched with water, and store. When you want to eat it, put it in a bowl and spread it out with a ladle, up to the edge of the bowl. Arrange olives and capers along the sides, and a pickled lime in the centre. Sprinkle on a little nigella for decoration. Pour some sweet olive oil over it. This dish goes off quickly, and does not keep. It is best eaten when it is still sweet. Remember this. It is eaten with a side of green onions. [Take tender green onions, strip away the outer peel, and wash them with salt. Then, wash them again with just water, and leave them to one side. When you want to eat it, take an onion in your hand and scoop up some *shīrāz* with it, as much as you like for each bite. Eat and enjoy, Allah the Exalted willing.][7]

5 Addition from Gayangos XVI (fol. 103r.).

6 The word is a borrowing from Persian (*shīr*, 'milk'; *āz*, 'greedy'), and referred to curd strained from the whey (Steingass 1892: 773). Ibn Janāḥ (2020: No. 830) said he was told by people 'from the East' that *shīrāz* is the same as *qanbarīs*. The latter appears in the *1001 Nights* (Mahdī 1984: I, 127) as well as in a number of cookery books, and denoted a yoghurt cheese which was usually dried. See Ibn Mubārak Shāh 2020: Nos. 181, 189; *Kanz*, Nos. 508, 515, 531. According to the author of *Wuṣla*, which has about ten recipes with *qanbarīs*, the best kind came from Baalbek (No. 8.55). In modern Arabic, cottage cheese is known as *aqiṭ*, though this is already mentioned by Ibn ʿAbd Rabbih (1983: VIII, 4) as one of the foods of the Bedouin Arabs, and was apparently mixed with *sawīq* (grain gruel). Ibn Zuhr (1992: 31; trans., 62) believed it to be harmful to the brain and nerves, whereas al Uryūlī (1983: No. 130) suggested counteracting its negative properties by eating *shīrāz* with olive oil and butter, and mixing it with the broth from plump chickens. It was available ready-made in the market, but, according to Ibn ʿAbdūn (Lévi-Provençal 1955: 44; trans., 73) should only be sold in skins (*ziqāq*), since they can be washed and cleaned each day; the use of earthenware jars would not protect against worms and mould. In BL Or5927, this recipe and the two that follow were wrongly bound in Section 7, with fol. 179v. being followed by fol. 174r.–v., which interrupts an aubergine recipe (No. 346).

7 The passage enclosed in brackets is an addition from BL Or5927 (fol. 174r.).

320. Recipe for making *khilāṭ*[8]

This is made in exactly the same way as *shīrāz*, except that you also require tender caper stalks, preserved in salt. Wash and cut them into small pieces, and then mix them in with the curdled milk. When this is done, pour it all in a bowl, and spread it out with a ladle. Garnish with olives and limes, and add a drizzle of olive oil. Eat and enjoy, Allah the Exalted willing.

321. Making curd with honey

Strain and curdle milk, as described above. If you want, you can curdle it with the flowers of wild artichokes, known as cardoon, which are suited to this. When the milk is curdling, sweeten it with as much honey dissolved in milk as you like, and then leave it. Eat it as you like, Allah the Exalted willing. When the curd is plain, it is eaten with good-quality figs.[9]

Chapter Two: on making curdled milk and extracting butter

322. Recipe for sieved curdled milk

Take as much of the above-mentioned curd as you want. Suspend[10] it in an esparto grass container in order to drain off most of the liquid. Take a horse-hair sieve and place it over a large bowl or earthenware pot. Put the curd in the sieve and rub it with your hands until it goes into the lower bowl. Once it is all in, add a sufficient amount of salt, and whisk to mix it well. Transfer to an earthenware bowl and eat it whenever you want, Allah the Exalted willing. [This is made like *shīrāz*, except that the whey of *shīrāz* is strained off, but in this recipe it is retained.][11]

---

8 See al-Warrāq 1987: 95; *Kanz*, Nos. 510–11. According to Ibn Zuhr (1992: 31; trans., 62), it is one of the most harmful and corrupting dairy products, and should not be consumed under any circumstances.

9 The recipe in Gayangos XVI (fol. 103r.) is highly abridged, and also has a different instruction: 'Put honey dissolved in milk when it is curdling, and then leave it until it is has curdled. It may be eaten with eggs, which is considered delicious.'

10 The translation is based on Gayangos XVI (fol. 103v.), as the other copies merely refer to the curd being 'placed' in the container.

11 Addition from Gayangos XVI (fol. 103v.).

323. Recipe for making curdled milk in a leather milk jug[12]

Take a tanned leather milk jug and repeatedly fill it with the liquid from yoghurt, which is called whey, to wash it until the skin no longer smells of tanning. Then, wash the jug with water, clean it and drain the water from it. Fill it up with strained milk and put it in a wooden pail with a lid. Make a hole in the pail with a drain so that the water can flow out when washing the jug. Place the pail in a place where it is out of the sun, or over an irrigation ditch,[13] and then cover the jug with green leaves, such as grape leaves, willow leaves, or something like that. Every day in the morning wash the leather jug and scrape it with the back of a knife, or with a wooden knife made especially for this purpose. Only a man or woman in a state of ritual purity is allowed to do this work. Swirl the jug around in the bucket, clean and wash it, and then change the leaves. Put the cover back on, and check it after three days; if you find that the milk has coagulated and curdled, scoop out as much as you want and put fresh milk in its place. If you want the curdled milk to be very thick, leave it until it acquires the desired consistency. Use it as a dip for grilled squabs or cockerels – in which case add olive oil and garlic – or gourd. When you remove the thick, curdled milk from the jug, make sure to always leave a little in the leather jug as yeast. Remember this. You should also take great care washing and cleaning it, because the curdled milk degrades very easily. If it is light, it can be used as a drink when eating bread. However, if it is thick and dense, it is used as described above, and can be made with some of the things you made with *shīrāz*[14] or *khilāṭ*.[15] Eat and enjoy, Allah the Exalted willing.

324. Recipe for extracting butter

Strain freshly milked milk, put it in an earthenware jar and let it stand for a day and a night. Afterwards, transfer it to a churn, suspend it, and vigorously shake it to mix the milk. When the cream separates and the

12 *qirba* (plural *qirab*), a receptacle made out of a single animal skin (usually sheep or goat) and sewn up at the back. It was also used to hold water, wine, oil, etc. already in Antiquity.

13 *sāqiya*; in the Mashriq, this denotes a water-wheel, but in Andalusian Arabic it referred to an irrigation canal or ditch. See Corriente 1997: 255; Dozy 1881: I, 665; Kazimirski 1860: I, 1110.

14 See recipe No. 319.

15 See recipe No. 320.

butter begins to form, take some fresh water and pour it into the milk. Shake it more vigorously until the butter coagulates, and then reach into the churn with your hand to remove the butter. You can drink the buttermilk that is left over in the churn, with the power of Allah the Exalted.

If you want – or need – to turn the clarified butter into butter again, take the clarified butter and wash it once or twice in hot water. Afterwards, put it in cold water and stir it continuously. Then take the butter out with your hand, put it in a jar, and serve, Allah the Exalted willing.

Chapter Three: on maturing[16] dry cheese in an earthenware jar, what is made with it, and restoring[17] butter and buttermilk

325. Recipe for preparing it[18]

Use cheese that was made in the second half of March or in April, salt it, and put it on a wooden board raised above the ground. It should be exposed to the air, but not to the sun. Continually wipe it down with a woollen cloth, and then coat with olive oil and salt until you can tell that it has absorbed the necessary salt, and all the moisture has dried out. This will be in the month of May. Then, take an earthenware jar in which olive oil has been stored, wipe it clean, but do not wash it with water. Once it is clean, put the oil-coated cheeses in side by side, without leaving any gaps in between, until the jar is full. Then cover it

---

16 *tahyī'a* ('preparing'); BL Or5927 (fol. 175r.) has the more technical *tarbiya* (from the verb *rabbā*, 'to grow', 'to preserve'), which is the more likely since *murabbā* denoted half-dry cheese in Andalusian Arabic. Lane 1863–74: III, 1023; Corriente 1997: 200.

17 The translation follows BL OR5927 (fol. 175r.), rather than the edition (2012: 220), which has 'extraction' (*istikhrāj*).

18 Physicians did not think highly of dry cheese. According to al-Uryūlī (1983: No. 133), dry cheese stimulates the appetite, but is not very nourishing, lingers in the stomach, and causes constipation. Ibn Biklārish (fols. 40v.–41r.) said that it is very constipating, and that eating it in large quantities gives rise to kidney stones and liver blockages. It is also difficult to digest and can cause colic, and is best made with milk from a young animal. Conversely, fresh cheese was praised because it was moist and nutritious, and for the speed with which it leaves the stomach. Ibn Jazla (fol. 53r.) commended the pleasant taste of fresh cheese, the best kind being made from sour milk.

and firmly seal the lid with mud. After leaving it alone for fifteen days, open the jar up and move the cheeses around; those that were on top should go on the bottom, and those that were at the bottom should now be on top. Re-cover the jar, and seal the lid. Leave the jar for a further ten days. Continue doing this until the cheeses are moist. You will know the cheeses are ready when you open the jar and notice perforations inside, filled with olive oil. Eat the cheese with good-quality bread and sweet grapes, throughout autumn, Allah the Exalted willing.

326. Dish made with dry cheese

Take as much cheese as you want, remove the rind, and then grate it into a fine powder. Next, boil cloves of garlic in water to soften them. Take them out and crush them in a wooden mortar before adding a pinch of salt. Then take hot water and dissolve the powdered cheese and garlic in it, making sure everything is mixed, and, finally, add good olive oil. Eat and enjoy, Allah the Exalted willing.

If you want to add crushed peeled walnuts to the cheese and garlic, feel free to do so, with the power of Allah the Exalted.

327. Another dish

Take some of the aforementioned cheese, put it in water to soften it, and then clean and cut it into thin squares. Next, put a sufficient amount of sweet olive oil in a clean pan and fry the cheese pieces in it, gingerly turning them whenever necessary so that they can brown on all sides. When the pieces are done, take them out and serve them in a bowl. Eat and enjoy, Allah the Exalted willing.

If possible, you should use sesame oil, which is particularly suited for this. It is said that fried cheese removes the odour of garlic and onion, Allah the Exalted willing.

328. Another dish[19]

Take some of the aforementioned cheese, remove its rind, and then cut it into small pieces. Thread them on a thin wooden stick, and roast them until they are golden brown on all sides. Eat and enjoy, Allah the Exalted willing.

---

19 BL Or5927 (fol. 175v.) and Gayangos XVI (fol. 105v.) have *naw'* ('type'), rather than *lawn* ('dish'), whereas the latter calls it *mashwī* ('roasted').

329. Restoring butter after it has gone off
Strain the water in which gum-cistus[20] has been cooked, and use it to boil the butter in, as a result of which it will become soft and tasty again, Allah the Exalted willing.

330. How to prevent milk from going sour quickly
To prevent milk from going sour, take fresh cheese and put it into the vessel with the milk. This prevents it from going sour.

20 *Shajar al-astab* (*Cistus ladaniferus*), which is found only in Gayangos XVI (*ibid.*), and can also denote rock-rose (*Cistus polymorphus*); Corriente 1997: 13. The edition (2012: 221) and BL Or5927 (fol. 175r.) have the unattested *shajar al-asīt*.

SECTION SEVEN

On vegetables and similar things

It consists of ten chapters.

Chapter One: on dishes made with gourd

331. Dish

Take a gourd, scrape the outside, clean out the inside, and boil in water with salt. When it is done, take it out of the pot and put it on a board to drain the water from it. Then take a clean frying pan and put it over a fire with olive oil. When the oil starts to boil, fry the pieces of gourd, after dredging them through flour. Turn them over in the pan until they are done and golden brown, and then transfer them to a ceramic bowl. Next, take a small pot with vinegar, pepper, salt, olive oil and a little water, and put it over a fire. When it comes to a boil, add a ladleful of fresh coriander juice and bring it to a boil again. Cut the fried gourd into medium-sized pieces and put them in the small pot. Take peeled crushed almonds, breadcrumbs and an egg yolk and beat it all together until everything is mixed. Take the broth from the small pot and pour it over the breadcrumbs mixed with the almonds and the egg yolk. Stir and then pour the mixture on the gourd in the pot. Remove the fire from underneath and leave it on embers to simmer down and to balance the flavours. Serve in a ceramic bowl. Eat and enjoy, Allah the Exalted willing.

332. Another dish

Take as many gourds as you like, scrape the outside, and clean out the insides. Cut each gourd into medium-sized pieces, and put them in a pot with water and salt. Place the pot over a fire and, when the gourd is done, take it out. Take a clean pot and put in a splash of water, olive oil, pepper, coriander seeds, vinegar, *murrī*, a sprig of oregano, garlic cloves and a bit of onion. Put the pot over a fire to cook and, when it has come to a boil, cut up the pieces of gourd some more, and throw them in the pot. Next, crush peeled walnuts[1] in a mortar with breadcrumbs and eggs, and add salt, a sufficient amount of pepper and a little ground saffron. Pour on some of the broth that is in the pot, and whisk everything together until it is all mixed, and then put it in the pot with the gourd. Remove the fire from under the pot and set it on embers while stirring it. Add egg yolks, and leave it until it sets and the flavours are balanced. Serve it in a ceramic bowl. Eat and enjoy, Allah the Exalted willing.

333. Another dish

Take as many gourds as you want, and proceed in the same manner as above. Then take a clean pot with water, salt, olive oil, coriander seeds, pepper and a bit of cut-up onion. Put it over a fire and, when it has come to a boil, add the gourd and then egg yolks. Next, crush pine nuts and breadcrumbs in a mortar, and add fresh coriander juice, egg whites, salt and pepper. Beat it all together, and pour on some of the broth from the pot. Stir well, and then tip the mixture into the pot. Remove the heat from under it and leave it on embers until the flavours are balanced. [Serve in a ceramic bowl, and][2] eat and enjoy, Allah the Exalted willing.

334. Another dish

Take as many gourds as you want, and do the same as you did before. Once the gourds have been boiled, squeeze out all of the water content. Pound them well in a mortar until you obtain a lump, and then add a sufficient amount of salt, as well as pepper and breadcrumbs. Next, break eggs and beat everything together, but make sure the mixture is not too runny. Put a clean frying pan with olive oil over a fire and, when the oil starts to boil, take the pounded gourd and shape it into discs, like those for *aḥrash*,[3] and fry them in the pan. Carefully turn them over so that they can brown on all sides. Whenever loaves are ready, transfer them to a ceramic bowl. Continue doing this until you

1 The translation is based on BL Or5927 (fol. 176r.) and Gayangos XVI (fol. 106r.), rather than the edition, which suggests 'almonds' (*lawz*), based on the unclear text in Wetzstein 1207 (fol. 73v.).

2 The section in brackets is taken from BL Or5927, fol. 176v.

3 See recipe No. 185.

finish the entire batch. Eat and enjoy, Allah the Exalted willing.

335. Another dish
Take as many gourds as you want, and do the same as before. Then take a new pot with water, salt, coriander seeds, pepper and a bit of cut-up onion. Put all of this in a pot over a fire to cook, and then add the chopped gourd. Next, take peeled almonds and crush them in a mortar with breadcrumbs, an egg and mint juice. Stir and mix it all together, and put it in the pot on a low fire until everything is done and the flavours are balanced. Serve in a ceramic bowl, and eat and enjoy, Allah the Exalted willing.

336. Another dish
Take as many gourds as you like, and proceed in the same manner as above, i.e. scrape and clean them. Next, cut them into small pieces and put them in a clean pot with salt, coriander seeds, pepper, caraway and a chopped onion. Put the pot over a fire and stir it carefully until the water from the gourd oozes out. Next, take some milk and add a sprinkling of *darmak* flour. Stir it, and pour it into the pot with the gourd, and add some good clarified butter. Cook it over a low fire, and gently stir until it is done. Serve in a ceramic bowl, and sprinkle on caster sugar. Eat and enjoy, Allah the Exalted willing.

337. Another dish
Take as many gourds as you want, and do the same as before. When you have boiled the gourds, take them out and thoroughly pound them in a mortar until you obtain a dough-like consistency. Add pepper, caraway, coriander seeds and fresh coriander juice. Beat it all together and put it in a clean pot with good clarified butter, milk and a little *murrī*. Put the pot over a moderate fire and gently cook everything, all the while stirring it so it does not burn. When it is done, serve it in a ceramic bowl, and sprinkle on cinnamon and pepper. Eat and enjoy, Allah the Exalted willing.

338. Another dish
Take as many gourds as you like, and do the same with each as you did previously, i.e. scrape, clean and wash them. Then cut them up, and

put the pieces in a clean pot with water and salt. Place the pot over a fire to cook and, when the gourd is done, take it out. Squeeze the water from the gourd pieces and rub them over a narrow-meshed sieve made of horse hair or esparto which has been put over a bowl to collect the gourd pieces. Next, take some curdled milk, like *shīrāz*[4] or leather jug curds,[5] and add as much cooked crushed garlic as you like. Pour this into the bowl with the gourd and thoroughly mix it all together. Serve up in a ceramic bowl and pour good olive oil over it. Eat and enjoy, Allah the Exalted willing.

339. Another dish

Take as many gourds as you want, and do the same with them as you did before. Cut each into long pieces, and boil them. When they are done, take them out and put them on a sieve or a board to drain the water. Next, break eggs into a bowl and add pepper, coriander seeds, caraway and a sprinkling of flour. Beat and mix everything well. Then take a clean frying pan and put it over a moderate fire with a drizzle of olive oil. When the oil starts to boil, throw in the gourd pieces, and turn them over to ensure that they brown on all sides. When they are done, take them out one by one, drag them through the egg batter, and fry them again. Do this several times, until the gourd is entirely surrounded by the batter and is no longer visible. When the gourd pieces are golden brown, remove them from the frying pan and serve them in a ceramic bowl. Sprinkle on a little *murrī* and chopped fresh coriander. Eat and enjoy, Allah the Exalted willing.

340. Another dish

Take as many gourds as you like, and do the same to it as you did before. Cut them lengthwise and put the pieces in a clean pot with water and salt. Place the pot over a fire and, when the gourd is done, take it out and put the pieces on a board to drain the water. Pour vinegar and olive oil into a ceramic bowl, and then put the gourd in. Eat and enjoy, Allah the Exalted willing.

If you want to include crushed garlic, cook it in vinegar first before adding it.

4 See recipe No. 319.
5 See recipe No. 323.

341. Recipe for a gourd *fālūdhaj*, which loosens the bowels[6]
Take skimmed honey and put it in a clean pot over a fire. When the honey has come to a boil, take as many gourds as you want, scrape the outside and remove the pith and seeds from the inside. Clean the gourds, cut them into small pieces, and put them in a clean pot with water over a fire. When the gourd is done, take it out and wash it in cold water, pressing it with your hands to squeeze the water out. Then pound it in a wooden mortar until it looks like dough. Take a bowl and place a fine-meshed horse-hair sieve over it on which to put the gourd, rubbing it with your hands so that pieces pass into the bowl. Next, colour it with a sprinkling of saffron, and put it in the pot with the honey. Stir so that the gourd blends with the honey, and cook over a moderate fire. When you see that the honey is about to thicken, gradually add good-quality clarified butter or olive oil, and let it be absorbed. If the mixture cannot absorb any more, remove the pot from the heat, and serve the contents in a ceramic bowl. Finally, sprinkle on pepper. This is a bowel-loosening and light dish. Eat and enjoy, Allah the Exalted willing.

Chapter Two: on what is made with aubergine[7]

342. Dish
Take as many aubergines as you want. Peel them and cut them into small round slices. Place them on a board, and sprinkle crushed salt in between each slice. Once you have finished doing this, put a stone or something else heavy on top to make the black aubergine juice ooze out. If you want to boil them over a fire with water and salt, put them in a clean pot and leave it until they start to cook, at which point you should take them out, wash them with hot water, and leave them until they have released all of their liquid. Next, take a clean pot and throw in vinegar, fresh coriander juice, olive oil, pepper, unpeeled garlic, peeled

6 The translation of the title is based on BL Or5927 (fol. 177v.) and Gayangos XVI (fol. 107r.); the edition (2012: 226) does not include this medical information in the title, but instead states that the dish 'is called *al-ṭalabiyya*'. Also see recipe No. 67.

7 Gayangos XVI continues with chapters on *jināniyya* (fols. 107v.–108r.), taro (fol. 108r.), broad beans and chickpeas (fols. 108r.–110r.), i.e. recipes Nos. 378 *et seq.* of the present text.

almonds, soaked chickpeas, a bit of cut-up onion, a sprig of oregano and a citron leaf. Put it over a fire to cook. Then take a clean frying pan and put it over a moderate fire with a drizzle of olive oil if the aubergines are boiled. If they have not been boiled, you should add some more olive oil. When the oil starts to boil, place the aubergine slices in the pan and thoroughly fry them. Once this is done, put them in the pot with the broth, and also add egg yolks. When the yolks have set, crack some more eggs [in a bowl] and add salt, pepper, ginger and a little ground saffron. Whip everything until it is blended, and then pour it into the pot (this will be the crusting). When it is ready, remove the pot from the heat and leave it on embers to balance the flavours. Serve in a ceramic bowl and then eat and enjoy, Allah the Exalted willing.

343. Another dish

Take as many aubergines as you want, peel them, and then throw them in a clean pot, which you put over a fire to cook. When the aubergines are done, take them out and squeeze out their juice. Thoroughly pound them in a wooden mortar, put the resultant mixture in a bowl, and then set it aside. Next, take a new pot with olive oil, *murrī*, salt and a little water, and place it over a fire. When it has come to a boil, put the aubergines in and gently stir them. When they are done, add egg yolks. Once these have set, take egg whites with breadcrumbs, pepper and ginger, and beat everything together. Use this mixture to crust the dish. When this is done, remove the fire from underneath the pot and leave it on embers until the flavours are balanced. Serve in a ceramic bowl, dusted with cinnamon. Eat and enjoy, Allah the Exalted willing.

344. Another dish

Take as many aubergines as you like, peel them and cut them into round slices. Put them in a pot with water and salt, and bring to a boil. When the aubergines are done, take them out and put them on a sieve or a board. Take a clean pot with some water, salt, olive oil, *murrī*, vinegar, pepper, coriander seeds, a little cumin, oregano, cloves of garlic and a bit of cut-up onion. Put it over a fire, and leave until it comes to a boil and everything is done. Next, take a clean frying pan with a sufficient amount of olive oil and put it over a fire. When the oil starts to boil, fry the aubergines, turning them over to brown them. Once they are done, take them out and put them in the pot with the seasonings, but first remove the cloves of garlic and the pieces of onion. Let it cook, and then add egg yolks and, once they have set, take eggs and whisk them with breadcrumbs and spices. Use this to crust the dish. When this is done, remove the fire from underneath the pot and leave it on embers until the flavours are balanced. Serve in a ceramic bowl, and sprinkle on pepper and cinnamon. Eat and enjoy, Allah the Exalted willing.

345. Another dish

Take as many aubergines as you like, and split them all the way up to the calyx. Stuff them with salt and put them in water. Leave them until they release their black juice, and then wash and clean them, squeezing out any remaining water. Next, take a clean frying pan, pour in some olive oil, and put it over a fire. When the oil comes to a boil, take the whole aubergines and fry them in the pan, turning them from time to time until they are fully fried and done. Remove them from the fire, and take a clean pot with vinegar, pepper, and coriander seeds, and put it over a fire. When it is boiling, throw in the aubergines and leave them until it comes to a boil again. Crust the pot with egg yolks, breadcrumbs and aromatic spices. Remove the fire underneath, and leave it on embers until the flavours are balanced. Serve in a ceramic bowl, and eat and enjoy, Allah the Exalted willing.

346. Another dish

Take as many aubergines as you like, peel them, and boil them in water and salt. When they are done, take them out, wash them with hot water and squeeze them until they release their juice. Thoroughly pound them, remove any bits that should not be there, and put them in a bowl with salt, pepper, cinnamon, ginger, olive oil and a sufficient amount of *murrī*. Crack in as many eggs as needed, and add breadcrumbs. Beat everything well, making sure the batter is not too light.[8] Next, take a clean frying pan, pour in olive oil, and put it over a fire. When the oil starts to boil, take the aubergines and make round, flat loaves,

8 The translation follows BL Or5927 (fol. 179r.) rather than the edition (2012: 229), which requires it to be light, i.e. runny, as this is less logical when the mixture needs to be shaped into loaves.

like *aḥrash*[9] discs. Fry them in the pan, turning them over so that they are golden brown on both sides. If you want to make a single loaf, put all of the pounded aubergines in the frying pan over a moderate fire. Gently and patiently fry until the loaf is cooked and browned on one side, before carefully turning it over. Once it is done and golden brown on both sides, put it in a ceramic bowl and sprinkle on cinnamon and pepper. Eat and enjoy, Allah the Exalted willing.

347. Another dish

Take as many aubergines as you like, peel them, and boil them in water and salt. Then take them out, wash them with hot water and squeeze them so that they release their juice. Then pound them well and remove any bits that should not be there. Put them in a bowl and add vinegar, olive oil and crushed cooked garlic. You can also add caraway if you like. Eat and enjoy, Allah the Exalted willing.

348. Another dish[10]

Take as many aubergines as you like, peel the rind, and cut them into four parts without, however, dividing them completely, and leave the calyces whole. Stuff them with salt so as to make them release their black juice. Afterwards, wash them, and throw them in a clean pot with water and salt. Put it over a fire to cook and, when the aubergines are done, take them out and squeeze out the liquid. Take the pulp, and put the calyces to one side. Put the pulp in a kneading tub, and knead it into a dough-like paste with your hands. If there are any aubergines left that require pounding, do so.[11] Next, pour some olive oil in a clean frying pan or a glazed earthenware casserole dish, put the aubergine in, and stir until they release no more liquid. If you want, you can leave them as they are, without frying them. Then put some breadcrumbs in a bowl, pour mint juice over them and crack in as many eggs as required. Set aside some egg yolks to garnish the casserole later on. Add salt, pepper, ginger, cinnamon, coriander seeds and a little crushed saffron to the

9 See recipe No. 185, though the form used here is vowelled as *aḥayrash*, which may either be a variant spelling or a colloquial plural form.

10 In Gayangos XVI (fol. 111r.), it is called *al-maḥshuw* ('stuffed').

11 The translation is based on Gayangos XVI (*ibid.*); both the edition (2012: 230) and BL Or5927 (fol. 179v.) have the nonsensical *al-ru'ūs* ('heads, calyces').

breadcrumbs and eggs, and whip it all with your hands so as to blend everything together well. Pour this batter onto the aubergines, and stir well until it coagulates into a single mass. Put it into a large, glazed casserole dish into which you have drizzled a little olive oil. Smooth the mixture out with your hands, and garnish the dish. [Take the calyces and dot them upright across the surface.][12] Under each calyx put a clove of cooked garlic and a piece of good-quality dry cheese.[13] Then pour a generous amount of olive oil on the surface, and dust with pepper and cinnamon before sending it to the oven. Place the dish away from the flames until it is set and golden brown. When it is ready, take it out and let it cool down. Eat and enjoy, Allah the Exalted willing.

349. Another dish[14]

Take as many aubergines as you like, and do the same with them as you did before. Use your hands to work the pulp into a dough, and set it aside. Next, peel and grate dry cheese until it looks like finely ground flour. Take garlic, and cook it in water until it is done. Pound it with the remaining ungrated cheese and add it to the aubergines, together with the powdered cheese. Add olive oil and thoroughly mix everything together with your hands [and also add crushed walnut kernels].[15] Put the mixture in a ceramic bowl. Place the aubergine calyces upright on the surface, sprinkle on as much powdered cheese as you want, and then [pour on plenty of] olive oil. Eat and enjoy, Allah the Exalted willing. If you feel that there is not enough cheese powder, add some more. The same applies to the olive oil.

350. Another dish[16]

Take as many aubergines as you want, and peel and slice them lengthwise, including the calyx. Make sure that the slices are thin. Throw

---

12 Addition from Gayangos XVI (*ibid.*).

13 The translation follows BL Or5927 (fol. 179v.), as the sentence in the edition has omissions and inaccuracies (e.g. *bayāḍ bayḍ*, 'egg-whites', instead of *ṭayyib*, 'good[-quality]').

14 In Gayangos XVI (*ibid.*), it is called *al-tūma*, which may be a colloquial pronunciation of *thūma* ('garlic clove'). Alternatively, it may refer to the Classical Arabic *tūma*, which denotes a large pearl and, by extension, an ostrich egg; Lane 1863–74: I, 323.

15 The passages in brackets are additions from Gayangos XVI (fol. 111v.).

16 The next recipe in Gayangos XVI (fol. 111v.) is *al-azaliyya* (see No. 360, below).

them in a clean pot with water and salt, and put it over a fire to cook. When the aubergine pieces are done, take them out of the pot and put them on a sieve to drain their juices. Next, take a large bowl and put in vinegar, *murrī*, pepper, coriander seeds, cumin, rubbed oregano, and both crushed and uncrushed garlic. Taste the aubergine and, if you find it is salty, rinse with water to get rid of the salt and gingerly squeeze the pieces with your hands. Immerse the pieces one by one in the sauce so they can fully absorb it. Take an earthenware casserole dish, pour in some olive oil, and then fill it up with the aubergine pieces. Pour in the rest of the sauce and plenty of olive oil as well. Put it in the oven away from the flames, and bake until the sauce dries out and only oil remains. When it is ready, take the dish out and let it cool down. Invoke Allah's name,[17] and then eat and enjoy, Allah the Exalted willing.

351. Another dish

Take as many small aubergines as you like. Peel and quarter them, but do not completely slice them through. Stuff them with salt, and put them in a bowl with a little water until the black liquid oozes out. Then, wash them in fresh water and throw them in a clean pot with water and salt. Put it over a fire and, when it has come to a boil, remove the aubergine pieces and transfer them to a sieve to drain off the broth. Next, put them in a clean pot and add water, olive oil, salt (if needed), pepper, coriander seeds and a little cumin. Put the pot over a fire to cook and, when the aubergines are done, add a sufficient amount of macerated *murrī*, and as much good vinegar as you want. When the pot comes to a boil, carefully remove the aubergine pieces so that they do not break up, and line them up in a casserole dish, with the calyces visible. Take some breadcrumbs and knead them with a little water, and as many eggs as the aubergines can hold. Throw in pepper, cinnamon, ginger, coriander seeds and crushed saffron, and beat well until everything is blended. Gently pour the mixture over the aubergines, covering all except the tips of the calyces. Garnish with egg yolks, pour in some of the strained broth, and add a bit more olive oil. Take the pot to the oven, but place it away from the flames until it is cooked through, the broth has dried out, and the surface of the dish has turned

17 *sammi Allāh*, which refers to uttering the so-called *bismillāh* ('in the name of Allah'), said by Muslims before eating or drinking anything.

golden brown. When it is ready, take it out and let it cool down. Eat and enjoy, Allah the Exalted willing.

If you want to make it with fresh coriander and mint juice, leave out the cumin, saffron and vinegar, and proceed with the power and strength of Allah.

352. Another dish

Take as many small aubergines as you like, do the same with them as you did before, and then put them in a clean pot with water, a lot of olive oil, pepper, coriander seeds, a little cumin, good *murrī*, unpeeled garlic and a bit of cut-up onion. Put the pot over a fire to cook and, when the aubergines are done, taste the saltiness. If they are not salty enough, add some more salt. Serve in a dish and drizzle on lime juice. Eat and enjoy, Allah the Exalted willing.

353. Another dish

Peel and chop up as many aubergines as you like. Put a lot of salt on them, and leave them in a bowl with a little water to make them release their black juice. Next, wash them in hot water to clean them and remove the salt. Dice a lot of onions, wash them with water and salt, and then rinse to clear away the salt. Put the onions in a clean pot with the aubergines, and add a little water and plenty of olive oil, as well as pepper, coriander seeds, a little cumin and some macerated *murrī*. Put the pot over a fire to cook and, when the aubergines and onions are done, serve them in a ceramic bowl. Eat and enjoy, Allah the Exalted willing. If you want, you can add suet or cook it with jerky.[18]

354. Another dish[19]

Take nicely formed aubergines and gently remove the calyces so that they retain their shape. Use a sharp knife to gingerly scrape out the insides from the area where the calyces were, but do not peel the aubergines. Boil what you have taken out with water and salt until done, and then throw the water out. Pound the aubergine in a casserole dish, as described above, and add grated breadcrumbs, eggs and spices. Stuff

18 *qadīd*; see recipe No. 466.

19 Except for the ending, this is identical to the recipe in *Anwāʿ* (144; BNF, fol. 53r.), where it is called *maḥshī* ('stuffed').

the mixture inside the hollowed-out aubergines. Return the calyces, secure them with thread, and layer the aubergines in the casserole. Pour the leftover filling and olive oil over them, and then put the casserole in the oven. Leave it until it thickens. This recipe can also be made with pounded meat, in which case the aubergines are stuffed with boiled or fried sparrow meat, the aubergine filling and boiled egg yolks. [The prettiest way to serve the aubergines is in a bowl (whole), looking as if nothing has been done to them. This is very tasty and exquisite. If you want, you can make this dish with coriander and mint juice, or leave it as it is.][20]

355. Another dish[21]

Take sweet aubergines and cut them in half without peeling them. Boil them in water and salt until they are done, and discard the water. Scoop out each aubergine half separately, making sure they retain their shape. Next, take their flesh and knead it with meat that has been cooked and pounded, as stated above. Beat everything together with eggs and spices, as described in the previous stuffed-aubergine recipe, and fill the empty halves with the mixture. Next, coat the aubergines with *darmak* flour, and fry them in a pan with olive oil until they are browned, all the while making sure that they retain their shape. They can be eaten like this, or you can serve them with a sauce like the one for fried aubergines, or one made with meat broth, vinegar, macerated *murrī*, and saffron. Brown the aubergines, as you would a *Burāniyya*.[22] It is wonderful.

---

20 The section enclosed in square brackets is included only in BL Or5927 (fol. 180v.).

21 The *Andalusian* contains a similar recipe, which does not, however, include the final serving suggestions; *Anwāʿ*, 144-5 (BNF, fol. 53r.).

22 See recipe No. 100.

356. Another dish, made like a *mughaffar*[23]

Take sweet aubergines and split them lengthwise and crosswise, into rectangles. Boil them in a pot with water and salt, and afterwards throw away the water. Take some *darmak* flour and mix it in a bowl with eggs, pepper, saffron, coriander seeds, coriander juice and just a drizzle of macerated *murrī*. When this batter has thickened and resembles a thick pottage, dip the aubergine pieces in it, and fry them in a pan with olive oil until golden brown. If you wish, you can either eat them like this, or[24] make an accompanying sauce, as described above.

357. Recipe for an aubergine omelette[25]

Peel sweet aubergines, and boil them in water and salt until they are done and thoroughly cooked.[26] Take them out of the water and knead them in a bowl with [grated] breadcrumbs, [eggs, olive oil],[27] macerated *murrī*, pepper, coriander seeds and cinnamon. Beat everything until you get a smooth batter and make it into thin round cakes, which you fry in a pan with olive oil until golden brown. Make a sauce for them by boiling vinegar, olive oil, *murrī* and crushed garlic. Pour it on the aubergine, and then eat.

---

23 This recipe is also found in the *Andalusian* (*Anwāʿ*, 145; BNF, fol. 53r.), where it is called *al-muʿaffar* ('covered with dust', from *ʿafr*, 'dust, earth'), which is the only occurrence to support Corriente's claim that it means 'basted (eggplant)' (1997: 358). In light of the different cooking methods of the *mughaffar* dishes in the present text, it may be speculated that there were, in fact, two different varieties, one called *mughaffar* (recipe No. 198), a chicken dish, and another, *muʿaffar*, to be applied to this recipe and Nos. 290 and 356, as they share the batter into which the main ingredient – fish and aubergine, respectively – is dipped before frying. More plausible, however, is that the form in *Anwāʿ* is a misspelling for *mughaffar* since the three recipes in the present text all specify that the main ingredient should be covered, and thus 'protected'. The dish has a number of interesting similarities with the Filipino signature dish *Tortang talong*.

24 The translation follows BL Or5927 (fol. 181r.), rather than the 'and' of the edition (2012: 234).

25 The similar recipe in the *Andalusian* (*Anwāʿ*, 146; BNF, fol. 53r.) has the more appropriate name of '*isfīriyyā* made with aubergine', since the dish is not actually an omelette.

26 BL Or5927 (fol. 181r.) suggests 'until they are dissolved' (*yanḥall*).

27 The words in brackets were taken from BL Or5927 (fol. 181r.), as they are omitted from the edition.

358. Recipe for aubergine sausages (*mirqās*)[28]

Take as many sweet aubergines as you want. Peel and boil them, and then add chopped suet, some macerated *murrī,* [eggs][29] and all the spices and ingredients you need to make *mirqās.*[30] Stuff the intestines with this mixture, as described above, but first add some eggs as this will keep the sausage together and prevent the filling from seeping out.

359. Another dish

Take as many aubergines as you like, and then peel and cut them into round slices. Salt them before pressing them down with a stone or something like that to make the aubergines release their black juice. When this is done, put the slices in hot water for a while, and then thoroughly wash them to get rid of the water and salt. Take a clean frying pan and drizzle in some olive oil. When the oil comes to a boil, fry the aubergine slices until they are done and golden brown. Then, remove them from the pan and serve them up in a ceramic bowl.

Feel free to add boiled vinegar with crushed and cooked garlic if you want.

Or, if you wish, you may include finely ground cheese with garlic and vinegar, added with a dribble of cooked olive oil. Eat and enjoy, Allah the Exalted willing.

360. A dish called *al-azaliyya*[31]

Peel and split aubergines one by one, but leave their calyces intact, and then cook them in a pot with water and salt until they are done. Squeeze[32] vinegar, *murrī,* pepper, coriander, cumin, grated oregano,

---

28 The *Andalusian* (*Anwāʿ*, 145; BNF, fol. 53r.) has a more expansive recipe, called 'recipe of *mirkās* [*sic*] sausages made with aubergine'.

29 Addition from Gayangos XVI (fol. 113v.).

30 The ones mentioned in *Anwāʿ* are *murrī,* pepper, cinnamon, spikenard, onion juice, coriander seeds and eggs, with everything being pounded in a mortar.

31 Recipes Nos. 358–61 are missing from BL Or5927. The name of the dish, which translates as 'the eternal', is most probably a misspelling of *al-arnabī,* which is the name of a somewhat similar aubergine dish in the *Andalusian* (*Anwāʿ*, 143; BNF, fol. 52v.), as well as of other dishes in the present book (see recipes Nos. 104, 302).

32 There is clearly a portion of the recipe missing that refers to the aubergines being boiled and then squeezed to release their black juice, after which the seasonings are added.

and crushed and uncrushed garlic in a bowl. Test[33] the saltiness of the aubergines, and take the pieces out of the sauce. Put them in a casserole dish already coated with olive oil, and pour the remaining sauce as well as a generous amount of olive oil on top. Cook in the oven, away from the flames until the liquid has dried out.

361. Another dish

Peel[34] small aubergines and scrape out the calyces. Slice each aubergine into four parts, but do not cut them all the way through. Boil, or stuff them with salt. Then, press them down with something heavy before washing and draining them. Next, boil them in a pot with water, salt (if required), olive oil, spices, cumin, vinegar and *murrī*. When they are done, remove them from the pot and place them in a casserole dish, with the stalks standing visibly upright. Dissolve breadcrumbs in water and beat with eggs – enough to cover them – spices and saffron. Gingerly pour the resulting batter over the aubergines until they are immersed and only the calyces are visible. Garnish with egg yolks and add the strained broth, as well as a splash of olive oil. Put the casserole in the oven until the batter is set and everything is done.

If you wish, you can add fresh coriander and mint juice, but in that case omit the vinegar, saffron, cumin and *murrī*.

362. Another dish

Peel aubergines and chop them up. Salt them and press them down with a weight. Throw on a large amount of salt and soak them in a bowl with a little water, or boil and wash them. Cut up a lot of onions and wash them twice before cooking them together with the aubergines in a pot with a little water, a generous amount of olive oil, pepper, coriander, a little cumin, and *murrī*. Let it cook over a fire for a sufficient amount of time [for it to be done], and then serve in a bowl. If you wish, you can also cook this recipe with meat and jerky.[35]

---

33 This is the word used in Gayangos XVI (fol. 111v.), while the edition (2012: 235) has 'remove'.

34 The translation is based on Gayangos XVI (*ibid.*); according to the edition (*ibid.*), they should be split.

35 See recipe No. 466.

363. Another dish

Take a moderately large aubergine and leave it whole with its skin on. Gently remove the calyx, but without deforming the aubergine. Use a thin knife to carefully scoop out the pulp from the site of the calyx until the inside of the aubergine is empty. Boil the pulp that has been removed in water and salt until it is done, and then throw out the water. Knead the pulp with grated breadcrumbs, beaten eggs and all the above-mentioned spices. Stuff this mixture inside the aubergine and then put the calyx back in, fastening it with strong twine. Do this with all of the aubergines you are using, until you get the required number. Layer the aubergines in a casserole dish, and pour the rest of the filling and olive oil over them. Bake them in the oven. If you like, you can mix the pounded meat from a ram or another animal, or cooked or fried sparrows, or boiled egg yolks with the aubergines, and use this as a stuffing. You could also make it green by adding coriander and mint juice. A prerequisite for this recipe is that the aubergines look pristine in shape, as if they are untouched, as this is what makes it truly exquisite.

364. Another dish[36]

Take as many aubergines as you like and put them in hot ashes, and also cover them with ashes. Put a fire on top and along the sides, and leave the aubergines until you know they are done. Then, take them out of the ashes and cut them up. Put olive oil and crushed cooked garlic in a bowl, and then take the aubergine pieces and remove the peels. Leave them, and then cut them up in the olive oil and garlic. Add salt and pepper and thoroughly mix everything together. Then eat and enjoy, Allah the Exalted willing. If you prefer to roast the aubergines in the *tannūr*, put them in the middle of the embers. If you want to use a brick oven, put the aubergine in an unglazed casserole dish and leave it until done. Then, take it out and eat, as described above, Allah the Exalted willing. Do not eat too much of this dish as it stirs up black bile.

36 This recipe is found only in BL Or5927 (fol. 181v.), though Gayangos XVI (fols. 113v.–114r.) includes an abridgement of the last paragraph as a separate recipe, titled 'a roast dish' (*mashwī*).

Chapter Three: on carrot dishes

365. [A dish][37]

Take thick and good-quality carrots, lightly scrape away the outer peel, and cut them lengthwise. Split the pieces in half again,[38] and remove the cores. Wash the carrot pieces well, put them in a clean pot with water and salt, and put it over a fire to cook. When they are done, gently take them out and put them on a sieve or board to drain. Take a clean frying pan, pour in sweet olive oil, and put it over a fire. When the oil has come to a boil, put the carrot pieces in and fry them until golden brown. When this is done, transfer them to a ceramic bowl and drizzle on boiled vinegar, cooked crushed garlic, and caraway. Eat and enjoy, Allah the Exalted willing. If you like, you can dispense with frying the carrot pieces. Alternatively, you can also dredge them in a *ṣināb* (mustard sauce),[39] especially as a garnish for stuffed meat dishes.[40]

Chapter Four:[41] on how to prepare truffles

366. A dish

Take some truffles known as *tirfās*,[42] thoroughly wash them, and then peel and break[43] them into small pieces with your hands, without using a knife. Put them in a clean pot with water and place it over a fire. Bring it to a boil once or twice, and then tip the truffles into a bowl. Briefly wash them in hot water. Take fresh cheese, crumble it into a bowl, and

37 The translation is based on the recipe in BL Or5927 (fols. 181v.–182r.) as it is much more detailed than that of the edition and Gayangos XVI (fol. 114r.): 'Cut the carrots into similar pieces without peeling them, clean the cores and split each piece in half. Boil them in salted water and then dry. Fry them in a pan with sweet olive oil. Add boiled vinegar, crushed garlic, and caraway. Any remaining pieces are left without frying, or used afterwards for garnishing the bowl.'

38 The text in Wetzstein 1207 ends here (fol. 77v.).

39 See recipes Nos. 409, 410.

40 *kawāmil* (plural of *kāmil*, 'complete'), though originally denoting a dish of stuffed lamb, the term also applied to other stuffed animal meat, such as chicken (Corriente 1997: 468). See recipe No. 148, above.

41 Chapters 4 until 9 are taken from BL Or5927 (fols. 182r.–183v.) as they are missing from the printed edition.

42 See recipe No. 127.

43 The text uses the verb 'cut'.

add broken eggs in proportion to the cheese and truffles. Scoop out the yolks, and then add pepper, ginger, cinnamon, coriander seeds, fresh coriander juice, mint juice and a bit of saffron. Thoroughly whisk it all together by hand, or with a ladle, until everything is blended. Mix with the eggs and truffles, blending everything well. Take a glazed casserole dish and pour in some olive oil. Throw in the mixture of the eggs, cheese and truffles, smooth everything out, and garnish with egg yolks. Sprinkle on pepper and coriander, as well as some more olive oil. Then, take the casserole to the oven and place it away from the flames, so the dish can thicken and brown. When it is ready, take it out and leave to cool down. Eat and enjoy, Allah the Exalted willing.

367. Another dish
Take as many truffles as you like, and do the same as before. When they are cooked, add some water and put in salt, pepper and ginger. Stir everything until it is all blended and then eat and enjoy, Allah the Exalted willing.

368. Another dish
Take as many truffles as you like, and do the same with them as you did before. Then, put them in a new pot with good-quality hot, strained butter, and leave it over a fire until cooked. When it is done, transfer to a ceramic bowl and sprinkle on a sufficient amount of salt and pepper. Eat and enjoy, Allah the Exalted willing.

369. Another dish
Take the largest truffles you can find, scrape them, and thoroughly wash and clean away any dirt, sand, etc. that sticks to them. Then, dry them with a towel. Take a linen cloth, moisten it with water, put the truffles in the middle of it and wrap them up. Put it on embers until you think they have been roasted, and then take them out and remove the cloth from the truffles. Wipe them down, quarter them with your hands, and then scatter on some salt and pepper and a sufficient amount of ginger. Eat and enjoy, Allah the Exalted willing. The best ovens for roasting truffles are those used for distilling rose water, so use one of those if you can. Bear this in mind.

Chapter Five: on what to do with asparagus, for which there is only one recipe[44]

370.

Take as much asparagus as you like, and clean it. Select the tender stalks and put them in a clean pot with water over a fire. Then take another pot with just water, and put it over a fire. When the asparagus has boiled three times or so, remove the water and pour on the hot water from the other pot. Put it over the fire again. Keep on doing this until their bitterness is gone. Then, wash the stalks with hot water and squeeze the asparagus to drain the moisture before serving it in a ceramic bowl. Drizzle on olive oil and vinegar, and garnish with split boiled eggs. Eat and enjoy, Allah the Exalted willing.

Chapter Six: on artichokes *(ḥarshaf)*, which are called *qannāriya*[45]

The best variety for cooking are the *afzān* artichokes.[46]

371. Dish

Take *afzān* artichokes, clean away their thorns and anything else that needs to be removed, and put them in a clean pot with water over a fire. When they have come to a boil once or twice, take them out of the pot, wash them with hot water, and leave them to rest. Take another pot, chop onions, and put them in it with a little water, salt, coriander seeds and pepper. Put it over a fire to cook. When the onions are done, take milk and add butter to it. Leave the pot on the fire until the milk comes to a boil. Then mash the artichokes in a mortar and put them in the pot with the milk and onions. Immediately afterwards, serve, and eat and enjoy, Allah the Exalted willing.

44 Also see recipe No. 122.

45 This is actually an Andalusian–Maghribi word for 'artichoke'. See Ibn Janāḥ 2020: No. 461; Corriente 1997: 153, 444; Dietrich 1988: III, 15; Dozy 1881: II, 411.

46 See recipe No. 126.

372. Another dish

Take any kind of artichokes you can, clean and cut them in round slices, and then boil them over a fire in water and salt. Next, rinse them and put them in a casserole dish with plenty of olive oil, purified vinegar, pepper, coriander seeds, cumin, crushed and whole garlic, hand-rubbed oregano, and citron leaves. Place the casserole over a fire to cook. When the artichokes are done and the liquid in the casserole has dried out and nothing but oil remains, remove it from the fire and leave to cool down. Invoke Allah's name, and then eat and enjoy, Allah the Exalted willing.

373. Another dish

Take any kind of artichokes you can, and do the same as in the previous recipe. Next, take a clean frying pan with olive oil and put it over a fire. Heat it until it starts to boil, and then fry the artichokes in it, turning them over so they can brown on all sides. Serve in a ceramic bowl and add vinegar, as well as crushed garlic cooked in water and vinegar. Invoke Allah's name, and then eat and enjoy, Allah the Exalted willing.

Chapter Seven: on what to do with mushrooms, for which there is only one recipe

374.

Take as many mushrooms, which are also called *fuqqaʿ*,[47] as you want, thoroughly wash them and chop them up. Put the pieces in a new pot and add a splash of water, salt, olive oil, chopped coriander seeds, cut-up onions, and pepper. Put the pot over a fire to cook. When the mushrooms are done, pour in a little vinegar and *murrī*, and crust the dish with two eggs and some flour, in the usual way. Leave on embers to thicken and to balance the flavours. Eat and enjoy, Allah the Exalted willing.

47 See recipe No. 239.

Chapter Eight: on what to do with spinach, leafy goosefoot, lettuce, and other similar things[48]

375. Dish

Take any of the vegetables mentioned, clean them, and put them in a clean pot over the fire. Bring to a boil once or twice, and then remove the vegetables from the pot. Put them on a wooden board and beat them with the back of a knife until you get a dough-like mixture which you put in a new pot with salt, sweet olive oil, coriander seeds, a bit of cut-up onion and a little water. Put the pot over a fire and, when it is boiling and the vegetables are done, take it down. If you leave them to boil, they will turn yellow.

If you like, you can put peeled and lightly pounded almonds in with the vegetables, as well as egg yolks and fresh butter. When everything is done, serve in a ceramic bowl. Eat and enjoy, Allah the Exalted willing.

376. Another dish

Take any of the vegetables mentioned, and clean them. If it is spinach, cut off the root only and leave the rest of it whole. The same applies to leafy goosefoot. If you are using lettuce, take only the inner leaves and those like them. Put whichever vegetables you have chosen in a clean pot with water and salt. Heat it over a fire to cook and, when the vegetables are done, remove them, squeeze out any moisture, and then serve in a ceramic bowl. Drizzle on olive oil and vinegar, and eat and enjoy, Allah the Exalted willing. Do the same with cabbages and turnips, and their leaves. If you want, you can add vinegar with cooked crushed garlic to cabbage, with the strength and power of Allah.

48 Gayangos XVI (fol. 114r.) only has the title, which is followed by that of Section Nine, whereas the two recipes in the chapter are located earlier in the text (fol. 107r.–v.), after the gourd *fālūdhaj* (recipe No. 341). The edition does not include them.

Chapter Nine: on cooking *jināniyya*[49]

377.

Take a tender, fresh gourd, scrape the outside, clean out the insides, and cut it up into small pieces. Wash them and put them to one side. Next, take small, tender and fresh aubergines, scrape out the calyces and remove the black peels before cutting them up into quarters, but do not slice all the way through so that they remain whole. Put them in a pot with water and salt over a fire. When it has boiled three times, take the aubergines out and wash them with hot water before placing them in a new pot. Add the gourd, as well as a sufficient amount of water, salt, plenty of olive oil, pepper, coriander seeds and a bit of cut-up onion, and then put the pot over a fire to cook. Take leafy goosefoot, purslane and any other vegetables that are available, such as serpent melon and cucumber shoots and tendrils, gourd tendrils, fresh coriander, and mint leafstalks. Thoroughly clean all of them, and cut as thinly as possible before putting everything in a clean pot [with water]. Bring it to a boil once or twice before removing it from the fire, and strain the water from the vegetables. Wash them with hot water, squeeze them to extract any remaining water, and then put them in the pot with the gourd and aubergines. Bring to a boil, and then take fresh coriander, which has been cleaned and crushed in a mortar, together with one or two cloves of garlic, before adding these also to the pot with the gourd and aubergine. Check on the gourd and aubergines and if you find that they are done, take small pieces of good-quality dry cheese and put them in the pot. Next, take another cheese, grate it to a fine powder, and set it aside. Transfer the contents of the pot to a large ceramic bowl and sprinkle on the grated cheese. Eat and enjoy, Allah the Exalted willing. Increase the amount of powdered cheese at will.

It has been mentioned that this dish can also be made with hogget lamb, in which case you should use the meat when it is freshly

49 The recipe in Gayangos XVI (fols. 107v.–108r.) is missing from the edition. The word *jinān* (plural of *janna*) usually means 'gardens', but in Andalusian Arabic also meant 'vegetable garden'. There is a similar dish in the *Andalusian* (*Anwāʿ*, 148–9; BNF, fol. 39v.), where the name is explained by the fact that it was customary to make it in vegetable and flower gardens.

slaughtered. The dish can be made with all manner of vegetables. Bear this in mind.

Chapter Ten: on [what is made with] taro [for which there is only one dish][50]

378.

Wash sweet and tender taro to get rid of the dirt. Remove the outer skin and cut the taro into thin slices. Lightly boil them in water and salt. Then, dry and fry in olive oil or suet until golden brown. Serve in a ceramic bowl, and drizzle on lime vinegar. [Eat and enjoy, Allah the Exalted willing.]

50 The passages in square brackets here and at the end of the recipe are additions from BL Or5927 (fols. 183v.–184r.).

SECTION EIGHT

On broad beans, chickpeas and the like

It consists of three chapters.

Chapter One: on fresh and dried broad bean dishes[1]

379. *Fustuqiyya*[2] dish (broad bean stew)
Take as many fresh broad beans as you want, peel them and wash them in fresh water, and then coat them with olive oil. Put them in a pot that has been smeared with olive oil, and add water, olive oil, coriander seeds and a cut onion. Put it over a fire and, when the beans are done and tender, remove any visible onion from the pot. Use a ladle to beat and mash the beans until everything is blended and you obtain a marrow-like consistency. Gradually season with purified crushed salt, stirring all the while and tasting to check whether it is salty enough. Next, crush fresh coriander in a mortar, squeeze out the juice, and put it in with the beans. Leave the pot over a low fire for a while, and then transfer to a ceramic bowl. Sprinkle on cumin and sweet olive oil, and eat and enjoy, Allah the Exalted willing. The beans can also be cooked with pounded fresh suet and coriander juice, or with the suet from the small intestines, cut as thinly as possible.

380. Another dish[3]
Take as many fresh broad beans as you like and peel their outer skin. Wash them and put them in a clean pot with fresh water over a fire to cook. When the beans are done, add salt and let it come to a boil. Then remove the pot from the fire and strain the water. Take a clean frying pan and pour in some olive oil before putting it over a fire. When the oil comes to a boil, add the broad beans and gently fry and stir them

---

1 BL Or5927 (fol. 184r.) has 'on what to do with fresh and dried broad beans'.

2 Also see recipe No. 140. The recipe in BL Or5927 (fol. 184r.), which does not have a title, has been used to complete the instructions.

3 The translation relies on the text in BL Or5927 (184r.–v.) as it is much more elaborate.

until they are browned, at which point remove them from the fire. Then crush garlic and put it in the frying pan together with the water left over from the beans, and leave until the garlic is cooked and the liquid has dried out. Add olive oil and return the broad beans to the pan, stirring them with the garlic and olive oil. When the oil comes to a boil, transfer the beans to a ceramic bowl and sprinkle on pepper. Eat and enjoy, Allah the Exalted willing.

If you want to, you can us macerated *murrī* and oregano instead of garlic and olive oil. Eat and enjoy, Allah the Exalted willing.

Equally, you could take the beans after boiling them and then fry them lightly. Take a small pot, put in a splash of water together with coriander seeds, macerated *murrī*, crushed garlic, a bit of cut-up onion and a generous amount of olive oil. Put the pot on the fire, and when the mixture comes to a boil add the broad beans and leave them in until the liquid has dried out and they are done. Serve and eat, Allah the Exalted willing.

If you wish, you can also prepare the two aforesaid recipes together, with germinated[4] broad beans which have sprouted, Allah the Exalted willing.

381. Another dish[5]

Take as many fresh broad beans as you wish and peel them. Add green garlic scapes,[6] cut off the leaves and throw them away. Put the beans and garlic scapes in a new pot with plenty of olive oil and a little water. Put it over a fire until the garlic and broad beans are cooked and the liquid has dried out, and only the oil is left. Transfer the contents to a ceramic bowl and sprinkle with pepper and salt. Eat and enjoy, Allah the Exalted willing.

---

4 *musammakh*, more correctly *muṣammakh* (Corriente 1997: 261, 310), with the verb according to Dozy (1881: I, 682) meaning to test seeds by growing them before sowing them, in order to ascertain healthy and bad ones.

5 The text in the edition was supplemented with instructions from BL Or5927 (fol. 184v.).

6 *'asālij* (sg. *'aslaj*), 'stalk' (of any plant), with *'asālij* also denoting mountain spignel (*Libanotis*). According to de Alcalá (1505: fol. 126v. [qVIv]), *'aslaj al-thūm* ('*alzluch aceum, acilich aceum*') meant *espigon de cabeça de ajos* ('garlic head spike'). See Dozy 1881: II, 128; Corriente 1997: 353.

382. Another dish[7]
Take fresh broad beans, peel their outer skins, wash them, and put them in a clean pot with fresh water. Place the pot on the fire to cook. When the beans are done, add salt and bring to a boil. Strain off the water and transfer the beans to a ceramic bowl. Season with salt and pepper, and then eat and enjoy, Allah the Exalted willing.

If you want, you can add vinegar and olive oil by way of a sauce. Eat and enjoy, Allah the Exalted willing.

383. Another dish
Take good-quality fresh, soft broad beans and leave their peels on. Put them in a large pot with fresh water and put it over a fire to cook. When the beans are done, pound some salt and pepper,[8] and then eat and enjoy, Allah the Exalted willing.

384. Another dish
Take good-quality fresh, soft broad beans and leave their peels on. Put them in a large pot with fresh water and put it over a fire to cook. When the beans are done, pound some salt and pepper, and put them in a bowl in front of you. Serve the beans in a large bowl and dip them in the picked-over salt and pepper when eating them, Allah the Exalted willing.

385. Another dish
Take germinated broad beans, wash them, and put them in a new pot with fresh water on the fire to cook. When the beans are done, strain off the water and transfer them to a ceramic bowl. Thoroughly pound salt and rue, and add them to the beans. Beat everything together, and eat and enjoy, Allah the Exalted willing.

If you want to add pounded cumin as well, feel free to do so. You could also take the broad beans after germination, peel them, and wash them in fresh water, before frying them in a pan with sweet olive oil

7 The translation of Nos. 382–5 is based on recipes found only in BL Or5927 (fol. 184v.–185r.), where they are fourth to seventh in the chapter. They are inserted here as both the edition and manuscript end this chapter with the same recipe.

8 As the recipe is clearly incomplete, it is impossible to tell whether it is a mere scribal duplication of the next recipe, or whether it was in fact meant to be a variation with different instructions.

over a gentle fire until they are golden brown. Sprinkle on salt, pepper, cinnamon and anything else you like to enhance the flavour. This is very good as a snack.[9] There is no harm in leaving the beans in water for a little while before frying them, as this will make them taste better.

386. Abridged dishes cooked with green broad beans[10]

In other recipes for cooking broad beans, they are cooked in water only. When they are done, pour out the water and season the beans with salt and pepper. Or you can make a sauce with vinegar and olive oil. You can also prepare the beans by cutting the ends of each pod with a knife and then frying them in a pan with olive oil. When serving, sprinkle on pepper, cinnamon and a pinch of salt. This dish is called 'the sparrow's head'. It is also made like this from sprouted broad beans.

You can also boil the beans whole in their pods just in water. Then shell the beans, and eat them sprinkled with crushed pepper and salt.

Another way is to peel sprouted broad beans and split the kernels in two before frying them in olive oil. Then season with spices and salt. This [method] is called 'the sparrow's head'.[11] After frying the beans, they may be put in rose water.

It is well known that sprouted broad beans are cooked in water. In fact, they should be cooked in just water, which is then thrown out. The beans are eaten with crushed garlic and rue, as well as, possibly, cumin, which is actually the best way to eat them.

---

9 *yuntaqil bihi*; the verb *intaqala* in this context refers to eating dried fruit (*naql*) as a snack when drinking wine. Dozy 1881: II, 716.

10 The title is taken from Gayangos XVI (fol. 109r.). This section is not found in BL Or5927, whereas in the edition (2012: 240) it is put under the heading of 'Another dish'.

11 The repetition of the name of the dish is probably due to the fact that the instructions were taken from different sources.

387. *Baysār* (mashed broad beans)[12]

Clean and wash dried beans[13] several times in hot water, until the liquid that comes out of them is entirely clear. Coat them with olive oil and put them in an oil-smeared pot. Pour in enough fresh water to immerse the beans, and add a split uncut onion, a whole head of garlic, cumin, coriander and fennel. Put everything in a pot to cook on the fire. When the beans are done, take a ladle and stir them until they fall apart and you are left with a single smooth mass with the consistency of marrow. Remove the garlic and onion from the pot. If the mixture is very thick, pour in a bit of hot water after having added some crushed salt to the pot. Put the salt in bit by bit until the beans are saturated, and leave the pot on a gentle fire until the liquid has dried out. Transfer to a ceramic bowl, and scatter a bit of cumin and olive oil on top of the bean mash. Let it cool down a bit, and then eat and enjoy, Allah the Exalted willing. If you like, you can eat it with rue, onions, or olives.

Chapter Two: on chickpea dishes

388. Dish[14]

[Take as many fresh green chickpeas as you want,] peel the outer skins and trim off the spiky ends. [Take a clean frying pan and pour in a sufficient amount of olive oil before putting it on the fire. When the oil comes to a boil, add chickpeas to the pan and gently fry them. Stir until they are done, and then transfer them to a small ceramic bowl.]

---

12 The translation has been supplemented with instructions from the (unnamed) recipe in BL Or5927 (fol. 185r.), which starts off slightly differently, instructing the cook to 'take as many ground dried broad beans as you like'. The dish could apparently also be cooked with butter and milk (Dozy 1881: I, 134). According to the tenth-century traveller al-Muqaddasī (1906: 183), the dish was an Egyptian speciality, though he also encountered it in Greater Syria. It probably originated in Egypt, as the name can be traced back to the Coptic *pesouro* (Darby *et al.* 1976: 683). Today, the dish (usually transliterated as *bissara* or *bessara*) is still a favourite in Morocco, where it is made with broad beans, garlic, olive oil and spices, and is often eaten for breakfast. Also see recipes Nos. 32, 89, 141.

13 *fayshār*, which is a variant of the more usual *faysār* (Corriente 1997: 410, 'cooked beans'). Dozy (1881: I, 134; II, 293) rightly points out that *faysār* is a variant spelling of *bayṣār* (or *baysār*).

14 This recipe and the following three have been augmented with instructions from BL Or5927 (fol. 185r.), enclosed in square brackets.

Add [macerated] *murrī*, pepper, [coriander] and cinnamon. [Eat and enjoy, Allah the Exalted willing.]

389. Dish of dried chickpeas

Clean and wash dried chickpeas, and soak them in fresh water, enough to immerse them. [When they are soft,] cook them in a [new] pot over a fire in the water in which they were soaked, together with sliced onion, pepper, coriander [seeds], and a little [crushed] saffron. When they are done, add a little [macerated] *murrī* and [a ladleful of good-quality] vinegar. [When the vinegar comes to a boil, remove the pot from the fire], and let it rest for a while before transferring the contents to a ceramic bowl. [Eat and enjoy, Allah the Exalted willing.] If you wish, rather than using vinegar and onion, you can drizzle [fresh] lime vinegar over the chickpeas when they are in the ceramic bowl. [Then eat with the strength of Allah the Exalted.]

390. Another dish

[Take as many white and black chickpeas as you like, and] clean and wash them. [Put them in a new pot] with enough [fresh] water to more than cover them, and leave them for an [entire] day [to soften them up].[15] Next, [put a pot over the fire and] boil them in the same water. Once they are done, add salt, pepper and ginger. [Pour the broth into a ceramic bowl, and drink it] for its well-known benefits, especially the one from black chickpeas. [If you want, you can eat the chickpeas, too.] Chickpeas are eaten to loosen the bowels, but excessive consumption fattens you up. [There are many benefits to them, especially the black ones. Remember this – success lies with Allah.]

Chapter Three: on lentil dishes

391.

[Take any kind of lentils you have to hand,] wash them, and cook them in a [new] pot with fresh water, olive oil, pepper, coriander [seeds] and sliced onions. When the lentils are done, add [a sufficient amount of]

15 According to Gayangos XVI (fol. 109v.), it is 'so as to release their beneficial properties'.

salt, a little [crushed] saffron, and [as much good] vinegar [as you want]. Break three eggs into the pot and leave it on the fire [until the eggs are set and the vinegar has come to a boil. Then remove the pot from the fire and transfer the contents to a ceramic bowl. Eat and enjoy, Allah the Exalted willing]. The lentils can also be cooked without onion, [with the strength of Allah the Exalted,] whereas those who wish can cook it with boiled and chopped taro.[16] Alternatively, the lentils can be cooked with water-dissolved yeast[17] added to the pot, over a low fire. When the mixture begins to thicken, add good clarified butter or sweet olive oil, as much as the lentils can absorb. When they can absorb no more, remove them from the fire, and serve sprinkled with pepper.

16 The recipe in BL Or5927 ends here.

17 The edition (2012: 242) has *jamīr*, which is an obvious misspelling of *khamīr*.

SECTION NINE[1]

On honeyed dishes and various kinds of sweets

It consists of seven chapters.

Chapter One: on *mu'assal* and *ghassānī*[2]

392. Making *mu'assal*[3]

Take as many *raṭls* of good-quality honey as you want, put it in an earthenware cauldron over a fire until it melts, and then strain it through a cloth made of wool or another fabric. Clean the cauldron, return the honey to it and put it on the fire again. Then, take good-quality dried starch and clean it. Put it in a bowl – apply a ratio of about two *ūqiyas* of starch for each *raṭl* of honey. Add peeled and split almonds and enough bloomed saffron to colour it, but take care you do not add too much, as this will alter [the taste of] the dish. Put the honey over a fire and, when it starts to heat up, add what is in the bowl bit by bit, stirring continuously to prevent crystallizing. Continue stirring until everything is blended and it begins to thicken. At that point, pour in a bit of olive oil, and stir until it is absorbed. Keep doing this for as long as the oil is being absorbed. When no more oil can be soaked up, this is a sign that the cooking is complete and it is ready. Remove from the fire, but leave the mixture in the pot. If you like, you can transfer it to a ceramic bowl. Smear a ladle with olive oil from the *mu'assal* vessel and use it to scoop as much, or as little, as you want into the bowls. Scatter on cinnamon,[4]

---

1 In Gayangos XVI (fol. 110r.), this section comes later (fol. 114r.–v.), and it continues with the aubergine chapter (see above).

2 The recipes in this chapter have been supplemented and amended with information in BL Or5927 (fol. 186r.), which is much more detailed than the printed edition.

3 *mu'assalāt* ('honeyed [dishes]'). Corriente (1997: 353) suggests that *mu'assal* referred either to *aruzz mu'assal* (rice with honey and milk boiled into a paste) or a sweetmeat of spiced starch with honey and almonds. The *Andalusian* has two similar recipes by this name (*Anwā'*, 198–9; BNF, fols. 69r.–v.), none of which corresponds to this one. As we have seen (recipe No. 150), there was also a meat *mu'assal*.

4 The edition is clearly corrupted here, as it refers to adding cinnamon and olive oil and stretching it little by little.

fānīdh[5] and ground sugar, and serve at the end of the meal, Allah the Exalted willing.

393. Making *ghassānī*[6]

Take as many *raṭls* of good-quality white honey and proceed in the same manner as described above. Then return it to the vessel in which it was thickened. Take white hulled sesame seeds in a ratio of three *ūqiyas* for each *raṭl* of honey. Apply the same ratio for split, peeled almonds. Take good-quality dried starch in the same quantity (as in the previous recipe) and dissolve it in fresh water before putting it in the vessel with the honey that is on the fire, together with the almonds and sesame. When you see that it is close to boiling, add the starch bit by bit, while stirring continuously, until you see that the mixture is on the verge of thickening. At that point, pour in the olive oil, as described above, until the honey mixture cannot absorb any more. Then, remove the vessel from the fire and let the pudding settle in it. When you want to serve it, do the same as explained above, Allah the Exalted willing.[7]

Chapter Two: on the various kinds of sweetmeats

394. Making a most amazing soft white sweet[8]

Heat as much good-quality honey as you like in a clean tinned cauldron over a low fire, continuously stirring it with a giant fennel stalk[9] or a sugar cane reed with a copper ring at the end. When it becomes too hot for the finger, remove the pot from the fire but keep on stirring

5 See recipe No. 413.

6 The *Andalusian* (*Anwāʿ*, 197; BNF, fol. 69r.) has a similarly named dish, which, however, corresponds to the meat *ghassāniyyya* of recipe No. 151.

7 The recipe in the printed edition simply has: 'It is made in the same way as *muʿassal*, except that you use good white honey and omit saffron. You also add sesame seeds and almonds, three *ūqiyas* of each for every *raṭl* of honey.'

8 The translations of this recipe and the next two incorporate instructions from BL Or5927, fols. 186v.–187r.

9 *kalkha*, the unit noun of *kalkh* (also *kalakh*), which was also known as *qanā*. could refer to a number of plants in the *Ferula* family. More unusually, it was sometimes equated with lovage (*kāshim*), and its resin with 'gum ammoniac' (*ushshaj*). In Andalusian Arabic, it could also denote the more general 'reed'. Ibn Janāḥ 2020: No. 460; Corriente 1997: 465; Dozy 1881: II, 482–3.

unremittingly, while the pot is on the floor. When it has cooled down, add four egg whites for each *raṭl* of honey, stirring the mixture until it turns into a single smooth mass without the eggs being visible. Then return the pot to a gentle fire and keep stirring until the mixture becomes very white and thickens. At this stage, you may add some picked-over walnuts or almonds, if you like, Allah the Exalted willing.

395. Making *fālūdhaj*[10]

Heat as much good honey as you want in a clean tinned cauldron over a fire until it has melted, and then strain it through a cloth made of wool or another fabric. After cleaning the cauldron, return the honey to it and then take good-quality dried starch in a ratio of one-and-a-half to two *ūqiyas* for each *raṭl* of honey, as well as a little saffron. Dissolve it in fresh water and add it to the honey. When the honey is on the verge of thickening,[11] pour in olive oil – four *ūqiyas* for each *raṭl* of honey – and half an *ūqiya* of yellow wax. When you see that the olive oil is no longer being absorbed,[12] add as many peeled and split almonds as you like. Put the cauldron over a gentle fire and keep on stirring until it is done. Add what you like by way of hulled sesame seeds. Then remove the pot from the fire and pour the mixture onto a marble slab or a smooth board, Allah the Exalted willing.[13] This concludes the preparation.

396. Another recipe[14]

Take as much good honey as you want and put it in a clean cauldron over a gentle fire. Once the honey has melted, strain it through a woollen cloth. Wash the cauldron, and then return the honey to it. Add dried starch – two-and-a-half *ūqiyas* for each *raṭl* of honey – and one *dirham* of ground saffron. Next, pour in olive oil in a ratio of four *ūqiyas* for each *raṭl* of honey. Put the pot over a low fire, stirring constantly with

---

10 Also see recipes Nos. 67, 339. There is a very similar recipe in the *Andalusian* (*Anwāʿ*, 207–8; BNF, fol. 72r.).

11 Or 'when it thickens', as in BL Or5927 (fol. 186v.).

12 The *Andalusian* (*Anwāʿ*, 207–8; BNF, fol. 72r.) recipe is more detailed here, and mentions that one should strain off the oil, but that the more is strained, the drier the sweet will become; if one does not strain it off, the pudding will remain moist.

13 The recipe in the *Andalusian* (*Anwāʿ*, 208) specifies that the confection is shaped in large or small round loaves or discs, as desired.

14 There is a second *fālūdhaj* recipe ('with sugar') following in the *Andalusian* (*Anwāʿ*, 208; BNF, fol. 72r.–v.) as well, but this one is very different from al-Tujībī's.

the above-mentioned cane reed. When the honey has thickened, add half a *raṭl* of peeled almonds, and then take the pot off the fire. Transfer the mixture to a marble kneading slab to cool down, until it becomes lukewarm. Then squeeze it with your hands to release the oil and shape the mixture into thin, round loaves, Allah the Exalted willing.

If you like, you can also add as many unhulled sesame seeds as you have to hand. When the pudding has thickened, remove the pot from the fire and spread out the mixture on a marble slab, as we have mentioned, with the strength of Allah the Exalted.

397. [Making] white *juljulāniyya* (white sesame nougat)[15]

[Take as much good honey as you want and put it in a cauldron over a fire until it melts.] Strain the honey [through a woollen cloth] as described above, [wash the cauldron and return the honey to it. Put it over a gentle fire] and stir. Use your finger to test the consistency and, when the honey no longer sticks, remove the pot from the heat, but stir constantly until it becomes lukewarm. Beat egg whites, using five egg whites for each *raṭl* of [red] honey, or four egg whites if it is white honey. [Beat them in a bowl until the foam rises on them.] Once the egg whites are foamy, pour them over the honey while it is lukewarm, and stir for a while. Return the cauldron to a [low] fire, stirring continuously with a reed until the mixture whitens and thickens. Add enough skinned sesame seeds, and stir until these are blended and the mixture has thickened. Then remove the pot from the fire, spread out the mixture on a marble kneading slab, and shape it into discs [of whatever size you prefer.][16]

15 There is a similar recipe (called 'white halva with sesame seeds') in the *Andalusian* (*Anwā'*, 209; BNF, fol. 72v.), though a tear in the manuscript means that half is missing. The translation passages in square brackets are additions from BL Or5927, fol. 187r. This sweet bears more than a passing resemblance to the modern Sicilian *cubbaita*, whose name, however, would appear to be derived from the next recipe.

16 According to the recipe in *Anwā'* (*ibid.*), the discs (though it uses the term 'loaves', *raghaf*) are cut into long strips with a knife, and once they become lukewarm they are broken off.

398. Making *al-Qubbayṭ al-majbūdh* (pulled honey taffy)[17]

Take as much good honey as you want and put it in a cauldron over a moderate fire until it melts. Strain the honey through a woollen cloth, as described above. [Wash the cauldron, return the honey to it, and put it over a fire. Stir it with the reed until it thickens, and then immediately test it on a marble kneading slab. If it thickens fast, that means that it is done, in which case remove the pot from the fire, and pour all of the honey on the slab.] Fix a large iron nail with a straight head into a wall. Hang the thickened honey on the nail and pull it. Fold and pull it several times, and if it cools down, bring it close to the fire to heat it up. Continue pulling until it whitens. Then, shape into *ka'k* rings the size of the palm of a hand. Place them on a glass or wooden tray in the shapes that you want. They are only good for one day, and are best when eaten immediately with plain biscuits (*ka'k*). Remember this and act accordingly, Allah the Exalted willing.

399. Making a *mukhammara* halva[18]

Take as much white honey as you want and put it in a cauldron over a moderate fire until it melts. Strain the honey through a woollen cloth as described above, then clean the cauldron, and return the honey to it

---

17 The translation incorporates the more detailed instructions in BL Or5927 (fol. 186v.), from which the word *qubbayṭ* was also taken, in preference to the edition's (2012: 245) *ghubbayṭ*, since the former form also appears in an incomplete recipe in the *Andalusian* (*Anwā'*, 209; BNF, fol. 72v.), entitled 'white halva pulled on a nail'. The pronunciation with 'gh' is also used by al-Uryūlī (1983: No. 145), who claimed that these kinds of sweets nourish the body without producing obstructions, because they are curdled without starch. Ibn al-Ḥashshā' (1941: 108, No. 1005) describes *qabābīṭ* as a kind of bread stuffed with sugar, almonds and pistachios. In al-Warrāq's cookbook (1987: 247, 248), this type of sweetmeat is referred to as *nāṭif al-mismār* or *nāṭif 'alā al-mismār* ('nail nougat'), but is also another name for the *fānīdh* of recipe No. 413. Al-Zubaydī (1999: II, 492), al-Lakhmī (2003: 81) and Ibn Khalṣūn (1992: 166; trans., 96) all give *qubbayṭ* (also spelled *qubbayd*) as a synonym of *nāṭif*. According to Ibn Khalṣūn, it was the only sweet that should come after a meal. The medieval *nāṭif* should not be confused, however, with the present-day Arab dip by the same name (known in English as *natef*), which is made with the root of soapwort and is used in the making of sesame halva.

18 This is taken from BL Or5927 (fol. 187r.–v), which has been used to supplement both this recipe and the next. The edition (2012: 245) has *muḥammara*, meaning 'roasted or browned'. Though usually meaning 'fermented', *mukhammara* can also refer to something that is 'veiled', or something that has a white head and black body, such as a ewe (Kazimirski 1860: I, 632).

over a moderate fire. Stir with a brass-tipped thick reed so that it does not burn. Then add egg whites – six for each *raṭl* of honey if you are using comb honey, or ten if it is non-comb honey. Beat the egg whites by hand until foam forms on them, stirring constantly until the honey becomes smooth. Throw the eggs in and return to the fire. Stir continuously with a reed until the mixture turns white and smooth, and then remove the cauldron from the fire. Next, clean a large frying pan or tinned copper pot and fill it with good-quality sweet olive oil. Bring to a boil and throw in the *khabīṣ* flatbreads, but take them out again quickly with a slotted ladle, just as one does when cooking syrups. If the *khabīṣ* sheets are whole, throw them in the pan one by one, and when they are fried put them on a board to dry and cool down before crumbling them like flour. Pour the cooked curdled honey – one *raṭl* of honey for two *raṭls* of *khabīṣ* crumbs – on top. Mix until it becomes a single smooth mass, and then allow it to cool down before serving. This completes the preparation.

Another way of making this is to thicken the honey with a lot of egg whites – around twenty or more – and instead of *khabīṣ* add a sufficient quantity of slightly roasted hulled sesame seeds to the honey, Allah the Exalted willing.

400. Making *khabīṣ* pudding[19]

Take four *raṭls* of good-quality white honey, and put it in a cauldron over a gentle fire until it melts. Strain the honey through a woollen cloth, as mentioned above. Wash the cauldron, return the honey to it, and put it over a fire. Continuously stir until it thickens. Then take a clean frying pan and pour in plenty of olive oil before putting it over a fire. When it comes to a boil, take one *raṭl* of *khabīṣ* broken up into crumbs and put them in the oil, little by little, so that they become soft and smooth. Then, quickly take them out and put them in the thickened honey, which should be piping hot.[20] Stir until the mixture is fully blended and smooth, and then serve, Allah the Exalted willing.

19 Also see recipes Nos. 63, 66.

20 The edition (2012: 246) adds here that 'the ratio should be one *raṭl* of *khabīṣ* crumbs for four of honey', which is clearly redundant at this stage.

401. Recipe for a *sukkariyya* halva[21]

Pound one *raṭl* of sugar and grate one-third of a *raṭl* of *darmak* breadcrumbs into a semolina-like consistency. Add six egg whites, and then heat up one *raṭl* of sweet olive oil in a cauldron. When it has come to a boil, throw in the sugar, breadcrumbs and egg whites. Stir the mixture continuously over a low fire until it is cooked and has thickened. Let it cool down, and sprinkle on sugar and spikenard.

402. Making sugar *muʿaqqad*[22] with almonds

Take one *raṭl* of sugar, and put it in a glazed earthenware casserole dish with enough rose water and water to cover it. Put it on a fire until the sugar melts and then strain it through a hair sieve. Wash the casserole, return the sugar to it, and put it over a moderate fire. Test it by using a spoon to scoop some of the mixture onto a marble kneading slab, and leave it to cool down. If it quickly thickens and becomes like a block, and you hear a ringing sound when you throw it on the slab, that means that it is ready. You will have taken a quarter of a *raṭl* of peeled almonds and cut them up, or crushed them in a mortar, which is even better. When the sugar is done, add the almonds and beat with a ladle until the mixture is thoroughly blended. Smear the kneading slab with sweet olive oil or sweet almond oil and put the *muʿaqqad* on it, piece by piece. Stretch it out with your hands and shape into flat discs.[23] The same recipe can be made with pine nuts or pistachios. This tastes very nice, Allah the Exalted willing.

---

21 The order of the instructions follows BL Or5927 (fol. 187v.) as it is more in keeping with those in other recipes. In the edition (2012: 246), it is called a '*sukkariyya* halva'. There is a similar recipe in the *Andalusian* (see: *Anwāʿ*, 210; BNF, fol. 73r.).

22 BL Or5927 (fol. 187v.) was used to complete the clearly defective recipe in the printed edition (2012: 246). The latter uses the variant *maʿqūd*, which could denote any kind of thickened sweetmeat made with honey (Kazimirski 1860: II, 314). There were two kinds of *muʿaqqad* (also *muʿqad*), one made with sugar and another with honey (recipe No. 405); see Corriente 1997: 359. A variant ('halva called *al-maʿqūda*') is found in the *Andalusian* (*Anwāʿ*, 211; BNF, fol. 73r.). This kind of confection also had an Egyptian equivalent, known as *ʿaqīd*. See Ibn Mubārak Shāh 2020: Nos. 160, 162; *Kanz*, Nos. 132, 138.

23 According to the *Andalusian* (*ibid.*), it can also be shaped into dates filled with almonds or pieces of *fānīdh*, or figs, grapes, raisins, and so on, while it is still hot.

403. Another similar recipe[24]

Dissolve one *raṭl* of sugar in two *raṭls* of [fragrant] rose water. Cook it over a low fire [until the sugar melts and then] strain [through a woollen cloth. Wash the pot and return the sugar to it. Put it over a fire and stir it continuously until it is fully done. Then remove it from the fire and] stir until it has cooled down [and is lukewarm]. [Thoroughly] beat twelve egg whites [with your hands] until they are foamy. Pour the mixture over the sugar, put it on the fire again, and [beat with a confectionery reed] until it becomes white and acquires the consistency of *'aṣīda*.[25] When it is done, remove from the fire and add half a *raṭl* of pistachios [if possible] or [the same amount of] peeled and crushed almonds, [as explained above, Allah the Exalted willing.]

404. Making *rukhāmiyya* ('marbled candy')[26]

Dissolve [good-quality] white sugar in a little water, [heat it up over a gentle fire, and skim off the froth]. Pound peeled almonds [and let them dry] until they resemble semolina. When the sugar is about to thicken, throw in the almonds (the equivalent of one-third of the amount of sugar) after having dissolved them in rose water, camphor, spikenard and cloves. Stir continuously until the mixture thickens, and then pour it on an oil-greased marble slab. Cover with a smooth, oil-greased board so that [the surface] becomes like a smooth cake. Cut with a knife in the shape of thin reeds, or any other shape you like. [Leave to cool down, and store.]

---

24 The parts enclosed in square brackets are taken from BL Or5927 (fol. 188r.). There is a similar recipe in the *Andalusian* (*Anwā'*,70; BNF, fol. 29r.). The result for both this recipe and No. 405 is a kind of nougat that is very similar to the modern Spanish *turron* or the Italian *torrone*.

25 See recipe No. 67.

26 The parts in brackets are additions in BL Or5927 (fol. 188r.–v.). The name of the dish is derived from *rukhām*, 'marble'. The recipe is a somewhat reduced version of the one in the *Andalusian* (*Anwā'*, 212; BNF, fol. 73v.), which specifies that the mixture needs to be kneaded while it is still warm. The Eastern cookery books have a number of recipes of meat stews by this name made with rice and milk. See Ibn Mubārak Shāh 2020: Nos. 44, 50, 234; al-Baghdādī 1964: 28 (trans., 46); *Waṣf*, 331–2, 342; *Kanz*, Nos. 64, Appendix 13; *Wuṣla*, No. 6.91; Ibn Jazla, fol. 107r.; *Taṣānīf*, fol. 77r.

405. Making honey *mu'aqqad*[27]

[Take as much good-quality honey as you want, put it in a clean cauldron over a fire until it melts, and] strain [through a thick cloth]. Wash the cauldron, return the honey to it, and] cook it over a moderate heat. Test it with your finger to see if it is done. If [the honey does not stick to your finger,] remove the pot from the fire [and let it simmer down until it becomes lukewarm]. Then take egg whites in a ratio of five for each *raṭl* of honey [if you are not using comb honey, and four if you are]. Beat them [well] until foam forms on them. [Put the egg whites in with the honey, and] beat [thoroughly] to mix it all. [Then put the cauldron over a gentle fire and continuously stir with a confectionery reed.] Patiently continue doing this until the mixture turns white and has thickened. Then add [one *raṭl* of crushed] peeled walnuts [and eat, Allah the Exalted willing].

Chapter Three: making[28] *Qāhiriyya* and *sanbūsak*

406. *Qāhiriyya* (marzipan biscuits)[29]

Take as much good-quality sugar as you like and the same amount in skinned sweet almonds. Thoroughly pound everything in a mortar until it starts to look like dough. Put the mixture in a large bowl and add rose water, cassia, cinnamon, spikenard, pepper, ginger, nutmeg, a sufficient amount of galangal, and a little camphor if you like. Knead all of this well until everything is blended and sticks together. Make sure the dough is somewhat tight. Make small rings out of it in the shape of *ka'k*. Then, take a sufficient amount of *darmak* flour, add sugar and almonds, and knead it into a slack dough with yeast and a little salt.

---

27 The *ma'qūd* of the edition was again corrected, while additions from BL Or5927 (fol. 188v.) are in square brackets.

28 This is based on BL Or5927 (fol. 188v.); the edition (2012: 248) has 'on…'.

29 The text of the edition (2012: 248) has a number of gaps in the instructions, and incorporates parts from another recipe (No. 412). As a result, the translation is based wholly on BL Or5927 (fol. 188v.), preserving only the title of the edition. The name of this sweet is derived from the Arabic word for the Egyptian capital, *al-Qāhira*, and thus translates as 'the Cairene (sweet)'. For other recipes, see: *Anwā'*, 67–8, 194-5 (BNF, fols. 28r.–v., 68r.–v.); *Wuṣla*, No. 7.71; Ibn Mubārak Shāh 2020: No. 150; *Kanz*, No. 322.

Set it aside and let it rest.[30] Then, take some starch, pound it into the dough, and work it. Take a clean frying pan and pour in sweet olive oil and, if you have it, sweet almond oil, as this is even better. Put it on the fire. When the oil starts to boil, take the rings one by one and dip them in the batter, until they are all coated with it. Fry them in the pan until they are done. As soon as one of them starts to brown, take it out quickly. Arrange all of them nicely in a bowl, pour on good-quality skimmed honey or some thickened rose-water syrup, and dust with caster sugar. Eat and enjoy, Allah the Exalted willing.

407. Another kind[31]

Take as much sugar and almonds as you like, and do the same as explained in the previous recipe, that is to say, crush them, knead into a dough and make into small rings, but smaller than the ones described above. Take the same amount of starch, and sift it. Then, take the rings one by one and sprinkle on enough of the starch until they are completely coated on all sides. Arrange them on an earthenware or iron *malla* and put it in the oven, away from the flames. Leave until they have set and begun to turn golden, at which point take them out and let them cool down before eating them, Allah the Exalted willing. In the absence of a *malla*, use a board, smear it with olive oil, and place the rings on it after sprinkling them with starch or *darmak* flour.

408. Another kind of *Qāhiriyya*[32]

Take two *raṭls* of good-quality sugar and dissolve it in fresh water or rose water. Put everything in a cauldron over a low heat, and skim off the sugar froth until the liquid thickens into syrup. Throw in two *raṭls* of finely ground peeled almonds and add one quarter of a *raṭl* of finely ground *darmak* flour. Knead it all until it forms a single mass and the oil

30 The Arabic text refers to letting it rise but, as becomes clear later, the biscuits are dipped into the mixture, which means it is a batter, rather than a 'dough'. The recipe also omits to include the crucial ingredient of water, irrespective of whether it is a dough or batter.

31 This recipe is misplaced in the printed edition as the second recipe in Chapter Five (2012: 250), and has thus been omitted there in the translation. It was supplemented with instructions from BL Or5927 (fols. 188v.–189r.).

32 A very incomplete version of this recipe appears as a separate entry (Chapter Five, recipe No. 3) in the printed edition (2012: 250–1). The translation relies heavily on the text in BL Or5927 (fol. 189r.).

is released (from the almonds). Leave for a while and add spikenard, cloves dissolved in rose water, and a little camphor, as much as you like. Knead and shape into large and small *ka'k* rings and let them dry a little. Next, dip them in a bowl containing thick water-dissolved starch coloured with saffron, though you can also omit the saffron and just leave it white. Remove the rings from the bowl and put them aside for a little while, before putting them in a pan with a generous amount of boiling olive oil. Be careful to leave them in for only a very short time, and take them out quickly, before they brown. Then, drench them in rose syrup, rose-water syrup or mastic syrup, before storing and using them, Allah the Exalted willing.

409. Making *sanbūsak*[33]

Take a sufficient quantity of good-quality sugar, dissolve it in rose water, and add almonds, pounded into a dough. Gingerly stir the mixture over a low fire until everything is blended together and looks like the *Qāhiriyya* filling. [Take it down from the fire and, once it is lukewarm][34] add crushed peeled almonds, spikenard, cloves, a little bit of mastic, and ginger. These spices should have previously been ground and dissolved in rose water infused with a little camphor and musk. [Beat everything together, and] knead the mixture until all the ingredients are thoroughly blended. Make thick discs with it, the size of the palm of a hand. This is the real *sanbūsak*; the one that the people of *Ifrīqiya* make, which is filled with [pounded] meat, is neither commendable nor delightful, [as it has no flavour or taste].

33 The edition has the misreading 'honey', rather than 'making' *sanbūsak*, and incongruously includes it at the end of Chapter 5 (2012: 251). It has been moved to this chapter as it appears in its title and is also located here in BL Or5927 (fol. 189r.). An identical recipe can be found in the *Andalusian* (*Anwā'*, 196; BNF, fol. 68v.), where it is called 'the royal *sanbūsak*'. The latter text explains that it used to be made in Marrakesh, at the court of the (Almohad) caliph Abū Yūsuf al-Manṣūr (1184–1199), and could be shaped like *ka'k* rings, oranges, apples or pears. As a result, it may be the ancestor of the Sicilian marzipan fruit, *frutta Martorana*. The savoury meat-filled variety referred to at the end is called the commoners' *sanbūsak* in the *Andalusian* (*Anwā'*, *ibid.*) and was the usual Near Eastern *sanbūsak*, which is closer to what today is known as samosa. See Ibn Mubārak Shāh 2020: 40–1; al-Dabbābī al-Mīsāwī 2017: 124–5.

34 The sections enclosed in brackets are based on BL Or5927.

Chapter Four: on making *jawzīnaq* and *lawzīnaq*[35]

410. Making *jawzīnaq* (walnut confection)[36]

Take as many freshly picked walnuts free from rot as you want. Break and remove their shells, and clean them. Soak half of them in boiling water and then skin them. Dry them with a cloth and leave them. Take the other half of the walnuts and pound them well so they release their oil, as described in another section of this book. When they release their oil, put it in a vessel. Take the first batch of walnuts and finely crush them. Transfer them to a kneading slab and pound them into a paste with a consistency that resembles brains. Take three parts of good-quality sugar and two parts of crushed walnuts, and pound everything together well. Taste it to see if it is sweet enough. Then take the oil released from the walnuts and smear it on the slab. Take sugar and walnuts and knead them together on the slab. Smooth the mixture out with your hands and cut it into pieces. Sprinkle on sugar, pepper, cinnamon and cassia, and then eat, Allah the Exalted willing.

If you like, you can make it with good-quality honey, which you put in a cauldron. Remove the froth after straining, and then stir over a fire. Once it thickens, add the crushed walnuts and stir until everything is mixed. Pour the mixture on a kneading slab smeared with the oil extracted from the walnuts. Spread out the dough on the slab and stretch it with your hands. Then, cut it into pieces, as described above, and sprinkle on the aromatic spices you have to hand. If you add camphor, this is the height of perfection, Allah the Exalted willing.

411. Making *lawzīnaq* (almond confection)[37]

[Take as much good-quality sugar as you want.] Dissolve it in [fragrant] rose water and fresh water, and strain, as mentioned before. Put it in a cauldron over a fire, [and when it comes to a boil and the sugar has dissolved, strain it] and add honey – one *ūqiya* for each *raṭl*

35 In the edition (2012: 252) it is Chapter Six.

36 Also see recipe No. 55. The recipe in this edition is clearly corrupted, as the second half reprises instructions for *fānīdh* (recipe No. 413) in BL Or5927. It has been amended and supplemented with the help of the latter.

37 This recipe is in Chapter Three in the printed edition (2012: 249), but clearly belongs in Chapter Six, as indicated by the title. The enclosed sections are additions from BL Or5927 (fol. 189v.).

of sugar. [Then, take peeled sweet almonds, thoroughly pound them, and put them in a jar to one side. Keep the sugar over a low heat until it is cooked and has thickened.] Once it is ready, remove the pot from the fire and add the crushed almonds – ten and a half *ūqiyas* for each *raṭl* of sugar. Stir the pot until everything forms a single mass, and then put the mixture on a kneading slab greased with almond oil. Cut into pieces and dust with sugar.

Chapter Five: on making sweet cane[38]

412. (Recipe)[39]
Take four *raṭls* of fresh milk, strain it, and add it to two *raṭls* of sugar. Put the mixture in a new earthenware or glazed casserole dish or a tinned cauldron over a moderate fire. Continuously, but gently, stir the mixture until it thickens and binds. Then put it on an oil-greased kneading slab and leave until it becomes lukewarm. Stretch pieces of it out to flat sheets four fingers in length, and then roll them up on top of sifted *darmak* flour so they look like cane tubes. Trim the ends even with a knife, serve on trays, and eat, Allah the Exalted willing.

Chapter Six: on making *fānīdh* and *ashqāqūl*[40]

413. Making *fānīdh* (pulled sugar taffy)[41]

38 In the edition (2012: 249), it is Chapter Four.

39 The *Andalusian* has a similar recipe (*Anwāʿ*, 70; BNF, fol. 28v.), entitled 'A preparation known as sweet cane', which has been used together with BL Or5927 (fol. 189v.–190r.) to supplement the one in the printed edition.

40 In the edition (2012: 250–1), this is Chapter Five.

41 The title of the recipe is missing from the edition (2021: 250, No. 1), but included in BL Or5927 (fol. 190r.), which is also the basis for the translation, as the edition is quite corrupted, and even includes instructions from another recipe (No. 404). In BL Or5927, this is the first recipe in its Chapter Four (fol. 190r.), which only has the two names in the title. The instructions are near-identical to half of those in the recipe for *jawzīnaq* (No. 410), as well as No. 398, of course, which is also for pulled taffy. The second recipe (with the variant spelling *ashqāqūr*) is similar to the *ashqāqūl* of the edition's Chapter Six, which also has a dish (*lawzīnāq*) in its title for which no recipe is included. The word *fānīdh* is a borrowing from the Middle Persian (Pahlavi) *pānīd*, meaning a sweet made from barley flour, lemon balm and sugar. The Arab

Take five *raṭls* of good sugar and put it in a tinned cauldron, adding enough fresh water to dissolve it. Put the cauldron over a moderate fire and, when it comes to a boil, skim off all the froth, making sure none of it remains. Leave the cauldron on the fire until it is done. Put an iron spoon in the cauldron and when you see that the sugar has hardened on it, drop the spoon; if you hear a cracking sound, this means that the sugar is cooked. Take a marble kneading slab and smear it with sweet olive oil or sweet almond oil. Pour the sugar mixture on it, and add a sufficient amount of mastic powder. Roll up the sugar mixture, hang it on a nail, and stretch it until it becomes white. If it cools down before it turns white, take the sugar close to the fire. Then resume the stretching until it turns white and smooth. Roll it in starch and spread out as much of the mixture as you need. Use scissors to cut it into pieces of the required size, big or small, and store them in a glass container or wooden bowl until such time as you wish to eat them, Allah the Exalted willing.

414. Making *ashqāqūl*[42]

Take as much sugar as you want, and do with it as described above until it comes to a boil. Then add pepper, cinnamon, ginger and a little pounded mastic. Smear the kneading slab with oil, and pour on the sugar mixture, bit by bit, in the quantity required to make flat, thin lozenges, both small and large. When they have cooled down, put them

---

fānīdh was usually made with sugar, water, honey and sweet almond oil, which, once cooked and made into a sticky dough, was stretched and made into elongated sweets, or shaped into figures, circles, triangles, etc. According to Ibn Jazla (fol. 161r.), the best *fānīdh* is the white one made from refined white sugar, and is useful against coughs and constipation. Al-Rāzī (1987: 155), for his part, claimed it was soothing for the throat, stomach and urethra. For other recipes (some of which are known as *ḥalwā yābisa*, 'dried sweet'), see *Anwāʿ*, 213 (BNF, fols. 73v.–74r.); *Waṣf*, 415–16, 455; al-Baghdādī 1964: 75 (trans., 98–9); *Wuṣla*, No. 757; *Kanz*, No. 265. Ibn al-Bayṭār 1992: III, 20, 30, 213. Also see Ouerfelli 2008: 314-315; Ibn al-Bayṭār 1992: III, 20, 30, 213; Nasrallah [al-Warrāq 2007]: 596-7; *idem* [*Kanz*, 2018]: 482-3; Steingass 1892: 233, 905; A. J. Marques da Silva, 'Du fanîd au penidios: Analyse comparée de recettes chrétiennes et maghrébo-andalouses de pénide (Moyen-âge et Renaissance)', in Stengel & Debbabi Missaoui 2020: 121-42. The same word could also refer to a type of refined sugar subjected to three firings, known as *sukkar sijzī* ('Sijistani sugar'), which was used as a laxative and carminative, or to refined sugar combined with sweet almond oil. See Sato 2015: 56, 164; Ouerfelli 2008: 525.

42 The more detailed instructions in BL Or5927 (fol. 190r.) have been incorporated in the translation. This recipe is very similar to one found in the *Andalusian* (*Anwāʿ*, 32; BNF, fol. 13r.).

in a glass or wooden vessel and eat, Allah the Exalted willing. If you like, you can, after the mixture has thickened, add fresh lime juice, and chew on the lozenges, which sweeten the breath and assist digestion.

Chapter Seven: on Eastern recipes

415. Recipe called al-Mutawakkil's brains[43]

Take four *raṭls* of good-quality honey and put it in a cauldron over a fire until it is dissolved. Strain it and return it to the cauldron after cleaning it. Add half a *dirham* each of ground spikenard and ground mastic. Then pound starch in the quantity of half that of the honey, and gradually add it to the cauldron, while stirring continuously until it thickens and forms a single smooth mass [less thick than *fālūdhaj*]. Then add a quarter of a *mudd* of hulled sesame seeds and two *ūqiyas* of peeled almonds. Add sweet olive oil so that the mixture does not stick to the sides of the pot, and keep stirring until it reaches the consistency of *fālūdhaj*.[44] Then, remove from the heat and store it in a glass or glazed earthenware container until required. [When you want to eat some, transfer the required amount to a ceramic bowl and] sprinkle on caster sugar and pounded almonds, walnuts [or pistachios]. [Eat and enjoy, Allah the Exalted willing.]

416. Recipe for *al-zumurrudī* ('emerald sweet')[45]

Take the same amount of honey as in the previous recipe, and proceed in the same way. When it is strained, add one half of a *dirham* each

---

43 The dish is named after the Abbasid caliph al-Mutawakkil (d. 861). In BL Or5927 (fol. 190v.), the recipe is called 'the brains of al-Wāthiq' (d. 847), who reigned before al-Mutawakkil. There are a few minor variations in the manuscript, which are set off in square brackets.

44 See recipes Nos. 337, 373.

45 It derives its name from the word for 'emerald', *zumurrud*, in reference to the colour of the dish. The translation is based on BL Or5927 (fol. 190v.), as the recipe in the edition (2012: 254; Gayangos XVI, fols. 119v.–120r.) is highly corrupted to the point of being unintelligible: 'Boil several *raṭls* of strained honey, as described above. Add cinnamon, spikenard and cloves – half a *dirham* of each – and grate one *raṭl*. It is eaten broken up, or peeled. It is sealed with clay so that it does not go off, and to prevent the air from entering the container.' It is followed by recipe No. 420 of the current translation.

of ground cinnamon, spikenard and cloves. Then, rub one *raṭl* of cold *darmak* flour breadcrumbs between your hands until they become like semolina. Then throw on half a *dirham* of saffron and the same amount of ground indigo.[46] Sprinkle on the crumbs with a bit of water, and rub the saffron and indigo with your hands until the colour turns green. Put it on the honey in the cauldron after boiling four *ūqiyas* of starch dissolved in a little water. When the honey has thickened, add the dyed breadcrumbs. When everything has become a single blended mass, pour in as much sweet olive oil as the mixture can absorb. Once it can no longer absorb anything and has gained the consistency of *fālūdhaj*, remove it from the fire and put it in a container. Sprinkle on sugar or coarsely chopped pistachios, or skinned almonds or walnuts. Eat and enjoy, Allah the Exalted willing.

417. Another recipe, called *qaṭā'if* halva[47]

Take good-quality honey, as described, and do the same things as before. After straining it, add one-half a *dirham* each of ground cinnamon, pepper and spikenard, and three-quarters of a *dirham* of ground saffron. When the honey starts to boil, add four *ūqiyas* of dried starch dissolved [in water]. Take one *raṭl* of cooked *qaṭā'if*,[48] cut them as thinly as possible, and add them to the honey. Stir[49] continuously until the *qaṭā'if* blends with the honey into a single smooth mass. Put both in a cauldron and pour on sweet olive oil, as much as can be absorbed. Stop doing this when it gains the consistency of *fālūdhaj*, and then take it down from the fire. Transfer it to a glass or earthenware container and, when you want to eat it, sprinkle on what is mentioned in the previous recipe. Eat and enjoy, Allah the Exalted willing.

---

46 *nīlaj*, a Middle Persian borrowing, which itself goes back to a Sanskrit word, and could denote both woad and indigo. In the pharmacological literature it was also known as *wasma*, *'iẓlim*, *ṭīn akhḍar* ('green clay'), and *al-'ayn al-khaḍrā'* ('green eye'), the last two referring to the colour of the dried sediment of fermented indigo leaves. The blue indigo dye was obtained by mixing this paste with lye. Ibn Janāḥ 2020: Nos. 297, 418, 701. Ibn Jazla (fol. 132v., 155r.) held that pounded indigo mixed with barley flour dissolves swellings when it is applied to them.

47 This recipe is found only in BL Or5927 (fol. 190v.–191r.).

48 See recipes No. 59, 60.

49 The manuscript adds the instruction to 'take the starch', which is clearly a scribal lapse, as the starch has already been used.

SECTION TEN

On various kinds of fermented condiments (*kawāmikh*),[1] on making vinegars and different kinds of *murrī*, on extracting oils and restoring oil that has gone bad, on restoring and replacing olive oil required for cooking by extracting oil from other seeds if it is not available, on improving food that has too much salt in it and malodorous meat, and other things like that.[2]

It consists of twelve chapters.

Chapter One:[3] on making *ṣināb*[4]

418. Recipe

Take fresh small-grained mustard imported from the land of the Christians, as this is the best. Take as much as you want and wash it repeatedly in hot water until all of the soil and dirt have been removed. Afterwards, put the seeds in a bowl. Then skin almonds – twice the amount of the mustard seeds – and mix the two together. Take a large mortar made out of wood (which is the best), stone, or copper, which is the worst of the three but can be used when you have nothing else. Take the mustard-and-almond mixture and gently crush it in the mortar until the almonds are crumbled. Put a bowl in front of you with vinegar and a little salt. Repeatedly put the hand you use for the mortar in the bowl and continue pounding until the almonds are completely dissolved. Scoop the mixture from the mortar with a ladle and put it in a container which you should cover so that dirt cannot get to it and spoil it. Then put another batch in [the mortar and continue] until you have finished all you need to crush, as described. Take as much as you want

1 On this term, which denoted milk-based preparations in Near Eastern cookery books, see Ibn Mubārak Shāh 2020: 79 (note 353). According to Corriente (1997: 467), it denoted a 'vinegar sauce' in Andalusian Arabic.

2 The title is based on BL Or5927 (fol. 191r.).

3 This chapter is missing from the edition, and has been added from BL Or5927, fol. 191r.

4 For other recipes, see al-Warrāq 1987: 94; *Kanz*, No. 468 (= al-Warrāq). According to Ibn Zuhr (1992: 65), it should be eaten by those complaining of cold stomachs.

of the grounds and return them to the mortar. Add very sour white vinegar bit by bit while stirring it with the pestle by hand to release the moisture from the almonds. There should not be a lot of vinegar so that the mixture does not become too runny. Next, take a close-meshed hair sieve and place it over an earthenware glazed or glass container, remove the *ṣināb* from the mortar and put it in the sieve. When you have finished sieving, transfer the liquid by itself to a jar. This is the first pressing. Return the *ṣināb* to the mortar and lightly pound it. Dilute it with vinegar and press it down on the sieve, as explained previously. Do this three or, if possible, four times to complete the task. If you like, you can mix the second pressing with the first, which improves its quality. Alternatively, you can leave each pressing by itself, and eat it with other dishes that are on the table, Allah the Exalted willing.

419. Another recipe[5]

Take as much of the aforementioned mustard[6] as you want, repeatedly wash the seeds with water, and then let them dry. Vigorously crush them in a mortar, and push the resulting paste through a hair sieve. Next, take peeled almonds and crush them before mixing them with the mustard and pounding them both together. Then press in order to release the oil from both the mustard and the almonds. Take the crumbs of *darmak* bread and put them in cold water. Gradually knead it into the mustard paste, and then pour in sour white vinegar into which you have previously dissolved a sufficient quantity of salt. Put in as much vinegar as desired. Thoroughly strain the paste through a cloth and add some honey in the process to temper the sourness. All of these recipes are good, Allah the Exalted willing.

5 This recipe is very similar to one found in the *Andalusian* (*Anwāʿ*, 32; BNF, fol. 13r.).

6 Here the author uses *ṣināb* in the Andalusian Arabic sense of 'mustard'.

Chapter Two: on pickling olives

420. Recipe[7]

Take as many large green olives harvested in the month of September[8] as you want, but carefully gather them with your hand to avoid damaging and spoiling them. Wash the dirt from them and slice them with a thin knife, but do not cut them all the way to the pit.[9] Make square or triangular incisions, depending on whether they are big or small. Put them in a glazed earthenware or glass container and immerse the olives in fresh water, but do not add salt. Leave them aside, as described above. Then take white salt, crush it, and put it in a bowl. Add enough fresh water to cover the olives. Use only a moderate amount of salt. Pour the salty water over the olives in the container, replacing the water in which they were previously. Cover for three days, but keep an eye on it and then taste the olives. If you find that they taste good, so much the better. If you think there is not enough salt and water, add some more. Use the olives when the taste is good, Allah the Exalted willing. If you like, once you have the right result, you can remove the water and cover the olives with olive oil.

421. Another recipe

Take medium-sized olives harvested in October, before they become ripe. Break them on a board to split [the flesh],[10] but do not remove it from the pit. Put the olives in fresh water and leave them, as described above. Change the water once, and then add water and salt. Leave them until they are pickled. When you want to use the olives, remove them from the container in which they are stored and transfer them to a small bowl. Grate on oregano and pour on a little oil. Whisk with your hands to mix the olives with the oregano and olive oil. Eat and enjoy, Allah the Exalted willing.

---

7 The first two recipes in this chapter are found only in BL Or5927 (fols. 191v.–192r.); they have been included at this point in the chapter since they precede the ones that are also in the printed edition.

8 This is the month that the olives begin to turn black; Ibn al-ʿAwwām 1802: II, 1, 418.

9 *ʿaẓm* (plural *ʿiẓām*), 'bone', but in North African dialects also 'pit' or 'stone', as well as 'egg', as it still is in present-day Tunisian Arabic. Dozy 1881: II, 142.

10 This is a speculative addition by analogy with the instructions in recipe No. 423, as the word is illegible due to damage to the manuscript.

If you like, you can keep the olives whole, in which case take a large, clean, pitch-coated earthenware jar, put the olives in it, pour on enough fresh water to immerse them, and then add an appropriate amount of salt. Taste it until it is to your liking. Cover the jar and leave it for ten days. Then open it and check the contents. If you find that it is not salty enough, add some salt and close the jar again, tightly sealing the lid with mud so that the air cannot reach the olives. Leave them like this until you know that they are done. When you want to use them, open the jar to remove the desired quantity, and then re-cover. If you wish, you can break some of the olives and add oregano and olive oil to them. However, you can also eat them whole if you like, Allah the Exalted willing.

422. Another similar recipe[11]

Take olives – both small and large – that are harvested in October and November,[12] and wash the [dirt away] before putting them in a large new pitch-coated earthenware jar that has been cleaned with water until the smell of pitch has gone. Put in a layer of olives and then another layer of a type of oregano known as *shardūn*;[13] keep on alternating the layers until the jar is full.[14] Then pour in enough fresh water to immerse the olives, and cover the jar, sealing it with mud. Leave it like this for a few days, and then open up the jar to check on the water level. If it is too low, add some more. Also taste it, and if it is lacking in salt, add some more. [Seal the lid with mud and leave to stand until you need

11 This would appear to be an abridged variant of a recipe found in al-Ṭighnarī (2006: 208–9), which is entitled *zaytūn muthmar* ('ripe olives'). An identically named, but completely different, recipe is found in Ibn al-ʿAwwām (2012: III, 531). The editor of the latter text has the vowelling *muthammar*, which is unclear in the context.

12 According to Ibn al-ʿAwwām (1802: II, 1, 418), the green olives used for preserving were harvested in October 'before they turn from green to yellow'.

13 Also *shardhūn*, known in English as conehead thyme, Persian hyssop or Spanish oregano (*Thymbra capitata, Thymus capitatus*). Al-Ishbīlī (2004–10: No. 3203) described it as a low bush, with very small leaves, almost invisible, greyish in colour, with small purple flower heads, with a spicy and somewhat bitter taste. He adds that he had personally tasted and collected it, and that it was known in Romance as *qumnāl*, 'which means little cumin, because of its power to open blockages and its acidity'. Also see Dietrich 1988: II, 384; Ibn Janāḥ 2020: Nos. 157, 365; Corriente 1997: 128, 279.

14 The translation of this passage relies on BL Or5927 (fol. 192v.) as it is very corrupted and incomplete in the edition.

them. Use them in a way you see fit, Allah the Exalted willing. If you like, you can break the olives before putting them in the jar.][15]

423. Another similar recipe[16]

Take as many fully ripe [black] olives – both large and small – as you like, wash off the dirt, and leave them to dry. Then take a board, put it in front of you, and place the olives onto it one by one. Strike the olives with another board, or in a wooden mortar in order to split the olives, but keep the flesh on the pits. You can also massage or crush them with your fingers. When this is done, take the olives and put them in a basket made from esparto [or another material, pack them tightly], and firmly tie some rope around it before weighing down the top with a stone or something else in order to make the olives release their juice. Leave them like this until all of their juice is gone and you can see the pits of the olives. Then open the basket, remove the olives, and transfer them to a large kneading tub. Add crushed salt, good-quality crushed oregano and olive oil, and mix everything together. Beat it with your hands until the salt, oregano and olives are all mixed, and then put the mixture in a glazed earthenware or glass container. Immerse the olives with good-quality olive oil [and seal the container with mud]. When you want to use some of them, scoop them out with a small ladle, but make sure that olives remain submerged in the olive oil so that the air cannot touch them, since they quickly get mouldy and spoilt. Remember this. Also, no woman or man in a state of impurity must be allowed to go near, or handle the olives. This is true for all fermented condiments (*kawāmikh*). Bear this in mind – Allah will grant you success in finding the right path.

---

15 The section in brackets is found only in BL Or5927, fol. 192v.

16 The recipe in the printed edition (2012: 255–6) was highly abridged, and so the translation is based on BL Or5927 (fol. 192v.). The passages in square brackets refer to supplementary information from the edition. A similar recipe is found in al-Ṭighnarī (2006: 210) but it does not, however, contain the opening instruction of breaking the olives.

Chapter Three: on pickling limes

424. Recipe[17]

Take [as many as you like] of the finest tender, fully ripe limes, picked in the season when they are at their best. After washing and drying them, slice and quarter them, without however cutting them all the way through and separating the pieces. Put them in a bowl as you go along, and continue until you have finished them all. Grind purified salt and fill the limes with it before placing them one by one in a glass container, until it is full. Take some more limes, cut them in half and squeeze out their juice into a bowl. The amount should be sufficient to immerse the limes that are in the container. Strain the juice through a cloth, and pour it on the limes, immersing them in it. Next, cover the container and put in a sunny place for three [four] days. Taste them, and if you find that there is not enough salt, add some, and then seal the mouth of the vessel containing the limes with crushed tragacanth gum[18] mixed with honey, as this is the best way to do it, but olive oil can also prevent them from becoming mouldy. Then, move the container out of the sun to somewhere that is airy and devoid of humidity.

If you like, you can mix the lime vinegar with water and salt. You could also substitute the lime vinegar for salt and water. Take enough fresh water to cover the limes and add salt to it. Taste it to see if the taste of salt is strong enough. If it is not, add some more, and then immerse the limes in the brine.

If you wanted, you could add honey to speed up the pickling process, or expose the limes to the sun. Make sure to move the container out of the sun as soon as it appears the limes are ready [to prevent spoiling them. Remember this and act accordingly, Allah the Exalted willing]. Some people make them in a different way, by first softening the limes in water for several days, then drying them, and throwing away the

---

17 The recipe in the edition (2012: 257) has been supplemented with information from BL Or5927 (fol. 193r.).

18 *kathīrā'* (also known as *qatād*), the sweet, translucent resin of bushes in the Astralagus family. It was used medicinally in a variety of applications, often for eye, urinary and intestinal illnesses, as well as coughs. Ibn Zuhr (1992: 91; trans., 112) recommended a tragacanth lambative (*la'ūq*) in the treatment of dysentery. Today it is used, for instance, in the dyeing, cosmetic and paper industries, and even in ice-cream. Ibn Sīnā 1999: I, 507–8, 520, 621; Lev & Mar 2008: 302–5.

water. Afterwards, they are scored, as described above, stuffed with salt, and placed in a glazed container one by one until it is full. Leave them like this, without adding any more water or vinegar, which will facilitate the pickling. This method is easier than the others.[19]

425. A similar recipe[20]

Wash large, fully ripe limes and split them, as explained above. Then pound good-quality sugar, and mix it with cinnamon, spikenard, ginger, pepper, cloves, a bit of mastic, galangal [and a little syrup]. Stuff this mixture in the limes and pack them one by one in a tall glass jar that can accommodate fifty limes, until it is full. Then, take other limes, halve them, and squeeze their juice into a bowl until you have the required quantity for the limes that are in the jar. Strain the juice and add salt to it, as much as required to enhance the flavour. Then pour the mixture on the limes in the jar, fully immersing them. Leave the jar in a place that is sunny for a day or two [or three]. Then, seal it off with sweet olive oil and move it to an airy location free from humidity. When you want to use the limes, scoop some out with a small spoon and serve them with what you have prepared, Allah the Exalted willing. Take care that the limes are not touched by anyone who is in a state of ritual impurity – Allah will grant you success.

19 The passages in brackets are additions from BL Or5927 (fol. 193r.), which omits the final section, after the invocation.

20 The text of the edition (2012: 258) has been amended with BL Or5927 (fol. 193r.–v.), while additions from the former are enclosed in brackets.

Chapter Four: on pickling capers[21]

426. [Recipe]

Clean tender caper stalks, pick them over, and wash them thoroughly with water. Then, take salt and clean it. Put the capers in a large new pitch-coated earthenware jar which has been used to store olive oil, and has been washed with water. Put a layer of salt followed by one with capers, and continue alternating them until the jar is completely full. Then take vinegar and fresh water in a ratio of one-third of water to two-thirds of vinegar, pour both in a tub, and whisk with your hands until they are blended. Pour the mixture on the capers in the jar, immersing them completely.

Cover the jar and leave it for three days. Then open the jar and, if you see that there is not enough liquid left, add some in the same proportions as above (one-third of water and two-thirds of vinegar). The same applies to the salt. Put the lid back on the jar and leave it for thirty days, after which check on the capers and top up the liquid if required. Reseal the jar with mud, and leave until the capers are fully done and ready to use, Allah willing. Eat them with vinegar and olive oil, or cut the stalks and put them in milk curds or cottage cheese (*shīrāz*),[22] as described in the first Chapter of the sixth Section of this book. Follow the same method for caper buds that have not yet opened, and for small berries[23] that are not fully grown and whose seeds are still growing.

---

21 BL Or5927 (fol. 193v.) adds 'in a variety of ways'. The translations in this chapter have been supplemented and amended with the manuscript versions (fols. 193v.–194r.), as the edition (2012: 259) is incomplete. In Eastern cookery books, too, there are a number of pickled caper recipes (al-Warrāq 1987: 99; *Wuṣla*, Nos 8.30–4; *Kanz*, No. 601), and even drinks (al-Warrāq 1987: 311–12). According to Ibn Rushd (1999: 422), capers are beneficial for the spleen, dense humours and toothaches, and also have diuretic and emmenagogic properties. Ibn Jazla (fol. 183r.) and Ibn Khalṣūn (1996: 163; trans., 92) added that they also have aphrodisiacal, anthelmintic and antidotal effects. According to the latter author, capers should be eaten with vinegar and sweet almond oil. Al-Razi (1987: 150) held that caper condiments (*kāmakh*) are bad for the stomach, arouse thirst, and emaciate the body.

22 See recipe No. 319.

23 *faqqūṣ* (also *faqqūs*); this word usually denotes a small serpent melon, also known as Armenian cucumber, and was associated with Egypt. Al-Bīrūnī (1973: 291; trans., 253) defined it as a green and raw watermelon, also known in Arabic as *ḥadaj* and in Persian as *safcha*, though the latter actually referred to an unripe gourd (Steingass 1892: 684). In the present text, it is short for *faqqūs al-kabbar*, a large caper. See

Remember this.

427. Another recipe, if you want the capers washed

Take caper stalks, as mentioned above, clean them, and put them in a basin with enough fresh water to immerse them. Change the water twice a day, in the morning and in the evening, until the capers lose their bitterness. Continue doing this for three or more days, and then taste to make sure they are ready; if they are, remove them from the basin, thoroughly wash them, and place them in a kneading tub. Next, sprinkle on the required quantity of salt, stir, and leave the capers without water for a while so that they can absorb the salt, before placing them in an earthenware jar. Mix water with vinegar and pour it over the capers, fully immersing them. Frequently check on them and if they lack water, add more. If you want the taste of vinegar to be predominant, add some more of it. When you want to use the capers, wash them and add olive oil and vinegar to them. Eat and enjoy, Allah the Exalted willing. You can use the same method for caper sprouts and berries. Remember this, and succeed with the power and strength of Allah.

Chapter Five: on pickling aubergines, onions, and turnips[24]

428. Pickling aubergines[25]

Peel fresh aubergines and scrape off the calyces. Split them lengthwise without dividing the pieces completely. If the aubergines are large, cut them into six or eight pieces; if they are small, into four, five or three. You can also slice them into rounds. Throw the pieces in a large pot with fresh water and salt, and place it over a fire. When it has come to a boil once or twice, remove it from the fire, take out the aubergine pieces, and leave them on a sieve or wooden board to drain off their water. Take an

---

Corriente 1997: 403; Ibn Mubārak Shāh 2020: 107 (note 497); al-Baghdādī 2021: 43.

24 This is the title in BL Or5927 (fol. 194r.); the printed edition omits the reference to onions and turnips.

25 There were some lacunae and omissions in the edition, which were supplemented with instructions from BL Or5927 (fol. 194r.–v.).

earthenware jar, which is pitch-coated or glazed both inside and outside, and put the aubergines in it. Taste it, and if you find that it is not salty enough, add some more, and then pour on vinegar and fresh water, as described above.[26] Keep an eye on the aubergines and if you see that the water has gone down, add some more. Cover and seal[27] with mud. If you want to cook the aubergines in, for instance, a *jarīriyya*[28] or a *Burāniyya*,[29] or any other vinegary dishes, take the aubergines out and wash them before cooking them in any way you like, Allah the Exalted willing. If you prefer, you can boil the aubergines and then add some crushed tender celery called parsley[30] in one half, and crushed fresh mint in the other half. This will give it a wonderful fragrance.

429. Pickling onions[31]

Take good-quality onions that have not been affected by rain (i.e. that are not soggy), and use your hands to pare off the roots and their thin peels. Next, take good honey, and put as much as you require in a kneading tub. Take vinegar and water in the previously mentioned proportions, and beat everything until it is all blended. Then taste and, if you find that sweetness prevails, add some vinegar, but not too much. Take nigella seeds, clean them, and add as many to the liquid as you like. Do the same with salt. Take a large earthenware pitch-coated or glazed jar and put the onions inside. Pour in the liquid until they are immersed, and then close off the jar, tying off the mouth with something that does not let the air through. Leave for three days, and then open it. If you see that there is not enough liquid left, add some more and taste it. If you find that it is lacking in honey, vinegar or salt, top

26 In the edition, the last section of the sentence reads: 'Afterwards, let them dry and put them in a varnished or glazed earthenware container, and add salt.'

27 From this point on, the text in the edition is much more abridged and incomplete, and continues as follows: '... until you want to eat them, as is done in al-Andalus or in Greece during the aubergine season. [...] Put crushed celery in the slits you have cut in the aubergine. [...] Then sprinkle on aromatic spices and serve. If you want to, you can bake them in the oven. The goal is for them to remain whole in the bowl, just as they are.'

28 I have not been able to identify this dish, and it cannot be excluded that it is a scribal error.

29 See recipe No. 100.

30 This is a reference to *karafs Rūmī* ('Roman celery') and *karafs waḥshī* ('wild celery'); Ibn Janāḥ 2020: Nos. 152, 447, 540.

31 Recipes Nos. 429–46 can only be found in BL Or5927, fols. 194r.–196v.

up with whichever is appropriate. Seal with clay and leave until it is required, at which time take the amount you want, and then tie off the jar again, Allah the Exalted willing.

430. Pickling turnips

Take good-quality tender turnips, clean them and completely remove the peels. When you have finished the peeling, cut them lengthwise into medium-sized pieces. Put a large pot or cauldron with water over a fire, and add salt and crushed safflower. When the water has come to a rolling boil, put the turnip pieces in, and leave them until they have boiled once or twice before lifting them out and transferring them to a kneading tub. Add crushed saffron and stir until everything is coloured. Take mustard seeds, crush them well, and add the grounds to the turnip pieces, rubbing them with both your hands. When you have finished this, cover the tub with a wooden board and let the turnips cool down. Then take off the board, examine the contents and rub the turnips; if you see that there is only a little mustard on them, add some more. Take good-quality sweet raisins, clean them and then pound finely. Knead them with a sufficient amount of good vinegar into a smooth mixture which should neither be too light nor too thick. Take a clean basin, put a fine-meshed sieve on top of it, and place the raisins in it. Press them with your hands until their juices are released into the basin. Take a fine-meshed animal-hair sieve and strain the liquid once or twice. Remove the turnips from the kneading tub and put them in a jar that is pitch-coated or glazed inside and outside. Pour on the raisin juice, stirring it with the turnips by hand or with a ladle, and immerse them in it. Cover the container and leave it for three days, after which open it, stir it and taste the liquid. If there is too little mustard, add some more after crushing it (as before). Do the same with saffron, or safflower if you do not have any saffron. Use the pickled turnips in whatever you have cooked, or eat them by themselves after adding some olive oil. Eat and enjoy, Allah the Exalted willing.

Chapter Six: on pickling fish

431. One kind

Take large or medium-sized fish of any variety you can find, clean them, split them open at the back, remove the bones, and gut them. Lightly boil them in hot water and salt, and wash them very well afterwards with cold water. If the fish are large, cut them up, but if they are medium size, leave them whole. Remove the insides and gills, and salt them. Take good-quality vinegar, but if it is very sour add enough water to break its sharpness, and also put in crushed oregano and nigella seeds. Put the fish in a clean vessel with salt and pour on enough of the pickling liquid to immerse them. Tie off the mouth of the vessel, and monitor it to make sure that there is always enough liquid. If you want to use the fish, take out the required quantity, Allah the Exalted willing.

432. Another kind[32]

This is used for making *murrī*, and is a fish known as *ṣīr* (salted sprats).[33] Take as many of the smallest fish you want, and put them in a jar after having washed them. Leave them like this, and add half the weight of the fish in salt. Put the jar in the sun and insert a reed to stir the contents three times a day, until the fish and salt are blended into a single smooth mass, like a dough, the smell of the fish has gone, and the liquid has a reddish colour. When this is the case, move the jar out of the sun and to a well-aired location free from humidity. If you like to make *murrī* from it, add *shardhūn* oregano, also known as *markīra*,[34] and mix it in well until you are happy with the oregano flavour in the *ṣīr*. Use it as I shall explain elsewhere in this book,[35] Allah the Exalted willing.

---

32 Also see recipe No. 461 ('fish *murrī*').

33 These small fish formed the basis for a condiment, known as *ṣaḥnāt* (this could also denote the fish), which Ibn Biklārish (fol. 103v.) and al-Isrā'īlī (1992: 509) state is the Syriac (*al-lisān al-Suryānī*) word for 'salted fish'. The term could denote a variety of fish. Also see Ibn Mubārak Shāh 2020: 60–1; *Kanz*, 275 (Appendix, No. 37); *Wuṣla*, Nos. 8.54, 8.64–5. It was especially associated with Egypt, where it was a staple in the commoners' diet, together with clams and cheese (al-Baghdādī 2021: 118; trans., 119). Salt-cured fish has remained a delicacy in the country to this day, and is known locally as *fisīkh* or (in Upper Egypt) *mulūḥa*, while the Egyptian colloquial *ṣīr* denotes either small fish or (as an adjective) 'heavily salted'.

34 This is a variant spelling of *marqīra*, which actually denotes Cretan spikenard (*Valerian phu*); Corriente 1997: 499. Also see recipe No. 422.

35 See recipe No. 461.

Chapter Seven: on making vinegars

433. Making grape vinegar

In order to make this type of vinegar, take good-quality fully ripe grapes and put the bunches into a clean jar until it is filled up. Leave for three days and then add more bunches until you have all the grapes you require. Next, take other grapes and use a press to squeeze their juice into the jar until you have filled it up. If you want the vinegar to be white, then use white grapes; if you want it to be red, take black grapes. Put five *raṭls* or so of fresh water in the jar, and on top of it put something that prevents animals from falling into it, but which does not prevent the vapours from escaping. When the vinegar is ready, take it out and replace it with hot water. If you like, you can remove the bunches of grapes, squeeze them with a press and put the resultant liquid in two jars. Pour in hot fresh water in a proportion of one quarter of the liquid. This will make it excellent vinegar, with the power of Allah the Exalted.

434. Another recipe (fig vinegar)

If there are no grapes, take fresh and dried figs and put them in a clean jar, filling it up halfway. Pour on hot water all the way to the top of the jar, and put it in a warm location so that it can heat up until the figs rot and become sour. Then strain the liquid, and the result will be pure vinegar, with the power of Allah the Exalted.

435. Another recipe

If you want the vinegar to be sweet and sour, take good-quality vinegar, as much as you like, and add freshly squeezed sweet grape juice. Take however much is required for the desired level of sweetness. Put everything in a jar, cover the mouth with bitumen, and let it stand for an entire month. When you open it at the end of this period, you will find that the vinegar is sweet and sour. It will stay like this until it runs out, with the power of Allah the Exalted.

You can also take a jar of the juice with two jars of good-quality vinegar and put both in a clean cauldron or, better still, a large earthenware pot. Put it over a fire to cook and, when it is done and it has been reduced by a third, strain it and put it in a clean, pitch-coated or glazed container. Tie off the mouth before letting it stand for twenty days, after which the liquid is ready for use and you will find that the vinegar is sweet and sour, with the power of Allah the Exalted.

Alternatively, you can mix a jar of vinegar with two jars of juice and three jars of water, and then boil everything in an earthenware container until the liquid reduces by a third. Strain and store it in jars, as described before. Let it stand for twenty days and you will find that the vinegar is sweet and sour, with the power of Allah the Exalted.

436. Another kind, known as pepper vinegar

This is very digestible and fragrant, and is made by taking twenty-five *raṭls* of good-quality, very sour vinegar and two *ūqiyas* of good pepper wrapped in a pouch. Hang the pouch in the jar with vinegar, making sure it is immersed in it. Seal off the mouth of the container with clay and let it stand for eight days. When you open it up, you will find that the vinegar has a peppery taste. Use it how you like, with the power of Allah the Exalted.

437. Restoring vinegar that has faded

Take grape dregs and dry them out. Take four *raṭls*, together with three bunches [of grapes], and put them in a jar of faded vinegar. Seal the mouth with clay and leave it for three days. When you open it up, you will find that the vinegar has become very sour and strong again, with the power of Allah the Exalted.

438. Another recipe

Take a jar of vinegar and divide its contents between three jars. Take the vinegar of two of the jars and cook it until it is reduced by one-third. Then transfer it to the jar with the remaining third that has not been cooked. Seal the jar with clay and leave it to stand for eight days. When you open it up, you will find that the vinegar has become very sour and strong again, with the power of Allah the Exalted.

439. Another recipe

Take chickpeas and cook them in fresh water until they are tender. Strain them, and then take one part of the chickpea water and put it in ten parts of vinegar. This will make the vinegar very sour and strong again, with the power of Allah the Exalted.

440. Another recipe

Take one part of water that is as bitter [as vinegar], like sea water, and add one part of good-quality vinegar. Next, take some barley and steep it in the water for three days, after which strain it off, and mix it with the vinegar in one container. Put a little bit of fried barley in the container. As a result, the vinegar will have the same taste and sourness it did before it faded, with the power of Allah the Exalted.

441. Making a vinegar yeast starter

Take one *raṭl* of good-quality raisins and remove their pips before crushing them in a mortar until they become like dough. Add one *raṭl* of honey, two *raṭls* of good vinegar, and two *raṭls* of sour grape vinegar. Mix everything together well and then pour the mixture into a glazed container. Seal it off tightly with clay so that the air cannot touch the contents. Put the container out in the sun for a period of ten days if you are in a hot country, and forty days if it is one with a temperate climate. When the period is over, and you want to open the container, move it out of the sun and let it stand for a few days before opening it. When you do open it, be careful not to expose your face to the heat coming out of the container. When you want to make vinegar, take one *raṭl* of the yeast starter and dissolve it in ten *raṭls* of hot water, whisking it over a fire until it changes colour. Then remove from the fire, let it cool down, and strain before use, Allah the Exalted willing.

442. Testing vinegar to see whether it has been watered down

Take vinegar that you have doubts about and put borax,[36] that is to say

36 *bawraq* (also *bawrāq* < Persian *bawrah*). The Greek word *nítron* is the etymon of the Arabic *nāṭrūn* (also *niṭrūn*), a mixture of salt and soda, typically associated with Egypt. This should be distinguished from today's borax (sodium borate), known in Arabic as *tinkār* (from the Persian *tangar*), which gave the English 'tincal' and 'tincar' (crude borax, formerly imported from Tibet), or as *liḥām al-dhahab* ('gold solder'), *lizāq al-dhahab* ('gold glue') – both of which are calques from the Greek *chrysocolla* – and *milḥ al-ṣāgha* ('goldsmiths' salt'). According to an eleventh-century Andalusian agricultural manual (López y López 1990: 109; trans., 186), borax was used to accelerate olive growth; after roasting, it was soaked in water until it acquired the consistency of honey. The resultant paste was rubbed on the plant and the buds once every eight days, until the buds sprouted. Borax was used in cooking in a variety of ways. The Greek botanist Theophrastus (d. 287 BCE) said that it was used when boiling cabbage to improve its flavour. In medieval Arab cuisine, borax served to assist the cooking of meat (Ibn Buṭlān recommended adding borax, as well as wax

natron, into the container with the vinegar. If it bubbles and foams, that means that it is pure, unadulterated. However, if it boils but there is no foam, that means that it is mixed with water. This is how vinegar is tested. Know this.

443. Making squill vinegar[37]

Take an earthenware container with a glazed exterior which is made with a partition inside. Then take squills, thoroughly clean away all the rotten and harmful bits, and cut them with a wooden stick, not with an iron one. Then take one squill, remove its outer peel, slice each layer into wide sections with a wooden knife, and thread them on a string with a wooden needle. When this is done, take some very sour vinegar and pour it into the container, making sure that there is a finger width between it and the partition. The quantity of vinegar should be the same in each container, and have a weight of four *raṭls*. Put in one-third of a *raṭl* of squill for each *qafīz* (of vinegar). Those who want to make it strong can do so by cutting up half an *ūqiya* of squill cores into the vinegar – but take care, since too much of it can make it bitter. Then take thin palm leaves, cut them up, and place the pieces over the partition to form a lattice. On top of it, layer lemon balm, mint, sweet marjoram and wild mint,[38] and stuff with pennyroyal or broad-leaved

---

and watermelon peel, to the pot), bread-making (as a glaze and leavening agent), and, more rarely, as an ingredient, in a *maḍīra* (see Nos. 168–9). It was also used to preserve colour, since some recipes recommend boiling turnip, beans, cabbage, wild mustard and chard with borax to keep them green. See Käs 2010: I, 325–37; Amar & Lev 118–20: Ibn Janāḥ 2020: Nos. 503, 538; Renaud & Colin 1934: 42 (No. 92), 173 (No. 473); *Wuṣla*, Nos. 5.76, 7.77; *Waṣf*, 321, 460; Ibn Mubārak Shāh 2020: 5 (note 8); Ibn Buṭlān 1990: 123; Dalby 2003: 234.

37 For another vinegar recipe with squill (also known as wild onion), see al-Warrāq 1987: 51; Ibn Jazla, fol. 86r. According to the latter, squill vinegar (preferably made with white squill) was useful for a variety of conditions, including sciatica, asthma, joint- and headaches, urethral stones and excess black bile, whereas gargling with it strengthens the teeth, improves the voice and removes foul breath. To obtain its beneficial effects, it should be drunk first thing in the morning on an empty stomach.

38 The Arabic *ghubayrā'* (*ghubayra*) – the diminutive of *ghabrā'* ('grey') – is usually a translation of Dioscorides's *glēkhon*, pennyroyal (*Mentha pulegium*), alongside *bulāyuh*, or its variant *fūlayū*, which appears later on in the sentence, and is sometimes equated with 'wild mint' (*fūdhanj barrī*). It may refer to a particular type of pennyroyal here. In the botanical literature, *ghubayrā'* could denote a wide variety of plants, including the sorb tree (*Sorbus domestica*), several species of *Cotoneaster* (for example, *atlanticus*, *nummularius*, *granatensis*), Assyrian plum (*Cordia myxa*),

thyme.[39] Take the pieces of squill that are on the string, put them on the fragrant herbs,[40] and layer some more of the latter on top. Then cover the container with an earthenware bowl, placing it over the mouth of the container in such a way that the air does not reach the contents. Let it stand for forty days. If you want, you can change the herbs after twenty days. At the end of the period, gingerly open the container and remove the herbs and the squill, leaving in the pieces of palm leaf. Strain the vinegar in a basket made of esparto grass after washing it in water to remove the smell. Store the vinegar in small, glazed earthenware or glass containers, and use it, for instance, when cooking aubergines, with fish, or anything else you like. Seal the containers with olive oil so as to protect the vinegar from the effects of the air, Allah the Exalted willing.

444. Sour grape vinegar

This type is made by taking as many unripe sour grapes as you want and crushing them well in a wooden or glazed mortar. Squeeze their juice until there is none left in them, and then strain it before putting it into glass containers. Put them in the sun and filter the liquid through a thick

Cretan dittany (*Origanum dictamnus*), hawthorn (*Crataegus monogyna*) and hogweed (*Heracleum sphondylium*). See al-Ishbīlī 2004–10: *passim*; Renaud & Colin 1934: 185–6 (No. 436); Dietrich 1988: II, 376-7 (No. III.30); al-Isrā'ilī 1992: 300; Ibn Janāḥ 2020: No. 1092. Al-Rāzī (1987: 155) said it had astringent and anti-emetic properties.

39 *nammām*, which was applied to multiple varieties of mint, and is often identified as spearmint (*Mentha spicata*), as well as wild thyme (*Thymus serpyllum*). According to Ibn al-Ḥashshā' (1940: 87, No. 811), it is a kind of basil known among the people of the Maghrib as sandalwood (*ṣandal*); it is similar to mint, and denotes whorled mint (*sīsanbar*). This is also reported by Ibn Janāḥ (2020: No. 645), who traced the name of the herb to the fact its sweet odour 'reveals' (*namma*) itself and the person perfumed with it. Al-Ishbīlī defined *nammām* as 'a species of mint (*na'na'*) and a variety of thyme (*sa'tar*). López y López 1990: 371–3; Meyerhof 1940: 125 (No. 255); al-Ishbīlī 2004–10: Nos. 196, 275, 3115; al-Dīnawarī 1973: No 557; al-Kindī 1948: 286–8.

40 *aḥbāq*, the plural of *ḥabaq* (a word of Syriac origin), refers to a generic class of odoriferous plants, mainly thyme, mint and basil varieties. Al-Ishbīlī (2004–10: Nos. 1632–53) identified nine broad *ḥabaq* categories, including *ḥabaq bustānī* (mint) and *ḥabaq turunjānī* (lemon balm). Ibn al-Bayṭār (1992: I, 254) suggests it corresponds to the Persian *fūtanj* (Arabic *fūdhanj*) – also a collective name for a number or aromatic species (mainly in the Lamiaceae family) – and resembles *nammām* (see recipe No. 443), which grows mainly in water. Ibn Luyūn 1988: 53; Corriente 1997: 114; López y López 1990: 279–80; Meyerhof 1940: 26 (No. 48); al-Dīnawarī 1974: No. 776; Lev & Amar 2008: 30.

cloth every three days. Add a little bit of good-quality salt. Continue to filter until you cannot see any dregs at the bottom of the containers. Leave the juice to ferment in the sun for forty days, and then seal the containers with olive oil and move them to an airy location, Allah the Exalted willing.

445. Another recipe

Take as many prime-quality unripe sour grapes as you want and proceed as described in the previous recipe. Strain the juice and put it in a large glazed pot over a moderate fire. Boil until the liquid is reduced by about a quarter, and then remove the pot from the fire. Leave it to cool down, and then strain the liquid. Transfer it to glass containers and seal with olive oil, Allah the Exalted willing.

446. Another recipe

If you need it more urgently at the start of the season, take bunches of unripe sour grapes and put them in a clean pot with enough water to cover them. Put the pot over a fire and, when it has boiled three times or so, take it down and squeeze the juice out of the bunches. Strain the liquid and pour it on meat, Allah the Exalted willing.

447. Lime vinegar[41]

Take fully ripe, good-quality limes and wash away the dirt and other impurities. Split them in half lengthwise and squeeze the [juice] into a bowl until you have as much as you want. Strain through a thin cloth, pour the liquid in glass containers, and add a sufficient amount of salt. Leave them somewhere in the sun, and then strain once or twice. Seal the containers with olive oil, and use any way you see fit afterwards, Allah the Exalted willing.

448. Mint vinegar

Take as much fresh and tender mint as you like. Clean and wash it in fresh water to remove all of the dirt and bad bits, before chopping it up and placing it in a kneading tub. Pour on its weight in good white

41 The translation of this recipe and the next includes instructions from the recipes in BL Or5927 (fols. 196v.–197r.), as they are more detailed than those of the edition (2012: 261).

vinegar, leave for a while, and then put it in the distilling flask (cucurbit),[42] as you do for rose water, and then tighten the top onto the cap (*anbīq*). Put it over a fire and leave it until distillation and the vinegar has dried out. Remove the distillate and then refill the distilling flask after washing it clean, and do the same as before. Strain the vinegar distillate and transfer it to glass containers. Use when you want to with roast meat, fish, and so on, Allah the Exalted willing. If you want, you can also use lemon balm (instead of mint).

Chapter Eight: on making macerated, cooked, and other kinds of *murrī*

449. Macerated *murrī*[43]

42 *qādūs al-taqṭīr* (lit. 'dripping'). The distillation process described here is done with an alembic, which is a corruption of the Arabic word *al-anbīq* (itself a transliteration of the Greek *ambix*). While today 'alembic' refers to the entire still, *al-anbīq* only denoted the cap placed on the vessel that is heated up, the 'cucurbit', known in Arabic as *qarʿa* ('gourd'), *qādūs* being the Andalusian term. The cucurbit contains a liquid (usually water) and the substance to be distilled (mint, in this case). The joint between the two components is sealed to make it airtight, and then the *anbīq* is connected with the 'recipient' (*qābila*) vessel into which the distillate will drip. Though invented in ancient Greece in the fourth century BCE, the instrument was perfected and used extensively by Islamic chemists and alchemists. Al-Ṭighnarī (2006: 398–402) discusses the composition of the best still. The word *qādūs* also denoted a water-wheel bucket, a frying dish (as well as the dish cooked in it), and a dry measure (*ca.* 16 pounds/4 kg). García Sánchez 1998: 135; Corriente 1997: 417; Sauvaire 1884: 517.

43 *murrī naqīʿ*; this recipe is very similar to al-Ṭighnarī's (2006: 119ff.). This type of *murrī* was the only one that found favour with the author of the *Andalusian*, because of its taste and benefits. In general, however, he advised against eating *murrī*, which explains why the book contains only one recipe. Less good, though still acceptable, is the *murrī* made from grape juice (see recipes Nos. 455–7, below) and aromatic spices but without burned bread. However, the one made with scorched honey and bread and other things should be avoided at all times since it causes black bile and has neither benefit nor flavour (*Anwāʿ*, 55; BNF, fol. 23v.). According to Ibn al-Ḥashshā' (1940: 27, No. 726), what was known in the Maghrib as *al-naqīʿ* is, in fact, Nabataean *murrī* (*murrī nabaṭī*). Ibn Biklārish (fol. 90v.), for his part, equated *murrī* with *murrī naqīʿ*, and says it is also known as *murdasana* and *murrī al-bawdhaq* – with *bawdhaq* (a variant of *būdhaj* – see below) being barley that has been kneaded and left to rot with fig leaves before mixing in wheat flour, salt and water, followed by salted bread and burnt bread. Afterwards, it is mashed. According to al-Uryūlī (1983: No. 101), it

This is made at the end of March (*Māris*) by grinding whole good-quality barley that is not smelly or rotten after leaving it out in the sun for a day.[44] Sift the bran out and knead into a firm dough without using salt. Shape the dough in the form of sugar loaves[45] and use your finger [or the handle of a ladle] to make a hole in the centre of each one. When this is done (make sure the dough is tight), take a large wooden board, which should be raised two spans off the ground, and throw on the bran. Next, take the loaves and wrap them in wild fig leaves, which you also stuff in the holes of the loaves. Arrange the loaves on the board, raised above the ground in a place where the air is dry but the sun cannot reach them. Sprinkle bran on them, and cover with wild fig leaves. Leave the loaves like this for twenty days, after which you flip them over on the board and add leaves and bran to the side which is now on top. Leave like this for another twenty days. Then remove the leaves and bran. The loaves will have dried out, and the sign that they have rotted is that they are covered in green mould tinged with red. This is the stage at which the loaves are called *būdhaq*.[46] Vigorously scrape them with a knife to clean away all the mould and other things from them. Break them up and pound them until you get something that looks like flour, and then sieve. Anything that does not pass through the sieve is pounded again until it has all turned into flour. Next, take sifted bran and half its quantity in pure ground white salt, as well as their combined weight in fresh water. Put everything in the kneading tub all at once, or in several stages, depending on how much

---

acts in a similar way to vinegar, warms the stomach, and dissolves the humours in it. For similar recipes, see *Kanz*, No. 150; Ibn Mubārak Shāh 2020: 44–5.

44 The second instruction is only found in the recipe in BL Or5927 (fol. 197r.–v.), which has been used to complement and amend the edition (2012: 262–3) where necessary, with variants being enclosed in square brackets.

45 *jamājim* (singular *jamjama*); the word also denoted pine cone, a measure for corn, etc., or a wooden bowl (whose capacity originally was that of the measure). See Lane 1863–74: II, 450; Corriente 1997: 101. Al-Ṭighnarī (2006: 119) has the equally plausible *jāmāt* (singular *jām*), which refers to a type of vase, as well as a (conical) sugar mould, also known as *ṭabarzad* (though in the Near East this referred to a high-quality white sugar). Al-Ḥashshā' 1932: 61 (No. 565); Dozy 1881: I, 168; Ibn Mubārak Shāh 2020: 17–18 (note 58).

46 A more usual form is *būdaj* (also *būdhaj*), which is how it appears in al-Warrāq, whereas al-Baghdādī (fol. 55r.) and *Waṣf* (404) have *fūdhaj*. This constitutes the basis for all kinds of fermented condiments, and can also be made with salty bread (al-Warrāq 1987: 98).

the tub can accommodate. Each time you finish a batch, decant it to a clean fragrant earthenware jar, which previously contained olive oil. This should be done in the evening. Fill the jar up to the neck so that the contents can 'boil' (i.e. ferment), and be stirred. Then put in anise, fennel seeds,[47] coriander seeds and nigella – four *ūqiyas* of each; half a *raṭl* of oregano leaves; a handful of royal oregano stems;[48] citron leaves; chopped fennel (leaves); wild fig leafstalks; and a pine cone from which the seeds have been removed.[49] Make sure the quantities are enough for one *rubʿ* of the barley flour, called *būdhaq*, and increase or reduce portions accordingly. Then pour olive oil into the jar, slightly more than the amount required to cover the dissolved flour, and also put in a three-pronged stick made from wood of the wild-fig tree. This is called a *dūṭabūl*[50] and is used for stirring the contents of the jar. Tie the mouth of the jar with a clean cloth, and cover it with the skin taken from a leather jug[51] that has had olive oil in it. Make sure that the part that has the hair on it is facing the cloth. Move the jar to a spot where the rising and setting sun shines on it. Stir it three times a day and leave it out for twenty days. At the end of this period take wheat flour that has had its bran sifted out, half of the quantity you took at the beginning, that is to say one-sixth of the present total amount. Divide into three parts, and knead one-third with yeast, but without salt. Leave it until it is about to bubble (i.e. ferment), and shape the dough into thin, round loaves with holes in them. Bake them in the oven until they set, but do not fully cook them. Remove them from the oven when they are still soft, and at that point crumble them into the jar, and quickly cover the mouth of the jar with the cloth and the leather skin to prevent the release of

47 The fact that the author uses the standard Arabic *rāziyānaj* for fennel, rather than the Andalusian *basbās*, which occurs throughout the text, is an indication of the foreign (Eastern) origin of this recipe.

48 The printed text has *lūlī*, rather than the correct *mulūkī*, which appears in BL Or5927. It is unclear which variety is intended here.

49 The ingredients and measures differ slightly from those by al-Ṭighnarī (2006: 121), who calls for a handful of crushed oregano; a handful of coriander, garlic, caraway, and citron leaves; one *ūqiya* of fennel; and half an *ūqiya* of nigella.

50 This term is missing from BL Or5927 (fol. 197v.), which simply refers to 'a stick that should have three branches'. It is a misspelling of *rū/uṭ<a>bāl*, an Andalusian Arabic word for 'rake'. See Marín in Monferrer-Sala & Al Jallad 2010: 45; Corriente 1997: 211.

51 *ẓarf*, a receptacle for holding liquids, made out of sewn-up goat's (or cow's) skin; Dozy 1881: II, 82–3.

steam. After leaving it for a day and a night, remove the cover and use your hands to rub the pieces inside until they dissolve and form one mass. Stir the jar, as you did before, for a further seven days. On the eighth day, knead the second third of the flour, as described, and also dissolve the pieces in the jar as you did before. Leave this for another seven days. On the eighth day, knead the remaining third of the flour, and once again proceed in exactly the same way. So, the loaves are added in three instalments over a twenty-one day period. Leave the jar for a further three days, and continue stirring as before.

Next, take an oblong, narrow-bottomed esparto-grass basket [three fingers wide at the bottom and three spans at the top], wash it with water, and put it out in the sun to get rid of the odour of the treated esparto grass. Attach handles to a basket, suspend it from a wooden beam, and put a tub underneath it. Pour everything that is in the jar into this draining vessel[52] to strain off the liquid. Once this is done, transfer all of it to glazed bowls which are placed in the sun – they should be covered at night and uncovered during the day – until a thickened layer of salt appears on the surface of the *murrī*, which is a sign that it is done. Gingerly remove the salt – this should be done either in the morning or in the evening – strain the *murrī* and put it in earthenware bowls that are glazed inside and out. Tie the mouths of the jars, and leave them out in the sun during the day, and cover them at night. Do this for five days, after which store them. This is the *murrī* base,[53] or 'first' *murrī*. Put the sediment back into the jar and pour on enough hot water. Stir it in the sun for ten days or more, three times a day. Add the loaves twice over a ten-day period, but make sure that this time they are fully baked until golden brown. Next, crush them to powder in a mortar and add this to the jar. After two days, empty the jar into the esparto filter and strain, as described, and then put the liquid in glazed vessels, which are placed in the sun. When the salt on top has thickened, remove it and strain the *murrī*. Transfer it to glazed vessels and leave it out in the sun until it is done before storing, Allah the Exalted willing. This is the 'second' *murrī*.

If you want, you can put some of the first *murrī* in a small oil-smeared [pitched] jar and add honey and crushed carob to it. This makes it

52 *maṣṣāl* ('dripper'); Corriente 1997: 504.
53 *ra's la-murrī*; Corriente 1997: 196.

utterly fragrant and delicious,[54] especially for those who serve it as a side, without cooking it (in a dish). Bear this in mind.

Some people also use a linen cloth as a strainer. If you use the esparto grass one, wash it first in water and dry it out in the sun before using it so as to get rid of any esparto treatment odours.[55] Remember this. Even the slightest inattention or rush in this respect will undo all of the work done. Also beware that one of the requirements for *murrī* is that no man or woman in a state of ritual impurity can take part in the making of it – including moving it from one place to another – or even go near when it is being made. Even a slight carelessness in this regard can spoil it. Remember this, and may Allah grant you success and strength.

450. Another kind

Take as much good-quality barley as you want, grind it, sift out the bran, and knead into a firm dough without salt. Shape the dough into round, flat loaves, two-and-a-half fingers thick and weighing twenty *ūqiyas*,[56] and puncture three holes in the centre of each. Spread the barley bran on a wooden board raised above the ground covered with wild fig leaves. Put the loaves on top, and then cover them with more wild fig leaves and bran. Place the board with the loaves in a place where it is exposed to dry air, but not to the sun. Leave them until they are dry and then remove the bran and leaves. Let the loaves dry and return the leaves on the sides, but remove those on top. When the loaves are completely dry [and mouldy], use a knife to thoroughly scrape away the leaves, bran and mould that are sticking to them. Make sure everything is removed, and no residue remains. Leave them for another three days until all the moisture has gone and they are completely dry. Next, crumble them with a pruning knife, until the pieces resemble chickpeas, and then grind and sift them to a flour. This is called *būdhaq*, the *murrī* base. Take as much of this as you want, add the same quantity of wheat flour with bran sifted out, and half that amount of purified crushed salt, that is to say one-fifth of everything.

54 *binna* (also *banna*), an Andalusian and North African Arabic term, which has survived in the Moroccan vernacular as *tbennen* ('to become tasty') and *bnīn* ('delicious'). Corriente 1997: 67.

55 This instruction appears here in BL Or5927 only, whereas the edition has it when the esparto basket is first mentioned.

56 One *raṭl* and a quarter according to BL Or5927, fol. 198r.

Put it all in a large earthenware jar that has had olive oil in it and has a fragrant smell. Place it in an elevated location, where the sun rises and sets on it. Take the flour and the salt, and beat everything on a leather ground cover[57] so that it is all mixed. Then put everything in the jar. This should be done in the evening. Pour fresh water in the jar until you obtain the consistency of *ḥarīra*.[58] Whip it with your hands until everything is dissolved and blended into a smooth mixture. Pour in enough good-quality olive oil to cover everything, and then add fennel stalks, a handful of oregano, two *ūqiyas* of nigella, half an *ūqiya* of citron leaves, fennel seeds and two pine cones. Insert a three-pronged stick made of wild fig-tree wood, as mentioned above, and use it to stir the contents of the jar twice a day, in the morning and evening, for seven days. Tie the mouth of the jar with a clean cloth, and cover it with the skin taken from a nice-smelling leather jug that has had olive oil in it, as described above. The jar should be filled up to the neck so the mixture can 'boil' (ferment). Bear this in mind. On the eighth day, take good-quality sifted wheat flour – half of what was mixed at the beginning – and split it into three parts. Knead the first third into an unleavened dough,[59] without salt, make medium-sized round loaves with it, and bake them in the oven. When they are close to being done, take them out and crumble them up and, while they are still hot, put them in the jar. Cover the mouth of the jar so as to trap the steam. Leave for three days. When you open the jar up on the fourth day, thoroughly mash the pieces with your hands and rub them along the walls of the jar until they are dissolved and the mixture looks like the one that was in the jar. On the fourth day, also take the second third of the above-mentioned flour, do what you did with the first batch, and leave for another three days. On the fourth day the bread pieces are uncovered and mashed, as mentioned.

The remaining third of the flour is used in exactly the same way as the first two batches. Continue to stir the jar with the stick, as you did

---

57 *naṭ'*, a piece of leather (often round), that served as a tablecloth, also known as *sufra*. Kazimirski 1860: II, 1284.

58 Ibn 'Abd Rabbih (1983: VIII, 5) defines this as 'soup made from fat and flour'. Today this denotes a spicy soup, which is very popular in North Africa (especially Morocco). Ibn Zuhr (1992: 14; trans., 50) claimed that, if it is made from wheat, it produces a heavy, crude humour; instead, it should be made with barley, sorghum or millet flour.

59 See recipe No. 4.

before, for forty days, twice a day, once in the evening and once in the morning. At the end of this period, take wheat flour that has also been sifted of its bran, but only half the same amount as before, and knead half of it into an unleavened dough, without salt. Shape this dough into round, flat loaves, each weighing about half a *raṭl*. Prick small holes in all of them, and then send them to the oven. Bake them at a very high temperature so that they turn deep brown or black, as the degree of baking will determine the colour of the *murrī*. Then take them out, and break them up, before grinding or pounding them into a flour-like consistency. Put the mixture in the jar and stir vigorously. Continue stirring the mixture twice a day, once in the morning and once in the evening, for a period of twenty days.

Then knead the second part of the flour, as mentioned above, and bake it at a very high temperature. If you want the *murrī* to be black, you should bake the bread until it turns black. If you prefer it to be light brown, then only bake it until it has turned golden. When this is done, add the bread to the earthenware jar and diligently stir it twice a day, in the morning and evening, until the end of autumn. When you want to use the *murrī*, first wash the esparto-grass strainer to get rid of any treatment odours, and then hang it out to dry, as mentioned above. Pour everything from the jar into it so that it can drip into a vessel underneath the strainer until only the sediment remains in the strainer. After carefully checking that it is well strained, transfer the liquid that has been collected to earthenware containers glazed inside and out, and seal with sweet olive oil, which can also be used, Allah the Exalted willing. Then return the sediment to the jar, and pour a sufficient quantity of hot water over it. Stir the jar three times a day over a period of eight days. Add baked, crumbled bread, as before, and leave for a further eight days, but do not be remiss in stirring it. Then strain it and use it in cooking, Allah the Exalted willing.

451. Cooked *murrī*[60]

Take one *mudd* of wheat or [and] barley flour, one *mudd* of ground salt, and a quarter of an *ūqiya* each of [crushed] coriander seeds, nigella,

60 The translations of recipes 451–4 are supplemented with instructions from BL Or5927 (fol. 199r.–v.), as it is more detailed than the edition (2012: 266–7). Variants are enclosed in brackets.

anise, and fennel seeds. Mix everything together with the flour and salt, knead into two round, flat loaves, and thoroughly bake them in the oven at a high temperature [until they are deep brown]. When they are done, crumble and grind them into a flour, and put it in a new pot with three *rubʿs* [three-quarters of a *rubʿ*] of fresh water, a pine cone emptied of its seeds, two *raṭls* of apples, two *raṭls* of cut and peeled quinces, and two *raṭls* of strained and skimmed honey. Bake the mixture in the oven overnight. In the morning, [vigorously] mash it and then leave it for two hours before straining it through a clean cloth and transferring it to a glazed container. This is the first *murrī*. Then, return the sediment to the pot and pour fresh water over it, half as much as the first time, and leave in the oven overnight. [Thoroughly] mash it as before [leave for an hour], and then strain and use, [Allah the Exalted willing].

452. Another kind

Take wheat and barley flour with its bran and crushed salt, one *mudd* of each [it is better to weigh than to measure], as well as crushed coriander seeds, nigella, fennel seeds and anise – one *ūqiya* of each. [Mix everything and] knead it very well [with a little water, and then shape the dough into two round, flat loaves. Take them to the oven and leave them until they are fully baked and have turned deep brown.] Take one of the loaves out of the oven just as it begins to roast, leaving the other until it is almost black. Then crumble them up, grind them as finely as flour, and put the crumbs in a new pot. Pour in one-and-a-quarter *raṭl* of honey and three-quarters of a *rubʿ* of [fresh] water. Cover [and seal] the pot [with clay] and leave it in the oven overnight. [Take it out in the morning and] mash what is in the pot, leave it for a while [until the sediment has settled], and then strain into glazed earthenware containers. Return the sediment to the pot with half as much water as you used the first time, and leave it in the oven overnight. Then strain and use, [Allah the Exalted willing]. If you like, you can colour it with ground saffron, [with the strength of Allah the Exalted].

453. Another kind

Take two *mudds* of good flour, one *mudd* of salt, and a handful each of nigella, anise and crushed coriander seeds. Vigorously knead everything, and shape the resultant dough into medium-sized round, flat loaves. Leave them to bake in the oven overnight. Take them out in the morning, and you will see that they are musk-coloured. Thoroughly pound the loaves until you get something resembling broad beans or chickpeas in size, and put them with everything else that was crushed in an earthenware pot filled with more fresh water than needed to cover the mixture. Also add a *raṭl* of honey, citron leaves, fennel stalks and oregano. Let is stand for a day, and then take it to the oven to bake. Leave it until it is done, and has thickened and changed colour. At that point, remove it, and then mash and strain it through a piece of fabric. Taste it and if you find that it lacks salt, add some, and then colour with some [one *dirham* of] crushed saffron. This is the first *murrī*. Put it aside. If you want to cook it at home, then you should boil it in a tinned cauldron or tinned pot over a fire until it has thickened, as described above. Then strain and store. Return the sediment to the pot and pour in a third [two-thirds] of the amount of water you used at the beginning. Cover and seal the pot, and leave it in the oven overnight. Take it out in the morning and strain it; this is the 'second' *murrī*. If you want to make a 'third' *murrī*, return the sediment to the pot and add half the amount of water that was used for the second *murrī*. Leave it in the oven overnight and, when you take it out in the morning, strain it and mix it with the second *murrī*. Return it to the pot and cook it until it thickens. Or, put this *murrī* in ceramic bowls out in the sun until it thickens and salt gathers on the surface. Then strain and put away, Allah the Exalted willing.

454. Another kind

Take three *raṭls* of wheat flour and one *raṭl* of salt. Knead them into a tight dough, shape into round, flat loaves, and bake them in the oven long enough for them to turn black. Remove them, pound them into flour, and put them in a new pot with twenty *raṭls* of fresh water and one *raṭl* of good-quality honey, as well as crushed coriander seeds, nigella and fennel – one *ūqiya* of each. Tie each of these spices into a cloth, and add them to the pot. Put a lid on the pot, seal it with clay, and leave it in the oven overnight. Remove it the following morning and thoroughly mash what is in the pot. Leave the mixture for an hour, and then strain and put aside. Return the sediment to the pot and add ten *raṭls* of water, half a *raṭl* of honey, half the weight of the spices, and some salt. Again leave in the oven overnight, mash what is in the pot, strain it, and then put aside. Use when needed, Allah the Exalted willing.

455. Making *murrī* with sweet must (freshly squeezed grape juice)[61]
Mix six *raṭls* of sifted barley flour with a third of that amount of salt. Knead them with water, and then work the dough in the shape of a bread loaf. Bake it in the oven until it browns and has the colour of musk.[62] Next, mix four *raṭls* of wheat flour with one-third of that amount of salt. Knead into a firm dough, and bake [the loaf] as you did before. When this is done, leave the loaf to cool down, and break it up into medium-sized pieces. Put everything into a large new pot and pour in enough sweet grape juice (the must) to cover the bread pieces by two-thirds of a hand span. Add ten citron leaves, carobs, quinces, apples, a pine cone and a fennel stalk. Make sure there is a distance of two-thirds of a span between the lid of the pot and the grape juice, so that it can boil without spilling over. Seal the mouth of the pot with clay, but leave a hole for it to breathe. Put the pot in the oven and leave it there overnight, away from the fire. Take it out in the morning, and strain it. Next, return the sediment to the pot, pour in another batch of must, and leave it to bake in the oven. Then, take it out and strain the *murrī*. If you see that it is too runny, resume cooking it at home until it thickens, and then transfer it to a glazed jar. Seal it with a generous amount of good-quality olive oil on top to prevent it getting mouldy. When you want to use it in something, employ all means to remove the olive oil so that nothing of it gets mixed into what you happen to be cooking, if it involves pure water, etc., Allah the Exalted willing.

61 *musṭār*, which goes back to the Latin *mustarium*, i.e. 'related to *vinum mustum* ("young wine")', probably via the Greek *moustárion*. In addition to 'must', *musṭār* denoted 'young wine' (Corriente 1997: 502). The title is that of the recipe in BL Or5927 (fols. 199v.–200r.), which has been used to complement the edition (2012: 267).

62 I follow BL Or5927 (fol. 199v.) here, which has *miskī* (as in recipe No. 453), rather than the clearly defective *washkī* (*al-lawn*) of the edition, which lacks the second half.

456. Another kind of must *murrī*[63]

Knead three *raṭls* of wheat flour into a firm dough, [shape into a loaf] and bake it at a high temperature in the oven until it turns black. Then mash it and put it in a [clean] pot with a *qadaḥ* of must [for each three *raṭls* of bread], as well as three-quarters of a *raṭl* of salt. Cover the pot with a perforated lid and add quinces, fennel seeds, nigella, a bunch of oregano, [two handfuls of oregano], and citron leaves to the must. Also add some honey if you want to increase the sweetness of the *murrī*. Bake it in the oven overnight, and [when you take it out in the morning,] strain the *murrī* [through a woollen towel] and put it aside. This is the *murrī* base. Taste it, and if you find that it lacks salt, add some. [If you see that it is too runny], pour it into bowls and place them out in the sun [until you are satisfied with the consistency.] Alternatively, you can cook it over a fire until it thickens, and then put it in a glazed container for storage. Return the sediment to the pot alongside salt and water, and put it in the oven overnight, as mentioned above, after which strain and use it.

457. Another similar recipe

Mix three *mudds* [of equal quantities] of wheat flour [and] of barley flour and one and a half *mudds* of salt. Knead this into a very firm dough, [shape it into a loaf,] and bake it in the oven until it is dark brown. Next, grind it until it becomes like flour, and put the mixture in a large [clean] pot with twenty-five *raṭls* of sweet must [or however much it can accommodate]. Add a bunch [handful] of oregano, a quarter of a *raṭl* [each] of fennel stalks, citron leaves, [crushed] coriander seeds, and nigella. [Put the pot over a fire] and cook until half of the must has evaporated. [Remove from the fire], mash what spices there are in it with the flour, and then strain [through a densely woven towel]. Store in a glazed container, and use after three months [, Allah the Exalted willing].

458. 'Instant' *murrī*, as a substitute for macerated *murrī*

[Take] one *raṭl* of wheat or barley flour, and put it in an earthenware casserole dish with two *ūqiyas* of salt and water. [Put it over a fire and

63 The parts enclosed in brackets in this recipe and the next two are additions from BL Or5927 (fol. 200r.–v.).

stir the flour until it turns brown and acquires the colour of musk. Then remove the pot from the fire and throw on two *ūqiyas* of crushed salt and enough fresh water to ensure the flour mixture is sufficiently liquid. Leave it to cool down, and] then thoroughly mash it with your hands. [Strain and put it to one side. Take a bit of] honey and put it in a [small] glazed earthenware casserole. [Cook it until it turns very black.] Strain, and add it to the previously strained liquid. Add [a cloth pouch containing] fennel, nigella, crushed coriander seeds, anise, oregano and cinnamon. [Then it is ready for use, Allah the Exalted willing.]

459. Another similar recipe[64]

Take one *raṭl* of honey, one of cut-up onion, and one of crushed salt dissolved in twice that amount of water (that is to say six *raṭls*). Bake it in a new pot in the oven overnight. Take it out in the morning, thoroughly mash and strain, and then use, Allah the Exalted willing. If it is runny, put it out in the sun in ceramic bowls until you are happy with its consistency. Know this and act accordingly, Allah the Exalted willing.

460. Another kind of *murrī*, made in a day and a night[65]

Knead two *raṭls* of barley flour with half a *raṭl* of salt, and bake it in the form of loaves until they are burnt. Then crumble everything and soak it in hot water (enough to cover it) for a day and a night, and then strain. Take a *raṭl* of raisins and the same amount of carob, together with nigella, fennel, sesame and anise – one *ūqiya* of each – a bunch of fennel stalks, a few citron leaves, pine nuts,[66] and a bit of pine-nut wood. Immerse everything in fresh water and boil until the essence of the ingredients is drawn out. Strain this liquid over the first one, and boil in a pot over a fire until it thickens and you are satisfied with the result.

64 The recipe has been amended with instructions from BL Or5927 (fol. 200v.).

65 This recipe is missing from BL Or5927.

66 The text has the clearly corrupted *laban* (*ṣanawbar*), which would translate as 'pine-nut milk'.

461. Fish *murrī*[67]

Take one *raṭl* of salted sprats (*ṣīr*)[68] [mentioned in the sixth Chapter of the tenth Section of this book] and put them in a sieve on top of a basin. Pour five [*raṭls*] of sweet must into it, a little at a time, all the while stirring it with your hand until all the liquid is strained through the sieve, and you are left with the sediment. Then, repeat with another load of sprats and must, until you have what you need. Make sure the sprats already contain *shardhūn* oregano. Put the *murrī* in a clean jar that has been used to keep olive oil. Then add cut quince and split onions which have been cut up without dividing the segments completely. Leave the jar so it can 'bubble' (ferment). Clean it every day, once in the morning and once at night, until it stops bubbling and all the sediment has settled at the bottom. If you want, you can put the *murrī* in jars that were used for oil, but cover them with olive oil and seal the lids with clay until such time as the contents are required in winter.

It is served by pouring it into a ceramic bowl, tipping sweet olive oil over it, and cutting up onions in it, if you like, but you can also add fried eggs, fried fish, and olives. Remember this. If you want the *murrī* to be red in colour, use black grape juice, whereas the white kind is made with white grape juice. Know this. If must is not available, the recipe can also be made with grape wine, in the same way as described, while the fermentation of the must will completely cancel out the effect of the wine. Bear this in mind.

---

67 The translation has been supplemented with information from BL Or5927 (fol. 200v.). Al-Uryūlī (1983: No. 102) claimed this type of *murrī* has warming and soothing properties, cleanses the stomach of phlegm and aids digestion of heavy food. According to Ibn al-Ḥashshā' (1932: 15, No. 132), fish *murrī* was called *bunn* (usually the word for coffee bean) and made from rotten fish, salt and grape juice, which is left until it takes on the colour and consistency of wine, without being intoxicating. He adds (*ibid.*, No. 128) that it is made with a small fish called *bunnī*, but that in the Maghrib it is made with a kind of large sardine (*sardhīn*), called *shaṭriyya*, and sometimes with other fish. Al-Ṭighnarī (2006: 123) also has a fish *murrī* recipe, which is, however, quite different, as it does not specify the fish, requires water (rather than must), oregano, fennel, coriander, and citron leaves, while the mixture is cooked over a fire several times. Al-Isrā'ilī (1992: 509) said that fish *murrī* is better – and less strong – than that made from barley, but that both are useful against dog bites.

68 The text has the diacritically defective *ṣabr*; the correct form is found in BL Or5291 (fol. 200v.), which begins the recipe with: 'Take *ṣīr* mentioned in the sixth Chapter of the tenth Section of this book.' See recipe No. 432.

462. Restoring [macerated] *murrī*[69]

If the macerated *murrī* shows signs of acidity – either because it has been in the sun only for a short time or because it has not been stirred enough – finely pound peeled walnuts, add them to the *murrī*, and stir it for several days. This gets rid of the acidity. If it is [too] salty, knead a loaf from unsalted wheat flour and bake it in the oven at a high temperature. Then crumble it up, pound it into flour, moisten with honey and knead finely. Put it in the *murrī*, leave for three days, and then strain. [Its saltiness will be gone, with the strength and power of Allah the Exalted.]

Chapter Nine: on making and restoring olive oil[70]

463. Making olive oil without olives, when olives are not available

Take terebinth (*buṭm*) – which is also known as *al-habba al-khadrā*'[71] – peeled walnuts and almonds, and sesame seeds, all in equal parts. Boil it all, and then squeeze out all the oil, and use instead of olive oil, after straining. [The sediment can be fed to cows, Allah the Exalted willing.]

---

69 Variants and amendments from BL Or5927 (fol. 200v.) are included in square brackets in this recipe and the next.

70 The title in BL Or5927 (fol. 200v.) is slightly different: 'On making olive oil without olives when they are not available, and on restoring olive oil if it is spoilt or its taste and odour have changed.'

71 *buṭm* (Dioscorides's *terminthos*) is the bitter fruit (nut) of the *Pistacia terebinthus* tree (*shajarat al-ḥabba al-khaḍrā'*), which extends from Morocco to the Hindu Kush. It was already eaten and pressed for oil by the Achaemenids and, before them, the ancient Mesopotamians (the Arabic word goes back to the Akkadian *buṭumtu*), who used it in one of their principal sweets, a dried fruit cake known as *mersu*. The tree (especially the related *Pistacia atlantica*) yields a fragrant resin (*'ilk*, *ṣamgh*), known as turpentine (from the Latin *terebinthus*), which was chewed as gum or used in perfumes. In ancient Greece, it was also added to wine. Terebinth was sometimes also known as *ḍirw* (*ḍarw*), though this actually denoted only the wild (*barrī*), rather than the cultivated (*bustānī*) variety. Like Dioscorides, Muslim physicians recommended terebinth as an aphrodisiac, while it was also thought to be beneficial for the spleen, and as a diuretic and emmenagogue. However, it was considered harmful to the stomach. Bottéro 1995: 23, 198; Ibn al-Bayṭār 1992: I, 134–5, II, 253; Ibn Jazla, fol. 40v.; Renaud & Colin 1934: 80–1; Dietrich 1988: I, 117–18; Dalby 1996: 323–4; Schmucker 1969: 115 (No. 130).

464. Restoring olive oil after it has gone bad[72]

Take salt and borax, finely grind them, and add enough of the grounds to a jar containing freshly pressed olive oil. This will restore the taste and smell of it. You can also add eight parts of sweet grape juice with a little liquorice in twenty parts of olive oil. Seal the containers with clay and leave them like this for ten days. When you open them, you will find that the oil tastes better, and that it has separated from the grape juice, which has become good wine.

If you fry citron roots in olive oil and add them to turbid olive oil, this clarifies it and improves its taste.

If you heat a brick on a fire until it turns red, and immediately break it into a bowl containing foul-smelling olive oil, it repairs the smell and clarifies the oil.

Or you can take one part of dry barley bread and the same amount in salt, pound them, and then put the grounds in a linen cloth. If you place this inside the container with spoiled olive oil, it will be restored.

You can also crush olive-tree bast, bark and its leaves, add a little roasted salt, and put all of it in a linen cloth, and then hang it inside the vessel containing the olive oil. Make sure it is immersed, and let it stand for three days. This will remove its cloudiness and improve its taste, with the power of Allah the Exalted. Or, if you use cumin and olive-tree bast and put it inside a container with spoilt olive oil, this will remove the foul odour and improve its taste, with the power of Allah the Exalted.

Chapter Ten: on extracting oils required for certain dishes[73]

465. Sweet almond oil

Crush good-quality [fresh] peeled sweet almonds in a mortar, until the mixture acquires the consistency of brains. Heat up fresh water

72 As the recipe in the edition (2012: 271) is corrupted, it was supplemented and amended with instructions from BL Or5927 (fol. 201r.–v.).

73 The title has been taken from BL Or5927 (fol. 201r.), which has also been used to complement the recipe here.

in a clean, glazed vessel and add one *ūqiya* of hot water for each *raṭl* of [pounded] almonds. Rub them vigorously with your hands until you see their oil come out from between your fingers. Then, put the almond mixture in a thick cloth, and gingerly squeeze it until all of the oil is released. Take the sediment and crush it again with a little hot water. Leave until the water has been absorbed, and then vigorously squeeze to express all the oil it holds. You should know that one *raṭl* of almonds yield a quarter or a third of their weight in oil, depending on the skill of the one performing the action. The same method is used to extract oil from walnuts, hazelnuts, pistachios, pine nuts and sesame seeds. Remember this. These oils are to be used in food only when they are fresh, as they quickly go off. Beware of this, and may Allah grant you success.

Chapter Eleven: on making jerky *(qadīd)*

466. [Recipe][74]

Take any kind of meat you like and cut it into strips, as thin and long as you can make them, and place them in a kneading tub with the requisite amount of very strong (sour) vinegar and enough crushed salt. Add the meat to the tub, and intermittently stir between early morning and noon prayer time, so that the meat can absorb as much of the vinegar and salt as possible. Then lift out the meat and sprinkle on pepper, coriander seeds, cumin, caraway and macerated *murrī*. Whisk the meat with the spices until they are all absorbed. Taste it, and if it lacks salt or anything else, add it. Leave the meat to marinate with the spices for a day, until the meat has fully acquired the flavours of the spices. If not, leave it overnight, and then hang it on a rope in the sun from morning

74 The recipe was completed with the help of BL Or5927, fol. 201v. Al-Rāzī (1881: 2–5) held that *qadīd* benefits the body, in that it safeguards against nausea caused by greasy food and excess consumption of wine, and also serves to suppress feelings of hunger, especially the 'false hunger' experienced by those who are inebriated. When one eats too much of it, though, it causes indigestion and thirst (alleviated by either oxymel or *jullāb*). According to a famous *ḥadīth* (al-Bukhārī 70:65), when the Prophet was served a meal of barley bread in a broth with gourd and jerky, he avoided the latter and ate only the gourd. Ibn ʿAbdūn ([Lévi-Provençal 1955]: 45) prohibited its sale 'as it has been prepared with poor-quality and decaying meat; it is of no benefit and is a deadly poison'.

until afternoon. Afterwards, take it down from the rope and put it on a sieve covered with something light. Put it back on the rope in the sun the next day, and continue doing this for several days, until the meat has dried out and lost all its moisture. At that point, transfer it to a vessel and put it somewhere airy, where it is not exposed to the sun or dampness. You can cook whatever you need, and use it just as you do fresh meat, Allah the Exalted willing. Bear this in mind. It can also be made with just water and salt, and then dried in the sun. Know this.

In Ibn Janāḥ's *Kitāb tafsīr al-adwiya* ('Treatise on the Explanation of the Medicines'),[75] I found a recipe the author calls *namaksūd*,[76] which is meat cured with crushed salt. The difference between this recipe and jerky is that *namaksūd* is made from a whole or split ram, while the meat stays moist and fatty. When you squeeze it, the grease gets onto your hands, and the knife cuts through it as if it were fresh meat. Also, it is not cut the way jerky is cut. Those who want to experience it

75 As mentioned in the Introduction, the book referred to here is, in fact, entitled *Kitāb al-talkhīṣ* ('The Book of Abridgement'). It was considered lost until a copy was identified in Istanbul in the late 1970s. The book is of huge significance, as it includes quotations from older sources that are no longer extant, and reveals an influence on major figures in medieval medicine and pharmacology, such as Maimonides. The text was recently edited by Bos *et al.* (2020), with a lengthy introduction on Ibn Janāḥ's life and works.

76 The word is a Persian borrowing, which literally translates as 'rubbed salt', but denoted salted beef. Ibn Janāḥ's text (2020: 784) reads as follows: '[*namaksūd*] is salted meat, since *namak* denotes "salt" in Persian and the meaning of *sūd* in this language is "the grinding". This meat is "ground" – that is to say rubbed — with salt. The difference between it and *qadīd* is the fact that *namaksūd* is put into the pickle as a whole or divided into two pieces only. The meat continues to be moist and greasy. If you touch it your hand becomes oily. A knife cuts through it as it does through fresh meat and it does not break into pieces, as *qadīd* does.' *Namaksūd* was a common travel food, and the tenth-century Abbasid traveller Ibn Faḍlān (Mackintosh & Montgomery 2014: 198) lists it, together with bread and millet, among basic travel provisions. The only other cookery book to contain a recipe is *Taṣānīf* (fol. 64r.–v.). Al-Warrāq mentions it, but only to discuss its medicinal properties: it is putrefying and, compared with other meats, less humid and hotter, while it spoils the blood (1987: 22). According to al-Rāzī (1881: 24–5), salting increases the benefit of dryness, heat and slowness in digestion. Ibn Jazla (fol. 230v.) describes it as meat which is sliced and then cured with salt and spices. The best variety is that which is fat and moist. It is beneficial for epileptics and those with phlegm and moistness. It is not very nutritious, and is harmful to colic sufferers. Its harmful effects are counteracted by cooking it in oil and milk. Interestingly enough, it was among the culinary recipes in Ibn Jazla's pharmacological encyclopedia to be translated into Latin in around 1300 (see Introduction), appearing as '*Nemehesuch*' (Iamobinus of Cremona, fol. 158v.).

should go ahead and make it – may Allah grant you success.

Chapter Twelve: on restoring food

467. If meat is too salty[77]

Knead flour without salt and cook it in the pot with the meat. Leave it for a while, and then take it out; the saltiness will have been removed from the meat, [Allah the Exalted willing].

468. If meat smells foul

[Take the meat and] prepare any dish [you like] that is easy for you to do, [and when you are heating it up over a fire] take a whole peeled almond or walnut, drill a hole in it [from top to bottom], and throw it into the pot. Once the meat is done, take out the walnut or almond, and the bad odour of the meat will be gone, [with the power and strength of Allah the Exalted].[78]

77 In the edition (2012: 274), both recipes in the chapter are joined, but the titles clearly mark them off as separate entries in BL Or5927 (fol. 201v.), which is why they appear as such here. Additions from BL Or5927 (fol. 201v.) are enclosed in square brackets in both. Other cookery books recommended dealing with excess saltiness by hanging a water-soaked cloth, bran (Ibn Mubārak Shāh 2020: 24) or a piece of papyrus (*Kanz* 1993: 6) in the pot.

78 The same method can be found in other culinary treatises as well, with walnuts (two) being preferred by Ibn Mubārak Shāh (2020: 24), and hazelnut shells by the author of *Kanz* (1993: 6). It was also recommended as a way of getting rid of offensive odours from cooking pots.

SECTION ELEVEN

Cooking grasshoppers, shrimp and snails[1]

469. [Preparing grasshoppers][2]

Take [the desired quantity of] large grasshoppers [of the variety known as *al-'Arabī* ('the Arab')] which appear in some years. [When they arrive, put them in a pot with hot water and let them] boil [once or] twice. [Then, take them out,] remove their wings and legs, and fry them in a [clean] pan [with olive oil until they are golden brown and] their moisture dries out. [Transfer them to a small ceramic bowl,] add *murrī*, cinnamon, and pepper, and serve them, [Allah the Exalted willing.] Even though the following is considered a bad fish that people shrink back from eating, I am mentioning it because many people do not find shrimp disgusting and look forward to them when they are in season. They are considered crustacean fish.[3]

---

1 The title has been taken from BL Or5927 (fols. 201v.–202r.), where this is Chapter Thirteen of Section Ten.

2 Variations in BL Or5927 (fol. 202r.) in this recipe and the next are enclosed in brackets. The consumption of *jarād* (which also denotes locusts) was first recorded among the ancient Babylonians, who considered pickled grasshoppers a delicacy, and whose main sauce/condiment, known as *shiqqu,* was made by fermenting fish, shellfish and grasshoppers (Bottéro 1985: 37). Grasshoppers/locusts were also eaten on the Arabian Peninsula, and are often mentioned in pre-Islamic poetry and proverbs, whereas their taste is described as being similar to the meat of scorpions. According to al-Rāzī (1987: 151) *jarād* are a harmful food and burn the blood. This was echoed by al-Isrā'īlī (1992: 573–4), who added that the meat of grasshoppers is extremely dry, and putrefies the blood. Ibn Jazla (fol. 53v.) advised against eating them for non-medicinal purposes, as they are lacking in nutrition and are harmful. Similarly, Ibn Zuhr (1992: 29–30; trans., 61) condemned *jarād* (the most common variety being the large and fast red ones) for generating noxious chyme (*kaymūs*), drying out the blood and causing illness. They are especially harmful for people with hot temperaments and phlegmatics. He said that people eat them cooked, fried or prepared in other ways, but added that the variety found in al-Andalus is not customary to eat, in any form. He even reports being told by Andalusians that it causes death. However, when *jarād* are eaten fermented in a condiment (*kāmakh*), they are less harmful. From a religious perspective, locusts were often associated with marine animals, and all religious schools except the Malikites consider them lawful food. Also see Marín 1994; Benkheira 2000: 67, 192–3; Waines 2011: 105–6 (L. Kopf).

3 The last sentence is only found in Gayangos XVI (fol. 133r.), but is omitted from the edition.

470. Preparing shrimp[4]

Take as many shrimps as you want, put them in a pot with water over a gentle fire, and bring it to a boil three times. Then remove the pot from the fire, pour away the water, and take the shrimps out. Sprinkle on crushed salt and oregano, and serve them. If you like, you can also fry them in a clean pan with olive oil until they are golden brown and [their moisture] has dried out. Transfer them to a small ceramic bowl, add macerated *murrī*, oregano, salt, pepper and cinnamon, and then serve, Allah the Exalted willing. This is the tastiest way to have them. These shrimps are plentiful in some large rivers, especially in the Seville region. They are also found in the river of Bijāya.[5] It is said that they are used specifically for breaking up calculi.

4 This recipe has been slightly amended with the text in BL Or5927 (fol. 202r.), most notably the fact that the shrimp should be brought to a boil three times, rather than for three hours. The Arabic word *qamarūn* (incorrectly vowelled as *qumrūn* in BL Or6927) is a borrowing from the Latin *cammarus* (< Greek *kámmaros*); Corriente 1997: 441; Dozy 1881: II, 404. Shrimp dishes are a rarity in the cookery books, and are only found elsewhere in al-Warrāq's, where they are called *rūbyān* (1987: 99, 122–3) and, in one recipe (a condiment), *rubaythā* (*ibid.*, 101), which, confusingly, is also the name of the condiment. Ibn al-Bayṭār's (1992: II, 430) definition of *rubaythā* refers only to the latter sense: 'an appetizer dip (*idām*) prepared by the inhabitants of Iraq from small fish, herbs and vinegar'. Ibn Zuhr (1993: 33; trans., 63) equates *rubaythā* with *qamarūn*, and says they are tasty and light, and increase sexual potency. More significantly, al-Uryūlī (1983: No. 116) quotes Ibn Zuhr as saying that the *qamarūn* came from a river in Seville, and is thus not a marine crustacean. Al-Rāzī praised the aphrodisiac properties of *rūbyān* and *rubaythā*, adding that the former are bloating but that the latter purify the stomach (1987: 149, 151). Al-Isrā'ilī (1992: 597) considered *rubaythā* another word for *arbiyān* (which is actually the Persian word), called *quraydis* (from the Greek *karídhes*) in Egypt. He warned that they should not be eaten salted or dried, since they dry out the stomach, though this can be counteracted by eating them with thyme, fresh rue, celery, washed olives, some nigella, and by drinking unadulterated wine afterwards. He claimed the best way to prepare them is fried in almond, sesame or olive oil. Ibn Jazla (fol. 105v.), for his part, made the distinction that *rubaythā* are hotter in temperament than *arbiyān* and invigorate coitus, but cause thirst. Ibn al-Ḥashshā' (1941: 52, No. 491) considered *rubaythā* and *qamarūn* two different – albeit similar – fish of the same genus. In light of the obvious confusion, it is perhaps more correct to refer to the former as 'prawns' and the latter as 'shrimp'.

5 This sentence and the previous one are missing from BL Or5927.

471. Preparing snails (*aghlāl*), which the Andalusians call qawqan[6]
[Take the required quantity and] repeatedly wash them in cold water until their slime is gone. Next, wash them [once or twice] in water and salt, and then just water. Throw them in a large pot filled with cold water and put it over a fire. When it comes to a boil, throw in water mint and citron leaves. Once they are cooked, add [a sufficient amount of] salt [and transfer them to a large bowl. Eat with bread and remove the snails (from their shells) with a citron thorn or something like it, Allah the Exalted willing.] This is a food that is considered disgusting, but most people eat it without loathing it because the snails feed a lot on wild herbs in spring.

6 This is the only snail recipe in the medieval Arab cookery books. The word *aghlāl* is of Berber origin. According to Ibn Jazla (fol. 73v.), snails extinguish heat in the blood and, when burnt, they are useful against eye ulcers. Archeological evidence reveals that snails were already eaten in ancient Greece in the Neolithic period, and later on were considered a powerful aphrodisiac. Galen even said that 'all Greeks eat snails on a daily basis'. See Powell 2003: 118; Dalby 1996: 38, 62; *idem* 2003: 305; Marín 1992; 16–17.

SECTION TWELVE

On hand-washing powders[1]

This consists of one chapter.

472. Hand-washing powder[2] to cleanse the hands, perfume the breath, soothe the mouth and gums, and remove the odours of greasy food

As for its composition, take one hundred *dirhams* of fine *bunk*,[3]

---

1 Recipes Nos. 472–8 are taken from the chapter devoted to hand-washing powders in Ibn al-Jazzār's book on aromatics and perfumes (2007: 117–20), with al-Tujībī retaining the same order. Both Ibn al-Jazzār and BL Or5927 (fol. 202r.–v.) were used to supplement the often-defective recipes in the edition, while variants are enclosed in square brackets.

2 *ushnān* denotes the ashes of saltwort, though it could also be made with various other plant species, such as *Anabasis*, *Arthrocnemum* (esp. *fruticosum*), *Atriplex*, *Halimione* or *Halogeton*, whereas al-Ishbīlī (2004–2010: No. 244) said it was a type of *ḥamḍ* (saltbush). It was already used by the ancient Sumerians, mainly for ritual washing, but they also mixed it with essential oils as treatment for headaches and abdominal cramps, and sometimes administered it as an enema. Owing to its widespread use for washing, *ushnān* was also known in Arabic as the generic *ghāsūl* ('washing substance'), as well as *ḥurd* and *qillī* (a borrowing from Akkadian *qīltu*, 'lye', and the etymon of the English *alkali*). Scholars identified a green-and-white variety, the best of which came from the region of Kufa. The biggest white ones were chosen as hand wash. According to Ibn Jazla (fols. 19v.–20r.), the bulbs are dried in the shade, and then ground and kneaded with rose water. This mixture is used to coat clay vessels and glass, and is then perfumed with agarwood, *nadd* (a compound incense comprising agarwood, ambergris, musk and frankincense) and camphor. Then it is re-ground to make it hard. In addition to being a purifier and cleanser, it was also recommended as an emmenagogue. Al-Ishbīlī identified a 'Persian' and 'Arab' variety, the latter being also known as *ushnān al-qaṣṣārīn*, 'the launderers' *ushnān*' (*ibid.*, Nos. 245–6). Also see Levey 1966: 231–2; Reinaud & Colin 1934: 38; Streck 2016–18: XII, 353–4 (C. Pappi), XV, 1–4 (D. Bawanypeck); Roth 1956–2010: XIII, 251; Ibn Sīnā 1999: I, 361; al-Rāzī 2000: 2932.

3 The printed edition has the unidentified *n.b.k.*, which was amended to *bunk* with the help of BL Or5927 (fol. 202r.). A similar misspelling is found in Yūḥannā Ibn Sarābiyūn (ninth century), who has *nabakh* (Guigues 1905: 332), which is actually the fruit of the jujube (*Ziziphus lotus*). Ibn al-Jazzār's text has *sukk* (see below). Medieval scholars such as Ibn Sīnā (1999: I, 394–5) or Ibn Jazla (fol. 43r.) held that *bunk* was brought from Yemen, and that it was the root of the gum Arabic tree (*umm ghaylān*, *Acacia nilotica/vera/gummifera*), which was also known as *al-ṭalḥ* in North Africa (Renaud & Colin 1934: 22–3, No. 46). It comes in yellow and white varieties,

together with red rose petals, lemongrass flowers,[4] dried marjoram, sandalwood, dried citron and fennel leaves[5] – ten *dirhams* of each; good-quality *sukk*,[6] unperfumed[7] agarwood, cloves, nutmeg, spikenard, and agarwood fruit[8] – three *dirhams* of each. Pound everything

the former of which is the best, since it is light and fragrant. Issa (1930: 2, 12) also identified it as *Acacia gummifera*. Many others, however, such as the twelfth-century Andalusian physician al-Ghāfiqī (fol. 68r.), believed it was a type of bast, similar to the bark of the mulberry tree from India that is burned for its sweet scent. Leclercq ([Ibn al-Bayṭār]: No. 359) and Steingass (1892: 203) equated it with Dioscorides's *nascaphthon*, whereas Ibn Janāḥ (2020: No. 162) said *bunk* was 'an aromatic' (*ṭīb*). *Bunk* has also been confused with *bunn* (coffee bean); Nasrallah [al-Warrāq] 2007: 766–9. The first to do so was the German botanist Leonhard Rauwolf (1535–96), who visited the Near East in 1573 and is responsible for the earliest description of coffee drinking (in Aleppo): 'There is a very good black beverage named *Chaube* [= *qahwa*, 'coffee'], which is black as ink and is very beneficial for ailments of the stomach. They drink it early in the morning, but also in public places, (...), as hot as possible, from hard and deep porcelain cups which they put often to their mouth, drinking small sips and passing the cup around as they sit in a circle. For this liquid, they use a fruit called *Bunnu* which on the outside in size and colour resembles a bayberry, with two thin skins, and is brought from India. (...). As they are similar in name and exterior to what *Avic.* [Ibn Sīnā] calls *Buncho* and *Rhazis ad Almons.* [= al-Rāzī, *Kitāb al-Manṣūrī*], *Bunca*, I take them to be the same, until such time as there is news to the contrary' (1582: 102–3). Also see al-Kindī 1948: 189–90; *EI*², s.v. 'qahwa' (C. Van Arendonk); Ukers 1922: 11–12.

4 *fuqqāḥ* ('flower') *al-idhkhir*, which was also known in the Maghrib as *tibn Makka* ('Mekkan straw'). Other names in Arabic include *ḥashīsh al-jamal* ('camel's hay') and the more intriguing 'Ma'mūn's toothpick'. This perennial grass can be found across the Arab world, and beyond, in India and Pakistan. Today, it is still used in folk medicine, mainly as an anti-inflammatory and diuretic. Amar & Lev 2008: 434–5; Meyerhof 1940: 8–9 (No. 8); Meyerhof & Sobhi 1932: 62–4; Ibn al-Bayṭār 1992: I, 21–2; Reinaud & Collin 1934: 18 (No. 34); Dietrich 1988: II, 100–1; Ibn al-Quff [H. Kircher 1967]: 70–1; al-Rāzī 2000: 2913.

5 BL Or5927 has dried bay leaves (*waraq rand*); Ibn al-Jazzār's recipe mentions neither fennel nor bay leaf here.

6 Lozenges shaped out of a paste made with violet and musk oil, and often a blend of aromatics, the principal component of which is *rāmik* (from the Akkadian *ramāku*, 'to bathe'), a compound including gallnut, cinnamon, ambergris, mastic, date syrup and honey. See Wiedemann 1914; al-Kindī 1948: 90–2 (recipes), 314–15, 329–31; Ducène 2016: 165; Engeser 1986: 136–7; Renaud & Colin 1934: 158 (No. 360); Roth 1956–2010: XIV, 111.

7 *muṭarrā* means 'mixed with aromatics', and in the case of agarwood involved soaking it in perfumed water prior to burning it; Kazimirski 1860: II, 80.

8 *harnuwa* (also *qarnuwa*), which was also known in North Africa as *flīfa*, that is to say *fulayfila*, the diminutive of *fulful* (pepper), in reference to the appearance of the fruit. See Renaud & Colin 1934: 58–9 (No. 127); Ibn al-Bayṭār 1992: 510. Lev & Amar (2008: 555) wrongly identify it as Guinea pepper (*Capsicum miminum*).

extremely well and then knead with rose water. Leave for one day and one night. Put it on a kneading slab and grind it until it is dry. Store, and wash your hands with it after eating. It is excellent in terms of its fragrance and benefits, Allah the Exalted willing.

473. Another excellent hand-washing powder[9]

It is more exquisite than the previous recipe. Take twenty *mithqāls* of *bunk*; dried melon peel, apple peels, dried citron peels, dried marjoram, dried storax, ten *mithqāls* of each; cyperus, sandalwood, sweet costus,[10] peeled St Lucie cherry,[11] four *mithqāls* of each; mace, cardamom, cubeb, cloves and agarwood, two *mithqāls* of each; and one *mithqāl* of camphor. Pulverize all of them and knead with good-quality red wine. Shape into discs and leave them to dry in the shade. Then, return them to the kneading slab, crush them with two *mithqāls* of excellent *sukk* and, finally, add camphor. You can also add some musk. This compound is delicious as well as being beneficial for the mouth and gums, Allah the Exalted willing.

9 Ibn al-Jazzār (2007: 118), who has musk instead of the *bunk* and *sukk* in this recipe, adds that he made it for the founder of the Fatimid caliphate, ʿAbd Allāh Ibn al-Mahdī billāh (d. 934).

10 *qusṭ ḥulw*; scholars generally identified three varieties of this aromatic root: *ʿArabī* (ʿArab'), which is white and also known as *baḥrī* ('marine'), or sweet costus; *Hindī* ('Indian'), which is black and bitter (hence also known as 'bitter costus', *qusṭ murr*); and *qaranfulī* ('clove costus'), a highly fragrant one, yellow in colour, from Syria. The white, sweet variety was considered the best, and is also the only one used in perfumes, etc. Medicinally, it was thought to be useful against chest pains and poisons, while its laxative and aphrodisiac properties are enhanced if it is taken with wine. Ibn Jazla, fols. 175v.176r.; Ibn Sīnā 1999: I, 648; Renaud & Colin 1934: 153 (No. 350).

11 *maḥlab*; its stones are cracked open to extract the seed of the fruit (also known as 'mahaleb or perfumed cherry'), which is then ground. In the medieval cookbooks, it was restricted to perfumes and hand-washing powders (see, for instance *Kanz*, Nos. 646-8), but Ibn al-ʿAwwām (1802: II, 380) reported that the seeds (*ḥabb*) were also eaten by old people, in which case they were boiled several times in water and then vinegar (to remove the smell and bitterness) before being cooked with dates and salt. The mixture is dried outside before being eaten with bread. Today, mahaleb is often used in food, particularly as a flavouring in sweets, or in bread-making.

474. Royal hand-washing powder[12]
Take thirty *dirhams* of *bunk*, as well as [fresh] good-quality agarwood, yellow sandalwood, Indian aloe fruit, cloves and nutmeg – three *mithqāls* of each. Pound it all together and sift it. Also take five *mithqāls* of *sukk*, three of *lakhlakha*,[13] and half a *dirham* [seven *dirhams*] of musk. Grind the musk and *sukk*, dilute with rose water, then add the *lakhlakha*, and mix all of this with the first mixture. Knead everything well, and leave to settle overnight. The next morning, put it on the kneading slab and pulverize. Store until you need to use it, Allah the Exalted willing.

475. Another [royal] compound which can be used instead of *ushnān*. It perfumes the breath and cleans away greasy odour and, if you swallow some of it, it does you no harm. It is beneficial for the teeth, and is used by kings to wash their hands with after dining.
As for its ingredients, take cinnamon and camphor, three *dirhams* of each; two *dirhams* of cloves; five *dirhams* each of frankincense, liquid storax, and lemongrass root; ten *dirhams* each of white sandalwood and cyperus; and thirty *dirhams* of nutmeg.[14] Pound and sift it all, and then use it. You can mix this with fifteen *dirhams* of toasted and slightly crushed Armenian clay. This is a well-known and tried recipe, Allah the Exalted willing.

476. Fragrant and highly beneficial hand-washing powder. It removes freckles and blemishes, and softens the limbs.
As for its ingredients, take barley flour, lentil flour and broad-bean

---

12 *ushnān mulūkī*; BL Or5927 titles it 'a kind of hand-washing powder used by kings', which is similar to the title of Ibn al-Jazzār's original recipe (2007: 118). Unsurprisingly, quite a few compounds laid claim to being 'royal', and there is a similarly named – but very different – recipe in *Kanz* (No. 649).

13 The word is Persian in origin (Steingass 1892: 1120), and referred to a perfume compound with varying ingredients which was used as a room freshener, and endowed with a number of health benefits. The recipe in a fourteenth-century Egyptian cookery book calls for rose water, borage water, clove water, agarwood, ambergris, musk, apple, cardamom and cubeb (*Kanz*, No. 671). Ibn al-Jazzār lists some twenty *lakhlakha* recipes (2007: 94–107) with a wide variety of aromatic ingredients.

14 BL Or5927 has the unidentified *jawz ḥamām* instead of the *jawz bawwā* ('nutmeg') of the edition and Ibn al-Jazzār.

flour – thirty *mithqāls* of each; dried myrtle[15] leaves, dried red roses, *bunk*, and dried marjoram – ten *mithqāls* of each; sweet costus and grated sandalwood, five *mithqāls* of each; *sukk*, cloves and cardamom – two *mithqāls* of each. Grind the medicinal ingredients, and then sift and knead them with the inner part of a melon rind.[16] Make discs with the mixture, and leave them to dry in the shade. Then grind them very finely and dilute with some camphor, if possible. If you do not have any to hand, perfume the compound with *nadd*[17] or *muthallatha*[18] while it is still moist. Use it to wash the hands. It is wonderful.

477. Another royal hand-washing powder for perfuming the hands[19] and breath, which also strengthens the gums

Take dried apple peels, dried citron peels, dried marjoram – of each twenty *mithqāls*; *bunk*, cyperus, lemongrass flowers, and red rose petals[20]– of each ten *mithqāls*; mace, cardamom, cubeb, agarwood fruit, cloves, cassia,[21] toothache tree bark,[22] cinnamon and grated sandalwood – of each two *mithqāls*; agarwood and camphor – of each one *mithqāl*. Pulverize it all, then sift and use to wash the hands. This is fragrant and beneficial, Allah the Exalted willing. Kings and nobles wash their hands with it after eating.

15 The edition has the erroneous reading *asriyās*, which should be corrected to *'ās yābis*, as confirmed by BL Or5927.

16 *shaḥm*, lit. 'fat'; Corriente 1997: 276.

17 A compound perfume used as incense; for recipes, see, for instance, *Wuṣla*, Nos. 1.8–9, 1.12, 1.17. According to al-Mas'ūdī (1861–77: I, 335), ambergris was also called *nadd* by druggists in Iraq and Persia.

18 Meaning 'trebled', this denoted a compound perfume of varying composition consisting of three ingredients. See al-Kindī 1948: 283.

19 The printed edition has the misreading *badan* ('body'), with the correct forms appearing in BL Or5927 (fol. 202v.) and Ibn al-Jazzār (2007: 120).

20 BL Or5927 (fol. 202v.) only lists 'dried citron leaves and dried marjoram'.

21 *salīkha*, a synonym of *dār ṣīnī*, which is the word used in Ibn al-Jazzār's recipe and here later in the list, but is sometimes also used for (true) cinnamon (*qirfa*) in the literature. See Lev & Amar 2008: 143–4.

22 *fāghira*; al-Ishbīlī (2004–10: No. 3795) describes its grain as being similar to the St Lucia cherry tree (see above), and adds that it is abundant on the North African coast. Ibn al-Jazzār's recipe (2007: 120) does not include this ingredient, but instead has *falanja*, another name for cubeb, which was also used to colour ointments (al-Ishbīlī 2004–10: No. 3737).

478. Hand-washing powder to clean the hands and eliminate greasy smells[23]

Take four *mithqāls* of cloves, one *ūqiya* of borax, and three *ūqiyas* of broad-bean flour. Finely grind everything, and wash your hands with it. It is very good and beneficial.

479. Another recipe

Grind and sift chickpeas, and use the powder to wash your hands after eating. It is very suited for this purpose. These are the hand-washing powders that people use.

480. Making *muṣannab* (mustard-flavoured grape juice)[24]

Take one pound of good mustard seeds for each twenty *rubʿs* of sweet grape juice. Crush the mustard seeds, sieve the grounds, and knead them with honey. Then take a new earthenware vessel which has been soaked in water for two or three days. Empty out the water and leave the vessel to air dry for a day. Smear the bottom and insides of the vessel with the mustard and honey paste, and leave aside for a day so as to allow the vessel to be permeated with it and absorb its flavours. Then, pour in sweet grape juice[25] after having strained it. If the vessel is filled up to the brim with the juice, the coating should also be applied

23 This recipe and the next are missing from BL Or5927, whereas No. 479 is not included in Ibn al-Jazzār's chapter either.

24 The edition (2012: 279) includes a very garbled version (incorrectly titled *ṣināb*) of the recipe in Gayangos XVI (fol. 134v.). It would appear to be orphaned from the opening chapter of Section Ten, which contains two other *ṣināb* recipes. A complete recipe can be found in Ibn al-ʿAwwām's book on agriculture (1802: II, 418–19), which contains three other *muṣannabs* (*ibid.* 414–18). He explains that mustard is added in order to preserve the sweetness of the grape juice. Ibn al-ʿAwwām gives Ibn Baṣṣāl as his source, and introduces the recipe as being another method of sweetening so that the result resembles a mixture of water and honey. The recipe can indeed be found in Ibn Baṣṣāl's text (1955: 18; trans., 231), in the final chapter (16), which deals with water, wells, the preservation of fruits, and other things farmers need to know. It appears after a recipe on making bouquets, and incongruously concludes the work, just as is the case here. The version in Ibn Baṣṣāl's edited text is unfortunately not complete either, but the similarities with al-Tujībī's text are such that the latter probably borrowed it from Ibn Baṣṣāl rather than from Ibn al-ʿAwwām, who is the only one to have a full version of the recipe. The translation relies on the recipes found in Gayangos XVI, Ibn al-ʿAwwām and Ibn Baṣṣāl. Also see Corriente 1997: 311.

25 The edition specifies that it should be ten *rubʿs* of juice; however, this is contradicted by the fact that the level of the juice varies according to the coating.

up to that level. If it is filled up halfway, or more or less than that, the juice should also reach the level of the mustard coating. This liquid will endure even when mixed with honey.

This will preserve the syrup, even if it is combined with grape juice mixed with honey. It will not taste bad, nor will it taste of mustard. It can be kept for a long time and preserves its sweetness. This recipe has been tried and tested. It is made like this in Sicily, and I have not seen anything like it that is better.[26]

THE END

God bless and save our lord Muḥammad,
his family and his companions

26 The last comment is mentioned by Ibn al-ʿAwwām as being the words of Ibn Baṣṣāl, though the edition of the latter's text does not contain it.

BIBLIOGRAPHY

I. Manuscripts

Andalusian → Anynomous: MSS G.S. Colin arabe 7009.

Anonymous: MSS G.S. Colin arabe 7009 Bibliothèque nationale, Paris [= *Andalusian*].

Anynomous: *Kitāb Waṣf al-aṭʿima al-muʿtāda*, Cairo, Dār al-Kutub, Ṣināʿa 51; Ṣināʿa 52; English translation, C. Perry, 'The description of familiar foods', in M. Rodinson *et al.* 2001: pp. 273–466 [= *Waṣf*].

Anonymous: *Taṣānīf al-aṭʿima,*: Wellcome (London), WMS Arabic 57.

al-Baghdādī, Muḥammad Ibn al-Ḥasan: *Kitāb al-ṭabīkh*, Ayasofia, 3710 (Istanbul).

al-Ghāfiqī, Abū Jaʿfar: *Kitāb al-adwiya al-mufrada*, Osler Library of the History of Medicine, McGill University (Toronto), MS 7508.

Iambobinus of Cremona: *Liber de ferculis et condimentis*, Bibliothèque nationale de France, lat. 9328.

Ibn Biklārish, Yūsuf Ibn Isḥāq, *Kitāb al-Mustaʿīnī*, Arcadia Library (London).

Ibn Jazla: *Minhāj al-bayān fīmā yastaʿmiluhu al-insān*, British Library, Or.7499.

Ibn Māsawayh, Abū-Zakarīyā Yūḥannā: *Fī dafʿ maḍārr al-aghdhiya*, Staatsbibliothek zu Berlin, Petermann I 370.

Ibn al-Raqqām: *Khulāṣat al-ikhtiṣāṣ fī maʿrifat al-qūwā wa 'l-khawāṣṣ*, University of Cambridge Library, MS Qq.54.

al-Rāzī: *Dafʿ Maḍārr al-Aghdhiyah*, Yale University, Beinecke Rare Book and Manuscript Library, Landberg MSS 473.

al-Shāṭirī, Muḥammad Ibn al-Ḥasan: *Sharḥ asmā' al-adwiya wa-ḥashā'ish al-mukhtalifa*, Universitätsbibliothek Leipzig, Vollers 772.

al-Tujībī, Ibn Razīn: *Faḍālat al-khiwān fī ṭayyibāt al-ṭaʿām wa 'l-alwān*, Staatsbibliothek zu Berlin, Wetzstein 1207; British Library, Or5927; Real Academia de la Historia (Madrid), Gayangos XVI.

Waṣf → Anynomous: *Kitāb Waṣf al-aṭʿima al-muʿtāda.*

II. Printed Materials

IN ARABIC AND PERSIAN

Abū 'l-Fidā' (1840): *Taqwīm al-buldān*, J. T. Reinaud & Mac Guckin de Slane (eds.), Paris: Imprimerie Royale.

Abū al-Ṣalt, ʿAbd al-ʿAzīz (2003): *Kitāb al-adwiya al-mufrada. Le livre des simples de Umayya b. ʿAbd al-ʿAzīz b. Abī al-Ṣalt al-Dānī al-Išbīlī*, Barbara Graille (ed./French translation), Damascus: Institut français du Proche-Orient.

Afshār, Īrāj (1360/1981): *Āshpaz-e dawra-ye Ṣafawi*, Tehran.

Ammar, Sleim (1994): *Ibn Al Jazzar et l'école médicale de Kairouan*, Tunis: Ben Arous.

Anonymous (2017): *al-Wuṣla ilā al-ḥabīb fī Waṣf al-ṭayyibāt wa 'l-ṭīb*, Charles Perry (ed./English translation), *Scents and Flavors. A Syrian Cookbook*, New York: New York University Press [= *Wuṣla*].

Anonymous (2010): *Anwāʿ al-ṣaydala fī alwān al-aṭʿima*, ʿAbd al-Ghanī Abū 'l-ʿAzm (ed.), Rabat: Mu'assasat al-Ghanī li 'l-Nashr [= *Anwāʿ*].

Anonymous (1993): *Kanz al-Fawā› id fī tanwīʿ al- Mawā'id* Manuela Marín & David Waines (eds.), Beirut/Stuttgart: Franz Steiner Verlag [= *Kanz*].

Anonymous (1961–62): 'Kitab al tabij fi-l-Magrib wa-l-Andalus fi ʿasr al-Muwahhidin, li-mu'allif mayhul (Un libro anónimo de la Cocina hispano-magribí, de la época almohade)', Ambrosio Huici Miranda (ed.), *Revista del Instituto de Estudios Islámicos* IX/X, pp. 15–256; English translation Charles Perry: *Anonymous Andalusian Cookbook*, http://daviddfriedman.com/Medieval/Cookbooks/Andalusian/andalusian_contents.htm.

al-Anṭākī, Dā'ūd (1890–91): *Tadhkirat ūli 'l-albāb wa 'l-jāmiʿ li 'l-ʿajab al-ʿujāb*, 2 vols., Cairo: Būlāq.

Anwāʿ → Anonymous (2010).

al-Baghdādī, ʿAbd al-Laṭīf (2021): *Kitāb al-Ifāda wa'l-i'tibār fi'l-umūr al-mushāhada wa'l-ḥawadith al-mu'āyana bi-arḍ Miṣr. A Physician on the Nile A Description of Egypt and Journal of the Famine Years*, Tim Mackintosh-Smith (ed./English translation), New York: New York University Press.

al-Baghdādī, Muḥammad Ibn al-Ḥasan (1964): *Kitāb al-ṭabīkh*, ed. Fakhrī al-Bārūdī, Damascus: Dār al-Kitāb al-Jadīd; English translation, Charles Perry: *A Baghdad Cookery Book*, Totnes: Prospect Books, 2005.

al-Bakrī, Abū ʿUbayd (2003): *Kitāb al-masālik wa 'l-mamālik*, 2 vols., Beirut: Dār al-Kutub al-ʿIlmiyya.

al-Bakrī, A. (1857): *Kitāb al-mughrib fī dhikr bilād Ifrīqiyā wa 'l-Maghrib*, MacGuckin de Slane (ed.), Algiers: Imprimerie du Gouvernement; French translation, M. de Slane, Description de l'Afrique septentrionale, Algiers: Adolphe Jourdain, 1913.

al-Bīrūnī (1973): *al-Ṣaydana fi 'l-ṭibb. al-Bīrūnī's book on pharmacy and materia medica*, H. M. Said & R. E. Elahie (ed./English translation), Karachi: Hamdard National Foundation.

Binsharīfa, Muḥammad (2009): *Ibn Razīn al-Tujībī, ḥayātuhu wa āthāruhu*, Casablanca: Maṭbaʿat al-Najāḥ al-Jadīda.

—(1982): 'Ḥawla Ibn Razīn mu'allif Kitāb al-Ṭabīkh', *Majallat Kulliyat al-Ādāb wa 'l-ʿUlūm al-Insāniyya bi-'l-Ribāṭ*, 8, pp. 95–118.

Būhīla, Idrīs (2012): *al-Jazā'iriyyūn fi Tiṭwān khilāl al-qarn 13/19*, Tetouan: Maṭbaʿat al-Hidāya.

al-Dabbābī al-Mīsāwī, Sihām (2017): *Mā'ida Ifrīqiyya. Dirāsa fī alwān al-ṭaʿām*, Tunis: Bayt al-Ḥikma.

al-Dimashqī, Abū 'l-Faḍl Jaʿfar (1999): *Kitāb al-ishāra ilā maḥāsin al-tijāra wa ghushūsh al-mudallisīn fīhā*, Beirut: Dār Ṣader.

al-Dīnawarī, Abū Ḥanīfa (1974): *Kitāb al-nabāt*, Bernhard Lewin (ed.), Wiesbaden: Franz

Steiner.

—(1973): *Kitāb al-nabāt; al-qism al-thānī min al-qāmūs al-nabātī*, M. Ḥamīdallāh (ed.), Cairo.

al-Farāhīdī, Khalīl (2008): *Kitāb al-ʿayn*, 8 vols., Mahdī al-Makhzūmī & Ibrāhīm al-Sāmarrāʾī (eds.), Cairo: Dār al-Hilāl.

al-Ḥimyarī, ʿAbd al-Munʿim (1984): *al-Rawḍ al-miʿṭār fī khabar al-aqṭār*, Iḥsān ʿAbbās (ed.), Beirut: Maktabat Lubnān.

Ibn ʿAbd Rabbih, Aḥmad (1983): *al-ʿIqd al-Farīd*, 9 vols., Mufīd Muḥammad Qamīḥa (ed.), Beirut: Dār al-Kutub al-ʿIlmiyya.

Ibn Abī Uṣaybiʿa (2020): *ʿUyūn al-anbāʾ fī ṭabaqāt al-aṭibbāʾ*, E. Savage-Smith, S. Swain & G. J. van Gelder (eds.), *A Literary History of Medicine*, Leiden: Brill.

Ibn al-ʿAwwām (2012): *al-Filāḥa al-Andalusiyya*, 7 vols., Anwar Abū Suwaylim, Samīr al-Darūbī & ʿAlī Arshīd Maḥāsina (eds.), Amman: Majmaʿ al-Lugha al-ʿArabiyya al-Urdunniyya.

—(1802): *Kitāb al-Filāḥa. Libro de agricultura*, 2 vols., J. A. Banquieri (ed./Spanish translation), Madrid: Imprenta Real; French translation, J.-J. Clément-Mullet, *Le Livre de l'Agriculture*, 2 vols., Paris: Librairie A. Franck, 1866.

Ibn Baṣṣāl (1955): *Kitāb al-filāḥa*, José Millás Vallicrosa & Mohamed Aziman (eds./Spanish translation), Tetuan: Maʿhad Mulay al-Ḥasan.

Ibn Baṭṭūṭa (1853–58): *Riḥla*, C. Defrémery & B. R. Sanguinetti (eds./French translation), *Voyages d'Ibn Batoutah*, 4 vols., Paris: Imprimerie Impériale.

Ibn al-Bayṭār, Abū Muḥammad (1992): *al-Jāmiʿ li-mufradāt al-adwiya wa 'l-aghdhiya*, Beirut: Dār al-Kutub al-ʿIlmiyya; French translation, Lucien Leclerq, 'Traite´ des simples par Ibn el-Beïthar', *Notices et extraits des manuscrits de la Bibliothèque nationale et autres bibliothèques*, 23: 1 (1877), 25: 1 (1881), 26: 1 (1883), Paris: Imprimerie Nationale.

Ibn Buṭlān (1990): *Taqwīm al-ṣiḥḥa. Le Taqwim al-Sihha (Tacuini Sanitatis) d'Ibn Butlan: un traité médical du XIe siècle*, Hosam Elkhadem (ed./French translation), Leuven: Peeters.

Ibn Ḥabīb, ʿAbd al-Malik (1992): *Mukhtaṣar fi 'l-ṭibb*, Camilo Alvarez de Morales & Fernando Girón Irueste (eds./Spanish translation), Madrid: Consejo Superior de Investigaciones Cientificas/Instituto de Cooperación con el Mundo Arabe.

Ibn al-Ḥashshāʾ (1941); *Mufīd al-ʿulūm wa mabīd al-humūm (wa-huwa tafsīr al-alfāẓ al-ṭibbiyya wa 'l-lughawiyya al-wāqiʿa fī Kitāb al-Manṣūrī li 'l-Rāzī)*, Georges Séraphin Colin & Henri-Paul-Joseph Renaud (eds.), Rabat: Imprimerie économique.

Ibn Iṣḥāq, Ḥunayn (1997): 'Kitāb al-Aghdhiya', Nina Garbutt (ed./English translation), PhD diss., University of Cambridge.

Ibn Janāḥ (2020): *Kitāb al-talkhīṣ*, Gerrit Bos, Fabian Käs, Mailyn Lübke & Guido Mensching (eds./English translation), *Marwān ibn Janāḥ: On the nomenclature of medicinal drugs (Kitāb al-talkhīṣ)*, 2 vols., Leiden: Brill.

Ibn al-Jazzār, Abū Jaʿfar (2007): *Kitāb fī funūn al-ṭibb wa 'l-ʿiṭr*, al-Rādī al-Jāzī & Fārūq al-ʿAsalī (eds.), Tunis: Bayt al-Ḥikma.

Ibn Juljul, Sulaymān Ibn Ḥassān (1992): *Maqāla fi 'l-tiryāq. Ibn Ŷulŷul. Tratado sobre los medicamentos de la tríaca*, I. Garijo Galán (ed.), Córdoba: Area de Estudios Arabes e Islámicos, Cátedra de Lengua y Literatura Arabes de la Universidad de Córdoba.

Ibn Khaldūn (2005): *al-Muqaddima*, 5 vols., 'Abd al-Salām al-Shadādī (ed.), Casablanca: Bayt al-Funūn wa 'l-'Ulūm; English translation, Franz Rosenthal, *The Muqaddimah: An Introduction to History*, 3 vols., London: Routledge & Kegan Paul, 1986.

Ibn Khallikān, Shams al-Dīn (1968–72): *Wafayāt al-a'yān wa-anbā' abnā' al-zamān*, 8 vols., Iḥsān 'Abbās (ed.), Beirut: Dār Ṣādir,

Ibn Khalṣūn (1996): *Kitāb al-Aghdhiya (Le livre des aliments)*, Suzanne Gigandet (ed./ French translation), Damascus: Presses de l'Ifpo.

Ibn al-Khaṭīb, Muḥammad Ibn 'Abd Allāh (1984): *Kitāb al-wuṣūl li-ḥifẓ al-ṣiḥḥa fī 'l-fuṣūl*, Maria de la Concepción Vázquez de Benito (ed./Spanish translation), Salamanca: Universidad de Salamanca.

Ibn al-Khūja, Muḥammad (1939): *Tārīkh ma'ālim al-tawhīd fī 'l-qadīm wa fī 'l-jadīd*, Tunis: al-Maṭba'a al-Tūnisiyya; 2nd edn., al-Jīlānī Ibn al-Ḥājj Yaḥyā & Ḥammādī al-Sāḥilī (eds.), Beirut: Dār al-Gharb al-Islāmī, 1985.

Ibn Luyūn (1988): *Kitāb ibdā' al-malāḥa wa inhā' al-rayāḥa fī uṣūl ṣinā'at al-filāḥa*, Joaquina Eguaras Ibáñez (ed./Spanish translation), Granada: Universidad Almería.

Ibn Mubārak Shāh (2020): *Zahr al-ḥadīqa fī 'l-aṭ'ima al-anīqa. The Sultan's feast: A Fifteenth-Century Egyptian cookbook*, Daniel L. Newman (ed./English translation), London: Saqi Books.

Ibn Qayyim al-Jawziyya (1927): *al-Ṭibb al-nabawī*, Aleppo: al-Maṭba'a al-'Ilmiyya.

Ibn Qutayba al-Dīnawarī, 'Abd Allāh (1925–30): *'Uyūn al-akhbār*, 4 vols., Cairo: Dār al-Kutub al-Miṣriyya.

Ibn Sa'īd al-Maghribī (1970): *Kitāb al-Jughrāfiyā*, Isma'īl al-'Arbī (ed.), Beirut: al-Maktab al-Tijārī li 'l-Ṭibā'a wa 'l-Nashr wa 'l-Tawzī'.

—(1953): *al-Mughrib fī ḥulā al-Maghrib*, Shawqī Dayf (ed.), 2 vols., Cairo: Maṭba'at Jāmi'at Fu'ād al-Awwal.

Ibn Sīnā (1999): *al-Qānūn fī 'l-ṭibb*, 3 vols., Muḥammad Amīn al-Dannāwī (ed.), Beirut: Dār al-Kutub al-'Ilmiyya.

Ibn al-Ukhuwwa, Muḥammad Ibn Aḥmad (1938): *al-Ma'ālim al-qurba fī aḥkām al-ḥisba*; Reuben Levy (ed./English translation), Cambridge: Cambridge University Press.

Ibn Wāfid, Abū 'l-Muṭarrif (1980): *Kitab al-wisād fī 'l-ṭibb*, Camilo Alvarez de Morales y Ruiz-Matas (ed./Spanish translation), *El libro de la Almohada de Ibn Wafid de Toledo (Recetario medico árabe del siglo XI)*, Toledo: Instituto Provincial de Investigaciones y Estudios Toledanos.

Ibn Waḥshiyya (1993): *al-Filāḥa al-Nabaṭiyya*, 2 vols., Tawfīq Fahd (ed.), Damascus: Institut Français de Damas.

Ibn Zuhr, Abū Marwān (1992): *Kitāb al-aghdhiya. Tratado de los Alimentos*, Expiración García Sánchez (ed./Spanish translation), Madrid: Consejo Superior de Investigaciones Cientificas.

al-Idrīsī, Muḥammad al-Sharīf (2002): *Kitāb nuzhat al-mushtāq fī ikhtirāq al-āfāq*, Cairo: Maktabat al-Thaqāfat a-Dīniyya.

—(1995): *Kitāb al-jāmi' li ṣifāt ashtāt al-nabāt wa-ḍurūb anwā' al-mufradāt. Compendium of the Properties of Diverse Plants and Various Kinds of Simple Drugs*, 3 vols., Fuat Sezgin, Mazen Amawī & Eckhard Neubauer (eds.), Frankfurt am Main: Institute for the History of Arabic Islamic Society.

—(1866): *al-Maghrib wa arḍ al-Sūdān wa Miṣr wa 'l-Andalus ma'khūda min Kitāb Nuzhat al-mushtāq fī ikhtirāq al-āfāq. Description de l'Afrique et de l'Espagne*, R. Dozy & M. J. de Goeje (eds./French translation), Leiden: Brill.

al-Ishbīlī, Abū 'l-Khayr (2004–10): *Kitāb 'umdat al-ṭabīb fi ma'rifat al-nabāt li-kull labīb. Libro base del médico para el conocimiento de la Botánica por todo experto*, Joaquín Bustamante, Federico Corriente & Mohand Tilmatine (eds./Spanish translation), 4 vols., Madrid: Consejo Superior de Investigaciones Científicas.

al-Isrā'ilī, Isḥāq b. Sulaymān (1992): *Kitāb al-aghdhiya wa 'l-adwiya*, Muḥammad al-Ṣabāḥ (ed.), Beirut: Mu'assasat 'Izz al-Dīn li 'l-Ṭibā'a wa 'l-Nashr.

al-Jāḥiẓ (1990): *Kitāb al-bukhalā'*, Cairo: Dār al-Ma'ārif; English translation, R. B. Serjeant, *The Book of Misers*, Reading: Garnet.

Kanz → Anonymous (1993)

al-Khaṭṭābī, Muḥammad al-'Arabī (1988): *al-Ṭibb wa 'l-aṭibbā' fi 'l-Andalus al-Islāmiyya*, 2 vols., Beirut: Dār al-Gharb al-Islāmī.

al-Kindī (1948): *Kīmiyā' al-'iṭr wa 'l-taṣ'īdāt. Buch über die Chemie des Parfums und die Distillationen. Ein Beitrag zur Geschichte des arabischen Parfumchemie und Drogenkunde aus dem 9. Jahrhundert*, Karl Garbers (ed./German translation), Leipzig: F. A. Brockhaus.

al-Lakhmī, Ibn Hishām (2003): *al-Madkhal ilā taqwīm al-lisān*, Ḥātim Ṣaliḥ al-Ḍāmin (ed.) Beirut: Dār al-Bashā'ir al-Islāmī.

Lévi-Provençal, Évariste (ed.) (1955): *Thalātha rasā'il Andalusiyya fī ādāb al-ḥisba wa 'l-muḥtasib*, Cairo: IFAO; (partial) French translation, Lévi-Provençal, *Séville musulmane au début du XIIe siècle. Le traite' d'Ibn 'Abdun sur la vie urbaine et les corps de métiers*, Paris: Maisonneuve & Larose.

López y López, Angel C. (ed./trans.) (1990): *Kitāb fī tartīb awqāt al-ghirāsa wa 'l-maghrūsāt*, Granada: Consejo Superior de Investigaciones Científicas.

Mackintosh-Smith, Tim & James Montgomery (eds./trans.) (2014): *Two Arabic Travel Books. Abū Zayd al-Sīrāfī: Accounts of China and India. Ibn Fadlān: Mission to the Volga*, New York: New York University Press.

Mahdī, Muḥsin (1984): *Alf Layla wa Layla*, 2 vols., Leiden: Brill.

Maimonides (1995): *Sharḥ Asmā' al-'Uqqār. Glossary of drug names*, Fred Rosner (ed./ English translation), Haifa: Maimonides Research Institute.

Makkī, Mahmūd 'Alī (ed.) (2003): *al-Sifr al-thānī min Kitāb al-muqtabas li-Ibn Ḥayyān al-Qurṭubī*, Riyadh: Markaz al-Malik Fayṣal li 'l-Buḥūth wa-l-Dirāsāt al-Islāmiyya.

al-Mālikī, Abū Bakr (1994): *Riyāḍ al-nufūs fī ṭabaqāt 'ulamā' al-Qayrawān wa Ifrīqiyya*, Bashīr al-Bakkūsh & Muḥammad al-'Arūsī al-Maṭwī (eds.), 2 vols., Beirut: Dār al-Gharb al-Islāmī.

al-Mannūnī, Muḥammad (1992): 'Dawr al-ḥarīr wa ṣinā'āt ukhrā bi-Tiṭwān al-qarn al-tāsi' 'ashar', in *Tiṭwān qabl al-ḥimāya (1860–1912)*, Tetouan: Maṭba'at al-Hidāya, pp. 21–31.

al-Maqqarī, Aḥmad Ibn Muḥammad (2012): *Nafḥ al-ṭīb min ghuṣūn al-Andalus al-raṭīb*, Iḥsān 'Abbās & Muḥammad Bin Sharīfa (eds.), 8 vols., Beirut: Dār al-Ṣādir.

al-Marrākushī, Abū 'Abd Allāh (2012): *al-Dhayl al-takmila li-kitābī al-mawṣūl wa 'l-ṣila*, 6 vols., Tunis: Dār al-Gharb al-Islāmī.

al-Mas'ūdī, 'Alī Ibn Ḥusayn (1861–77): *Murūj al-dhahab wa ma'ādin al-jawhar*, Barbier de Meynard & Pavet de Courteille (eds./trans.), 9 vols., Paris: Imprimerie Nationale.

al-Muqaddasī (1906): *Aḥsan al-taqāsīm fī maʿrifat al-iqlīm*, M. J. de Goeje (ed.), Leiden: Brill.

al-Qumrī, Abū Manṣūr (1991): *Kitāb al-tanwīr fi 'l-iṣṭilāḥāt al-ṭibbiyya*, Riyadh: Maktab al-Tarbiyya al-ʿArabiyya li-Duwal al-Khalīj.

al-Rāzī, Abū Bakr Muḥammad Ibn Zakariyyā (2000): *al-Ḥāwī fi 'l-ṭibb*, Beirut: Dār al-Kutub al-ʿIlmiyya.

—(1987): *Kitāb al-Manṣūrī fi 'l-ṭibb*, Ḥāzim al-Bakrī al-Ṣiddīqī (ed.), Kuwait: Maʿhad al-Makhṭūṭāt al-ʿArabiyya.

—(1881): *Manāfiʿ al-aghdhiya wa-dafʿ maḍarrihā*, Cairo: al-Maṭbaʿ al-Khayriyya.

al-Samarqandī, Najīb al-Dīn (2016): *Kitāb al-aghdhiya wa 'l-ashriba*, Juliane Müller (ed./German translation), Leiden/Boston: Brill.

al-Saqaṭī, Abū ʿAbd Allāh (1931): *Kitāb fī ādāb al-ḥisba*, G.-S. Colin & E. Lévi-Provençal (eds.), Paris: Ernest Leroux.

al-Shayzarī, ʿAbd al-Raḥmān (n.d.): *Kitāb nihāyat al-rutba fī ṭalab al-ḥisba*, Muḥammad Ḥasan Muḥammad Ḥasan Ismāʿīl & Aḥmad Farīd al-Mizyudī (eds.), Beirut: Dār al-Kutub al-ʿIlmiyya; English translation, Ronald Buckley, *The Book of the Islamic Market Inspector*, Oxford: Oxford University Press, 1999.

al-Thaʿālibī (1900): *Ghurar akhbār mulūk al-Furs wa sayruhum*, H. Zotenberg (ed.), Paris: Imprimerie Nationale.

al-Ṭighnarī, Muḥammad Ibn Mālik (2006): *Kitāb zuhrat al-bustān wa nuzhat al-adhhān*, Expiración García Sánchez (ed.), Madrid: Consejo Superior de Investigaciones Cientificas.

al-Tujībī, Ibn Razīn (2012): *Faḍālat al-khiwān fī ṭayyibāt al-ṭaʿām wa 'l-alwān*, Muḥammad Ibn Shaqrūn (ed.), Beirut: Dār al-Gharb al-Islāmī.

al-Ṭūsī, Naṣīr al-Dīn (2014): *Kitāb albāb al-Bāhiyya wa 'l-tarākīb al-sultāniyya. The Sultan's Sex Potions: Arab Aphrodisiacs in the Middle Ages*, Daniel L. Newman (ed./English translation), London: Saqi Books.

al-ʿUmarī, Shihāb al-Dīn (2010): *Masālik al-abṣār fī mamālik al-amṣār*, 27 vols., Kāmil Salmān al-Jabbūrī & Mahdī al-Najm (eds.), Beirut: Dār al-Kutub al-ʿIlmiyya.

al-ʿUqbānī, al-Tilimsānī, Muḥammad (1965): '*Tuḥfat al-nāẓir wa-ghunyat al-dhākir fī ḥifẓ al-shaʿāʾir wa-taghyīr al-manākir*', Ali Chenoufi (ed.), *Bulletin des Études orientales*, XIX, pp. 133–344.

al-Uryūlī [= al-Arbūlī] (1981–83): '*al-Kalām ʿalā 'l-aghdhiya*. Un tratado Nazari sobre alimentos', Amor Díaz García (ed./Spanish translation), *Cuadernos de estudios medievales y ciencias y técnicas historiográficas*, 6–7 (pp. 5–37), 10–11 (pp. 5–91).

al-Warrāq, Abū Muḥammad al-Muẓaffar Ibn Naṣr Ibn Sayyār (1987): *Kitāb al-ṭabīkh wa 'l-iṣlāḥ al-aghdhiyya al-maʾkūlāt wa ṭayyib al-aṭʿima al-maṣnūʿāt*, Kaj Öhrnberg & Sahban Mroueh (eds.), Helsinki, Finnish Oriental Society; English translation Nawal Nasrallah, *Annals of the Caliphs' Kitchens: Ibn Sayyâr al-Warrâq's Tenth-Century Baghdadi Cookbook*, Leiden: Brill, 2007.

Wuṣla → see Anonymous (2017).

Yāqūt al-Ḥamawī (1977): *Muʿjam al-buldān*, 5 vols., Beirut: Dār Ṣādir.

al-Zubaydī, Abū Bakr Muḥammad Ibn al-Ḥasan (1999): *Mukhtaṣar kitāb al-ʿayn*, 2 vols.,

'Abd Allāh Ibn Nāṣir al-Qarnī (ed.), Mekka: Umm al-Qurā University,

IN EUROPEAN LANGUAGES

Ahlwardt, W. (1889–99): *Verzeichnis der arabischen Handschriften*, 10 vols., Berlin: A. Asher & Co.

Ahsan, Muhammad Manazir (1973): 'Social Life under the Abbasids (170–289/786–902)', PhD diss., University of London.

Alpert, Michael (2001): *Crypto-Judaism and the Spanish Inquisition*, Basingstoke: Palgrave.

Álvarez Millán, Cristina & Claudia Heide (eds.) (2008): *Pascual de Gayangos: A Nineteenth-Century Spanish Arabist*, Edinburgh: Edinburgh University Press.

André, Jacques (1981): *L'Alimentation et la cuisine à Rome*, Paris: Les Belles Lettres.

Arié, Rachel (1974–75): 'Remarques sur l'alimentation des musulmans d'Espagne au cours du bas Moyen Âge', *Cuadernos de Estudios Medievales*, 2–3, pp. 289–312.

Arranz-Otaegui, Amaia, Lara Gonzalez Carretero, Monica N. Ramsey & Tobias Richter (2018): 'Archaeobotanical evidence reveals the origins of bread 14,400 years ago in northeastern Jordan', *Proceedings of the National Academy of Sciences*, 115: 31, pp. 7925–930.

Asín-Palacios, Miguel (1919): *La escatologia musulmana en la Divina Comedia*, Madrid: Real Academia Española.

Aubaile-Sallenave, Francoise (1992): 'Zanbo'a, un citrus mysterieux chez les arabes medievaux d'Al-Andalus', in Expiración García Sánchez (ed.), *Ciencias de la naturaleza en Al-Andalus*, Granada: CSIC-I.C.M.A., pp. 111–33.

Bearman, P. J., *et al.* (1960–2005), *Encyclopædia of Islam*, 2nd edn., 12 vols., Leiden: E. J. Brill.

Benkheira, Mohammed Hocine (2000): *Islam et interdits alimentaires. Juguler l'animalité*, Paris: Presses Universitaires de France.

Berenson, Amira (2016): *The Almoravid and the Almohad Empires*, Edinburgh: University of Edinburgh Press.

Bolens, Lucie (1980): 'Pain quotidien et pains de disette dans l'Espagne musulmane', *Annales: Économies, Sociétés, Civilisations*, 35: 3–4, pp. 462–76.

Bottéro, Jean (1995): *Textes Culinaires Mesopotamiens. Mesopotamian Culinary Texts*, University Park, PA: Eisenbrauns.

Brisville, Marianne (2020): 'Et le Moyen Age inventa le couscous', *l'Histoire*, 472, pp. 69–70.

—(2018a): 'L'alimentation carnée dans l'Occident islamique médiéval. Productions, consommations et représentations', 2 vols., PhD diss., Université Lumière-Lyon 2.

—(2018b): 'Meat in the Urban Markets of the Mediaeval Maghrib and al-Andalus. Production, Exchange, and Consumption', *Food and History*, 16: 1, pp. 3–20.

—(2017): 'Plats sûrs et plats sains dans l'Occident musulman médiéval. La *harīsa* comme contre-exemple?', in Bruno Laurioux (ed.), *L'acquisition des aliments: de la nature à la table au Moyen Âge*, Paris: CTHS, pp. 107–18.

—(2013): 'Le gout de la viande chez les élites dans l'Occident musulman medieval, l'exemple du *Kitāb al-Ṭabīẖ, Horizons Maghrébins. Le droit à la mémoire*, 69, pp. 14–20.

Brunschvig, Robert (1940–47): *La Berbérie orientale sous les Ḥafṣides des origines à la fin du XV siècle*, 2 vols., Paris: Adrien-Miasonneuve.

—(1936): *Deux récits de voyage inédits en Afrique du Nord au XVe siècle. Abdelbāsit B. Khalil et Adorne*, Paris: Larose.

—(1935): 'Mesures de capacité de la Tunisie médiévale', *Revue Africaine*, 77: 3–4, pp. 86–90.

Burton, Sir Richard Francis (1893): *Personal Narrative of a Pilgrimage to Al-Madinah and Meccah*, 2 vols., London: Tylston and Edwards.

Carabaza Bravo, Julia M., *et al.* (2004): *Árboles y arbustos en Al-Andalus*, Madrid: Consejo Superior de Investigaciones Científicas.

Chalmeta, P. (1970): 'La Hisba en Ifriqiya et Al-Andalus: Étude Comparative', *Cahiers de Tunisie*, 18: 69–70, pp. 87–105.

Collins, Roger (2012): *Caliphs and Kings Spain, 796–1031*, Chichester: Wiley-Blackwell.

Constable, Olivia Remie (1994): *Trade and Traders in Muslim Spain: The Commercial Realignment of the Iberian Peninsula, 900–1500*, Cambridge: Cambridge University Press.

Cook, Michael (2004): *Commanding the Right and Forbidding Wrong in Islamic Thought*, Cambridge: Cambridge University Press.

Corominas, Joan, & José A. Pascual (1984): *Diccionario crítico etimológico castellano e hispánico*, 4 vols., Madrid: Gredos.

Corriente, Federico (2008): *Dictionary of Arabic and Allied loanwords: Spanish, Portuguese, Catalan, Galician and Kindred Dialects*, Leiden/Boston: Brill.

—(1997): *A Dictionary of Andalusi Arabic*, Leiden: Brill.

Crum, Walter Ewing (1939): *A Coptic Dictionary*, Oxford: The Clarendon Press.

Curtis, Robert I. (1991): *Garum and Salvamenta. Production and Commerce in Materia Medica*, Leiden: Brill.

Dalby, Andrew (2003): *Food in the Ancient World from A to Z*, London: Routledge.

—(1996): *Siren Feasts: A History of Food and Gastronomy in Greece*, New York: Routledge.

Dankoff, Robert, & Sooyong Kim (2011): *An Ottoman Traveller. Selections from the Book of Travels of Evliya Çelebi*, London: Eland Publishing.

Darby, William J., Paul, Ghalioungui & Louis Grivetti (1977): *Food: Gift of Osiris*, 2 vols., London: Academic Press.

De Alcalá, Pedro (1505): *Vocabulista aráuigo en letra castellana*, Granada: Juan Varela de Salamanca.

De Casteau, Lancelot (1604): *Ouverture de Cuisine*, Liège: Leonard Streel.

de Epalza, Miguel, & Ramón Petit (eds.) (1973): *Recueil d'études sur les Moriscos andalous en Tunisie*, Madrid: Instituto Hispano-Arabe de Cultura.

Dietrich, Albert (1993): *Die Ergänzung Ibn Ǧulǧuls zur Materia medica des Dioskurides*, Göttingen: Vandenhoeck & Ruprecht.

—(1991): *Die Dioskurides-Erklärung des Ibn al-Baitār. Ein Beitrag zur arabischen Pflanzensynonymik des Mittelalters*, Göttingen: Vandenhoeck & Ruprecht.

—(1988): *Dioscurides triumphans. Ein anonymer arabischer Kommentar (Ende 12. Jahrh.*

N.Chr.) zur Materia medica, 2 vols., Göttingen: Vandenhoeck & Ruprecht.

Douglas, Mary (2001): *Implicit Meanings: Selected Essays in Anthropology*, 2nd edn., London/New York: Routledge.

Dozy, Pieter Reinhart (1881): *Supplément aux dictionnaires arabes*, 2 vols., Leiden: Brill.

—(1861) *Histoire des musulmans d'Espagne: jusqu'à la conquête de l'Andalousie par les Almoravides (711–1110)*, 4 vols., Leiden: Brill; partial English translation, Francis Griffin Stokes, *Spanish Islam*, London: Chatto & Windus, 1913.

Dozy, P. R., & W.H. Engelmann (1869): *Glossaire des mots espagnols et portugais dérivés de l'arabe*, Leiden: E. J. Brill.

Dozy, R. & Charles Pellat (1961): *Le Calendrier de Cordoue [de l'année 961]. Texte arabe et ancienne traduction latine*, Leiden: Brill.

de Eguílaz y Yanguas, Leopoldo (1886): *Glosario etimológico de las palabras españoles (castellanas, catalanas, gallegas, mallorquinas, portuguesas, valencianas y bascongadas) de orígen oriental (árabe, hebreo, malayo, persa y turco)*, Granada: La Lealtad.

EI[2], see Bearman, P. J., *et al.* (1960–2005).

EI[3], see Fleet, Kate (2007–).

Ellis, A. G., & Edward Edwards (1912): *A Descriptive List of the Arabic Manuscripts Acquired by the Trustees of the British Museum since 1894*, London: British Museum.

Engeser, Marianne (1986): *Der 'liber servitoris' des Abulkasis (936–1013)*, Stuttgart: Deutscher Apotheker Verlag.

Erman, Adolf, & Hermann Grapow (1971): *Wörterbuch der aegyptischen Sprache*, 7 vols., Berlin: Akademie Verlag.

Fleet, Kate, *et al.* (2007–): *The Encyclopaedia of Islam: Three*, Leiden: Brill.

Fraenkel, Siegmund (1886): *Die aramäischen Fremdwörter im arabischen*, Leiden: E. J. Brill.

García Sánchez, *Expiración (2007): 'La diététique alimentaire arabe, reflet d'une réalité quotidienne ou d'une tradition fossilisée ? (IXe–XVIe siècles)'*, in Françoise Sabban & Frédérique Audoin-Rouzeau (eds.), *Un aliment sain dans un corps sain: Perspectives historiques*, Tours: Presses universitaires François-Rabelais, pp. 65–92.

—(2004): 'Especias y condimentos en la sociedad andalusí: Prácticas culinarias y aplicaciones dietéticas', in Antonio Garrido Aranda (ed.), *El sabor del sabor: hierbas aromaticas, condimentos y especias*, Córdoba: Universidad de Córdoba, pp. 71–96.

—(2001): 'Las fuentes citadas en el tratado agrícola de al-Tignari', *Dynamis: Acta Hispanica ad Medicinae Scientiarumque Historiam Illustrandam*, 21, pp. 205–31.

—(1998): 'Les techniques de distillation de l'eau de rose à al-Andalus', *Res Orientales*, XI, pp. 125–40.

—(1997): 'La consommation des épices et des plantes aromatiques en al-Andalus', *Médiévales*, 33, pp. 41–53.

—(1995a): 'La gastronomía andalusí', in El Legado Andalusí (ed.), *El zoco: vida económica y artes tradicionales en al-Andalus y Marruecos*, Barcelona: Lunwerg Editores.

—(1995b): 'La traducción catalana medieval del *Kitāb al-Agḏiya* (Tratado de los alimentos) de Avenzoar ', in *Colloqui d'Història de l'Alimentació a la Corona d'Aragó*, Lérida: Institut d'Estudis Ilerdencs, I, pp. 363–86.

—(1990a): 'Agricultura y legislación islámica: el prólogo del *'Kitāb zuhrat al-bustān* de al-Ṭiġnarī', in E. García Sánchez (ed.), *Ciencias de la Naturaleza en al-Andalus. Textos y Estudios*, I, Granada: CSIC/EEA, pp. 179–93.

—(1990b): 'Los cultivos de Al-Andalus y su influencia en la Alimentación', in *Aragón vive su historia : [actas de las] II Jornadas Internacionales de Cultura Islámica, Teruel 1988*, Madrid: Al-Fadila Instituto Occidental de Cultura Islámica, pp. 183–92.

—(1988): 'Al-Tignari y su lugar de origen', *Al-Qantara*, 9: 1, pp. 1–12.

—(1987–88): 'El Tratado Agrícola Del Granadino Al-Ṭiġnarī', *Quaderni di Studi Arabi*, 5/6, pp. 278–91.

—(1986): 'La alimentación en la Andalucía islámica. Estudio histórico y bromatológico. II: Carne, pescado, huevos, leche y productos lácteos', *Andalucía Islámica. Textos y Estudios*, 4–5 (1983–86), pp. 237–78.

—(1981–82): 'La alimentación en la Andalucía islámica. Estudio histórico y bromatológico. I. Cereales y leguminosas', *Andalucía Islámica. Textos y Estudios*, 2–3, pp. 139–79.

—(1980): 'Ibn Azraq: Uryúza sobre ciertas preferencias gastronómicas de los granadino', J. Bosch Vilá & W. Hoenerback (eds.), *Andalusia Islamica, Textos y Estudios*, Granada: Universidad de Granada, I, pp. 141–63.

García Sánchez, Expiración & Luis Ramón-Laca (2001): 'Sebestén y zumaque, dos frutos importados de Oriente durante la Edad Media', *Anuario de Estudios Medievales*, 31:2, pp. 867-881.

García, Expiración, & Julia María Carabaza (2009): 'Studies on the Agronomy of Al-Andalus', *Revue des mondes musulmans et de la Méditerranée*, 126.

García-Sanjuán, Alejandro (2008): 'Jews and Christians in Almoravid Seville as Portrayed by the Islamic Jurist Ibn 'Abdūn', *Medieval Encounters*, pp. 78–98.

Gaul, Anny (2018): 'Seven Centuries of Bstila', *Cooking with Gaul*, https://cookingwith-gaul.com/2018/02/25/seven-centuries-of-bstila/.

George-Tvrtković, Rita (2012): *A Christian Pilgrim in Medieval Iraq: Riccoldo da Montecroce's Encounter with Islam*, Turnhout: Brepols.

Gerli, Michael E., & Ryan D. Giles (2021): *The Routledge Hispanic Studies Companion to Medieval Iberia: Unity in Diversity*, London/New York: Routledge.

Ghazi, M. F. (1959): 'Un groupe sociale: les "raffinées" (*Ẓurafā'*)', *SI*, XI, pp. 39–71.

Gitlitz, David M., & Linda Kay Davidson (2000): *A Drizzle of Honey. The Life and Recipes of Spain's Secret Jews*, New York: St Martin's Griffin.

Gilli, Patrick (1984): 'Les Traités de cuisine dans la *péninsule ibérique:* 13e et 16e siècles', MA diss., Université de Paris I.

Glick, Thomas F. (1979): *Islamic and Christian Spain in the Early Middle Ages*, Princeton, NJ: Princeton University Press.

Gobert, Ernest (1955): 'Les références historiques des nourritures tunisiennes', *Cahiers de Tunisie*, 12, pp. 501–42.

Goody, Jack (1996): *Cooking, Cuisine and Class: A Study in Comparative Sociology*, Cambridge: Cambridge University Press.

Grainger, Sally (2021): *The Story of Garum: Fermented Fish Sauce and Salted Fish in the Ancient World*, London/New York: Routledge.

Guigues, Pierre (1905): 'Les noms arabes dans Serapion, "Liber de simplici medicina":

essai de restitution et d'identification des noms arabes de médicaments usités au moyen âge', *Journal Asiatique*, 5 (10ème serie), pp. 49-112.

Hamarneh, Sami (1975): *Catalogue of Arabic Manuscripts on Medicine and Pharmacy at the British Library*, Cairo: Les Editions Universitaires d'Egypte.

Harrell, Richard S., Thomas Fox, Mohammed Abu-Talib *et al.* (2007): *A Dictionary of Moroccan Arabic. Moroccan-English*, Washington D.C.: Georgetown University Press.

Harvey, Leonard Patrick (2005): *Muslims in Spain, 1500 to 1614*, Chicago: University of Chicago Press.

Hernández Bermejo, J. Esteban, & Expiración García Sánchez (2009): 'Tulips: An Ornamental Crop in the Andalusian Middle Ages', *Economic Botany*, 63: 1, pp. 60–6.

Hernandez Bermejo, J. E. & García Sánchez, E. (1988): *La Figura de Ibn al-Awwam y el Significado de su 'Tratado de Agricultura' dentro de la Escuela Agronómica Andalusi*, Madrid: Ministerio Agricultura, Pesca y Alimentacion.

Hinz, Walther (1955): *Islamische Masse und Gewichte*, Leiden: E. J. Brill.

Issa Bey, Ahmed (1930): *Dictionnaire des noms des plantes en Latin, français, anglais et arabe*, Cairo: Imprimerie Nationale.

Isidorus (1911): *Etymologiarum sive originum*, W. M. Lindsay (ed.), Oxford: Clarendon Press; English translation, Stephen A. Barney *et al.*, *The Etymologies of Isidore of Seville*, Cambridge: Cambridge University Press, 2006.

Jayyusi, Salma Khadra (ed.) (1992): *The Legacy of Muslim Spain*, 2 vols., Leiden: E. J. Brill.

Jónsson, Már (2007). 'The Expulsion of the Moriscos from Spain in 1609–1614: The Destruction of an Islamic Periphery', *Journal of Global History*, 2: 2, pp. 195–212.

Käs, Fabian (2010): *Die Mineralien in der arabischen Pharmakognosie: Eine Konkordanz zur Mineralischen Materia Medica der klassischen arabischen Heilmittelkunde nebst überlieferungsgeschichtlichen Studien*, 2 vols., Wiesbaden: Otto Harrassowitz.

Kazimirski, A. de Biberstein (1860): *Dictionnaire arabe-français, contenant toutes les racines de la langue arabe, leurs dérivés, tant dans l'idiome vulgaire que dans l'idiome littéral, ainsi que les dialects d'Alger et de Maroc*, 2 vols., Paris: Maisonneuve.

Kircher, Heidi Gisela (1967): 'Die "Einfachen Heilmittel" aus dem "Handbuch der Chirurgie" des Ibn al-Quff', Ph.D. diss., Rheinische Friedrich-Wilhelms-Universität (Bonn).

Kuhne Brabant, Rosa (1995): 'La fruta, ¿alimento o medicamento? Reflexiones sobre la presencia de la fruta en la farmacopea árabe medieval', *Anaquel de estudios arabes*, VI, pp. 69–86.

—(1995): 'Reflexiones sobre un tratadito dietético prácticamente desconocido, el *Tafḍīl al-'asal 'alà l-sukkar* de Abū Marwān b. Zuhr', in Concepción Castillo Castillo *et al.* (eds.), *Homenaje al profesor José María Fórneas Besteiro*, Granada, Universidad de Granada, II, pp. 1057–67.

Kuhne Brabant, Rosa & Monique da Silva (1997): 'Le sucre et le doux dans l'alimentation d'al-Andalus', *Médiévales*, 33, pp. 55–67.

Kulikowski, Michael (2004): *Late Roman Spain and Its Cities: Ancient Society and History*, Baltimore: Johns Hopkins University Press.

Lane, W. E. (1863–74): *Arabic-English Lexicon Derived from the Best and the Most Copious Eastern Sources; Comprising a Very Large Number of Words and Significations Omitted in the Kámoos, with Supplements to Its Abridged and Defective Explanations, Ample Grammatical and Critical Comments, and Examples in Prose and Verse*, 5 vols., London: Williams and Norgate (vols. 6–8, ed. Stanley Lane Poole, London, 1877–93).

Latham, J. D. (1957): 'Towards a Study of Andalusian Immigration and Its Place in Tunisian History', *Cahiers de Tunisie*, pp. 203–52.

Laurioux, Bruno (2005): *Une histoire culinaire du moyen âge*, Paris: Honoré Champion.

—(1983): 'De l'usage des épices dans l'alimentation médiévale', *Médiévales*, 5, pp. 15–31.

Lev, Efraim, & Zohar Amar (2007): *Practical Materia Medica of the Medieval Eastern Mediterranean According to the Cairo Genizah*, Leiden: Brill.

Levey, Martin (1973): *Early Arabic pharmacology / An introduction based on ancient and medieval sources*, Leiden: E. J. Brill.

—(1966): *The Medical Formulary or Aqrabīdhīn of al-Kindi*, Madison/ Milwaukee: University of Wisconsin Press.

—(1961): 'Ibn Māsawaih and His Treatise on Simple Aromatic Substances: Studies in the History of Arabic Pharmacology I', *Journal of the History of Medicine and Allied Sciences*, 16: 4, pp. 394–410.

Lévi-Provençal, E. (1932): *L'Espagne musulmane au Xe siècle. Institutions et vie sociale*, Paris, Maisonneuve & Larose.

Lewicka, Paulina B. (2011): *Food and Foodways of Medieval Cairenes: Aspects of Life in an Islamic Metropolis of the Eastern Mediterranean*, Leiden: Brill.

Lirola Delgado, Jorge (ed.) (2004–17): *Biblioteca de Al-Andalus*, 9 vols., Almería: Fundación lbn Tufayl de Estudios Árabes.

Löw, Immanuel (1881): *Aramaeische Pflanzennamen*, Leipzig: Wilhelm Engelmann.

Magirus, Antonius (1612): *Koocboec oft familieren keukenboec*, Leuven: Iohannes Christophorus Falvius; 3rd edn., Antwerp: Martinus Verhulst, 1663.

Maíllo Salgado, Felipe (1991): *Los arabismos del Castellano en la baja edad media. Consideraciones históricas y filológicas*, Salamanca: Universidad de Salamanca.

Marín, Manuela (2010): 'Words for Cooking: The Culinary Lexicon in Ibn Razīn's *Fudālat al-khiwān*', in Juan Pedro Monferrer-Sala & Nader Al Jallad (eds.), *The Arabic Language Across the Ages*, Wiesbaden: Otto Harrassowitz, pp. 37–48.

—(2004): 'From Al-Andalus to Spain: Arab Traces in Spanish Cooking', *Food & History*, 2, pp. 35–52.

—(1997): 'Cuisine d'Orient, cuisine d'Occident', *Médiévales*, 33, pp. 9–21.

—(1994): 'Nota sobre *ğarād*', *Al-Qanṭara*, 15, pp. 253–6.

—(1981): 'Sobre Būrān y Būrāniyya', *Al-Qantara*, 2, pp. 193–207.

Marín, M. & David Waines (eds.) (1994): *La alimentacion en las culturas islamicas*, Madrid: Agencia Espagniola de Cooperación Internacional.

Martellotti, Andrea (2001): *Il* Liber de ferculis *di Giambonino da Cremona. La gastronomia araba in Occidente nella trattatistica dietetica*, Fasano: Schena.

May, Robert (1685): *The Accomplisht Cook, Or the Art and Mystery of Cooking*, London: Obadiah Blagrave.

Menocal, María Rosa, Raymond P. Scheindlin & Michael Sels (2000): *The Cambridge History of Arabic Literature: The Literature of al-Andalus*, Cambridge: Cambridge

University Press.

Meyerhof, Max (1940): 'Un glossaire de matière médicale, composé par Maïmonide: *Šarḥ asmāʾ al-ʿuqqār* (l'explication des noms de drogues)', *Mémoires Présentés à l'Institut d'Egypte,* 41, Cairo: Imprimerie de l'Institut Français d'Archéologie Orientale.

Meyerhof, M. & G. P. Sobhi (1932): *The Abridged Version of the 'Book of Simple Drugs' of Aḥmad ibn Muḥammad Al-Ghâfiqî by Gregorius Abû-lFarag (Barhebraeus),* Cairo: El Ettimad.

Newman, Daniel L. (2018): 'Arabic Travel Writing', in Das Nandini & Tim Youngs (eds.), *The Cambridge History of Travel Writing,* Cambridge: Cambridge University Press, pp. 143–58.

Ouerfelli, Mohamed (2008): *Le Sucre. Production, Commercialisation et Usages dans la Méditerranée médiévale,* Leiden/Boston: Brill.

Panayi, Panikos (2014): *Fish and Chips: A History,* London: Reaktion Books.

Powell, Owen (2003): *Galen: On the Properties of Foodstuffs* (*De alimentorum facultatibus*), Cambridge: Cambridge University Press.

Rauwolf, Leonhard (1582): *Aigentliche beschreibung der Raiß/so er vor diser zeit gegen Auffgang in die Morgenländer/fürnemlich Syriam, Iudæam, Arabiam, Mesopotamiam, Babyloniam, Assyriam, Armeniam etc. nicht ohne geringe mühe vnnd grosse gefahr selbs volbracht,* Lauingen: Leonhard Reinmichel.

Renaud, H., & G. S. Colin (eds./trans.) (1934): *Tuḥfat al-aḥbāb: Glossaire de la matière médicale marocaine,* Paris: Paul Geuthner.

Reynolds, Dwight F. (2021): *The Medical Heritage of al-Andalus,* London: Routledge.

—(2008): 'Al-Maqqarī's Ziryāb: The Making of a Myth', *Middle Eastern Literatures,* 11: 2, 2008, pp. 155–68.

Riley-Smith, Jonathan (1987): *The Crusades: A Short History,* New Haven, CT: Yale University Press.

Roden, Claudia (2000): *The New Book of Middle Eastern Food,* New York: Alfred A. Knopf.

Rodinson, Maxime (2005): 'Les influences de la civilisation Musulmane sur la civilisation Européenne médiévale dans les domaines de la consommation et de la distraction : l'alimentation', *Food & History,* 3:1, pp. 9–30.

—(1962): 'La *ma'muniyyat* en orient et en occident', Études *d'Orientalisme dédiées à la mémoire de Lévi-Provençal,* II, Paris pp. 733–47.

—(1949): 'Recherches sur les documents arabes relatifs à la cuisine', *Revue des Études Islamiques,* pp. 95–165.

Rodinson, Maxime, A. J. Arberry & Charles Perry (eds.) (2001): *Mediaeval Arab Cookery,* Totnes: Prospect Books.

Rodríguez Lorente, Juan José, & Salvador Fontenla Ballesta (1988): 'Contribución al estudio de la metrología hispano-árabe. La plata nasri', *Al-Qantara,* IX, pp. 475–87.

Roth, Martha T. *et al.* (eds.) (1956–2010): *The Assyrian Dictionary of the Oriental Institute of the University of Chicago,* 28 vols., Chicago: University of Chicago.

Rouighi, Ramzi (2005): 'Mediterranean Crossings, North African Bearings: A Taste of Andalus in Bejaia (1250–1400)', PhD diss., Columbia University.

Sato, Tsugitaka (2015): *Sugar in the Social Life of Medieval Islam,* Leiden: Brill.

Sauvaire, M. H. (1884): 'Arab Metrology. V. Ez-Zahrâwy', *Journal of the Royal Asiatic Society of Great Britain and Ireland*, 16: 4, pp. 495–524.

Sbath, Paul (1936): 'Traité sur les substances simples aromatiques par Yohanna Ben Massawaïh', *Bulletin de l'institut égyptien*, 19: 1 pp. 5–27.

Scappi, Bartolomeo (1570): *Opera*, Venice; English translation, Terence Scully, *The Opera of Bartolomeo Scappi (1570). L'arte et prudenza d'un maestro cuoco (The Art and Craft of a Master Cook)*, Toronto: University of Toronto Press, 2011.

Schiaparelli, Celestino (1871): *Vocabulista in arabico, pubblicato per la prima volta, sopra un codice della biblioteca Riccardiana di Firenze*, Florence: Le Monnier.

Schmucker, Werner (1969): *Die pflanzliche und mineralische Materia medica im Firdaus al-Ḥikma des Ṭabarī*, Bonn: Selbstverlag des Orientalischen Seminars der Universität Bonn.

Shafer-Elliott, Cynthia (2013): *Food in Ancient Judah: Domestic Cooking in the Time of the Hebrew Bible*, Sheffield: Equinox.

Shoshan, Boaz (1993): *Popular Culture in Medieval Cairo*. Cambridge: Cambridge University Press.

Siggel, Alfred (1958): *Das Buch der Gifte des Gābir Ibn Ḥayyān*, Wiesbaden: Franz Steiner Verlag.

Steingass, Francis Joseph (1892): *A Comprehensive Persian–English Dictionary, Including the Arabic Words and Phrases to Be Met with in Persian Literature*, London: Routledge & K. Paul.

Stengel, Kilien, & Siham Debbabi Missaoui (eds.) (2020): *La cuisine du Maghreb n'est-elle qu'une simple histoire de couscous?*, Paris: L'Harmattan.

Streck, Michael P. *et al.* (2016–18): *Reallexikon der Assyriologie und Vorderasiatischen Archäologie*, 15 vols., Berlin: De Gruyter.

Terés Sádaba, Elías (1975): 'Los códices árabes de la colección Gayangos', *Al-Andalus*, 40, pp. 1–52.

Ukers, William H. (1922): *All About Coffee*, New York: Tea and Coffee Trade Journal Company.

Unvala, J. (ed./trans.) (1921): *The Pahlavi Text 'King Husraw and His Boy'*, Paris: n.p.

Vallve'Bermejo, Joaquín (1984), 'Notas de metrología hispano-árabe. III. Pesos y monedas', *Al-Qantara*, V, pp. 147–69.

—(1977): 'Notas de metrología hispano-árabe. II. Medidas de capacidad', *Al-Andalus*, 42: 1, pp. 61–110.

—(1976): 'Notas de metrología hispano-árabe. El codo en la España musulmana', *Al-Andalus*, 41: 2, pp. 339–54.

van Gelder, Jan (2000): *Of Dishes and Discourse: Classical Arabic Literary Representations of Food*, Richmond: Curzon.

Vehling, Joseph Dommers (trans.) (1977): *Cookery and Dining in Imperial Rome: A Bibliography, Critical Review and Translation of the Ancient Book Known as Apicius de re Coquinaria*, Dover Publications.

Vilar, Juan Bautista (1997): 'El viaje de Pascual de Gayangos a Marruecos en 1848 en busca de manuscritos y libros árabes', *Boletín de la Biblioteca Menéndez* Pelayo, 73, pp. 29–41.

von Grunebaum, Gustav E. (1953): *Medieval Islam*, Chicago: University of Chicago Press.

Waines, David (ed.) (2012): *Food Culture and Health in Pre-Modern Islamic Societies*, Leiden: Brill.

—(ed.) (2002): *Patterns of Everyday Life*, Aldershot: Ashgate.

—(1992): 'The *darmak* decree', *Al-Qantara*, 13, pp. 263–5.

Watson, Andrew M. (1983): *Agricultural Innovation in the Early Islamic World. The Diffusion of Crops and Farming Techniques, 700–1100*, Cambridge: Cambridge University Press.

Weiss Adamson, Melitta (2006): 'Ibn Ǧazla auf dem Weg nach Bayern', in Andreas Speer (ed.), *Wissen* über *Grenzen. Arabisches Wissen und lateinisches Mittelalter*, Berlin: de Gruyter, pp. 357–74.

Wenzel, Catherina (2014): *Verdammt und Vollkommen Muhammad in Dantes Divina Commedia*, Münster: LIT Verlag.

Wiedemann, Eilhard (1914): 'Über arabische Parfüms', *Archiv für Geschichte der Medizin*, 8: 2/3, pp. 83–8.

Yaacob, Ahmad Bin Che (1996): 'The Development of the Institution of Hisba in Medieval Islam', PhD diss., University of Edinburgh.

Yungmann, Limor (2020): 'Les livres de cuisine du Moyen-Orient médiéval (IVe–Xe/ Xe–XVIe)', PhD diss., École des Hautes Études en Sciences Sociales.

Ziolkowski, Jan M. (2015): *Dante and Islam*, New York: Fordham University Press.

INDEX OF PEOPLE AND PLACES

ʿAbd al-Basīṭ Ibn Khalīl (15th c.) 26–7
ʿAbd al-Raḥmān I (756–88) 1, 3
ʿAbd al-Raḥmān II (822–52) 2, 3
al-ʿAbdarī, Muḥammad (d. 1289) 15
Abū 'l-Fidā (d. 1331) 13
Alfonso X (1221-1284) 11–12
ʿAlī Ibn Abī Ṭālib (656-661) 11
Almería (al-Mariyya) 3, 12, 14
Almohads (*al-Muwaḥḥidūn*) 6–7, 12, 14, 28
Almoravids (*al-Murābiṭūn*) 6–7, 12
ʿAmrūs Ibn Yūsuf al-Muwallad (8th/9th c.) 233
al-Andalus (Muslim Spain) 1, 3, 5–8, 12, 14, 17, 24, 27–28, 31, 36, 39, 42, 48, 50, 54, 60, 63–64, 67, 69, 72, 111, 116, 118
al-Anṭākī, Dāwūd (d. 1599) 49
Aquinas, Thomas (d. 1274) 9
Avicenna → see Ibn Sīnā

Bacon, Roger (d. 1292) 9
ʿAbd al-Laṭīf al-Baghdādī 189
al-Baghdādī, Muḥammad Ibn al-Ḥasan al-Kātib (d. 1239–40) 3, 46
al-Bakrī, Abū ʿUbayd (d. 1094) 42
Berbers 1, 103
Bijāya (Béjaïa) 14–15, 381
Bonaventura da Siena (13th c.)
Būrān 82

Charles of Anjou (d. 1285) 16
Córdoba (Qurṭuba) 1–3, 7, 12–13, 36, 45

Dante Alighieri (1265–1321) 11

Francis of Assisi (d. 1226) 9

al-Ghāfiqī, Abū Jaʿfar (d. 1165) 384
Grosseteste, Robert (d. 1253) 9
Granada (Gharnāṭa) 7, 12, 23, 28

Ḥafṣid 14, 15, 71
Hārūn al-Rashīd (766-809) 26
al-Ḥimyarī, ʿAbd al-Munʿim (14th c.) 43

Ibn ʿAbd al-Ra'ūf (10th c.) 31
Ibn ʿAbdūn al-Tujībī (12th c.) 10
Ibn Abī Uṣaybiʿa (d. 1270) 5
Ibn al-ʿAwwām, Abū Zakariyā (*fl.* 12th c.) 23, 48, 50, 68
Ibn al-Azraq, Abū ʿAbdallāh (1428–69) 28, 36
Ibn al-Bayṭār, Abū Muḥammad (d. 1248) 30
Ibn Baṣṣāl, Abū ʿAbd Allāh (11th c.) 3, 5, 23, 46
Ibn Baṭṭūṭa, Abū ʿAbdallāh (d. 1369) 28
Ibn Biklārish, Yūsuf (Yūnus) b. Isḥāq al-Isrā'īlī (*fl.* late 11th – early 12th c.) 59
Ibn Buṭlān, Ibn ʿAbdūn (1001–1064) 134, 283, 357
Ibn Ḥabīb, ʿAbd al-Malik (790–853) 127
Ibn Ḥayyān al-Qurṭubī (d. 1076) 2
Ibn Janāḥ, Abū 'l-Walīd Marwān (*fl.* first half 11th c.) 23, 378
Ibn al-Jazzār, Abū Jaʿfar (d. 1005) 23
Ibn Jazla (d. 1100) 11
Ibn Juljul, Sulaymān Ibn Ḥassān (10th c.) 5
Ibn Khalṣūn al-Andalusī (13th c.) 39, 52–3, 67
Ibn al-Khaṭīb, Muḥammad Ibn ʿAbd Allāh (d. 1374) 48
Ibn al-Khūja, Muḥammad (1869–1943) 29
Ibn Luyūn (14th c.) 91, 155
Ibn Mardanīsh (d. 1172) 12, 68
Ibn Māsawayh, Abū-Zakarīyā Yūḥannā (d. 857) 53
Ibn Maymūn → see Maimonides
Ibn Qayyim al-Jawziyya (d. 1350) 92
Ibn Qutayba (d. 889) 183, 205, 219
Ibn al-Raqqām (*ca.* 1250–1315) 50
Ibn Rushayd, Muḥammad (d. 1321) 15
Ibn Saʿīd al-Maghribī (1214–1286)
Ibn Sīnā (980–1037) 4–5, 11
Ibn al-Ukhuwwa (1258–1328) 32
Ibn Waḥshiyya (10th c.) 95, 171
Ibn Wāfid, Abū 'l-Muṭarrif (d. 1067) 3
Ibn Zuhr, Abū Marwān ʿAbd al-Malik (d. 1162) 4–5, 22, 33, 39, 43, 50, 61–2, 65–6
Ibrāhīm Ibn al-Mahdī (779–839) 2–3, 38

Ifrīqiya 100, 338
al-Idrīsī, al-Sharīf (d. 1165) 9, 13, 43
al-Ishbīlī, Abū 'l-Khayr (*fl.* 11th–12th c.) 49–50
al-Isrā'ilī, Isḥāq (d. *ca.* 955) 52

Jaén (Jayān) 7

Latini, Brunetto (1220–1294) 11
Louis IX (1240–1270) 16

Malaga (Malāqa) 28, 33
al-Ma'mūn (813–833) 4, 82
Maimonides (d. 1204) 4
al-Mālikī, Abū Bakr (*flr.* 1061–81) 7
al-Manṣūr (d. 1002) 3
al-Maqqarī, Shihāb al-Dīn (d. 1632) 28
Marrakech (Marrākush) 6, 22
al-Mas'ūdī, 'Alī Ibn Ḥusayn (d. 956) 53, 59
al-Mawṣilī, Ibrāhīm (d. 804) 2
al-Mawṣilī, Isḥāq (d. 850) 2
al-Muqaddasī, Shams al-Dīn (2nd half of the 10th century) 324
Murcia (Mursiyya) 7, 12–14, 36, 68, 71, 118
al-Mustanṣir (1249–77) 16, 71
Peter the Venerable (ca. 1092–1156) 10

al-Qumrī [al-Qamarī], Abū Manṣūr (*fl.* 10th century) 52

al-Rāzī, Abū Bakr Muḥammad Ibn Zakariyyā (d. 925 or 935) 4, 30, 39, 48, 51–2, 65
Riccoldo da Monte Croce (1243–1320) 10
Robert of Ketton (d. 1157) 10

Saint Louis → see Louis IX
Ṣalāḥ al-Dīn al-Ayyūbī (1137–1193) 11
al-Samarqandī, Najīb al-Dīn (d. 1222) 45, 47
Ṣanhāja 6
al-Saqaṭī (11th – 12th c.) 33, 54, 61
Seville (Ishbiliyya) 5, 7, 10, 12–13, 15, 22, 30, 381
al-Shāṭirī, Muḥammad Ibn al-Ḥasan (*fl.* 1731–32) 191
al-Shayzarī, 'Abd al-Raḥmān Ibn Naṣr (13th c.) 32
Sicily 9, 15–16, 43, 389
Ṭāriq Ibn Ziyāḍ (7th – 8th c.) 1
Theophrastus (d. 287 BCE) 357
al-Ṭighnarī, Muḥammad Ibn Mālik (11th – 12th c.) 23, 50
Toledo (Ṭulayṭula) 3, 6, 9, 11, 35, 54
al-Tujībī, Ibn Razīn (13th c.) 3, 5, 10, 13–15, 17–26, 29, 32, 34–38, 40, 42–43, 45–48, 50, 54–60, 62–68, 71
Tunis 7, 14–16, 26, 29, 33, 42, 71, 100

al-'Umarī, Shihāb al-Dīn (1301–1349) 54
al-'Uqbānī al-Tilimsānī (d. 1467) 33
al-Uryūlī, Abū Bakr (15th c.) 57

Valencia (Balansiyya) 6–8, 12, 36, 54, 68, 118
al-Warrāq, Ibn Sayyār (10th c.?) 38, 43, 59

Yāqūt al-Ḥamawī (d. 1229) 13

Ziryāb, Abū 'l-Ḥasan 'Alī Ibn Nāfi' (*ca.* 790-852) 2–3

GENERAL INDEX

abū khuraysh → see borage
acorn (*ballūṭ*) 34, 45, 51, 247–8
afzān → see artichoke
agarwood (*'ūd; Aloexylon agallochon* Lour.) 52–53, 99, 120, 384–7
agarwood fruit (*harnuwa*) 384, 387
aḥrash 209, 218, 264, 299, 305
aknāf 40, 195
almonds (*lawz*; *Prunus amygdalus*) 25, 50–1, 56, 63, 100–1, 104–6, 116, 119, 121–5, 129, 133, 136–9, 157, 161–3, 166–7, 170, 173, 181, 187, 192, 197–199, 201, 203–6, 208, 211, 214, 219, 222, 226–7, 229–30, 234, 237–8, 240–2, 247–8, 250–1, 253–4, 256–7, 264–5, 272, 274, 276–9, 288, 298, 300, 303, 318, 328–31, 334–8, 340, 342–5, 375–7
ambergris, 52–4, 66, 184
almond oil (*duhn al-lawz*) 129, 334, 337, 340–1, 376
anchovy (*shaṭṭūn; Engraulis encrasicolus*) 42, 269
anise (*anīsūn*; *Pimpinella anisum*) 364, 369, 373
apples (*tuffāḥ, Pyrus malus*) 45, 48, 184, 264, 281, 369, 371
'aqīd 63
'arabī 12, 60, 192, 380
arnabī 163, 283
artichoke (*ḥarshaf, khurshūf*; *Cynara cardunculus, var. scolymus*) 21, 30, 46, 86, 182, 293, 316–17
ashqāqul 87, 340, 341
'aṣīda 36, 135, 335
asparagus (*asfarāj, hilyawn*; *Asparagus officinalis*) 2, 21, 45–6, 86, 178–80, 316
aubergine (*bādhinjān*; *Solanum melongena*) 21, 31, 45–6, 50, 71, 86, 95–6, 111–12, 148–49, 158–9, 168, 217, 264, 283–4, 302–13, 319, 352–3, 360

badawiyya 238
badī'ī 200, 208, 291
balāja (tripe casserole) 24, 198
barkūs 117
barley (*sha'īr*; *Hordeum vulgare*) 29, 34, 36, 44–5, 57, 66, 82, 118, 154, 358, 363–4, 366, 368–9, 371–3, 376, 386
basbāsiyya (fennel stew) 173, 275
bay leaf (*rand*; *Laurus nobilis*) 53
baysār 112, 150, 190, 325
bāzīn 153
beef (*laḥm baqarī*) 21, 38–9, 57, 66, 84–5, 95, 148, 151, 153–4, 157–8, 160, 162–5, 264
borage (*lisān al-thawr*; *Borrago officinalis*) 175
borax (*bawraq*) 358, 376, 388
bovine antelope (*baqar waḥsh*) 37, 208
box (*buqs*; *Buxus sempirverens*) 155
brains (*dimāgh*) 63, 238, 339, 342, 376
bran (*nukhāla*) 33, 50, 116–18, 133, 363–4, 366, 368–9
bread (*khubz*) 21, 24–6, 30, 33–6, 40, 57, 61, 70–2, 82, 85, 89–92, 94–101, 103, 107–8, 111–12, 114–15, 127, 131, 153, 165, 193, 203, 207, 225, 237, 242, 260, 278, 288, 294, 296, 299, 304, 334, 345, 367–8, 371–2, 376, 382
bread crumb (*lubāb*) 237
breadcrumbs 35–6, 40, 62, 92, 97–8, 102, 105–7, 109, 112–15, 133, 136, 149, 195, 199, 203–5, 222, 234, 236, 246, 254, 257, 265, 272, 277–9, 283, 288, 298–300, 303–8, 310, 312–13, 334, 343
briar wood (*khalanj*; *Erica arborea*) 72
brisket 95, 163
broad beans (*fūl*; *Vicia faba*) 21, 46, 48, 87, 98, 112–113, 147, 150, 190–191, 208, 321–325, 370
bunk, 383, 385–7
broad-leaved thyme (*nammām*; *Thymus pulegioides*) 46, 52, 183–4, 220, 347, 360, 381
bulyāṭ 154
būdhaj 362, 363
bunk 383, 385–7
Būrāniyya 160, 182

butter (*zubd*) 21, 26, 39, 59–60, 86, 94, 97–9, 102–9, 113, 115, 124, 127–30, 132, 135–8, 141–3, 145–6, 148–51, 153–6, 201, 206–7, 213, 240–1, 252, 288, 293–5, 297, 300, 302, 315–16, 318, 327
buttermilk (*laban makhīḍ*) 206, 295

cabbage (*kurunb; Brassica oleracea*) 30, 95, 147, 153–5, 169–70, 264–5, 318
camphor (*kāfūr*; *Cinnamomum camphora*) 52–3, 64, 66, 119, 184, 226, 238, 240, 335–6, 338–9, 385–7
capers (*qubbār*; *Capparis spinosa*) 68, 292, 351–2
capon (*khaṣī*; *makhṣī*) 37, 40, 97–100, 110, 237, 247
caraway (*karāwayā*; *Carum carvi*) 52, 54, 56–7, 105, 115, 169, 188–9, 214, 227, 242–3, 245–6, 248, 281, 284, 300–1, 305, 314, 377
cardamom (*hāl; Elettaria cardamomum*) 53, 238–9, 274, 276, 387
cardoon (*laṣīf*; *Cynara cardunculus*) 182, 293
carob (*kharnūb*; *Ceratonia siliqua*) 30, 365, 371, 373
carrots (*jazar*; *Daucus carota*) 45, 102, 147, 181, 264, 314
cassia (*dār ṣīnī*; *Cinnamomum cassia*) 52, 54–5, 136–7, 144, 336, 339, 387
caul fat 112, 194, 266
cauliflower (*qunnabīṭ*; *Brassica oleracea var. botrytis*) 28, 46, 48, 172
celery (*karafs*; *Apium graveolens*) 273, 275, 353
chard → see Swiss chard
cheese (*jubn*) 21, 27, 43, 48, 56, 58–2, 66, 69, 84–6, 98, 100, 105, 110–12, 117, 119, 142–6, 156, 176, 189, 200–1, 204, 208, 212–13, 224, 248–9, 270, 290–2, 295–7, 306, 311, 314–15, 319, 351
chestnuts (*qasṭal*) 34, 45, 51, 247–248, 251
chicken (*dajjāj*) 21, 26, 37–41, 59, 61–2, 69, 71, 85, 97–107, 110–11, 114, 146, 148, 151, 153, 159, 165, 167–8, 185, 201, 210, 221, 225–38, 240–52, 261, 264–6
chickpeas (*ḥimmiṣ*; *Cicer arietinum*) 21, 46, 66, 87, 96, 99–102, 105–6, 157, 161–3, 173, 180–1, 191–3, 197–8, 208, 211, 227, 229–31, 253, 264, 289, 303, 321, 325–6, 357, 366, 370, 388
cinnamon (*qirfa*; *Cinnamomum zeylanicum*) 52, 54–7, 60, 64, 93–8, 100–2, 104–5, 107–8, 114–15, 119, 122–3, 128–31, 133, 136–9, 141–3, 145–6, 148–9, 151, 154, 157–8, 160, 162, 168, 170–2, 178–80, 184–6, 192, 198–9, 201–2, 204–5, 210–12, 215, 219, 221–3, 225, 227–9, 233–5, 238–9, 242–5, 247, 250–2, 254, 257–61, 265–6, 270–2, 274, 276–8, 281, 283, 285–9, 291, 300, 303–6, 310, 315, 324, 326, 328, 336, 339, 341, 343, 350, 373, 380–1, 386–7
citron (*utrujj*; *Citrus medica*) 48–50, 96, 101, 157–8, 161, 163, 178–81, 192, 197–8, 208, 226–31, 241, 253, 264, 268, 274–6, 281, 303, 317, 364, 367, 370–3, 376, 382, 384–5, 387
clarified butter (*samn*) 59–60, 94, 97, 99, 102, 104–5, 109, 113, 115, 127–30, 132, 135–8, 141–2, 145, 148–51, 153–5, 241, 288, 295, 300, 302, 327
cloves (*qaranful*; *Syzygium aromaticum*) 41, 51–6, 102, 104–5, 112, 119, 129, 137, 144, 157, 161–3, 168, 170–1, 178–9, 181, 197, 211, 213, 215, 219, 222, 227, 229–30, 238, 240, 247, 249, 253, 255–6, 259–60, 264–5, 267, 269, 272, 276, 278–81, 283, 285–6, 289, 296, 298, 303–4, 319, 335, 338, 343, 350, 384–8
cockerel 249, 251, 294
comb honey (*shuhd*) 125, 132, 135, 333, 336
coriander (*kuzbara*; *Coriandrum sativum*) 43, 45, 51–2, 54–7, 62, 69, 92, 94–103, 105–7, 111–12, 114–15, 117, 136–7, 142, 144–7, 151, 153–5, 157, 161–5, 167–76, 178–81, 183–90, 192–3, 196–8, 200–9, 211–14, 217, 219, 222, 225–30, 232–8, 241–8, 251–7, 259, 261, 263–6, 268–9, 272, 274–81, 283–9, 291, 298–305, 307–13, 315–19, 321–2, 325–6, 364, 368–70, 372–3
coriander seeds (*kuzbara yābisa*) 52, 92, 94–6, 102, 106, 136–7, 147, 161–5, 167, 170, 172–6, 178–81, 183–90, 192–3, 196–8, 200, 202–3, 205, 207–9, 211–12, 214, 222, 225–30, 232–8, 241–5, 247–8, 251, 253–7, 259, 261, 263–6, 268–9, 272,

274–81, 283–5, 287–9, 291, 298–301, 303–5, 307–8, 310, 315–19, 322, 364, 368–70, 372–3
costus (*qusṭ*) 52, 385, 387
couscous (*kuskusū*) 25, 27–8, 59, 69, 99, 147–51
cubeb (*kabāba*; *Piper cubeba*) 385, 387
cucumber (*khiyār*; *Cucumis sativus*) 45, 111, 319
cucurbit 362
cumin (*kammūn*; *Cuminum cyminum*) 27, 46, 51–2, 54–7, 95, 101, 107, 112, 157, 161–3, 170, 178–81, 184, 190–2, 197, 200, 208–9, 211–12, 215, 226, 228, 230, 237, 253, 256, 268–70, 272, 274–5, 278, 280–1, 284–5, 287, 289, 303, 307–8, 311–12, 317, 321, 323–5, 376–7
curd (*ʿaqīd*) 21, 48, 59, 86, 132–3, 290, 292–3, 301, 351
curdled milk (*rāʾib*) 139, 249, 293–4, 301
cyperus (*suʿd*; *Cyperus longus*) 52, 385–7

darmak (fine white flour) 34–5, 89, 106, 109, 114, 119, 121–5, 128, 130, 135–6, 138–9, 141, 143–6, 160, 192, 217–18, 250, 270, 276–7, 279, 287, 289, 300, 309–10, 334, 336–7, 340, 343, 345
dates (*tamr*, *ruṭab*; *Phoenix dactylifera*) 17, 48, 63, 120, 138
deer (*ayyal*) 37, 208
donkey (*ḥimār*) 169

eel (*silbāḥ*) 42, 280
eggs (*bayḍ*) 21, 41, 43–4, 47, 61–2, 66, 74, 84, 86, 100–2, 104–9, 135–7, 141, 145–6, 157–8, 160, 166, 168, 170–1, 177–81, 193, 197–206, 211, 215–20, 222–3, 227–31, 233–8, 241–8, 251–4, 257–8, 260, 263, 265–6, 272, 277–9, 283, 285–9, 291, 299, 301, 303–13, 315–17, 327, 330, 333, 374
emmer wheat (*quṭniyya*) 34, 156
esparto (*ḥalfāʾ*; *Lygeum spartum*) 132, 207, 290, 292–3, 301, 348, 360, 365–6, 368

faḥṣī 185, 231
fālūdhaj 29, 59, 63–4, 66, 134, 302, 330, 342–3
fānīdh 3, 87, 329, 340
faṭīr (unleavened bread) 35
fennel (*basbās*, *nāfiʿ*, *rāziyānaj*; *Foeniculum vulgare*) 26, 45, 52, 55, 91, 96, 98, 101, 115, 118, 121, 147, 157–8, 161, 163, 173, 179–81, 191–2, 194, 197–8, 204, 207–8, 227, 230, 253, 264, 271, 274–5, 325, 329, 364, 367, 369–73, 384
fenugreek (*ḥulbā*; *Trigonella foenum-graecum*) 45, 117–18
fidāwsh 24, 150–1
figs (*tīn*; *Ficus carica*) 45, 48, 57, 291, 293, 356
flour (*daqīq*) 32–6, 44, 47, 59, 61, 64, 73–4, 89, 91, 96, 101, 103, 106, 109, 114–25, 128, 130, 133, 135–6, 139–41, 143–7, 149–50, 152, 154, 160, 192, 202, 217–18, 221, 238, 250, 254, 270, 273, 276–7, 279, 287, 289, 298, 300–1, 306, 309–10, 317, 333, 336–7, 340, 343, 363–73, 375, 379, 386–8
fuqqaʿ → see mushroom
furn 35, 70–1, 89
fustuqiyya 51, 190, 208, 321

galangal (*khūlanjān*; *Alpinia galanga*) 52, 54, 57, 274, 336, 350
garden artichoke (*qannāriyya*, *Cynara scolymus*) 182
garlic (*thūm*; *Allium sativum*) 43, 45, 57–8, 96, 100–1, 110, 112, 115–16, 156–8, 161–5, 178–81, 191, 197, 208–13, 215–16, 219, 224, 227, 229–30, 238, 245, 248–50, 253, 255–62, 264, 267, 269–76, 278–82, 284–7, 289, 294, 296, 298, 301–8, 310–14, 317–19, 322, 324–5
garniture 70, 166, 193, 198
gazelle (*ghazāl*) 33, 37–38, 121, 208
gazelle's ankles 121–2
ghaḍāra 72
ghāliya (perfume compound) 53
ghassānī 87, 149, 328–9
ghassāniyya 197
ghiḍāra → see *ghaḍāra*
giant fennel (*kalkha*; *Ferula communis*) 329
gilt-head bream (*jarrāfa*) 268
ginger (*zanjabīl*; *Zingiber officinale*) 41, 43, 46, 52–7, 62, 95–6, 100–2, 104–5, 107, 114–15, 119, 121, 139, 148, 151, 154, 157–8, 160, 162, 167–8, 170–2, 178–81, 183–7, 198–9, 201, 205, 211, 213, 215, 219, 222–3, 225, 227–9, 231, 233–4, 238, 245,

247, 250, 252, 254, 257–61, 265, 270–2, 274–8, 283, 285–6, 303–5, 307, 315, 326, 336, 338, 341, 350
***gizzard*, 101, 105–6, 136, 223, 228–9, 236, 241–6, 257**
goose (*iwazz*) 21, 37, 85, 222–4, 237, 241–2, 264
gourd (*qarʿ, yaqṭīn; Lagenaria siceraria*) 21, 46, 66, 95–6, 111–12, 147, 149, 153, 155, 177, 183, 232, 256, 294, 298–302, 319
grapes (*ʿinab*; *Vitus vinifera*) 45, 48, 57, 156, 210, 232, 296, 356–7, 360–1
grasshopper 21, 38, 88, 380
gum-cistus (*Shajar al-astab*; *Cistus ladaniferus*) 297

hand-washing powder → also see *ushnān*
hare (*arnab*) 37, 39–40, 111, 208–9, 211–13, 264
ḥarīra 367
harīsa (porridge) 24–5, 32, 38, 59, 66, 84–5, 155, 199, 220–1
hazelnuts (*bunduq*; *Coryllus avallana*) 51, 144, 377
hedgehog (*qunfudh*) 37, 208
ḥiṣrimiyya (verjuice stew) 232
honey (*ʿasal*) 32, 36, 61–5, 107–8, 113, 120, 122–46, 152–3, 155–6, 164, 196–7, 203, 250, 269, 282, 284, 291–3, 302, 328–33, 336–7, 339, 342–3, 345, 349, 353, 358, 365, 369–70, 372–3, 375, 388–9
ḥūtiyya ('the fishy one') 229
ḥuwwārā (prime-quality flour) 102, 149, 238

Ibn al-Waḍīʿ's chechia 98
Ibrāhīmiyya 238
indigo (*nīlaj*; *Indigofera tinctoria*) 343
intestines 38, 41, 44, 69, 94, 112, 166, 186, 190, 194, 197–8, 200–1, 205, 216–17, 235, 266, 311, 321
isfanj (doughnuts) 32, 59, 62, 85, 119, 140–2, 144, 221
isfīriyya (*isfiriyya, isfāriya*) 223, 228–9, 244, 248, 254, 285
iṭriyya (noodles) 35, 66, 84, 152

jaʿfariyya 230
jalīdiyya 237
jalja (sauce) 68, 165, 166
jamalī 157, 166, 216, 224, 262, 275
jashīsh 36
jawzīnaq 2, 64, 87, 125–6, 339
jerky (*qadīd*) 41, 66, 84, 308, 312, 377–8
jināniyya 319
jūdhāba 66, 133, 239
juljulāniyya (sesame nougat) 63, 331

kāfūriyya (camphor stew) 226
al-kaḥlāʾ 278
kāmakh 351, 380
kāmil 195
kaʿk (ring-shaped biscuits) 62–4, 69, 71, 119–21, 123, 138, 141, 146, 204, 218, 290, 332, 336, 338
kānūn 71
khabīṣ 59, 63, 128, 131–134, 251, 333
kid goat 94, 290
khilāṭ 293–4
kubbād → see *zanbūʿ*
kunāfa 34 63, 69, 74, 126, 127, 134
kurunbiyya (cabbage stew) 169
kūsha 71

lakhlakha 386
lakhṭij 24, 116
lamb (*kharūf*) 25, 36–9, 41, 66, 71, 84–5, 97–8, 103, 148–9, 153, 200–8, 238, 254, 290, 319
laqāniq (sausages) 41, 217, 242–4, 264
lawzīnaq 2, 64, 87, 126, 339
lawziyya 187, 225–6
leafy goosefoot (*yarbūz*; *Blitum virgatum*) 86, 176, 207, 318–19
lemon (*laymūn*; *Citrus limon*) 31, 45, 50, 57–8, 164, 174, 207, 232, 259, 359, 362
lemon balm (*turunjān*; *Melissa officinalis*) 45, 207, 232, 259, 359, 362
lemongrass (*idhkhir; Andropogon Schoenanthus*) 384, 386–7
lentils (*ʿadas*; *Lens culinaris medik*) 21, 326–7
lettuce (*khass*; *Lactuca sativa*) 45, 86, 98, 147, 176–7, 207, 318
liquorice (*ʿūd al-sawsan*; *Glycyrrhiza glabra*) 53, 376
liftiyya (turnip stew) 170
lime (*līmū; Citrus aurantiifolia* [*Chrstm.*]

Swingle) 50, 57, 100, 185, 187–8, 195, 210, 220, 226, 235, 241, 263–4, 270, 282, 292–3, 308, 320, 326, 342, 349–50, 361
locust 38
lovage (*kāshim*; *Levisticum officinale*) 52

mackerel 272
madhūn (type of flour) 131
maḍīra 59, 206
maḥshī 260, 263
maghmūm 189
maghmūma 189
mahaleb cherry → see St Lucie cherry
makhāriq 143
Malabar plum (*Eugenia jambosa*) 49
malla 35, 71–2, 90–1, 99, 103, 105, 109, 121, 130, 146, 271, 337
maqdūnis → see parsley
maqrūḍ (fried semolina pastry) 64, 138
marjoram (*marzanjush*; *Origanum majorana*) 359, 384, 387
marrow (*mukhkh*) 96, 101, 110, 112, 116, 120, 138, 142, 145, 150, 159, 176, 187, 190, 206, 215, 233, 240, 243, 275, 321, 325
mastic (*maṣṭikā'*; *Pistacia lentiscus*) 41, 52–3, 56–7, 114–15, 120, 130, 148–9, 213, 215, 219, 225, 235, 247, 265, 268, 270–2, 274–6, 278, 283, 285–6, 338, 341–2, 350
melon (*biṭṭīkh*; *Cucumis melo*) 111, 319, 385, 387
milk (*laban ḥalīb*) 25, 39, 41, 47, 58–60, 73–4, 86, 97, 103, 108–9, 113, 116, 118, 123, 129, 139, 142–4, 152, 154–5, 168, 206–7, 234, 249, 290, 293–5, 297, 300–1, 316, 340, 351
millet (*banīj*, *jāwars*; *Panicum miliaceum*, *Pennisetum typhodeum*) 29, 34, 36, 91, 117
mint (*na'na'*; *Mentha arvensis*) 45, 52, 55–7, 105, 112, 115, 136–7, 142, 144–6, 158, 160, 168, 170–1, 174–5, 178, 190, 194, 201, 204–5, 207, 216, 219, 223, 225, 227, 229–36, 241, 245–7, 257–9, 264, 266, 270–1, 273, 275–6, 285–6, 289, 291, 300, 305, 308–9, 312–13, 315, 319, 353, 359, 361–2, 382
mirqās (sausages) 32, 41, 84–5, 215–18, 245, 264–5, 311
mountain goat (*wa'l*) 37, 208
mu'aqqad 63, 334, 336
mu'allak 201
mu'allaka 153
mu'assal 63, 334, 336
muballaqa 207
mufarrij 164, 231, 256, 259
mufattit 227
mughaffar 228, 277, 310
muḥammiṣ (coarse couscous) 117
mujabbana (fried cheese buns) 21, 24, 27, 58, 60–2, 69, 85, 119, 125, 142–6, 291
mukhallal 24, 67, 227
mullet (*būrī*; *Mugil cephalus*) 267–8, 274
muqawwara 123–4
murakkaba 137
murawwaj 269
murūziyya 161, 231
murrī (fermented condiment) 32, 34, 44, 51–2, 57–8, 62, 67, 87, 100, 104, 107, 137, 157, 160, 162–4, 178–81, 183, 185–6, 189, 192, 194–5, 197, 200, 202–5, 207–15, 217–19, 222–4, 227–31, 236–7, 241–6, 248–50, 252–6, 260–1, 263–4, 266–71, 273–8, 280–1, 284–7, 289, 298, 300–1, 303–4, 307–12, 317, 322, 326, 344, 355, 362, 365–6, 368–75, 377, 380–1
musammana 99, 130
muṣannab 388
mushahhada 103, 128
mushamma' 24, 282
mushāsh 138
mushrooms (*fuqqa'*, *fuṭr*) 317
musk (*misk*; *Moschus moschiferus*) 33, 52–4, 64, 66, 123–4, 184, 240, 338, 370–1, 373, 385–6
musṭ 68, 371–2, 374
mustard (*khardal*; *Sinapis alba*) 39, 45, 52, 66, 68, 193–4, 216–17, 314, 344–5, 354, 388–9
al-Mutawakkil's brains 63, 342
muṭajjan 179
muthallath 67, 160, 166, 277
muthallatha 387
mutton (*ghanam*) 37–39, 41, 96–7, 148, 151, 153–4, 159, 161, 164, 167, 221, 264, 275
muwarraqa 130, 143
myrobalan plum (*ihlīlaj*; *Prunus cerasifera*) 161
myrtle (*'ās*; *Myrtus communis*) 53, 194, 387

na'na'iyya (mint stew) 259
nadd 387
namaksūd 378
narjisiyya 62, 181, 236
Nayrūz 110–11
nigella (*shūnīz*; *Nigella sativa*) 45, 52, 292, 353, 355, 364, 367–70, 372–3
nīmbirisht (poached eggs) 287
nutmeg (*jawz bawwā*; *Myristica fragrans*) 53–5, 64, 336, 384, 386

olive oil (*zayt zaytūn*) 31, 33, 43–4, 58, 61–2, 65, 70, 74, 87, 92, 94–6, 98–107, 110–15, 117, 119–31, 133–4, 136–7, 139–47, 150–1, 153–64, 167, 169–70, 172–6, 178–81, 183–7, 189–93, 196–205, 207–15, 217–19, 221–4, 226–8, 230–65, 267–89, 291–6, 298–9, 301–30, 333–4, 337–8, 341–4, 346–52, 354, 360–1, 364, 367–8, 371, 374–6, 380–1
olives (*zaytūn*; *Olea europaea*) 44, 50, 56, 68, 71, 87, 100, 113, 195, 235, 264, 292–3, 325, 346–8, 374–5
omasum (*qibā*) 219
omelette (*'ujja*) 59, 62, 107–8, 228, 285, 288, 310
onion (*baṣal*; *Allium cepa*) 25, 30, 44–6, 92, 94–107, 111–15, 117, 136–7, 147, 151, 153–5, 157, 161–4, 167, 169–70, 172–6, 178–81, 183–7, 190–3, 197–8, 200, 202, 204–9, 211–12, 214–17, 220, 222, 225–7, 229–30, 232–8, 241–7, 251–3, 255–7, 259, 261–6, 268–71, 274–5, 278, 283–4, 289, 292, 296, 298–300, 303–4, 308, 312, 316–19, 321–2, 325–7, 352–3, 373–4
orache (*qaṭaf*; *Atriplex hortensis*) 176
oregano (*ṣa'tar*; Origanum vulgare) 44–45, 54–5, 163, 177, 184, 189, 194–5, 208–9, 213, 224, 236–7, 241–2, 248–50, 269, 272, 274–6, 279, 286, 298, 303, 307, 311, 317, 322, 346–8, 355, 364, 367, 370, 372–4, 381

parsley (*baqdūnis, maqdūnis*; *Petroselinum macedonicum*) 69, 165, 213, 273, 353
partridge (*ḥajal*) 21, 37, 41, 61, 85, 100, 111, 253–4, 264
peach (*khawkh*; *Persica vulgaris*) 45
pellitory (*'āqir qarḥā*; *Anacyclus pyrethrum*) 199
pennyroyal (*fulāyū*; *Mentha pulegium*) 359
pepper (*fulful*; *Piper nigrum*) 39, 46, 51–7, 62, 64, 92, 94–108, 111–12, 117, 119, 121, 125–7, 129, 133, 135–7, 139, 144–5, 147–148, 151, 153–5, 157–8, 160–5, 167–76, 178–81, 183–6, 188–206, 208–215, 219, 222–4, 226–39, 241–8, 250–7, 259–66, 268–72, 274–81, 283–9, 291, 298–308, 310–13, 315–17, 319, 322–4, 326–7, 336, 339, 341, 343, 350, 357, 377, 380–1
pigeon (*ḥamām*) 37, 40–1, 61, 111, 256
pine cone (*jamjamat al-ṣanawbar*) 364, 367, 369, 371
pine nut (*ṣanawbar*) 45, 51, 121–125, 136–137, 145, 219, 247–8, 251, 254, 265, 272, 278–9, 299, 334, 373, 377
pistachios (*fustuq*; *Pistacia vera*) 51, 125, 136–7, 145, 238, 334–5, 342–3, 377
plum (*'ayn al-baqar*; *Prunus domestica*) 48–9, 68, 161–2, 281
pomegranate (*rummān*; *Punica granatum*) 3, 45, 48, 188
pomelo (*zanbū'*; *Citrus maxima*) 49
poussin 37, 102–3, 232
pullet (*farrūj*, pl. *farārīj*) 37, 41, 167, 195, 225–7, 232, 235, 239, 248, 250
purslane (*rijla; Portulaca oleracea)* 177, 207–8, 319

qadīd → see jerky
Qāhiriyya 64, 87, 336–8
qaliyya 200
qar'iyya (gourd stew) 177, 183, 232, 256
qaṭā'if (crêpes) 34, 58, 63, 69, 71, 103–4, 128–9, 343
qayḥāṭa 143
qidr 52, 69, 186
qubbayṭ majbūdh (pulled honey taffy) 63, 332
quince (*safarjal*; *Cydonia oblonga*) 44–5, 48, 185, 246, 264, 369, 371–2, 374
qunnabīṭiyya (cauliflower stew) 172
Qurashiyya 237

Ra's Maymūn ('the blessed head') 24, 63, 135, 166, 197
rabbit (*qunilya*) 37, 39–40, 111, 208–9, 211–13, 264
rāhibī ('the monk's dish') 68, 163, 216, 224,

231, 256, 262, 274, 282, 284
rā'ib (curdled milk) 249
raisins (*zabīb*) 25, 57, 161, 233, 237, 354, 358, 373
ram (*kabsh*) 37, 39–41, 50, 71, 93, 112, 167, 169–170, 172–8, 180–97, 203, 216, 265–6, 313, 378, 385
rāmik (perfume compound) 384
rāyib → see *rā'ib*
rennet (*minfaḥa*) 290
rice (*aruzz*; Oryza *sativa*) 31, 36, 45, 58–9, 87, 118, 152–4, 181, 221
rice pudding (*al-aruzz bi 'l-laban al-ḥalīb*) 36, 58–9, 87, 152
rijliyya (purslane stew) 177
rose (*ward*) 14, 52–4, 64, 66, 70, 119–21, 123–5, 129–30, 137, 143, 164, 184, 203, 212, 215, 226, 238–40, 250–1, 315, 324, 334–9, 362, 384–7
rose jam 164
rose syrup (*sharāb al-ward*) 129, 238, 240, 338
rose water (*mā' al-ward*) 52, 54, 64, 66, 70, 119–21, 123–5, 129, 137, 143, 164, 184, 203, 212, 215, 226, 238–40, 250–1, 315, 324, 334–9, 362, 385–6
rose-water syrup (*jullāb*) 125, 130, 337–8
rue (*fayjan, sadhāb*; *Ruta graveolens*) 45, 193, 245, 273, 323–5
rukhāmiyya 63, 335
ruqāq (thin flatbread) 33, 133, 143–4, 239

sabāt 100
safflower (*'uṣfur*; *Carthamus tinctorius*) 354
saffron (*za'farān*; *Crocus sativus*) 31, 43, 45, 52–8, 96–7, 101, 105, 107, 118, 132–5, 146, 149, 157, 160–4, 166, 178–82, 184, 189, 192, 195–9, 201–2, 204, 207–8, 211–12, 214, 220, 222–3, 226–8, 230–1, 234–5, 237–8, 240–1, 244, 246–7, 253–4, 257, 264, 268, 270, 272–7, 280–1, 283–5, 289, 291, 299, 302–3, 305, 307–10, 312, 315, 326–8, 330, 338, 343, 354, 369–70
ṣaḥnāt (fish condiment) 355
St Lucie cherry (*maḥlab; Prunus mahaleb*) 385
salt (*milḥ*; *Sodium chloride*) 32–3, 35, 46, 51–2, 55–7, 60, 73, 89, 91–2, 94–107, 109–15, 117–19, 121, 124–5, 128–30, 135–7, 140–3, 145–8, 150–5, 157–65, 167–81, 183–94, 196–213, 215–17, 219, 222–30, 232–9, 241–8, 250–7, 259–66, 268–89, 291–3, 295–6, 298–305, 307–27, 336, 344–55, 361, 363–73, 376–9, 381–2
saltwort (*ushnān*; *Salsola kali*) 53
samīd (*samīdh*) → see semolina
samn (clarified butter) 59–60
sanbūsak 25, 87, 336, 338
sandalwood (*ṣandal*; *Santalum album*) 52–3, 384–7
Ṣanhājī 19, 21, 26, 37, 86, 264 266
sardine (*sardīn*; *(Sardina pilchardus Walbaum*) 270–1, 276, 284
sausage → see *mirqās, laqāniq*
seabass (*manānī*) 267
semolina (*samīd*) 27, 32–3, 35–6, 73–4, 89–90, 93, 99–101, 103, 105–6, 109–10, 114, 127–30, 133–5, 137–8, 140–3, 147, 150–3, 197, 207, 217, 222, 241, 334–5, 343
serpent melon (*qiththā'* ; *Cucumus melo flexuosus*) 111, 319
sesame (*simsim, juljulān*; *Sesamum indicum*) 26, 32, 58–9, 66, 84, 91, 139, 204, 296, 329–31, 333, 342, 373, 375, 377
sesame oil (*zayt al-simsim*) 26, 32, 58–9, 296
shad (*shābal*) 267–8, 271
shaddock → see pomelo
shardhūn (type of oregano; *Thymbra capitata*) 355, 374
shīrāz (cottage cheese) 249, 292–4, 301, 351
shrimp 21, 380–1
shiwā' 186
shiwā' qidr (pot roast) 186
silqiyya (chard stew) 173
ṣināb (mustard-and-raisin dip) 52, 216, 314, 344–5
ṣinābī 193
snails (*aghlāl, qawqan*) 41–2, 380, 382
soapwort (*ṣābūniyya*; *Saponaria officinalis*) 332
sorghum (*dhura, dukhn*; *Sorghum bicolor*) 31
sour grapes (*ḥiṣrim*) 45, 48, 57, 210, 232, 360–1
sparrow (*'uṣfūr*; pl. *'aṣāfīr*) 21, 37, 41, 85, 100, 102, 146, 195, 204, 221, 262–4, 309, 313, 324

spikenard (*sunbul hindī*; *Nardostachys jatamansi*) 41, 51–6, 64, 100, 102, 104–5, 119, 129, 133, 136–7, 148–9, 157, 168, 170–1, 213, 215, 219, 222, 229, 238–41, 243, 247, 265, 272, 274, 276–8, 283, 285–6, 334–6, 338, 342–3, 350
spinach (*isfānākh*; *Spinachia oleracea*) 21, 86, 94, 175–6, 207, 318
ṣīr (salted sprats) 355, 374
squab (*farkhat al-ḥamām*) 33, 37, 41, 85, 100, 105–8, 136–7, 195, 204, 241, 245–6, 251, 255–8, 260, 264–6, 294
squill 57, 284, 359–60
starch (*nashā, lubāb*) 36, 47, 127, 129, 133–4, 196, 328–30, 337–8, 341–3
starling (*summān*) 21, 37, 85, 146, 204, 261–2, 264
storax (*mayʿa*) 52, 385–6
sturgeon (*shūlī*) 267
suckling kid (*jadī raḍīʿ*) 98, 167–8, 177, 201, 207, 264
suet (*shaḥm*) 138, 149, 152, 165–6, 168–71, 173–5, 178, 185–7, 189–90, 194, 196, 208–9, 215–19, 221, 240, 308, 311, 320–1
sugar (*sukkar*; *Saccharum officinarum*) 3, 26–27, 31, 45, 47, 50, 56, 60, 63–5, 97, 108–9, 113, 119, 121–6, 128–30, 136–9, 142–3, 145–6, 152, 155, 198, 203, 226, 238, 240, 242, 251, 300, 329, 334–43, 350, 363
sugar cane (*qaṣab*) 3, 45, 64, 136, 329
sukk (perfume compound) 52–3, 384–7
sukkariyya 334
sumac (*summāq*; *Rhus coriaria*) 55, 57, 232–3
summāqiyya (sumac stew) 232
summer savory (*shaṭriyya*; *Satureja hortensis*) 184
sweet basil (*bādharuj, ḥabaq*; *Ocimum basilicum*) 171
sweet costus (*qusṭ ḥulw*; *Saussurea costus* [Falc.] Lipsch.) 385, 387
sweet marjoram (*marzanjūsh, Origanum majorana*) 359
Swiss chard (*silq*; *Beta vulgaris*) 173
syrup (*sharāb*) 20, 64–5, 125, 129–30, 238, 240–1, 269, 284, 333, 337–8, 350, 389

ṭabāhijiyya 188–9
tafāyā 2, 25, 52, 55, 67, 167, 174, 207, 225, 274
ṭalabiyya 302
ṭājin 69
tallow 131
taltīn 154
tannūr 35, 40, 70–1, 89–91, 93, 97, 100, 112, 149, 164, 194–5, 205–6, 208–10, 249, 313
taro (*qulqās*; *Colocasia esculenta*) 21, 28, 46, 86, 188, 320, 327
terebinth (*buṭm*; *Pistacia terebinthus*) 375
tharīda 2, 21, 24–5, 56–7, 59, 66, 72, 85, 89, 92–104, 106–13, 147
thūmiyya 238
ṭifshīla 192
tirfās 183, 314
toothache tree (*fāghira*; *Xanthoxylon/Fagara avicennae* Lam.) 387
tragacanth gum (*kathīrā'*; *Astragalus tragancantha*) 349
tripe (*karsh*) 38, 86, 93, 95, 112, 150, 157–8, 163, 166, 194, 198, 200–1, 206, 219–20, 264–6
truffles (*kam'*; *Terfezia spp.*) 21, 45–6, 98, 183, 202, 208, 314–15
tuffāḥiyya 185
tuna (*tunn*) 42–3, 57, 280–4
al-Turkiyya ('the Turkish one') 235
turnip (*lift*; *Brassica rapa*) 48, 113, 147, 153, 160, 170–1, 188, 264, 318, 352, 354
turtledove (*yamāma*) 21, 37, 41, 85, 195, 204, 241, 258–62, 264
turunjāniyya (lemon-balm stew) 174

ushnān → see saltwort
'uṣub (tripe sausages) 94, 150

veal 168, 170, 172, 181–2, 184–5, 193, 220
verjuice (*mā' ḥiṣrim*) 48, 232, 263, 282
vinegar (*khall*) 21, 24, 33, 38, 43–4, 48, 50–2, 57–8, 62, 68, 73, 82–3, 87, 96, 100–1, 105, 107, 114, 149, 157, 160–6, 178–82, 184–6, 189, 191–5, 197, 200, 202–3, 208–19, 223, 226–31, 233, 236–8, 242–6, 248, 251, 253–4, 256–7, 263–4, 267–70, 273–8, 280–2, 284–7, 289, 298, 301–5, 307–12, 314, 316–18, 320, 323–24, 326–7, 344–5, 349–62, 377

walnuts (*jawz*; *Juglans regia*) 45, 51, 56, 62, 64, 100, 110, 123–5, 139, 145, 237, 244,

247–8, 268, 274, 288, 296, 299, 330, 336, 339, 342–3, 375, 377
water mint (*ḍawmarān*; *Mentha aquatica*) 382
wheat (*qamḥ*, *ḥinṭa*; *Triticum durum*) 16, 25, 29, 32–6, 45, 91, 115, 117–18, 132, 134, 150, 155–6, 221, 364, 366–72, 375
whey 292–4
wild fig (*dhukkār*; *Ficus carica silvestris*) 363–4, 366–7

al-Yahūdiyya ('the Jewish one') 234
yearling ram (*kabsh thanī*) 167, 176–8, 183–4, 186–7, 190–5
yeast (*khamīra*) 35, 64, 89–90, 96, 101, 105, 108, 110, 115–16, 119, 121, 123–5, 128–30, 135, 137–41, 144, 146, 153–4, 206, 217, 234, 250, 285, 294, 327, 336, 358, 364
yoghurt 59, 258, 294

zabzīn 24, 117, 151
zanbū' → see pomelo
zīrbājiyya 226
zulābiyya 27, 32, 59, 63, 139–40
zumurrudī 63, 342